# *Banking Law and Regulation*

# *BANKING LAW AND REGULATION*

***Second Edition***

**JONATHAN R. MACEY**
J. DuPratt White Professor of Law
Cornell University

**GEOFFREY P. MILLER**
Professor of Law
New York University

ASPEN LAW & BUSINESS
A Division of Aspen Publishers, Inc.

ISBN 1-56706-518-X



Permissions
Aspen Law & Business
A Division of Aspen Publishers, Inc.
1185 Avenue of the Americas
New York, NY 10036

2 3 4 5

*For our children—*
*Jason and Forrest*
*(G. M.)*
*Ally and Josh*
*(J. M.)*

# *SUMMARY TABLE OF CONTENTS*

# CONTENTS

## 2. ENTRY INTO THE BUSINESS OF BANKING 87

## 3. REGULATION OF THE BANKING BUSINESS 123

# PREFACE

This is a book about banking law and regulation. By "banking law" we mean not only the law applicable to traditional commercial banks, but also the pattern of regulation governing other depository institutions (institutions that accept checking account deposits from customers) such as savings and loans, savings banks, and credit unions. Reference will also occasionally be made to other types of financial institutions such as securities firms, pension funds, and life insurance companies, which are increasingly offering "bank-like" services. Accordingly, the scope of the book is broader than traditional commercial banks.

At the same time, we do not treat all legal issues affecting the business of depository institutions. Banks and thrifts confront many thorny questions in the handling of negotiable instruments such as checks. We leave the legal rules applicable to negotiable instruments to courses on the Uniform Commercial Code. Banks also face a variety of legal problems in making and collecting on loans; for the most part these problems are also outside the scope of this book, although we do treat the question of lender liability in Chapter 3. Finally, banks, like other firms, must comply with all sorts of federal and state regulations applicable to businesses generally, such as rules regulating securities issuance, prohibiting discrimination in employment, governing relationships with unions, and much more. These topics are treated in the relevant substantive law courses such as securities regulation, employment discrimination, and labor law.

This book is structured as follows. Chapter 1 provides an introduction and overview, including a discussion of banking history, which in our opinion is essential to an understanding of the current structure of banking regulation. Chapters 2 and 3 consider the regulations governing entry into the business of banking and regulatory limitations on the business operations of banking institutions. Chapter 4 expands the coverage to consider the regulation of bank holding companies and their affiliates. Chapter 5 treats geographic restrictions on bank expansion.

Chapter 6 discusses the securities powers of banks, one of the most controversial contemporary issues in bank regulation. Chapter 7 examines regulatory enforcement powers, and Chapter 8 looks at bank failure. Finally, Chapter 9 addresses the topic of international banking and the ever-increasing "globalization" of financial institutions law.

Accompanying this book is a statutory supplement. Because banking law is so heavily statutory in focus, frequent reference to the governing legislation is essential. Although the casebook quotes key language from the most important provisions, a full understanding of banking law requires close reading of all the relevant statutes. Accordingly, we encourage students to study the statutory language carefully as well.

Most casebook authors can look forward to the second edition with calm assurance that not much is really going to change. A new case here, a doctrine created or destroyed there, maybe even some minor statutory amendments—nothing drastic or extraordinary. Not so for banking law—ignore it for a few months and it seems like a new country. The changes that have occurred in the law since the first edition, a mere five years ago, range from the profound (for example, the Riegle-Neal Interstate Banking and Branching Efficiency Act of 1994, which fundamentally alters the ground rules on geographic expansion) to the trifling, with many, many changes in between. Moreover, as this revision is being written, Congress threatens to repeal the Glass-Steagall Act, thus obviating nearly all of our Chapter 6. Although we have made every effort to update this book as completely as possible, the pace of change in the law is so great that at least some of the book is sure to be out of date even before it appears. (For this reason, among others, we strongly encourage you to utilize the statutory and case supplement.)

In revising this book, we were struck by the extraordinary help we have received from readers—students and colleagues both—who drew our attention to areas where the book needed improvement or correction. From a list of helpers too numerous to mention, we would like to single out for special thanks Howard Cayne, Derek Bush, Patricia McCoy, Eric Posner, and Peter Swire. Comments on this second edition are eagerly invited. Finally, we thank our editors at Aspen Law & Business; our research assistant, Daniel Frommer; our secretaries Linda Gilich, Jennifer Larmour, and Kathy Wimsett; and, as always, our families.

*Jonathan R. Macey*
*Geoffrey P. Miller*

February 1997

# ACKNOWLEDGMENTS

We wish to thank the following copyright holders who kindly granted permission to reprint excerpts from the following materials.

Aspinwall, On the "Specialness" of Banking, 7 Issues in Bank Reg. 16 (1983). Copyright © 1983 by Issues in Bank Regulation, Bank Administration Institute. Reprinted by permission.

Fischel, The Economics of Lender Liability, 99 Yale L.J. 131, 141-142, 145 (1989). Copyright © 1989 by the Yale Law Journal Co., Inc. Reprinted by permission of the Yale Law Journal Co., Inc. and Fred B. Rothman & Co.

Fischel, Rosenfield, & Stillman, The Regulation of Banks and Bank Holding Companies, 73 Va. L. Rev. 301, 302, 314, 324-325, 326-327 (1987). Copyright © 1987 by the Virginia Law Review Association. Reprinted by permission of the Virginia Law Review Association and Fred B. Rothman & Co.

Garten, Banking on the Market: Relying on Depositors to Control Bank Risks, 4 Yale J. on Reg. 129, 131-132 (1986). Copyright © 1986 by the Yale Journal on Regulation, Box 401A Yale Station, New Haven, CT 06520. Reprinted from Volume 4 by permission. All rights reserved.

Hu, Misunderstood Derivatives: The Causes of Information Failure and the Promise of Regulatory Incrementalism, 102 Yale L.J. 1457 (1993). Copyright © 1993 by The Yale Law Journal Company. Reprinted by permission of The Yale Law Journal Company and Fred B. Rothman & Company from The Yale Law Journal, vol. 102, pages 1457-1513.

Macey, Special Interest Groups and the Judicial Function: The Dilemma of Glass-Steagall, 33 Emory L.J. 1 (1983). Copyright © 1983 by the Emory Law Journal. Reprinted by permission.

Macey & Miller, The Community Reinvestment Act: An Economic Analysis, 79 Va. L. Rev. 291 (1993). Copyright © 1993 by the Virginia Law

Review Association. Reprinted by permission of the Virginia Law Review Association and Fred B. Rothman & Co.

Macey & Miller, Nondeposit Deposits and the Future of Bank Regulation, 91 Mich. L. Rev. 237 (1992). Reprinted from Michigan Law Review, November 1992, vol. 91, no. 2. Copyright 1992 by The Michigan Law Review Association.

Miller, The Future of the Dual Banking System, 53 Brooklyn L. Rev. 1 (1987). Copyright © 1987 by the Brooklyn Law Review. Reprinted by permission.

Render, Virtual Payments Systems: Legal Issues of Electronic Cash (1995). Unpublished. Copyright © 1995 by Paula Wilson Render. Quoted by permission.

Scott, In Quest of Reason: The Licensing Decisions of the Federal Banking Agencies, 42 U. Chi. L. Rev. 235 (1975). Copyright © 1975 by the University of Chicago Law Review. Reprinted by permission.

Swire, Safe Harbors and a Proposal to Improve the Community Reinvestment Act, 79 Va. L. Rev. 349 (1993). Copyright © 1993 by the Virginia Law Review Association. Reprinted by permission of the Virginia Law Review Association and Fred B. Rothman & Co.

# *BANKING LAW AND REGULATION*

# 1 INTRODUCTION AND OVERVIEW

## A. INTRODUCTION

The world of banking—commercial banks, savings and loans, savings banks, and credit unions—is a world in upheaval. New products are introduced at dizzying speed. Distinctions among institutions that once made all the difference now make very little difference at all. Geographic restrictions that once contained banks within limited markets are falling before a tidal wave of deregulation. Banks that once were prohibited from paying interest on checking accounts now compete vigorously for deposits. Securities firms and other institutions are encroaching on the once-sacrosanct turf of deposit banking. Banks are expanding outward into all sorts of nonbanking activities. Some banks have grown huge. Others have failed; the failure rate for both banks and savings and loans was higher during the 1980s than at any time since the Great Depression. And these are just the most visible effects of a market revolution that has shaken the foundations of banking over the past decade.

All market changes spawn legal problems; revolutionary changes tax the legal system to its limits. So it is with banking. Stimulated by changing markets and fluctuating political pressures, the law governing depository institutions has itself undergone a revolution. Since 1980 Congress has passed a half dozen important banking statutes; courts have issued many decisions on issues of first impression; and bureaucratic agencies have promulgated scores of important regulations. Even so, the legal system seems to lag behind impetuous marketplace changes.

The revolution in banking today presents both a challenge and an opportunity for the student and the practitioner of banking law. The challenge is to keep abreast of fast-paced developments in the law and the marketplace. The opportunity is to think creatively about how banking law is evolving in order to assist clients in protecting their interests and positioning themselves to take advantage of new market opportunities. Although much is uncertain about banking law, one thing we do know: The field will continue to generate interesting and complex issues for many years to come.

## B. HISTORICAL OVERVIEW

Few fields of American law are more heavily influenced by history than banking law. Without an understanding of banking history, many elements (a cynic might say *most* elements) of banking regulation appear arbitrary, capricious—even perverse. Why should we have a "dual banking system" with overlapping state and federal chartering? Why an elaborate regime of geographic and product-line restraints on bank activities? Why is banking segmented into different institutions—commercial banks, savings and loans, savings banks, credit unions? Why do we have a confusing, balkanized, Rube Goldberg structure of regulation, with three or more regulators involved in many transactions?

American banking law is undoubtedly quirky, and many oddities can be explained only on historical grounds. History is valuable not just for understanding the oddities in banking law, but also for placing current controversies and debates in context and obtaining an overview of the revolutionary changes that are today revamping the system top to bottom. Accordingly, we believe that some understanding of banking history is an essential prerequisite to grasping the structure and content of current banking law.

### 1. *Bank of the United States*

We begin our history—somewhat arbitrarily—with the formation of the First Bank of the United States. Banking in the colonies had been rudimentary, largely because the needs of commerce at the time did not require banks in the modern sense. Soon after Cornwallis's surrender at Yorktown in 1781 the Continental Congress established a Bank of North America, under national charter, in an attempt to cope with the financial disarray that attended the recently ended hostilities. The following year, however, the Bank of North America reincorporated under a Pennsylvania charter. It soon became just one of several state banks that sprang into being in the years following the Revolutionary War.

The Constitution of 1787 contained a number of clauses designed to control the nation's chaotic fiscal affairs. It denied states the power to issue coin or paper money and gave the federal government the power to issue coin. (Because circulating bank notes were not considered to be paper money at the time, but rather paper convertible into money, they were not affected by these provisions.) In response to other trade barriers, the Constitution gave the federal government the power to regulate commerce. On the question of whether the government would have the power to incorporate a bank or other corporation, the Constitution was silent. However, under the doctrine that powers not expressly granted in a Constitution are denied, silence was generally understood to mean that no such power existed.

The genesis of the Bank of the United States was Treasury Secretary Alexander Hamilton's "Report on a National Bank," submitted to Congress in 1790. The report borrowed Adam Smith's description of the Bank of England to make the case that a national bank could augment the productive capital of society and thus help create a strong and prosperous nation. The report further argued that the bank could aid in the administration of public finances by facilitating the collection of taxes and by making loans to the Treasury. Moreover, it could provide a uniform paper currency good for all payments due the government.

Hamilton's proposal called for an authorized capital of $10 million, enough to support an extensive note circulation. The government would subscribe $2 million, paying with its debt. The public would subscribe the rest, paying one-fourth in specie, thus assuring adequate reserves, and three-fourths in the government's 6 percent obligations, thus supporting the government's credit by increasing the demand for its debt. Finally, Hamilton's proposal called for private management of the bank with government oversight. This scheme was designed to increase public faith in the bank's notes: Government oversight would prevent the management from running amok; private management would prevent legal suspension of redemptions in the face of imagined exigencies.

Hamilton's bank met with considerable opposition. James Madison, who had played a seminal role in drafting the Constitution, led those in Congress who believed the bank was unconstitutional. The Constitution, he argued, had granted the federal government only certain specific powers. The power to incorporate a bank was not one of them. Moreover, the bank would interfere with the states' sovereign rights to decide for themselves whether to establish or prohibit banks. Others in Congress opposed the bank on much simpler grounds. These were the agrarians, who believed that all corporations were evil instruments of a small elite.

Despite the opposition, the bank garnered a two-thirds majority in each congressional house, with northerners and Federalists voting overwhelmingly for it and southerners and Republicans voting overwhelmingly against. The charter was more detailed and restrictive than prior state bank charters. Along with the provisions already mentioned, prohibitions were placed on trading in goods and on holding land in excess of forfeited collateral. The charter was for a 20-year life.

President Washington was troubled by the bill he received from Congress. His secretary of state, Thomas Jefferson, urged that while the bank was arguably a convenience, it was certainly not a necessity, and hence was unconstitutional. Treasury Secretary Hamilton countered that the purpose of the Constitution was to set up a workable government and that any means "fairly applicable" to that end could be employed. The difference between Jefferson and Hamilton was simple but fundamental. Jefferson feared concentrated power in any form; Hamilton feared the lack of it. Jefferson wanted a weak government that would leave the people to their own devices; Hamilton wanted a strong government that would lead the nation to prosperity. Hamilton won the battle (and ultimately the war). In 1791 Washington signed into law the charter for the Bank of the United States.

In December of 1791, following a heavy oversubscription of its public capital, the Bank of the United States opened its doors in Philadelphia, then still the seat of the federal government. Eventually it opened eight branches in spite of Hamilton's protestations that dividing the bank's operations would weaken it. Some branches met with hostility; Georgia imposed a tax on the Savannah branch and forcibly entered the bank's vaults to collect it. The bank sued to regain its specie, but lost on jurisdictional grounds. Bank of the United States v. Deveaux, 9 U.S. (5 Cranch) 61 (1809).

Viewed as a commercial bank, the Bank of the United States was managed conservatively. This was in part because it needed to keep available a large reserve of specie to insure the government a ready source of loans. Conservative management was also intended, initially, to reduce state bank hostility by minimizing interference with state bank business. This second rationale failed; due to the sheer size of its capital, the bank quickly came to dominate commercial lending.

In its "official" functions the bank was an unqualified success. It efficiently managed tax collections, government disbursements, and foreign exchange, and by issuing 20 percent of all the notes in circulation, provided a uniform currency for all transactions with the government. It enjoyed a near monopoly in government loans, though the Treasury occasionally spread tokens to state banks. This monopoly was ever less important, however, because the government began retiring its debt after 1800, resulting in the bank's holding fewer and fewer government obligations. Indeed, the government became the bank's largest net depositor. Thus, one of the bank's originally intended functions—bolstering of the government's credit—ultimately proved unnecessary.

The bank's main success, however, was its evolution into a central bank. This had neither been anticipated nor intended. Indeed, in 1791, there was no real necessity for a central bank. There was no need to regulate the nation's money supply. The Constitution, in giving Congress the power to coin money and set its value, envisioned self-adjusting specie mechanism that was inconsistent with outside monetary control.

Nevertheless, the Bank of the United States became a central bank. Two factors were critical in this development: the proliferation of state banks, which transformed American banking into a single system, and the size of the Bank of the United States, which enabled it to play the central role in that system. The proliferation of state banks caused a large and continuous flow of state bank notes to come into the bank. This permitted it to regulate national credit. When the bank wanted to restrain credit, it redeemed the notes it received promptly, thereby forcing other banks to keep greater specie reserves to meet the redemptions. Conversely, when the bank wanted to stimulate credit, it showed forbearance. It complemented this strategy by decreasing or increasing its own level of loans, as the case required, and because it controlled so much specie (by 1811 fully 50 percent of bank-held specie) this had a great added effect. Needless to say, the bank's activities, while useful, made it few friends among state bankers.

The national political scene changed dramatically during the bank's 20 years. Republicans replaced Federalists in power. Nevertheless, the bank flourished. Jefferson, who never waivered in his dislike for the bank, chose simply to ignore it as president, delegating all responsibility for it to his Treasury Secretary Albert Gallatin. When the time came for the bank's recharter, James Madison, who had succeeded Jefferson as president, actually led the fight for the bank. He argued that history had proved the bank to be more than an expediency, indeed a near necessity, and that 20 years of annual legislative acts tacitly recognizing it had persuaded him of its constitutionality. The bank had some friends in Congress who agreed with Madison. Their advocacy, however, was uninspiring: "near necessity" is a pale rallying cry when the opposition screams "abomination." Meanwhile, the advocacy of bank insiders was nonexistent. The bank's directors were politically inept; they did not feel it their duty to lobby for the bank. The bank's shareholders were overwhelmingly foreign; they believed that prudence dictated silence.

The bank's opponents, however, felt no such restraints. Some were hardened agrarians venting their usual rage. Most were businessmen with interests in state banks. They argued that the landscape had changed since 1791. Now there were state banks everywhere capable of providing the government with any service that the Bank of the United States provided. Thus by definition the bank was unnecessary. The aim of these businessmen was mercenary; they knew that the bank's business would have to go to state banks. Moreover, they knew that without the bank's interference there would be less credit restraint, less competition, and more state bank profitability. The states joined in with the businessmen;

they held large ownership stakes in their banks and coveted the windfalls that would be realized after the destruction of the federal bank.

The congressional debates of early 1811 suppressed the real issues in favor of the idealism of constitutionality. Fully 35 of the 39 speeches on the bank's recharter centered on the constitutional issue. Congress also focused on the bank's usurpation of a central banking role and its alleged interference with state banks and state rights. A final theme was the claimed dominance of the bank by its British stockholders, this despite the fact that foreign stockholders were barred from voting their shares. Vote or no, the foreigners were the beneficiaries of a government monopoly, and the dividends paid them were but a degrading tribute.

A bill for recharter was tabled indefinitely by a one-vote margin in the House. A similar bill was defeated by a one-vote margin in the Senate. Given the virulence of the antibank rhetoric, the bank won a moral victory. But moral victories mean little. The bank's protestations notwithstanding, dissolution commenced almost immediately. The bank was dead.

## 2. *The Second Bank: 1816-1836*

The bank was dead, but banking flourished. Many of the bank's operations continued in private hands after 1811. The Philadelphia office, acquired by businessman Stephen Girard, remained in business as a private banking firm housed in the same building and operated by the same staff. At the same time, entrepreneurs opened many new banks under state charter. Accordingly, the total volume of banking operations increased dramatically in the interregnum between the two United States banks. Bank notes in circulation and commercial loans more than doubled between 1811 and 1816.

But the new banking system soon ran into trouble. When the British raided Washington in 1814, banks across the country experienced runs on specie and stopped paying it out. In the absence of a federal regulator, the state authorities proved unable or unwilling to force banks to pay out specie or close. The result was a loss for bank customers and noteholders but a boon for bankers who no longer had to maintain large specie reserves. Bank notes in circulation became the equivalent of interest-free, indefinite loans from the public to the banks.

Predictably, suspension of specie redemption depreciated bank notes in circulation, which already traded at all sorts of discounts from par depending on location and the identity of the issuing bank. Commerce suffered, and the federal government, forced to accept depreciated state bank notes as payment for taxes, defaulted on some of its bonds. Government debt now depreciated as well, with the Treasury experiencing severe difficulty in finding any takers for new bond issues.

These chaotic conditions stimulated renewed calls for a national bank. Investors in government bonds favored such a bank as enhancing their prospects of repayment. State bankers opposed the measure, which they feared would end the suspension of specie redemption and increase competition in the banking industry. The practical necessity of a federal bank being manifest, however, the state banks lacked the political muscle to prevent the rechartering of the Bank of the United States, which Congress authorized in 1816 for a 20-year period.

The bank was dead; long live the bank. The second bank was just as powerful as the first and quite a bit bigger. Moreover, the national economy was now firmly embarked on a period of vigorous expansion and industrialization. The demand for the bank's services could only increase. Its rechartering after 20 years seemed inevitable.

But things quickly soured. The bank's original directors were incompetent or worse. All sorts of financial chicanery, insider loans, and outright frauds took place in the bank and its branch offices. The worst abuses occurred at the Baltimore branch, where the cashier, one James McCulloch, lent himself half a million dollars on no collateral as part of a fraudulent conspiracy that eventually cost more than $1.5 million.

By 1818—a mere two years after its resurrection—the bank was financially prostrate and politically unpopular. State governments began to enact punitive taxes on the bank or its branches, with the evident purpose of driving the bank out of business or at least out of state. McCulloch, whose misdeeds at the Baltimore branch had yet to be exposed, refused to pay the Maryland tax and was promptly sued by the state for nonpayment.

The case eventually reached the Supreme Court in one of the leading constitutional decisions of the nineteenth century. McCulloch v. Maryland, 17 U.S. (4 Wheat.) 316 (1819). Chief Justice Marshall's opinion sustaining the power of Congress to charter a bank, and denying Maryland the authority to tax a bank so chartered, is best known today for its sweeping interpretation of the federal commerce power. At the time, however, the opinion was equally important for its practical consequences. If a state could tax the bank or its branches, then the bank could not survive as a national institution. The *McCulloch* decision granted the bank a reprieve from execution at the hands of the state governments.

Eventually the bank came under responsible management. Frauds and chicanery ceased. The bank evolved into a central bank in the modern sense under the leadership of the brilliant but politically inept Nicholas Biddle, who became its president in 1823. Under Biddle's guidance the bank regulated the money supply by redeeming state bank notes for specie. It stabilized the currency, protected credit markets, and assisted the Treasury Department's operations. It encouraged state banks to maintain adequate specie reserves, thus assuming a de facto regulatory role in the banking system nationwide.

Despite these accomplishments—or perhaps because of them—the bank remained unpopular in many circles. State bankers, financial speculators, and business entrepreneurs saw the bank as a threat to profits and as a stumbling block to economic growth. Western farmers who had purchased land on credit blamed the bank for their difficulties in repaying the loans even though the loans usually had been extended by state banks. State politicians saw the bank as an unwarranted intrusion of federal power into areas reserved for state autonomy.

These interests had little in common other than dislike of the bank. For several years opposition was sporadic and disorganized. When Andrew Jackson assumed the presidency, however, the bank's foes gained a powerful leader whose courage and determination were exceeded only by his implacable hatred of the bank.

Congress passed legislation rechartering the bank in 1832, but Jackson vetoed the bill, issuing in the process a statement destined to become one of the leading state papers in American history. For all its fame, Jackson's veto message appears today as a confused jumble of contradictory ideas and distorted analysis. The bank was unconstitutional as an infringement on state's rights, said the president—despite Supreme Court decisions and decades of nearly universal consensus to the contrary. The bank was a tool of the rich—even though most influential opponents of the bank were as rich or richer than the bank's shareholders. The bank was not to be trusted to serve American interests because "more than a fourth part of the stock is held by foreigners"—even though foreign investors had no vote under the bank's charter. Whatever its analytical merits, the veto message was a political triumph. The bank's days were numbered.

Jackson followed his advantage by withdrawing government deposits from the bank and placing them in specially favored state-chartered banks. The bank, mortally wounded, died quietly in 1836 when its charter expired. Its principal office in Philadelphia continued under Biddle's leadership with a state charter, but after initial successes the successor bank failed in 1841, leaving Biddle a disgraced and pathetic figure.

## *3. Free Banking Era: 1836-1863*

With the fall of the Bank of the United States, the nation embarked on a period of banking without a central bank. The loss of a central bank had two principal effects. First, it unleashed powerful entrepreneurial forces eager to enter the lucrative banking business. These entrepreneurs pressed for state legislation allowing "free banking"—that is, easy entry into banking without the need for special legislative charter. More than half the states between 1837 and 1863 passed such free banking statutes, resulting in many new banks being formed during this period. The second consequence of the bank's demise was that responsibility for supervising the safety and soundness of banks passed to the states. Although some states such as New York proved effective regulators, other states were much less capable.

The combination of free entry and state regulation gave shape to the era between 1836 and 1863, commonly known as the "free banking era." Perhaps the most prominent feature of this period was the state of the national currency, which consisted of the circulating notes of state-chartered banks. Although such notes in theory were instantly redeemable in specie, the practical reality was different. To obtain redemption in specie it was necessary to deliver the note to the offices of the issuing bank, a task that was by no means trivial if the issuing bank happened to be located outside the major cities. Moreover, even if a note were presented, the holder could have no assurance that the bank would honor its promise to redeem in specie. The bank might have failed while the note was in circulation or might be operating under suspension of redemption. In either case, specie would not be forthcoming.

Accordingly, bank notes in circulation traded at discounts from par value reflecting the location and credit of the issuing bank. In 1845, for example, New York bank notes traded in Philadelphia at near par—with a discount of only .75 percent—but notes of some Michigan banks traded at a discount of 65 percent off par. These discounts were published in "bank note reporters" showing the current value of state bank notes in different financial centers. The lack of a single defined currency trading at par created obvious difficulties for trade, because for each transaction merchants had to calculate into the price the value of the currency with which payment was to be made.

The problem of currency values was aggravated by the phenomenon of "wildcat banking." Wildcat banks were so named because they were established so far out of the path of civilization that the only noises to be heard in their offices were the cries of the wildcat and other forest denizens. The owner of a wildcat bank would issue a flood of bank notes backed by minimal specie, calculating that few noteholders would ever find their way out to the wilderness to redeem the obligations. Although wildcat banking was possible under the old system of special charters, it was much easier to accomplish in free banking states because the entrepreneur did not have to convince the state legislature of his financial probity in order to obtain a charter. Not surprisingly, the failure rate among wildcat banks was high compared to that of their domesticated cousins in the financial centers.

Until recently, most historians have judged the free banking era a failure. They point to the problems of currency valuation as well as the large incidence of free bank failures. In Indiana, for example, 86 of the

104 free banks opened between 1852 and 1862 failed; even in New York, generally regarded as the most successful free banking state, 160 of 449 banks established between 1838 and 1863 failed.

Some revisionist scholars have debunked this negative view of the free banking era. They observe that although the failure rate was indeed high during the period, noteholders usually were paid in full. One study estimates that the total losses from bank failures in free banking states between 1837 and 1860 were less than $2 million, of which more than half the losses occurred in only one state, Michigan. Some have also claimed that wildcat banking was not nearly as serious a problem as many believed.

The debate between traditional and revisionist historians of the free banking era has obvious implications for banking policy today. If the free banking era is seen as a failure, as in the traditional view, the argument for governmental intervention and regulation of banking today is considerably stronger than if the era is seen as a moderate success, as in the revisionist view.

## 4. *National Bank Act: 1863-1864*

Whatever its merits as a means of providing private banking services, free banking was not well equipped to aid in the financing of government operations. After a period of unsatisfactory dealings with state banks, the federal government withdrew from the banking system altogether in 1846. The independent treasury system, established in that year, prohibited the government from using bank notes and mandated that public funds be kept in the custody of government officials rather than deposited in banks.

The independent treasury system served the nation's fiscal needs adequately in a period of domestic tranquillity and limited, passive government. With the outbreak of the Civil War, however, the system's defects as a means of financing a modern state became manifest. President Lincoln found no money at all in the Treasury when he took office in 1861. Worse, the federal government was blocked by law from turning to banks for emergency credit. Lincoln's treasury secretary, Salmon P. Chase, obtained congressional authorization to borrow $150 million from northern banks, but then considered himself bound by law to demand payment in specie rather than bank credit, thus stimulating massive hoarding of gold and constricting the money supply, a monetary effect exactly opposite to what was required to sustain the Union through an extended and costly conflict. Eventually, the shortage of gold and silver forced the banks and the federal government to suspend specie payments altogether.

Chase responded to the crisis by proposing a system that combined aspects of the old Bank of the United States and state free banking statutes. He advocated, essentially, a regime of federal free banking, with federally chartered institutions authorized to issue a uniform national currency. The proposal did not affect the legal status of the existing state-chartered banks, but the expectation was that all or nearly all state banks would convert over to federal charters if the measure passed. State banks were less than enthusiastic about the proposal, which they saw, correctly, as the approaching wedge of federal regulation. The measure, however, was politically popular both because the public believed it necessary to finance the war, and because businessmen were fed up with the inconveniences incident to the system of circulating state bank notes.

The measure—known as the National Bank Act—passed in 1863 and was amended in 1864. Contrary to Chase's expectations, however, state-chartered banks did not rush to convert over to federal charters; the vast majority of national banks chartered in the first few years were new start-ups rather than state conversions. Something of the stick was needed to supplement the carrot. Congress provided the stick in 1865 by imposing a punitive and constitutionally suspect 10 percent tax on state bank notes. State banks challenged the tax in court, but the Supreme Court sustained it in 1869, thus establishing an important constitutional precedent for the power of the federal government to discriminate against an otherwise lawful industry for regulatory purposes. Veazie Bank v. Fenno, 75 U.S. (8 Wall.) 533 (1869). Salmon Chase—now Chief Justice—wrote the Court's opinion sustaining the tax notwithstanding the fact that four years earlier he had been chiefly responsible for the enactment of the statute under review.

## 5. *From the Civil War to the Federal Reserve Act: 1865-1913*

Over the next half-century the banking industry evolved into an organization marked by three fundamental features: (1) dual banking—the system of overlapping state and federal chartering; (2) unit banking—the principle that banks should conduct their business out of only one office or, at most, out of a small number of geographically proximate offices; and (3) market segmentation—the splintering of the banking market into commercial banks, on the one hand, and thrift institutions (savings and loans and savings banks), on the other. None of these features represented any conscious or deliberate choice by the political system; once in place, however, they became deeply embedded political realities that have fundamentally structured the regulation and politics of banking up to the present day.

### a. The Dual Banking System

The tax on state bank notes sustained in *Veazie Bank* threatened the very existence of state-chartered banks because it effectively precluded them from issuing notes. It looked for a while as if state banks would indeed be extirpated. The number of national banks grew from 66 in 1863 to 1,640 in 1868, while state banks fell in number from 1,466 to 247 during the same period. Ultimately, however, the federal tax proved completely ineffectual. By the 1860s banks had developed the checking account as an effective substitute for circulating notes. When making a loan a bank could simply record a credit in the borrower's checking account instead of issuing bank notes to the borrower. The borrower could then transfer funds to others by means of the personal check instead of passing on bank notes. The check, like the bank note, was redeemable at the bank on demand (provided the customer had not overdrawn). The checking account represented an advance over the bank note because it offered greater security and flexibility for the customer. And because checks in circulation were not bank notes, they were not subject to the prohibitory 10 percent tax.

Thus even after *Veazie Bank* many banks continued under state charter through the simple expedient of replacing circulating notes with checking accounts. After a low point in 1868 the number of state banks rebounded rapidly until, by the 1890s, the number of state and federal banks were roughly equal. States won the race for new banking charters because they offered more desirable terms to banking entrepreneurs: minimum capital requirements in many states were much lower than for national banks; national banks were subject to minimum reserve requirements whereas most state banks were not; and state banks were not subject to the burdensome investment restrictions applicable to national banks, especially restrictions on the power of a bank to extend credit on the security of real property. By 1914 there were 14,512 state banks as compared with 7,518 national banks.

Thus the quite unintended consequence of the National Bank Act was to establish a "dual banking system"—a system of overlapping state and federal chartering, in which banks enjoy the choice of chartering agencies and in which state and federal authorities compete to attract bank charters. The dual system has remained a pervasive feature of American banking law and regulation up to the present day, although by now the accident of its birth is often forgotten.

### b. Unit Banking

The early history of banking in the United States would not have suggested that the industry would coalesce into a system of unit banking.

As we have seen, the Bank of the United States operated a nationwide branching system. At the state level the history was mixed. Branching was virtually unknown in New England. In the South many banks operated branches in the modern sense, although the number of branches was never very large. In the western (now midwestern) states of Indiana, Missouri, Ohio, and Iowa, state banks were established with monopoly powers and extensive branching networks; the State Bank of Ohio, established in 1845, operated 36 branches by 1863. Unlike branch banking as we understand it today, however, in which the branches are simply arms of the main bank, these early branching networks appear to have been loose confederations of institutions that, although denominated as "branches," actually enjoyed considerable autonomy in organization, capitalization, and operation. These western branching networks may have functioned as de facto cartels, with the authority of the central bank being exercised for the purpose of restricting interbank competition and maintaining monopoly profits.

Thus at the outbreak of the Civil War, branching practice was divided into three broad regions: the Northeast, where branching was unknown; the West, where branching took the form of loose confederations of local institutions; and the South, where banks tended to operate limited networks of branches of a type recognizable today. Laws specifically outlawing branch banking, however, were uncommon.

The National Bank Act profoundly changed this arrangement. The Act contained two provisions that seemed to require that the business of a national bank be conducted in a single location. In fact these provisions were not intended to outlaw branching, but rather to suppress wildcat banking by requiring banks to have a fixed and permanent abode. Nevertheless, the comptroller of the currency quickly ruled that the National Bank Act prohibited branching by national institutions.

The Act did not prohibit branching by state banks and, as amended in 1865, allowed state banks converting to national charter to retain their branching networks. As a practical matter, however, the statute extinguished the state branching networks as well. The Civil War destroyed the state banks in the South and with them, their existing branch networks. The new banks that appeared were established under federal charter and accordingly could not branch. In the West, the system of national chartering destroyed the monopoly position—and therefore the raison d'être—of the state branch banking networks. Most branch banks in the western states declared their independence and converted to federal charter. In the North, where branching had never taken hold, unit banking remained the norm among state banks after the Civil War, as it had been before.

The unit banking system, like the dual banking system, appears to have been born literally by accident. Yet as in the case of the dual banking system, unit banking, once established, created vested interests that in subsequent years would vigorously contest legislative efforts to change the status quo. Smaller institutions, mostly operating under state charter, came to fear competition from the big "money center" banks. They developed an ideology of the independent local bank that, they asserted, would serve the financial needs of small communities much better than the urban leviathans, whose sole interest would be to maximize profits and to drain capital out of local communities.

A coalition of country bankers expressed their views on the subject at an American Bankers Association convention in 1902. Branch banking by national banks, they said, would

> create a brood of two hundred or three hundred great central banks, with 10,000 to 15,000 branches in large cities as well as small, and as such branches would have no capital and only figure-head management, individualism in management would cease, local taxes [would] be evaded, [there would be] no home distribution of profits, local progress [would be] retarded, in short, the great central banks would skim the cream from the whole country to enrich [their own] exchequers.

This ideal of local autonomy became a fundamental tenet of banking policy and exerts a powerful influence even today in the politics of banking law and regulation.

The charge that big-city banks would drain capital out of rural areas was probably well-founded since the most efficient—and therefore the most profitable—use of capital at the time was in the burgeoning cities. However, the claim that capital would not be siphoned away from rural areas under the unit banking system was specious. Smaller banks tended to have a net capital surplus: More funds were brought in than could profitably be invested in the locality. A system of correspondent banking evolved to transfer and allocate capital across the nation. Smaller banks developed relationships with big urban banks in which some of the smaller bank's funds would be deposited at the large bank, and the large bank, in return, would provide check-clearing, investment brokerage and advice, and other services for the smaller institution. The result was a capital outflow from small-town and rural areas to the cities—exactly what the unit banking interests claimed would occur if branching were allowed.

The unit banking system—coupled with the low minimum capital requirements typically required for state-chartered banks—profoundly affected the structure of the American banking industry by decentralizing it and multiplying the number of banks, as shown in the table below.

| *Year* | *Number of Banks* |
|---|---|
| 1865 | 1,643 |
| 1880 | 2,696 |

| Year | Number of Banks |
|---|---|
| 1890 | 5,585 |
| 1900 | 8,100 |
| 1910 | 19,304 |
| 1914 | 22,030 |

The American system of decentralized small banks stood in sharp contrast to the system developing in other countries such as Canada, whose banking industries were dominated by a small number of large institutions operating nationwide branching networks.

### c. Market Segmentation

The period from 1865 to 1913 witnessed the growth of a new "species" of banking institution. For whatever reason, banks had long defined their role as serving the needs of commerce. The banking needs of individuals—other than the wealthy and privileged few—were not adequately served by banks in the nineteenth century. The thrift industry developed to make up for this deficiency and to help the less privileged classes realize the American dreams of financial security and home ownership.

As originally conceived, the thrift institution served a charitable rather than a profit-making purpose. The goal was social welfare, not private wealth. Traditional thrift values are classically displayed in Frank Capra's 1946 movie *It's A Wonderful Life*, in which Jimmy Stewart, as the local building and loan president, struggles to assist the working class and to fend off the greedy machinations of the local commercial banker.

Two types of thrift institutions developed in the nineteenth century. Savings banks—located principally in the Northeast—arose to help workers save a portion of their wages by providing depository services for small savers. Savings and loans (or building and loans) developed to help people of limited means save enough money to purchase a home. Both types of institution were typically held in "mutual" form—they were owned by depositors rather than shareholders. Although savings banks and savings and loans were established for different purposes (saving versus home acquisition), the functional distinction between them was never clear-cut. The distinction, however, became deeply embedded in the regulatory system, so that in important respects the legal regulations applicable to savings banks were different than those governing savings and loans.

The first savings bank was established in 1819 and the first savings and loan in 1831, but the growth of thrift institutions occurred after the Civil War. By 1887 there were more than 500 thrifts nationwide; by 1900 there were more than 5,000. The thrift industry became a political interest group with its own sophisticated lobby, seeking special regulatory favors not available to commercial banks (such as federal and state tax exemptions). The segmentation of the banking industry into commercial banks and thrifts has had a profound effect on the politics and economics of banking regulation, an effect that continues to influence developments in the banking industry today.

## 6. *Federal Reserve Act of 1913*

The National Bank Act established national banks and allowed the government to maintain a national currency. The comptroller of the currency exercised some regulatory authority over the banking system as the supervisor of federally chartered institutions. However, the country still lacked a central banking function of the sort that had been exercised by the Bank of the United States. Possibly as a result of the lack of a central authority controlling the money supply, the economy was subject to periodic panics. Financial crises occurred in 1873, 1884, 1890, 1893, and 1907. These panics were marked by bank runs, chaotic conditions in money markets, and, sometimes, serious long-run economic downturns. While farmers were especially hard-hit, the adverse effects of the panics were felt throughout the economy.

Blame for the panics was cast about widely, but the principal suspects were Wall Street bankers who, it was said, speculated with the public's money and with the interbank balances of small banks. Congress attempted to remedy the situation in 1913 with the Federal Reserve Act, the most revolutionary development in banking regulation since the National Bank Act of a half century earlier. Like the National Bank Act, the Federal Reserve Act did not create a new central bank such as the Bank of the United States, but instead drew on a less controversial model: bankers' clearinghouses, which were private arrangements among money center banks designed to facilitate check clearing and to provide emergency liquidity assistance to member banks. The Federal Reserve Act established a clearinghouse-type arrangement of 12 regional Federal Reserve banks, which were mixed public and private institutions enjoying some autonomy but supervised by a board of governors appointed by the president. All national banks were required to join the system and to keep a portion of their reserves on deposit with a Federal Reserve bank. State banks were permitted but not required to join. The system established a means of providing emergency liquidity assistance to banks experiencing runs, facilitated efficient check clearing by means of bookkeeping entries at the Federal Reserve banks, and provided some federal control over the money supply, especially after the Federal Reserve began to engage in coordinated open-market operations in the early 1920s.

The Federal Reserve Act significantly affected the balance of power under the dual banking system. National banks were forced to become members of the Federal Reserve System, but state banks were not. Complete success of the system depended on state banks voluntarily becoming members. The architects of the Federal Reserve Act confidently expected state banks to join in order to take advantage of check clearing and emergency liquidity assistance. But state banks resisted joining the system because doing so would subject them to federal regulation and inspection and to higher minimum reserve requirements. Only 17 state-chartered banks entered the system in its first year; and although by 1922, 1,648 state banks had joined, 19,566 state banks remained outside. After 1922 state bank membership declined again, falling to 1,177 in 1929. Thus the Federal Reserve System was unable to achieve effective control over the vast majority of smaller banks. Because large numbers of state banks remained outside the system, the correspondent banking arrangements that the Federal Reserve Act was designed to supersede remained a dominating force in American banking.

## 7. *Industry Consolidation: 1914-1933*

During the period from 1914 to 1933, powerful economic and political forces were pressing for consolidation in the banking industry. Unit banking, even supplemented with a developed system of correspondent relationships, was simply not as efficient a means of conducting many banking operations as was an integrated system of geographically dispersed offices under common ownership and control. Banking consolidation offered economies of scale, including internalized check clearance, that were probably more efficient than the correspondent banking system. Further, customers could benefit from consolidation to the extent that it allowed them to transact their banking business at a variety of different locations. Consolidation may also have offered banks the benefit of a diversified portfolio of assets: Unit banks that made almost all their loans in a given community were heavily dependent on the fortunes of that particular community, whereas banks with more extensive operations could diversify their risk by investing in a variety of different communities. The forces for banking consolidation paralleled in some respects the contemporaneous "chain store" movement, in which local grocery stores were supplanted by big firms with many retail outlets.

Not surprisingly, banking consolidation posed a severe threat to unit banks. Like local grocers, unit banks feared competition from big, geographically diversified rivals, and they exercised their considerable political muscle to prevent consolidation from occurring. The unit banking forces were able to maintain many of the existing legal impediments to banking consolidation. They were not, however, able to suppress the economic pressures for consolidation, any more than King Canute was able to command the tides. When the irresistible force of consolidation met the immovable obstacle of unit banking, something had to give. The clash between these contradictory forces resulted in a number of compromise formations, of which the most important were (1) state branch banking, (2) chain banking, (3) group banking (bank holding companies), and (4) bank mergers.

### a. Branch Banking

By the turn of the century it was evident that national banks would not be able to exercise special branching privileges under the dual banking system. But if authorized by state law, state banks could establish branches. Although opposition to branching remained strong, and many states enacted antibranching statutes, a few states began to permit branching for state institutions relatively early in the century. Support for these branching statutes came from state-chartered city banks that wanted to establish branches to reach retail customers within their home cities. Although rural banks continued to oppose branching in order to insulate themselves from competition, their opposition was muted to some extent by the fact that the institutions they perceived as the greatest threat—the big national banks—would not be permitted to branch if the state liberalized its own branching laws. Among the early states permitting some form of branching were California, Delaware, Florida, Georgia, Maine, Massachusetts, and New York.

After a slow start, branch banking grew rapidly. The brilliant California banker, A.P. Giannini, spectacularly demonstrated the advantages of branch banking by building up the Bank of Italy (later the Bank of America) into one of the nation's largest financial institutions by means of extensive statewide branching. By the 1920s branch banking expanded rapidly; the total number of bank branches increased from 1,281 in 1920 to 2,525 in 1925 to 3,522 in 1930.

The growth of state branch banking destabilized the dual banking system. Heretofore, state banks had been small unit banks. Now, in states permitting branching, state banks were growing rapidly in size and enjoyed a competitive edge over their national bank rivals that were not permitted to branch. To use a traditional metaphor of banking politics, the playing field was no longer level. The branch banking movement, accordingly, posed a severe threat to the national banking system and to the Federal Reserve Board, for if the inequality continued it was predictable that federally chartered institutions would start to convert over to state charters and leave the Federal Reserve System. National banks sought authority to branch but were stoutly resisted by state banking interests.

In 1927, after an extended legislative battle, Congress passed the McFadden Act, which authorized national banks to establish branches in their home office cities if state law granted similar privileges to state banks. Although the McFadden Act as originally drafted did not return national banks to competitive equality as regards branching (because they were not permitted to branch outside of their home cities), the regulatory disparity was sufficiently alleviated to stem the erosion of the national banking system.

### b. Chain Banking

Where branching was prohibited, or made difficult by statutory or regulatory restrictions, there was an obvious alternative available to the enterprising banker: rather than own a bank with branches, simply own a number of separate banks. This type of arrangement came to be known as "chain banking." Individual ownership of numerous banks was not an ideal substitute for branching because of legal requirements that the corporate enterprises be kept separate. However, a considerable overlap of operations could be achieved at the practical level if all banks in the chain were wholly owned by a single individual or entity (so that fiduciary duties to minority shareholders did not have to be considered).

Extensive chains developed rather early in postbellum banking history. The major chains were in the Midwest, Pacific Northwest, and South. Some of these banking chains grew very large; one, the Whitham-Manley chain, contained over 180 banks at its peak in the early 1920s. Chain banking, however, was largely a rural and small town phenomenon and did not catch on in the big financial centers. This limited success was due to several defects inherent in the chain banking form. Because chain banking involved individual ownership of banks, it did not provide ready access to capital markets nor did it offer easy opportunities for banking firms to become directly involved in nonbanking businesses. Moreover, chain banking was not particularly conducive to centralized management because in form the banking chain was a set of entirely independent institutions united only by common individual ownership.

### c. Group Banking (Bank Holding Companies)

Group banking—banking through the use of bank holding companies—offered a more flexible structure for bank expansion. A bank holding company is simply a corporation that owns one or more banks. Like chain banking, group banking allowed banking institutions to circumvent restrictive rules against branch banking. But the bank holding company provided better access to capital markets since the holding company was a corporation with shares that could be sold to the public. In addition, the holding company could conduct operations of a nonbanking sort, either directly or through a subsidiary. Accordingly, the bank holding company allowed banking firms to circumvent restrictive rules on the types of business in which banks could engage. Finally, the bank holding company was much more suitable to centralized management than was the banking chain because the holding company—usually under the domination of a central "lead" bank—could oversee and guide the operations of all the subsidiary banks.

Bank holding companies developed somewhat later than chain banks, largely because many early state corporate laws prohibited one corporation from owning stock in another corporation. Bank holding companies grew dramatically in the 1920s, however, as a result of the same underlying economic forces that stimulated the growth of branch banking during this period. Where branching was restricted or prohibited, the economies of scale were best achieved through expansion by means of holding companies.

### d. Bank Mergers

Consolidation in banking also occurred via the bank merger, which became increasingly popular after 1920. One hundred eighty-three banks were absorbed by other banks in 1920, 356 in 1925, and 698 in 1930. During the period from 1921 to 1931, more than 5,000 banks were absorbed. Many of these mergers were between smaller institutions, but some involved large financial center banks; in one 1930 merger, the Chase bank consolidated with two other institutions to form what at the time was the largest financial institution in the world.

No single cause appears to have been responsible for these bank mergers. In some states, notably California, mergers were a means by which an expansion-minded bank could circumvent state rules prohibiting the establishment of de novo branches in communities where other banks were in operation. Elsewhere mergers occurred to achieve economies of scale, to rescue failing institutions by consolidating them with healthy ones, or to close down solvent but unprofitable institutions. Many politicians and scholars also charged, especially after the banking crisis of 1933, that banks had consummated mergers to increase their size and prestige without regard to the financial soundness of the transaction.

Taken together, branch banking, chain banking, group banking, and bank mergers contributed to a significant consolidation in the banking industry. Bank mergers and bank failures soon outpaced the rate of new bank formation: The number of commercial banks in the United States grew from 24,514 in 1910 to 30,390 by 1920, but thereafter fell to 28,442 in 1925, 23,679 in 1930, and 15,478 in 1935. Moreover, these statistics understate the actual amount of consolidation in the industry because they do not include instances of de facto consolidation through group, chain, and branch banking. By 1929 the structure of American banking was very different from what it had been at the turn of the century.

## 8. The Banking Crisis: 1929-1933

Although by the late 1920s the banking industry appeared to be generally healthy, even a roaring bull market could not disguise its underlying weaknesses. For reasons already discussed—the diseconomies of scale and lack of asset diversification of small unit banks—the bank failure rate was significant during this period. Five hundred and one banks failed in 1921, representing 1.6 percent of all banks in operation; in 1926, the worst failure year prior to the stock market crash of 1929, 956 banks failed, representing 3.4 percent of banks in operation. Failures were common in the thrift industry as well. Thus even before the onset of the Depression the public had reason to doubt the soundness of the banking system.

Prior to 1930, bank failures tended to be isolated (albeit increasingly common) events. In 1930, however, a rash of bank failures in the Midwest and South sparked what economists Milton Friedman and Anna Schwartz call a "contagion of fear" among depositors. Waves of generalized bank panics took place in each of the following years: 1,345 banks failed in 1930, 2,298 in 1931, and 1,456 in 1932. Congress attempted to remedy the situation in 1932 by establishing the Reconstruction Finance Corporation to loan funds to banks experiencing liquidity problems. The measure was only partially successful.

Early in 1933 the public lost all remaining confidence in the banking system. Bank panics occurred in state after state, forcing state governments to declare banking "holidays," an ironic misnomer for governmentally imposed suspensions of payouts to depositors. But while banking holidays might temporarily relieve the pressure on banks in one state, they increased the pressure on the system as a whole as depositors in other states rushed to withdraw their funds in anticipation that a bank holiday would be declared in their state. By March 1933 over half the states had declared banking holidays.

Finally, the unimaginable happened: The banking system collapsed. President Roosevelt, who had taken office just two days earlier, declared a nationwide banking holiday on March 6, 1933. The cessation of banking activities was complete: Unlike in earlier panics, in which banks ceased paying out deposits or notes but otherwise continued in operation, all banking stopped in the catastrophe of 1933. Banks began to reopen after about a week, but approximately 5,000 were unable to do so immediately, and over 2,000 never reopened.

Public opinion at the time blamed the disaster on Wall Street. Large banks and securities firms were alleged to have engaged in reckless speculation with the public's money and to have fallen prey to numerous conflicts of interest stemming from affiliations between commercial and investment banks. More recently, some scholars have questioned the view that malfeasance and breaches of trust by Wall Street money men caused the crisis, instead attributing much of the disruption to government incompetence. According to Milton Friedman and Anna Schwartz, for example, the banking holiday of 1933 "came close to being worse than the disease." They fault the Federal Reserve for failing to supply the banking system with sufficient liquidity in the years 1929-1933.

Whatever its causes, the disaster of 1933 swept away the political opposition that had stymied earlier movements for banking reform. Congress quickly passed the Banking Act of 1933, or Glass-Steagall Act, a fundamental piece of legislation that remains, in modified form, the centerpiece of American banking policy. The Banking Act of 1933 contained five provisions that are of special interest in the history of banking law.

### a. Separation of Investment and Commercial Banking

Responding to political charges that the Depression had been caused by bank speculation in securities, the Glass-Steagall Act separated commercial banking from investment banking. Securities firms were not to accept deposits or affiliate with deposit-taking institutions; and commercial bank members of the Federal Reserve System were barred from participating, either directly or indirectly, in many aspects of the securities business.

### b. Federal Deposit Insurance

The statute established a program of federal deposit insurance. A number of states—principally rural states with strong unit banking interests—had implemented deposit insurance systems prior to 1933; although these systems could not withstand the national banking crisis, they provided a model for the federal legislation. In this respect the federal legislation of 1933 resembles the earlier statutes of 1913 and 1863, which also drew heavily on prior state experience. The Banking Act of 1933 provided federal deposit insurance for qualified members of the Federal Reserve System and established the Federal Deposit Insurance Corporation (FDIC) to oversee the system. The purpose of deposit insurance was to preclude bank runs by assuring depositors that even if their banks failed their funds would be secure.

### c. Limitations on Deposit Interest

The 1933 legislation prohibited the payment of interest on checking accounts and permitted regulation of the interest paid on time and savings deposits. These measures were designed to reduce the cost of funds for banks by suppressing ruinous competition for deposits.

### d. Holding Company Regulation

The legislation for the first time regulated bank holding companies at the federal level by requiring multibank holding companies to obtain Federal Reserve approval before they could vote stock in subsidiary banks if any subsidiary bank was a member of the Federal Reserve System. In addition, the statute limited transactions between member banks and affiliates, including holding company affiliates. A 1935 amendment exempted one-bank holding companies (holding companies that owned only one bank) from these rules.

### e. Branch Banking

Finally, the Banking Act of 1933 amended the McFadden Act to expand the branching privileges of national banks. The McFadden Act had allowed national banks to branch only within their home cities, even in states where state-chartered institutions enjoyed broader branching privileges. Congress rectified this competitive inequality by giving national banks the same branching rights as state-chartered banks in the jurisdiction. Thus, national banks could branch at any location within their home state that would be permitted to similarly situated state banks under state law. National banks were barred from branching across state lines, however. The principle thus established—that of "competitive equality"—has been a shibboleth of dual banking ever since.

The Banking Act of 1933 profoundly influenced the structure and politics of banking. The pros and cons of its various provisions continue to be hotly debated. There are two principal views. One perspective sees the legislation as serving important public interests in preventing bank failures and bank panics, deterring speculation and conflicts of interest, and suppressing unhealthy competition. A second point of view sees the statute as principally serving the narrow economic interests of the affected industries: The divorce of investment and commercial banking protected each industry from competition by the other; the regulation of interest on deposits created a government-sponsored and government-enforced cartel fixing the price for deposits; and deposit insurance represented a victory for the politically powerful unit banks, which were much more failure-prone than their big-city rivals.

The Depression also spawned fundamental legislation for the thrift industry. In 1932 Congress created the Federal Home Loan Bank System. Modeled on the Federal Reserve System, the Home Loan Bank System included 12 regional Home Loan Banks and the Federal Home Loan Bank Board (FHLBB), a federal agency with functions similar to those of the Federal Reserve's Board of Governors. In 1933 Congress passed the Home Owner's Loan Act, allowing the FHLBB to charter mutual savings and loan associations. The following year, in the National Housing Act, Congress established the Federal Savings and Loan Insurance Corporation (FSLIC) to administer a federal deposit insurance scheme for savings and loans. Also in 1934 Congress passed the Federal Credit Union Act, authorizing the federal chartering of credit unions.

## 9. *Years of Stability: 1934-1980*

After 1934 the banking system settled into an extended period of relative stability. Between 1934 and the late 1970s, there were no fundamental changes in the structure of bank regulation. The changes that did occur tended to be preventive in nature—that is, the regulatory system acted to maintain the status quo against marketplace forces that were threatening to disrupt existing relationships.

Three principal reasons explain this long period of stability. First, the political accommodations of the Depression era legislation proved remarkably durable. The limitations on deposit interest insulated banks and thrift institutions from any urgent need to compete for funds; the separation of commercial and investment banking benefited the banking and the securities industries by prohibiting them from competing with each other; and the separate regulatory schemes for thrift institutions proved congenial to both thrifts and banks because each industry obtained a regulatory authority that was responsive to its particular needs and interests. The industries did not want to upset this stable—and profitable—arrangement.

Second, the Depression's trauma created a culture of risk-aversion in the banking industry. The stuffy, white-shirted banker of popular imagination was an exaggerated caricature of emblematic attitudes actually displayed by many bankers. A wit once defined a banker as someone who never does anything for the first time—a definition that had considerable substance during these years.

Third, the problem of bank failure largely disappeared. The massive failures of 1930-1933 weeded out the most inefficient banks. Meanwhile, federal deposit insurance proved remarkably successful at preventing runs, especially after Congress authorized state banks that were not members of the Federal Reserve System to obtain deposit insurance. From the end of World War II through the late 1970s, the average failure rate for commercial banks was less than .1 percent: Fewer than one bank in a thousand failed in a given year. Banks that failed or disappeared through merger were replaced by an approximately equal number of new banks. Between 1933 and 1970 the number of commercial banks in the country fluctuated in a narrow range between approximately 13,000 and 14,000. Failures in the thrift industry were infrequent as well, although the rate was somewhat higher than for commercial banks. Only 120 savings and loans failed between 1935 and 1979.

The stability in the system during these years did not signal a complete lack of political controversy, however. Simmering beneath the surface were disputes over issues of geographic bank expansion, either by branching or by holding companies. Further, the later years of this period saw important developments in two other areas: consumer regulation and the growth of thrift institutions.

### a. Geographic Bank Expansion

#### *i. Branch Banking*

As noted above, in the early years of the century many states opted for unit banking—a policy that each bank could have one and only one deposit-taking facility. A large number of these unit banking states amended their laws during the Depression to allow branch banking, either on a statewide basis or limited to defined regions within a state. Support for liberalized branching came from the weaker unit banks that would have to close unless they could merge with a stronger institution. Antibranching laws impeded this kind of "rescue" merger because the acquiring bank could not operate the office of the acquired bank as a branch. Ironically, therefore, the very forces that had campaigned most strongly for unit banking—small or inefficiently managed local banks—eventually supported modification of the unit banking rules.

Unit banking gradually gave way to branch banking. During the 1930s, 18 states authorized limited or statewide branching, and, as shown below, the trend continued thereafter.

| *Year* | *% of Banks Operating Branches* |
|---|---|
| 1920 | 1.7 |
| 1930 | 3.2 |

| Year | % of Banks Operating Branches |
|---|---|
| 1940 | 6.6 |
| 1950 | 8.8 |
| 1960 | 17.3 |
| 1970 | 29.2 |
| 1979 | 44.7 |

Despite the rapid increases in branching, domestic banks were not permitted to branch across state lines. Due to a gap in the statutory framework, however, foreign banks were not so restricted. They could establish branches in many states and engage in deposit-collection and lending activities indistinguishable from those of domestic banks. In the 1970s foreign banks rushed to exploit this special status, with predictable political consequences: Domestic banks cried "foul!" Congress responded with the International Banking Act of 1978, which eliminated most of the interstate branching privileges previously enjoyed by foreign banks.

### *ii. Bank Holding Companies*

In addition to the gradual increase in branch banking, the years 1933-1979 witnessed significant increases in the number of banks held in holding company form. However, unlike branch banking, where the statutory changes occurred at the state level, the holding company issue generated important federal legislation.

In the years following passage of the Banking Act of 1933, the Federal Reserve Board lobbied for federal legislation regulating companies holding banks that were not members of the Federal Reserve System. The Federal Reserve was anxious to expand its regulatory authority as well as to remove the incentive for holding companies to escape federal regulation by having their subsidiary banks leave the Federal Reserve System. Joining the Federal Reserve in the request for new legislation were smaller banks that feared competition from the big "money center" banks. These big banks could circumvent the rules against interstate branching by establishing holding companies and opening subsidiary banks in other states; since these were not "branches," they were not barred by the McFadden Act.

Congress responded in 1956 with the Bank Holding Company Act, which extended federal regulation to all bank holding companies, whether or not their subsidiary banks were members of the Federal Reserve System. The so-called Douglas Amendment prohibited interstate acquisitions of banks by bank holding companies unless specifically authorized by a statute in the state where the acquired bank was located. Further, the 1956 statute limited the types of nonbanking activities a bank holding company could engage in to activities "of a financial, fiduciary, or insurance nature" that were "so closely related to the business of banking . . . as to be a proper incident thereto." Each of these provisions has been important in the subsequent development of banking structure in the United States.

The Bank Holding Company Act expressly exempted one-bank holding companies, which at the time were mostly small institutions in unit banking states. Although the one-bank holding company exemption was adopted at the behest of the unit banking interests, it provided a regulatory loophole that was eventually exploited by urban banks. A bank could engage (indirectly) in nonbanking businesses of all sorts simply by transforming itself into a subsidiary of a one-bank holding company and causing the holding company to engage in nonbanking activities either directly or through a separately incorporated subsidiary. After a relatively slow start, banks began to form one-bank holding companies at an accelerating pace in the late 1960s.

Smaller banks, joined by multibank holding companies and the Federal Reserve, launched a legislative campaign to regulate one-bank holding companies, claiming, among other things, that if banks were allowed to affiliate with nonbanking businesses, the consequence would be the development of a Japanese-style "zaibatsu" system of large banking-industrial conglomerates (this being prior to the Japanese "economic miracle" of the 1970s, it was assumed that a zaibatsu-type system would be undesirable). Congress passed legislation in 1970 regulating one-bank holding companies and tightening up the test for nonbanking activities permitted to any holding company by requiring that nonbanking activities not only be closely related to banking, but also that the public benefits of such activities outweigh the expected adverse effects.

Despite these regulations, bank holding companies have increased in size and importance after 1970. By 1978 the bank holding company form was the dominant structure in the entire banking industry, with approximately 71 percent of total domestic banking deposits controlled by subsidiaries of bank holding companies.

The holding company movement affected the thrift industry as well, although the rate of holding company formation for thrifts was lower than for banks. In 1955 Lehman Brothers, an investment banking house, established the first savings and loan holding company. This was an obvious attempt by the investment banking industry to cross over the Great Wall of the Glass-Steagall Act and invade the hinterlands of banking. Congress responded in 1959 with the Savings and Loan Holding Company Act, which provided that firms owning more than one thrift institution could engage in nonthrift activities only as permitted by the FSLIC. As in the case of commercial banks, however, "one-thrift" holding companies were exempted (provided the subsidiary savings and loan held a specified percentage of its assets in home mortgages).

### b. Consumer Protection and Antidiscrimination Regulation

The flowering of the consumer movement in the 1970s resulted in extensive regulation of bank activities. Underlying these changes was a perception that banks frequently took advantage of small or unsophisticated customers by imposing "hidden" fees and interest charges. Banks were also accused of "redlining"—drawing a "red line" around impoverished urban areas and refusing to make any loans to borrowers located within the areas so marked.

Congress responded with a plethora of new laws. Three statutes are particularly important in the area of consumer protection: (1) the Truth-in-Lending Act of 1968, requiring standard form disclosure for many types of consumer credit; (2) the Fair Credit Reporting Act of 1970, protecting individuals against false or outdated information circulated by credit rating agencies and giving individuals rights of access to report information; and (3) the Right to Financial Privacy Act of 1978, giving individuals a right to notice when government agencies request access to their financial records.

In the antidiscrimination area, Congress also passed three important statutes: (1) the Equal Credit Opportunity Act in 1975, prohibiting discrimination against women and other groups in the allocation of credit; (2) the Home Mortgage Disclosure Act of 1975, requiring financial institutions to maintain records from which patterns of redlining can be determined, and (3) the Community Reinvestment Act of 1977, requiring regulatory agencies to encourage the provision of credit to local communities.

### c. Growth of the Thrift Industry

Beginning in about 1960 the thrift industry, long the poor cousins of commercial banks, began a period of rapid expansion that lasted until the mid-1980s. This growth spurt appears to have been caused by a number of factors: the remarkable rate of new home construction during these years; the growth in personal income and wealth, especially in the middle-class market segment traditionally served by the thrift industry; the breakdown of the charitable ethic of thrift management and its replacement with a commercial profit motive; and, especially in later years, easy entry into the thrift business that allowed a number of unsavory or unqualified individuals to acquire and operate thrifts.

All thrift institutions grew rapidly during this period. Perhaps the most remarkable success story, however, was the credit union movement. Credit unions have been around since early in the century. They sprang from the same public-spirited impulse that had earlier given rise to the savings bank and the savings and loan. But while the savings bank was intended to encourage thrift, and the savings and loan to facilitate home ownership, the credit union was intended to facilitate the supply of consumer credit to workers, farmers, and other worthy borrowers whose credit needs were not being adequately served by existing banking facilities.

Unlike other bank-like institutions, the credit union grew up around the workplace. Employers actively supported the establishment of credit unions among their workers as a means of improving the welfare, morale, and reliability of their workers. Credit unions grew at a phenomenal pace, as shown in the table below.

| *Year* | *Total Assets (in billions)* |
|---|---|
| 1960 | $ 7 |
| 1965 | 11 |
| 1970 | 18 |
| 1975 | 38 |
| 1980 | 73 |

By the close of 1979 the thrift industry represented a significant portion of the nation's total financial intermediation. Problems in the thrift industry, accordingly, represented a threat to the economy as a whole—as would be demonstrated in the savings and loan crisis of the 1980s.

## 10. *The Revolution: 1979 to the Present*

The period of banking stability that followed the Depression came to a crashing halt in the late 1970s. Since 1979 banking has undergone a revolution as profound and wrenching as any prior period in history. Every element of the banking structure established in 1933 has been dismantled or severely modified. This banking revolution has been accomplished by agency action, judicial decision, and six important statutes: the Depository Institution Deregulation and Monetary Control Act of 1980 (DIDMCA); the Depository Institutions Act of 1982 (Garn-St Germain Act); the Competitive Equality Banking Act of 1987 (CEBA); the Financial Institutions Reform, Recovery and Enforcement Act of 1989 (FIRREA); the Federal Deposit Insurance Corporation Improvement Act of 1991 (FDICIA); and the Riegle-Neal Interstate Banking and Branching Efficiency Act of 1994. Above all, however, the revolution in banking has occurred outside the legal system through the medium of fast-paced developments in the marketplace.

Fundamental questions are again raised about the nature and purpose of banking regulation. If their predecessors never did anything for the first time, today's bankers do almost everything for the first time. The new era in banking has been equally challenging for bank lawyers, who must adjust the advice they give their clients to account for rapid changes in statutes, regulations, and business conditions.

The recent upheavals in banking have fundamentally altered every aspect of the industry. The most salient areas of change, however, are these: (1) deposit interest rates have been deregulated; (2) geographic restraints on bank expansion are being dismantled; (3) massive breaches have been opened in the Glass-Steagall "wall" between banking and securities activities; (4) differences between different categories of financial institution—commercial banks, savings and loans, credit unions, even securities firms, life insurance companies, and pension funds—have become less important; and (5) bank failure has again become a serious problem, especially in the savings and loan industry, where a wave of failures during the 1980s imposed hundreds of billions of dollars in costs on the nation's taxpayers. We discuss these different elements of the revolution in turn.

### a. Deregulation of Deposit Interest Rates

As was the case for the Depression-era banking revolution, the banking revolution of the 1980s and 1990s is first and foremost the product of unusual macroeconomic conditions. The extraordinary increase in world oil prices during the 1970s caused a serious inflation in the American economy during 1978-1979. In October 1979, the Federal Reserve Board adopted tight monetary policies in an attempt to curb the price spiral. The policies were ultimately successful, but in the short term the restriction in the money supply, coupled with the natural effects of inflation, drove interest rates to record levels, peaking above 21 percent for the prime rate in 1980.

The sudden rise in interest rates threatened the structure of deposit interest regulation. The Banking Act of 1933 prohibited the payment of interest on checking accounts, and the Federal Reserve Board's Regulation Q placed a ceiling on the interest rates banks and thrift institutions could pay on time and savings accounts. This was fine when interest rates were low, as was the case for most of the period from 1933 to 1978. Depositors did not incur any great costs placing their funds with a bank or thrift institution; and although depository institutions could not engage in direct price competition, they engaged in vigorous "nonprice" competition for deposits, for example by offering "free" checking or by giving prizes of various sorts for opening accounts. When nominal interest rates soared in the late 1970s, however, the opportunity cost to the customer of placing funds on deposit at a bank or thrift became very large. Customers were no longer willing to leave their funds in low interest bank accounts when they could earn 14 or 15 percent through some other investment.

The result was massive "disintermediation," a long word that means simply that customers withdrew their funds from banks and invested them elsewhere. The asylum of choice for banking refugees was the money market mutual fund, a professionally managed investment pool holding a diversified portfolio of money market investments, such as commercial paper (short-term unsecured corporate debt) and government securities. The money market fund offered a safe, high-yield investment, in many cases with limited checking privileges. During the late 1970s money market funds grew at a phenomenal pace, with assets increasing from less than $4 billion in 1978 to over $60 billion in 1980. Most of these funds came from commercial banks and savings and loans.

Although minor episodes of disintermediation had occurred earlier (late 1960s, 1973-1974) with little lasting effect, the hemorrhage of funds in 1978-1980 drove the banking industry into crisis. The Regulation Q price ceiling, long the banker's friend because it suppressed competition, now became the banker's enemy. Desperate for deposits, depository institutions sought ways around the regulation. Banks offered unregulated large-denomination certificates of deposit (CDs) at market rates. Savings and loans entered the checking business with the negotiable order of withdrawal (NOW) account. Eventually Congress acted, passing the DIDMCA, which mandated the phase-out of interest rate ceilings and authorized the payment of interest on checking accounts. Two years later Congress sped the process along in the Garn-St Germain Act, which authorized depository institutions to offer insured money market funds, eliminated the "thrift differential" in Regulation Q (under which thrift institutions were allowed to pay slightly higher interest on time and savings accounts than could banks), and authorized "Super-NOW" accounts with deregulated interest rates. Today interest rates are effectively deregulated throughout the banking industry.

### b. Dismantling of Geographic Restraints on Bank Expansion

All of the geographic barriers that once segmented the banking market are rapidly being dismantled. The changes have occurred both within states, with the rapid elimination of most unit banking rules, and nationwide, with the remarkable growth of interstate banking.

### i. Branch Banking

The advent of the Automatic Teller Machine (ATM) posed a challenge to unit banking legislation in many states. ATMs offer great convenience since they allow the customer to conduct routine banking transactions at all hours and in a variety of locations. Public as well as industry demand during the 1970s and 1980s generated legislation in many states liberalizing branching rules to allow banks to operate remote ATMs. But branching through ATMs increased competition for banking services, thus undermining the basic function of branching restrictions in general. Accordingly, the political coalition in favor of unit banking rules began to disintegrate in many states, leading to widespread liberalization of branching rules. Although branching rules still exercise an important influence on some banking markets, the trend nationally is towards statewide branching.

### ii. Interstate Banking

Even more significant than the liberalization of branching rules within states has been the breakdown of the barriers that cabined banks within the borders of a single state. Interstate banking, once the exception, is now the norm. During the 1970s and 1980s banks found any number of means of operating interstate, including nonbank holding company subsidiaries, "loan production offices," "consumer" or "nonbank" banks, international banking subsidiaries, credit card operations, ATM networks, interstate acquisition of failing institutions, deposit solicitation, and much more. All of these devices permitted banks to circumvent the apparently hard and fast rules against interstate banking.

Even more important than these various devices were acquisitions by bank holding companies pursuant to the Douglas Amendment to the Bank Holding Company Act, which allowed interstate acquisitions only if specifically authorized by legislation in the acquired bank's state. For many years small bank interests blocked attempts in state legislatures to authorize interstate expansion. In 1982, however, states in the New England region invented the "regional banking compact," which is simply an informal agreement among states to open their banking markets to each other but to exclude other states. From the perspective of banks in states authorizing such legislation, regional banking compacts had the great advantage of excluding states such as New York, Illinois, and California that are home to the so-called money center banks.

The Supreme Court upheld regional banking legislation in Northeast Bancorp v. Board of Governors of the Federal Reserve System, 472 U.S. 159 (1985), sparking a nationwide wave of interstate banking legislation. Some states permitted full nationwide banking through holding companies, some permitted full nationwide banking at a certain date in the future, some permitted interstate banking within a specified region, and one or two continued to prohibit all interstate banking. The trend, however, was in the direction of free interstate banking at the holding company level.

In 1994 Congress dramatically changed the ground rules for interstate banking by enacting the Riegle-Neal Interstate Banking and Branching Efficiency Act. This statute repeals the Douglas Amendment to the Bank Holding Company Act and provides instead that, subject to certain exceptions, the Fed may approve interstate acquisitions by adequately capitalized and adequately managed bank holding companies "without regard to whether such transaction is prohibited under the law of any State." The statute permits interstate bank mergers as of June 1997, subject to the power of states to opt out or accelerate the effective date. Interstate *branching,* as opposed to holding company acquisitions or mergers, is also authorized, but to a more limited extent: a bank may branch into another state, but only if the host state has enacted a law that expressly permits all out-of-state banks to open branches within its borders. Foreign banks are given the same interstate branching rights as those enjoyed by national banks located in the same home state. The Riegle-Neal Act constitutes a new charter for geographic bank expansion; it is likely, over the coming years, to facilitate even greater consolidation in the industry than has been observed already.

One consequence of the interstate banking movement has been to create so-called super-regional banks, institutions located outside the money center cities of New York, Chicago, and Los Angeles that have grown large through mergers and acquisitions. Super-regional banks have proved vigorous competitors for the big money center banks.

### c. Breakdown of the Glass-Steagall Wall

The once-sacrosanct wall between investment and commercial banking is also crumbling and seems ready to fall. Nonbanks invaded the commercial banking turf by offering money market funds with checking privileges. Customers can conduct a variety of banking activities through money market funds, although usually they are not allowed to draw small checks and often cannot withdraw cash. Securities firms also invaded the core banking market of making commercial loans by means of the commercial paper market. Because interest rates on commercial paper are lower than rates on bank loans, many corporations have taken to placing commercial paper for their short-term financing needs, thus "eliminating the middle man" (the bank) and saving money. Banks have counterattacked by invading the securities business. They now serve as investment advisors to mutual funds, act as stock brokers, and compete with securities firms in the market for placing commercial paper with buyers. Even more significantly, securities subsidiaries of bank holding companies have been allowed to engage in the full range of traditional securities activities, including the underwriting of corporate debt and equity issues.

### d. Breakdown of Distinctions Among Financial Institutions

One of the most remarkable features of the 1980s revolution in banking was the blurring of distinctions among types of financial institutions. The differences between banks and thrift institutions are rapidly diminishing. These days the notion of a thrift institution as a quasi-charitable enterprise for the benefit of the working and immigrant classes is completely outmoded. Thrifts, like banks, are profit-seeking providers of financial services. For the most part, bank customers today do not care—and often do not know—whether they are using a bank or a thrift institution for their banking needs. Thrifts are now permitted to offer interest-bearing checking accounts and, because of deregulation at the state and federal level, now have broad powers to make commercial loans and acquire other assets outside of their traditional portfolios of home mortgages and government securities.

In some respects the 1989 FIRREA statute further blurred the distinction between banks and thrifts by permitting thrifts to recharter as banks and by permitting bank holding companies to acquire healthy thrifts. In one other respect, however, this statute reinforced the traditional distinction between banks and thrifts by requiring savings associations to maintain a relatively large proportion of their assets in the form of home mortgages or risk being treated as banks for regulatory purposes. Some have prophesied that these strict rules on thrift investments, coupled with relatively harsh minimum capital standards and higher insurance assessments also mandated by FIRREA, will eventually spell the doom of the thrift industry as a distinct line of commerce, as thrift institutions will either go out of business or consolidate with commercial banking organizations. At present, however, it is too early to foretell how these changes will affect the thrift industry—beyond the indubitable proposition that the impact will be profound and long-lasting.

Just as distinctions between thrifts and commercial banks are vanishing within the banking industry, so are the differences between these traditional depository institutions and other providers of financial services. As we have noted, banks and thrifts have entered the securities business, and securities firms have invaded banking. To be sure, it is still possible to tell a securities firm like Merrill, Lynch, Pierce Fenner & Smith from a commercial bank like Citibank. But in many respects the operations of these two financial giants are overlapping, and the areas of overlap are surely going to expand over the coming years. Somewhat further afield, but still highly relevant, are the life insurance companies and the pension funds, institutions that do not usually offer depository or transactional services but nevertheless perform the bank-like function of financial intermediation—pooling assets and investing them in portfolios of securities and commercial loans.

The blurring of distinctions among financial institutions poses important challenges for the regulatory system. For while the market distinctions disappear, the regulatory schemes applicable to different types of institution remain separate and in many respects inconsistent. Eventually the nation may evolve towards some kind of unified regulatory structure for financial institutions. The development of such a structure, however, is still years in the future, and whatever statutory evolution occurs undoubtedly will be profoundly influenced by the effects of political lobbying by the various interest groups in the financial services industry.

#### e. The Problem of Bank Failures

The revolution of the 1980s was accompanied by a bank failure rate unequalled since the Depression. From 1946 to 1984 the average annual failure rate for banks was only .07 percent, but from 1984 to 1987 the figure increased five-fold to .37 percent. One hundred twenty banks failed in 1985, 145 in 1986, 184 in 1987, 206 in 1989, 168 in 1990, and 124 in 1991. Moreover, these failures were not restricted to small banks. One of the nation's largest banks, Continental Illinois National Bank, failed in 1984 and required a federal bailout; the large Bank of New England failed in 1991, and rumors of troubles at other big banks swept through the financial markets from time to time during this period. Unexpected weaknesses in commercial banks during 1991—especially in the New England region—drove the FDIC Bank Insurance Fund into near-insolvency, requiring a $70 billion federal bailout in the Federal Deposit Insurance Corporation Improvement Act (FDICIA).

The situation was even grimmer in the savings and loan industry, in which approximately a third of the nation's thrifts became insolvent or financially troubled in the 1980s. The issue of thrift institution insolvency became one of the more intractable political issues of the 1980s. Congress provided short-term relief in 1987 when it authorized a recapitalization for the FSLIC, but the funds authorized were grossly inadequate to accomplish the task of returning the FSLIC and the thrift industry to solvency. In 1989 Congress responded to the thrift crisis by enacting FIRREA, which provided for the rescue of the thrift insurance fund and abolished the FHLBB and the FSLIC, vesting responsibility for deposit insurance in the FDIC and responsibility for supervision and enforcement in a newly created Office of Thrift Supervision (OTS) in the Department of the Treasury. The legislation also established the Resolution Trust Corporation (RTC) to handle disposition of billions of dollars in assets of failed thrift institutions. Estimates of the cost of this federal bailout of the thrift industry have gone as high as $500 billion (interest included), or about $150 billion in present value terms.

During the 1990s, the banking industry returned to financial health, and many institutions reported record profits. The FDIC's list of problem institutions shrank dramatically, and the number of bank failures fell to levels close to those observed prior to the crisis. Nevertheless, the trauma of the 1980s remains in the banking industry, much as the trauma of the 1930s lingered on well past the end of the Depression. Banking has been fundamentally changed as a result of the recent events, and it will be many years, if ever, before it returns to the old system of stable institutions and reliable profit margins.

This brings us to the present. Although the restructuring to the banking industry over the past decade has been revolutionary, even more profound changes are being proposed. The structure of bank holding company regulation may be changed; bank powers may be liberalized; and the allocation of regulatory powers among banking regulators may be reshuffled once again.

### f. The Future

From today's perspective, we see banking—and banking law—in the midst of radical changes. The future remains cloudy, but the direction of change appears certain. The distinctions among banks, thrifts, and other types of financial institutions will continue to break down, leading eventually to a more unified financial services industry. The regulatory structure will need to be updated to account for these ongoing marketplace changes. At the same time the geographic restraints on banking will continue to crumble, leading eventually to nearly universal nationwide and even worldwide banking. The number of banks will decrease as banks fail or are acquired through merger. The size of the largest institutions will increase. American banks will increasingly function in a unified worldwide financial marketplace and will face intense competition in that marketplace from vigorous banking institutions located in Europe, Japan, and elsewhere.

These changes are sure to bring political strains and public policy debates of their own. How those debates play themselves out in the arenas of law and legislation remains to be seen.

In a widely reported speech at the Federal Reserve Bank of Chicago's

Bank Structure conference in May 1993, Fed Chairman Alan Greenspan voiced concern about troubles to come in the industry. Consider the following selection from Chairman Greenspan's speech.

## Remarks by Alan Greenspan Chairman, Board of Governors of the Federal Reserve System

*May 6, 1993*

While the short- to intermediate-term prospects for the [banking] industry should not give us cause for concern, I am less sanguine about the long run. Bank commercial and industrial lending as a percentage of total borrowing by nonfinancial businesses has been declining for several decades. This trend is disturbing for reasons that go beyond contemporary concerns about the causes of the recent credit crunch. American businesses increasingly are borrowing directly from investors in the form of commercial paper and other debt obligations, or they are borrowing from nonbank financial institutions. Viewed in this light, the issue becomes one of the future role of U.S. banks in the overall provision of financial services, not just loans.

This challenge to banks has occurred largely as a result of the technological changes that have permitted investors to make their own evaluations regarding credit and market risk, thereby allowing investors to lend directly to larger borrowers. To some extent, banking organizations have responded to these changes by participating themselves in the increase in direct investor-borrower deals. The Board has acted, within the confines of existing law, to allow banks to evolve along with technological change. Nevertheless, the restrictions of Glass-Steagall, in the absence of significant reform legislation, imply that the challenge to banks' role in financial intermediation will continue to be driven to a substantial degree by artificial legislative constraints, not market conditions. Besides Glass-Steagall, other legal impediments to needed structural reform in banking—such as restrictions on interstate branching—remain firmly in place.

Public policy, in my view, *should* be concerned with the decline in the importance of banking. To the extent that market forces are displacing the intermediation functions of banks, economic efficiency is not being impaired: but to the extent that unnecessary laws and regulations are responsible for the decline, there is a significant reduction in allocative efficiency associated with preventing banking companies from fully exercising their abilities to underwrite and manage risk. As the nonbanking sector expands relative to the banking sector—because of artificial legal barriers to bank expansion—human resources, physical assets, and capital must be reallocated to the nonbank sector. The "transaction costs" of this reallocation are not trivial. Further, the banking sector loses the opportunity to fully diversify its activities in a way that may permit it to move toward the risk-return frontier rather than remain inside it. Finally, and most importantly, the consumers of financial services are denied the lower prices, increased access, and higher quality services that would accompany the increased competition associated with permitting banking companies to expand their activities.

The debate over the repeal of Glass-Steagall provides an interesting and instructive case study of the difficulty in achieving legislative reform. The possibility of repeal of Glass-Steagall has been raised many times over the last two decades, but, each time, the opponents of repeal have mustered arguments to defeat such proposals. Recently for example, in 1991, when the recommendations of the Treasury Department regarding expanded powers were being considered (and ultimately rejected in the final FDICIA legislation), a popular argument against reform was that banks were in trouble with low earnings and high loan loss provisions. Expanded powers at that time, it was argued, would only lead to additional risk that could cause more bank failures. Now, in 1993, opponents of reform argue that bank profits are at historically record levels: therefore, expanded powers are not needed by the banks to maintain their profitability.

Apparently, there is *no* good time for reform. This line of argument is disturbing. We cannot afford to be complacent regarding the future of the U.S. banking industry. The issues are too important for the future growth of our economy and the welfare of our citizens. I trust that Congress will see FDICIA . . . not as an end in itself, but as providing a vehicle for allowing needed restructuring of our banking industry. Equally important, I would hope that our experiences with the portions of FDICIA that impose excessive burdens on banks have taught us that existing and proposed banking laws must be evaluated to determine their likely impacts on the soundness and competitiveness of our banking system. And, once legislation is passed, it must be implemented in a way that preserves the value-added of the banking system, by not confining banks in a regulatory straitjacket that stifles innovation and prudent risk management. Further, this must be done in a way that properly balances the banks' role as risk-takers and risk managers with the public policy concerns of bank safety and protection of the taxpayer. By doing this, we can greatly assist in the process of achieving a healthy and dynamic economy.

## Macey & Miller, Nondeposit Deposits and the Future of Bank Regulation

***91 Michigan Law Review 237 (1992)***

[The authors describe various forms of "nondeposit deposit," by which they mean an instrument or account that fulfills the functional purposes of a checking account deposit but is not treated as a deposit for purposes of federal deposit insurance, Federal Reserve Board reserve requirements, or both. One example of a nondeposit deposit is an account in a money market mutual fund, which offers consumers a low-risk checking account outside the banking system. The authors argue that] the nation has already entered with a vengeance into the era of nondeposit deposit banking. The traditional bank deposit against which reserves must be held and deposit insurance paid is suffering encroachment from a wide variety of competitive instruments and arrangements, all of which, to one degree or another—often to a substantial degree—serve a function economically similar to that of the checking account at a depository institution.

The dramatic growth of nondeposit deposits . . . represents a development of profound importance for the future of the U.S. banking industry. Because these instruments can function as partial, or, in some cases, nearly complete substitutes for the traditional checking account balance, they are likely to grow relative to bank deposits to the extent that the latter will operate under costly regulatory constraints not applicable to [uninsured] depository institutions.

In the long run, the traditional banking function of matching checking account deposits against portfolios of commercial loans will probably become significantly less important. Banks—especially big banks—are already in the process of altering their balance sheets on the liability side to include a greater percentage of nondeposit deposits relative to traditional checking accounts. This process will probably accelerate.

At the same time, nonbanks will increasingly intrude on the core banking business of offering transaction services. The regulatory and cost advantages enjoyed by many of the nondeposit deposit instruments that nonbanks can presently offer, and those that will likely be developed in the future, are nearly certain to induce further nonbank expansion into this service market. The result will be further blurring of the distinctive characteristics that through the years have allegedly made banks "special" institutions deserving unique regulatory treatment.

Perhaps the most important consequence of the growth of nondeposit deposits for the long-range prospects and stability of the banking system is that they promise to convert federal deposit insurance from an essentially mandatory form of social insurance, which persons wishing to consummate economic transactions are forced to accept without any real choice as to whether the benefits of the insurance are worth the costs, into an optional system that consumers can utilize if they wish or can avoid if they are willing to incur the risks of conducting their affairs through higher yielding, but uninsured, transaction accounts.

We believe that real reform of our system of deposit insurance can only come by means of such marketplace evolution, rather than social engineering through the political process. If deposit insurance can be made essentially a voluntary program, the costs of such insurance can then be better imposed on those wishing to obtain its benefits. In such a world, deposit insurance will survive if its benefits exceed its costs; but if the costs of deposit insurance—in terms of the moral hazard and subsidization of risk-taking that it creates and the elaborate regulatory constraints that must be instituted to correct for these problems—turn out to exceed the benefits, then deposit insurance will wither away to a largely vestigial—and therefore socially unproblematic—program. . . . If the nondeposit deposit moves the financial services industry forward into more competitive and efficient forms, the result will benefit consumers of banking services and the American economy as a whole.

## NOTE ON BANKING IN CYBERSPACE

As you might have expected, banking has begun to explore the information superhighway in order to develop new market opportunities. In fact, the Internet is already being used to carry out payment and clearance functions that are no different in principle from checks or that formerly cutting-edge technology, electronic funds transfer. Start-up firms with names like First Virtual Holdings, Cybercash, DigiCash, and Netscape Communications are seeking to exploit the fact that, as of 1995, about thirty million households and three million merchants in the United States enjoyed access to the Internet. Already, merchants are meeting customers—and each other—across this data highway. There is even an Internet Shopping Network.

In 1996 Internet transactions were growing by an estimated 1 percent *a day,* or 365 percent a year. One study estimates that by the year 2000 some $600 billion worth of goods and services will be purchased over the Internet. While it might be easy to dismiss such claims as visionary, there is no doubt that commercial usage of the information superhighway is exploding.

One problem with trade over the Internet is the payments system. If the openness and availability of the Internet has been its strength, it is also a weakness as far as payments are concerned. There is always a risk that third parties will gain access to credit card numbers or other financially sensitive information used for making payments for goods or services obtained over the Internet. A great deal of thought, energy, and research is going into means for protecting the system against these hazards.

By the mid-1990s, banks were entering cyberspace with a vengeance, especially in the area of credit card processing. One Internet entrepreneur, Cybercash Inc., has been marketing services to banks willing to accept payment from the cardholder's home computer on credit cards the banks had issued. Under one agreement with First National

Bank of Omaha, Cybercash will give more than 44,000 merchants access to its service, which uses data encryption to prevent credit card fraud on the Internet.

One of the most intriguing developments in this area is the creation of "electronic cash," which can be used to effect transactions over the net. Consider the following description.

## Render, Virtual Payment Systems: Legal Issues of Electronic Cash (1995)

Electronic cash, as envisioned by one of its pioneers, is a form of scrip that may be downloaded from a participating bank and transmitted to participating vendors much as electronic mail messages are currently sent. Electronic cash may be exchanged for U.S. currency at any time. The proposed systems secure the transmission of this scrip with encryption technology and ensure anonymity for the consumer through the use of blinding factors. . . .

[An example of the way in which electronic cash payments over computer networks operate is DigiCash®, an electronic cash pioneer.] DigiCash B.V. of Amsterdam offers electronic cash for use in buying and selling information, goods, and services over computer networks like the Internet. Electronic cash, or "ecash®," is created by the consumer using DigiCash software, and validated by an Internet ecash bank. Ecash uses encryption techniques that provide transmission security, integrity, and authentication. . . . DigiCash has also introduced the use of blinding factors, so that a user may spend ecash as anonymously as he or she spends cash today. . . .

To use DigiCash, a user must have a connection to the "World Wide Web," . . . a graphic-oriented overlay on the Internet that provides users with an easy, "point-and-click" means of accessing Internet services. The user may download DigiCash's ecash software via the Web, free of charge. The first time the user runs the ecash software, the software assists him or her through the process of opening an account at an Internet ecash bank. . . . DigiCash is negotiating with national banks to provide real ecash banking services.

The user makes a withdrawal from the ecash bank much as a bank customer might make a withdrawal from an ATM. The difference is that the ecash bank does not dispense traditional cash. Instead, it sends an amount of electronic cash to the ecash software on the user's PC. The ecash stays on the user's PC until she spends it.

The ecash software remains active while the user is accessing the World Wide Web, as a button bar that the user can move around on the screen. The user then navigates the Web to find a vendor who is selling something the user wants and who accepts ecash. When the user decides to make a purchase from a vendor who accepts ecash, he or she fills in the vendor's form. The user chooses to pay for the purchase using ecash by clicking on a field in the vendor's form. Clicking on this field activates the ecash software. A dialog box appears asking the user to confirm that payment should be made in the specified amount. The user clicks on the "yes" choice, and the ecash is transferred from his or her PC to the vendor who sends them on to an account at the ecash bank. The button bar reflects the balance on the user's PC.

A seller accepts ecash using the same software on a Web server. The ecash software the users download from DigiCash's "home page" on the Web includes the programs a vendor needs to create a shop that buyers can access via the Web. The vendor makes information or services available via a Web server. When ecash buyers access their sites, the vendor accepts their ecash via the Web server. Therefore, if a company already had a site on the Web, it could begin accepting ecash by registering with DigiCash and downloading the ecash software, a process that in full operation might require no more than a few hours.

## C. WHAT IS A BANK?

We have talked at some length about the history of banking. In so doing, we left open the question of how our topic is to be defined. We now consider that basic issue.

What is a bank? Most people think they know one when they see one; as one of our friends replied when we asked the question, "It's the dinky little place where I put my dinky little savings to earn some dinky little interest." This might be a perfectly serviceable definition for most practical purposes, but it won't do for the study of banking law. We need something more specific.

### 1. *Three Definitions*

But what is it, exactly, that distinguishes a bank from other types of economic enterprise? We might think of three ways of defining a bank: (1) with reference to the *legal regulation* within which the institution functions; (2) with reference to the *services* banks offer to customers; and (3) with reference to the *economic function* that a bank performs in the society.

### a. Legal Form

Perhaps the simplest way to define a bank is to look at its legal form. If the institution has a state or federal charter to operate as a commercial bank, then it is a bank. This approach has the merit of being simple and clear, but it is grossly underinclusive for most purposes. To be sure, institutions with state or federal commercial banking charters are banks, but so are many other institutions operating under different legal frameworks. In particular, thrift institutions—savings and loans, savings banks, and credit unions—are virtually indistinguishable from commercial banks for many purposes. Without some good reason to do so, it would be arbitrary to exclude thrifts from our definition. And, as we shall see, many other institutions—such as money market mutual funds—are also acting like banks today. To the extent they act like banks, should they not be included in our definition of a bank? These considerations suggest that defining a bank with sole reference to its legal form may not be wholly satisfactory.

### b. Services

An alternative way to define a bank is by the *services* that it offers its customers. One might say, like our friend, that the distinguishing feature of a bank is the fact people put their savings there in order to earn interest. More precisely, we can define a bank as an institution that accepts deposits subject to check and makes loans. This definition will do nicely for many purposes—indeed, as we will see, it is a rough approximation of the definition used by Congress in key legislation.

But this definition too is imperfect. People put their savings in all sorts of investments other than bank accounts; corporate, federal, and municipal bonds, purchase money mortgages, and other investments all have this feature. Other types of institutions—notably money market mutual funds—offer checking privileges. And all sorts of nonbank firms—life insurance companies, mortgage companies, pension funds, consumer finance firms—make loans. There is no one service or group of services that banks alone offer their customers. Accordingly, while a definition in terms of bank services has much to recommend it, it is not entirely satisfactory either.

### c. Economic Function

Finally, it may be fruitful to define a bank more generally in terms of economic function. Each of the specific services offered by banks—

accepting deposits, offering checking privileges, and making loans—is part and parcel of a bank's role of being a *financial intermediary* providing *transactional services* to customers. Let us unpack these concepts.

### *i. Financial Intermediation*

Financial intermediaries are institutions that take money from investors, pool it, and invest the pooled funds in other enterprises. These institutions are referred to as *intermediaries* because they occupy a position between the investor and the ultimate investment. The investor in a financial intermediary has a claim only against the intermediary and not against the firms or other ventures in which the intermediary invests. In this respect financial intermediaries are to be distinguished from institutions such as securities brokerage firms, which do not act as intermediaries but rather assist the customer in making direct investments. Financial intermediaries include depository institutions, life insurance companies, mutual funds, and pension funds.

Why would investors use financial intermediaries? After all, the intermediary demands a fee for its services—either an express management fee, in the case of mutual fund advisors, an interest rate spread, in the case of banks, or some other form of compensation. Why not "eliminate the middle man" by placing funds directly in profit-making ventures? The answer is that financial intermediaries offer a number of important benefits that customers cannot obtain by direct investment.

First, financial intermediaries offer *diversification*. Other things equal, investors prefer to hold a diversified portfolio of assets because by doing so they can greatly lower the risk of their investments. If all of your money is tied up in one investment, you will be wiped out if that investment fails. If, on the other hand, you hold many different investments, the failure of one firm in your portfolio will not be very significant. Diversification becomes easier as the size of the investment portfolio grows. Thus a financial intermediary can diversify its pool of funds more easily and cheaply than can an individual investor. Accordingly, unless the individual has a fortune to invest, intermediation may be an efficient way to achieve diversification of the individual's investment portfolio.

Second, financial intermediaries offer *expertise*. Bank loan officers, for example, are (in theory) highly skilled at identifying good, profitable uses for the depositors' funds. It is easy to see why customers would be willing to pay for receiving the benefit of investment expertise. Even if an individual were willing to incur the nondiversified risk of making a commercial loan, few have the market savvy to distinguish a good loan from a bad one. By placing their money in a bank they in effect hire the bank to use its expertise in identifying good investment opportunities.

Bank customers need not—in fact almost never do—know anything about the markets in which the bank invests its assets. Because depositors don't need to gain the expertise themselves, they can spend their time doing more enjoyable things—playing golf, watching "Wheel of Fortune," studying banking law.

Third, financial intermediaries allow investors to take advantage of *economies of scale*. Many investments are simply out of reach of the ordinary mortal, even if the investor were otherwise willing to incur the nondiversified risk and had the expertise to evaluate the prospect. Commercial bank loans often run seven figures or more, and even some securities investments—notably commercial paper issued by large corporations—are available only in denominations that foreclose the market to most individuals. Because financial intermediaries pool funds from numerous investors, they are able to participate in the market for these large scale investments.

Fourth, some financial intermediaries—banks in particular—convert *illiquid investments* into *liquid ones*. Other things equal, every one would prefer to be able to cash in their investments quickly in order to meet sudden demands for funds, thus making a liquid investment more desirable than an illiquid one. But illiquid investments typically offer greater return simply because they *are* illiquid and therefore less desired by investors. A financial intermediary can invest in a portfolio of illiquid assets and then offer its own investors liquid claims on its own assets. This conversion of illiquid investments into liquid ones represents a significant benefit for investors. At the same time, banks also convert illiquid assets of their borrowers into liquid ones. Consider a manufacturing firm that has a plant worth $1 million. This firm has a $1 million asset, but it cannot use any of this value to pay current operating expenses: The asset is illiquid. If, however, the firm obtains a mortgage from a bank secured by the plant, it can convert a substantial portion of the plant's value into liquid form—and can do so without having to sell the plant.

For these and perhaps other reasons financial intermediaries have survived and prospered even though intermediation is costly to the customer. This is not to say, of course, that customers always prefer intermediated investments. This is obviously not the case: Although financial intermediaries hold a substantial amount of the nation's securities and dominate loan markets, direct (nonintermediated) investments are at least as important in the economy. Very large investors are less likely to use financial intermediaries because they can bring the intermediary's services "in house." And investors of all sorts are less likely to use a financial intermediary to the extent that the market in which they are investing is efficient. As markets become more efficient, the value of expertise declines. The intermediary's knowledge is less valuable in an efficient market like the New York Stock Exchange than it is in a relatively inefficient market like the market for commercial loans.

### ii. *Transaction Services*

Banks are financial intermediaries that provide *transaction services.* Any society needs a mechanism by which wealth can be transferred from one party to another to consummate an economic transaction. Primitive societies might work with a barter system, by which goods of different sorts are exchanged at a ratio determined by bargaining among the parties. All developed societies use money, which is far more efficient than barter because it does not require that each party to a transaction have some good that the other wants.

Money can be in the form of currency—some tangible medium of exchange that is accepted in the society as a temporary abode of purchasing power. For many purposes, however, currency is not the most efficient means of transferring wealth in developed societies. It is often more efficient to use an accounting system in which wealth transfers are accomplished through bookkeeping entries: debits and credits to the accounts of buyer and seller. An accounting system of exchange usually operates in tandem with a currency medium, but it need not do so; in theory an accounting system could operate without any physical medium of exchange at all. Banks provide such an accounting system, or means of transferring wealth through bookkeeping entries.

An accounting system works by each party to an economic transaction having an account at a bank. When the parties consummate the deal, the buyer of goods or services instructs her bank to debit her bank account and credit the seller's bank account (this may be accomplished by check, but any method of conveying instructions to the buyer's bank would do). For example, assume Buyer has an account for $5,000 at Bank B, Seller has a stereo system worth $500 and an account for $20,000 at Bank S, and Bank B has an account for $1,000 at Bank S. There are four relevant actors: Buyer, Seller, Bank B, and Bank S; their respective balance sheets (greatly simplified) look like so:

**Buyer**

| *Assets* | | *Liabilities/Net Worth* | |
|---|---|---|---|
| B Bank Account | $5,000 | Net Worth | $5,000 |

**Bank B**

| *Assets* | | *Liabilities/Net Worth* | |
|---|---|---|---|
| S Bank Account | $1,000 | Buyer's Account | $5,000 |
| Loans, etc. | 4,000 | | |

**Seller**

| Assets | | Liabilities/Net Worth | |
|---|---|---|---|
| S Bank Account | $20,000 | Net Worth | $20,500 |
| Stereo | 500 | | |

**Bank S**

| Assets | | Liabilities/Net Worth | |
|---|---|---|---|
| Loans, etc. | $21,000 | Bank B Account | $ 1,000 |
| | | Seller's Account | 20,000 |

Buyer and Seller agree on a purchase price of $500 for the stereo. How will Buyer transfer wealth to Seller to effect the transaction? Buyer instructs Bank B to debit her account $500 and credit Seller with $500. Bank B can't directly credit Seller with $500 because Seller has no account at Bank B. But Seller has an account at Bank S, and so does Bank B. Accordingly, Bank B can arrange with Bank S to debit Bank B's account at Bank S for $500. Bank S can then credit $500 to Seller's account. After all these bookkeeping entries, the balance sheets look like so:

**Buyer**

| Assets | | Liabilities/Net Worth | |
|---|---|---|---|
| B Bank Account | $4,500 | Net Worth | $5,000 |
| Stereo | 500 | | |

**Bank B**

| Assets | | Liabilities/Net Worth | |
|---|---|---|---|
| S Bank Account | $ 500 | Buyer's Account | $4,500 |
| Loans, etc. | 4,000 | | |

**Seller**

| Assets | | Liabilities/Net Worth | |
|---|---|---|---|
| S Bank Account | $20,500 | Net Worth | $20,500 |

**Bank S**

| Assets | | Liabilities/Net Worth | |
|---|---|---|---|
| Loans, etc. | $21,000 | Bank B Account | $ 500 |
| | | Seller's Account | $20,500 |

A review of these simple balance sheets reveals that the banks have provided a transaction service whereby wealth is transferred from buyer to seller by means of bookkeeping entries. No currency is necessary for this transaction to take place; currency need not enter the picture at all as long as there is some measure of price in the society against which the bookkeeping entries may be pegged.

Notice that the transaction described above works only because Bank B has an account at Bank S that could be debited in order to transfer funds between the banks. In a system with many banks it would be inconvenient indeed if each bank had to maintain an account relationship with each other bank. The problem can be mitigated if the jurisdiction supports a central bank with which all other banks maintain an account; transfers of wealth among banks can then be accomplished by debiting and crediting their respective accounts at the central bank. In the United States this service is provided by the Federal Reserve System.

### *iii. Relationship Between Intermediation and Transaction Services*

We have defined a bank in functional terms as a financial intermediary that offers transaction services. Thus banks provide two different services: They act as financial intermediaries and they facilitate wealth transfers by bookkeeping entries. What connection, if any, is there between these services?

It is quite possible to imagine a financial intermediary that does not offer transaction services. Indeed, thousands of such intermediaries exist right now; life insurance companies, pension funds and other institutions do not provide transaction services. It is also possible to imagine a company that provides transaction services without intermediation. Such a firm would act essentially as a broker, arranging for the transfer of direct claims on assets from buyer to seller. In the illustration above, for example, a transaction servicing company could arrange for the transfer to the Seller of $500 worth of securities owned by the Buyer. If the Seller didn't want Buyer's securities, the transaction servicing company could sell the securities on the market for Buyer's account and buy for the Seller's account an equal value of other securities more desired by the Seller. No intermediation would be involved.

As a practical matter, however, the function of providing transaction services is closely linked with financial intermediation. The most efficient way to provide transaction services is apparently to hold customer accounts at the servicing company. Thus firms that provide transaction services tend to hold deposits from customers. Once they hold depositors' accounts, firms find it profitable to invest these funds in securities and productive ventures pending demand on the funds by the customer.

Hence all, or virtually all, companies providing transaction services are also financial intermediaries. According to our functional definition, institutions that provide both services are banks.

*QUESTIONS AND COMMENTS*

1. The Bank Holding Company Act of 1956 once defined a "bank" as "any institution organized under the laws of the United States [or] any State of the United States . . . which (1) accepts deposits that the depositor has a legal right to withdraw on demand, and (2) engages in the business of making commercial loans." What do you think of this definition? Can you think of ways to avoid being classified as a "bank" while still engaging in essential banking functions?

In 1987 Congress redefined the term "bank" in the Bank Holding Company Act to include (1) any institution insured by the Federal Deposit Insurance Corporation, whether or not it takes demand deposits or makes commercial loans, or (2) any other institution that both accepts demand deposits or similar transaction accounts and engages in the business of making commercial loans. See 12 U.S.C. §1841(c)(1).

2. How would you define a "bank" if you were drafting the law?

## 2. *Demand Deposits and Fractional Reserves*

We now want to explore some of the ramifications of our functional definition of a bank as a financial intermediary offering transaction services. Two matters in particular deserve attention at this juncture: the duration of a bank's liabilities, and the means a bank uses to ensure that it will be able to honor its commitment to repay depositors.

### a. Demand Deposit Banking

The nature of a bank as a provider of transaction services implies that customer accounts will be extremely short-term in nature. The reason is simple. It simply would not do if people had to wait days or weeks before they could consummate economic transactions (why not?). An efficiently functioning transaction service must be able to move funds rapidly. For this reason an institution offering transaction services must provide customers with accounts that can be accessed instantly—or at least very quickly. A customer must be able to withdraw funds "on demand." All institutions that fall within our functional definition of a bank offer demand deposit accounts.

This function of offering demand deposit accounts distinguishes banks from other financial intermediaries that do not offer transactional services. Consider closed-end mutual funds. Investors in closed-end funds obtain "shares" that they can hold or sell on the market. They cannot, however, redeem shares from the fund itself. A closed-end fund's balance sheet, accordingly, is financed principally with "equity"—that is, by ownership interests—which can be conceived of as a liability with indefinite duration.

Consider life insurance companies. These firms receive funds in the form of premiums that, like other financial intermediaries, they invest in securities, loans, and other productive ventures. A very high percentage of their liabilities consist of reserves for payment to beneficiaries upon death of insureds. These liabilities are not indefinite—everyone dies—but they are long-term in nature—most people don't expect to die soon. Some life insurance policies may be redeemed on demand for their cash surrender value, but these are unusual.

Pension funds fall on the same continuum. Their liabilities are shorter-term than those of life insurance companies—most people retire and draw pensions before they die—but nevertheless their liabilities are still long-term in the scheme of things because pension fund investments are made over the course of many years before the employee begins to draw benefits.

Institutions that satisfy the functional definition of a bank do offer demand accounts. The paradigmatic case is the commercial bank, which has been offering demand accounts (or demand notes, which amount to much the same thing) for hundreds of years. Consider also thrift institutions, institutions that traditionally have not been considered banks. They did not offer full-scale transaction services: If Buyer wanted to purchase a stereo from funds held at a savings and loan, Buyer would have to go in to the institution with a passbook, withdraw the funds in the form of cash or teller's check, and physically transfer the funds to Seller. In line with this traditional "nonbank" role, thrift institutions did not offer demand accounts. They offered time and savings accounts under which (in theory) the institution could demand a substantial notice period before allowing withdrawals. Today, however, thrift institutions provide transactions services equivalent to those offered by banks, accomplished by means of checking accounts in which the depositor has power to withdraw funds on demand. Whatever the case may have been in years past, it is clear that today thrift institutions satisfy our functional definition: They are "banks" in every relevant economic sense of the word.

We should also mention one other important financial intermediary, the open-end mutual fund. Open-end funds accept money from customers, which they then invest in a portfolio of securities. They stand ready to redeem their shares for customers at any time, and allow such redemption in the form of checks written on the fund and payable to third parties. Thus an open-end fund, like a traditional bank, is a financial intermediary offering transaction services through the medium of demand accounts. In functional terms, open-end funds *are* banks, although the transaction services they offer are often limited in extent (the customer, for example, may be allowed to write checks only above some relatively large minimum amount).

There is, however, one key functional difference between open-end funds and traditional banks: Demand accounts at banks are in the form of *demand debt*—the bank contractually agrees to repay a sum certain—whereas demand accounts at open-end mutual funds are in the form of *demand equity*—the mutual fund does not agree to pay back a sum certain, but only to pay the depositor a fractional share of the fund's current net asset value. As we will see, the fact that open-end funds are not financed by demand debt has important practical consequences. Because of these different functional consequences, and because open-end mutual funds are subject to quite different legal regulation, we limit further discussion in this book to banks and thrifts except as otherwise specifically mentioned.

### b. Fractional Reserves

Financial intermediaries offering demand deposit accounts operate according to the principle of *fractional reserves.* This simply means that the institution does not keep enough money on hand to pay out all depositors at the same time.

In some respects every business enterprise operates according to a fractional reserve principle. Every business must make sure it has enough funds on hand to pay debts as they become due; otherwise it will be forced into insolvency. On the other hand, no business keeps all its funds on hand in a drawer. Businesses keep only enough funds on hand in liquid form to pay off the demands of creditors as they arise. In this sense every commercial enterprise—indeed, every economic actor including ordinary people like all of us—operates through the use of fractional reserves.

Although the fractional reserve principle, broadly defined, operates throughout the economy, banks differ from other firms in the method they use to ensure they will have sufficient funds on hand to pay off liabilities as they come due. Nonbank institutions can know for sure how much money they will need to have on hand to pay off liabilities as they mature because their liabilities are in the form of debt with stated maturities. They can safely tie up the rest of their assets in all sorts of illiquid projects, keeping only enough money on hand to pay off their maturing debt.

Banks, however, cannot know for certain how much of their debt will be due on any given day because most of their debt is in the form of deposits payable on demand. They could, of course, keep enough cash in their vaults to cover all demand debt, but then they would never be able to invest more than a small percentage of their assets in profit-making ventures (such as making commercial loans). The rest of their assets would be tied up in cash, which pays no interest at all. Banking would not be very profitable under these conditions.

Thousands of years ago bankers discovered a wonderful secret. They realized that it is not necessary for them to keep enough cash on hand to pay off all demand deposits because the law of large numbers makes it extremely improbable that all deposits will be called in at the same time. Bankers need to keep on hand only enough cash to pay off the fraction of deposits that are likely to be demanded on a given day. They can loan out the rest at interest.

This is the core principle of fractional reserve banking: Banks need to keep only a fraction of total deposits on reserve as cash, relying on the law of large numbers to ensure that no more than a small percentage of deposits are cashed in at any given time. They invest the remainder in loans or other illiquid but profitable ventures. It is only because of fractional reserves that banking is—or can be—a highly profitable business.

What about bank customers? Are they helped or harmed by fractional reserve banking? Much of the distrust of banks one finds in popular culture is based on uneasiness with the fractional reserve principle. There is a natural tendency to believe that if you deposit your funds in a bank, the bank should hold them for you and not give them out to somebody else. Yet from an economic point of view, customers benefit from fractional reserve banking. It is only because banks hold fractional reserves that they can invest customer's funds in productive ventures, and pass a portion of those profits back to the customer in the form of services (such as free checking) and interest.

## D. BANK RUNS, THE MONEY SUPPLY, AND THE PAYMENTS SYSTEM

It is sometimes said that banks are "special." They are not like ordinary business organizations such as manufacturing firms. They are different, unusual, even unique. But why? Banks, like every other business enterprise, are operated for profit. They offer a product—or perhaps more accurately, a bundle of services—to the public and charge a fee for doing so. Like most large businesses, they are typically structured as corporations, with shareholders, boards of directors, and all the rest. To be sure, their businesses differ in obvious ways from other businesses; a bank is not a pencil factory. But all business enterprises differ in the nature of their product, their markets and so on. What, if anything, is it about banks that sets them apart from all other enterprises? Why is this business different from all other businesses?

There are, in fact, at least three important ways in which banks differ from other businesses. The special features of banks are these: (1) their susceptibility to runs and panics; (2) their role in the money supply; and (3) their role in the payments system. Each of these special features, as we will see, is directly related to the functional definition of a bank as a financial intermediary maintaining a system of accounts by which transfers of wealth are carried out with bookkeeping entries.

## 1. Bank Runs and Panics

First, individual banks are uniquely susceptible to runs, and the banking industry as a whole is uniquely susceptible to panics. Why?

To illustrate a bank run, let us conjure up a world similar to our own except that there is no deposit insurance. A rumor begins to circulate in this world that a particular bank—we'll call it the Prudential Bank—is in trouble. Some cautious depositors go to the Prudential to withdraw their funds. Others see them entering the bank and, fearing that the bank will have insufficient funds to pay everyone, decide that they, too, had better get their funds out. The line at the teller's window grows. Soon it extends out the door and into the street. Frenzied depositors, panicked by the thought that if they wait the bank's resources will be drained by other depositors, drop everything to get in line, desperately hoping that they will be able to withdraw their savings before the bank closes. And of course eventually the Prudential *does* close, if only because no bank has enough cash on hand at any given moment to pay off more than a fraction of its depositors.

Other people in town have their savings elsewhere—say at the Hometown Savings & Loan and the Main Street Bank. They have no reason to fear a run on the Prudential Bank. But as they see the crowd milling outside the Prudential building they might begin to wonder about their banks as well. The more cautious among them decide that they might as well withdraw their cash and put it under a mattress until the problem at the Prudential blows over. Lines begin to form at Hometown and Main Street banks as well. Soon all the banks in town are undergoing full-blown runs. The bank run turns into a bank panic—a generalized loss of confidence in the banking system.

Bank runs and bank panics are frightening events, even when they occur, as they do today, largely in the form of electronic or mail withdrawals placed from remote locations rather than by means of panicky mobs.

Perhaps the most disturbing feature of a bank run is its odd juxtaposition of mass irrationality with individual rationality. A bank run is in no one's best interest. Even if the bank has become insolvent, everyone would be better off if closure occurred through an orderly process in which the bank could maximize the value of its assets rather than selling them at "fire sale" prices in order to satisfy depositor demands. Nevertheless, once a bank run begins it is in everyone's individual interest to participate in the run. If they sit on the sidelines they are sure to lose their savings, but if they join the run they at least have a chance of recovery.

We mentioned that bank runs and panics are rare today. The reason is federal deposit insurance, which covers accounts at insured banks and thrift institutions up to $100,000 per depositor per institution. Even the rich and famous, if they exercise the remotest degree of care, can place their funds at banks without a twinge of fear that they will have to give up their lifestyles due to bank failure.

Yet even today runs and panics are not unknown. One of the largest banks in the country, Continental Illinois National Bank, failed in 1984 after a run by uninsured depositors (with accounts exceeding $100,000). Nor has the concern for bank panics evaporated. Federal regulators handling the Continental Bank insolvency were acutely aware of the possibility that failure of one of the nation's largest banks could lead to generalized panic. And panics have indeed occurred in recent years. In the early 1980s depositors at certain state-chartered thrift institutions in Maryland and Ohio discovered to their dismay that their accounts were not insured by any governmental agency; their response was to run all the nongovernmentally insured institutions in these states.

Why does the banking system (in the absence of deposit insurance) appear so susceptible to runs and panics? The answer has to do with the economic function of a bank as an institution with demand debt and fractional reserves. Imagine rumors starting about the financial condition of a manufacturer of lead pencils. Could investors in the pencil manufacturer start a run? No. They couldn't start a run because the liabilities of ordinary industrial firms are not demand instruments. Shareholders could do nothing in the short run but sell their shares on the market; and debtholders ordinarily would have no recourse but to wait until the debt becomes due, so long as the firm keeps up with its interest payments. A run is not possible because the pencil manufacturer's liabilities are relatively long-term.

In the case of a bank, however, depositors have a right to withdraw on demand. If they hear rumors about the bank, they can take their funds out in a matter of minutes. Moreover, the principle of fractional reserves states that banks will never have more than a small portion of depositors' funds on hand in the form of cash. Thus if a run starts and many depositors demand withdrawal, the bank will certainly not be able to satisfy its customers. The law of large numbers fails and with it, the bank. In the absence of emergency liquidity assistance (such as loans from the Federal Reserve) no bank, however solvent and well-managed, can withstand a run.

In considering bank runs and panics, it is necessary to distinguish commercial banks and thrifts, on the one hand, from open-end mutual funds, on the other. Although open-end mutual funds fit the functional definition of a bank we proposed above, they are not subject to runs in the same way as banks are. The reason is two-fold. First, we observed that the liabilities of open-end funds are in the form of demand equity rather than demand debt. Because the fund pays out investors based on net asset value, there is virtually no chance that the fund will become economically insolvent as a result of investor withdrawals. Each investor will simply receive her or his pro rata share of the fund's assets. There is little reason, accordingly, to rush to withdraw funds.

It remains theoretically possible that an open-end fund would suffer a temporary or "liquidity" insolvency if depositors demanded withdrawal more quickly than the fund could liquidate its assets to pay them. This possibility, however, is virtually eliminated by the second feature that distinguishes open-end funds from commercial banks and thrifts. The assets of an open-end fund are typically devoted almost entirely to short-term securities with ready markets. These assets can be converted to cash in a matter of hours. Thus even if unusual conditions caused a sudden unexpected surge in withdrawals, an open-end fund could almost certainly cover the demands within a very short time. For both of these reasons—that an open-end fund's liabilities are in the form of equity rather than debt and that its assets are in highly liquid short-term securities—runs on open-end funds are virtually nonexistent despite the fact that they do not carry federal deposit insurance.

### *QUESTIONS AND COMMENTS*

1. Given that banks are subject to runs, why would customers (in the absence of deposit insurance) ever put their money in a bank?

2. Why were bank buildings once constructed out of beautiful marble in imitation of classical Greek temples?

## *2. Role of Banks in the Money Supply*

Banks play a key role in the creation and destruction of money. The reason for their central role is that they offer demand accounts that are the functional equivalent of money—indeed, that *are* money according to standard economic definitions of the term. Again, this particular role for banks is a function of the fact they are financed by demand deposits: It is these demand deposits that have the characteristic of money.

It is not intuitively obvious why demand deposit or checking accounts are money. A natural assumption is that the only "real" money is cash or coins, but this assumption is false. We think of cash as money only because it performs certain functions: It is a medium of exchange and store of value. But checking accounts are also media of exchange and stores of value—perhaps not as universally accepted as cash (a merchant wants some identification before accepting a personal check), but still widely used. For most purposes a personal check is quite equivalent to currency as a means of consummating economic transactions.

Where does the money in checking accounts come from? In large part, it is created (and destroyed) by banks themselves. Banks create money when they make loans, and destroy it when they accept repayment of loans. To understand how banks create and destroy money, it is useful to consider two situations: first, a world in which banks do not keep any reserves against deposits; and second, a world in which banks do keep reserves against deposits.

Let's assume (contrary to fact) that banks lend out all their assets without retaining any reserves against deposits. Say a bank gives you an unsecured loan of $1,000 to help buy a personal computer. The loan is evidenced by your promissory note, and the bank gives you deposit credit of $1,000 on which you can draw a check. At this point the books look like this:

***You***

| *Assets* | | *Liabilities/Net Worth* | |
|---|---|---|---|
| Checking account | $1,000 | Note to Bank | $1,000 |

***Bank***

| *Assets* | | *Liabilities/Net Worth* | |
|---|---|---|---|
| Note from You | $1,000 | Checking account | $1,000 |

Before the loan goes through you have no money. After the loan, you have $1,000 in the form of a bank account. Meanwhile, the bank has not had to give out any cash: It has simply created a credit in your name on its books. Of course, you might write a check for $1,000 immediately to the computer store and exhaust your account; but now the computer store has a check for $1,000 to deposit in *its* account. The $1,000 remains in the system. Amazingly, it looks as if there is now $1,000 more in the economy than was present before the loan. And if the bank can lend a thousand dollars to you, it can lend a million—or a billion—to others. It is literally creating money out of nothing!

Now bankers obviously cannot create money forever. That privilege is reserved to counterfeiters and the federal government. Banks' ability to create money is limited by a number of factors, practical as well as legal.

First, fractional reserve banking implies that banks must keep at least some assets on reserve in the form of cash in order to pay out depositors who demand cash. Second, banks are required by law to maintain a certain percentage of reserves against deposits in the form of vault cash or on account at the Federal Reserve. Third, banks must, as a practical matter, maintain excess reserves beyond those required by law in order to ensure that checks drawn by their depositors and deposited in other banks do not cause their reserves to drop below the level required by law.

Accordingly, let's now adopt the more realistic assumption that banks need to keep some level of reserves against deposits. The necessity that a bank maintain reserves limits its ability to create money. Posit that a bank is subject to a fractional reserve requirement of 10 percent. Assume further that banks always lend up to their reserve limits. A bank with no reserves to start with could make no loans at all. Let us say, however, that the Federal Reserve buys $1,000 worth of securities on the market, and that the seller of these securities deposits the government's check to an account at Bank A. Now Bank A has legal reserves of $1,000 (since the funds received upon clearing the government's check count as legal reserves). How much money will the banking system create?

To start with, the purchase of securities by the Federal Reserve creates $1,000 in new money. But this is not the end of the story. Bank A will not let the $1,000 lie idle. Instead, it will lend out $900, retaining $100 to satisfy the 10 percent reserve requirement. We will assume that this $900 loan is immediately transferred by the borrower to some other bank, Bank B. Bank A's books now look like this:

***Bank A***

| *Assets* | | *Liabilities/Net Worth* | |
|---|---|---|---|
| Reserves | $100 | Deposits | $1,000 |
| Loans | 900 | | |

Bank A has created $900 in money, while just managing to stay within its 10 percent reserve requirement by holding $100 against $1,000 in deposits. So now a total of $1,900 in money has been created as a result of the initial Federal Reserve infusion of $1,000.

But will only $1,900 be created? No. Bank B, to which the borrower from Bank A has transferred the bank credit, now has $900 in excess reserves against which it can make loans. Bank B will make new loans of \$810, keeping \$90 in reserves to satisfy the 10 percent reserve requirement:

**_Bank B_**

| *Assets* | | *Liabilities/Net Worth* | |
|---|---|---|---|
| Reserves | \$ 90 | Deposits | \$900 |
| Loans | 810 | | |

This process will repeat itself from bank to bank until there are no excess reserves left in the system. At the end of the process, the banking system as a whole will have created \$10,000 in new money:

**_Banking System_**

| *Change in Deposits* | *Change in Loans* | *Change in Reserves* |
|---|---|---|
| +\$10,000 | +\$9,000 | +\$1,000 |

In reality the situation is not this simple because the banking system does not continue to make loans until all excess reserves are exhausted. As noted already, banks need to hold some excess reserves to ensure that their reserve levels do not fall below the legal minimum as a result of deposit outflows. Further, the money creation process will screech to a halt if a borrower decides to hold loan proceeds as cash rather than depositing them in a checking account.

Nevertheless the principle remains valid: When the Federal Reserve introduces cash or Federal Reserve account credit into the banking system, the effect is to create new money at a multiple of the amounts introduced. By the same token, when cash or federal reserve credit is removed from the banking system, money is destroyed at a multiple of the reserves that are removed.

Obviously, cash and Federal Reserve accounts are different from ordinary money. They are *high-powered money* because their introduction into the banking system creates money in a multiple of their face amount, and their removal from the system destroys money according to the same multiplier.

The Federal Reserve uses high-powered money to control how much money the banking system creates or destroys. The Fed pumps high-powered money into the economy by several mechanisms. First, it purchases securities on the open market, the effect being to increase the amount of high-powered money in the banking system, and thus, to increase the money supply. Contrariwise, open-market sales of securities by the Federal Reserve remove high-powered money from the system, thus decreasing the money supply. Second, the Federal Reserve loans money to banks, increasing the supply of high-powered money, or accepts repayment of loans from banks, decreasing the supply of high-powered money. Third, the Federal Reserve increases the money supply by reducing the required reserve ratio and decreases the money supply by increasing the required reserve ratio. All of these devices intimately involve the banking industry. For this reason, banks are sometimes called the "transmission belts" of monetary policy.

The close relationship between banks and the money supply has important consequences for public policy. If, for whatever reason, the banking system breaks down, the money supply will certainly be affected. In the view of some economists, the Great Depression of the 1930s was closely connected with the breakdown of the American banking system in 1933, which caused a massive contraction in the money supply as customers rushed to withdraw funds from banks. The banking system's relationship with the money supply suggests reasons for concern about a possible breakdown of the system in the future.

## 3. *Role of Banks in the Payments System*

In addition to their unique susceptibility to runs and their role in the creation and destruction of money, banks are often deemed special in their role (in partnership with the Federal Reserve) as guardians and operators of the "payments system"—the system by which checks are cleared. More generally, banks operate a system by which transfers of wealth—which may or may not involve the creation of pieces of paper known as checks—are carried out through bookkeeping entries.

Banks dominate the payments system in this country. When you write a check to your landlord, the landlord deposits the check in her bank. The landlord's bank then sends the check to your bank through some clearance mechanism, usually by means of a local "clearing house" where local banks exchange checks drawn on other local banks. The banks transfer the amount of your rent check from your bank to the landlord's bank by netting out all the checks drawn on each other and accounting for the remainder by crediting or debiting accounts the banks have with each other or with the Federal Reserve.

So, for example, if on a given day your bank presents a total of $10,000 in checks drawn on your landlord's bank, and your landlord's bank presents $8,000 of checks drawn on your bank (including your rent check), the two banks might settle up at the end of the day by recording a debit of $2,000 to an account that your landlord's bank holds at your bank. That settles things between the banks. The banks then settle things with their customers: Your bank debits your account by the amount of the rent check and your landlord's bank credits her account.

You would never bounce a check, of course, but if you did overdraw, your bank would return the check to the landlord's bank marked "NSF" (not sufficient funds) and the landlord's bank would send it to the landlord, who would then call you with a gentle request for an explanation. All the provisional settlements would be readjusted to account for the fact that the check failed to clear.

If you write a check for a pair of blue jeans to the L.L. Bean Company of Freeport, Maine, and you happen to live in Detroit, the clearance mechanism will be slightly different. Your check will probably be cleared by means of a courier service operated by the Federal Reserve. In this case the funds are likely to be transferred from your bank to Bean's bank by means of credits and debits to accounts held by the respective banks at the Federal Reserve. Alternatively, your check might be cleared through a large bank that operates a courier service for interstate clearance. In any case, however, clearance will be handled within the banking industry.

These days transfers are increasingly being made electronically, by means of so-called EFT (electronic funds transfer) technology. EFT avoids the inefficiencies and delay associated with the physical transport of checks. Although we are still far from the "checkless society" that had been predicted for EFT, electronic transfer is steadily gaining importance. Again, however, the process of electronic clearance is dominated by the banking industry.

Why do banks dominate the payments system? No law says they must. It is possible to imagine a system in which clearance occurs outside the banking industry. An established national courier system such as Federal Express could, in theory, enter the clearing business. When Bean's receives your check in the mail for the blue jeans, it could give the check to Federal Express for clearance rather than depositing the check to its bank account and letting banks handle the transaction. Federal Express could physically transport the check to your bank, and present it for payment in cash; Federal Express could then present an equal amount of cash to Bean's to complete the transaction.

Although nonbank clearance is conceivable, it is apparently impracticable—otherwise we would see courier services offering the service already! Why don't we observe nonbank check clearance?

First, customers prefer bank clearance. Because funds are deposited directly in their accounts, customers avoid the step of handling the funds when they are received. Some customers also apparently feel more comfortable when their funds are "in the bank"—a psychological factor that may explain the continued popularity of walk-in bank services despite the convenience, reliability, and ready availability of banking by mail. Second, clearance through the banking system provides some assurances against fraudulent endorsements since banks often maintain long-standing checking account relationships with customers that include accounts that can be debited if things go wrong. Third, banks usually do not charge separately for clearance fees (why not?), so a nonbank competitor would not be able to offer customers immediate savings in any event.

Bank domination of the payments system creates the potential for severe economic disruption in the event of widespread bank failure. What happens to checks in transit when the bank having custody over them fails? Is there a danger that checks will not be paid? In fact, very few problems have occurred as a result of individual bank failures. But the failure of a very big institution might cause disruption. More troublesome still is the prospect of a banking panic. If the nation's banking system becomes paralyzed by a panic, what happens to the payments system? In fact, the payments system did suspend for approximately a week during the "bank holiday" of 1933, causing widespread hardship. The prospect of such a catastrophe recurring is a principal concern driving the choice of regulatory policies in the banking area.

*QUESTIONS AND COMMENTS*

A friend writes you a check on his bank for $150. You show up at his bank (where you don't have an account), endorse and present the check, and ask the teller to give you cash. Is the teller likely to cooperate? Why not?

### 4. Model Bank Balance Sheet

The concept of a bank as a financial intermediary offering transaction services implicitly refers to the two sides of a bank's balance sheet. Transaction services, as we have seen, entail that a bank is financed largely by demand deposits. Such deposits dominate the liability side of the balance sheets of most banks. The idea of a financial intermediary suggests that the asset side of the balance sheet will reflect investments in other productive enterprises rather than activities that are directly productive in their own right.

Thus we can reduce our functional model of a bank to a greatly simplified model balance sheet.

***First National Bank***

| *Assets* | | *Liabilities/Net Worth* | |
|---|---|---|---|
| Cash | $ 100 | Deposits | $1,000 |
| Fixed rate mortgages | 1,000 | Equity | 100 |

We see immediately that this institution is a financial intermediary: It does not engage directly in productive activity but rather provides funds to other enterprises. The bank is capitalized principally through demand deposits. It operates with fractional reserves, retaining only $100 in cash, just enough to satisfy a 10 percent reserve requirement on deposits of $1,000.

Two other points about this balance sheet deserve mention: the amount of leverage, and the relative duration of assets and liabilities.

### a. Leverage

Leverage simply refers to the ratio of debt to equity on the liability side of a company's balance sheet. The more debt relative to equity, the more highly "leveraged" a company is.

The metaphor of leverage refers to the impact of debt on profits. Debt has the effect of increasing (or decreasing) the return on equity for any given level of return on assets. It is like a lever, which transmutes a small amount of force exercised over a large distance into a large amount of force exercised over a small distance (the British have a similar metaphor; they call the ratio of debt to equity "gearing").

Why does the debt-equity ratio affect the return on equity? Assume that a firm starts with $1,000 in equity raised from investors. It invests in productive enterprises that generate an annual net income of $150. The return on equity from this investment is 15 percent—not bad. But now let's say the firm retires $500 in equity (for example, by buying back its stock) and takes out a bank loan of $500 at 10 percent. Now the firm must pay $50 per year in debt service, so the net return from its investments is reduced from $150 to $100. However, the equity has been reduced as well, from $1,000 to $500. The return on equity has increased from 15 percent to 20 percent ($100 net profit on equity of $500). The return on equity has been leveraged through the addition of debt. The more debt, the more leverage. If the loan is increased to $900 and equity reduced to $100, the return on equity increases to 60 percent—and so on.

This sounds too good to be true, and it is. There is a dark side to the force of leverage. Let's say our loan of $500 was at an interest rate of 20 percent rather than 10 percent. Now our net return on equity after debt service goes *down* rather than up, to 10 percent. And as we increase the leverage we become increasingly worse off. If we finance our firm with $900 in debt at 20 percent and $100 in equity, our return on equity is −30 percent. A relatively profitable venture when financed all with equity has turned into a serious money loser.

What is the turning point at which leverage ceases to benefit equity holders and begins to penalize them? The key is the relationship between the return on assets free and clear of debt and the interest rate that must be paid on the debt. If the assets return 15 percent free and clear of debt, then leverage will benefit the equity holder so long as the interest rate is less than 15 percent (we ignore here the effect of taxes, which have important consequences in the real world). If, on the other hand, the interest rate exceeds 15 percent, then leverage will hurt the equity holder. And the degree to which the equity holder is benefited or hurt is proportional to the amount of leverage.

Banks tend to be highly leveraged relative to industrial companies. Book value leverage (the ratio of debt to total liabilities and capital) for industrial firms has traditionally run at between 33 and 40 percent. But industrial firms are nowhere close to the leverage ratios at banks. The ratio of debt to total liabilities and capital at commercial banks is over 90 percent, more than double the ratio for industrial firms. The leverage ratio at the First National Bank in our example is approximately average for commercial banks.

What accounts for this dramatic contrast in leverage ratios between banks and industrial companies? A number of explanations have been proposed. First, banks can predict their return on assets much more precisely than can industrial firms. The customer who borrows from a bank promises to pay a stated interest rate at stated times. The bank knows that (barring customer default) it will receive the proceeds on the due date. Industrial companies, in contrast, cannot know how their assets will perform. A recession could stifle sales, causing prices and profits to plummet. New competition could appear with the same effect. Unexpected technological developments could cause a plant to become obsolete. Consumer tastes could shift. Because return on assets is uncertain for industrial companies, they need to keep a higher percentage of their capitalization in the form of equity in order to avoid the risk of bankruptcy.

Second, banks enjoy ready access to sources of loans on a short-term basis if the need arises. They can borrow excess reserves from other banks in the "federal funds" market. Or they can obtain liquidity loans from the Federal Reserve. These sources of liquidity are not available to industrial firms. Banks, accordingly, can take on high levels of demand debt with fairly good assurance that if they are temporarily unable to meet their debt service obligations internally, they will be able to borrow enough money to do so.

Finally, federal deposit insurance may enhance a bank's ability to borrow money from the public in the form of bank deposits. Lenders to industrial firms are likely to demand that the firms maintain a reasonably large "cushion" of equity in order to provide assurances against bankruptcy. As a firm's leverage grows it must usually pay higher and higher interest rates to compensate lenders for the increased bankruptcy risk. In the case of banks, however, the public is more or less indifferent to leverage ratios because deposits (up to $100,000 per depositor per institution) are protected by federal guarantee. Accordingly, banks do not find it difficult to attract new depositors no matter how high their leverage ratios might be.

The high leverage ratios at banks raise concerns about bank failure.

We saw that bankruptcy risk increases with leverage because the equity cushion is correspondingly small. Further, we saw that leverage can be extremely disadvantageous to the equity holder if the interest rate on the debt exceeds the return on assets free and clear of debt. If banks get into this situation—if their cost of deposits exceeds their return on assets free and clear of debt—they will lose money rapidly and the equity cushion will disappear. This is exactly what happened to many banks and savings and loans in the late 1970s and early 1980s. As a result, federal regulators have moved aggressively to increase capital ratios—sometimes in the face of determined political opposition from the banks themselves.

### b. Asset-Liability Structure

Another important feature of the First National Bank's balance sheet is the comparative duration of assets and liabilities. This bank faces a gross mismatch between the duration of its assets—long-term mortgages held in inventory—and the duration of its liabilities—short-term demand deposits. The mismatch, in turn, creates severe interest rate risk.

Assume that short-term interest rates, which historically have been 5 percent, suddenly rise to 20 percent. The interest rate of the mortgages held by the bank naturally stays the same at 10 percent. Thus the bank must now pay 20 percent for funds in the deposit market in order to support assets paying only 10 percent. This is buying high and selling low—never a profitable strategy. Moreover, even if the bank could unload its mortgages, it could do so only at a loss (assuming long-term rates have risen as well) because the capital value of a fixed rate mortgage goes down as interest rates go up. In a highly leveraged firm like our bank, the losses stemming from high interest rates will quickly erode the equity and cause the bank to fail.

Banks today are acutely sensitive to interest rate risk, and employ a variety of strategies for avoiding it: decreasing the duration of their assets, increasing the duration of their liabilities, or ensuring that a high percentage of their loans pay at adjustable rates. Banks can also hedge against interest rate risk in the financial futures markets. Interest rate risk remains a problem nevertheless, especially in the savings and loan industry where customers have resisted paying variable interest rates on home mortgages.

Further, the interest rate risk in a mismatched balance sheet *could* be quite profitable. If rates *fall,* instead of rise, the bank will make high profits. An insolvent or nearly insolvent institution might deliberately expose itself to interest rate risk in hopes that rates will fall, generating high profits and returning the institution to solvency. If rates rise, of course, the institution will fail, but because the institution is already near insolvency the losses from failure will fall on the government's deposit insurance funds rather than the bank's shareholders. This incentive towards excessive risk-taking is a major concern in the regulation of insolvent or failing banks.

*QUESTIONS AND COMMENTS*

1. Why might savings and loan regulators favor the enforceability of "due-on-sale" clauses that allow home mortgage lenders to call in a loan prematurely upon sale by the homeowner? See Fidelity Federal Savings & Loan Association v. De La Questa, 458 U.S. 141 (1982).

2. Can you think of any reasons other than those suggested above why banks have higher leverage ratios than do industrial firms?

3. "As the distinctions between banks and other firms disappear during the 1990s, so will the disparity in leverage ratios between banks and other firms." Do current developments tend to bear out this prediction? Do you think the prediction will hold in the long term?

4. Consider the following epigram: "The difference between banks and industrial firms amounts to this: Banks are sure of their return on assets but unsure of the duration of their liabilities; industrial firms are sure of the duration of their liabilities but unsure of their return on assets." How much of the distinction between banks and industrial firms do you think this adage captures?

## NOTE ON THE FUNCTIONAL DEFINITION OF A BANK

The material above has focused on a "functional" definition of a bank. Consider, in this regard, the following analysis by the Supreme Court of the distinctions between banks and other firms.

> Commercial banks are unique among financial institutions in that they alone are permitted by law to accept demand deposits. This distinctive power gives commercial banking a key role in the national economy. For banks do not merely deal in, but are actually a source of, money and credit; when a bank makes a loan by crediting the borrower's demand deposit account, it augments the Nation's credit supply. Furthermore, the power to accept demand deposits makes banks the intermediaries in most financial transactions (since transfers of substantial moneys are almost always by check rather than by cash) and, concomitantly, the repositories of very substantial individual and corporate funds. The banks' use of these funds is conditioned by the fact that their working capital consists very largely of demand deposits, which makes liquidity the guiding principle of bank

lending and investing policies; thus it is that banks are the chief source of the country's short-term business credit.

United States v. Philadelphia National Bank, 374 U.S. 321, 326 (1963).

## E. STRUCTURE OF BANKING REGULATION

We now turn away from the industry itself to look briefly at its regulators. The structure of banking regulation is heavily influenced by the structure of banking *regulators*. In the historical section of this chapter we have seen that from time to time Congress has established new regulatory bodies. Just as the United States has opted for a highly diffuse, localized structure of banks, it has chosen to vest regulatory authority in a number of different institutions. We first outline the different regulatory agencies, then step back to assess the pros and cons of the American regulatory structure.

### 1. *Bank Regulatory Agencies*

#### a. Federal Reserve System

The Federal Reserve System is comprised of 12 Federal Reserve banks and a 7-member board of governors. Members of the board are appointed by the president for 14-year terms, subject to Senate confirmation. The president also appoints a chairman and vice-chairman for 4-year terms, again subject to Senate approval. Although the chairman is in theory only "first among equals," as a practical matter the chairman acts as principal spokesperson for the entire system and often exercises considerable influence over the other governors.

The Federal Reserve is said to be an "independent agency." The president cannot fire members of the board except for cause, a limitation that in practice gives the Federal Reserve considerable insulation from presidential influence in policy-making. In addition, the Federal Reserve is substantially insulated from congressional influence because, unlike almost every other federal agency, it does not require appropriations. It supports itself with interest earned on its holdings of government bonds—indeed, viewed as a private enterprise the Federal Reserve would be one of the most profitable businesses in the world.

The Federal Reserve performs both monetary and regulatory functions. In its role as the nation's central bank it controls the money supply through its Open Market Committee. In its role as a regulator the Federal

Reserve oversees all of the nation's bank holding companies as well as member banks in the Federal Reserve System. It also exercises broad-ranging miscellaneous supervisory powers, including regulation under various consumer-protection statutes. Much of this regulatory responsibility is delegated to the 12 Federal Reserve banks, but major questions of policy are determined by the board of governors.

#### b. Comptroller of the Currency

The Comptroller of the Currency has principal supervisory authority over national banks. The Comptroller issues charters for new national banks and supervises the operations of existing national banks through a corps of bank examiners.

The Comptroller's legal status within the executive branch is somewhat ambiguous. The Office of the Comptroller is housed within the Department of the Treasury, suggesting that the Comptroller is a subordinate official within a chain of command extending up to the president. However, Congress also stipulated that the Comptroller be appointed by the president for a 5-year term, subject to Senate confirmation, and that the Comptroller may not be removed except for cause, a provision generally thought to create independence from executive oversight and supervision. In practice the Comptroller exercises a considerable degree of autonomy both from the president and from the secretary of the treasury.

#### c. Federal Deposit Insurance Corporation

The Federal Deposit Insurance Corporation (FDIC) is an independent agency headed by a five-person board of directors. Two board members are the Comptroller of the Currency and the director of the Office of Thrift Supervision (see below) serving ex officio. The other three members are appointed by the president for six-year terms, subject to the advice and consent of the Senate.

The FDIC, through the Bank Insurance Fund, provides federal deposit insurance to all national banks and virtually all state-chartered commercial banks, as well as small numbers of thrift institutions. In addition, it provides deposit insurance to virtually all of the nation's savings and loans and savings banks through the Savings Association Insurance Fund, which is separate from the Bank Insurance Fund for accounting purposes but which is also administered by the FDIC. Until 1989 the Federal Savings and Loan Insurance Corporation (FSLIC) provided federal insurance for most of the nation's savings and loans and savings banks. However, the FSLIC was abolished in 1989 by the Financial

Institutions Reform, Recovery and Enforcement Act (FIRREA), with its deposit insurance functions being taken over by the FDIC. The FDIC inspects institutions it insures. It handles failures of insured institutions, and has authority to act as conservator of institutions that are in danger of default and as receiver of failed institutions. The FDIC's authority over the resolution of troubled depository institutions was significantly enhanced in the 1991 FDICIA legislation.

### d. Federal Home Loan Bank System

The Federal Home Loan Bank System, modeled after the Federal Reserve System, consists of 12 regional Federal Home Loan banks, the member savings and loan associations, and a five-member Federal Housing Finance Board, an independent agency consisting of four members appointed by the president with the advice and consent of the Senate and the secretary of the Department of Housing and Urban Development serving ex officio. Members of the Federal Housing Finance Board serve for seven-year terms; one must be from an established organization representing consumer or community interests. The former governing agency, the Federal Home Loan Bank Board (FHLBB), was abolished by the FIRREA in 1989.

### e. Office of Thrift Supervision

Established by the FIRREA in 1989, the Office of Thrift Supervision (OTS) is charged with supervising and regulating the savings and loan industry. The OTS is not an independent agency, but rather is a subsidiary office within the Department of the Treasury. However, the secretary of the treasury has only limited authority to direct the activities of the OTS.

### f. National Credit Union Administration

The National Credit Union Administration (NCUA) is an agency in the executive branch, headed by the National Credit Union Board consisting of a chairman, a vice chairman, and a third member, each appointed by the president with the advice and consent of the Senate. The NCUA charters and supervises federal credit unions. Through the National Credit Union Share Insurance Fund (NCUSIF), the NCUA provides federal deposit insurance for national and qualified state-chartered credit unions.

#### g. State Regulators

State-chartered commercial banks, savings and loans, savings banks, and credit unions are supervised, examined, and regulated by a variety of state agencies.

#### h. Department of Justice

The antitrust division of the Department of Justice regulates parts of the bank merger process by passing on applications for consolidations or mergers of banks under the federal antitrust laws. The department's criminal division prosecutes criminal violations of federal law by bank officers. The department's attorneys litigate some banking cases on behalf of the federal agencies and represent the federal government before the U.S. Supreme Court.

### 2. *Pros and Cons of the American System*

It is not obvious that different segments of the financial services industry should be regulated by separate agencies. Consider Japan, where one agency, the Ministry of Finance, oversees not only all banking institutions but also securities firms. The Ministry's broad mandate gives it a systematic overview of the Japanese economic system in general, while its regulatory jurisdiction over a variety of competing industries seems calculated to induce responsible policies that don't unduly favor one industry over another. This is not to paint too idealized a picture of the Japanese system, which is no doubt subject to many imperfections, but merely to suggest a possible model for regulation that has intellectual plausibility and differs markedly from our own system.

Especially when viewed in comparison with a regulatory system such as Japan's, the American system does appear complex, even baroque. And indeed, the system is frequently criticized on this ground—with the most vocal objections often coming from people serving in high-level administrative positions. The U.S. system is accused of suffering from jurisdictional overlaps that induce excessive, duplicative, or conflicting regulation, distort economic behavior, increase transactions costs, delay desirable transactions, and unfairly favor some institutions over others.

From time to time over the past 50 years blue-ribbon panels have recommended fundamental changes in the bank regulatory structure. A recent, comprehensive set of high-level recommendations is contained in the Treasury Department's legislative proposals, which were submitted to Congress in 1991. Yet commendable as these studies and recommendations have been, they have had very little effect to date. Indeed, just as efforts to simplify the tax code seem inevitably to make it more complex, each new piece of federal banking legislation seems to add an additional level of intricacy to the system.

The unusual structure of the American system of bank regulation is partly a function of banking politics. As new areas of activity came under regulation, each affected industry segment pushed for a regulator of its own, in the belief that a regulator with a narrow mandate would be more responsive to industry needs than a regulator with a broad mandate. For example, savings and loans may have believed that a regulator of savings and loans would be more responsive to their needs than would a generalized banking regulator, since an agency with a more general regulatory portfolio might become dominated by commercial banks. The splintering of banking regulation may also have been appealing to members of Congress because a variety of smaller agencies might be more responsive to congressional influence than would a single large agency like the Japanese Ministry of Finance.

The fact that American banking regulation may be politically expedient does not in itself justify the system as representing sound public policy. Are there justifications for the U.S. bank regulatory structure apart from politics? Consider the following arguments:

First, a splintered regulatory system may actually be a safeguard against excessive regulation. If one banking agency imposes excessively burdensome or inefficient regulations on its industry segment, the effect will be to give a competitive advantage to institutions regulated by other agencies. Institutions subject to the first agency will be driven out of business or will attempt to place themselves under a different regulator. Thus if the Comptroller of the Currency imposes overly burdensome regulations on national banks, the affected institutions can relinquish their national bank charters and recharter under state law, escaping the Comptroller's writ. This phenomenon has happened repeatedly in the history of American banking regulation.

Second, the incessant turf battles incident to the American system are the regulatory equivalent of competition in the private sector; they induce regulators to be diligent and competent in order to maintain their "market share" in competition with other regulators. Although it is difficult to judge these things, most observers would probably agree that banking agencies display a higher-than-average level of competence and diligence when compared with government agencies in general.

Third, the splintering of banking regulation is analogous to the splintering of American politics into numerous interest groups. The pluralist theory of democracy, which sees the competition among interest groups as conducive to the public interest, can be modified to justify a plural regulatory system. Thus, conflict among bank regulators may result in policies that are desired by none of the contestants but that actually serve the public interest quite well.

## *QUESTIONS AND COMMENTS*

1. Consider the following quote from the Bush Task Force Report (the blue-ribbon report on regulation of financial services prepared by a task force under the direction of then-Vice President George Bush):

> Throughout American history, no single government authority has ever been entrusted with regulatory authority over all American banks. Such an unprecedented concentration of regulatory power in the hands, ultimately, of a single individual or board could have a variety of deleterious effects, including a significant erosion of the dual banking system and a possible increased risk of unanticipated supervisory problems affecting all banks. These factors suggest strongly that more than one federal bank regulator should continue to be maintained.

Blueprint for Reform: The Report of the Task Group on Regulation of Financial Services 46 (1984). Do you agree?

2. In 1993 the Clinton administration submitted an equally blue-ribboned report to Congress. While past blue-ribbon proposals had come to naught, this one would surely be different. Eerily echoing Marx's aphorism that "the philosophers have only interpreted the world, in various ways; the point, however, is to change it" Karl Marx, Theses on Feuerbach, in Karl Marx & Friedrich Engels, 1 Selected Works 15 (Moscow, 1969), the administration proclaimed that "we have studied enough. Now it is time to act."

The administration proposed to reinvent banking regulation through a number of reforms. Most importantly, it would establish a Federal Banking Commission, an independent agency that would regulate all FDIC-insured depository institutions and their holding companies and other affiliates and would exercise all the depository institution regulatory functions of the Comptroller of the Currency, the Federal Reserve Board, the FDIC, and the OTS. The FDIC would continue to insure deposits and to act as conservator or receiver of failed depository institutions. The Federal Reserve Board, as the nation's central bank, would continue to conduct monetary policy, administer the payments system, and provide liquidity for financial markets through its discount window. The states would remain the primary regulator of the banks they charter, "thus preserving the integrity of the dual banking system."

The Clinton administration proposal—tidy, sensible, well-researched, and cogently argued—received the same treatment as all the other blue-ribbon commissions. It was publicized, distributed, applauded, vetted—and ignored.

3. Is it not anomalous that the Federal Reserve Board should exercise powerful regulatory functions as well as operate the nation's central bank? In particular, do you see any necessary connection between the

Federal Reserve's role in controlling the money supply and its power to control the affairs of bank holding companies?

## 3. *Banking Politics*

Few industries are as politically active as banking. The industry is divided into organized interest groups along a number of fault lines—small banks/large banks, thrifts/commercial banks, banks/nonbanks, and more. These interest groups are highly effective legislative lobbyists at both the state and federal level. They participate regularly in important administrative proceedings. In addition, especially in recent years, they have become sophisticated litigators, adapting techniques of "test case" litigation to the financial services arena. As we will see, many of the most important banking cases of the past decade have involved interest groups as parties on one or both sides of the issue.

Among the oldest associations in the banking field is the American Bankers Association, representing commercial banks generally. The nation's biggest banks are also politically active on their own behalf at both the state and the federal levels. Bank holding companies are members of the Association of Bank Holding Companies. Smaller and unit banks find their voice in the Independent Bankers Association of America. Savings institutions are politically organized in the U.S. League of Savings Associations and a variety of other organizations. Federal credit unions are served by the National Association of Federal Credit Unions. The list could be extended. In addition to these national organizations, the banking industry is also comprehensively organized into state associations.

Organized lobbies serve the interests of nonbank financial intermediaries as well. The Securities Industry Association represents the majority of the nation's securities brokers and investment banks. The Investment Company Institute performs a similar role for the mutual fund industry, as does the American Council of Life Insurance for the life insurance industry.

In addition to interest groups representing industry segments, the regulators themselves maintain a powerful political presence. The major federal banking agencies and the Securities and Exchange Commission are continuously involved in legislative politics; an important part of the job of any agency head is to cultivate influence with members of Congress and staffers on the key banking committees. State bank regulators seek power in numbers: the Conference of State Bank Supervisors, the National Association of State Savings & Loan Supervisors, and the National Association of State Credit Union Supervisors represent state commercial bank, savings & loan, and credit union regulators, respectively. Insurance regulators are organized as the National Association of Insurance Commissioners. State securities regulators are represented by the North American Securities Administrators Association.

The massive organization of banking into political interest groups has made legislative compromise difficult to achieve. Banking legislation tends to remain in a state of impasse, the result of forces powerful enough to block any legislation inimical to their interests, but not powerful enough to obtain desired legislation over the opposition of other groups. The legislative logjam breaks only during times of crisis, as in the banking revolution of the 1980s. But this legislation was enacted only because of compelling need. In the absence of a crisis situation, it is doubtful that major new banking reforms would have been implemented in the 1980s.

### *QUESTIONS AND COMMENTS*

1. It is hard to measure the degree of political activity within an industry, but it does appear that banking is as politically active as any American industry. Why should this be so?

2. Develop an argument that the pervasive influence of interest groups in the politics of banking may be an effective means of obtaining socially desirable legislation in the area. What are the strengths and weaknesses in the argument?

## F. BASIC RATIONALES FOR BANK REGULATION

At first glance the case for regulating banks appears overwhelming. Banks are among the most regulated industries of all, not only in the United States but worldwide. This is nothing new: Banks have always been heavily regulated. Even during the American "free banking" era, states imposed capital requirements and inspected the operations of state-chartered banks.

This banking history suggesting the value of government regulation of banks is buttressed by impeccable intellectual authority. Adam Smith, who was in general no fan of government controls, believed strongly that banks should be regulated to prohibit issuance of low-denomination notes and to require that all notes be redeemed in specie on demand. Smith's distinguished intellectual descendant Milton Friedman, also no fan of regulation, speaks in glowing terms about the benefits of federal deposit insurance and professes admiration for the punitive tax imposed on state bank notes after the Civil War. If scholars of such unimpeachable free-market credentials favor bank regulation, who could be against it?

Of course, the fact that banks have been heavily regulated in the past does not necessarily mean that they should *continue* to be regulated; perhaps regulatory programs of years past were ill-considered. Further, it should be noted that Smith and Friedman were not in favor of *all* forms of banking regulation. Their concern was to maintain a stable money supply, and they understood that banks play a key role in the process by which money is created and destroyed. These scholars—and many others—find much to criticize about other forms of banking regulation. Accordingly, it may be worthwhile to step back for a moment and consider in general terms the basic rationales for banking regulation. We hope to identify the underlying justifications for the multitude of rules and regulations that we will encounter in the remainder of this book.

So: What is special about banks that requires that they be subject to a unique regulatory structure? We have seen three distinctive features of banking, each of them related to banks' role as financial intermediaries providing transaction services with demand debt: susceptibility to runs, participation in money creation and destruction, and custodianship of the payments system. These are important differences between banks and other firms. The question from the perspective of public policy is this: For what purposes do these differences *make* a difference?

The public policy issue is crystallized in the longstanding debate over whether or not banks are "special." Some commentators claim that banks are special, even unique. Others retort that they aren't really very special after all. In reality, the debate concerns a somewhat different question: whether banks should receive unique regulatory treatment from the government. The claim that banks are "special" stands as a proxy for the argument that banks require unique regulatory treatment.

In this respect the claim that banks are special has a curious dual feature. On the one hand, it justifies all sorts of regulatory intervention into banking markets that are uncommon or unknown in other markets. Few other businesses are subject to the same level of pervasive governmental controls. In this respect banks could be said to be specially *disfavored* because their freedom of action is profoundly constrained by government regulators.

On the other hand, the claim to specialness also justifies all sorts of regulatory *favors* for banks. In particular, no other business can offer its investors the same level of protection against default risk in the form of government deposit insurance. And few, if any, other businesses have benefited as handsomely from government policies suppressing competition. Thus banks have found Big Brother to be jealous and watchful, but also generous and forgiving.

In light of the foregoing, consider the following selections, one by a prominent official at the Federal Reserve and the other by an executive at one of the nation's largest banks.

## Corrigan, Are Banks Special?

***Federal Reserve Bank of Minneapolis 1982 Annual Report***

### Introduction

The recent evolution of the financial structure in the United States has produced two competing points of view regarding the proper direction for further change. On the one hand, there is the view that the "financial services industry"—encompassing banks, thrifts, brokers, investment banks, and insurance companies—should be looked at as a single entity. According to this view, efforts to distinguish among kinds of institutions are both futile and unnecessary. This view of the financial services industry is based on the belief that many financial services offered by various classes of institutions are so complementary to (or such close substitutes for) one another that institutional distinctions are rendered useless. Implicit in this view is the assumption that banks are not special.

The competing, if not opposing, view is that banks are indeed special. This view holds that specialization of financial institutions has worked well and, at least in some cases, specialization may still be more efficient and also better serve the public interest. This view is associated with the historical separation of banking from commerce and from investment banking. In general, this "separation doctrine" in banking grew out of concerns about concentration of financial power, possible conflicts of interest, and the appropriate scope of risks banks should incur in the face of the special trusteeship falling on institutions that engage in the lending of depositors' money. In a shorthand way, as pertains to banks and the banking system, these concerns are typically captured by the phrase, "safety and soundness."

These two points of view do not necessarily represent mutually exclusive approaches to financial market structure. For example, in the context of a large financial services holding company, banks could be legally separated from nonbanks, but it is not clear that such separation would necessarily provide the kinds of protections that are currently built into federal banking laws.

Thus, assessing the merits of these two competing views must start with some very basic questions: Are banks "special" or are they simply another provider of financial services? Does it matter what kinds of risks banks incur? Does it matter who owns banks? Is "safety and soundness" a cliche, or should it have genuine and substantial meaning for banks, for bank regulators, and for the public at large?

While banking practices have naturally evolved over time, recently a combination of events has shifted that process to one of an almost revolutionary character. Amidst this process of rapid change, with market innovation and new sources of competition, there is a perception that banks' competitive position—and presumably their market share—has slipped. Casual observation of the growth of the commercial paper market, the thrift industry, money market mutual funds (MMMFs), and the de facto trend toward ownership of banks by securities firms and commercial enterprises, tends to support that perception. Indeed, there are numerous instances in which nonbanks have been able to provide "bank-like" services at a lower cost (or a higher rate of return) to the individual or corporate customer, thereby drawing business away from banking institutions.

High on the list of reasons that are cited for this perceived shift of market position from banks to nonbank competitors is the extra burden of regulation on banks. The fact of a heavy regulatory burden on banks is beyond dispute, but in some cases it is also true that regulation—relating to, for example, deposit insurance or access to the discount window—provides powerful incentives for individuals and businesses to maintain relationships with banks. . . .

Despite these regulatory restraints, banks have not stood still in the face of changing financial markets and new sources of competition. By using the flexibility provided by the Bank Holding Company Act, by developing sophisticated liability management techniques, by major expansions abroad, and by creative and innovative adaptations of "conventional" banking services, banks have actually fared rather well in terms of preserving their overall market position. . . . The analysis does not, however, imply that heavy regulation has not constrained the growth of banks and their market share, for it is quite possible that absent such regulations, banks' position would have risen rather than essentially held steady. Nor does the analysis indicate whether a rising or falling bank share is good, bad, or indifferent from the perspective of the public interest. To some extent these issues depend upon whether, in fact, there is something special about banks that is worth preserving. Indeed, if banks are special, it would not be in the public interest for the features or functions that make banks special to be eroded by competitive, regulatory, or legislative forces. By the same token, if what is special about banks dictates a *relatively* heavy dose of regulation, public policymakers should not be goaded into eliminating *necessary* regulation simply because bank market share might grow to some higher level without that regulation.

### What Makes Banks Special?

Reduced to essentials, it would appear that there are three characteristics that distinguish banks from all other classes of institutions—both financial and nonfinancial. They are:

1. Banks offer transaction accounts.
2. Banks are the backup source of liquidity for all other institutions.
3. Banks are the transmission belt for monetary policy.

These three essential bank characteristics and the interrelationships between them are discussed below. Of necessity, the discussion treats each factor separately. However, it is clear that these essential characteristics are highly complementary and furthermore that it is the relationship among them that best captures the essence of what makes banks special.

### Issuance of Transaction Accounts

Only banks issue transaction accounts; that is, they incur liabilities payable on demand at par and are readily transferable by the owner to third parties. The owner of a transaction account can demand and receive currency in the face amount deposited in the account; write a check in the full amount of the account; or, perhaps most importantly, the owner of the account can transfer the full amount of the account to a third party almost instantaneously by wire transfer. The liquidity, mobility, and acceptability of bank issued transaction accounts permit our diverse economic and financial system to work with the relative ease and efficiency to which we are accustomed. Moreover, in periods of financial stress, the capacity to quickly move transaction account balances to third parties takes on special significance by providing elements of flexibility and certainty in making and receiving payments that help to insure that financial disruptions do not spread. Individual banks can also create these highly liquid and mobile balances through their lending function. The capacity to "create" liabilities with these characteristics is vital to the ongoing needs of commerce, but it takes on special significance in periods of financial stress. . . .

Looked at in this perspective, the critical difference between banks and other classes of financial institutions rests with the capacity of banks to incur (and to create) liabilities that are payable on demand at par and that are readily transferable to third parties. The resulting mismatch of the maturities of assets and liabilities makes banks particularly vulnerable to sudden drains on deposits that can jeopardize their solvency. In practice, depositors—reinforced by the public policy safety net—have demonstrated tendencies to drain deposits from particular banks only when confronted with the reality or the perception of losses growing out of asset management problems and/or poor management of banking organizations. Thus, while the deposit taking function of banks is what makes them unique, the integrity of that process depends upon the risks, real and perceived, associated with the lending and related activities of the banking system as a whole and its capacity to absorb shocks in the short run.

### Backup Sources of Liquidity

As discussed above, the fact that banks issue transaction deposits is the key factor that distinguishes them from other classes of financial and nonfinancial institutions. However, experience also suggests that public confidence in the ability of banks to meet their deposit obligations is ultimately related to the quality of bank assets and to the overall financial condition of the bank. This relationship takes on additional importance when it is recalled that banks can also create, through their lending activities, transaction deposits. Indeed, in a very real way, banks are the primary source of liquidity for all other classes and sizes of institutions, both financial and nonfinancial. . . .

Looked at in this light, the ability of banks to fulfill their role as standby sources of liquidity and credit rests importantly on the quality and consistency of credit judgments made by banks. This is particularly true in periods of stress when banks may be called on to supply credit to borrowers who, for one reason or another, temporarily do not have access to other sources of funds or to make the even more difficult decisions as to which borrowers are experiencing problems of a fundamental or irreparable nature. It is in these particular circumstances that banks must be in a position to make rigorous, impartial, and objective credit decisions, because it is precisely in such circumstances that the potential for compromise in the impartiality of the credit decision making process is greatest and the potential for asset quality deterioration is the largest. It is in this light that considerations about the commingling of banking and other interests and concerns about the ownership and control of banks become compelling.

To summarize, virtually all other financial markets and other classes of institutions are directly or indirectly dependent on the banking system as their standby or backup source of credit and liquidity. Banks can fulfill this function for a variety of reasons, including their relative ease of access to deposit and nondeposit sources of funding. However, experience suggests that the capacity to provide this function or, more directly, to provide access to these markets and sources of funding—like the integrity of the deposit taking function—is ultimately related to the overall financial strength of banks and the quality of bank assets. This role of banks as a standby source of liquidity takes on special significance in periods of stress and in this light underscores the importance of rigorous and impartial credit judgments by banks. This, in turn, provides a particularly relevant context in which concerns about the commingling of banking and other interests should be evaluated.

### Transmission Belt for Monetary Policy

As the preceding discussion suggests, there is a direct link between banks and the central bank arising in part from the central bank's lender of last resort function. More broadly, the fact that banks are subject to reserve requirements places the banking system in the unique position of being the "transmission belt" through which the actions and policies of the central bank have their effect on financial market conditions, money and credit creation, and economic conditions generally. To put it somewhat differently, the required reserves to the banking system have often been described as the fulcrum upon which the monetary authority operates monetary policy. The reserves in the banking system also serve the complementary purpose of providing the working balances which permit our highly efficient financial markets to function and to effect the orderly end-of-day settlement of the hundreds of billions of dollars of transactions that occur over the course of each business day.

Some have argued that neither monetary policy nor the payments mechanism are dependent on the relationship between reserves and the banking system. There have been, or are, schemes for conducting monetary policy and operating a payments mechanism that do not use bank reserves and the banking system in the way the U.S. system currently operates. However, it is also true that any of these alternative arrangements would entail major institutional changes and run the risk that they might not work as efficiently as the current framework or the possibility that they might not work at all. In short, to justify departure from the current arrangement the weight of evidence should be overwhelming that the current system is not working or that some alternative system would work decidedly better. . . .

As suggested above, these and other forces may already be working to introduce a larger margin of slack into the transmission belt. While the slack evident today is of manageable proportions, the future design of the banking and financial system must leave intact a strong yet adaptable mechanism through which monetary policy and the payments mechanism can function. This imperative underscores the case for attempting to segregate essential banking functions into an identifiable class of institutions and seeking to ensure that these institutions have the financial strength and vitality to perform their essential functions and to absorb changes in the credit market and economic conditions associated with periods of monetary restraint. . . .

## Aspinwall, On the "Specialness" of Banking

***7 Issues in Bank Reg. 16 (1983)***

The assertion that banks are special and therefore require special regulatory treatment is back. . . . Once again, specialness (largely a Federal Reserve doctrine) is being invoked to justify the continuation, if not the extension, of elements of commercial bank regulation not now imposed on competing institutions.

Application of the Federal Reserve's "specialness" line of thinking is exemplified by a recent statement by Gerald Corrigan entitled "Are Banks Special?" In essence, Mr. Corrigan's position is that banks play a unique role in the economy, and this requires distinctive regulatory treatment. While he concedes that heavy regulation in the past may have constrained the growth of banks and the market share of banks, since:

> if banks are special, it would not be in the public interest for the features or functions that make banks special to be eroded by competitive, regulatory, or legislative forces. By the same token, if what is special about banks dictates a *relatively* heavy dose of regulation, public policy makers should not be goaded into eliminating *necessary* regulation simply because bank market share might grow to some higher level without that regulation. [Emphasis original.]

This line of reasoning raises two basic questions. The first is whether the specialness argument squares with reality. The second is whether the policy prescription of reregulation (as suggested above) necessarily follows. In other words, on what principles should changes in banking-type regulation be judged?

Briefly, this article advances two principal arguments. First, banks are not "special" by any criteria that justify the extent of current regulation. Indeed, virtually all financial services furnished by nonbanks are subject to substantially less regulation than applicable to banks—so far without the adverse consequences that "reregulators" fear would follow reduced bank regulation. Second, the improvement of financial services and the strengthening of financial entities require fewer (not more) restrictions on pricing, service lines and location.

## The Meaning of "Special"

In each of the major categories of financial services, . . . , several kinds of institutions are "special" in that they are significant factors that are highly important in economic activity. As with parents' claims for their children, however, if all entities are special, no one is. While this does not diminish the importance attaching to finance functions, it makes the policy implications attaching to a claim of specialness highly ambiguous. In fact, given the increased feasibility of new alternative financial services, persistent regulatory burdens in one sector virtually assure a competitive decline for the regulated. The experience with money market mutual funds during the past decade is clear on this point.

In Mr. Corrigan's view three characteristics make banks special. These are: 1) Banks offer transaction accounts, 2) banks are the backup source of liquidity for all other institutions and 3) banks are the transmission belt for monetary policy. These are reviewed briefly in turn.

*Transaction Services.* There are two major components to transaction services—clearing and settlement. Transfers of financial information are, in effect, clearings. They move quickly from one party to another, either within the same institution or between institutions, largely by check, telephone or electronic device. In the past, clearing was a function of commercial banks, clearing houses (groups of banks) and the Federal Reserve. In recent years, however, thrift institutions have gained direct access to bank clearing houses (directly and through jointly owned clearing banks) and to the Federal Reserve. In addition, nondepository financial institutions have acquired thrifts as well as limited purpose commercial banks. A small number (so far) of retailing and manufacturing concerns have done the same. The increasing role of credit card systems, such as Visa, in clearing services should be added to this list. Consequently, clearing access is now available to an ever-widening range of institutions. New technological applications are also facilitating clearing outside traditional channels. The so-called "smart card" is one example. In terms of clearing, therefore, the distinctive role of commercial banks is clearly eroding.

A second characteristic of transaction services is the existence of instruments having a cash or near-cash property that is compatible with the funds clearing process. In addition to funds transferable at par and on demand, there are also those readily marketable at a minimal differential from par. Instruments that are not directly transferable may serve a funds transfer role if, after conversion costs, there is a higher net return to users than recourse to "traditional" funds transfer arrangements.

Mr. Corrigan tends to ignore the practical implications of growing nonbank involvement in the clearing process per se. In fact, while he refers to transaction accounts, his major preoccupation seems to be with transactable funds—that is, funds that are easily accessible for the purpose of transfer to others. He asserts that transaction accounts should be redefined to include not only demand deposits, NOW accounts and share drafts, but possibly also money market deposit accounts, money market mutual funds and other nonbank institutional arrangements offering so-called check writing capabilities.

The immediate regulatory implications include a recasting ot what is a demand deposit (relating to the definition of a bank under the Bank Holding Company Act) and a broader application of reserve requirements. In essence, virtually anything that is liquid appears to need reserves (if not other forms of regulation). Mr. Corrigan stops short of extending this net to market securities, but that is a natural extension of this line of reasoning. Indeed, this approach is only the latest of an endless process of reclassification, as experience over the past 15 years has shown. Incentives to develop new instruments or new ways to process old instruments invariably stem from the burdens of regulation applying to established arrangements or institutions.

*Liquidity Backup.* Access to liquid assets is a form of liquidity that is of considerable importance in the structuring of assets and liabilities by every class of economic unit. This access affects spending decisions, consumption versus saving and the kinds of borrowing vehicles employed. Banks are not the only source of such backup. All entities engaged in lending offer customers credit access that may constitute a reserve resource. Examples of other sources include insurance companies, brokers and nonbank issuers of credit cards. Moreover, an increasing amount of direct credit market financing, such as commercial paper issuance, is only partially tied to lines of credit and the like. Mr. Corrigan's unqualified emphasis on bank liquidity service is somewhat misleading. During periods of monetary stringency in the past, the Federal Reserve has cautioned banks to restrain their "backup" and commitment activities at the very time, according to Mr. Corrigan, when banks have a "special" role.

*Transmission Belt for Monetary Policy.* Mr. Corrigan contends banks have a unique role as the vehicle through which actions of the Federal Reserve affect financial markets, money and credit creation, and economic conditions generally. This is nothing more than a revised version of the long-discredited Federal Reserve membership argument. While monetary policy is executed largely through open market transactions with large dealers in Government securities, that is a process reflecting the limited number of participants that are large enough to handle large-size transactions effectively, rather than banking distinctiveness per se. Indeed, a number of Government securities dealers are not banks, and, taken literally, Mr. Corrigan's argument implies that they should be subjected to banking-type regulation. Moreover, the financial market manifestations of monetary policy are interest rate movements, which influence the spending, saving and balance sheet decisions of all economic units—bank and nonbank alike.

## Rationalization of Regulation

Specialness in the sense invoked by Mr. Corrigan (among others) implies an ability to compartmentalize financing functions that is at variance with the dynamic behavior of many classes of institutions (financial and nonfinancial) offering financial services. Indeed, reregulators seem to demonstrate unshakable faith in three propositions: 1) The financial services industry can be compartmentalized, 2) depository institutions can be assigned certain compartments and no others, and nonbanks can be assigned other compartments but not those (or some of those) assigned to banks and 3) to the extent depository institutions are handicapped in the assignment of their compartments, that is the price to be paid for being a bank in the first place.

Forces for change reflect the joint effects of regulatory constraints, new technology and increased incentives for regulatory avoidance (largely reflecting higher interest rates and shifts in intermediation risks). Many regulators fail to take adequate account of these effects.

To be sure, while the "specialness" arguments advanced by Mr. Corrigan are open to question, it is obvious banks do play a major role in providing financial services. Objectives of banking-type regulation should be shaped to meet public needs. While this is a truism, it does not suggest which direction is better than the extent of present regulation—more or less. In this connection, broadly speaking, nonbank firms engaged in investment, insurance and securities activities are subject chiefly to the following:

- Disclosure
- Consumer protection and fairness
- Avoidance of conflicts of interest
- Standards of competence and conduct
- Capital adequacy
- Asset valuation
- Avoidance of portfolio concentrations

At the same time, liabilities arising from many of these activities are Federally insured. Examples include coverage of pension benefits by the Pension Benefit Guaranty Corporation Act and of claims on brokerage firms by the Securities Investor Protection Corporation. Neither in connection with such insurance nor with other nonbank activities are nonbank institutions subjected to the degree of regulation as that applicable to commercial banks. Those differential constraints include:

1. Limitations on range of permitted financial services—especially those imposing restrictions on insurance, securities underwriting and ownership of thrift institutions.
2. Severe limitations on interstate operations.
3. Pricing limitations relating to demand and savings deposit interest and size minima and prepayment penalties applying to time deposits.
4. Reserve requirements and ownership of Federal Reserve stock—both of which impose material opportunity costs.
5. Adherence to more rigorous anti-trust standards.
6. Requirement that regulators receive prior notice in advance of virtually any expansion representing a previously authorized activity.
7. On-site examination.

Banking regulatory authorities currently face four alternatives. First, they may do nothing. This means permitting less regulated entities to take what they may, with authorities playing a relatively passive role in avoidance innovation by the regulated. Structural changes when they become sizably enough would be validated. Second, Congress may strive to rebuild the *status quo* pattern of institutions and services of some previous period by seeking to unwind, through forced divestiture, most structural changes of the past decade. This is not likely to be feasible with technological change driving costs of entry and transactions ever lower. Third, they may extend the regulatory net covering the "most regulated" entities to all entities. Fourth, they may seek to enhance, rather than distort, processes of change. This would mean eliminating regulation that tends to weaken traditional intermediaries (or make them more susceptible to risk) and strengthening regulations aimed to avoid actionable problems.

Only the last of these seems to offer an even-handed opportunity for financial strengthening. On the one hand, reduced regulation of bank services and branching would furnish opportunities to develop greater operating efficiencies and more diverse kinds of business risks. This may entail processing savings relating to packages containing broader ranges of services and lower-cost methods of delivering services. In the process, users of financial services would benefit from improved alternatives.

On the other hand, in addressing a more rational regulatory policy, the broad range of regulatory objectives identified above must be kept in mind. That is, there is a strong case that a prerequisite to further deregulation is a more rational treatment of risk-taking by banking institutions under their present operating powers (as well as any new ones). As a prime example, the present structure of fixed-rate premiums for deposit insurance has tended to encourage some managers of banks and thrift institutions to increase the riskiness of their activities.

A system of risk-adjusted deposit premiums is needed to place the insurance system on a more rational basis. Such a step would shift a greater share of the insurance burden to those entities engaging in relatively riskier activities. To be sure, in practice serious obstacles confront the implementation of such a program. For example, risk attributes will differ over time and among institutions in different markets. Current bank examination procedures are not an adequate source of risk assessment. Moreover, it is not feasible to impose premiums of a size sufficient to cover, on an actuarial basis (assuming one exists), a bunching of failures reflecting common macroeconomic forces. Finally, a serious risk exists that a structure of risk-related premiums would eventually degenerate into a politically-based tax system.

Greater disclosure is also a central factor in highlighting differences in risk characteristics among institutions. Such a step would include more detail on matters such as the duration characteristics of assets and liabilities and activities of nonbank holding company subsidiaries. Moreover, a program of enhanced disclosure should also include estimates of current market valuations for assets and liabilities. Changes along these lines would constitute new disincentives for a variety of the risks that, after the fact, many banking institutions are perceived to have taken in recent years.

In a similar vein, as the permissible range of services broadens, so too does the risk of improper tying arrangements, conflicts of interest and other similar abuses. Disclosure is one technique for avoiding problems such as these. The bank holding company structure also provides a vehicle that may help to separate certain functions so as to reduce the incidence of such abuses.

Anther prerequisite to further deregulation is the reorientation of the structure of regulatory agencies in order to accord a greater priority for competition. This does not necessarily point to the abandonment of policies relating to safety and soundness, but it would require a more open trade-off in the design of regulatory policies. Indeed, the decline of compartmentalization—accompanied by regulatory jostling for turf—increases the need for a new evaluation of regulatory-agency organization.

## Conclusion

The degree of institutional specialization and compartmentalization that tended to characterize financial markets in the past is diminishing. Indeed, the pace of change appears to be accelerating. These changes reflect a number of forces, one of which is differences among classes of institutions in regulatory constraints.

The dynamic process of change in financial markets constitutes an effective shift in the application of regulation, although not necessarily in regulatory objectives themselves. In order to extend old regulations to new institutions or their services, there is a burden to show that these objectives are not being served. The fact of regulatory avoidance is not even prima facie evidence. Essentially, the pro-regulation argument is that the existence of regulation under the status quo ante is sufficient to warrant new extension of regulation.

Those asserting that banks are so special as to require special regulation seek to resist shifts of activity from the regulated to the less-regulated. This response aims to increase regulation on those services increasingly offered by the less-regulated—if not to increase direct regulation on the less-regulated per se.

The case on the other side is that extended operating powers and few restrictions are likely to enhance institutional resiliency, leading to improved services for users. In a competitive environment, the most efficient will survive. Thus, the regulatory objective of safety and soundness is likely to be served, not jeopardized, by a regulatory structure imposing fewer impediments on banking operating powers.

*QUESTIONS AND COMMENTS*

1. Economists have few models to draw on when they imagine a system of laissez-faire banking, simply because banking has been so heavily regulated throughout history. The closest model may be the banking industry in Scotland in the late eighteenth and early nineteenth centuries, which was characterized by free entry, no monetary policy, and the virtual absence of political regulation. If the Scottish experience is a model, laissez-faire banking would look quite a bit like regulated banking: Scottish banks issued short-term debt securities that were redeemable in specie and circulated as currency, operated with fractional reserves, and loaned funds to merchants and manufacturers much like their more heavily regulated English counterparts. Unlike American free banks, however, which were mostly unit banks, Scottish banks maintained extensive branching networks.

Many commentators from Adam Smith on have judged the Scottish experiment in laissez-faire banking a success. The money supply remained stable. The failure rate was low—lower than in England—and failures that did occur did not spark panics. Meanwhile, the Scottish economy flourished—an economic boom that some have attributed in part to the existence of vigorous competition in the banking industry. See generally L. White, Free Banking in Britain: Theory, Experience, and Debate, 1800-1845 (1984).

2. Who do you think has the better of the argument on the specialness of banks, Corrigan or Aspinwall? Might the truth lie somewhere in between?

3. Why might it be in the interest of the Federal Reserve Board to claim banks are special? Why might it be in the interest of a large bank to think otherwise? What position do you think the nation's smaller banks might take on this question? What about securities firms?

# 2 ENTRY INTO THE BUSINESS OF BANKING

## A. INTRODUCTION

A team of entrepreneurs or business professionals wishing to form a general, nonbanking corporation may do so at will in any state in the union. They simply must file articles of incorporation with the appropriate state official. Obtaining such a certificate of incorporation requires that incorporators fill out a form, select a corporate name, and pay a fee. After that, corporate life begins. Once these routine steps are completed, state officials have no authority to deny a certificate of incorporation to the incorporators.

There is a burgeoning literature on the competition among states to obtain the chartering business of corporations. A great deal of this literature, particularly that emanating from the law and economics movement, is devoted to showing that the competition among states for corporate charter revenues (which come in the form of franchise taxes and other fees charged to incorporating firms) furthers shareholders' interests. The competing view is that the competition among the states is harmful to the American system of corporate governance because it advances the interests of incumbent management at the expense of shareholders.

The means for obtaining a corporate charter is very different for banks than it is for nonbanking firms. First, while a general corporate charter may only be obtained from the appropriate state regulatory authority, banks may be incorporated either by an individual state or by the federal government. (Recall our discussion of America's "dual banking system" in Chapter 1.) But as will be seen, the fact that banks may obtain charters either from state governments or from the national government does not mean that they have a wider range of choices than do general corporations. A general corporation, unlike a bank, may obtain its corporate charter in one state—say Delaware—but conduct all of its business outside of that state. Thus general corporations may choose among all 50 states when selecting a set of corporate laws by which to be bound. By contrast, the traditional rule in banking has been that a bank's principal place of business must be in the state of its incorporation. This rather unique set of chartering procedures distinguishes banking from any other form of U.S. corporation.

But perhaps the most significant difference between the chartering process for banks and that for general corporations is that entering the business of banking requires a special charter—it is not a matter of right. Rather, it is up to the discretion of the appropriate state or federal regulator to permit new entry. Those who wish to organize a national bank must obtain their special charter from the primary regulator of national banks, the Comptroller of the Currency. Those who wish to organize a state-chartered bank must obtain their charter from the appropriate state regulatory authority in whatever state the bank is to operate in.

This chapter looks at the two features distinguishing entry into the banking business. First comes a consideration of the chartering process, the key elements of which are (1) the formal legal criteria for obtaining a bank charter, and (2) the ability of the regulators to make discretionary judgments about those trying to obtain such a charter. Second is an examination of the American dual banking system in which we will discuss whether this system serves as a source of weakness or of strength for U.S. banks.

## B. THE CHARTERING PROCESS

### 1. *Practical Problems in the Formation Process*

Like all other corporations, banks are established by promoters. Typically, promoters of banks are not visionary entrepreneurs or hard-driving takeover artists; banks are usually formed by well-financed, established entities. But banks can be formed by an individual or group of individuals, and many charters are granted to such applicants every year. At the promotion stage, the organizers have considerable flexibility about the form their institution will take. They can elect to form a commercial bank or a thrift institution, and they can opt for federal or state charter. They can determine the area or community, in which the new institution will have its principal place of business. All these issues should be weighed carefully and in depth by the promoters before they begin the actual process of establishing the institution, because it will be difficult to change course after the initial application is made.

Once the form and location of the new depository institution are selected, the promoters and their counsel should make every effort to contact the institution's future regulator and build constructive relationships with its representatives. Regulators like to be consulted, and those forming the new institution should assume that their relationships with the regulator will be constructive. The regulator's staff may prove to be useful resources who can help move the application along with minimum difficulty. Relations with the regulator may not, of course, always run smoothly—sometimes they don't—but it is important to start out on a good footing. Problems can be dealt with later if they arise.

Preapplication consultation is especially important when the contemplated transaction is unusually complex. Meetings provide the organizers' counsel with an opportunity to explain the proposal to the regulatory staff while giving the promoters an early indication of whether the regulators are likely to approve the application.

Once the regulatory approval process is under way, the promoters can prepare to open the new institution—leasing space, contracting with providers of goods and services, hiring staff, and so on. What is the status of these contracts? Three stages of the chartering process can be distinguished, each with potentially different legal consequences.

First comes the period before the articles of incorporation have been filed. The promoters may make contracts at this point on behalf of a corporation "to be formed," or words to that effect. As in corporation law generally, these preincorporation contracts present difficulties of interpretation and enforcement. If the contract is breached by the promoters—say, the proposed bank is never established—can the counterparty look to the promoters as a group, or to any of them, to fulfill the obligation? Since there is no corporation in effect when the contract is signed, there is no limited liability; therefore, the persons who act for the future corporation are arguably liable on the contract. The promoters as a group may be characterized as a general partnership, with each promoter being jointly and severally liable. On the other hand, if the counterparty has clearly indicated that it intends to look only toward the future corporation for performance of the contract, then the promoters may be able to avoid this exposure.

The second stage is after articles of incorporation have been filed with the appropriate regulator but before the institution has received a charter to do business as a depository institution. Most difficulties arise at the second stage, since the regulator may take a substantial period of time to investigate the charter application, especially if it is contested. At this point, a corporation has been established, presumably with limited liability, but it has not been authorized to engage in the banking business. What kinds of contracts can the firm enter into at this point, and what happens if the contract is outside the firm's corporate powers? The bank in formation, and those who deal with it, must be careful to ensure that the institution does not overstep the bounds of permissible activities.

The third stage, of course, is when the corporation has received permission from the regulator to enter the banking business.

The original National Bank Act provided that "no [national bank] shall transact any business, except such as is incidental and necessarily preliminary to its organization, until it has been authorized by the Comptroller of the Currency to commence the business of banking." This provision, eliminated in 1933, created serious problems because parties dealing with a bank in formation might find that their contracts made in good faith were declared ultra vires and unenforceable. See McCormick v. Market Bank, 165 U.S. 538 (1897)(long-term lease with a bank in formation was declared unenforceable to recover anything beyond the value of what the bank in formation had actually received and enjoyed). Despite the elimination of the original National Bank Act provision, it is clear that a bank in formation cannot engage in the business of banking until the charter has been granted; see 12 C.F.R. §5.20(f). The extent to which long-term contracts by a bank in formation, such as the long-term lease at issue in the *Market Bank* case, are enforceable today is not entirely clear.

## 2. *Federal Banking Agencies*

### a. The Comptroller and the National Bank Act

The National Bank Act itself appears to give the Comptroller of the Currency very little discretion regarding whether to issue a charter for a proposed new bank, 12 U.S.C. §§21-27. A new bank must be formed by at least five natural persons who draft articles of association detailing "in general terms the object for which the association is formed, and may contain any other provisions not inconsistent with the law, which the association may see fit to adopt for the regulation of its business and the conduct of its affairs." 12 U.S.C. §21. The incorporators of a bank must also draft an organization certificate containing the name of the putative bank, which must include the word "national," the place where its "operations of discount and deposit" are to be carried on, the amount of capital stock and the number of shares into which the stock is to be divided, and the names and addresses of the shareholders along with the number of shares held by each of them. 12 U.S.C. §22.

Section 26 of the National Bank Act requires that the Comptroller investigate the condition of a bank whenever the statutory requirements for forming a bank have been met. These statutory requirements include transmitting an organization certificate to the Comptroller of the Currency and obtaining payment for the bank's capital stock. Most interestingly, §27 states that

> If, upon a careful examination of the facts so reported (under Section 26), and of any other facts which may come to the knowledge of the Comptroller . . . , it appears that such association is lawfully entitled to commence the business of banking, *the Comptroller shall give to such association a certificate* . . . that such association has complied with all the provisions required to be complied with before commencing the business of banking and that such association is authorized to commence such business.

12 U.S.C. §27 (emphasis supplied). See also City National Bank v. Smith, 513 F.2d 479, 480-481 & n.6 (1975). The statute further emphasizes the Comptroller's limited discretion to deny bank charters by narrowly defining the circumstances under which the Comptroller may deny such charters:

> the Comptroller may withhold from an association his certificate authorizing the commencement of business, whenever he has reason to suppose that the shareholders have formed the same for any other than the legitimate objects contemplated by this chapter.

12 U.S.C. §27.

This lack of discretion in the Comptroller was widely recognized in the period immediately following the Civil War up until the turn of the century. During this era, charters were freely available to any qualifying group. R. Robertson, The Comptroller and Bank Supervision 66-69 (1968). Issuing charters became more tightly controlled in the early part of the twentieth century following the panic of 1907. Nonetheless, the Comptroller did not obtain a strong statutory foundation for exercising discretion over the bank chartering process until the Federal Deposit Insurance Corporation (FDIC) was created by the Banking Act of 1935. See Scott, In Quest of Reason: The Licensing Decisions of the Federal Banking Agencies, 42 U. Chi. L. Rev. 235, 240 (1975) excerpted infra.

The Comptroller requires minimum capital greatly in excess of the statutorily defined minimum capital requirements contained in the National Bank Act. The minimum capital requirements under the National Bank Act range from a low of $50,000 to a high of $200,000 depending on the size of the community in which the bank is to be located. By contrast, under the Comptroller's regulations, there is a minimum net capital requirement of $1 million, subject only to special waiver. 12 C.F.R. §5.20(d)(3)(iii).

The Comptroller's stated goals are to fulfill its responsibility to determine whether a proposed bank is likely to (1) be operated in safe and sound manner, (2) possess reasonable prospects for success, and (3) meet the credit needs of the community. In its attempt to meet these goals, the Comptroller considers the following factors when deciding whether to approve or decline a bank application:

1. the bank's future earnings prospects;
2. the general character of its management;
3. the adequacy of its capital structure;
4. the convenience and needs of the community to be served by the bank;
5. the financial history and condition of the bank; and
6. whether or not it has complied with all the provisions of the National Bank Act and whether or not its corporate powers are consistent with the purposes of the Federal Deposit Insurance Act.

12 C.F.R. §5.20(c).

The Office of the Comptroller has made it clear that it views the above criteria as enabling rather than restrictive in the sense that the criteria expand rather than contract the scope of the Comptroller's discretion. In addition, the Comptroller takes the view that these six factors must be viewed as part of an integrated whole. Thus

> the appraisal of each of the elements of the operating plan and the appraisal of the organizing group are evaluated together in light of the Office's experience in chartering national banks. That experience has shown that an organizing group and its operating plan must be stronger in markets in which economic conditions are marginal, or in which competition is intense.

12 C.F.R. §5.20(d)(1)(ii). In addition, "[d]eficiencies in one factor may be compensated for by strengths in one or more of the other factors." 12 C.F.R. §5.20(d)(1)(i). On the other hand,

> deficiencies in certain factors, such as unrealistic earnings prospects, tend to reflect negatively on other factors, such as capital adequacy or community service, and may result in denial. In addition, each element of the operating plan reflects either positively or negatively on the organizing group and will influence the appraisal of the organizing group's acceptability. For example, if any aspect of the operating plan is inappropriate in the context of the market to be served, it reflects negatively on the organizing group's ability to operate a successful bank.

Id.

### b. Director of the Office of Thrift Supervision and FIRREA

The Financial Institutions Reform, Recovery and Enforcement Act of 1989 (FIRREA) significantly changed the dynamics of the chartering game. Prior to the passage of FIRREA, federal savings and loan institutions (also known as savings associations) were chartered and insured by a single entity, the Federal Home Loan Bank Board (FHLBB). The FHLBB was abolished under FIRREA, and the responsibility for chartering and insuring savings and loans was split between two agencies. The Federal Deposit Insurance Corporation (FDIC) assumed control of the bankrupt savings and loan insurance fund and transferred it to the newly created Savings Association Insurance Fund (which was kept separate and distinct from the Bank Insurance Fund, the fund that insures bank deposits). A newly created arm of the Treasury Department, the Office of Thrift Supervision (OTS), assumed all of the FHLBB's regulatory responsibilities, which include examining and regulating all savings and loans and chartering federal savings and loans.

Section 5 of the Home Owners Loan Act of 1936 authorized the FHLBB to "give primary consideration (when granting a charter) to the best practices of thrift institutions in the United States." The same charge is given to the director of the OTS now that the FHLBB is no longer in business. In addition, like its predecessor the FHLBB, the OTS may grant a thrift charter only:

> (1) to persons of good character and responsibility, (2) if in the judgment of the Director [of the Office of Thrift Supervision] a necessity exists for such an institution in the community to be served, (3) if there is a reasonable probability of its usefulness and success, and (4) if the association can be established without undue injury to properly conducted existing local thrift and home financing institutions.

12 U.S.C. §1464(e).

Despite the differences in statutory language between the chartering standards used by the Comptroller of the Currency for granting charters to banks and the chartering standards used by the OTS for granting charters to thrifts, the substantive standards are much the same. As Professor Kenneth Scott observed when discussing the Comptroller and the FHLBB,

> [b]y different routes, the two agencies emerge at about the same point. Both face a short list of general standards in the relevant statutes for charter approvals . . . Furthermore the charter standards are either too narrow or too unspecified to serve as much of a guide for or restraint upon the exercise of (agency) discretion.

Scott, In Quest of Reason: The Licensing Decisions of the Federal Banking Agencies, 42 U. Chi. L. Rev. 235 (1975).

Professor Scott goes on to discuss in some detail the six factors the Comptroller is supposed to consider when deciding whether to grant or deny a bank charter. Professor Scott's article presents a valuable picture of the internal workings of the licensing decisions of the federal banking agencies.

## Scott, In Quest of Reason: The Licensing Decisions of the Federal Banking Agencies

***42 U. Chi. L. Rev. 235, 242 (1975)***

. . . .

The process formally begins when an "Application to Organize a National Bank" is filed with the Regional Comptroller. This is a short form containing little more than the proposed name, locations, and initial capital of the new bank, together with rather long and detailed biographical and financial statements by each of the organizers. The applicant is separately required to submit additional information, primarily on the issue of profitability: the location chosen, the population and economic character of the area the bank will serve, competing financial institutions in that area, and projections of deposit and loan growth and of income and expenses. This information is frequently provided in the form of a "market survey" prepared by a consulting firm.

The application is then assigned to a national bank examiner for a field investigation. His comments and findings are rendered in two parts, the "Examiner's Report of an Investigation," which is available to the public, and the "Confidential Memorandum" to the Comptroller, which is not. The Examiner's Report summarizes some of the application information and gives a brief economic description of the service area and community, but contains little in the way of evaluation. That is provided in the Confidential Memorandum, on a number of topics. The examiner gives his views on how much initial capital the bank should have; he checks on the biographical and financial data furnished by the principal figures in the proposed bank and offers his conclusions about whether they are acceptable persons; and he answers questions such as these:

4. Is there a public need for the proposed bank or is the area reasonably well served by existing banks and branches? . . .
5. Is it reasonable to expect that the available banking business will be adequate to support the proposed bank, if established, together with existing competitive banks and branches, or will an overbanked situation be created? Indicate whether a healthy or unhealthy degree of competition will accrue.

He concludes by recommending either approval or denial of the application. Neither the form nor any standard instructions provide criteria by which these judgments and conclusions are to be reached; consequently, they rest largely on the personal attitudes of the examiner to whom the application was assigned.

The applicant has to publish notice of the filing of the charter application, and it is permissible, though uncommon, for objectors to request a hearing. Otherwise, the application simply proceeds along a recommendation chain. . . .

*Decision Grounds.* What can be said about the Comptroller's decision process and grounds for decision, as set forth in the application files? First of all, it is worth noting what factors do *not* seem significant in most cases. Consider the factors enumerated in section 1816 of title 12 of the United States Code, which constitutes the statutory framework for the Comptroller's exercise of chartering discretion:

> [1] The financial history and condition of the bank, [2] the adequacy of its capital structure, [3] its future earnings prospects, [4] the general character of its management, [5] the convenience and needs of the community to be served by the bank, and [6] whether or not its corporate powers are consistent with the purposes of [the statute].

The first and second factors amount, in the case of a newly chartered bank, to its initial capitalization. In none of the sample cases was inadequate capitalization mentioned as an adverse factor or reason for denial, and for a rather simple reason: The applicants will generally either conform their application to the amount of initial capital which the agency indicates it deems desirable, or abandon the application as not feasible under the circumstances. . . . In effect, . . . this issue is disposed of at an early stage and is not reflected in the final figures.

The fourth factor, the general character of management, was mentioned in some cases, but in fact was rarely determinative. A lot of the charter application routine bears on this factor—the long biographical and financial questionnaires required of the organizers and principal stockholders and proposed managing officers, and the investigation reports made on them by the field examiner. It is generally understood, however, that if the agency objects to any of these persons, he will be replaced or dropped from the applicant group, so this factor too does not often determine the final outcome.

The sixth factor, corporate powers consistent with the purposes of the act, to the extent it has any meaning at all, is satisfied by the use of a prescribed form of articles of incorporation. It was never referred to in any way in any sample case.

That leaves factors three and five, future earnings prospects and the convenience and needs of the community; as already noted, these were the central points of disagreement in the recommendation change. . . . [T]he issue was . . . often cast in terms of whether there was a "need" for a new bank. Analytical distinctions between the two factors were not clearly made, however. The discussion of community needs sometimes, though not often, involved an assertion that the new entry would cause injury to existing banks . . . , but the argument shaded into the argument that there was not enough business of the new bank . . . to be profitable in the near future.

Most of the Comptroller's decisions, therefore, seem to turn on assessments of "need" and "profitability," and it is these two factors that warrant closer scrutiny. As it stands, each participant in the recommendation chain forms his own judgment as to profitability and reflects his own concept of need; there is no discussion of, or explicit agreement on, the underlying premises. Unless that consideration is systematically undertaken and articulated, the Comptroller's decision process will never be comprehensible, either internally or externally.

To afford an illustration of what would be entailed, let us explore these concepts somewhat further, from a critic's standpoint. What does it mean to inquire whether the community "needs" a new bank . . . ? How is the public need for any new facility or service determined, whether it be a bank or a department store or supermarket? The answer for most products and services is whether the public is willing to patronize it enough and pay enough for it to be supplied at a profit—in other words, profitability is a measure of the extent of "need." It ensures that the social value of what is being provided, as measured by the public itself and what it is willing to pay, exceeds the social costs of supplying it. It is not apparent why this is not the standard of need to apply to banking offices as well. In the Comptroller's files there are numerous examples of the use of much cruder standards—for instance, whether there are other banking offices that customers can go to without incurring what is, in the examiner's opinion, too much inconvenience, or whether a casual interview process with local businessmen turned up statements that they wanted a new bank. It is not at all clear that the "need" criterion does not resolve itself into the other key issue of profitability.

But why should the Comptroller be concerned with profitability? That factor is usually the worry of those who are financing a new venture; they have the most at stake and every reason to go into the matter as carefully as they can. It is hard to see why either superior sources of information or superior thoroughness of analysis would characterize the Comptroller's office as it grinds through hundreds of applications each year. It is as if a Washington agency had to approve each decision of a grocery chain concerning location of new outlets. A presumed agency expertise must find some rational foundation it its actual capacities, or it is an empty shibboleth.

But suppose we put aside the question of whether the agency or the applicant is in the better position to make judgments about the profitability of a particular location, and assume that applicants will make more mistakes than the agency will—how is the public interest thereby threatened? A bank simply closes down a branch that does not become profitable; rather than attempting to second-guess the bank's profitability estimate, the Comptroller could merely ascertain whether the bank could afford the cost of an error. Similarly, in the case of a new charter, the Comptroller could merely require that the amount of initial capital be sufficient to cover several years of reporting losses.

A familiar rejoinder would be that we are concerned about the effects of a mistaken judgment, not merely or even primarily on the applicant, but on other institutions. In the jargon of the business, the concern is that new entry would lead to an "overbanked" condition. In more general terminology, the argument is that errors of entry judgment (which by assumption are made more often by applicants than by the agency) will at times produce excess capacity. Although long run excess capacity in an industry is normally corrected by elimination of the industry's less efficient facilities or firms, the argument continues, banking is a special case because the contraction may involve bank failure. At this point the argument tends to become either emotional or obscure.

To some, the very words conjure up the collapse of the 1930s and the thought is unacceptable, though the fact is that several hundred banks have failed since the 1930s. To others, apparently, a policy of preventing bank failures is viewed as having major benefits but not costs.

A less extreme position would be that, while entry controls and a policy of failure prevention do have costs, they are outweighed by the benefits. But that position too is open to criticism on both theoretical and empirical grounds. For example, to what extent do entry controls actually prevent bank failure? At best (or worst), entry controls can confer a protected monopoly position on certain firms; that may be reflected in the present market value of the firm, but they do not constrain the future operations and policies of risk-acceptance by the firm. Nor is it easy to see the large metropolitan centers and national banking markets, in which the big banks operate, as protected monopolies; there are too many substantial competing firms. To the extent entry controls have successfully created monopoly positions (or "prevented overbanking," the preferred phrase), it is probably in local markets and smaller towns. Is the purpose of entry controls mainly to prevent the failure of small banks? Why, and for whose benefit? Presumably, it is not to protect the stockholders; that is the very risk they undertake to bear. Perhaps to protect the depositors? But most of them are covered by deposit insurance; the smaller the bank, the higher tends to be the percentage of its deposits that are insured. Deposit insurance merely transfers the loss to the FDIC, so perhaps the need is to protect the insurance fund? But the failure of small banks is the kind of event that the FDIC and FSLIC insurance funds can most easily handle, and there is little reason to doubt their adequacy for this purpose.

In short, the reasons for the Comptroller's concern with entry controls, and with overriding applicants' estimates of need and profitability, are by no means self-evident or self-validating. If it is to protect banks and their stockholders from losing money on poor site selections, it seems unwarranted. On this score, it also seems unsound, for it is hard to give credence to the proposition that on the whole the Comptroller's staff in Washington or in the field can judge the business potential of different locations across the entire United States better than the applicants can. If it is to protect depositors, or really the deposit insurance funds, from losses due to failures caused by "unhealthy" competition, it seems unnecessary on the one hand and largely impossible on the other. Among other things, there are too many sources of competitive pressure quite outside the Comptroller's control—not only state banks, and savings and loan associations, but also, increasingly in recent years, other investment media (such as mutual funds and direct investment in the capital markets) and other sources of loans (such as insurance companies, or direct access to the capital markets through commercial paper or variable-rate notes). It is not surprising, therefore, to find that economists have become dubious about the justification and effects of entry controls in banking.

The foregoing discussion is not intended to reach a conclusion or be definitive, but merely to open up the kind of issues that the Comptroller should be facing in his administration of entry controls for national banks. What are the justifications and objectives of entry controls that the Comptroller believes have current validity? What determinations, concerning need or profitability or unhealthy competition or whatever, is he thereby required to make? On what sort of findings of fact are those determinations to be based?

The answers to those questions will not be obtained by opening up the "confidential" part of the Comptroller's files, as some of the cases sought to do, for they cannot be found there either. So far as an examination of over a hundred branch and charter files reveals, the problem is one of developing explicit answers and standards; they simply do not now exist.

Although this discussion has centered on the Comptroller, its applicability is not confined to him. In its essential characteristics, the branch and charter decision process of the Federal Home Loan Bank Board [now the OTS] has the same shortcomings. . . . The purpose has been not to single out the Comptroller, but to use his procedures as a way of developing in some depth the problems presented by all the federal banking agencies in their licensing decisions.

*QUESTIONS AND COMMENTS*

1. In the absence of deposit insurance, what justifications would the Comptroller have for denying a bank charter to a group of entrepreneurs who wished to establish a bank? Suppose a particular bank did not meet the necessary criteria for obtaining a charter. Would it make sense to allow the Comptroller discretion to issue a charter anyway on the condition that the bank pay a higher premium to the FDIC for its insurance than other banks? What is Professor Scott's perspective? After reading his article do you think Scott would object to removing the banking agencies' regulatory authority to deny licenses to people who would like to obtain bank charters? What would be likely to happen if bank charters were granted as a matter of right like general corporation charters are?

2. As Professor Scott indicates, one consequence of the vague standards available to the licensing agencies is that decisions can be made on a case-by-case basis. What are the pros and cons of granting such discretion to the Comptroller?

3. Are there any benefits from not requiring the Comptroller to hold a hearing on charter applications if he chooses not to? Put another way, isn't Professor Scott really saying that the burden of persuasion should be on the regulatory agency, not on the party seeking to obtain the charter? Would this be the case if the charter application did not permit the bank to obtain deposit insurance?

4. How much weight do you give to the fact that the federal licensing agencies are supposed to have particularized expertise in banking and, therefore, should be able to judge how likely a proposed new bank's success is? What incentives does a regulator have to grant a new bank charter? To deny one?

5. Turning to Professor Scott's statistical picture, he finds that the Comptroller rejected 40 percent of applications for new national banks and the FHLBB rejected 61 percent of the applications for new federal savings and loans. Of what significance is the fact that the Comptroller and the FHLBB each rejected a substantial number of applications during the time period studied? One way to look at this large number of denials is simply to conclude that the Comptroller was harming consumers by restricting entry. Another way to look at the same numbers is to conclude that the Comptroller and the FHLBB were acting to retain an optimal number of banks, so that bank solvency would not be threatened by "destructive competition."

6. Professor Scott studied the decisions of the Comptroller between 1969 and 1973. In more recent years the Comptroller has been even more liberal in granting charters. In 1985 the Comptroller approved 264 applications for national bank charters and denied 81 applications, a

denial rate of 23 percent. In 1986 the Comptroller approved 66 charters and denied 17, for a denial rate of 20 percent. In 1987 the Comptroller denied only 13 percent of the applications upon which he acted, approving 68 applications and turning down only 10. Notice that the total number of applications declined in each of these years. Why do you think this might be the case?

7. Regardless of what the licensing agencies *thought* they were doing, in light of the large numbers of bank failures in recent years, isn't it clear that they were woefully unsuccessful in keeping poorly managed banks out of the industry or in protecting existing banks from "destructive competition"? In light of the fact that the savings and loan industry got into even more difficulty than the commercial banking industry, isn't it instructive that the FHLBB rejected a far higher percentage of applications than did the Comptroller of the Currency?

8. But is that the only way to look at these numbers? One might also draw the inference that the FHLBB was "captured" by the existing group of savings and loans to a greater extent than was the Comptroller by the existing commercial banks. As a consequence of being captured by the firms it was supposed to regulate, might not the FHLBB have denied charter applications from proposed new entrants in order to protect existing firms from competition?

9. In examining bank entry restrictions between 1936 and 1962, Sam Peltzman concluded that legal barriers to entry caused there to be 2,200 fewer banks chartered than there otherwise would have been. Peltzman, Entry into Commercial Banking, 8 J. L. & Econ. 11 (1965). The United States has more commercial banks in relation to its population than any other country in the world. Can it be, as Peltzman suggests, that in fact the country has too *few* banks? Or perhaps we have too many banks, but the ones we have are run by the wrong people? How might this problem be addressed?

10. Professor Scott also notes that personal characteristics of the applicant group, such as their reputation, financial strength, and experience, were rarely the determinative factor in the grant or denial of a charter application. What is the explanation for this? Professor Scott found that most of the Comptroller's decisions seem to turn on assessments of community need and profitability. Could it be that these determinations are made with one eye toward future litigation?

11. Professor Scott criticizes the Comptroller's definition of what it means for a community to "need" a new bank. What is Professor Scott's definition, and how does it differ from the Comptroller's practice? Scott further criticizes the Comptroller's concern with profitability and makes it clear that he thinks that the individuals financing a new venture are likely to be better equipped than the Comptroller to judge whether a new bank is likely to succeed or to fail. Scott bases his argument on the logic that because those organizing a new bank generally are putting

their own money up to capitalize the venture, they have strong incentive to make sure that their project fares well.

But doesn't the existence of FDIC insurance change this analysis significantly? Consider this: Bank organizers are likely to have a higher tolerance for risk than bank regulators. In return for putting up money to start a bank, those who organize a bank typically receive stock in the new venture. These shareholders capture all of the gains if the bank does well, but their losses are capped at the amount of their initial investments. By contrast, the FDIC insurance fund captures none of the gains if the bank does well, but bears all of the costs of depositors' losses. Thus regulators have good reason to be concerned with business ventures that appear to be exceptionally risky, do they not?

12. What effect would fully risk-based deposit insurance have on the analysis in Note 11 above?

13. Another criticism of the banking regulators' discretionary powers, one not discussed by Scott, is that these powers invite political intrigue and even corruption. Do you view this as a serious concern?

We now turn from our consideration of the internal workings of the Comptroller's Office to a consideration of the appropriate standard of review for the Comptroller's decisions.

## Camp v. Pitts

***411 U.S. 138 (1973)***

PER CURIAM.

In its present posture this case presents a narrow, but substantial, question with respect to the proper procedure to be followed when a reviewing court determines that an administrative agency's stated justification for informal action does not provide an adequate basis for judicial review.

In 1967, respondents submitted an application to the Comptroller of the Currency for a certificate authorizing them to organize a new bank in Hartsville, South Carolina. . . . On the basis of information received from a national bank examiner and from various interested parties, the Comptroller denied the application and notified respondents of his decision through a brief letter, which stated in part: "[W]e have concluded that the factors in support of the establishment of a new National Bank in this area are not favorable." No formal hearings were required by the controlling statute or guaranteed by the applicable regulations, although the latter provided for hearings when requested and when granted at the discretion of the Comptroller. Respondents did not request a formal hearing but asked for reconsideration. That request was granted and a supplemental field examination was conducted, whereupon the Comptroller again denied the application, this time stating in a letter that "we were unable to reach a favorable conclusion as to the need factor," and explaining that conclusion to some extent.[2] Respondents then brought an action in federal district court seeking review of the Comptroller's decision. The entire administrative record was placed before the court, and, upon an examination of that record and of the two letters of explanation, the court granted summary judgment against respondents, holding that de novo review was not warranted in the circumstances and finding that "although the Comptroller may have erred, there is substantial basis for his determination, and . . . it was neither capricious nor arbitrary." 329 F. Supp. 1302, 1308. On appeal, the Court of Appeals did not reach the merits. Rather, it held that the Comptroller's ruling was "unacceptable" because "its basis" was not stated with sufficient clarity to permit judicial review. 463 F.2d 632, 633. For the present, the Comptroller does not challenge this aspect of the court's decision. He does, however, seek review here of the procedures that the Court of Appeals specifically ordered to be followed in the District Court on remand. The court held that the case should be remanded "for a trial de novo before the District Court" because "the Comptroller has twice inadequately and inarticulately resolved the [respondents'] presentation." The court further specified that in the District Court, respondents "will open the trial with proof of their application and compliance with the statutory inquiries, and proffer of any other relevant evidence." Then, "[t]estimony may . . . be adduced by the Comptroller or intervenors manifesting opposition, if any, to the new bank." On the basis of the record thus made, the District Court was instructed to make its own findings of fact and conclusions of law in order to determine "whether the [respondents] have shown by a preponderance of evidence that the Comptroller's ruling is capricious or an abuse of discretion." 463 F.2d, at 634.

We agree with the Comptroller that the trial procedures thus outlined by the Court of Appeals for the remand in this case are unwarranted under present law.

Unquestionably, the Comptroller's action is subject to judicial review under the Administrative Procedure Act (APA), 5 U.S.C. §701. But it is also clear that neither the National Bank Act nor the APA requires the

2. The letter reads in part:

> On each application we endeavor to develop the need and convenience factors in conjunction with all other banking factors and in this case we were unable to reach a favorable conclusion as to the need factor. The record reflects that this market area is now served by the Peoples Bank with deposits of $7.2MM, The Bank of Hartsville with deposits of 12.8MM, The First Federal Savings and Loan Association with deposits of $5.4MM, The Mutual Savings and Loan Association with deposits of $8.2MM and the Sonoco Employees Credit Union with deposits of $6.5MM. The aforementioned are as of December 31, 1968.

Comptroller to hold a hearing or to make formal findings on the hearing record when passing on applications for new banking authorities. . . . Accordingly, the proper standard for judicial review of the Comptroller's adjudications is not the "substantial evidence" test which is appropriate when reviewing findings made on a hearing record, 5 U.S.C. §706(2)(E). Nor was the reviewing court free to hold a de novo hearing under §706(2)(F) and thereafter determine whether the agency action was "unwarranted by the facts." It is quite plain from our decision in Citizens to Preserve Overton Park v. Volpe, 401 U.S. 402 (1971), that de novo review is appropriate only where there are inadequate factfinding procedures in an adjudicatory proceeding, or where judicial proceedings are brought to enforce certain administrative actions. Id., at 415. Neither situation applies here. The proceeding in the District Court was obviously not brought to enforce the Comptroller's decision, and the only deficiency suggested in agency action or proceedings is that the Comptroller inadequately explained his decision. As *Overton Park* demonstrates, however, that failure, if it occurred in this case, is not a deficiency in factfinding procedures such as to warrant the de novo hearing ordered in this case.

The appropriate standard for review was, accordingly, whether the Comptroller's adjudication was "arbitrary, capricious, an abuse of discretion, or otherwise not in accordance with law," as specified in 5 U.S.C. §706(2)(A). In applying that standard, the focal point for judicial review should be the administrative record already in existence, not some new record made initially in the reviewing court. Respondents contend that the Court of Appeals did not envision a true de novo review and that, at most, all that was called for was the type of "plenary review" contemplated by *Overton Park,* supra, at 420. We cannot agree. The present remand instructions require the Comptroller and other parties to make an evidentiary record before the District Court "manifesting opposition, if any, to the new bank." The respondents were also to be afforded opportunities to support their application with "any other relevant evidence." These instructions seem to put aside the extensive administrative record already made and presented to the reviewing court.

If, as the Court of Appeals held and as the Comptroller does not now contest, there was such failure to explain administrative action as to frustrate effective judicial review, the remedy was not to hold a de novo hearing but, as contemplated by *Overton Park,* to obtain from the agency, either through affidavits or testimony, such additional explanation of the reasons for the agency decision as may prove necessary. We add a caveat, however. Unlike *Overton Park,* in the present case there was contemporaneous explanation of the agency decision. The explanation may have been curt, but it surely indicated the determinative reason for the final action taken: the finding that a new bank was an uneconomic venture in light of the banking needs and the banking services already available in the surrounding community. The validity of the Comptroller's action must, therefore, stand or fall on the propriety of that finding, judged, of course, by the appropriate standard of review. If that finding is not sustainable on the administrative record made, then the Comptroller's decision must be vacated and the matter remanded to him for further consideration. It is in this context that the Court of Appeals should determine whether and to what extent, in the light of the administrative record, further explanation is necessary to a proper assessment of the agency's decision.

The petition for certiorari is granted, the judgment of the Court of Appeals is vacated, and the case is remanded for further proceedings consistent with this opinion.

It is so ordered.

## *QUESTIONS AND COMMENTS*

1. What sort of information did the Comptroller give the parties in this case when he notified them that he had denied their application for a new bank charter? Would this be sufficient under current rules that state "[w]hen an application is disapproved, the Office [of the Comptroller] sends a letter containing the basis for the disapproval to the spokesperson (a member of the organizing group and director of the proposed bank who is designated to correspond with the office on matters relating to the application) and other interested parties to the application"? 12 C.F.R. §5.20(d)(iii).

2. Recall the six criteria to be used in deciding whether to approve an application for a new bank charter: future earnings prospects; general character of a bank's management; the adequacy of the bank's capital structure; the convenience and needs of the community to be served by the bank; the financial history and condition of the bank; and whether the applicant has complied with the provisions of the relevant banking statutes. In light of the vague, open-ended nature of these criteria, won't any litigation turn on the issue of who has the burden of proof, regardless of the degree of deference to be accorded to the Comptroller?

3. As indicated above, the Office of the Comptroller has made it clear that it believes it has substantial discretion to interpret even these vague criteria. The Comptroller stresses that its office's responsibilities involve a "rigorous appraisal and a weighing of the relevant statutory factors in the context of the economic and competitive conditions in the community (market) to be served." 12 C.F.R. §5.20(d). This suggests that applicants should not expect to be given the benefit of the doubt in licensing applications. Furthermore, decisions about applications are based on both objective facts and subjective judgments because of the "complex relationships among the factors." Id.

4. Professor Scott suggested that the decision to grant or deny a

bank's charter application is likely to turn more on the general philosophical orientation of the regulators than on objective criteria specific to the applicant. Thus a Comptroller who values the efficacy of free competition is more likely to approve bank charters than one who believes that excessive competition poses dangers to the banking system. Professor Scott's evidence supports this conclusion, at least to some extent—he is able to show that the Comptroller often disagrees with the field agent who does the actual field examination and who thus has specific information about the nature of the applicant. Indeed, Scott shows that the Comptroller disagrees with the person on the scene much more often than he disagrees with higher-ranking subordinates, who have no personal knowledge of the applicant.

5. Suppose that you agree with the proposition that the general philosophy of the Comptroller is the most important variable under the current statutory framework. Would this conclusion lead you to believe that reviewing courts ought to be more or less deferential to the Comptroller's judgments than current law dictates?

6. As footnote two of the *Camp* opinion indicates, the Comptroller apparently viewed the fact that the community was being served by several banks already as evidence of a lack of a need within the community. Can the Comptroller really base a conclusion on the "convenience and needs" issue solely on the presence or absence of other banks serving the community? Wouldn't it be useful to know how quickly the community has been growing or how profitable the existing banks have been? Suppose the applicant could show that the existing banks had been making very large profits. What difference might that make in the Comptroller's analysis? Should a finding that the existing banks are losing money or barely breaking even be dispositive?

7. Do you think the Comptroller should be required to hold a hearing or make formal findings of fact on proposals for new bank charters? In the absence of either of these, how is it possible for a court to determine whether the Comptroller's decision was arbitrary, capricious, or an abuse of discretion? What recourse does the court indicate is available to plaintiffs who wish to challenge the Comptroller's decisions? Note that the Court permits the administrative agency whose licensing decision is being challenged to explain its actions "either through affidavits or testimony" if additional explanations for its actions are considered necessary. Would this holding allow an administrative agency to reach an arbitrary conclusion and later justify its result after the fact?

8. What significance does the court assign to the fact that the Comptroller gave a contemporaneous explanation of its decision in this case? Does this create an incentive for the Comptroller to explain its actions? Or does it have the opposite effect?

9. Clearly, the philosophy within the Office of the Comptroller regarding the appropriate degree of scrutiny of bank charter applicants

has changed over time. In October 1980, for example, the Comptroller amended 12 C.F.R. §5.20 and liberalized its chartering policy so that would-be bankers who wished to organize a new bank in an already competitive market would find it easier to obtain a charter than in the past. Subsequent to that determination, however, there have been a well-publicized rash of bank failures, and the federal deposit insurance fund has come under increasing pressure. (Chapter 8 discusses this in greater detail.) Consequently, the Comptroller may be less inclined than previously to approve new bank charters in competitive markets.

10. Another obstacle to obtaining a national bank charter is imposed by the Community Reinvestment Act. 12 U.S.C. §§2901-2906. The Community Reinvestment Act requires the Comptroller to determine whether any proposed new bank will be able to meet the credit needs of the bank's proposed new community, including low- and moderate-income neighborhoods. Thus every application for a national bank charter must contain a Community Reinvestment Act statement. We discuss the CRA at length in Chapter 3.

11. Are charters being rejected for the same reasons now as in the period studied by Professor Scott? Although no one has replicated Professor Scott's detailed statistical analysis, it appears from a review of more recent decisions that the needs test, while still very important, is no longer the sole meaningful reason for rejecting an application. In contrast with the period studied by Professor Scott, in more recent years the character and fitness of management have been grounds for rejecting a surprising number of applications. The other major impediment to charter approval in recent years is failure to serve the credit needs of communities under the Community Reinvestment Act.

To give the flavor of some of these decisions, here is the OCC's synopsis of certain decisions in April-June 1988:

> On April 25 the Office denied an application to charter a national bank in Dewey, Oklahoma. The application was denied due to weaknesses in the operating plan compounded by expected poor economic conditions in the proposed service area. The Office did not believe that the organizing group possessed sufficient strengths to offset the weaknesses identified in the operating plan.
>
> On May 23 the Office denied a proposal to charter a new national bank in Brunswick, Georgia. The Office's denial was based upon the less than satisfactory qualifications of the organizing group and their proposed chief executive officer, and the fact that the organizers were not knowledgeable about the operating plan. The Office determined the prospects of success for the proposed new bank in this competitive market were weak.
>
> On June 17, 1988, an application to establish a national bank in West Sacramento, California, was denied. The proposed new bank was denied due to deficiencies in the operating plan, the lack of involvement by the organizing group in developing the operating plan, minimally acceptable

capital, and the group's unacceptable approach to the Community Reinvestment Act.

On the basis of these decisions, what would you advise promoters of a new national bank to do in order to maximize the probability of obtaining charter approval?

12. If for some reason or another the Comptroller is not inclined to approve charter applications, those who wish to open banks will look for business organizations that are useful alternatives or close substitutes. One possibility would be to obtain a charter from the Office of Thrift Supervision, which charters savings and loan associations (also known as thrift institutions). As noted above, the chartering requirements for thrifts are as vague and open-ended as the chartering requirements for banks.

Still another option would be to organize a credit union. Like a bank, a credit union takes deposits and makes loans. A likely problem here, however, is that both borrowers from and depositors in credit unions must be members of the union, and membership is limited to individuals who have some sort of existing relationship with one another or with a particular geographical area. As with savings and loan associations, credit unions generally are limited to consumer lending and noncommercial deposit takings, and they generally "specialize in providing more modest financial services to member/customers delineated in relatively narrow terms." M. Malloy, I The Corporate Law of Banks, 17 (1987).

But still another alternative exists: obtaining a state bank charter.

## 3. *Chartering Process for State Banks*

The most obvious alternative for would-be bankers unable to obtain a charter from the Comptroller is to obtain a state bank charter. As a practical matter of competitive necessity, however, our bankers would have to obtain deposit insurance from the FDIC if they want to be successful in attracting deposits. Virtually all state-chartered banks have opted to obtain deposit insurance. Report of the Task Group on Regulation of Financial Services 18 n.6 (1984). The factors that the FDIC considers in granting insurance include the same factors that the Comptroller of the Currency uses in considering whether to grant a new national bank charter. In addition, the FDIC must determine "upon the basis of a thorough examination of such bank that its assets in excess of capital requirements are adequate to enable it to meet all of its liabilities to depositors and other creditors as shown by the books of the bank." 12 U.S.C. §1215(a). Obviously this last criterion was designed to deal with existing banks applying to obtain FDIC insurance for the first time; these provisions have virtually no applicability to an application for a new bank charter.

The details of the chartering process vary from state to state. The basic criteria for obtaining a state commercial banking charter are similar to the federal procedures. For example, when applying for a charter in California, one files an application with the state's Superintendent of Banking, who then makes an investigation and examination of the application for the purpose of ascertaining the:

> (1) character, reputation, and financial standing of the organizers and their motives in applying for the charter; (2) need for the proposed bank or trust company in the community to be served; (3) likely economic viability of the proposed bank or trust company; and (4) character, financial responsibility, banking or trust experience, and business qualifications of the proposed officers of the bank or trust company.

Michael Malloy, I The Corporate Law of Banks, 115 (1987). In California the presumption is against the granting of a new charter. California law specifically requires disapproval unless the Supervisor finds that:

> (1) public convenience and advantage would be promoted by establishment of the proposed bank or trust company; (2) conditions of the locality to be served afford a reasonable promise of successful operation; (3) formation of the proposed bank is "for no other purpose than the legitimate objects contemplated" by the statute; (4) the proposed capital structure is adequate; (5) proposed officers and directors have sufficient banking or trust experience, ability, and standing to afford a reasonable promise of successful operation; (6) the name of the proposed bank will not be confusing in relation to the name of any other current or former bank or trust company; and (7) the applicant has complied with all applicable provisions of the statute.

Id. at 116-117.

In Florida, applications for state bank charters are filed with the Department of Banking and Finance. The department investigates (1) the character, reputation, financial standing, business experience, and qualifications of proposed officers and directors; (2) the need for the proposed bank in the primary service area where it will be located; and (3) the economic viability of the proposed bank, as well as the effect on existing facilities in the area. Fla. Stat. Ann. §658.20(1) (1984). Interestingly, as part of its investigation, the Department of Banking and Finance is required by law to contact the National Crime Information Center and the Florida Department of Law Enforcement to determine whether any of the bank's proposed officers and directors have criminal records.

In deciding whether to approve an application for a charter, the state banking department determines whether the new bank will promote "public convenience and advantage," has a "reasonable promise of successful operation for the proposed bank and existing financial institutions in the primary service area," has adequate capital, and has officers with suitable "experience ability, standing and reputation." Fla. Stat. Ann. §558.21(2), (3) (1984). At least one of the outside directors of the new bank must "have had direct experience as an officer or director of a financial institution within three years of the date of the application." Fla. Stat. Ann. §658.21(4) (Supp. 1986).

In Florida if the bank board approves the application, the proposed bank must apply for FDIC insurance within six months of the approval date. This may be done either by applying directly to the FDIC for insurance or by applying for membership in the Federal Reserve System. If a bank does not apply for insurance within the six-month period, or if either the FDIC or the Federal Reserve System deny membership to the new bank, the applicant's Florida bank charter will be revoked and terminated. Id.

*QUESTIONS AND COMMENTS*

1. In light of the requirement in Florida that banks whose applications are approved at the state level must apply for membership in the Federal Reserve System or the FDIC within six months, why is it necessary that states play any role at all in the application process? Indeed, what is the local interest in chartering a bank when local depositors are protected by FDIC insurance up to $100,000 in losses?

2. The California and Florida statutes specifically state that it is within the discretion of the state regulatory agency to grant or withhold a charter to a new banking organization. How much discretion do these state statutes give to the relevant state banking officials? Given that the state licensing rules apparently vary little from the federal rules in terms of how much discretion they accord to the licensing agencies, what factors do you think influence an applicant's decision about whether to apply for a state or federal charter?

Just as there are few cases challenging the Comptroller's decisions to grant or deny a charter to a would-be national bank, litigation at the state court level challenging charter decisions by state banking officials also has been rare.

## State Banking Board v. Allied Bank, Marble Falls

***748 S.W.2d 447 (Tex. 1988)***

PER CURIAM.

[The Texas banking board approved a charter application for a new state bank to be called the United Bank Horseshoe Bay. A rival bank, Allied Bank Marble Falls, sued to overturn the agency's decision. At issue was §16(b) of the Texas Administrative Procedure and Texas Register Act, which states that final decisions of regulatory agencies "must include findings of fact and conclusions of law separately stated. Findings of fact, if set forth in statutory language, must be accompanied by a concise and explicit statement of the underlying facts supporting the findings. . . ."]

[The state appellate court held that the order approving the charter application failed this standard. It observed that "[t]he chief characteristic of [the board's] purported findings of underlying fact is that they are equivocal, undecided, or mere summaries of the evidence interwoven with expositions about the contentions of the parties. The entirety . . . is dominated by such phrases as 'the protestant urged,' 'the testimony reflects,' 'it is suggested,' the witness 'expressed the opinion,' and the witness 'testified.' The [relevant portions of the opinion] do not constitute 'findings' of any kind for they do not even purport to declare the truth, as to the adjudicative facts in issue, which the Board might have determined from the evidence adduced. They do not satisfy the requirements of . . . §16(b)."]

The issue presented in this appeal is whether the court of appeals properly reviewed findings of fact rendered by the State Banking Board. The proposed directors of United Bank Horseshoe Bay filed an application for a new state bank charter with the Board. A majority of the Board approved United's application. Allied Bank Marble Falls, which has opposed United's charter application, sued in the district court seeking a judicial review of the Board's order. The district court affirmed the Board's order. The court of appeals reversed and remanded. . . . We reverse the judgment of the court of appeals and render judgment for United.

United filed its application with the State Banking Board in July of 1984. After due and proper notice of this filing, Allied, along with several other banks, filed a protest. On October 11 and 12, 1984, and again on July 9, 1985, hearings were conducted. At these hearings, testimony and evidence were presented by both the applicants and the protestants.

On December 12, 1985, the Board met to consider United's application. By a two-to-one vote, the Board approved the application, and in support of its conclusions of law, made the following ultimate findings of fact:

1. A public necessity exists for the proposed bank;
2. Their proposed capital structure is adequate;
3. The proposed bank's anticipated volume of business is such as to indicate profitable operation;
4. The proposed officers and directors have sufficient banking experience, ability and standing to render success of the proposed bank profitable; and
5. The applicants are acting in good faith. . . .

In Texas Health Facilities Comm'n v. Charter Medical-Dallas, Inc., 665 S.W.2d 446 (Tex. 1984), this court established the standard to be employed by reviewing courts pursuant to §16(b) [of the state's administrative proceeding act].

In *Charter Medical,* this court reviewed certain fact findings entered by the Texas Health Facilities Commission. . . . Based upon this extensive review, we held that an administrative agency's findings of fact, in order to comply with the mandates of §16(b),

> should be clear, specific, non-conclusory, and supportive of the ultimate statutory finding. Mere recitals of testimony or references to or summations of the evidence are improper. Such findings should be stated as the agency's findings. The findings should relate to material basic facts and should relate to the ultimate statutory finding that they accompany. In general, the findings of fact required by [§16(b)] should be sufficient to serve the overall purposes evident in the legislative requirement that they be made.

*Charter Medical,* 665 S.W.2d at 452. In spite of this pronouncement, we acknowledge that this court has "neither the right nor the authority to lay out a *precise* form of findings to be made" by administrative agencies. Id. (emphasis added).

This, however, is exactly what the court of appeals had done in the instant case. While the court's opinion purports to apply the standard from *Charter Medical,* a closer reading exposes a complete rejection of that standard. By dissecting the board's valid final order and subjecting the selected component parts to a newly-minted, hypertechnical standard of review under §16(b), the court of appeals has not only misapplied established precedent, it has invaded the Board's fact finding authority. . . . The Board's final order clearly satisfies the purposes behind §16(b) in that it (1) indicated that the Board fully considered all of the evidence and facts, (2) informed Allied of the facts found so that it could intelligently prepare and present an appeal, and (3) assisted this court in *properly* exercising its function of reviewing the order.

Therefore, pursuant to Tex. R. App. P. 133(b), a majority of this court grants United's writ of error, and without hearing argument in this case, reverses the judgment of the court of appeals and renders judgment for United.

## *QUESTIONS AND COMMENTS*

One factor that prospective incorporators should consider in deciding whether to seek a state or federal bank charter is the amount of time involved in obtaining regulatory approval. Another factor should be the reputations of the state and federal regulators involved and of the federal regulators in Washington. After reading these cases, do you think an additional factor to consider should be the rights provided under the state's administrative law? What about the attitudes of the judiciary towards judicial review of agency rulemaking? If so, would you be more likely to seek a state bank charter in Illinois or in Texas? Why?

## C. THE DUAL BANKING SYSTEM

The above discussion raises two questions concerning our nation's dual banking system. The first is whether the necessity of obtaining federal deposit insurance mitigates the degree to which states compete with the federal government for the privilege of providing bank charters. The second issue, which we will consider more closely in this section, is why banks that qualify for FDIC insurance should ever be denied a bank charter under state law.

### Miller, The Future of the Dual Banking System

***53 Brooklyn L. Rev. 1 (1987)***

Ever since the Civil War, the American banking industry has operated under a system of overlapping state and federal regulation. Unique among the nation's private industries, banks and thrift institutions can be chartered either by a state or by the federal government. By selecting one chartering authority rather than another, depository institutions can, to a substantial extent, determine the nature of the regulations to which they will be subject, as well as the identity of the government agency that exercises the regulatory function. Furthermore, the choice is a continuing one, in that a depository institution dissatisfied with its regulator can, for a nominal expense, convert from federal to state charter or vice versa.

The "dual banking system" has long been a sacred cow in the American political tradition. Politicians may complain about aspects of the overlapping regulatory scheme and may attempt to adjust the balance of power between the states and the federal government in minor respects, but questioning the underlying premise of the dual banking system has traditionally been outside the borders of permissible political discourse. Today, however, the dual banking system is undergoing powerful and as yet largely unrecognized strains. The nation's financial system is in a state of rapid evolution, even of revolution. The fundamental changes that are occurring in the banking industry have profound consequences for the future of the dual banking system.

In this article I argue that the dual banking system is largely premised on the existence of a state of affairs that is eroding as the financial marketplace changes. Dual banking functioned effectively in an era of competitively restricted and geographically limited banking; but the introduction of intense competition and interstate banking has dramatically altered the ground rules. It is doubtful that the dual banking system can survive in its present form as the financial services marketplace undergoes this rapid transformation. Eventually, we may see banking develop towards the pattern that is familiar for other industries: chartering by states, not by the federal government; high mobility by firms in terms of choosing where to charter; and regulation by the federal government to the extent necessary to protect the federal interest.

### A. *JUSTIFICATION FOR THE DUAL BANKING SYSTEM*

Perhaps the most noteworthy feature of the dual banking system—often obscured in the debate about minor controversies arising within the system—is the highly anomalous character of the system itself. Virtually all private business enterprises, other than depository institutions, are chartered at the state level. Federal chartering is generally reserved for enterprises that are partially or wholly devoted to serving a governmental interest. Yet in banking we see a very different pattern, one of federal chartering of institutions that are both privately owned and devoted to the pursuit of profit for the owners. What is it about banks that justifies this apparently bizarre deviation from our normal system of state chartering?

It has long been argued that banks are "special" and, therefore, subject to unique regulatory requirements and safeguards, such as the federal deposit insurance program. The "specialness" of banks suggests the possibility that the dual banking system can be justified as being required by those features of banking that are not present in more typical business enterprises. This thesis, however, does not withstand analysis. Banks are special, first, because of the high levels of demand debt in their balance sheets that renders them uniquely subject to destabilizing runs; and, second, because of their critical role in the creation and regulation of the nation's money supply. Yet neither of these features of banking has much, if anything, to do with the dual banking system. National and state banks are equally subject to runs; and (these days at least) the Federal Reserve Board has plentiful authority to control the money supply regardless of whether the nation's banks are chartered by the states or by the federal government. There is, accordingly, little merit to the thesis that the "specialness" of banks provides a justification for the dual banking system.

A modern rationale for national chartering, . . . is that competition among regulatory agencies causes the regulatory system as a whole to move in the direction of policies that allow broader operating authority and impose fewer constraints on profitability. For a believer in the free market, this spells a desirable trend towards economic efficiency. The dual banking system, therefore, can be justified today as a means of providing that depository institutions will not be trapped by a regulator and subjected to unnecessary, burdensome, and inefficient regulations.

[This] thesis was a powerful one at [one] time and continues to have considerable validity. But it is important to note that the thesis is implicitly premised on the existence of geographically limited banking. Why, under the [pro-competitive] hypothesis, are banks different from other firms? Because banks are trapped—forced to charter—in the state in which they have their depository business. They cannot reincorporate in some other state if they dislike the policies imposed on them by the bank examiner of their home state. In this respect banks are different from other firms, because other firms, if they dislike the regulations imposed by their chartering state, can simply reincorporate in some other state at minimal cost. This is the reason commonly given for Delaware's dominance in the market for corporate charters—that Delaware provides the mix of regulations that is most desirable to major business corporations or at least to the managers who make the decision about where to incorporate. If banking resembled other industries, banks would not need the dual banking system to escape bondage to their chartering authority; they could simply reincorporate in some other state offering less onerous regulations.

But the interstate banking environment that characterizes the world of competitive banking is one in which banks are much less trapped within their chartering state. Banks can conduct many of their operations in other states free of the oversight of the chartering authority. Citibank, for example, can move its credit card operations to South Dakota by establishing a limited service bank in that state as a subsidiary of the parent holding company. Even if a bank is required to retain its charter in the state where it has its principal operations, it can shop around for more favorable regulatory environments for many of its operations. This trend can only accelerate in the future as interstate banking becomes more and more of a reality [as happened in 1994 with the enactment of the Riegle-Neal Interstate Banking and Branching Efficiency Act].

In a world of interstate branching, banks would operate like other firms. If they disliked the regulations imposed by their chartering state, they could simply recharter in another state without having to alter the substantive nature of their operations. [Full-scale] interstate branching is still far in the future, but it does seem to be a logical stopping point for the trend towards geographic bank expansion that we are seeing today.

Accordingly, [the competitive] thesis, the most viable contemporary justification for the dual banking system, is being progressively eroded by marketplace changes. As banks move interstate, federal chartering will no longer play a crucial role as a means of avoiding burdensome regulation. Thus, one principal facet of the dual system—the existence of federal chartering authority—rests on increasingly shaky ground in an era of competitive banking.

### B. STATE SAFETY AND SOUNDNESS REGULATION

A second aspect of the dual banking system is coming under increasing strain as a result of the developments outlined above: the state system of safety and soundness regulation. For many years, state banking supervisors have comprehensively supervised and regulated the activities of state-chartered institutions in the interest of protecting the financial integrity of those institutions. This is not only a regulatory system, but also a powerful political interest spearheaded by the Conference of State Bank Supervisors, a trade group and lobbying organization that exercises considerable clout on Capitol Hill and in state legislatures.

In looking at state safety and soundness regulation it is useful to evaluate how the relative state and federal interests have changed as a result of the marketplace evolution from cartel to competitive banking. The states' justification for regulating state-chartered depository institutions is the interest in protecting depositors who are located in the state. That interest may have been worthy of respect in the era of cartel banking; almost all depositors in state-chartered institutions were from the chartering state, and the state did not have many competing interests that could interfere with its mission of depositor protection. Moreover, some states maintained at least the pretense of exercising a deposit insurance function, although in fact many were merely supervising the activities of private deposit insurers rather than putting the state's full faith and credit behind these nonfederal deposit insurance funds.

The states' justifications for imposing safety and soundness regulations on state-chartered banks are considerably less compelling in a competitive banking environment. First, the states can no longer claim to have any role in deposit insurance. The disasters of state-sponsored private insurance funds in Maryland and Ohio during the 1980s have in effect destroyed the viability of private deposit insurance for all institutions other than credit unions. Second, the deposit market is becoming increasingly an interstate market. Many depositors are coming into banks from other states, often through the offices of professional deposit brokers. The state's interest in protecting in-state depositors is correspondingly reduced. Third, the increase in the federal deposit insurance ceiling to 100,000 dollars per depositor per bank has meant that most individual depositors are protected by federal deposit insurance and have no need of an additional layer of state safety and soundness protection. Depositors who have uninsured balances are the ones most likely to be from other states or foreign countries—depositors in whose interests the state cannot be said to have a strong concern.

At the same time, the events of recent years have created a countervailing set of interests that have nothing to do with safety and soundness regulation. State legislators respond to pressures from in-state interest groups other than banks—consumers, homeowners, nonbank institutions, and more. These interest-group pressures may result in state regulation that is not in the best interests of bank safety and soundness. Homeowners, for example, may press for state legislation outlawing devices such as due-on-sale clauses, despite the contribution that due-on-sale clauses make to protecting banks against interest-rate risk. Moreover, now that interstate banking is a reality, states are becoming interested in attracting banks to their borders in order to create jobs within the state or to enhance their revenue bases. In recent years, states have begun to offer expanded powers to out-of-state depository institutions on the condition that they come into the state and provide jobs for its citizens, sometimes on the express understanding that the out-of-state banks will not compete with existing in-state banks. And because of increased competition and risk in the financial services industry, state-chartered depository institutions are being pressured to engage in a wide range of activities not permitted to institutions operating under federal charter. Accordingly, state authorities face countervailing pressures that may render suspect, in some instances, the efficacy of the state's safety and soundness regulation.

Economists use the phrase "moral hazard" to denote a condition in which the knowledge that a third party will bear the costs of some harm creates a risk that the actor may fail to take due precautions against occurrence of the harm. The deposit insurance system is often said to create moral hazard on the part of depository institutions by giving them an incentive to take excessive risks with the knowledge that the costs of unsuccessful risk-taking will be borne by the deposit insurance funds, while the benefits will be captured by the banks. Thus, the existence of deposit insurance creates a tendency towards the very action that one wants to protect against. It is not as commonly recognized, however, that state regulators are also subject to moral hazards stemming from deposit insurance. States may have an incentive to permit or even encourage risky activities by state-chartered banks, since the benefits of those activities will in many cases inure to the states, but the costs of the activities, if they go badly, will be borne by the federal insurance funds. This moral hazard has been significantly increased by the move from cartel to competitive banking, since the destabilizing effects of competitive banking create both opportunities for states to compete with other states for banking business by offering regulatory relief, and corresponding dangers that, if a state does not offer such relief, it will lose business to other states that will.

Finally, the state interest in safeguarding the safety and soundness of state-chartered depository institutions is undermined by the reduced efficacy of state supervision in an interstate banking environment. A state-chartered bank that is part of an interstate holding company structure is inevitably going to depend largely on the well-being of the whole structure. Although the requirement of separate chartering provides a measure of continuing power to state authorities, the fact remains that it will be increasingly difficult for state banking authorities to supervise the activities of banks that are part of interstate networks. If the system evolves to allow interstate branching, the efficacy of state safety and soundness regulation will be reduced still further.

Turning now to the federal interests, we find quite a different calculus of interests. One primary characteristic of competitive banking is increased risk of bank failure, which in turn places pressure on the federal deposit insurance funds. Accordingly, the federal government has a much greater interest in ensuring bank safety and soundness than at any time since the establishment of cartel banking. That interest will often run directly contrary to state regulation. . . .

### Conclusion

The continued role for state regulation is problematic. In an era of competitive banking the federal interest in protecting the deposit insurance funds is necessarily paramount, while the state interest in protecting depositors will be more and more chimerical. Eventually the banking system may evolve towards a more rational arrangement—one in which the states charter all depository institutions; where such institutions can branch freely across state lines; where banks and thrift institutions, like other firms, can recharter in some other state without excessive cost; where the federal role is limited to activities reasonably necessary to carry out the responsibility of providing deposit insurance; and where the federal function is not impeded by the states and is limited to the area in which the federal government has a compelling regulatory interest.

## *QUESTIONS AND COMMENTS*

1. Professor Miller observes that the dual banking system is a "sacred cow in American political life," and that challenging its legitimacy "has traditionally been outside the borders of permissible political discourse." Why do you suppose this is the case? One explanation is that a dual banking system causes state and federal regulators to compete for bank charters in order to retain market share. It is argued that this competition serves as a constraint on the abuse of regulatory discretion and leads to more efficient bank regulation. On the other hand, there are others who question whether the current system has any beneficial

effects. For example, when Arthur Burns was the chairman of the board of governors of the Federal Reserve System he observed that the competition among state and federal regulators led to a "competition in laxity" because the regulators must promulgate lax regulations and have lax enforcement procedures in order to attract chartering business. Address of Arthur Burns to the American Bankers Association Convention, Honolulu, Hawaii, Oct. 21, 1974. Chairman Burns also observed that "sometimes regulatory agencies are played off against one another" by bankers seeking to obtain regulatory forbearance. Id.

Proponents of the value of the dual banking system respond to this argument by saying that bank owners have an economic incentive to maximize the value of the firm and therefore will select the set of regulations that achieves that goal. See Scott, The Dual Banking System: A Model of Competition in Regulation, 30 Stan. L. Rev. 1 (1977). These arguments track the traditional corporate law arguments, outlined in the introduction to this chapter, about the value of jurisdictional competition for corporate charters. See generally Baysinger & Butler, The Role of Corporate Law in the Theory of the Firm, 28 J.L. & Econ. 179 (1985).

2. In evaluating the merits of each side in this debate, one must consider why the state and federal regulatory agencies are concerned with their share of the market for corporate charters. There is some reason to doubt that they do care. Private firms are interested in attracting new customers, but regulatory agencies lack the same economic incentives as private firms since the people making the decisions are supposed to be doing something other than maximizing profits. Banking regulators should be rewarded if they take steps that will facilitate a safe and sound banking system. It is not generally thought that they are rewarded simply for attracting new business. Certainly the evidence reported in the last section concerning the high number of bank charters denied by the Comptroller supports the position that the goal of banking regulators is not simply to attract new chartering business.

Further doubts about the validity of the argument that a dual banking system creates healthy competition are raised in the Butler & Macey article discussed in Note 6 below.

3. Professor Miller points out a major difference between the competition among states for the privilege of issuing general corporate charters and the competition between the states and the federal government to issue bank charters. What is the nature of this difference?

4. One primary purpose of banking regulation is to improve the safety and soundness of the nation's banking system. Is a dual banking system likely to further this end? What are the costs and benefits to a state from granting a charter to a bank that is highly risky because it plans to specialize in making speculative development loans? If this bank fails, who will be responsible for seeing that the insured depositors are compensated? What does Professor Miller say about whether there is a

legitimate state interest in promoting the safety and soundness of banks? What do these observations suggest about the viability of a dual banking system?

5. What is the "calculus of interests" that exists at the federal level, according to Professor Miller? Couldn't the federal government protect its interests in the integrity of the nation's financial system without interfering with the states' ability to grant bank charters simply by refusing to give federal deposit insurance to institutions it believes are likely to fail?

6. Whereas Professor Miller took the position that a dual banking system is somewhat passé, Professors Henry Butler and Jonathan Macey argue that competition among the states is virtually nonexistent. See Butler & Macey, The Myth of Competition in the Dual Banking System, 73 Cornell L. Rev. 677 (1988).

Butler and Macey argue that competition in the dual banking system is more imagined than real because the federal government can invoke the commerce clause and the supremacy clauses of the U.S. Constitution to preempt state laws whenever state law gives state-chartered banks a meaningful advantage over federal banks.

Butler and Macey, like Miller, recognize that the historical record provides little evidence for the proposition that regulators were trying to foster healthy competition among themselves in order to further the public interest. In fact, the existence of the dual banking system is a historical accident. Congress passed the National Bank Act of 1863 authorizing the establishment of national banks not to provide a source of competition for state banks, but rather to provide the nation with a stable system of currency to replace the existing system of notes issued by state banks, and to provide a ready market for the new bonds being issued by the federal government to finance the Civil War. The drafters of the National Bank Act anticipated that state banks would exchange their state charters for national charters and that a dual banking system would exist only during a brief transition period.

Congress imposed a punitive tax on state bank notes when state banks showed a reluctance to give up their state bank charters. This ploy failed as state banks began offering checking accounts as low-cost substitutes for the bank notes they previously had issued. Thus the real rationale for the dual banking system, according to Butler and Macey, is Congress's desire to capture some of the advantages associated with being the monopoly provider of bank charters.

As noted above, Butler and Macey argue that the generally accepted theory of competition in the dual banking system is flawed because of the ability of the federal government to trump conflicting state regulations whenever doing so furthers its interest. In addition, as a matter of competitive necessity, both state and national banks must obtain deposit insurance from the federal government, and the FDIC requires that banks obtaining such insurance comply with its uniform regulations regardless of contrary provisions in the laws of individual states.

Butler and Macey argue that the lack of competition in the dual banking system is not such a bad thing because state banking regulation plays no productive role in making banks safer. The existence of federal deposit insurance deprives the states of the argument that state regulation is necessary to protect local depositors. Indeed, the presence of deposit insurance may make state competition undesirable since state regulators have incentives to adopt regulations that allow local bankers to take excessive risks. The benefits associated with this risk-taking are felt within the states with permissive regulations, as loans are freely made to create new jobs and economic expansion. The costs associated with such permissive regulations, however, are borne nationally since the federal government is the entity that must step in to pay off the debts incurred by bankers taking advantage of lenient state banking laws.

To illustrate the point of their article, Butler and Macey examine the history of reserve requirement regulations on state and national banks. Reserve requirements consist of bank assets that must be held in the form of vault cash or deposits with one of the regional Federal Reserve banks or with banks approved by the board of governors of the Federal Reserve System. Reserve requirements obligate the banks that are subject to such requirements to hold a certain percentage of their liabilities in cash or cash equivalents in order to ensure that they will be able to meet the liquidity needs of depositors. Until 1980 only federally chartered banks were subject to the reserve requirements imposed by the Federal Reserve Board. State banks that did not choose to become members of the Federal Reserve System were subject only to the reserve requirements imposed by state regulators. These state reserve requirements were considerably lower than the reserve requirements imposed by the Federal Reserve. The federal response was to pass the Depository Institutions Deregulation and Monetary Control Act of 1980, which imposed the federal reserve requirements on all banks, thereby eliminating a major dimension of the competition within the dual banking system.

Because reserve requirements are equivalent to a tax—assets held in reserve earn little or no interest—the lower reserve requirements that existed for state nonmember banks were very popular and were one of the main reasons cited for the departure of many medium-sized banks from the Federal Reserve System prior to 1980. Moreover, many state regulators allowed the state banks to meet their reserve requirements by holding assets in interest-bearing securities, thereby further reducing the relative cost of state-composed reserve requirements.

Butler and Macey argue that Congress's decision to impose standardized minimum reserve requirements was clearly inconsistent with the idea of competition in the dual banking system. They also argue that the decision was fully justified in light of federally sponsored deposit insurance:

> The ability of state banking authorities, before 1980, to relieve banks of onerous reserve requirements gave state nonmember banks additional leeway to engage in excessive risk-taking (in the form of extremely illiquid asset portfolios) at the expense of the federal banking authorities. Put another way, the ability of state banking authorities to set the reserve requirements for federally insured banks created a negative externality. All of the costs of the low state reserve requirements were borne at the federal level because riskier state banks placed an added burden on either the Federal Reserve as lender of last resort or the federal insurance fund. In contrast, all of the benefits of the low reserve requirements were enjoyed at the state level in the form of additional local loans at lower interest rates, higher interest rates for local depositors, and greater returns to shareholders in state-chartered, nonmember banks. Thus, not only does the dual banking system not function as envisioned, it does not appear that permitting states to regulate federally-insured banks is particularly desirable in the presence of fixed-premium, federally-sponsored deposit insurance. Such state regulation will likely permit state banks to engage in excessive risk-taking at the expense of the federal deposit fund. . . .

73 Cornell L. Rev. 677, 696 (1988).

Despite the extension of minimum reserve requirements to state banks, the Federal Reserve Board would still prefer that the Fed pay interest on the reserves it holds from commercial banks. Otherwise, it recognizes that commercial banks are likely to engage in transactions or arrangements which are functionally similar to checking accounts but which do not qualify as reserves for Federal Reserve Act purposes. The Fed also worries that the reserve requirement is placing banks at a disadvantage to other institutions, most notably to foreign banks with respect to offshore deposits and to money market mutual funds, both of which can offer the equivalent of transaction services but do not have to hold reserves at the Fed.

In 1994 Congress instructed the Federal Reserve to study the whole question, including the necessity of requiring sterile reserves for monetary policy purposes, the appropriateness of paying a market rate of interest on reserves, or paying the equivalent of a market rate of interest into the federal deposit insurance funds, the monetary impact that the failure to pay interest has had on depository institutions, and the impact that the failure to pay interest on reserves has had on the ability of the banking industry to compete with nonbanking providers of financial services and with foreign banks. Section 329 of the Riegle Community Development and Regulatory Improvement Act of 1994, Pub. Law 103-325. This provision is apparently part of a campaign by the Fed to start paying interest on reserves, despite the budgetary impact on the federal government that would be caused by the change.

7. Both Miller, and Butler and Macey recognize that the dual banking system is a political sacred cow. Why do you think this is the case? Under Butler and Macey's hypothesis, what reason do state regulators have to maintain the dual banking system? Is it possible to reconcile the arguments that Butler and Macey make with the arguments made by Miller in the previous article?

8. Butler and Macey argue that there is no efficiency or safety-and-soundness reason why obtaining a bank charter could not become a matter of right, provided other specified public objectives are met. How would it be possible to meet these other public policy objectives?

9. Note that Butler and Macey do observe some evidence of the competition between state and federal regulators that is supposed to characterize the dual banking system. In particular, they note that at one time, the states had more liberal rules regarding reserve requirements than the federal government. Was this evidence of "healthy" or "unhealthy" competition between the regulators?

10. In light of the analysis presented in this chapter, what, if anything, do you think is accomplished by the presence of a dual banking system?

11. In the FDICIA legislation of 1991, Congress provided that an insured state bank may not engage as principal in any type of activity that is not permissible for a national bank unless the FDIC determines that the activity would pose no significant risk to the deposit insurance fund and the state bank complies with applicable capital standards. Arguably the extensive preemption of state-chartered bank and thrift powers contained in the 1991 legislation further supports the Butler-Macey claim that the dual banking system is largely a myth because of the power of Congress to preempt state legislation under the Supremacy Clause of the Constitution.

12. On the other hand, some prominent commentators argue that important aspects of the dual banking system survive these changes. Although the new statute limits the activities in which insured state-chartered banks may engage as principal, it does not similarly restrict the powers of state banks as agents. Brokerage and other agency activities are perhaps the most significant nonbank activity engaged in by state banks.

13. For more extended discussion on the status of the dual banking system after FDICIA, see, e.g., Melanie Fein, FDICIA Imposes New Limits on State Banks, Commercial Law and Practice Course and Handbook Series: The FDIC Improvement Act of 1991: What Banks and Thrifts Need to Know Now (1992); James B. Watt, After the FDICIA, Is There Life for Dual Banking?, 11 Banking Policy Report (1992).

# 3 REGULATION OF THE BANKING BUSINESS

In this chapter we assume that problems of entry into the banking industry have been solved: The institution has been duly chartered and legally constituted to do business as a commercial bank or thrift. This, of course, is not the end of the story, but rather the beginning. Once a bank is established, it must face multiple and complex questions about the outer limits of its powers.

This chapter begins our exploration of the nature of those limits. We begin by returning briefly to the topic of the dual banking system, and exploring the degree to which states may regulate the activities of federally chartered institutions. We then turn to the regulatory system's attempt to define the "business of banking" and to confine banks to activities falling into that definition. We proceed to examine limitations on bank investments, depository activities, and capital adequacy.

Reserved for a later chapter (Chapter 6) is the special and important topic of securities activities by banks and bank holding companies.

## A. THE DUAL BANKING SYSTEM: A REPRISE

We have already discussed the dual banking system in general terms (in Chapter 2). We now return to that subject in a more applied setting. Questions of bank powers inevitably involve an initial determination of applicable law: Is a federal rule applicable to a particular issue, or is the governing principle to be found in state law?

It might seem as if the answer to this question should be simple: We simply ask whether the institution is state-chartered or federally chartered, and apply the law accordingly. The reality is not that simple. Federally chartered banking institutions are subject to state laws in many respects. Conversely, state-chartered institutions are also sometimes subject to federal law.

The methodology for resolving these questions is one of preemption. Congress clearly has plenary authority, subject only to constitutional constraints, to regulate the affairs of national banks and federally chartered savings institutions. Nor is there much question, at least these days, as to the power of the federal government to set rules for the operation of *state*-chartered institutions. The federal government *could,* if it wanted, preempt state power in this area and apply its own rules. The issue in a concrete case is thus not whether the federal government has power to preempt state rules, but rather whether it has done so *in fact.*

Many years ago the Supreme Court set out standards, still generally applicable, for evaluating whether state or federal rules apply to the operations of national banks. First, it is clear that national banks are subject to state law with respect to many of their operations. In National Bank v. Commonwealth, 76 U.S. (9 Wall.) 353, 362 (1869), the Supreme Court observed that national banks are

> governed in their daily course of business far more by the laws of the State than of the Nation. All their contracts are governed and construed by State laws. Their acquisition and transfer of property, their right to collect their debts, and their liability to be sued for debts are all based on state law.

However, it is equally clear that state law must give way to overarching federal interests in some cases. In Davis v. Elmira Savings Bank, 161 U.S. 275, 283 (1896), the court characterized national banks as

> instrumentalities of the federal government, created for a public purpose, and as such necessarily subject to the paramount authority of the United States. It follows that an attempt, by a State, to define their duties or control the conduct of their affairs is absolutely void, wherever such attempted exercise of authority expressly conflicts with the laws of the United States, and either frustrates the purpose of the national legislation or impairs the efficiency of these agencies of the Federal government to discharge the duties, for the performance of which they were created. These principles are axiomatic, and are sanctioned by the repeated adjudications of this court.

In evaluating challenges to the application of state law to federally chartered banks and savings associations, a court today will first inquire as to whether there is an explicit statutory preemption of state authority. If there is no such preemption, there may nevertheless be an express *regulatory* preemption. Such preemption will be upheld if reasonably within the scope of the powers granted by Congress to the federal regulatory agency. See Fidelity Federal Savings & Loan Association v. de la Cuesta, 458 U.S. 141 (1982) (upholding FHLBB regulation preempting state laws restricting the use by federal savings and loans of due-on-sale clauses in mortgages).

If there is no express preemption either in a statute or a regulation, the question becomes whether the state rule in issue interferes impermissibly with the federal regulatory scheme. There have been a number of cases in recent years holding state authority to be impliedly preempted in various respects. See, e.g., National State Bank of Elizabeth v. Long, 630 F.2d 981 (3d Cir. 1980) (reporting and disclosure requirements of state anti-redlining statute held invalid as applied to national banks on the ground that they were inconsistent with the Home Mortgage Disclosure Act of 1975). Most of these cases infer preemption from a statute. While federal agency regulations may also be deemed implicitly preemptive, courts are quite wary of doing so. See Hillsborough County v. Automated Medical Labs, 471 U.S. 707, 717 (1985) ("[a]s a result of their specialized functions, agencies normally deal with problems in far more detail than does Congress. To infer preemption whenever an agency deals with a problem comprehensively is virtually tantamount to saying that whenever a federal agency decides to step into a field, its regulations will be exclusive. Such a rule, of course, would be inconsistent with the federal-state balance embodied in our Supremacy Clause jurisprudence.").

Most preemption cases consider the effect of state regulation on federal statutes or regulations. However, in the bank failure context the federal courts have developed an extensive jurisprudence that applies a preemptive federal common law to the rights of federal banking agencies in dealing with failed institutions. See D'Oench, Duhme & Co. v. FDIC, 315 U.S. 447 (1942). These issues are discussed at length in Chapter 8.

Preemption analysis also applies to determine whether federal law has ousted state regulation of *state*-chartered institutions. It would appear that courts are more willing to defer to state authority when the institution in question operates under a state charter for the obvious reason that Congress probably does not intend to displace state authority over state-chartered institutions unless doing so is clearly necessary to prevent interference with a federal regulatory scheme. However, courts do not hesitate to displace state regulation where a congressional intent to preempt is clear or where the state regulation in issue is inconsistent with the otherwise applicable federal rule.

These issues of preemption play a role not only in the analysis of bank powers treated in the present chapter, but also in many other issues of banking law. Accordingly, we will return to them from time to time in the remainder of the book.

## Barnett Bank of Marion County v. Nelson

*116 S. Ct. 1103 (1996)*

Breyer, J.

The question in this case is whether a federal statute that permits national banks to sell insurance in small towns pre-empts a state statute that forbids them to do so. To answer this question, we must consider both ordinary pre-emption principles, and also a special federal anti-preemption rule, which provides that a federal statute will not pre-empt a state statute enacted "for the purpose of regulating the business of insurance"—unless the federal statute "specifically relates to the business of insurance." McCarran-Ferguson Act, 15 U.S.C. §1012(b). We decide that the McCarran-Ferguson Act's special anti-pre-emption rule does not govern this case, because the federal statute in question "specifically relates to the business of insurance." We conclude that, under ordinary pre-emption principles, the federal statute pre-empts the state statute, thereby prohibiting application of the state statute to prevent a national bank from selling insurance in a small town.

### I

In 1916 Congress enacted a federal statute that says that certain national banks "may" sell insurance in small towns. It provides in relevant part: "In addition to the powers now vested by law in national [banks] organized under the laws of the United States any such [bank] located and doing business in any place [with a population] . . . [of not more than] five thousand . . . may, under such rules and regulations as may be prescribed by the Comptroller of the Currency, act as the agent for any fire, life, or other insurance company authorized by the authorities of the State . . . to do business [there], . . . by soliciting and selling insurance . . . Provided, however, That no such bank shall . . . guarantee the payment of any premium . . . And provided further, That the bank shall not guarantee the truth of any statement made by an assured [when applying] . . . for insurance." Act of Sept. 7, 1916, 39 Stat. 753, 12 U.S.C. §92.

In 1974 Florida enacted a statute that prohibits certain banks from selling most kinds of insurance. It says: "No [Florida licensed] insurance agent . . . who is associated with, . . . owned or controlled by . . . a financial institution shall engage in insurance agency activities. . . ." Fla. Stat. Ann. §626.988(2)(Supp. 1996). The term "financial institution" includes "any bank . . . [except for a] bank which is not a subsidiary or affiliate of a bank holding company and is located in a city having a population of less than 5,000. . . ." §626.988(1)(a).

Thus, the State Statute says, in essence, that banks cannot sell insurance in Florida—except that an unaffiliated small town bank (i.e., a bank that is not affiliated with a bank holding company) may sell insurance in a small town. Ibid.

In October 1993 petitioner Barnett Bank, an "affiliated" national bank which does business through a branch in a small Florida town, bought a Florida licensed insurance agency. The Florida State Insurance Commissioner, pointing to the State Statute (and noting that the unaffiliated small town bank exception did not apply), ordered Barnett's insurance agency to stop selling the prohibited forms of insurance. Barnett, claiming that the Federal Statute pre-empted the State Statute, then filed this action for declaratory and injunctive relief in federal court.

The District Court held that the Federal Statute did not pre-empt the State Statute, but only because of the special insurance-related federal anti-pre-emption rule. The McCarran-Ferguson Act, which creates that rule, says:

"No act of Congress shall be construed to invalidate, impair, or supersede any law enacted by any State for the purpose of regulating the business of insurance, or which imposes a fee or tax upon such business, unless such Act specifically relates to the business of insurance. . . ." McCarran-Ferguson Act (or Act), §2(b), 59 Stat. 34, 15 U.S.C. §1012(b).

The District Court decided both (1) that the Federal Statute did not fall within the McCarran-Ferguson Act's exception because it did not "specifically relate to the business of insurance"; and (2) that the State Statute was a "law enacted . . . for the purpose of regulating the business of insurance." Barnett Banks of Marion County, N. A. v. Gallagher, 839 F. Supp. 835, 840-841, 843 (M.D. Fla. 1993) (internal quotation marks omitted). Consequently, the McCarran-Ferguson Act, in the District Court's view, instructs courts not to "construe" the Federal Statute "to invalidate" the State Statute. 15 U.S.C. §1012(b). The Eleventh Circuit Court of Appeals, for similar reasons, agreed that the Federal Statute did not pre-empt the State Statute. Barnett Bank of Marion County, N. A. v. Gallagher, 43 F.3d 631, 634-637 (1995).

We granted certiorari due to uncertainty among lower courts about the pre-emptive effect of this Federal Statute. . . . We now reverse the Eleventh Circuit.

**II**

We shall put the McCarran-Ferguson Act's special anti-pre-emption rule to the side for the moment, and begin by asking whether, in the absence of that rule, we should construe the Federal Statute to pre-empt the State Statute. This question is basically one of congressional intent. Did Congress, in enacting the Federal Statute, intend to exercise its constitutionally delegated authority to set aside the laws of a State? If so, the Supremacy Clause requires courts to follow federal, not state, law. U.S.

Const., Art. VI, cl. 2; see California Fed. Sav. & Loan Assn. v. Guerra, 479 U.S. 272, 280-281 (1987) (reviewing pre-emption doctrine). Sometimes courts, when facing the pre-emption question, find language in the federal statute that reveals an explicit congressional intent to pre-empt state law. . . . More often, explicit pre-emption language does not appear, or does not directly answer the question. In that event, courts must consider whether the federal statute's "structure and purpose," or nonspecific statutory language, nonetheless reveal a clear, but implicit, pre-emptive intent. Id., at 525; Fidelity Fed. Sav. & Loan Assn. v. De la Cuesta, 458 U.S. 141, 152-153 (1982). A federal statute, for example, may create a scheme of federal regulation "so pervasive as to make reasonable the inference that Congress left no room for the States to supplement it." . . . Alternatively, federal law may be in "irreconcilable conflict" with state law. . . . Compliance with both statutes, for example, may be a "physical impossibility," . . . or, the state law may "stand as an obstacle to the accomplishment and execution of the full purposes and objectives of Congress." . . .

In this case we must ask whether or not the Federal and State Statutes are in "irreconcilable conflict." The two statutes do not impose directly conflicting duties on national banks—as they would, for example, if the federal law said, "you must sell insurance," while the state law said, "you may not." Nonetheless, the Federal Statute authorizes national banks to engage in activities that the State Statute expressly forbids. Thus, the State's prohibition of those activities would seem to "stand as an obstacle to the accomplishment" of one of the Federal Statute's purposes—unless, of course, that federal purpose is to grant the bank only a very limited permission, that is, permission to sell insurance to the extent that state law also grants permission to do so.

That is what the State of Florida and its supporting amici argue. They say that the Federal Statute grants national banks a permission that is limited to circumstances where state law is not to the contrary. In their view, the Federal Statute removes only federal legal obstacles, not state legal obstacles, to the sale of insurance by national banks. But we do not find this, or the State's related, ordinary pre-emption arguments convincing.

For one thing, the Federal Statute's language suggests a broad, not a limited, permission. That language says, without relevant qualification, that national banks "may . . . act as the agent" for insurance sales. 12 U.S.C. §92. It specifically refers to "rules and regulations" that will govern such sales, while citing as their source not state law, but the federal Comptroller of the Currency. Ibid. It also specifically refers to state regulation, while limiting that reference to licensing—not of banks or insurance agents, but of the insurance companies whose policies the bank, as insurance agent, will sell. Ibid.

For another thing, the Federal Statute says that its grant of authority to sell insurance is in "addition to the powers now vested by law in national [banks]." Ibid. In using the word "powers," the statute chooses a legal concept that, in the context of national bank legislation, has a history. That history is one of interpreting grants of both enumerated and incidental "powers" to national banks as grants of authority not normally limited by, but rather ordinarily pre-empting, contrary state law. See, e.g., First Nat. Bank of San Jose v. California, 262 U.S. 366, 368-369 (1923) (national banks' "power" to receive deposits pre-empts contrary state escheat law); Easton v. Iowa, 188 U.S. 220, 229-230 (1903) (national banking system normally "independent, so far as powers conferred are concerned, of state legislation"); cf. Waite v. Dowley, 94 U.S. 527, 533 (1877) ("Where there exists a concurrent right of legislation in the States and in Congress, and [when] the latter has exercised its power, there remains in the States no authority to legislate on the same matter"). Thus, this Court, in a case quite similar to this one, held that a federal statute permitting, but not requiring, national banks to receive savings deposits, pre-empts a state statute prohibiting certain state and national banks from using the word "savings" in their advertising. Franklin Nat. Bank v. New York, 347 U.S. 373, 375-379 (1954) (Federal Reserve Act provision that national banks "may continue . . . to receive . . . savings deposits" read[s] as "declaratory of the right of a national bank to enter into or remain in that type of business"). See also De la Cuesta, supra, at 154-159 (1982) (federal regulation permitting, but not requiring, national banks to include in mortgage contracts a debt accelerating "due on sale" clause, pre-empts a state law forbidding the use of such a clause). . . .

In defining the pre-emptive scope of statutes and regulations granting a power to national banks, these cases take the view that normally Congress would not want States to forbid, or to impair significantly, the exercise of a power that Congress explicitly granted. To say this is not to deprive States of the power to regulate national banks, where (unlike here) doing so does not prevent or significantly interfere with the national bank's exercise of its powers. See, e.g., Anderson Nat. Bank v. Luckett, 321 U.S. 233, 247-252 (1944) (state statute administering abandoned deposit accounts did not "unlawfully encroach on the rights and privileges of national banks"); McClellan v. Chipman, 164 U.S. 347, 358 (1896) (application to national banks of state statute forbidding certain real estate transfers by insolvent transferees would not "destroy or hamper" national banks' functions); National Bank v. Commonwealth, 76 U.S. 353, 9 Wall. 353, 362 (1870)(national banks subject to state law that does not "interfere with, or impair [national banks'] efficiency in performing the functions by which they are designed to serve [the Federal] Government").

Nor do these cases control the interpretation of federal banking statutes that accompany a grant of an explicit power with an explicit statement that the exercise of that power is subject to state law. See, e.g., 12 U.S.C. §36(c) (McFadden Act) (authorizing national banks to operate branches, but only where state law authorizes state banks to do so); §92(a) (Comptroller of Currency may grant fiduciary powers "by special permit to national banks applying therefor, when not in contravention of State or local law"). Not surprisingly, this Court has interpreted those explicit provisions to mean what they say. See, e.g., First Nat. Bank in Plant City v. Dickinson, 396 U.S. 122, 131 (1969)(under McFadden Act, state branching restrictions apply to national banks); First Nat. Bank of Logan v. Walker Bank & Trust Co., 385 U.S. 252, 260-261 (1966) (same); see also Van Allen v. Assessors, 70 U.S. 573, 3 Wall. 573, 586 (1866) (enforcing 1864 amendments to National Bank Act expressly authorizing state taxation of national bank shares).

But, as we pointed out, . . . where Congress has not expressly conditioned the grant of "power" upon a grant of state permission, the Court has ordinarily found that no such condition applies. In Franklin Nat. Bank, the Court made this point explicit. It held that Congress did not intend to subject national banks' power to local restrictions, because the federal power-granting statute there in question contained "no indication that Congress [so] intended . . . as it has done by express language in several other instances." 347 U.S. at 378, and n. 7. . . .

The Federal Statute before us, as in Franklin Nat. Bank, explicitly grants a national bank an authorization, permission, or power. And, as in Franklin Nat. Bank, it contains no "indication" that Congress intended to subject that power to local restriction. Thus, the Court's discussion in Franklin Nat. Bank, the holding of that case, and the other precedent[s] we have cited above, strongly argue for a similar interpretation here—a broad interpretation of the word "may" that does not condition federal permission upon that of the State. . . .

In light of these considerations, we conclude that the Federal Statute means to grant small town national banks authority to sell insurance, whether or not a State grants its own state banks or national banks similar approval. Were we to apply ordinary legal principles of pre-emption, the federal law would pre-empt that of the State.

## III

We now must decide whether ordinary legal principles of pre-emption, or the special McCarran-Ferguson Act anti-pre-emption rule, governs this case. The lower courts held that the McCarran-Ferguson Act's special anti-pre-emption rule applies, and instructs courts not to "construe" the Federal Statute to "invalidate, impair, or supersede" that of the State. 15 U.S.C. §1012(b). By its terms, however, the Act does not apply when the conflicting federal statute "specifically relates to the business of insurance." Ibid. In our view, the Federal Statute in this case "specifically relates to the business of insurance"—therefore the

McCarran-Ferguson Act's special anti-pre-emption rule does not apply. . . .

For these reasons, the judgment of the Court of Appeals is reversed.

*QUESTIONS AND COMMENTS*

1. As of 1995, sixteen states had denied national banks licenses to sell insurance (what interests do you think promoted these decisions?). The principal case holds that §92 displaced the state regulation because it satisfies both the normal standard for preemption and specifically relates to the business of insurance, thus falling outside the special preemption rule of the McCarran-Ferguson Act.

2. In some cases a state's regulation may be characterized as either a banking regulation or a regulation of insurance. In such cases, there may be an issue under the McCarran-Ferguson Act as to whether the state (as opposed to the federal) rule is a regulation of the business of insurance. If not, the state statute would not qualify for reverse preemption under the McCarran-Ferguson Act in any event. See Owensboro National Bank v. Stephens, 44 F.3d 388 (6th Cir. 1994) (concluding that the state statute at issue did not regulate insurance, thus obviating the effect of the McCarran-Ferguson Act).

3. For background on the McCarran-Ferguson Act, see Jonathan R. Macey and Geoffrey P. Miller, Costly Policies: State Regulation and Antitrust Exemption in Insurance Markets (AEI Press 1993).

## B. ACTIVITIES RESTRICTIONS

Let us now consider the specific regulatory limits on bank powers. A longstanding principle of bank regulation holds that banks should be in the business of banking, and not in any other business. Banks should be banks, and nothing else. But like most principles—especially those that can be expressed in four words or less—the maxim that banks should be banks is easier to state than to explain or to apply. Two questions seem particularly pressing. First, saying that banks should be banks makes sense only if we know what banks *are*—a question that we discussed in Chapter 1 but that we return to briefly here. Second, we will ask *why* the activities of banking firms should be restricted to the "business of banking." What would be so terrible if banks became homebuilders or manufacturers of lead pencils?

## 1. National Banks

Section 24 of title 12 of the United States Code sets forth the powers of national banks. The first six powers are standard for all corporations: powers to make contracts, engage in litigation, appoint officers and directors, prescribe bylaws, remain in existence indefinitely, and so forth. These are not problematic.

The same cannot be said, however, for Clause Seventh. The essence of §24 (Seventh) is simple: A national bank shall have power to exercise *"all such incidental powers as shall be necessary to carry on the business of banking"* (emphasis added). This is an incidental powers clause (note the similarity in language and function to the Necessary and Proper Clause of the Constitution). As a matter of logic, the clause would seem to establish two zones of permissible activities for national banks: first, the "business of banking" strictly construed; and second, other activities that, while not part of the "business of banking," are nevertheless necessary to carry on the business of banking. This second category is evidently broader than the first; how much broader is a matter of debate.

Congress has provided some guidance as to the types of activities authorized by §24 (Seventh). They include "discounting and negotiating promissory notes, drafts, bills of exchange, and other evidences of debt; . . . receiving deposits; . . . buying and selling exchange, coin, and bullion; . . . loaning money on personal security and . . . obtaining, issuing, and circulating notes." The problem in interpreting this language, however, is that the activities mentioned do not seem to be "incidental" powers in any respect. They represent the essence of traditional commercial banking: receiving deposits, making loans, issuing notes. If these are incidental powers, it is difficult to see what "business of banking" they could possibly be incidental to!

Perhaps by specifying incidental powers that sound like banking per se, Congress intended virtually no leeway for activities outside the commercial banking business in its most traditional form. On the other hand, the quoted language might provide guidance as to the nature of the "business of banking," not to the types of powers that are incidental to that business. Then, however, the identification of permissible incidental powers is left entirely up to interpretation, either by banking agencies, courts, or banks themselves. Moreover, it is not clear whether Congress intended to "fix" the business of banking for all time in the mold of the mid-nineteenth century, when the statute was first passed, or whether the phrase allows room for evolution as banking markets develop.

It should already be evident that §24 (Seventh) poses more questions than it answers. In this regard, consider the following judicial opinion, which offers an influential and important approach to the interpretive difficulties discussed above.

### a. Travel Agency Services

## Arnold Tours, Inc. v. Camp

*472 F.2d 427 (1st Cir. 1972)*

HAMLEY, Circuit Judge.

This class action involves the authority of national banks to engage in the travel agency business. The plaintiffs are Arnold Tours, Inc., and forty-one other independent travel agents of Massachusetts engaged in the travel agency business.

One of the defendants is William B. Camp, Comptroller of the Currency (Comptroller), whose office has issued rulings and regulations to the effect that national banks may engage in that business. The other defendant is South Shore National Bank (South Shore), a national banking association chartered by the United States Government, with a principal place of business in Quincy, Massachusetts, and with twenty-seven branch offices throughout Massachusetts. South Shore has been engaged in the travel agency business, operating it as a department of the bank, since November, 1966, after having bought out the fourth largest travel bureau in New England. Plaintiffs asked for declaratory and injunctive relief, the effect of which would be to force South Shore out of the travel business. . . .

The parties are in agreement that if there is any statutory authority for national banks to engage in the travel agency business, it is to be found in the following language contained in 12 U.S.C. §24, Seventh, a provision of the national Bank Act (Act):

> Seventh. To exercise . . . all such incidental powers as shall be necessary to carry on the business of banking. . . .

The Comptroller relied upon the quoted statutory words in his 1963 ruling that national banks could engage in the travel agency business. Thus, paragraph 7475 of the Comptroller's Manual for National Banks (1963), which is now codified as 12 C.F.R. §7.7475, reads:

> *§7.7475 National banks acting as travel agents*
> Incident to those powers vested in them under 12 U.S.C. 24, national banks may provide travel services for their customers and receive compensation therefor. Such services may include the sale of trip insurance and the rental of automobiles as agent for a local rental service. In connection therewith, national banks may advertise, develop, and extend such travel services for the purpose of attracting customers to the bank.

In holding that 12 U.S.C. §24, Seventh, did not authorize national banks to engage in the travel agency business the district court, in its opinion, first focused attention on the nature of South Shore's travel agency operation. The court relied upon the graphic description of a modern agency operation given by Charles F. Heartfield. Heartfield had served as vice-president of South Shore, in charge of its travel department, from November 1, 1966 to 1970. His description of a modern agency operation is set out in the margin.[4]

The district court then observed that

> To say that conduct of a business of the nature and type described by Mr. Heartfield is a *sine qua non* to the successful operation of a national bank is a self-refuting proposition, especially in view of the fact that on the defendants' own claim only 122 national banks out of the many hundreds if not thousands in existence were providing travel agency services in 1967.

338 F. Supp. at 723.

The Comptroller argues that the district court applied an erroneous legal standard in reviewing the Comptroller's construction of the "incidental powers" clause of the National Bank Act (12 U.S.C. §24, Seventh), as indicated by the court's above-quoted use of the term sine qua non.

We are in agreement with the Comptroller that a sine qua non standard would be an inappropriate measure of a national bank's incidental powers under 12 U.S.C. §24, Seventh. While the pertinent language of that section refers to all such incidental powers "as shall be necessary to carry on the business of banking" we do not believe "necessary" was there used to connote that which is indispensable.

But we believe that, read in context with its entire opinion, the district court's reference to the concept of sine qua non was not intended to state the test for determining whether a particular bank activity is authorized as an incidental power. What seems to us to be a more reliable gauge of the district court's rationale is its discussion immediately following the sine qua non statement quoted in the margin.

The district court therein indicated that its chief concern was

4. Heartfield said:

> A travel department is a functioning complete travel service bureau within the confines and control of the bank. It is a department store of travel—staffed by knowledgeable people—trained in the techniques of selling every mode of transportation—air, rail, steamship, U-drive car. It is a staff acquainted with thousands of hotels and resorts—proficient in the intricacies of foreign customs and regulations, health requirements and languages, accustomed with tipping customs, foreign exchange, conversant with foreign representatives and hotel managers, tour operators and tour guides, knowledgeable in the history and geography of our own great United States—as well as the rest of the shrinking world, constantly aware of changing tarrifs [sic] and schedules, well acquainted with over 60 airlines throughout the world, 40 domestic and international railroads, and numerous motorcoach lines, steamship companies, etc. . . .
>
> To sum it up—a good travel department is a personalized department store of travel.

whether a travel agency business primarily involves the performance of financial transactions pertaining to money or substitutes therefore. If not, the court in effect ruled, that business was not within the normal and traditional range of the monetary activities of a national bank, and thus not encompassed by the "incidental powers" provision of 12 U.S.C. §24, Seventh. It was on this basis that the district court distinguished the travel agency business from such approved "incidental powers" of national banks as those employed in selling travelers' checks or foreign currency, issuing letters of credit, or making travel loans.

But the Comptroller and South Shore do not agree that the "incidental powers" of national banks should even be restricted to the performance of financial transactions pertaining to money or substitutes therefor or that only such transactions lie within the normal traditional range of the activities of a national bank. . . .

The most reliable guides as to what is encompassed in the term "the business of banking" are the express powers of national banks as set out in the National Bank Act. And when one looks at past decisions it becomes apparent that the activities of national banks which have been held to be permissible under the "incidental powers" provision have been those which are directly related to one or another of a national bank's express powers. . . .

In our opinion, these decisions amply demonstrate that a national bank's activity is authorized as an incidental power, "necessary to carry on the business of banking," within the meaning of 12 U.S.C. §24, Seventh, if it is convenient or useful in connection with the performance of one of the bank's established activities pursuant to its express powers under the National Bank Act. If this connection between an incidental activity and an express power does not exist, the activity is not authorized as an incidental power.

This brings us to a consideration of the question of whether the operation of a travel agency business, such as that conducted by South Shore, may reasonably be said to be convenient or useful in connection with the performance of one of the bank's established activities in the exercise of its express powers.

While the Comptroller and South Shore do not concede that such a relationship between an incidental and an express power must exist, they suggest ways in which they believe a travel agency business is directly related to a national bank's normal banking operations. In presenting this view, they pursue two lines of argument. One of these is an effort to equate the basic functions performed by travel agencies with functions which have historically been performed by banks. The other is based on the premise that a substantial number of banks have, for a long time, been providing travel agency services.

With regard to the first of these contentions, defendants assert that the basic functions performed by travel agencies consist of: (1) procuring carrier passage and other travel accommodations by acting as agent for passengers and carriers, and (2) providing various informational services to the traveler. Defendants then assert that both of these "basic" travel agency functions are only particular applications of the broad agency and informational services which banks traditionally offer among their "congeries of services."

In our view this analysis unrealistically minimizes the basic functions of a travel agency business and unjustifiably exalts the agency and informational functions of national banks.

The operation of a travel agency in the United States today is a highly complex activity. See note 4 above. Some of the aspects of that business are closely regulated under the supervision of the Civil Aeronautics Board, the Interstate Commerce Commission, and the Federal Maritime Commission. It is true that a travel agent acts as an agent for the traveler, but it also acts as an agent for carriers. A travel agency provides informational service for the traveler, but it also solicits travel business, advertises and in general promotes the interests of its carrier principals. More importantly, the agency and informational services a bank travel agency renders are pursuant to its own interest in making its travel department profitable, wholly apart from the bank's normal banking operations.

On the other hand, while national banks provide certain agency and informational services they are normally of a kind which are germane to the financial operations of the bank in the exercise of its express powers. There are, of course, instances in which banks have, as a convenience to their regular customers, and without additional compensation, obtained railroad, steamship or airline tickets for such customers, or provided information helpful to such customers in connection with their travels. But incidental good will service of this kind cannot reasonably be equated with the operation of a modern travel agency for profit. In short, there is a difference between supplying customers with financial and informational services helpful to their travel plans and developing a clientele which looks to the bank not as a source of general financial advice and support but as a travel management center.

The Comptroller asserts that one of the central purposes of the National Bank Act, enacted during the Civil War, was to serve as a unifying force to the nation and that the draftsmen of the Act contemplated that the Act would fulfill its unifying purpose by, among other things, facilitating interstate commerce and "facilitating travel."

As a reading of these documents demonstrates, the objective of establishing a "unifying force" and "facilitating travel" were viewed in those early years, not as being attainable through the operation of a banking travel service, but as being attainable through the establishment and circulation of a national currency. Prior to the National Currency Act of 1863, now also known as the National Bank Act, there was no national currency and financial transactions were largely conducted through the medium of bank notes issued by state banks. The establishment of a national currency provided a form of legal specie acceptable throughout the country, and it was this which provided the desired "unifying force" and assisted in "facilitating travel."

South Shore asserts that banks in the United States have been offering travel services to their customers since at least 1865, when the Security National Bank in Sheboygan, Wisconsin, formally established its bank travel department. According to South Shore, in the ensuing years of the nineteenth century and the period preceding World War I, numerous other banks began to offer travel services largely to accommodate the great number of immigrants arriving in this country. The travel service then rendered by banks involved assisting immigrants in remitting money to families in their native lands, obtaining steamship tickets for relatives, and transmitting these prepaid tickets to foreign addresses. Immigrants during this period made periodic trips "home" and needed travelers' checks, letters of credit, foreign currency and other banking assistance.

The limited and largely uncompensated services of this kind, rendered by banks during this period, bear very little resemblance to the functioning of a modern travel agency. Moreover, it was not until 1959 that the Comptroller of the Currency ruled that national banks could engage in a regular travel agency business. . . .

Despite the Comptroller's sanction, since 1959, of the operation of travel agency businesses by national banks, only one hundred twenty-two out of about four thousand seven hundred national banks were engaged in that business in 1967, when this action was brought. This is far from persuasive evidence that the operation of travel service departments is useful and convenient to the functioning of normal banking services under the express powers granted by the National Bank Act. . . .

In view of the many considerations which lead to a contrary conclusion, as reviewed above, the lack of essential articulation supporting the Comptroller's 1963 ruling, issued without opinion or accompanying statement, and in the light of the lack of uniformity in the Comptroller's own interpretation of the statute, we conclude that the Comptroller's current interpretation, as embodied in 12 C.F.R. §7.7475, is not entitled to dispositive deference. . . .

We conclude that the district court did not err in entering a declaratory judgment to the effect that it is illegal for a national bank to operate a full-scale travel agency since such an operation is not an exercise of the incidental powers referred to in 12 U.S.C. §24, Seventh. For the same reason the district court did not err in determining that 12 C.F.R. §7.7475 is invalid to the extent that it is construed by the Comptroller as authorizing a national bank to operate a full-scale travel agency. These determinations in no way limit banks in rendering banking services for travelers, such as the sale of travelers' checks and foreign currency, the making of travel loans, issuance of letters of credit, and providing gratis travel information. . . .

*QUESTIONS AND COMMENTS*

1. The court suggests that a permitted incidental activity must be "convenient or useful in connection with the performance of one of the bank's established activities pursuant to its express powers under the National Bank Act." Even though the court ruled that operating a full-service travel agency fell outside a national bank's incidental powers, isn't the articulated test too lenient? The statute requires that the activities in question be *necessary* to carry on the business of banking. The court states that a permitted incidental activity must be *convenient or useful* in connection with the performance of a national bank's express powers. Something that is convenient or useful is often not necessary. Can you reconcile these?

2. Note that the court permits banks to provide free travel information. Why is it incidental to the business of banking if a bank offers travel information for free, but not incidental to the business of banking if a bank charges a fee?

3. Is the court saying that the "business of banking" is broader than the express powers of a national bank under the National Bank Act? But then what guidance does it offer to identifying what the "business of banking" is? Or does the court's test make it unnecessary to identify the "business of banking"?

4. What is the relevance of the fact that only a small percentage of national banks had taken advantage of the Comptroller's action permitting banks to operate travel agencies? Would the analysis have been different if many banks had entered the business? What would this show other than that travel agency operation is a profitable business for banks?

5. What, given the court's articulated test, is the relevance of the historical experience of national banks in the travel business? If the key is the "express" powers under the National Bank Act, then the historical experience of banks in the travel business would be irrelevant, would it not? Consider the court's language again: There must be a connection between a given activity and "one of a bank's established activities pursuant to its express powers under the National Bank Act." On rereading, does this language suggest anything further about the relevance of history?

6. Why didn't the court defer to the decision of the Comptroller, a presumably "expert" official, concluding that offering travel agency services was incidental to the business of banking? What does the court know that the Comptroller doesn't know? Footnote 12 of the court's

opinion, not reproduced in the text, contains a long discourse on the fact that many other rulings of Comptroller Saxon had been reversed in court.

7. Why might this suit have been brought as a class action of travel agents in Massachusetts, rather than as a challenge to the Comptroller's regulation by a national association of travel agents in federal court in Washington, D.C.?

8. What social policy is served by keeping national banks out of the travel agency business?

### b. Personal Property Leasing

## M & M Leasing Corp. v. Seattle First National Bank

*563 F.2d 1377 (9th Cir. 1977), cert. denied, 436 U.S. 956 (1978)*

SNEED, Circuit Judge:

Appellees, Seattle First National Bank (Seafirst) and Peoples National Bank of Washington, are engaged in the leasing of motor vehicles and other personal property. Appellants, M & M Leasing Corporation, Goodway Leasing, Inc., Bill Pierre Leasing, Inc., and Budget Rent-a-Car of Washington-Oregon, Inc., are independent corporations engaged principally in motor vehicle leasing. Defendant-cross-appellant is the Comptroller of Currency of the United States.

Appellants, plaintiffs in the trial court, sought a declaration that the appellees' leasing of motor vehicles and other personal property was not authorized by 12 U.S.C. §24 (Seventh), despite the fact that it is sanctioned by the Comptroller of the Currency.[2] Appellants also requested an injunction barring appellees and their subsidiaries from further motor vehicle leasing activities. Moreover, appellants asserted that, even if the Comptroller's rulings relied upon to sanction appellees' activities are

2. The authorization appears in 12 C.F.R. §7.3400 and is as follows:

> A national bank may become the owner or lessor of personal property acquired upon the specific request and for the use of a customer and may incur such additional obligations as may be incident to becoming an owner and lessor of such property. Lease transactions do not result in obligations for the purpose of 12 U.S.C. 84. Since the lease payments are in the nature of rent rather than interest, 12 U.S.C. 85 and 86 are not applicable.

12 C.F.R. §7.7376 authorizes an operating subsidiary of a national bank to "lease property."

valid, such activities exceeded the authorization the rulings provided and should be enjoined to that extent.

The trial court in an able opinion distinguished between motor vehicle lease transactions in which the banks *do not* assume the risk of residual value fluctuation upon termination of the lease (so-called "open end" leases) and those in which the banks *do* assume such risk (so-called "closed end" leases). In its initial judgment the trial court enjoined the appellees "from engaging in motor vehicle lease transactions in which the banks assume the risk of residual value fluctuation upon termination of the lease" and declared the Comptroller's interpretive rulings, 12 C.F.R. §§7.3400 and 7.7376, invalid to the extent they authorized such leases.

None of the parties was entirely satisfied by this disposition of their dispute. The appellee banks moved to clarify the opinion and judgment to remove "closed end" leases in which there is to be a "full payout" prior to termination of the lease from the scope of the trial court's injunction and to delete the words "motor vehicle" from the language of the injunction. The appellants thought the court's injunction should embrace all leasing and the Comptroller of Currency indicated displeasure with the restrictiveness of the trial court's opinion and injunction.

The trial court in due course amended its injunction to delete the words "motor vehicle" so that it currently reads "from engaging in lease transactions in which the banks assume the risk of residual value fluctuation upon termination of the lease." Also, by order, the trial court construed its opinion and judgment as follows:

> Lease transactions in which the lessor bank, during the initial lease term, is repaid the cost of the property leased, plus the cost of financing the transaction, in the form of rentals, tax benefits and/or the guarantee of a financially responsible guarantor, are neither disapproved in the Court's opinion nor enjoined by the judgment entered herein.

These modifications satisfied the appellees but, of course, neither the appellants nor the Comptroller. Hence, this appeal was taken by them. We affirm in part and reverse in part.

In essence, we view the trial court's holding as correct, so far as it goes, but somewhat more restrictive than the law requires. As we see it, the "business of banking," which 12 U.S.C. §24 (Seventh), authorizes the appellees to conduct, includes leases of personal property when, in the light of all relevant circumstances, the transactions constitute the loan of money secured by the properties leased. A transaction may be so characterized, in our opinion, even if it is designed so that the lessor bank does not recover during the initial lease term every penny of the cost of the leased property plus its financing costs. A lease ceases to be a secured loan when the lessor assumes material burdens other than those of a lender of money and is subject to significant risks not ordinarily incident to a secured loan. The bright line traced by the trial court provides a sound guide by which leases can be kept within the scope of the "business of banking." We are not, however, prepared to say that the trial court's bright line constitutes the precise outer limit of the "business of banking."

To support our holding, we first will describe the nature and scope of national banks' involvement in the leasing of personal property, we will next analyze the term "business of banking" and apply the analysis to such leasing, and, finally, we will identify some of the characteristics of leases which lie beyond the outer limits of the "business of banking."

### I. Leasing By National Banks

The record of this case indicates that the role of national banks, such as Seafirst and Peoples, in personal property leasing generally is essentially that of a financing agency. To illustrate this it is useful to divide personal property leases into motor vehicle leases and leases of aircraft, ships and other so-called "big ticket" items.

Motor vehicle leases usually, but not invariably, are generated by automobile dealers. Particular dealers will enter into an agreement with a bank under which dealers will lease automobiles to their customers. The major terms of a lease, *i.e.*, make, model, accessories, term, and payment schedule, are fashioned by the dealer in a manner that fits his and the customer's interests and conforms to the lease design envisioned by the dealer's arrangement with the bank. To protect itself against improvident leases the bank possesses the right to review both the substantive terms of a lease and the credit-worthiness of the lessee before accepting the lease. The crucial items reviewed are the credit rating of the customer and the vehicle's residual value. Upon accepting the lease the lessee-customer is notified and instructed to make lease payments to the bank. The title of the vehicle shows the bank as the legal owner, while the customer is listed as registered owner and lessee. Customers who approach the bank initially are usually referred to dealers with whom the bank has leasing arrangements.

The bank functions somewhat differently with respect to "big ticket" items. With respect to them, generally the customer calls the bank directly and expresses an interest in leasing particular personal property. This contact essentially is to inquire about the availability of credit. The bank performs no procurement function. The customer chooses the property he wishes to lease, selects a vendor and negotiates with him the terms of the purchase. Assuming the bank finds the customer an acceptable credit risk, it then purchases the property and leases it to the customer. Delivery by the seller is made directly to the customer-lessee who makes the lease payments to the bank.

Both motor vehicle leases and "big ticket" leases provide that the burdens of operating costs and risks are borne by the lessee. Thus, the lessee agrees to purchase insurance sufficient to cover the bank's interest, to pay all repairs and maintenance, and to assume the risk of loss or damage.

Motor vehicle leases and "big ticket" leases frequently differ, however, in certain important respects. Foremost is the difference in the lessee's responsibility at the expiration of the initial term of the lease. Motor vehicle leases, for example, include a guarantee by the lessee that the vehicle will have a certain residual value at the expiration of the usual two or three year term.

This residual value is simply the anticipated resale value of the vehicle at the lease's termination. Should resale value in fact be less than the guaranteed residual value, the lessee must pay the difference. Should it be more, the excess when realized is refunded to the lessee. "Big ticket" item leases, on the other hand, normally impose no residual value guarantee on the lessees. The need for such guarantees is reduced, if not eliminated, by the fact that such leases typically are for a term which approximates the economic life of the properties. Leases in which there is a residual value guarantee are designated, in the language of commerce, as "open end" leases, while those in which no such guarantee exists are designated "closed end" leases.

Closed end leases, therefore, do impose on the lessor bank a risk not borne in the case of open end leases. In the former the lessor bank must absorb any difference between the estimated residual value at the end of the lease and a lesser actual resale price. In the open end lease, on the other hand, any such difference is guaranteed by the lessee. It is this distinction between the two types of lease that, as already noted, strongly influenced the trial court's disposition of this case.

Notwithstanding this difference between open end and closed end leases, the lessor bank under each type of lease realizes on the property at the expiration of the lease in a substantially similar manner. Thus, at the lease's end the lessor bank will dispose of the property in the simplest possible manner. Should the lessee not purchase the item, either for the estimated residual value or for a mutually agreeable price, the lessor bank will dispose of it by sale or by way of a new lease. Motor vehicles not sold to the lessee, for example, are either resold to the dealer, sold in the wholesale market, or leased to another customer. Moreover, the record of this case does not reveal that closed end leases as a class impose significantly more onerous economic burdens on banks than do open end leases. This is not surprising because leases of "big ticket" items, leased under closed end terms, generally provide for the bank's investment plus interest to be returned by way of lease payments prior to the expiration of the lease.

From the standpoint of a bank the advantages of leasing, as opposed to traditional lending on chattel security, are said to be numerous. Certain tax benefits pertaining to depreciation and the investment tax credit are said to be available under leasing but not under lending. Leasing, it is pointed out in the record of this case, permits the avoidance of usury laws and increases the demand for credit by eliminating the need for down payments by the customer.

Lessees also may derive advantages from leasing not available when conventional borrowing is employed. A lease obligation may be reflected on the balance sheet more favorably than an indebtedness, and leasing may permit avoidance of limitations on the lessee's ability to borrow.

In any event, leasing yields to the banks a rate of return that compares favorably to that of lending. A portfolio of prudently-arranged leases imposes no greater risks than one of equally prudently-arranged loans. It is small wonder, therefore, that today over 1000 national banks are engaged in the leasing of personal property which has an aggregate value in excess of $2 billion. Thus, although much of this growth has occurred in the 1970's and resulted from the entrance of national banks into the field of motor vehicle leasing, it is clear that leasing at present is a significant part of the business of national banks.

## II. The "Business of Banking"

While the importance of leasing to the business of national banks is relevant to determining the extent to which such activity is useful and convenient, it does not alone establish that leasing is within the "business of banking" as authorized by 12 U.S.C. §24 (Seventh). In construing the scope of the authority established by this statutory provision, we adopt the approach employed by the First Circuit in Arnold Tours, Inc. v. Camp, 472 F.2d 427, 431-32 (1st Cir. 1972). That is, for an activity to be pursuant to an incidental power "necessary to carry on the business of banking" it must be "convenient or useful in connection with the performance of one of the bank's established activities pursuant to its express powers under the National Bank Act." *Id.* at 432. Thus, leasing must be convenient or useful to business *expressly* authorized by 12 U.S.C. §24 (Seventh). As indicated above, we hold that leasing, when in the light of all relevant circumstances the transaction constitutes a loan of money secured by the leased property, is incidental to the "loan of money on personal security," an activity expressly authorized by the National Bank Act.

In reaching this conclusion we draw comfort from the fact that commentators uniformly have recognized that the National Bank Act did not freeze the practices of national banks in their nineteenth century forms. Indeed, many contend that the powers of national banks "are not confined to the powers specified in the National Bank Act and those necessary to carry out those specific powers." Trimble, The Implied Power of National Banks to Issue Letters of Credit and Accept Bills, 58 Yale L.J. 713, 721 (1949). We prefer, however, the *Arnold Tours, Inc.* formulation of the scope of "incidental" powers; but, whatever the scope of such powers may be, we believe the powers of national banks must be construed so as to permit the use of new ways of conducting the very old business of banking. Those who would reject such new ways should recall that Chief Justice Holt's efforts in Clerke v. Martin, 2 Ld. Raym. 757 (1702) to deny the negotiability of promissory notes payable to a named payee or order was overturned by statute several years later. 3,4 Anne c.9 (1704). As Holdsworth put it, Chief Justice Holt's mistake was to believe that "the most correct technical reasoning could stop the development of the new machinery rendered necessary by the new needs of an expanding trade." Holdsworth, History of the Engish Law VIII, 175-76 (1926). Unless compelled by higher authority, which we would then believe to be misguided, we do not wish in the context of this case to repeat Chief Justice Holt's mistake.

Appellants would have us follow in Holt's footsteps by emphasizing that secured lending to permit the acquisition of property can be accomplished through traditional forms. A loan secured by a chattel mortgage or a conditional sales contract provides the proper means, they insist, by which a "loan of money on personal security" ought to be accomplished. A lease which serves the same purpose is impermissible. Particularly is this true, they assert, when both the lessor bank and the lessee customer distinguish the lease from a loan, and third parties, including various government agencies, treat the two quite differently.

Appellants are correct in stating that functionally interchangeable leases and secured loans are regarded as distinct in both the rhetoric and regulation of this form of commerce. However, it is their functional interchangeability that is the touchstone of our decision. To ignore that in the interpretation of 12 U.S.C. §24 (Seventh), is figuratively to reject, as did Chief Justice Holt, something "invented in Lombard Street." Clerke v. Martin, supra. Whether third parties in other contexts should treat leases that are equivalent to loans as nonetheless distinct and separate is not at present before us. Whatever might be the proper dispositions of such issues, they should not influence our opinion in this case.

### III. The Limits of the "Business of Banking"

It should be clear that our holding is not without limits. It does not embrace the view that national banks may compete with appellants in the daily or short-term car rental business. Nor does it permit national banks to become self-financing automobile dealers, utilizing their unique position to acquire an inventory of automobiles at advantageous prices to lease at going market rates to customers. Neither activity is a means by which a bank makes a "loan of money on personal security." Each is a business distinct from banking.

A national bank also leaves the business of banking when it undertakes, as a "service" to its customers, to pass on to them any price reductions which its marketing power can extract from sellers of automobiles or other personal property. There may be a place for a "buyer's cooperative" in automobile marketing, but that place is not in a national bank. Such a cooperative, whether in substance or in form, is not the business of banking.

It is also clear that national banks cannot provide operational services such as repairs, maintenance, spare parts, insurance coverage, license renewals, etc. Such services are not those of a bank. This proscription shapes the duration of a lease that a national bank property can employ. Short term leases which inescapably thrust upon the bank significant service responsibilities impose non-banking responsibilities. As previously indicated, leases of automobiles for two or three years do not necessarily entail nonbanking responsibilities; and, of course, a lease for the economic life of the property also does not.

Proscribed operational services, also, do not include the functions incident to the disposal of the property at the expiration of the lease as described [earlier in] this opinion. So long as these activities constitute only the orderly liquidation of the banks' security they remain within the business of banking.

Finally, our holding manifestly is not intended to authorize leases which impose significant financial risks on national banks more onerous than those incident to loans. Therefore, it is necessary that the lessor bank look primarily to the obligations of the lessee for the entire return of its advances. It is the lessee's credit worthiness, not primarily the market value of the leased property, to which the bank must look for its return. No banker, however, ignores the borrower's collateral; nor must he when the loan is cast in lease form. Our point, put differently, is that a lease, which from its inception inevitably must be repeated or extended to enable the bank to recover its advances plus profit, is not a "loan of money on personal security." Such leases indicate a rental business, not the business of banking. To engage in the business of renting personal property would permit the assumption of risks not permitted national banks. An impermissible assumption of risks is not indicated, however, either by an open end lease, in which the bank's entire advance is guaranteed by the lessee, or a closed end lease, in which the residual value of the leased property at the expiration of the lease contributes insubstantially to the bank's recovery of its advances plus interest.

### IV. Role of the Comptrollers

We recognize our observations do not provide a comprehensive charter by which the appellee banks may guide their steps. For example, we have not dealt with the type of advertising that is compatible with leasing activities of national banks that are within their statutory authority. Nor do we comment on the appropriateness of a subsidiary of a national bank acquiring a dealer's license from the state and maintaining a garage for storing previously leased automobiles.

Preparation of a comprehensive charter is a function that belongs to the Comptroller. It is his duty to promulgate reasonably detailed regulations which will confine leasing within the channels of the "business of banking." We do not believe that 12 C.F.R. §§7.3400 and 7.7376 adequately perform this duty. . . .

## *QUESTIONS AND COMMENTS*

1. Underlying the decision in this case is the court's perception that leasing motor vehicles and other personal property can in many circumstances be functionally similar to a loan for the purchase of personal property and secured by the property in question.

Assume, for example, that a commercial airline wants to purchase a jet aircraft. The traditional form of bank financing would be a loan to the airline backed by a security interest in the aircraft. The bank would receive payments from the airline for interest and return of principal; if the airline defaulted, the bank could obtain the aircraft and sell it, using the proceeds to cover its loan.

Alternatively, however, the transaction could be structured so that the bank is the legal owner of the aircraft, rather than a lender with a security interest. The bank would then "lease" the aircraft to the airline, with the airline agreeing to make regular payments on the lease and to cover all expenses of insurance, maintenance, and repair. If the airline fails to make the lease payments, the bank as owner can terminate the lease and obtain possession of the aircraft, which it could then sell or lease to another customer.

These transactions seem different, but in economic terms they are similar. In each case the bank provides the money for the purchase of the aircraft; in each case the airline obtains the right to use the property, subject to a requirement that payments be made to the bank. In each case the bank looks to the property for security in the event the airline defaults on the payment obligation.

Why then use a lease instead of a standard bank loan? A number of benefits of leases are set forth in the case. By far the most important force driving leasing, however, is (or, somewhat more accurately, was) the tax code. If the airline could not use the tax benefits of ownership—that is, accelerated depreciation and investment credits—the deal could be made sweeter for both parties if those tax benefits could be transferred to a lessor that could use them. Because a leveraged lease vested formal ownership rights in the bank (or other lessor), the bank could claim the tax benefits on its return.

The kicker in all this—and the matter that troubles the court in *M & M Leasing*—is the allocation of residual ownership rights. The court disapproves lease arrangements as not incidental to banking if the bank incurs substantial ownership risks at the end of the lease period. Thus, if the leased property has any significant value at the end of the lease, the bank must be able to look to the customer to make good the loss if the actual residual value of the property turns out to be less than the residual value that had been anticipated at the outset.

You may wonder why this matter of residual value is of any importance to banks. It is very doubtful that banks actually wanted to incur ownership risks at lease-end. They did so because of tax considerations. At the time of the *M & M Leasing* case the Internal Revenue Service insisted that a lease arrangement of this sort must allocate to the lessor some economically valuable residual ownership rights. Otherwise the transaction would be recast as a secured loan and the tax benefits would be lost. *M & M Leasing,* however, imposes a nearly opposite requirement, namely that if the activity is to be permitted to national banks, it must involve no substantial residual ownership risk to the bank. The case thus posed a challenge for tax and banking lawyers to guide their national bank clients between the Scylla of the tax code and the Charybdis of the National Bank Act.

A variety of developments in the years since *M & M Leasing* have fundamentally altered the legal landscape. Most importantly, as a result of the Tax Reform Act of 1986 the value of lease financing is substantially lessened by a variety of rules restricting or penalizing the transfer of tax benefits. In addition, Congress amended the National Bank Act in 1987 to permit national banks to lease personal property for financing purposes, without regard to the risk of fluctuations in residual value, so long as the arrangements are net leases (in which the lessee pays the expenses of maintenance, insurance, and upkeep) and the investment does not exceed 10 percent of a bank's assets. 12 U.S.C. §24 (Tenth). The Comptroller of the Currency has adopted a consolidated rule on lease financings, incorporating both *M & M Leasing* and 12 U.S.C. §24 (Tenth). 12 C.F.R. part 23. As a result of these changes in tax and banking law, the situation today is that banks may engage rather freely in lease financing deals, but the benefits of such deals have been substantially eroded by changes in the tax law.

It is evident, therefore, that *M & M Leasing* has been largely superseded by subsequent events. The case nevertheless remains an important legal precedent for the light it sheds on the incidental powers of national banks.

2. The court explicitly endorses the *Arnold Tours* approach to inci-

dental powers. However, does the opinion actually apply a slightly different test? Consider in this regard the court's repeated reference to Chief Justice Holt's mistake. What was Holt's mistake, and why did the court not want to repeat it?

3. In any event, is the analogy to Chief Justice Holt apt? Holt decided a question of common law that was later overturned by statute. Judge Sneed addresses a pure question of statutory law. If the law is to be changed, shouldn't that function be up to Congress?

4. Perhaps Judge Sneed answers this objection by saying that the "National Bank Act did not freeze the practices of national banks in their nineteenth century forms." In other words, Judge Sneed sees the National Bank Act as adopting an evolving standard of the "business of banking." What evidence does he adduce to show that Congress intended an evolving standard? What implications for interpreting a regulatory statute flow from the conclusion that a legislature adopted an evolving standard?

5. In the end, doesn't Judge Sneed fall prey to Chief Justice Holt's mistake after all? If the standard is an evolving one, why not conclude that it has evolved to the point where banks can offer leases in which they maintain residual ownership risk? This was evidently the direction the industry was heading (because of the tax considerations discussed above). Doesn't Judge Sneed stop progress in its tracks in just the same manner as Justice Holt did in 1702?

6. Judge Sneed seems to make an implicit distinction between changes that merely alter the form, but maintain the substance, of a bank transaction, on the one hand, and changes that go to the substance of a bank's activities, on the other. But is this distinction really viable? How easy is it to tell the difference between form and substance? And isn't there some tension between the distinction and Judge Sneed's suggestion that the National Bank Act adopts an evolving standard for the business of banking?

7. What would you say, in this regard, about Justice Holt's mistake—is the negotiability of a note payable to order a matter of mere form, or one of substance? What about leases themselves, even ones where the bank incurs no residual ownership risk? To be sure, such leases are functionally similar to secured loans; but secured loans do not involve the de facto sale of tax benefits. Does the fact that tax benefits are transferred in a lease financing make the distinction between leases and secured loans one of substance? Judge Sneed says that "functional interchangeability . . . is the touchstone of our decision." But isn't it perfectly clear that lease financings and secured loans are *not* functionally interchangeable?

8. Can a national bank pool home mortgages, assign them to a trust, and sell "pass-through" certificates to the public representing a fractional undivided interest in the pool of mortgages? See Securities Industry Association v. Clarke, 885 F.2d 1034 (2d Cir. 1989), *cert. denied,*

110 S. Ct. 1113 (1990) (activity was incidental to the bank's power under §24 (Seventh) to "negotiat[e] promissory notes . . . and other evidences of debt").

9. Does a bank take on any extra risks if it structures a financing transaction as a lease rather than a secured loan? Consider the facts of Midwest Precision Services, Inc. v. PTM Industries Corp., 887 F.2d 1128 (1st Cir. 1989). A bank agreed to provide lease financing for a piece of machinery. It issued a purchase order to the seller with instructions that the machinery was to be shipped directly to the lessee. The lessee rejected the shipment as defective and refused to accept any cure. Seller sued the lessee and the bank. The court of appeals held that the bank was a "buyer" under U.C.C. §2-103(a), that it had delegated to its lessee the responsibility to comply with its contractual obligations as buyer, and that it was accordingly liable to the seller for the lessee's wrongful refusal to accept delivery or to allow cure. For discussion of some of the problems in this area, see Boss, Panacea or Nightmare? Leases in Article 2, 64 Boston Univ. L. Rev. 39 (1984).

### c. Data Processing Services

## National Retailers Corp. of Arizona v. Valley National Bank

***411 F. Supp. 308 (D. Ariz. 1976), aff'd, 604 F.2d 32 (9th Cir. 1979)***

BOLDT, Senior District Judge, Sitting by Designation.

#### I. STATEMENT OF THE CASE

This is an action for a declaratory judgment and injunctive relief against the defendant, James E. Smith, Comptroller of Currency (hereafter Comptroller). Plaintiff seeks a declaratory judgment that a ruling, 12 C.F.R. §7.3500, *Use of data processing equipment and furnishing of data processing services,* issued by the Comptroller is unlawful and should be set aside as arbitrary, capricious and an abuse of discretion, contrary to constitutional rights, power, privilege or immunity and, in excess of statutory jurisdiction, authority or limitations. Injunctive relief is sought to enjoin the Comptroller from issuing any opinion, rule or regulation permitting national banks to perform computer data processing services for any person unless the data processing services are directly "incidental" to the express powers of the bank under the National Bank Act. 12 U.S.C. §24.

The factual pattern within which plaintiff seeks the declaratory and injunctive relief involves plaintiff, National Retailers Corporation of

Arizona (hereafter NRCA) an Arizona corporation that has been offering data processing services to retailers and others in Arizona since 1966. The data processing services offered by plaintiff require the use of a cash register and computer sold by National Cash Register (NCR). The cash register produces a magnetic tape which can be fed into the NCR computer to produce computer print-outs reflecting various aspects of the customer's business. One of plaintiff's customers, a subsidiary of Hart, Schaffner & Marx, was Hanny's, a retail clothing merchandiser with a substantial number of stores in Arizona and in the Phoenix area. Prior to October 1, 1971, Hanny's was obtaining data processing services from plaintiff. On or about October 1, 1971, Hanny's obtained almost identical services from Valley National Bank (hereafter VNB). The data processing services offered by the VNB to Hanny's and the public, also utilized an NCR cash register and computer combination. The contested service which VNB offers pursuant to the Comptroller's ruling is called a Retail Information System (hereinafter RIS). The retailer's sales transaction data, when recorded on NCR cash registers and processed through an NCR computer owned by VNB, can be assembled and compiled into numerous different reports which provide the retailer with information regarding various aspects of his business. A retailer whose sales data has been processed by VNB has the option of purchasing some or all of the reports made available to VNB's data processing service. . . .

The bank charged Hanny's substantially lower rates than those of plaintiff for essentially the same services.

[The applicable regulation, 12 C.F.R. §7.3500, reads as follows:]

> (a) A national bank may use data processing equipment and technology to perform for itself and *others* all services expressly or incidentally authorized under the statutes applicable to national banks. For example, as part of its banking business and incidental thereto, a national bank may collect, transcribe, process, analyze, and store, for itself and *others*, banking, financial, or related economic data. In addition, incidental to its banking business, a national bank may (1) market a by-product (e.g., program, output, etc.) of an above-described data processing activity; and (2) *market excess time* on its data processing equipment so long as the only involvement by the bank is furnishing the facility and necessary operating personnel.
>
> (b) The provision of data processing services by a national bank to others is subject to the prohibitions contained in 12 U.S.C. 1972 concerning tying arrangements, reciprocal dealing, and price discrimination. In particular, a national bank may not require any party who is or proposes to be a customer for any service or product of the bank to utilize any data processing service offered by the bank, and the bank may not fix or vary the consideration for any extension of credit, lease, or sale of property or provision of another service on the condition or requirement that a customer utilize a data processing service offered by the bank.

(Emphasis added.) . . .

For this Court to apply the *Arnold Tours* standard, which this Court approves and adopts, the relevant express powers of the National Bank Act must be compared to the activity alleged by defendant to be within the incidental powers of national banks, i.e., the RIS provided by VNB. Having done so, the Court must decide whether the service in question is "convenient or useful" to the performance by the VNB of express powers stated in the National Bank Act. If so, it is within the incidental powers of a national bank. Defendant contends the RIS is very useful to the VNB and national banks in general when considering and processing applications for loans on accounts receivable or for operating capital. National banks lending money for operating capital or on accounts receivable is a function clearly within the express powers under the National Bank Act. 12 U.S.C. §24 (Seventh). Upon a thorough examination of the evidence and authorities presented this Court is satisfied that the RIS of the VNB is not "convenient or useful" to the performance by the VNB of express powers under the *Arnold Tours* standard. Nor is the offering of the RIS without limitation permissible under any reasonable interpretation of the incidental powers provision of the National Bank Act. Therefore, the RIS of the VNB is not a proper or legal activity within the statutory context of 12 U.S.C. §24 (Seventh) and to the extent the Comptroller's ruling and comments authorizes or permits without limitation the public marketing of the RIS by the VNB or other national bank, the Comptroller's ruling and comments are found to be contrary to law and in excess of his delegated authority and are hereby declared invalid.

If the reports available from the RIS service were limited to the *processing* of applications for accounts receivable or operating capital loans by the VNB this Court would not hesitate to find such activity sufficiently related to the express powers of national banks and within the standard of *Arnold Tours,* and would hold that the RIS as limited was within national bank incidental powers. However, the facts of this case are otherwise. VNB did not limit or intend to limit the RIS to producing information and reports useful in processing and considering loan applications from persons or businesses participating in the RIS. It is because of this wide latitude in the range of persons offered the RIS which is not specifically limited by or excepted from the Comptroller's interpretive ruling, that this Court finds the ruling to be beyond the authority of the Comptroller and contrary to the law as interpreted by this court. . . .

## *QUESTIONS AND COMMENTS*

1. What is the problem with banks offering data processing services to merchants? What public policy benefits might be obtained if such services were allowed?

2. Banking is a highly data-intensive industry; banks must have the ability to access and manipulate information on customers' accounts, loans, interest rates, and much more. Assume that data processing is

characterized by high fixed costs and low marginal costs, so that a bank that has purchased sophisticated computer equipment to perform its own data processing can offer excess capacity on the system to others at low cost. This seems to have been the case for Valley National Bank. Since performing data processing for a bank's own purposes is no doubt essential to modern banking, why is offering excess capacity to third parties not a proper incidental function, especially since the effect of the activity will be to reduce a bank's own cost for computation services?

3. Can a national bank sell computer hardware to other banks as part of a package of correspondent services? See Office of Comptroller of the Currency, Letter No. 345, reprinted in Fed. Banking L. Rep. (CCH) ¶85,515 (July 9, 1985) (concluding that one can).

### d. Insurance Agency Activities

## NationsBank of North Carolina v. Variable Annuity Life Insurance Co.

***115 S. Ct. 810 (1995)***

GINSBURG, J.:

These consolidated cases present the question whether national banks may serve as agents in the sale of annuities. The Comptroller of the Currency, charged by Congress with superintendence of national banks, determined that federal law permits such annuity sales as a service to bank customers. Specifically, the Comptroller considered the sales at issue "incidental" to "the business of banking" under the National Bank Act [12 U.S.C. §24 Seventh]. The Comptroller further concluded that annuities are not "insurance" within the meaning of [12 U.S.C. §92]; that provision, by expressly authorizing banks in towns of no more than 5,000 people to sell insurance, arguably implies that banks in larger towns may not sell insurance. . . . We are satisfied that the Comptroller's construction of the Act is reasonable and therefore warrants judicial deference. . . .

### I

Petitioner NationsBank of North Carolina, N. A., a national bank based in Charlotte, and its brokerage subsidiary sought permission from the Comptroller of the Currency . . . for the brokerage subsidiary to act as an agent in the sale of annuities. Annuities are contracts under which the purchaser makes one or more premium payments to the issuer in exchange for a series of payments, which continue either for a fixed period or for the life of the purchaser or a designated beneficiary. When a purchaser invests in a "variable" annuity, the purchaser's money is invested in a designated way and payments to the purchaser vary with investment performance. In a classic "fixed" annuity, in contrast, payments do not vary. Under the contracts NationsBank proposed to sell, purchasers could direct their payments to a variable, fixed, or hybrid account, and would be allowed periodically to modify their choice. The issuers would be various insurance companies. . . .

The Comptroller granted NationsBank's application. He concluded that national banks have authority to broker annuities within "the business of banking" under 12 U.S.C. §24 Seventh. He further concluded that §92, addressing insurance sales by banks in towns with no more than 5,000 people, did not impede his approval; for purposes of that provision, the Comptroller explained, annuities do not rank as "insurance." . . . Respondent Variable Annuity Life Insurance Co. (VALIC), which sells annuities, challenged the Comptroller's decision. . . .

## II

### *A*

. . . . As the administrator charged with supervision of the National Bank Act, . . . the Comptroller bears primary responsibility for surveillance of "the business of banking" authorized by §24 Seventh. . . . Under the formulation now familiar, when we confront an expert administrator's statutory exposition, we inquire first whether "the intent of Congress is clear" as to "the precise question at issue." Chevron U.S.A. Inc. v. Natural Resources Defense Council, Inc., 467 U.S. 837, 842 (1984). If so, "that is the end of the matter." Id. But "if the statute is silent or ambiguous with respect to the specific issue, the question for the court is whether the agency's answer is based on a permissible construction of the statute." Id. at 843. If the administrator's reading fills a gap or defines a term in a way that is reasonable in light of the legislature's revealed design, we give the administrator's judgment "controlling weight." Id. at 844.

In authorizing NationsBank to broker annuities, the Comptroller invokes the "power [of banks] to broker a wide variety of financial investment instruments," . . . which the Comptroller considers "part of [banks'] traditional role as financial intermediaries," . . . and therefore an "incidental power . . . necessary to carry on the business of banking." . . . The Comptroller construes the §24 Seventh authorization of "incidental powers . . . necessary to carry on the business of banking" as an independent grant of authority; he reads the specific powers set forth thereafter as exemplary, not exclusive.

VALIC argues that the Comptroller's interpretation is contrary to the clear intent of Congress because the banking power on which the Comptroller relies—"brokering financial investment instruments"—is not specified in §24 Seventh. . . . According to VALIC, the five specific activities listed in §24 Seventh after the words "business of banking" are exclusive—banks are confined to these five activities and to endeavors incidental thereto. . . . VALIC thus attributes no independent significance to the words "business of banking." We think the Comptroller better comprehends the Act's terms.

The second sentence of §24 Seventh, in limiting banks' "dealing in securities," presupposes that banks have authority not circumscribed by the five specifically listed activities. Congress' insertion of the limitation decades after the Act's initial adoption makes sense only if banks already had authority to deal in securities, authority presumably encompassed within the "business of banking" language which dates from 1863.[2]

### *B*

As we have just explained, the Comptroller determined, in accord with the legislature's intent, that "the business of banking" described in §24 Seventh covers brokerage of financial investment instruments, and is not confined to the examples specifically enumerated. He then reasonably concluded that the authority to sell annuities qualifies as part of, or incidental to, the business of banking. National banks, the Comptroller observed, are authorized to serve as agents for their customers in the purchase and sale of various financial investment instruments, . . . and annuities are widely recognized as just such investment products. . . .

By making an initial payment in exchange for a future income stream, the customer is deferring consumption, setting aside money for retirement, future expenses, or a rainy day. For her, an annuity is like putting money in a bank account, a debt instrument, or a mutual fund. Offering bank accounts and acting as agent in the sale of debt instruments and mutual [funds are] familiar parts of the business of banking. . . .

In sum, modern annuities, though more sophisticated than the standard savings bank deposits of old, answer essentially the same need. By providing customers with the opportunity to invest in one or more annuity options, banks are essentially offering financial investment instruments of the kind congressional authorization permits them to broker. Hence, the Comptroller reasonably typed the permission NationsBank sought as an "incidental power . . . necessary to carry on the business of banking."[4]

2. We expressly hold that the "business of banking" is not limited to the enumerated powers in §24 Seventh and that the Comptroller therefore has discretion to authorize activities beyond those specifically enumerated. The exercise of the Comptroller's discretion, however, must be kept within reasonable bounds. Ventures distant from dealing in financial investment instruments—for example, operating a general travel agency—may exceed those bounds.

4. Assuring that the brokerage in question would not deviate from traditional bank practices, the Comptroller specified that NationsBank "will act only as agent, . . . will not have a principal stake in annuity contracts and therefore will incur no interest rate or actuarial risks." . . .

### III

#### A

In the alternative, VALIC argues that 12 U.S.C. §92 bars NationsBank from selling annuities as agent. That section provides: "In addition to the powers now vested by law in [national banks] . . . any such [bank] located and doing business in any place the population of which does not exceed five thousand inhabitants . . . may . . . act as the agent for any fire, life, or other insurance company authorized by the authorities of the State in which said bank is located to do business in said State, by soliciting and selling insurance and collecting premiums on policies issued by such company. . . ."

The parties disagree about whether §92, by negative implication, precludes national banks located in places more populous than 5,000 from selling insurance. We do not reach this question because we accept the Comptroller's view that, for the purpose at hand, annuities are properly classified as investments, not "insurance."

Again, VALIC contends that the Comptroller's determination is contrary to the plain intent of Congress, or else is unreasonable. In support of its position that annuities are insurance, VALIC notes first that annuities traditionally have been sold by insurance companies. But the sale of a product by an insurance company does not inevitably render the product insurance. For example, insurance companies have long offered loans on the security of life insurance, . . . but a loan does not thereby become insurance. . . .

VALIC further argues that annuities functionally resemble life insurance because some annuities place mortality risk on the parties. Under a classic fixed annuity, the purchaser pays a sum certain and, in exchange, the issuer makes periodic payments throughout, but not beyond, the life of the purchaser. In pricing such annuities, issuers rely on actuarial assumptions about how long purchasers will live.

While cognizant of this similarity between annuities and insurance, the Comptroller points out that mortality risk is a less salient characteristic of contemporary products. Many annuities currently available, both fixed and variable, do not feature a life term. Instead they provide for payments over a term of years; if the purchaser dies before the term ends, the balance is paid to the purchaser's estate. Moreover, the presence of mortality risk does not necessarily qualify an investment as "insurance" under §92. . . .

#### *B [omitted]* . . .

We respect as reasonable the Comptroller's conclusion that brokerage of annuities is an "incidental power . . . necessary to carry on the business of banking." We further defer to the Comptroller's determination that 12 U.S.C. §92 is not implicated because annuities are not insurance within the meaning of that section.

## *QUESTIONS AND COMMENTS*

1. This case introduces us to the conflict between the banking and insurance industries, a conflict that is likely to characterize much of the politics of banking law during the last half of the 1990s. The insurance lobby—especially the independent insurance agents—has proven itself to be a match, or even more than a match, for the awesome political clout of the banking industry. While other limits on banking powers have been dismantled in recent years, Congress has adhered rather steadfastly to limits on banks' or holding companies' entering the insurance agency business. Still, the insurance industry's power is much less when it comes to influencing banking regulators such as the Comptroller of the Currency—as we see from the facts of this case.

2. What construction of §24 (Seventh) did VALIC put forward? What construction of the statute did the Court adopt? Can any clear-cut test be discerned from Justice Ginsburg's opinion?

3. What is the impact of this case on decisions such as *Arnold Tours*? Recall Judge Hamley's test in that case—that an activity is part of a national bank's incidental powers if it is "convenient or useful in connection with the performance of one of the bank's established activities pursuant to its express powers under the National Bank Act." Does that test remain good law after *NationsBank*?

4. Wasn't VALIC correct that the annuities in question in this case had an insurance element? If the annuity were to be paid to the contract holder for the extent of his or her natural life (or for a period measured by the life of another), then the person's expected mortality would be a crucial factor in valuing the instrument. Someone who buys an annuity is hedging against the risk of long life, just as someone who buys life insurance is hedging against the risk of a short one. In either case, mortality risk is a paramount concern. And this is the type of risk that insurance is all about, is it not?

5. Given that annuities are a traditional product sold by insurance companies, how could a unanimous Supreme Court have reasonably concluded that they are not "insurance"?

6. Do you detect a somewhat different judicial attitude toward the Comptroller of the Currency in this opinion than in the previous cases? The Supreme Court here seems inclined to uphold the Comptroller's interpretations so long as they have a reasonable basis in the statute—an application of the familiar *Chevron* test of judicial review of administrative interpretations of governing statutes. Is that the test we find applied in *Arnold Tours* or *National Retailers*—or even *M & M Leasing*?

7. For a time it appeared that the whole question of the interpretation of §92 might be moot. It turns out that Congress, apparently accidentally, left out a comma when it enacted a comprehensive revision of the federal statutes in 1918, the inescapable logical effect of which was to repeal §92. Although the repeal was, to all appearances, completely inadvertent, one federal appeals court concluded that the meaning of the statute was plain and that federal courts had no discretion to look behind the plain language to salvage the apparent congressional intent. The Supreme Court unanimously reversed. United States National Bank of Oregon v. Independent Insurance Agents of America, Inc., 508 U.S. 439 (1993). Justice Souter's opinion observed that "a purported plain-meaning analysis based only on punctuation is necessarily incomplete and runs the risk of distorting a statute's true meaning. Along with punctuation, text consists of words living [in] 'a communal existence,' in Judge Learned Hand's phrase, the meaning of each word informing the others and 'all in their aggregate taking their purport from the setting in which they are used.' Over and over we have stressed that 'in expounding a statute, we must not be guided by a single sentence or member of a sentence, but look to the provisions of the whole law, and to its object and policy.' No more than isolated words or sentences is punctuation alone a reliable guide for discovery of a statute's meaning. Statutory construction 'is a holistic endeavor,' and, at a minimum, must account for a statute's full text, language as well as punctuation, structure, and subject matter. Here, though the deployment of quotation marks in the 1916 Act points in one direction, all of the other evidence from the statute points the other way. It points so certainly, in our view, as to allow only the conclusion that the punctuation marks were misplaced. . . ."

8. How would you analyze a national bank's power to offer a "retirement certificate of deposit," with the following features. The retirement CD is offered to individuals who open an account by making a deposit at the bank. The customer chooses a maturity date. The account earns interest on a tax-deferred basis, and additional deposits can be made until maturity. At maturity, the customer can elect to withdraw up to two-thirds of the principal and accrued interest. The balance is distributed to the customer in fixed periodic amounts, including interest, for the remainder of the customer's life. Technically, interest ceases to accrue at maturity, but the bank calculates an imputed interest rate to be set at competitive levels and applied in the calculation of the payout. The principal and interest are insured until maturity by the FDIC. Is this straightforwardly permitted by the principal case? Or can you perceive a difference—is a bank acting as an agent in the retirement CD?

9. Retirement CDs have been enormously controversial, largely because they represent a major intrusion by banks into a core business of the insurance industry. Some of the bloom may have come off the rose, however, with the IRS's announcement early in 1995 that it was

considering regulations that would deny bank-issued retirement CDs the same tax-deferral on income that is enjoyed by similar instruments issued by insurance companies.

10. Suppose a given state changed its law to prohibit banks from offering retirement CDs. Recall the issues presented in the *Barnett Bank* case earlier in this chapter. Should the state regulation prohibiting retirement CDs be considered prohibited under the National Bank Act, even though there is no express provision in federal law authorizing national banks to offer such products? If the National Bank Act is preemptive, should the preemption be effective given the special rules relating to insurance under the McCarran-Ferguson Act, since the incidental powers clause of §24 (Seventh) does not appear to relate specifically to the business of insurance? Is the McCarran-Ferguson Act even relevant here, given the analysis in the principal case that variable annuities are not "insurance" within the meaning of §92? Is the concept of "insurance" under §92 the same as "insurance" under the McCarran-Ferguson Act?

11. Because it concluded that annuities are not insurance for purpose of the relevant statute, the Court in *NationsBank* left open a question with enormous practical implications—whether §92 allows a national bank located in a town of not more than 5,000 persons to sell insurance outside the local community. The Court of Appeals for the District of Columbia Circuit addressed that issue in 1993. Its opinion is excerpted immediately below.

## Independent Insurance Agents of America v. Ludwig

***997 F.2d 958 (D.C. Cir. 1993)***

BUCKLEY, J.:

This case is before us on remand from the Supreme Court [in United States National Bank of Oregon v. Independent Insurance Agents of America, Inc., 113 S. Ct. 2173 (1993)]. It concerns the interpretation of section 92 of the National Bank Act, which authorizes any bank located in a community with a population of 5,000 or less to sell insurance, subject to the regulations of the Comptroller of the Currency. The Comptroller determined that section 92 imposes no geographic limit on the insurance market so that, as long as it is located in a small town, a bank is free to solicit and serve insurance customers everywhere. We uphold the Comptroller's interpretation as permissible. . . .

[In 1986 the Senior Deputy Comptroller of the Currency for National Operations wrote a letter concluding that] "a national bank or its branch which is located in a place of 5,000 or under population may sell insurance to existing and potential customers located anywhere. In other words, bank branch must be located in a small town, it can sell insurance to persons and businesses located outside that town. . . . ["]

The precise question before us is whether section 92 places any limitations on the geographical scope of the insurance business that may be conducted by a national bank located in a community having a population of 5,000 or under. It is not relevant, for this purpose, that the bank in question is a subsidiary of a major banking corporation.

In examining the Comptroller's interpretation of the National Bank Act, we apply the principles set forth in Chevron U.S.A. Inc. v. NRDC, 467 U.S. 837, 842-45 (1984). . . . Section 92 provides that a national bank located and doing business in a community having a population of not more than 5,000 may "act as the agent for any . . . insurance company . . . by soliciting and selling insurance and collecting premiums." 12 U.S.C.S. §92. These words evince no unambiguous command that the banks may sell insurance only to local townspeople. . . .

[The court analyzed the legislative history and found little evidence of legislative intent on the question at issue. W]e find nothing in this history to suggest an unambiguous congressional intent on the precise question at issue. Furthermore, it is not our job to divine how legislators would have responded to hypotheticals, . . .—particularly where the question is as unknowable as the reaction of 1916 legislators to a world of microchips, communication satellites, fax machines, direct mail and telephone solicitation, and all the other technologies and techniques that now enable a nationwide business to be conducted from any hamlet. We decline appellants' invitation to recast the statute to fit contemporary circumstances; when time and technology open up a loophole, it is up to Congress to decide whether it should be plugged, and how.

[The court concluded that the Comptroller's interpretation of the statute was reasonable enough to satisfy the *Chevron* standard.] Congress expressly permitted small town banks to sell insurance, and the Comptroller has concluded that it did not impose a geographic limit on the insurance business they are allowed to conduct. . . .

*QUESTIONS AND COMMENTS*

1. U.S. Bancorp, which was seeking to market insurance nationwide from a small town, has more than $7 billion in assets. This is hardly the kind of struggling small-town institution that Congress probably had in mind when it passed §92 in 1916, is it? How persuasive do you find Judge Buckley's statement that the size of the institution involved is irrelevant?

2. Assuming that this opinion represents the law of the land, aren't its implications quite stunning? Given the technological advances cited

by Judge Buckley in his opinion, it would appear quite simple for a bank to establish a very large insurance agency business in a small town and sell policies nationwide. What is this going to do to the nation's independent insurance agents?

3. Judge Buckley may have been right that under *Chevron* the court's duty was to sustain the Comptroller's action. But how impartial do you think the Comptroller was in this case? Isn't the Comptroller likely to favor the interests of national banks over independent insurance agents? Anyway, how reliable is the agency's action when it came in the form of a letter signed by a subordinate agency official? This isn't the kind of formal, notice-and-comment rulemaking based on a comprehensive agency record that you might expect for a decision of this magnitude, is it? Why do you think the Comptroller's office acted in such a low-key fashion?

4. Some states allow their state-chartered institutions to exercise insurance agency functions from towns of more than 5,000 inhabitants. What if a state-chartered institution in such a state, which operates insurance agencies in towns over 5,000, seeks to convert over to national bank charter? Must it divest itself of these agencies, or can it continue to operate them under §92 even after it has become a national bank? In 1995, the Comptroller permitted such a charter conversion and allowed the new national bank to keep its agencies. Comptroller of the Currency, Corporate Decision 95-55 (Nov. 15, 1995).

#### e. Risk-Bearing Activities

The preceding subsection discusses whether a national bank can act as an insurance agent; we explored the question whether national banks may do so in very small towns. An insurance agent is a broker; it does not itself bear the risk insured against. What about a bank providing insurance directly or, more generally, agreeing to act as a specialized third-party risk-bearer to protect others against future harms? It might seem in the abstract that if a bank cannot act as an insurance agent, it certainly could not provide insurance directly since doing so is far more risky than a mere agency function. Standard hornbook law agrees. A bank, it is frequently said, may not act as a guarantor for the performance of a contract made by another. The reality, however, is not that simple. The fact is that national banks do act as specialized third-party risk-bearers in a variety of different situations, and that their activities in this regard are consistent with the restrictions in the National Bank Act.

Consider in this regard the standby or "guaranty" letter of credit, the validity of which under the National Bank Act is discussed in the following case.

## Republic National Bank of Dallas v. Northwest National Bank of Fort Worth

***578 S.W.2d 109 (Tex. 1978)***

McGee, Justice.

The Republic National Bank of Dallas sued Northwest National Bank of Fort Worth on an instrument entitled "IRREVOCABLE LETTER OF CREDIT." The disposition of this appeal hinges on the enforceability of that instrument.

The facts of the case are virtually undisputed. In December of 1968 Ronald Hughes, Dudley Hughes, Sr., and Dudley Hughes, Jr., became interested in purchasing the stock of Crown Hill Memorial Park, Inc., corporate owner of a north Dallas cemetery. As required by the law of this state, Crown Hill had a perpetual care fund held in trust for the purpose of maintaining and caring for the grounds and physical plant of the park. American Cities Trust Company was the trustee of the fund at that time. Among the assets, and constituting a major portion of the fund, was a $50,000 promissory note made payable to the fund's trustee in five equal installments by B&H Amusement Rides, Inc. The prospective purchasers of Crown Hill were wary of this particular note and refused to close the sale as long as it was a fund asset. Consequently, on February 28, 1969, B&H caused Northwest National Bank to issue an instrument in favor of the trustee which provided:

THE NORTHWEST NATIONAL BANK
7820 White Settlement Road
Forth Worth, Texas

Speegle Berry
President

IRREVOCABLE LETTER OF CREDIT
Non-Transferable

February 28, 1969

American Cities Trust Company
1815 South Montclair, Oak Cliff
Dallas, Texas,
and/or its successor as Trustee
of the Perpectual Care Fund of
Crown Hill Memorial Park,
a Perpetual Care Cemetery.

Gentlemen:

We hereby open our irrevocable credit in your favor, available in the following manner and on the following terms:

1. *Transferability.* The credit is nontransferable.

2. *Drafts.* Your single draft drawn on Northwest National Bank of Fort Worth, at ten (10) days' sight, in the amount of the unpaid principal, interest and attorneys' fees then due and payable after default, pursuant to the terms of a certain Promissory Note executed January 12, 1968, by B&H Amusement Rides, Inc., payable to the order of American Cities Trust Company, which draft must state upon its face: "Drawn under Letter of Credit of the Northwest National Bank of Fort Worth, Texas, dated February 21, 1969."

3. *Total.* The draft must not exceed Fifty Thousand and no/100 Dollars ($50,000.00).

4. *Purpose.* To be applied to the balance remaining on a certain loan evidenced by a certain Promissory Note executed January 12, 1968, by B&H Amusement Rides, Inc., payable to the order of American Cities Trust Company, secured by a security interest in and upon the inventory of B&H Amusement Rides, Inc.

5. *Documents.* The required documents are:

(a) Original Promissory Note, executed January 12, 1968, by B&H Amusement Rides, Inc., payable to the order of American Cities Trust Company.

(b) Copy of letter advising B&H Amusement Rides, Inc. of default in the payment of the said note executed January 12, 1968, said advice letter being addressed to B&H Amusement Rides, Inc., showing receipt and being dated not less than twenty (20) days in advance of the date of Sight Draft.

(c) Copy of letter advising E.L. Baker, Jr., Jerome I. Weiner, and Henry W. Simon, Jr., of default in the payment of the said Note executed January 12, 1968, said advice letter being addressed in care of Simon & Simon, attorneys, 816 First National Building, Fort Worth, Texas, and being dated not less than twenty (20) days in advance of the date of Sight Draft.

(d) Copy of letter which advised owners of B&H Amusement Rides, Inc. property of default in payment and resulting acceleration of the said Promissory Note dated January 12, 1968, said letter being dated not less than twenty (20) days prior to the date of Sight Draft.

6. *Obligation of issuer.* The Northwest National Bank of Fort Worth, Texas, agrees with American Cities Trust Company, and/or its successor as Trustee of the Perpetual Care Fund of Crown Hill Memorial Park, a Perpetual Care Cemetery, to duly honor a proper draft drawn and negotiated in compliance with the terms of this Letter of Credit upon presentation to the office of the bank.

7. *Rules applicable.* The Credit, except as otherwise provided,

is to be governed by the Uniform Commercial Code in force in the State of Texas on the date of its issuance.

Yours very truly,

NORTHWEST NATIONAL BANK

By: /s/ Speegle Berry
(Authorized Signature)
President

After consulting with legal counsel and the Commissioner of the Texas State Banking Department, the purchasers accepted the letter of credit and closed the sale of Crown Hill.

After making a few payments, B&H defaulted on the note. The successor trustee, Republic National Bank, thereupon presented all the required documents along with a draft in the amount of $45,104.75 to Northwest National Bank. It is undisputed that this presentment was in full compliance with the letter of credit terms, but Northwest nonetheless refused to honor the draft. Republic then filed suit to recover damages, alleging its demand and Northwest's dishonor. . . .

The central issue presented is whether the instrument issued by Northwest is a valid and intra vires letter of credit or an ultra vires guaranty agreement. Since we have been unable to locate any Texas case law pertinent to this particular question, we will freely consult decisional authority from other jurisdictions in addition to the guidance provided by Chapter 5 of the Texas Business and Commerce Code.

Republic National Bank, as our petitioner, contends that the instrument is a valid and intra vires letter of credit, and that, even if it should be found that the instrument is a guaranty, it nonetheless should be enforced against Northwest. Northwest National Bank replies that the instrument is unenforceable as a guaranty because paragraph 4 essentially provides that the purpose of the credit is to guarantee an existing note and to protect payment in the event of default. As such, Northwest reasons that the issuance of the instrument was an ultra vires act since traditional thought has been that national banks are without authority to act as a guarantor or surety for the performance of contracts made by others. . . . Inasmuch as we hold that the instrument in question qualifies as an enforceable and intra vires letter of credit, we deem it unnecessary to express a further opinion as to whether a guaranty made by a national bank may be enforced against it.

Generally, a true letter of credit is the third contract in a complex of three independent contracts. The first contract is the agreement between parties to the underlying obligation; typically, this is the contract between the obligor and obligee. The second contract is ordinarily between the bank or other person (the issuer) and the obligor (the account party), which precipitates the issuance of the letter of credit. The third contract, or the letter of credit, is between the issuer and the obligee (the beneficiary), which provides that the issuer will make payments to the beneficiary upon presentation of a draft and certain documents (a documentary draft) or simply upon the presentation of a draft (a clean letter). . . .

By some estimates the "traditional credit" or "commercial credit" has been in use in one form or another since 1100 A.D., finding its impetus in the insecurity surrounding international sales of tangible goods. . . . Since its genesis, however, the use of letters of credit has expanded far beyond this tangible-goods-in-sales context. One particular development has been the "standby credit" or "guaranty credit" whereby the issuer agrees to pay the beneficiary upon presentment of documentation indicating that the account party has defaulted on a payment obligation. Distinguished from the traditional credit, the standby credit is used primarily to finance or secure an underlying intangible or money indebtedness undertaken by the account party such as a promissory note. . . .

Standby credits have also been recognized as an incident of the banking business by the Comptroller of the Currency, 12 C.F.R. §7.1160(a)-(b) (1978), the Board of Governors of the Federal Reserve System, Id. §208.8(d)(1)-(2), and the Federal Deposit Insurance Corporation, Id. §337.2(a)-(b). Any troubling economic problems presented by a bank's issuance of these credits appear to be resolved by applicable federal regulations. For example, standby credits are regarded as the functional equivalent of loans and are expressly made subject to the bank's statutory lending limitations. Id. §§7.1160(b); 208.8(d)(2); 337.2(b). Additionally, Federal Reserve regulations require that the issuing bank undertake a credit analysis of the account party "equivalent to that applicable to a potential borrower in an ordinary loan situation." Id. §208.8(d)(2)(ii). Therefore, the risk to the issuing bank's shareholders and depositors appears to be no more dangerous than the risk incurred by the making of a normal loan. . . .

It has been suggested that while a standby or guaranty credit may meet the formal requisites of a letter of credit, such an instrument is in substance a guaranty or suretyship contract and, thus, under traditional analysis beyond the bank's power to issue. . . . Although it is true that every letter of credit appears to function as a guaranty, there are several subtle but important distinctions. A true guaranty creates a secondary obligation whereby the guarantor promises to answer for the debt of another and may be called upon to perform once the primary obligor has failed to perform. Since a guaranty is ancillary to the underlying contract, a dispute as to the rights and obligations of the guarantor can only be resolved by a factual determination of the rights and obligations of the parties to the underlying contract. A bank that issues a credit, however, acts as a principal, not as an agent of the account party, and it engages its own credit. Thus, upon the issuance of a credit, the bank assumes a primary obligation independent of the underlying contract and engages that it will pay upon the presentation of documents required by the instrument. If a conforming presentation of documents is made, the issuer of a credit is obligated to pay without reference to the rights and obligations of the parties to the underlying contract. . . .

This is not to say, however, that a national bank is without limit to issue instruments under the guise that they are credits. In Wichita Eagle & Beacon Publishing Co. v. Pacific National Bank, 493 F.2d 1285 (9th Cir. 1974), a letter of credit was issued in favor of certain lessors by Pacific National Bank providing that the bank would pay against a draft and documents indicating that the lessees had failed to complete construction of a parking garage. After default Wichita Eagle presented the draft and required documents but the presentment was dishonored. The district court held the instrument to be a valid credit but the circuit court reversed, holding that the instrument was an ordinary guaranty. The court noted that its disposition of the appeal was not predicated on the fact that payment was triggered by default, but rather, the instrument involved strayed too far from the basic purpose of a credit. Id. at 1286. Instead of requiring the mere examination of documents to ascertain liability, the credit required the bank to undertake actual determinations of fact regarding the underlying obligation. This, the court concluded, invited the very evil that letters of credit were designed to avoid—protracted, expensive litigation. Id. at 1286-87.

We are persuaded by these authorities and therefore hold that under Chapter 5 of our commercial statutes the test of a true letter of credit may be stated as follows: The engagement is a letter of credit if the issuer has a *primary* obligation that is dependent *solely* upon presentation of conforming documents and not upon the factual performance or nonperformance by the parties to the underlying transaction. . . .

Northwest's instrument is labeled "IRREVOCABLE LETTER OF CREDIT." Paragraph 6 expressly provides that Northwest will duly honor a draft properly drawn and in compliance with the terms of the instrument. Paragraph 2 requires that the draft state a proper recital along with the amount due and payable after default. Paragraph 5 lists the required documents to be attached. A fair and reasonable reading of paragraph 4 in relation to the rest of the instrument reveals that the purpose of the letter of credit is to pay principal, interest and attorney's fees pursuant to the terms of the *enclosed* note. While it is true that the instrument refers to the underlying transaction, it has been held that such general references may be disregarded as surplusage unless they impose some condition to the issuer's liability. Nowhere does it appear that Northwest was required to go outside the presented draft and documents to determine its liability. To the contrary, the instrument contains only two conditions precedent to payment: (1) presentation of a properly drawn draft; (2) presentation of four specific documents.

Finally, we are not persuaded by Northwest's argument that the present instrument is a guaranty because it secures an existing promissory note. Since by its very nature a letter of credit is a separate contract independent of the underlying transaction, it necessarily follows that there is no legal distinction between a letter of credit issued before, after, or concomitantly with the consummation of the underlying transaction. As aforementioned, the issuer of a true letter of credit creates a primary obligation dependent solely upon presentation of conforming documents.

Having fully considered the policy behind our commercial statutes along with all relevant authorities, we conclude as a matter of law that the instrument before us is a valid, intra vires, and enforceable letter of credit. The judgments below are reversed and judgment is rendered for Republic National Bank of Dallas.

*QUESTIONS AND COMMENTS*

1. As the court observes in *Republic National Bank,* a letter of credit is part of a three-corner commercial transaction. Underlying the letter of credit is a contract between two parties. In *Republic National Bank* the contract was the $50,000 note made by B&H Amusement Rides and payable to the trustee of the Perpetual Care Fund of Crown Hill Memorial Park. Now as a result of negotiations for the sale of the cemetery, B&H obtains (for a suitable fee) a "standby" letter of credit (see discussion that follows) from Northwest National Bank guaranteeing that B&H will pay on the note. (In all probability the real party in interest here was not B&H but rather the cemetery owners who wanted the letter of credit to satisfy the buyers' demand for assurances that B&H would pay on the note.) In this transaction B&H is called the "account party" (because it is assumed to have an account at the bank), and the bank is called the "issuer" of the letter of credit. The bank issues the letter of credit in favor of the "beneficiary" (here, the trustee). The bank thereby commits itself to make good on the note if the beneficiary presents the prescribed documentation.

2. This case involves the "standby" or "guaranty" letter of credit, which although similar in form to traditional letters of credit, actually has a somewhat different function. Under a traditional letter of credit the bank essentially advances a loan to the account party by agreeing to pay drafts as presented. The bank expects to have to pay off the drafts, and the beneficiary does not look to the bank as being secondarily liable in the event the account party defaults. In a standby letter of credit, in contrast, the bank expects and hopes not to have to pay off the draft, and the beneficiary looks to the bank as a guarantor that will be responsible to pay only if the account party defaults. This difference accounts for the

controversial nature of the standby letter of credit as compared with the traditional letter of credit.

3. Standby letters of credit have become quite significant instruments in the economic system. They are frequently used to guarantee commercial paper (short-term notes of blue-chip companies), a market that totals over $400 billion in outstanding securities. They are also often used to back up municipal and corporate bonds. Standby letters of credit issued by U.S. commercial banks increased from approximately $5 billion outstanding in 1973 to over $200 billion in 1991.

4. As the court observes in *Republic National Bank,* federal banking agencies have approved standby letters of credit as appropriate banking activities. The Comptroller of the Currency's regulation provides that a national bank may issue letters of credit, which "[a]s a matter of sound banking practice" should be issued in conformity with the following criteria:

> (a) [e]ach letter of credit should conspicuously state that it is a letter of credit or be conspicuously entitled as such; (b) the bank's undertaking should contain a specified expiration date or be for a definite term; (c) the bank's undertaking should be limited in amount; (d) the bank's obligation to pay should arise only upon the presentation of a draft or other documents as specified in the letter of credit, and the bank must not be called upon to determine questions of fact or law at issue between the account party and the beneficiary; (e) the banks' customer should have an unqualified obligation to reimburse the bank for payments made under the letter of credit.

12 C.F.R. §7.7016. The FDIC generally prohibits insured institutions from guaranteeing the obligations of others, but exempts letters of credit issued in the ordinary course of business. 12 C.F.R. §332.1(d). Included within the exemption are standby letters of credit, which the FDIC defines as

> any letter of credit, or similar arrangement however named or described, which represents an obligation to the beneficiary on the part of the issuer (1) to repay money borrowed by or advanced to or for the account of the account party, or (2) to make payment on account of any indebtedness undertaken by the account party, or (3) to make payment on account of any default (including any statement of default) by the account party in the performance of an obligation.

12 C.F.R. §337.2.

5. Standby letters of credit are one example of a broader class of modern "off-balance sheet" activities by banks. Other significant off-balance sheet activities include loan commitments (commitments to make a loan in the future); forward, futures, and options contracts; and interest rate and currency swap transactions. Among other advantages from the

point of view of banks, such off-balance sheet activities historically have not been subject to minimum bank capital requirements (though as we discuss below, this advantage has now been substantially eroded by new capital guidelines that take explicit account of the risk of some off-balance sheet activities). In addition, standby letters of credit and other off-balance sheet activities, because they do not tie up capital, do not need to be funded by deposits against which a bank must hold costly reserves and on which it must pay deposit insurance premiums.

6. Is it not perfectly clear that the transaction at issue in *Republic National Bank* was a guarantee? The bank promised the trustee that if B&H did not pay the bank would. What is this in substance other than a guarantee of B&H's obligation?

7. What do you think of the court's distinction between a standby letter of credit and a "true" guarantee—that in a true guarantee the guarantor must investigate and determine the rights of the parties to the underlying contract, whereas in a letter of credit the only issue is whether the beneficiary has presented documents conforming with the letter? This is a standard view among commentators that letters of credit are not guarantees. But is it right? The court says that the function of a guarantee is to "answer for the debt of another and . . . to perform once the primary obligor has failed to perform." Why is an issuing bank any less a guarantor merely because it can determine the scope of its liability by an examination of the documentary record?

8. The court suggests that the rationale behind the rule that the bank's obligations must be determined solely from the documentary record is that otherwise there could be "protracted, expensive litigation." Is the court right that the bank's unconditional commitment to pay upon receipt of the specified documents is sufficient to prevent litigation? What if the account party attempts to enjoin payment before the documents are presented? Although UCC §5-114(2) sets forth a strict standard for such actions, there has been considerable litigation. See Thorup, Injunctions Against Payment of Standby Letters of Credit: How can Banks Protect Themselves?, 101 Banking L.J. 6 (1984).

9. In any event, is avoiding litigation what the rule against bank guarantees was designed to avoid? Isn't it more realistic to say that the purpose of the rule was to prevent the bank from incurring large and risky contingent liabilities—liabilities that are made larger and more risky if the bank is deprived of the opportunity to assert the account party's defenses in an action on the letter of credit by the beneficiary?

10. Although the issue of bank standby letters of credit was highly controversial at the time of the *Republic National Bank* decision, the matter has not been heavily litigated. Why not? Is it significant that this case involved a questionable attempt by the issuing bank to avoid paying out on a deal that had turned sour?

11. A bank establishes a subsidiary to offer municipal bond insur-

ance to qualified credit risks in the form of "standby credits." Under the terms of this insurance, if the issuer defaults, the bondholders would present documentary proof on nonpayment to the subsidiary, which would then be obligated to pay the principal and interest due the bondholders, becoming thereby subrogated to the rights of bondholders against the issuer. Is this activity permissible? See American Insurance Association v. Clarke, 865 F.2d 278 (D.C. Cir. 1988) (upholding Comptroller's approval of such a program).

12. Why not let banks make as many guarantees as they want without regulatory intervention, on the theory that the bank has a better sense of its own welfare than does the regulatory system? In thinking about this question, consider why banks might tend to underprice—and therefore overproduce—standby letters of credit. Consider also the effect of standby letters of credit and other contingent liabilities on bank risk.

## 2. *Other Depository Institutions*

So far we have discussed activities restrictions on national banks. Activities restrictions apply also to state-chartered banks. For the most part these restrictions track those applicable to national banks, but some significant differences may exist. Usually where there are differences the state-chartered banks have greater freedom of operations. For example, banks chartered in California may provide electronic data processing services to the public for a fee. Cal. Fin. Code Ann. §778. South Dakota permits state-chartered banks to operate travel agencies on bank premises, S.D. Laws §51-18-1.2, and to "engage in all facets of the insurance business," id. §51-18-1.3. New York and other states expressly authorize banks to act as commercial factors (that is, to purchase open accounts of merchants). E.g., McKinney's Consol. N.Y. Banking Law Ann. §96.

Prior to 1991, state banks were not significantly restricted by federal law with respect to their activities, although if the bank was operated in an unsafe or unsound manner it stood to forfeit its federal deposit insurance coverage. The Federal Deposit Insurance Corporation Improvement Act of 1991 (FDICIA) imposed significant restrictions on insured state-chartered banks, however. An insured state bank "may not engage as principal in any type of activity that is not permissible for a national bank" unless the state bank is in compliance with applicable capital adequacy standards and "the [FDIC] has determined that the activity would pose no significant risk to the appropriate deposit insurance fund." 12 U.S.C. §1831a(a).

This general rule allows the FDIC to make exceptions for well-capitalized institutions when the activity in question does not pose a significant risk to the deposit insurance fund. However, a number of other sections impose flat prohibitions that cannot be altered by administrative action. In a major victory for the insurance industry, for example, insured state banks are absolutely prohibited from engaging in insurance underwriting except to the extent that activity is permissible to national banks. Id. §1831a(b)(1). Insured state banks are also generally prohibited from acquiring or retaining any equity investment of a type that is not permissible for a national bank, except that an insured state bank may acquire or retain an equity investment in a subsidiary of which the state bank is majority owner. Id. §1831a(c).

The FDICIA also imposed restrictions on the activities of subsidiaries of state-chartered insured banks, which are similar to the restrictions applicable to the state-chartered banks themselves. See id. §24(d).

The activities powers of federally chartered savings and loans are set forth in 12 U.S.C. §1464; for the most part, however, nontraditional activities of federally chartered savings and loans have been delineated by FHLBB (now OTS) regulations. Until relatively recently the powers of federal savings and loans were quite narrowly confined to accepting time and savings deposits and making home mortgage loans. These institutions did not engage in substantial fee-generating activities. More recently, and especially in the 1980s, however, the FHLBB began to allow federal savings and loans to enter a variety of new lines of business, including data processing services and property leasing. FIRREA authorized the FDIC to prohibit activities by members of the Savings Association Insurance Fund that pose a serious threat to the assets of the fund. 12 U.S.C. §1828(m)(3).

State-chartered savings associations (savings and loans and savings banks) have in some instances been granted activities powers even greater than those enjoyed by federal savings and loans. However, 12 U.S.C. §1831e(a) provides that federally insured state-chartered savings associations "may not engage as principal in any type of activity . . . that is not permissible to a Federal savings association" unless the FDIC determines that the "activity would pose no significant risk to the affected deposit insurance fund" and the state association complies with federal capital adequacy rules. If the activity in question is permissible for a federal savings association, §1831e permits state-chartered savings associations to engage in the activity in an amount greater than that which would be permitted to federal associations provided that the institution meets federal capital adequacy standards and the FDIC has not determined that engaging in that amount of the activity poses any significant risk to the affected deposit insurance fund. In addition, if a savings association fails to qualify as a "qualified thrift lender," it must comply with rules applicable to national banks (as well as those applicable to thrifts) with respect to new activities and investments. A qualified thrift lender is a savings association that maintains a specified percentage of its assets in certain (mostly housing-related) assets.

Among all the banking institutions treated in this book, credit unions have the most restricted powers. A provision of the Federal Credit Union Act, 12 U.S.C. §1757, sets forth a limited range of authorities for federally chartered credit unions. Section 1757(17) provides that a federal credit union shall have "such incidental powers as shall be necessary or requisite to enable it to carry on effectively the business for which it is incorporated." Although this incidental powers clause seems to hold the potential for expanded credit union activities powers, it has not been used for this purpose to date. The NCUA has not been vigorous in attempting to expand the activities powers of credit unions by regulation, probably because its constituent credit unions have not lobbied for increased powers. The powers of state-chartered credit unions are set forth in state law and generally track those of federal credit unions.

## C. LIMITATIONS ON INVESTMENTS

The previous section discussed limits on a bank's *activities*—that is, restrictions on the types of goods or services that a bank may offer directly to customers. Now we turn our attention to limits on bank *investments,* where the bank itself is not directly providing a good or service but rather is investing funds in enterprises operated by others.

The distinction between activities and investments is somewhat artificial, in that bank resources are committed to the function we have called activities no less than to the function we have called investments. Despite this artificiality, the distinction between activities and investments seems pretty clear for most purposes and tracks important differences in legal treatment.

One key difference between activities and investments is that activities do not generally show up on a bank's balance sheet. They are "off-balance sheet" functions. With respect to activities, a bank's profit comes from the fees earned by the activity, which the bank hopes will be enough to cover the full costs of the activity in question. Investments, on the other hand, appear explicitly on the asset side of a bank's balance sheet. As we saw in Chapter 1, a bank is a financial intermediary that takes funds from depositors (and other sources), pools those funds, and invests them in various productive ways. The bank's profit from investments is based on the "spread" between the income returned by its investments and the amount the bank must pay to obtain funds from depositors and other sources.

Unlike a typical business enterprise, which is subject to few limitations on its investments, banks are heavily regulated in their investment options. Certain investments (such as direct equity interests in real estate ventures or the purchase of corporate equity securities) have traditionally been out of bounds for banks. The structure of regulation strongly directs a bank towards a principal focus on lending, since loans are not categorically foreclosed to banks. But even bank loans are subject to pervasive restrictions. Banks are limited in the extent to which they may extend credit to insiders or invest more than a fraction of their assets in any one borrower. Bank loans are scrutinized under a variety of federal statutes designed to protect consumers or to ensure that credit is made available to local communities. And loans may involve the bank in potential liability either to the borrower or to third parties. This subsection accordingly looks first at various forms of impermissible investments, and then turns to an analysis of the various restrictions on a bank's lending function.

## 1. *Impermissible Investments*

Some bank investments simply are not permitted. These include most direct equity investments in real property as well as various forms of securities investments.

### a. Real Estate Investments

Despite the fact that a substantial part of the assets of commercial banks are devoted to loans secured by real property, the power of banks to own and possess real estate is heavily circumscribed by restrictive legislation. In the case of national banks, the relevant statute, 12 U.S.C. §29, establishes a general presumption against banks purchasing, holding, or selling real property. The statute admits only two significant exceptions.

First, national banks may hold real estate obtained in satisfaction of debts or purchased at foreclosure sales. 12 U.S.C. §29 (Second, Third, Fourth). This exception is necessary in order to allow banks to exercise their rights of foreclosure and to buy in at foreclosure sales. If banks were not permitted to buy in at foreclosure sales and take possession of the property, they would not be able fully to protect their security interest since the chances are high that other bidders at the foreclosure sale would not offer a fair market value or even, in many cases, a value equal to the amount of the outstanding lien. Section 29 provides, however, that banks may hold such property only for a limited period of time, generally not to exceed five years.

Second, a national bank is permitted to acquire and hold such real property "as shall be necesary for its accommodation in the transaction of its business." 12 U.S.C. §29 (First). This is an authorization for banks to own their premises and related properties, either directly or by means of a subsidiary bank premises corporation. This exception creates an obvious potential for use as a means of circumventing the restrictions on real estate ownership; in theory, a bank might acquire an entire block of Manhattan real estate, declare it a "premises," and then lease out vast amounts of space to unrelated entities. This potential is limited, however, by 12 U.S.C. §371d, which generally prohibits national and state member banks from making investments in bank premises or in corporations owning the bank premises that exceed the amount of the bank's capital stock. Further, the purchase of real estate must be reasonably necessary to carry on the business of banking; the Comptroller of the Currency or Federal Reserve Board might well look askance at efforts by banks to circumvent the general restriction on real estate holdings by purchasing property grossly in excess of the bank's current needs. Nevertheless there is some opportunity for national banks to engage in general real estate operations by means of the premises exception.

Banking institutions other than national banks are also constrained in various ways in their ability to obtain equity interests in real estate. State member banks are subject to the limitation applicable to national banks under which the amount invested in bank premises is limited to the amount of the bank's capital stock. 12 U.S.C. §371d. However, nonmember banks in some states may be permitted a broader range of real estate investments depending on the provisions of state law. These rules appear to be preempted, though, by 12 U.S.C. §1831a(c), which provides that "[a]n insured State bank may not, directly or indirectly, acquire or retain any equity investment of a type that is not permissible for a national bank." More generally, 12 U.S.C. §1831a(a) provides in pertinent part that "an insured State bank may not engage as principal in any type of activity that is not permissible for a national bank unless (1) the [FDIC] has determined that the activity would pose no significant risk to the appropriate deposit insurance fund; and (2) the State bank is, and continues to be, in compliance with applicable capital standards prescribed by the appropriate Federal banking agency."

Federal savings and loan institutions are permitted to invest in real estate to be used for office and related facilities. State savings and loans were once permitted much broader real estate investment powers under the terms of state statutes, but FIRREA limits them now to the same equity investment rules that apply to federal thrift institutions. 12 U.S.C. §1831e(c)(1). Moreover, 12 U.S.C. §1467a(m), §303 of FIRREA, provides that savings associations that do not qualify as a "qualified thrift lender" must comply with real estate investment restrictions (and other investment and activities restrictions) applicable to national banks, in addition to whatever retrictions may exist as a result of their status as thrift institutions.

In general, credit unions have not engaged to any discernible extent in direct real estate investment.

## *QUESTIONS AND COMMENTS*

1. The Supreme Court has explained the restrictions on national bank ownership of real estate as follows: "The object of the restrictions was obviously threefold. It was to keep the capital of the banks flowing

in the daily channels of commerce; to deter them from embarking in hazardous real-estate speculations; and to prevent the accumulation of large masses of such property in their hands." Union National Bank v. Matthews, 98 U.S. 621, 626 (1878).

2. National Bank X comes to you for advice. It plans to purchase a newly constructed office building from a builder and then lease it to a customer on a 30-year net lease, under which the customer incurs all costs of management, maintenance and repair, and pays all applicable taxes. The lease payments include one substantial lump-sum payment up front, with the remaining payments being the same as the payments on a market rate 30-year declining balance mortgage, in the amount of the bank's purchase prices less the first lease payment. At the end of the lease period the customer has the option to purchase the property from the bank for $10. Would this arrangement be permissible under the National Bank Act?

### b. Securities Investments

In addition to making permissible real estate investments, banks typically invest a substantial fraction of their assets in various forms of securities. Securities investments by banks, however, are heavily regulated by law. In the case of national banks and state bank members of the Federal Reserve System, the permitted investments (sometimes called "bank-eligible" investments) are set forth in 12 U.S.C. §24 (Seventh), which is made applicable to state member banks by 12 U.S.C. §335.

The general rule, as we will see in more detail in Chapter 6, is that national banks and state member banks may not deal in, underwrite, or purchase securities of any sort. Securities activities are strictly limited to "purchasing and selling . . . securities and stock without recourse, solely upon the order, and for the account of customers." 12 U.S.C. §24 (Seventh).

This is not the end of the story, however, for §24 (Seventh) goes on to establish a variety of exceptions to the general rule that national and state member banks may act only as securities brokers and may not deal in or underwrite securities or acquire these investments for their own account. Federal law, as interpreted by the Comptroller of the Currency, divides securities investments into several different categories.

So-called Type I securities are those that a bank may deal in, underwrite, purchase and sell for its own account without limitation. These include obligations supported by the full faith and credit of the United States, obligations of any state or political subdivision backed by the full faith and credit of the state or subdivision, and certain other securities identified in 12 U.S.C. §24 (Seventh). The general authorization for national banks and state member banks to underwrite and acquire these

Type I securities enables banks to become dealers in government obligations.

Other securities, denominated Type II securities, may be handled by national and state member banks on more limited terms. Specifically, a national and state member bank may deal in, underwrite, or acquire or sell for its own account these securities subject to the limitation that the total amount of these securities of any one issuer held by a bank for its own account may not exceed 10 percent of its capital stock and surplus. Type II securities include obligations of a variety of federal instrumentalities, as well as "obligations issued by any State or political subdivision . . . for housing, university, or dormitory purposes." 12 C.F.R. §1.3(d).

Type III securities include "marketable obligations, evidencing indebtedness of any person . . . or corporation in the form of bonds, notes and/or debentures commonly known as investment securities." 12 U.S.C. §24 (Seventh). National banks and state member banks are permitted to acquire and sell these securities for their own accounts, subject to the requirement that the total amount of these securities of any one issuer not exceed 10 percent of the bank's capital and surplus. Type III securities are distinguished from Type II securities in that banks may not underwrite or deal in them.

Essentially, Type III securities are investment grade corporate debt. The Comptroller permits a national bank to purchase such securities for its own account if "in its prudent banking judgment . . . it determines that there is adequate evidence that the obligor will be able to perform all that it undertakes to perform in connection with the security, including all debt service requirements, and that the security is marketable, that is, that it may be sold with reasonable promptness at a price which corresponds reasonably to its fair value." 12 C.F.R. §1.5(a). Accordingly, the Comptroller essentially formulates a two-part test, requiring first that there be a reasonable assurance of repayment, and second that the security be marketable on some relatively efficient market. In the absence of a specific ruling by the Comptroller, a bank must more or less decide for itself whether particular debt securities satisfy the requirements of 12 C.F.R. §1.5.

What about investments in equity securities? In general, national banks and state member banks are prohibited from purchasing, selling, dealing in, or underwriting any equity securities at all. 12 U.S.C. §24 (Seventh). However, these institutions can make limited investments in certain defined types or classes of equity securities. They may, for example, invest in corporations or partnerships established pursuant to certain federal or state housing statutes. Id. They may also invest in banks or bank holding companies established to provide services exclusively to banks ("bankers banks"). Id.

National and state member banks are generally permitted to invest up to 10 percent of their capital and surplus in the stock of "bank service corporations"—usually wholly owned subsidiaries—which are authorized to provide services to depository institutions and to engage in other nondepository activities that are deemed "so closely related to banking or managing or controlling banks as to be a proper incident thereto." 12 U.S.C. §§1843(c)(8), 1864(f). Approval of a federal banking regulator is typically required before a bank may invest in a service corporation or before a service corporation may engage in a nonbanking activity. Many banks have used this authority to establish service corporations engaging in a variety of different activities.

An increasingly important exception to the rule against bank equity investments permits national banks and state member banks (where permitted under state law) to acquire shares of stock in small business investment companies (SBIC's) in an amount up to 5 percent of the bank's capital and surplus. 15 U.S.C. §682(b). Effectively, §682(b) permits banks or bank holding companies to establish venture capital subsidiaries that may then make equity investments in all sorts of enterprises, subject only to the Small Business Administration's rather generous interpretation of what constitutes a "small business." If the bank or bank holding company is large—for example, a Citibank/Citicorp—§682(b) permits investments in "small businesses" that reach well into seven figures.

So far we have been discussing the securities investments permitted to national and state member banks. What of state banks that are not members of the Federal Reserve System? Such banks, as a practical matter, must obtain insurance from the FDIC, and the FDIC may suspend or terminate the insurance of any insured bank that engages in "unsafe or unsound practices" or that is in an "unsafe or unsound condition." 12 U.S.C. §1818(a) (we discuss this enforcement power in Chapter 7). Ordinarily, the FDIC does not suspend or terminate deposit insurance, however, so the principal restraints on state nonmember bank securities investments arise under state law. Many states permit their banks to invest in corporate debt but prohibit most equity investments. Other states, however, permit their banks to obtain significant equity interests. In California, for example, state-chartered commercial banks are permitted, subject to regulations of the state banking superintendent, to "invest in the capital stock, obligations, or other securities of one or more corporations" (other than corporations in the insurance business). Cal. Fin. Code Ann. §772. State bank securities powers, however, appear to be constrained by 12 U.S.C. §1831a(a), which generally prohibits insured state-chartered banks from engaging as principal in any activity that would not be permissible for a national bank unless the FDIC has determined that the activity would pose no significant risk to the deposit insurance fund and the institution is itself in compliance with applicable capital regulation. The securities powers of state banks are also apparently constrained by 12 U.S.C. §1821a(c), which generally prohibits insured state banks from directly or indirectly acquiring an equity investment of a type that is not permissible for a national bank, and by 12 U.S.C. §1831a(f)(1), which extends most national bank restrictions on common and preferred stock investments to insured state banks.

The thrift industry is typically more constrained in its securities activities. Subject to certain exceptions and limitations, federally chartered thrift institutions are permitted by 12 U.S.C. §1464(c) to invest in U.S. government securities, certain government agency securities, securities of states or political subdivisions of states, mortgage-backed securities, and certain other securities. They may invest in, hold, or sell commercial paper and corporate debt securities as defined and approved by the Office of Thrift Supervision. 12 U.S.C. §1464(c)(2)(D). Federal associations may also invest in service corporation subsidiaries. 12 U.S.C. §1464(c)(4)(B). Such service corporations may engage in activities approved by the Office of Thrift Supervision that would not be permitted to a federally chartered association itself. See Securities Industry Association v. FHLBB, 588 F. Supp. 749 (D.D.C. 1984) (upholding service corporation's provision of limited brokerage and investment advisory services).

State-chartered savings associations may invest in securities as permitted by state law. However, as already mentioned, 12 U.S.C. §1831a severely limits the investment powers of federally insured state thrifts by providing that state-chartered savings associations may not engage as principal in activities not permitted for federally chartered associations, unless the FDIC has determined that the activity would pose no significant risk to the federal deposit insurance fund and the savings association is in compliance with federal capital adequacy guidelines. If the activity in question is permitted to a federal association, a state-chartered association may engage in that activity in an amount that is not permissible for federal associations if the FDIC has not determined that engaging in that amount of the activity poses a significant risk to the deposit insurance fund, and the savings association complies with federal capital adequacy guidelines. As regards investments in equity securities, 12 U.S.C. §1831e(c)(1) provides generally that "a savings association chartered under State law may not directly acquire or retain any equity investment of a type or in an amount that is not permissible for a Federal savings association."

## *QUESTIONS AND COMMENTS*

1. The dramatic growth of the junk bond (or "high yield debt") market in the 1980s strained the concept that banks should invest in debt and not equity because debt investments are less risky. Junk bonds of shaky companies are often more risky than equities of blue chip companies. Thus depository institutions that wanted to increase their risk exposure in order to earn greater returns on their investments began

to acquire large amounts of junk bonds for their portfolios. In 1985 the Office of the Comptroller of the Currency issued a policy statement declaring that "[c]orporate debt securities used to finance corporate take-overs are generally considered to be predominantly speculative with limited marketability. Accordingly, national bank commitments to acquire such 'Junk Bonds' will be viewed as violations of [12 U.S.C. §24]." Office of the Comptroller of the Currency, Banking Bulletin 85-12 (May 31, 1985). Federally insured savings associations are prohibited from investing in junk bonds by 12 U.S.C. §1831e(d), which provides that "no savings association may . . . acquire or retain any corporate debt security not of investment grade."

2. How effective do you think the prohibition on junk bond investments will be? Doesn't the prohibition simply encourage banks to fund leveraged buyouts or other corporate takeovers by means of bank loans rather than junk bond acquisitions? Why isn't it more advantageous to allow financing through junk bonds because sale of these securities on developed capital markets may tend to improve the efficiency of the capital formation process? And doesn't the rule against junk bonds effectively foreclose the business of funding corporate takeovers to smaller banks, thus artificially favoring the interests of the big money center institutions?

3. What public policy is served by encouraging banks to use depositors' funds to make loans rather than to buy securities?

## 2. *Restrictions on the Extension of Credit*

So far we have considered types of investments that are subject to categorical restrictions—equity interests in real estate and interests in different types of securities. Now we consider the regulation of the lending function, which, of course, is the traditional form of bank investment.

The lending function is hedged in by restrictions intended to achieve a number of different public policy objectives. Insider loan restrictions and lending limits are designed to prevent banks from investing their assets in excessively risky or inappropriate ways; the regulations protect depositors and the federal deposit insurance funds. A different group of restrictions on lending activity is designed to protect the interests of borrowers. One such restriction—the prohibition of usury—has an exceedingly ancient lineage in banking history; the remaining restrictions we discuss in this section are products of the last few decades. Still another form of regulation is designed to ensure that credit is made available to local communities and not denied to members of particular groups on invidious grounds. Finally, an increasingly important new form of regulation of a bank's lending function is so-called lender liability principles, which are sometimes intended to protect the public at large from the harmful consequences of a bank's lending activities.

### a. Regulations Intended to Ensure Bank Safety and Soundness

Now let us consider a group of regulations generally intended to ensure that a depository institution does not make its lending decisions in an unsafe or unsound fashion. These include restrictions on loans to insiders, which in the absence of regulation might be made on unduly favorable terms, or without adequate analysis of the borrower's creditworthiness. Another regulation in this category is that limiting the amount a depository institution can lend to a single borrower; the purpose of this regulation is to prevent the institution from tying its activities too heavily with the fortunes of any single borrower. A third regulation falling under this general heading is the "qualified thrift lender" test, which generally limits most savings institutions investments to traditional housing finance activities, partly on the theory that housing finance activities of this sort are less risky than other activities recently engaged in by many thrift institutions.

#### *i. Insider Loans*

First, consider the danger that a bank will make excessive loans to its own officers, directors, or employees. Because these are pure self-dealing transactions, the danger of abuse is evident. Especially in smaller institutions, which tend to be dominated by a single individual or control group, the temptation to grant loans on favorable terms—or based on inadequate security—to insiders, their families, or their friends may prove irresistible in the absence of strict regulation.

In light of these obvious dangers, one might think that the best regulatory approach is simply to prohibit loans to insiders altogether. This has not proved to be the case. Under 12 U.S.C. §375a, a national or state member bank may make loans to its executive officers, subject to the following limitations: (1) the bank would be authorized to make the loan to borrowers other than its officers; (2) the loan is on terms not more favorable than those afforded other borrowers; (3) the officer has submitted a detailed current financial statement; and (4) the loan be on condition that it shall become due and payable on demand at any time when the officer becomes indebted to any other bank or banks in an amount greater than the amount of credit of the same category that could be extended to him by the bank of which he is an officer. The statute specifically approves the extension to executive officers of first mortgage residential loans and educational loans; other loans are permitted, under the Comptroller's regulations, in an amount up to the higher of $25,000 or 2.5 percent of capital and surplus, but not to exceed $100,000. 12 C.F.R. §31.2(a).

Additional limitations on insider loans are found in 12 U.S.C. §375b. This provision places limits on loans to bank officers, bank directors, persons who directly or indirectly or in concert with others own or control 10 percent of any class of voting stock of the bank, and companies or political campaign committees controlled by or operating for the benefit of such bank insiders. The statute generally prohibits member banks from making loans to insiders as there defined that (1) aggregate more than the institution's capital and surplus; (2) exceed for any one borrower an amount set by the appropriate banking agency unless the loan is approved in advance by a vote of the bank's board of directors with the interested party not participating; (3) are not made on substantially the same terms, including interest rate and collateral, as those prevailing at the time for comparable transactions with other persons or present more than normal credit risk; or (4) exceed the limits on loans to one borrower for national banks. The Comptroller's regulations implement the limitation on loans to any one borrower by requiring board approval for loans that exceed the higher of $25,000 or 5 percent of the bank's capital and surplus up to $500,000. 12 C.F.R. §31.2(b).

For comparable provisions governing other financial institutions than national banks, see 12 U.S.C. §1828(j) (other insured state banks) and 12 U.S.C. §1468 (federal and state thrifts).

## *QUESTIONS AND COMMENTS*

1. Jane Jones is president of First National Bank and a longtime client. She comes to you with the following proposal: First National Bank will make large loans to insiders at Second National Bank, and in return Second National Bank will informally agree to make extensive loans to insiders at First National Bank. She says she sees nothing wrong with the idea personally but wants to know if it is legal. Is it? See 12 U.S.C. §1972(2) (prohibiting the extension of credit to insiders of a bank that another bank has a correspondent relationship with unless the credit is extended on essentially the same terms and conditions as apply to other customers).

2. Jesse Jones, Jane Jones' father, applies to the bank for a loan of $150,000. Assume that Jane Jones has no knowledge of the loan application and that the loan to Jesse would be on substantially the same terms and conditions as apply to other borrowers. Can the bank extend the loan?

3. Jane Jones is prominent in Republican politics and has been

mentioned as a possible candidate for an ambassadorial post. Barny Smith, Republican candidate for the Senate, applies to the bank for a $1 million loan for his campaign committee. The loan would be adequately secured and on no more favorable terms than loans to other customers. May the bank advance the money? What if Jane Jones called up the head of the bank's loan committee and told her that "I can personally vouch for Barny Smith"?

4. Jane Jones comes to you visibly upset. She has just received news that Prudential Bank is about to launch an unfriendly offer for any and all shares of First National. She asks about the legality of her bank's adopting the following plan: In the event that First National Bank is acquired by any other institution, and any officer or director of First National Bank ceases thereafter to be affiliated with the successor institution, the First National Bank commits to extend $10 million in bank credit to that individual for a ten-year period, the interest rate to be the lowest prime rate prevailing at any time during the five years before the party draws down the credit. The proposed agreement would expressly state that it is binding on the bank's successors and assigns. Assume that $10 million would be well within the limit on loans to a single borrower. Can First National Bank adopt the plan?

5. First National Bank discovers during a routine audit that it has advanced loans to an officer, Jerry Black, that exceed the limits of 12 U.S.C. §375a. It asks Black to repay the loan, but he refuses on the grounds that he "doesn't have the money." What course of action would you recommend that the bank pursue? Can it declare the loan in default and seek to accelerate the repayment obligation?

6. Why should banks be allowed to make loans to insiders at all? Given the danger of abuse, isn't the safest course to exclude them altogether?

7. If there is a sound public policy justification for allowing some loans to insiders, why insist that they be on terms no more favorable than those given to other customers? After all, waiters and waitresses get discounts on dinners at their restaurants, department store employees get discounts on store merchandise, and so on. Why couldn't favorable loans to insiders be justified as a means of improving employee loyalty and morale? Why can't they be justified as based on a bank's superior knowledge about the reliability and credit history of its insiders?

### ii. Lending Limits

The second major limitation on lending powers intended to ensure safety and soundness is the limitation on loans to any single customer. The purpose behind lending limits seems rather clearly to require asset diversification. If a bank invests too much in a single borrower, default by that borrower will severely impair the bank's safety and soundness. Lending limits require banks to "spread the wealth" and thus diversify their asset portfolios. A secondary purpose might be to mitigate the bad effects of "sweetheart" deals that don't fall within the limitations on insider loans discussed above.

The lending limits for national banks are set forth in 12 U.S.C. §84. The basic statutory scheme is as follows. First, the statute limits total loans outstanding to any "person." What is a "person" under §84? The statute defines the term to mean "an individual, sole proprietorship, partnership, joint venture, association, trust, estate, business trust, corporation, sovereign government or agency, instrumentality, or political subdivision thereof, or any similar entity or organization." 12 U.S.C. §84(b)(2).

Second, the statute imposes two limits on loans to any person. Loans that are outstanding and not fully secured by collateral "shall not exceed 15 per centum of the [bank's] unimpaired capital and unimpaired surplus." 12 U.S.C. §84(a)(1). But a national bank may make loans in excess of this limit up to 10 percent of its unimpaired capital and surplus, provided that such loans are "fully secured by readily marketable collateral having a market value, as determined by reliable and continuously available price quotations, at least equal to the amount of the funds outstanding." Thus, a national bank can make a maximum loan to any person equal to 25 percent of its capital and surplus, provided that part of the loan representing at least 10 percent of the bank's capital and surplus is fully collateralized.

The statute proceeds to list a number of exceptions under which national banks can make loans that otherwise would violate the general loan limits. Among the more important such exceptions are loans secured by U.S. government obligations, loans secured by a segregated deposit account at the lending bank, loans arising from the discount of commercial paper, and the purchase of acceptances issued by other banks. The statute is implemented by regulations of the Comptroller of the Currency.

An obvious way around the loan limitations is to make loans to a group of ostensibly discrete persons when the loans themselves are aggregated as a matter of real economic function. Section 84 authorizes the Comptroller of the Currency to issue regulations on this topic. 12 U.S.C. §84(d)(2). The Comptroller's regulation, 12 C.F.R. §32.5, provides that as a general rule, loans or extensions of credit to one person will be attributed to other persons when (1) the proceeds of the loans or extensions of credit are to be used for the direct benefit of the other person or persons, or (2) a "common enterprise" is deemed to exist between the persons. Whether or not two or more persons are engaged in a common enterprise depends on a realistic evaluation of the facts and circumstances of each case. However, the Comptroller generally takes the view that common enterprise exists where the expected source of repayment for each loan is the same for each person, or where loans are made to persons who are related through common control. A common enterprise is also deemed to exist when separate persons borrow from a bank for the purpose of acquiring a business enterprise of which those persons will own more than 50 percent of the voting stock. The regulation contains other specific rules on loans to corporations, partnerships, and foreign governments.

For parallel provisions governing financial institutions other than national banks, see 12 U.S.C. §1464(u) (thrift institutions); 12 C.F.R. §563.93 (same); 12 C.F.R. pt. 215, subpt. A, App. (member banks of the Federal Reserve System).

What are the consequences if a national bank has exceeded its lending limits under §84? In particular, what is the exposure of bank directors who cause or knowingly allow the extension of credit in violation of the lending limit in cases where the loan subsequently goes bad? The following case addresses this problem.

## Del Junco v. Conover

***682 F.2d 1338 (9th Cir. 1982), cert. denied, 459 U.S. 1146 (1983)***

FLETCHER, Circuit Judge:

In December 1979, a periodic examination by the Comptroller of the Currency ("Comptroller") of the Los Angeles National Bank ("Bank") disclosed a possible violation of the provisions of 12 U.S.C. §84. . . . At issue was whether three of the Bank's loans were really to the same entity and whether, when added together, they exceeded the bank's legal lending limit.

The loans were to Rehbock Lewis ("Lewis"), President of Fame Furniture Co., Inc.; Fame Furniture Co., Inc. ("Fame"); and Ralph Ware ("Ware"), Treasurer of Fame. The chart below sets forth the date, borrower, and amount of each loan, as well as the legal lending limit of the bank at the time of each loan and the amount by which the loans, when aggregated, exceeded the legal lending limit:

| *Date Granted* | *Borrower* | *Amount* | *Lending Limit* | *Excess Amount* |
|---|---|---|---|---|
| 1/19/79 | Lewis | 225,000 | | |
| 5/9/79 | Fame | 225,000 | | |
| | SUBTOTAL | 450,000 | 272,866 | 177,134 |
| 6/11/79 | Ware | 125,000 | | |
| | PRESENT BALANCE | 575,000 | 277,108 | 297,892 |

The legality of the Lewis loan for $225,000 has never been at issue, as that loan did not exceed the legal lending limit of the bank when it was made. However, if the Lewis, Fame, and Ware loans could be aggregated, then the latter two loans would exceed the Bank's lending limit.

The Comptroller first requested the Directors of the Bank to indemnify the Bank for any losses sustained as a result of the two excess loans; the Directors refused. The Comptroller then began a formal cease and desist action against the Directors and the Bank by issuing a Notice of Charges. The Bank and Directors answered, and the Comptroller moved for summary judgment in an agency proceeding.

In the agency proceeding, the Bank and Directors admitted that they knew that the proceeds of the Fame and Lewis loans were to be used for the benefit of Fame. On these facts, the Administrative Law Judge (ALJ) ruled that it was proper to aggregate the Lewis and Fame loans so as to constitute a violation of 12 U.S.C. §84. He also ruled, however, that an evidentiary hearing would be necessary to determine whether the proceeds of the Ware loan were actually used for the benefit of Fame, an element that had to be satisfied if the Ware loan could be added to the Fame loan. Such an evidentiary hearing was then held, and the ALJ determined that the Ware loan was used for the benefit of Fame. Accordingly, the ALJ recommended that the Comptroller issue a cease and desist order, that the Directors indemnify the Bank for the Fame and Ware loans, that the Bank recover costs of collection fees, and that the Bank recover attorneys' fees that it had paid for the Directors' defense.

[The court concluded that there was sufficient evidence to support the ALJ's ruling that the Lewis, Fame, and Ware loans should be aggregated and that the latter two loans exceeded the bank's lending limit.]

The Directors' potential liability is limited to $350,000—the difference between the total credit extension to Fame ($575,000) and the amount of the legal Lewis loan ($225,000). The Comptroller takes the position that the Directors' potential loss of $350,000 cannot be reduced by recoveries until the legal loan to Lewis has been repaid with interest.

In the instant case, the purpose underlying 12 U.S.C. §84—protection of a bank's assets—will be furthered if the Directors are not allowed to extinguish their liability until the legal Lewis loan, which is unsecured, is fully repaid. The policy of protecting bank assets would be frustrated if the Directors were allowed to make, as they did, an unsecured but legal loan to the borrower, then to use, or agree to the use of, the borrower's assets to secure further credit extensions that are illegal. Such a procedure would permit the Directors to protect themselves fully against any exposure resulting from the illegal loans while substantially increasing the risk that the bank would be unable to recover the amount of its legal loan. The fiduciary responsibility of the Directors of the bank precludes them from protecting themselves against liability at the bank's expense. The security arrangement was in derogation of that responsibility. Thus, the Directors may not use the borrower's assets to extinguish their own liability to the bank.

Here, the Directors ignored the recommendation of the Comptroller and the bank president's advice that the first loan to be paid off should be that of Rehbock Lewis and not Fame Furniture, since the stockholders might claim that this loan was paid to limit the liabilities of the Directors. The Comptroller's remedy is appropriate, because any other remedy could create a conflict of interest between the Bank and its Directors.

In light of the Comptroller's broad discretion to fashion an appropriate remedy, we conclude that the remedy he selected was lawful. It serves to protect the bank's assets, to insure that the Directors fulfill their fiduciary duty, and to prevent the Directors from insuring themselves against liability for their wrongful act at the Bank's expense. . . .

*QUESTIONS AND COMMENTS*

1. FIRREA provided explicit authority for banking agencies to issue cease-and-desist orders requiring institution-affiliated parties (including bank directors) to "make restitution or provide reimbursement, indemnification, or guarantee against loss if . . . the violation or practice involved a reckless disregard for the law or any applicable regulations or prior order of the appropriate Federal banking agency." 12 U.S.C. §1818(b)(6)(A)(ii). Cease-and-desist orders are discussed in Chapter 7.

2. Section 301(5)(u) of FIRREA generally makes savings associations subject to the same limits on loans to one borrower as apply to national banks. However, a savings association may make loans to one borrower for any reason up to $500,000 or make loans to one borrower to develop residential housing, not to exceed the lesser of $30 million or 30 percent of the association's capital and surplus, subject to certain conditions and requirements. The director of OTS may impose stricter regulations on a case-by-case basis in order to protect an institution's safety and soundness.

3. How effective do you think lending limits are at ensuring a bank's portfolio diversification? They seem well designed to protect against defaults arising from individualized credit risk. Bus is this sufficient to ensure a diversified loan portfolio?

4. Consider in this regard the fact that many of the problems in the banking industry during the 1980s arose because banks specialized too heavily in real estate lending, energy lending, agricultural lending, or less-developed country sovereign lending. Do lending limits protect against this lack of diversification?

5. Are there any efficiency costs of lending limits? Why not leave it up to bank officers and directors to determine for themselves exactly how much loss exposure they are willing to take on from a given bor-

rower? Other than the possible desire to do favors for friends, what incentives do bank officers and directors have to make excessively undiversified loans?

6. How do lending limits affect the structure of the banking industry? Consider the fact that some profitable loan markets, such as construction lending or merger and acquisition lending, require minimum loan amounts in excess of seven figures.

7. As we will see below, the federal banking agencies have adopted risk-based capital standards. Do lending limits have any continuing function once bank capital is adjusted to account for the riskiness of a bank's loan portfolio?

### *iii. Qualified Thrift Lender Test*

We turn now to a rule that is not so much a restriction on the allocation of credit as a requirement that credit be allocated in certain ways. This is the "qualified thrift lender" (QTL) test applicable to thrift institutions, which came into the law in the Competitive Equality Banking Act of 1987 and was comprehensively revised in §303 of FIRREA and §§437-441 of FDICIA. The general purpose of the QTL test is to encourage—even to force—thrift institutions to remain principally within their historical role of providing housing finance. The underlying premise of the rule is that the thrift crisis of the late 1980s arose largely as a result of thrift institutions' risky ventures into nontraditional lines of business.

The current QTL rules set forth a complex formula that essentially requires savings institutions to maintain a certain percentage of assets in housing finance and related activities. A thrift institution will qualify as a QTL only if its qualified thrift (i.e., housing related) investments are at least equal to 65 percent of its total portfolio assets on a monthly average basis in 9 out of every 12 months. The consequences of failing to satisfy the QTL test are severe. Essentially, a thrift that fails the QTL test must either become a bank or be treated both as a bank *and* a thrift for most regulatory purposes. In addition, the nonqualifying savings association loses its eligibility to obtain loans from a Federal Home Loan Bank. Holding companies that control a nonqualifying savings institution are required to register as bank holding companies.

#### *QUESTIONS AND COMMENTS*

1. How effective do you think the QTL test will be at controlling risk-taking by savings associations? The savings industry tends to view the test as punitive and unwise because it strongly discourages asset

diversification that, other things equal, would seem to be risk-reducing. Do you agree?

2. What do you see as the effect of the QTL test on the thrift industry? Some have argued that the QTL rules, coupled with additional unfavorable regulatory provisions—higher insurance assessments and stricter capital standards—will force most of the remaining solvent thrift institutions to merge with a commercial banking organization or to convert over to banking charter. The fact that the federal thrift regulator—the director of the Office of Thrift Supervision—is no longer head of an independent agency but rather a subordinate official in the Department of the Treasury (albeit one exercising a considerable degree of administrative autonomy) may reduce administrative opposition to such a withering away of the thrift industry as a distinctive set of financial institutions. Do you see such a withering away as likely? Would it be a good thing if it happened?

### b. Regulations Intended to Protect Borrowers

#### *i. Usury*

Usury traditionally understood is nothing other than the taking of interest. For reasons that remain obscure, usury has been prohibited throughout much of the history of civilization. Despite these restrictions, interest has always been a component of commercial dealings for the obvious reason that no one would lend money unless he or she received some compensation for doing so. All sorts of arrangements grew up to disguise interest payments and thus permit commercial relations to exist in ostensible compliance with the usury prohibition.

Eventually Western societies dropped their outright prohibition on taking interest. Instead, they sought to place limits on the amount of interest that could be taken. Usury came to be defined not as the taking of interest per se, but rather as taking interest beyond the limits allowed by law. In this form we still have usury limits in banking law today.

The law of usury in the United States is today an enormously complicated, uncertain, and rapidly shifting field. In large measure the current uncertainty is due to the unusual credit market conditions of the late 1970s, which placed tremendous strains on the viability of traditional usury ceilings. As interest rates became more volatile the notion of a fixed cap above which a loan became usurious became harder to sustain. These marketplace strains prompted some preemptive federal intervention into state usury law, a development that has added further complexity to the area.

*Usury Limits: State Rules.* Despite this federal intervention, which we will discuss anon, the basic law of usury remains state law. There is no uniform state law in this area. Different states impose different interest rate ceilings. Some states exempt categories of borrowers, such as corporations; others do not exempt corporations; still others exempt corporations unless the corporate form is being used as a means of avoiding usury ceilings. Many states provide one "legal" rate of interest and another rate for interest specified in written contracts. Interest-like fees and charges—such as points and commitment fees—may or may not fall within a particular state's usury rules. Some states adopt special rules for interest charged on real estate mortgages or in consumer credit transactions; others do not. It is, accordingly, impossible to do much more than warn the student or practitioner that state rules on usury must be carefully consulted before a bank client (or any other client, for that matter) enters a transaction that has the appearance or substance of being a loan at an unusually high interest rate.

*QUESTIONS AND COMMENTS*

1. Borrower and lender, both located in State X, stipulate that their loan agreement is to be governed by the laws of State Y. The interest rate is usurious under the laws of State X but permissible under the laws of State Y. Is the loan usurious? Do you need more facts to answer the question? See National Surety Corp. v. Inland Properties, Inc., 286 F. Supp. 173, 187 (E.D. Ark. 1968), *aff'd*, 416 F.2d 457 (8th Cir. 1969) (under state's conflict of law principles, parties may contract as to governing law as long as the chosen body of law bears a reasonable relationship to the contract).

2. A merchant gives customers a choice of how to make payment for goods. They may pay a cash price immediately, or they may use credit and pay a higher price later. Does the difference between the immediate cash purchase price and the time purchase price represent interest subject to state usury laws? Most states exclude merchant credit of this sort (the "time-price differential") from usury prohibitions. See, e.g., Sliger v. R. H. Macy & Co., Inc., 59 N.J. 465, 283 A.2d 904 (1971). But see State v. J. C. Penney Co., 48 Wis. 2d 125, 179 N.W.2d 641 (1970).

3. Do you see any difference in substance between an arrangement under which a merchant charges a higher price for credit sales than cash sales and an arrangement under which a lender advances credit to a customer for the purchase of merchandise, with the customer agreeing to repay the credit with interest on a subsequent date?

4. What do you think of the traditional justification for the time-price differential doctrine, namely that a higher price for credit sales than for cash sales is not a "loan" or a "forbearance"? Some courts have suggested that the rationale for the time-price differential doctrine is that

usury statutes apply only to the loan of money, not to the loan of goods. Does this explanation fare any better?

5. Can you formulate a justification of the time-price differential doctrine that draws on the consumer-protection rationale for usury statutes?

6. What is the impact of the time-price differential doctrine on the competitive position of banks vis-à-vis other lenders? Why has this doctrine shown such a high degree of political stability and such widespread acceptance among the states? Is it significant that merchants have been selling goods on credit free of usury limitations for at least 150 years?

7. Should the interpretation of state usury laws turn in part on whether the borrower is the sort of "necessitous debtor" whom the usury laws are supposedly designed to protect? See Stoddard v. Stoddard, 641 F.2d 812 (9th Cir. 1981).

*Usury Limits on National Banks.* Usury limits for national banks are contained in 12 U.S.C. §85. Section 85 permits national banks to charge the greater of three rates: (1) the rate allowed by the laws of the state where the national bank is located, except that where a state sets a different rate for state-chartered banks, this rate is allowed for national banks; (2) 1 percent above the discount rate on 90-day commercial paper in effect at the Federal Reserve bank in the district where the bank is located; or (3) 7 percent if no interest rate is fixed by state law.

Of these provisions, the most controversial has been the one allowing national banks parity with state-chartered institutions. The problems in this area parallel in some respects the problems of branching for national banks under the McFadden Act, discussed in Chapter 5, which also looks to state regulation of state banks to determine regulations applicable to national banks. However, unlike the case of branching, where the governing principle (at least until recently) has been one of "competitive equality" between national and state banks, in the case of usury regulation it has always been clear that national banks enjoyed special privileges not available to state institutions.

## Tiffany v. National Bank of Missouri

***85 U.S. 409 (1874)***

[A national bank had loaned money at 9 percent; the laws of the state limited state-chartered banks to 8 percent but allowed other lenders to charge up to 10 percent.]

The provisions of the thirtieth section of the [National Bank Act], under which the suit was brought, are as follows:

> Every association organized under this act, may take, receive, reserve, and charge on any loans . . . *interest at the rate allowed by the laws of the State or Territory where the bank is located, and no more;* except that where, by the laws of any State, a different rate *is limited* for banks of issue organized under State laws, the rate *so limited* shall be allowed every association organized in any such State under this act. And when no rate is fixed by the laws of the State or Territory, the bank may take, receive, reserve or charge a rate not exceeding 7 per centum. . . .

Justice STRONG delivered the opinion of the court.

The position of the plaintiff is, that the general provision of the act of Congress that National banking associations may charge and receive interest at the rate allowed by the laws of the State where they are located, has no application to the case of these defendants, and that they are restricted to the rate allowed to banks of issue of the State, that is, to 8 per cent. This, we think, cannot be maintained. The act of Congress is an enabling statute, not a restraining one, except so far as it fixes a maximum rate in all cases where State banks of issue are not allowed a greater. There are three provisions in section thirty, each of them enabling. If no rate of interest is defined by State laws, 7 per cent. is allowed to be charged. If there is a rate of interest fixed by State laws for lenders generally, the banks are allowed to charge that rate, but no more, except that if State banks of issue are allowed to reserve more, the same privilege is allowed to National banking associations. Such, we think, is the fair construction of the act of Congress, entirely consistent with its words and with its spirit. It speaks of allowances to National banks and limitations upon State banks, but it does not declare that the rate limited to State banks shall be the maximum rate allowed to National banks. There can be no question that if the banks of issue of Missouri were allowed to demand interest at a higher rate than 10 per cent. National banks might do likewise. And this would be for the reason that they would then come within the exception made by the statute, that is, the exception from the operation of the restrictive words "no more" than the general rate of interest allowed by law. But if it was intended they should in no case charge a higher rate of interest than State banks of issue, even though the general rule was greater, if the intention was to restrict rather than to enable, the obvious mode of expressing such an intention was to add the words "and no more," as they were added to the preceding clause of the section. The absence of those words, or words equivalent, is significant. Coupled with the general spirit of the act, and of all the legislation respecting National banks, it is controlling. It cannot be doubted, in view of the purpose of Congress in providing for the organization of National banking associations, that it was intended to give them a firm footing in the different States where they might be located. It was expected they would come into competition with State banks, and it was intended to give them at least equal advantages in such competition. In order to accomplish this they were empowered to reserve interest at the same rates, whatever those rates might be, which were allowed to similar State institutions. This was considered indispensable to protect them against possible unfriendly State legislation. Obviously, if State statutes should allow to their banks of issue a rate of interest greater than the ordinary rate allowed to natural persons, National banking associations could not compete with them, unless allowed the same. On the other hand, if such associations were restricted to the rates allowed by the statutes of the State to banks which might be authorized by the State laws, unfriendly legislation might make their existence in the State impossible. A rate of interest might be prescribed so low that banking could not be carried on, except at a certain loss. The only mode of guarding against such contingencies was that which, we think, Congress adopted. It was to allow to National associations the rate allowed by the State to natural persons generally, and a higher rate, if State banks of issue were authorized to charge a higher rate. This construction accords with the purpose of Congress, and carries it out. It accords with the spirit of all the legislation of Congress. National banks have been National favorites. They were established for the purpose, in part, of providing a currency for the whole country, and in part to create a market for the loans of the General government. It could not have been intended, therefore, to expose them to the hazard of unfriendly legislation by the States, or to ruinous competition with State banks. On the contrary, much has been done to insure their taking the place of State banks. The latter have been substantially taxed out of existence. A duty has been imposed upon their issues so large as to manifest a purpose to compel a withdrawal of all such issues from circulation. In harmony with this policy is the construction we think should be given to the thirtieth section of the act of Congress we have been considering. It gives advantages to National banks over their State competitors. It allows such banks to charge such interest as State banks may charge, and more, if by the laws of the State more may be charged by natural persons.

The result of this is that the defendants, in receiving 9 per cent. interest upon the loans made by them, have not transgressed the act of Congress, consequently they are under no liability to the plaintiff.

Judgment affirmed.

## *QUESTIONS AND COMMENTS*

1. *Tiffany* established the principle, which remains valid today, that national banks enjoy "most favored lender" status under state law: They may take advantage of the highest rate allowed to lenders under state law even if state-chartered banks are restricted to lower rates.

2. See the statutory supplement accompanying this casebook for the current text of §85.

3. Why do you think Congress might have specially provided for a situation where more stringent usury limits apply to state-chartered banks than for other lenders in the state?

4. What policy did the Court discern underlying the National Bank Act regarding the competitive positions of state and national banks?

5. Reconsider the history recounted in Chapter 1. Was there anything about the nation's banking structure at the time of this decision that might have influenced the Court's analysis?

6. Assume a state sets a general usury ceiling of 10 percent, a usury ceiling for commercial banks of 8 percent, and a usury ceiling for consumer finance companies of 12 percent. What is the ceiling for national banks?

7. 12 U.S.C. §1831d(a) provides that

> [I]n order to prevent discrimination against State-chartered insured banks, . . . with respect to interest rates, if the applicable rate prescribed in this subsection exceeds the rate such State bank . . . would be permitted to charge in the absence of this subsection, such State bank . . . may, notwithstanding any State constitution or statute which is hereby preempted for the purposes of this section . . . charge on any loan . . . interest at a rate of not more than 1 per centum in excess of the discount rate on ninety-day commercial paper . . . or at the rate allowed by the laws of the State, territory, or district where the bank is located, whichever may be greater.

A federally insured, state-chartered bank makes a loan at an interest rate that is prohibited to banks under the state's usury statute but that would be permissible for certain other lenders. Is the loan valid? See Vander-Weyst v. First State Bank of Benson, 425 N.W.2d 803 (Minn.), *cert. denied,* 488 U.S. 943 (1988) (insured state-chartered banks enjoy most-favored lender status).

8. Section 85 was adopted in an era of relatively localized banking. Today, however, banks can easily solicit loans on a nationwide basis by the use of the mails or other media. This activity raises the question of how §85 applies to loans issued by a national bank in State A to customers in other states. If State A allows a much higher interest rate than that allowed by State B, where a bank's borrower is located, which interest rate controls under §85? Consider the following case:

## Marquette National Bank of Minneapolis v. First of Omaha Service Corp.

*439 U.S. 299 (1978)*

Justice BRENNAN delivered the opinion of the Court.

The question for decision is whether the National Bank Act, Rev.

Stat. §5197, as amended, 12 U.S.C. §85, authorizes a national bank based in one State to charge its out-of-state credit-card customers an interest rate on unpaid balances allowed by its home State, when the rate is greater than that permitted by the State of the bank's nonresident customers. The Minnesota Supreme Court held that the bank is allowed by §85 to charge the higher rate. 262 N.W.2d 358 (1977). We affirm.

I

The First National Bank of Omaha (Omaha Bank) is a national banking association with its charter address in Omaha, Neb. Omaha Bank is a card-issuing member in the BankAmericard plan. This plan enables cardholders to purchase goods and services from participating merchants and to obtain cash advances from participating banks throughout the United States and the world. Omaha Bank has systematically sought to enroll in its BankAmericard program the residents, merchants, and banks of the nearby State of Minnesota. The solicitation of Minnesota merchants and banks is carried on by respondent First of Omaha Service Corp. (Omaha Service Corp.), a wholly owned subsidiary of Omaha Bank.

Minnesota residents are obligated to pay Omaha Bank interest on the outstanding balances of their BankAmericards. Nebraska law permits Omaha Bank to charge interest on the unpaid balances of cardholder accounts at a rate of 18% per year on the first $999.99, and 12% per year on amounts of $1,000 and over. Minnesota law, however, fixes the permissible annual interest on such accounts at 12%. To compensate for the reduced interest, Minnesota law permits banks to charge annual fees of up to $15 for the privilege of using a bank credit card.

The instant case began when petitioner Marquette National Bank of Minneapolis (Marquette), itself a national banking association enrolled in the BankAmericard plan, brought suit in the District Court of Hennepin County, Minn., to enjoin Omaha Bank and Omaha Service Corp. from soliciting in Minnesota for Omaha Bank's BankAmericard program until such time as that program complied with Minnesota law. Marquette claimed to be losing customers to Omaha Bank because, unlike the Nebraska bank, Marquette was forced by the low rate of interest permissible under Minnesota law to charge a $10 annual fee for the use of its credit cards. . . .

II . . .

Omaha Bank is a national bank; it is an "instrumentalit[y] of the Federal government, created for a public purpose, and as such necessarily subject to the paramount authority of the United States." Davis v. Elmira Savings Bank, 161 U.S. 275, 283 (1896). The interest rate that Omaha Bank may charge in its BankAmericard program is thus governed by federal law. See Farmers' & Mechanics' Nat. Bank v. Dearing, 91 U.S. 29, 34 (1875). The provision of §85 called into question states:

> Any association may take, receive, reserve, and charge on any loan or discount made, or upon any notes, bills of exchange, or other evidences of debt, interest at the rate allowed by the laws of the State, Territory, or District *where the bank is located*. . . . and no more, except that where by the laws of any State a different rate is limited for banks organized under State laws, the rate so limited shall be allowed for associations organized or existing in any such State under this chapter. (Emphasis supplied.)

Section 85 thus plainly provides that a national bank may charge interest "on any loan" at the rate allowed by the laws of the State in which the bank is "located." The question before us is therefore narrowed to whether Omaha Bank and its BankAmericard program are "located" in Nebraska and for that reason entitled to charge its Minnesota customers the rate of interest authorized by Nebraska law.[19]

There is no question but that Omaha Bank itself, apart from its BankAmericard program, is located in Nebraska. Petitioners concede as much. The National Bank Act requires a national bank to state in its organization certificate "[t]he place where its operations of discount and deposit are to be carried on, designating the State, Territory, or district, and the particular county and city, town, or village." Rev. Stat. §5134, 12 U.S.C. §22. The charter address of Omaha Bank is in Omaha, Douglas Country, Neb. The bank operates no branch banks in Minnesota, nor apparently could it under federal law. See 12 U.S.C. §36(c).

The State of Minnesota, however, contends that this conclusion must be altered if Omaha Bank's BankAmericard program is considered: "In the context of a national bank which systematically solicits Minnesota residents for credit cards to be used in transactions with Minnesota merchants the bank must be deemed to be 'located' in Minnesota for purposes of this credit card program."

We disagree. Section 85 was originally enacted as §30 of the National Bank Act of 1864. The congressional debates surrounding the enactment of §30 were conducted on the assumption that a national bank was "located" for purposes of the section in the State named in its organization

19. We have no occasion in this case to parse the meaning of the phrase in §85 "associations *organized or existing* in any such State. . . ." (Emphasis added.) This phrase occurs in the "except" clause of §85, which, at least since Tiffany v. National Bank of Missouri, 18 Wall. 409 (1874), has been interpreted as an "enabling" clause. "If there is a rate of interest fixed by State laws for lenders generally, the banks are allowed to charge that rate, but no more, except that if State banks of issue are allowed to reserve more, the same privilege is allowed to National banking associations." Id., at 411. Since there is in this case no allegation or proof that Minnesota state banks are "allowed to reserve more" than the rate of interest "for lenders generally," we need not determine the relationship of the phrase "organized or existing" to the term "located."

certificate. Omaha Bank cannot be deprived of this location merely because it is extending credit to residents of a foreign State. Minnesota residents were always free to visit Nebraska and receive loans in that State. It has not been suggested that Minnesota usury laws would apply to such transactions. Although the convenience of modern mail permits Minnesota residents holding Omaha Bank's BankAmericards to receive loans without visiting Nebraska, credit on the use of their cards is nevertheless similarly extended by Omaha Bank in Nebraska by the bank's honoring of the sales drafts of participating Minnesota merchants and banks. Finance charges on the unpaid balances of cardholders are assessed by the bank in Omaha, Neb., and all payments on unpaid balances are remitted to the bank in Omaha, Neb. Furthermore, the bank issues its BankAmericards in Omaha, Neb., after credit assessments made by the bank in that city.

Nor can the fact that Omaha Bank's BankAmericards are used "in transactions with Minnesota merchants" be determinative of the bank's location for purposes of §85. The bank's BankAmericard enables its holder "to purchase goods and services from participating merchants and obtain cash advances from participating banks throughout the United States and the world." Minnesota residents can thus use their Omaha Bank BankAmericards to purchase services in the State of New York or mail-order goods from the State of Michigan. If the location of the bank were to depend on the whereabouts of each credit-card transaction, the meaning of the term "located" would be so stretched as to throw into confusion the complex system of modern interstate banking. A national bank could never be certain whether its contacts with residents of foreign States were sufficient to alter its location for purposes of §85. We do not choose to invite these difficulties by rendering so elastic the term "located." The mere fact that Omaha Bank has enrolled Minnesota residents, merchants, and banks in its BankAmericard program thus does not suffice to "locate" that bank in Minnesota for purposes of 12 U.S.C. §85.

### III

Since Omaha Bank and its BankAmericard program are "located" in Nebraska, the plain language of §85 provides that the bank may charge "on any loan" the rate "allowed" by the State of Nebraska. Petitioners contend, however, that this reading of the statute violates the basic legislative intent of the National Bank Act. At the time Congress enacted §30 of the National Bank Act of 1864, so petitioners' argument runs, it intended "to insure competitive equality between state and national banks in the charging of interest." This policy could best be effectuated by limiting national banks to the rate of interest allowed by the States in which the banks were located. Since Congress in 1864 was addressing a financial system in which incorporated banks were "local institutions," it did not "contemplate a national bank soliciting customers and entering loan agreements outside of the state in which it was established." Therefore to interpret §85 to apply to interstate loans such as those involved in this case would not only enlarge impermissibly the original intent of Congress, but would also undercut the basic policy foundations of the statute by upsetting the competitive equality now existing between state and national banks.

We cannot accept petitioners' argument. Whatever policy of "competitive equality" has been discerned in other sections of the National Bank Act, §30 and its descendants have been interpreted for over a century to give "advantages to National banks over their State competitors." Tiffany v. National Bank of Missouri, 18 Wall. 409, 413 (1874). "National banks," it was said in *Tiffany,* "have been National favorites." The policy of competitive equality between state and national banks, however, is not truly at the core of this case. Instead, we are confronted by the inequalities that occur when a national bank applies the interest rates of its home State in its dealing with residents of a foreign State. These inequalities affect both national and state banks in foreign State. Indeed, in the instant case Marquette is a national bank claiming to be injured by the unequal interest rates charged by another national bank. Whether the inequalities which thus occur when the interest rates of one State are "exported" into another violate the intent of Congress in enacting §30 in part depends on whether Congress in 1864 was aware of the existence of a system of interstate banking in which such inequalities would seem a necessary part.

Close examination of the National Bank Act of 1864, its legislative history, and its historical context makes clear that, contrary to the suggestion of petitioners, Congress intended to facilitate . . . a "national banking system." . . .

Petitioners' final argument is that the "exportation" of interest rates, such as occurred in this case, will significantly impair the ability of States to enact effective usury laws. This impairment, however, has always been implicit in the structure of the National Bank Act, since citizens of one State were free to visit a neighboring State to receive credit at foreign interest rates. This impairment may in fact be accentuated by the ease with which interstate credit is available by mail through the use of modern credit cards. But the protection of state usury laws is an issue of legislative policy, and any plea to alter §85 to further that end is better addressed to the wisdom of Congress than to the judgment of this Court.

Affirmed.

### *QUESTIONS AND COMMENTS*

1. Assume the same facts as the principal case, except that the Marquette National Bank solicits Nebraska customers for its BankAmeri-

card program by means of a loan production office located in Omaha. The loan production office solicits new accounts, but card approval and billing services are run out of Minneapolis. Could the Marquette bank charge its Nebraska customers the rate permitted under Nebraska law? See Fisher v. First National Bank of Chicago, 538 F.2d 1284, 1291 (7th Cir. 1976), *cert. denied,* 429 U.S. 1062 (1977) (national bank may charge the higher rate); Fisher v. First National Bank of Omaha, 548 F.2d 255, 258 (8th Cir. 1977) (ditto).

2. Banks chartered in State X are permitted to charge out-of-state borrowers interest rates up to the limit allowed by the borrowers' home states. May national banks located in State X do the same? The Comptroller's Office says yes. Letter of Peter Liebesman, reprinted in Fed. Banking L. Rep. (CCH) ¶85,495 (1985-1987 Transfer Binder).

3. What do you think of the Court's argument that "[i]f the location of the bank were to depend on the whereabouts of each credit-card transaction, the meaning of the term 'located' would be so stretched as to throw into confusion the complex system of modern interstate banking. A national bank could never be certain whether its contacts with residents of foreign States were sufficient to alter its location for purposes of §85." Couldn't a national bank have determined the applicable rates from the billing addresses of its customers?

4. What effect does *Marquette National Bank* have on a state's ability to enforce its usury statute?

5. Economists tend to be skeptical about the efficacy or desirability of usury limits. They observe that usury limits reduce the supply of credit to those who might need credit the most—persons whose financial position makes them questionable credit risks. Such people can obtain credit only by paying a high interest rate to compensate the lender for the risk of default. But if the interest rate is high enough it will run afoul of the usury limit. The supply of legitimate credit to such borrowers will be cut off, and the individuals will either have to do without credit, or go to loan sharks or other less reputable sources of credit. And because loan sharks operate outside the law, they demand even higher interest rates than would a bank in the absence of usury limits, since they must be compensated not only for the risk of borrower default but also for the risk that they will be apprehended and punished. Thus the economic case for usury as a consumer protection measure is not clear-cut. For debate on this question, compare Comment, Usury Legislation—Its Effects on the Economy and a Proposal for Reform, 33 Vanderbilt L. Rev. 199 (1980) with Wallace, The Uses of Usury: Low Rate Ceilings Reexamined, 56 Boston Univ. L. Rev. 451 (1976).

6. High nominal interest rates in the late 1970s severely strained the regime of state usury statutes. In some instances credit dried up because market rates exceeded the usury ceilings. Congress entered the picture with legislation overriding state usury ceilings in some circumstances, thus allowing both state and national banks to charge rates that

otherwise would be prohibited. The most important of these provisions were contained in the Depository Institutions and Monetary Control Act of 1980, which preempted all usury ceilings on first mortgage loans (subject to state override within three years) and allowed all federally insured depository institutions to charge the rates permitted to national banks under §85 (also subject to state override).

7. What is the penalty for a national bank that violates §85? Section 86 of title 12 provides that "[t]he taking, receiving, reserving, or charging a rate of interest greater than is allowed by [§85], when knowingly done, shall be deemed a forfeiture of the entire interest which the note, bill, or other evidence of debt carries with it, or which has been agreed to be paid thereon. In case the greater rate of interest has been paid, the person by whom it has been paid . . . may recover back . . . twice the amount of the interest thus paid."

## Smiley v. Citibank (South Dakota)

***116 S. Ct. 1730 (1996)***

Justice Scalia delivered the opinion of the Court.

Section 30 of the National Bank Act of 1864, Rev. Stat. §5197, as amended, 12 U.S.C. §85, provides that a national bank may charge its loan customers "interest at the rate allowed by the laws of the State . . . where the bank is located." In Marquette Nat. Bank of Minneapolis v. First of Omaha Service Corp., 439 U.S. 299 (1978), we held that this provision authorizes a national bank to charge out-of-state credit-card customers an interest rate allowed by the bank's home State, even when that rate is higher than what is permitted by the States in which the cardholders reside. The question in this case is whether §85 also authorizes a national bank to charge late-payment fees that are lawful in the bank's home State but prohibited in the States where the cardholders reside—in other words, whether the statutory term "interest" encompasses late-payment fees.

Petitioner, a resident of California, held two credit cards—a "Classic Card" and a "Preferred Card"—issued by respondent, a national bank located in Sioux Falls, South Dakota. The Classic Card agreement provided that respondent would charge petitioner a late fee of $15 for each monthly period in which she failed to make her minimum monthly payment within 25 days of the due date. Under the Preferred Card agreement, respondent would impose a late fee of $6 if the minimum monthly payment was not received within 15 days of its due date; and an additional charge of $15 or 0.65% of the outstanding balance on the Preferred Card, whichever was greater, if the minimum payment was not received by the next minimum monthly payment due date. Petitioner was charged late fees on both cards.

These late fees are permitted by South Dakota law, see S. D. Codified Laws §§54-3-1, 54-3-1.1 (1990 and Supp. 1995). Petitioner, however, is of the view that exacting such "unconscionable" late charges from California residents violates California law, and in 1992 brought a class action against respondent on behalf of herself and other California holders of respondent's credit cards, asserting various statutory and common-law claims. Respondent moved for judgment on the pleadings, contending that petitioner's claims were pre-empted by §85. The Superior Court of Los Angeles County initially denied respondent's motion, but the California Court of Appeal, Second Appellate District, issued a writ of mandate directing the Superior Court to either grant the motion or show cause why it should not be required to do so. The Superior Court chose the former course, and the Court of Appeal affirmed its dismissal of the complaint. . . . The Supreme Court of California granted review and affirmed, two Justices dissenting. . . . We granted certiorari. . . .

**II**

In light of the two dissents from the opinion of the Supreme Court of California, . . . and in light of the opinion of the Supreme Court of New Jersey creating the conflict that has prompted us to take this case, it would be difficult indeed to contend that the word "interest" in the National Bank Act is unambiguous with regard to the point at issue here. It is our practice to defer to the reasonable judgments of agencies with regard to the meaning of ambiguous terms in statutes that they are charged with administering. See Chevron U.S.A. Inc. v. Natural Resources Defense Council, Inc., 467 U.S. 837, 842-845 (1984). As we observed only last Term, that practice extends to the judgments of the Comptroller of the Currency with regard to the meaning of the banking laws. "The Comptroller of the Currency," we said, "is charged with the enforcement of banking laws to an extent that warrants the invocation of [the rule of deference] with respect to his deliberative conclusions as to the meaning of these laws." NationsBank of N. C., N. A. v. Variable Annuity Life Ins. Co. [115 S. Ct. 810] (1995). . . .

On March 3, 1995, which was after the California Superior Court's dismissal of petitioner's complaint, the Comptroller of the Currency noticed for public comment a proposed regulation dealing with the subject before us, see 60 Fed. Reg. 11924, 11940, and on February 9, 1996, which was after the California Supreme Court's decision, he adopted the following provision:

"The term 'interest' as used in 12 U.S.C. §85 includes any payment compensating a creditor or prospective creditor for an extension of credit, making available of a line of credit, or any default or breach by a borrower of a condition upon which credit was extended. It includes, among other things, the following fees connected with credit extension or availability:

numerical periodic rates, late fees, not sufficient funds (NSF) fees, overlimit fees, annual fees, cash advance fees, and membership fees. It does not ordinarily include appraisal fees, premiums and commissions attributable to insurance guaranteeing repayment of any extension of credit, finders' fees, fees for document preparation or notarization, or fees incurred to obtain credit reports." 61 Fed. Reg. 4869 (to be codified in 12 CFR §7.4001(a)).

Petitioner proposes several reasons why the ordinary rule of deference should not apply to this regulation. First, petitioner points to the fact that this regulation was issued more than 100 years after the enactment of §85, and seemingly as a result of this and similar litigation in which the Comptroller has participated as amicus curiae on the side of the banks. The 100-year delay makes no difference. To be sure, agency interpretations that are of long standing come before us with a certain credential of reasonableness, since it is rare that error would long persist. But neither antiquity nor contemporaneity with the statute is a condition of validity. We accord deference to agencies under Chevron, not because of a presumption that they drafted the provisions in question, or were present at the hearings, or spoke to the principal sponsors; but rather because of a presumption that Congress, when it left ambiguity in a statute, meant for implementation by an agency, understood that the ambiguity would be resolved, first and foremost, by the agency, and desired the agency (rather than the courts) to possess whatever degree of discretion the ambiguity allows. See Chevron, supra, at 843-844. Nor does it matter that the regulation was prompted by litigation, including this very suit. Of course we deny deference "to agency litigating positions that are wholly unsupported by regulations, rulings, or administrative practice," . . . The deliberateness of such positions, if not indeed their authoritativeness, is suspect. But we have before us here a full-dress regulation, issued by the Comptroller himself and adopted pursuant to the notice-and-comment procedures of the Administrative Procedure Act designed to assure due deliberation, see 5 U.S.C. §553. . . . That it was litigation which disclosed the need for the regulation is irrelevant.

Second, petitioner contends that the Comptroller's regulation is not deserving of our deference because "there is no rational basis for distinguishing the various charges [it] has denominated interest . . . from those charges it has denominated 'non-interest.' " . . . We disagree. As an analytical matter, it seems to us perfectly possible to draw a line, as the regulation does, between (1) "payment compensating a creditor or prospective creditor for an extension of credit, making available of a line of credit, or any default or breach by a borrower of a condition upon which credit was extended," and (2) all other payments. . . .

In any case, we do not think that anything which can accurately be described as a change of official agency position has occurred here. . . .

In addition to offering these reasons why 12 CFR §7.4001(a) in particular is not entitled to deference, petitioner contends that no Comptroller interpretation of §85 is entitled to deference, because §85 is a provision that pre-empts state law. She argues that the "presumption against . . . pre-emption" announced in Cipollone v. Liggett Group, Inc., 505 U.S. 504, 518 (1992), in effect trumps Chevron, and requires a court to make its own interpretation of §85 that will avoid (to the extent possible) pre-emption of state law. This argument confuses the question of the substantive (as opposed to pre-emptive) meaning of a statute with the question of whether a statute is pre-emptive. We may assume (without deciding) that the latter question must always be decided de novo by the courts. That is not the question at issue here; there is no doubt that §85 pre-empts state law. In Marquette Nat. Bank of Minneapolis v. First of Omaha Service Corp., 439 U.S. 299 (1978), we dismissed petitioners' argument that the "exportation" of interest rates from the bank's home State would "significantly impair the ability of States to enact effective usury laws" with the observation that "this impairment . . . has always been implicit in the structure of the National Bank Act. . . . The protection of state usury laws is an issue of legislative policy, and any plea to alter §85 to further that end is better addressed to the wisdom of Congress than to the judgment of this Court." Id., at 318-319. What is at issue here is simply the meaning of a provision that does not (like the provision in Cipollone) deal with pre-emption, and hence does not bring into play the considerations petitioner raises.

## III

Since we have concluded that the Comptroller's regulation deserves deference, the question before us is not whether it represents the best interpretation of the statute, but whether it represents a reasonable one. The answer is obviously yes.

Petitioner argues that the late fees charged by respondent do not constitute "interest" because they "do not vary based on the payment owed or the time period of delay." . . . We do not think that such a limitation must be read into the statutory term. Most legal dictionaries of the era of the National Bank Act did not place such a limitation upon "interest." . . . The definition of "interest" that we ourselves set out in Brown v. Hiatts, 82 U.S. 177, 15 Wall. 177, 185 (1873), decided shortly after the enactment of the National Bank Act, likewise contained no indication that it was limited to charges expressed as a function of time or of amount owing: "Interest is the compensation allowed by law, or fixed by the parties, for the use or forbearance of money or as damages for its detention." . . .

Petitioner suggests another source for the asserted requirement that the charges be time- and rate-based: What is authorized by §85, she notes, is the charging of interest "at the rate allowed" by the laws of the bank's home State. This requires, in her view, that the interest charges be expressed as functions of time and amount owing. It would be surprising to find such a requirement in the Act, if only because it would be so pointless. Any flat charge may, of course, readily be converted to a percentage charge—which was indeed the basis for 19th-century decisions holding that flat charges violated state usury laws establishing maximum "rates." . . . And there is no apparent reason why home-state-approved percentage charges should be permissible but home-state-approved flat charges unlawful. In any event, common usage at the time of the National Bank Act prevents the conclusion that the Comptroller's refusal to give the word "rate" the narrow meaning petitioner demands is unreasonable. . . .

Finally, petitioner contends that the late fees cannot be "interest" because they are "penalties." [But i]n §85, the term "interest" is not used in contradistinction to "penalty," and there is no reason why it cannot include interest charges imposed for that purpose. . . .

. . . . Because the regulation is entitled to deference, and because the Comptroller's interpretation of §85 is not an unreasonable one, the decision of the Supreme Court of California must be affirmed.

### *QUESTIONS AND COMMENTS*

1. Consider the material on the dual banking system in Chapter 2 of this book. What impact do you think the *Smiley* case will have on state regulation of late fees and other charges for *state*-chartered institutions?

2. Notice that cases such as *Marquette* and *Smiley* appear to give national banks a significant advantage over merchants with respect to the administration of credit card programs, since banks located in states offering favorable regulations on interest rates and fees can take advantage of the preemptive effect of §85 and obtain better terms than a merchant offering credit to its customers. How might merchants respond? Large merchants can take advantage of the power to open special purpose "credit card banks," operating under national bank charters, which can be located in a favorable jurisdiction and which can administer the merchant's credit card system. Unlike ordinary commercial banks, such credit card banks can be owned by nonfinancial institutions. See 12 U.S.C. §1841(c)(2)(F).

#### *ii. Modern Consumer Protection Rules*

Consumer protection rules in banking are a combination of the very old (usury) and the very new. Congress has been indefatigable in creating new rights and causes of action for consumers in connection with the provision of credit. Although generalizations about these new statutes are difficult, it would probably be fair to say that while usury rules are designed to police the substantive fairness of the bargain under which credit is supplied, the newer rules tend to regulate the procedures for the supply of credit, especially the disclosures required for banks and other lenders. A brief discussion of the more important federal statutes follows.

The most important of these new statutes is undoubtedly the Truth in Lending Act (TILA), 15 U.S.C. §§1601-1665, 1671-1677. This is a pure disclosure statute applicable to consumer credit and consumer lease transactions; it does not impose any particular terms or set interest rates. The underlying philosophy is that informed consumers will be able to judge for themselves whether a particular credit transaction is in their interests, and that standardization of disclosure will enable consumers to comparison shop for the most favorable terms. Detailed regulations governing TILA disclosures are set forth in the Federal Reserve Board's Regulation Z, 12 C.F.R. part 226. The Fair Credit and Charge Card Disclosure Act of 1988, Pub. L. No. 100-583, amends the Truth in Lending Act to require new disclosures in connection with applications and solicitations for all credit and charge cards, including disclosures of annual percentage rates, periodic membership fees, minimum finance charges, and the type of balance calculation method used. The act preempts state legislation in the field. The TILA has been a fertile source of litigation in the federal courts, stimulated largely by a provision that creditors who fail to comply with the act or with Regulation Z may be liable for a reasonable attorneys' fee.

In addition to the TILA, several specialized statutes govern credit disclosures and other consumer rights in real estate transactions. The Interstate Land Sales Full Disclosure Act, 15 U.S.C. §§1701-1720, imposes securities law-type disclosure obligations on the sales of large parcels of unimproved land in interstate commerce. It was designed to deter the type of abuses that have occurred from time to time in the sale of Florida and sunbelt real estate. The Real Estate Settlement Procedures Act, 12 U.S.C. §§2601-2617, requires that residential mortgage lenders must provide buyers with a uniform settlement statement with itemized costs and charges. The Home Equity Loan Consumer Protection Act of 1988, Pub. L. No. 100-709, requires lenders to disclose significant details about the terms of open-end home equity loans, including a notice that default under the loans could result in loss of the house. Lenders are also prohibited from unilaterally changing the terms of a home equity loan agreement or, with certain exceptions, from unilaterally terminating an open-end home equity loan.

The FDICIA of 1991 extended the reach of consumer laws in the area of deposit-taking. Subtitle F of FDICIA, the "Truth in Savings Act," establishes rules of disclosure for terms and conditions of interest paid and fees charged on deposit accounts, modeled generally on the Truth in Lending Act. The disclosure rules are backed up by provisions that subject depository institutions to damages liability (not to exceed $500,000 in the case of class actions) plus costs and attorneys' fees.

In addition, the FDICIA legislation reduces the insurance assessment for "lifeline" checking accounts designed to serve the needs of low-income people, FDICIA §232, and provides a credit against assessments to depository institutions that increase their services to distressed communities, FDICIA §233. The statute also instructs the FDIC to offer single-family homes under its control to qualifying individual households or public agencies or nonprofit organizations that agree to make the property available for occupancy by low-income families. FDICIA §241.

Several statutes are intended to prevent abuses in the investigation of consumer credit or the collection of debts. The Federal Fair Credit Reporting Act, 15 U.S.C. §§1681-1681t, regulates the preparation and distribution of reports by consumer reporting agencies regarding a customer's creditworthiness or general reputation. The act requires that "obsolete" information be deleted from credit reports and provides consumers with the right to be informed of the nature and substance of the reports on their credit. The act provides procedures for consumers to dispute reports they believe to be inaccurate or unfair. The Fair Debt Collection Practices Act, 15 U.S.C. §§1692-1692o, prohibits harassing or abusive tactics in the collection of debts. Although banks are largely exempt from the coverage of this statute, they have tended to use its standards as guidelines for their efforts to collect on their own loans.

Several statutes govern access by government agencies to individual financial records. Congress in these statutes attempted to balance the government interest in law enforcement against the privacy interests of individuals whose financial records might be opened to a government investigation. The Bank Secrecy Act, codified at various sections of titles 12 and 31 of the U.S. Code, requires reporting and record keeping for certain bank transactions in order to assist criminal, tax, or regulatory investigations or proceedings. The Bank Secrecy Act authorizes the secretary of the treasury to establish uniform rules on the maintenance of records by financial institutions, and to require reports on large currency transactions and maintenance of foreign bank accounts. The secretary of the treasury has promulgated regulations under the statute that require, *inter alia,* that banks must report all currency transactions with a monetary value in excess of $10,000. See generally 31 C.F.R. §103. The Supreme Court upheld the Bank Secrecy Act against constitutional attack in California Bankers Association v. Shultz, 416 U.S. 21 (1974).

The Right to Financial Privacy Act of 1978, 12 U.S.C. §§3401-3422, limits the power of government agencies to obtain access to individual financial records. Bank customers are given rights to notice of governmental demands for information and are allowed to use specified procedures to contest the government's claim of access to their records. If a bank customer makes a prima facie showing that the governmental demand is improper, the government must justify its demand by demonstrating that it has objective reason to believe that disclosure of the records will aid in a legitimate law enforcement investigation within the agency's jurisdiction. More recently Congress gave the government greater rights of access to certain information as part of the Anti-Drug Abuse Act of 1986, Pub. L. No. 99-570.

Congress has also acted to protect consumers in the area of check clearance. Banks were often accused of "holding" consumer deposits far longer than was necessary to effect actual clearance; the bank earned a "float"—interest on the funds—for the period after clearance and before the funds were credited to the customer. Congress responded to these charges with the Expedited Funds Availability Act of 1987. This statute sets specific and detailed schedules for the clearance and settlement of checks.

### *QUESTIONS AND COMMENTS*

1. Why do you think that Congress has entered the picture so vigorously in the past 20 years or so after remaining virtually quiescent on consumer protection issues in credit markets for so many years?

2. Is consumer protection legislation of this sort best achieved at the federal as opposed to the state level?

3. Why do you think these statutes are mostly enforceable through private litigation rather than by means of a federal agency empowered to supervise the practices of the nation's providers of consumer credit? Which mechanism—private litigation or government agency—do you think is best suited to achieving the statutory goals? Do you see any dangers with either mechanism?

4. Banks that are not permitted to "hold" checks for substantial periods after clearance will no longer earn a "float" on the funds. This may be good for consumers, but won't banks just pass the costs on to consumers in a different way, for example by increasing minimum required balances for checking accounts or charging explicit check-clearance fees?

### c. Regulations Intended to Ensure Credit Availability

We now turn our attention from legislation designed to protect consumers against abuse or to inform them of their rights to legislation designed to ensure that such credit as is provided will be offered on free and equal terms to all qualified applicants.

### *i. Antidiscrimination Rules*

The leading federal statute in this area is the Equal Credit Opportunity Act (ECOA), 15 U.S.C. §§1691-1691f. This statute prohibits discrimination by any creditor with respect to any aspect of a credit transaction on the basis of race, color, religion, national origin, sex, marital status, or age. Creditors subject to the statute include, inter alia, anyone who "regularly extends, renews, or continues credit." The statute is fleshed out in detail in the Federal Reserve Board's Regulation B, 12 C.F.R. part 202.

#### *QUESTIONS AND COMMENTS*

1. The Federal Reserve Board takes the position that the ECOA adopts an "effects" test. 12 C.F.R. §202.6. An Official Staff Interpretation states that

> [t]he Act and regulation may prohibit a creditor practice that is discriminatory in effect because it has a disproportionately negative impact on a prohibited basis, even though the creditor has no intent to discriminate and the practice appears neutral on its face, unless the creditor practice meets a legitimate business need that cannot reasonably be achieved as well by means that are less disparate in their impact. For example, requiring that applicants have incomes in excess of a certain amount to qualify for an overdraft line of credit could mean that women and minority applicants will be rejected at a higher rate than men and nonminority applicants. If there is a demonstrable relationship between the income requirement and creditworthiness for the level of credit involved, however, use of the income standard would likely be permissible.

Official Staff Commentary on Regulation B §202.6(a)(2), reprinted in Fed. Res. Reg. Serv. §6-180.

2. Lawyer Wilson has a mixed practice of matrimonial and general litigation. Ninety-five percent of Wilson's matrimonial clients are male, while the general litigation clients are about half men and half women. Wilson's policy is to require a full retainer in advance for matrimonial cases but to bill general litigation clients at the end of the month. Has the ECOA been violated?

3. Sanchez, a Mexican citizen lawfully residing in the United States, applied to a bank for credit but is rejected on the ground that he is "not

a U.S. citizen." Has the bank violated the ECOA? See Bhandari v. First National Bank, 808 F.2d 1082, 1100-1101 (5th Cir.), *vacated on other grounds*, 492 U.S. 901 (1989) (concluding that discrimination on the basis of alienage is permissible under the ECOA).

4. Assume that older people have a better record of repaying debts than younger people. Can a bank consider the fact that an applicant is on in years as a factor in favor of extending credit? See 12 C.F.R. §202.6(b)(2) (age may be a predictive variable if used in an empirically derived, statistically sound credit scoring system so long as "the age of someone who is elderly (62 or older) is not given a negative value"). Does this sound like a fair interpretation of the statute?

5. The statute provides an exemption, inter alia, for "special purpose credit programs" offered by profit-making organizations to "meet special social needs" if such programs satisfy standards prescribed by the Federal Reserve Board. 15 U.S.C. §1691(c). Imagine a company that develops a program to sell kitchen equipment to young, unmarried females, but that treats males and married persons less favorably in the allocation of credit. It claims that young women between 18 and 21 have traditionally been excluded from credit markets. Assume there is validity to this claim. Does its program violate the ECOA? See United States v. American Future Systems, Inc., 743 F.2d 169 (3d Cir. 1984).

6. The statute provides that "any creditor . . . who fails to comply with any requirement imposed under this subchapter shall be liable to the aggrieved applicant for punitive damages." 15 U.S.C. §1691e(b). Does this mean that punitive damages *must* be awarded even if the defendant has not acted maliciously or intentionally? See Fischl v. General Motors Acceptance Corp., 708 F.2d 143, 148 (5th Cir. 1983) (punitive damages may be awarded if the creditor's conduct is "wanton, malicious or oppressive" or "in reckless disregard of the applicable law").

7. Can a bank refuse to extend credit to lawyers on the ground that they tend to be litigious and make trouble? Should it be able to do so?

## United States of America v. Chevy Chase Federal Savings Bank

***D.D.C. 1994***

### [Consent Decree]

This decree is entered, upon consent of the parties, to resolve claims of the United States that Chevy Chase Federal Savings Bank and the B.F. Saul Mortgage Company . . . violated the Fair Housing Act, 42 U.S.C. §§3601-3619, and the Equal Credit Opportunity Act, 15 U.S.C. §§1691-1691f, by discriminating on the basis of race in home mortgage financing and other types of credit transactions in the Washington, D.C. metropolitan area. The United States contends that the Bank and Mortgage Company have considered the racial composition of residential areas in determining where to market their products, and have avoided doing business in areas where African American persons reside. The United States further alleges that the challenged practices and policies are intended to deny, and have the effect of denying, an equal opportunity to residents of African American neighborhoods, on account of the racial identity of the neighborhood, to obtain mortgage financing and other types of credit transactions. The totality of the policies or practices challenged are commonly referred to as redlining. . . .

By this decree, the Bank and Mortgage Company have committed to a remedial plan by which they will take all reasonable actions to obtain a market share of mortgage loans in African American neighborhoods, that is comparable to the Bank and Mortgage Company's market share in white residential areas. The Bank and Mortgage Company's plan to achieve this objective includes opening another three mortgage offices in African American residential neighborhoods of the Washington, D.C. metropolitan area in the near future, which will provide some banking services by automated teller machines (ATM's). . . . Promptly upon receipt of regulatory approval from the Office of Thrift Supervision, the Bank will open a branch in the Anacostia area of Washington, D.C. and the Bank expects to open additional branches in African American residential neighborhoods of Washington, D.C. and Prince George's County, Maryland during the term of this consent decree.

The Bank and Morgage Company will invest $11,000,000.00 in the African American community of the Washington, D.C. metropolitan area during the five year consent decree period to settle the claims of the United States for the damage caused by the alleged redlining, and in furtherance of their commitment to better serve this community. This investment will be undertaken through a combination of subsidized lending programs directed to Washington, D.C. metropolitan area African American neighborhoods, and the opening of new bank branches and mortgage offices in these neighborhoods. Specifically, over five years the Bank and Mortgage Company will provide at least $7,000,000.00 in lending subsidies for the special home mortgage loans, which may be increased depending on the number of bank branch/mortgage office locations to be opened during the consent decree period.

Chevy Chase and the Mortgage Company adamantly deny that any act or omission on their part as alleged in the government's complaint . . . as violative of federal law was motivated in any way by discriminatory intent or racial bias. The Bank and the Mortgage Company have agreed to the undertakings set forth in the Consent Decree to settle the government's claims against them and because they believe the affirmative lending actions and practices described will enable them to better serve the African American community.

*QUESTIONS AND COMMENTS*

1. The government's case against Chevy Chase was apparently sparked by a report in the Washington Post that accused Washington, D.C., area lending institutions, especially Chevy Chase, of systematically discriminating against African Americans in the extension of credit. Joel Glenn Brenner and Liz Spayd, A Pattern of Bias in Mortgage Loans; Statistics Show Blacks at a Disadvantage, Washington Post, June 6, 1993, at A1.

2. Notice that there were no allegations that Chevy Chase had deliberately discriminated against any single individual. The government's entire case was premised on the theory that Chevy Chase had violated the ECOA by shunning heavily African American neighborhoods in favor of heavily European American ones. This was an unprecedented application of the statute, and the legality of the government's theory has yet to be definitively resolved in court since the excerpted case settled.

3. The Justice Department's news release on the settlement stated: "Broadening its approach to ending lending discrimination, the Justice Department today settled an unprecedented case against a Washington, D.C. area bank for refusing to make its services available in predominantly African American neighborhoods. The case, against Chevy Chase Federal Savings Bank and its wholly owned subsidiary, B.F. Saul Mortgage Company, is the first lending discrimination suit focussing solely on a bank's refusal to market its services in minority neighborhoods. 'To shun an entire community because of its racial makeup, is just as wrong as to reject an applicant because they are African American,' said Attorney General Janet Reno. 'Some neighborhood banks may turn away blacks because of their race, but other neighborhoods may not even have banks to which blacks can turn.' "

4. The Justice Department's use of the ECOA to combat alleged redlining drew howls of outrage from bankers and other critics. It even sparked an unusual display of disunity within the Clinton administration, as the acting director of the Office of Thrift Supervision went public with the claim that the Justice Department's theory was mistaken.

5. Officials at Chevy Chase vehemently denied that they had ever engaged in discrimination on the basis of race, and claimed that they settled the case only because of overwhelming pressure from the government. In interviews with the press, they claimed that 79 percent of the mortgage and home improvement loans the bank made in the District in fact went to applicants from the areas it allegedly had shunned, that

it had an excellent lending record in the largely African American Prince George's County, that it was barred by law from opening branches in the District until 1986, that it had twice attempted to open a branch in a predominantly African American neighborhood in the District during the 1990s, only to be turned down by the OTS, and that according to poll results African Americans in Prince George's County were equally likely to recommend Chevy Chase to a friend as any other institution. Jaret Seiberg, Maryland Thrift in Redlining Settlement Insists That It Had Done Nothing Wrong, American Banker, August 25, 1994.

6. How would you decide the question at issue in the *Chevy Chase* case?

### *ii. Community Reinvestment Rules*

Congress has also acted in other ways to ensure that the supply of credit is not cut off to particular communities, especially low-income areas. A number of federal statutes are designed to discourage and deter banks from redlining, no matter whether they do so as a matter of policy or of practice.

The most important such statute is the Community Reinvestment Act (CRA),12 U.S.C. §§2901-2906. The CRA requires "appropriate Federal financial supervisory agencies," in connection with their examination of financial institutions, to "assess the institutions' record of meeting the credit needs of its entire community, including low- and moderate-income neighborhoods, consistent with the safe and sound operation of such institution" and to "take such record into account in [the agency's] evaluation of an application for a deposit facility by such institution." 12 U.S.C. §2903. Applications for deposit facilities include new charters, deposit insurance, merger with or acquisition of another bank, establishment of a branch, or relocation or a branch or a home office. A bank must therefore consider its community investment policies whenever it wants to make any substantial business changes or to expand its operations in significant ways.

The Home Mortgage Disclosure Act, 12 U.S.C. §§2801-2810, serves parallel purposes to the CRA. This statute applies to depository institutions with home or branch offices in cities that satisfy certain criteria. The act requires these institutions to compile a variety of statistics about home mortgage lending. This statute is fleshed out under the Federal Reserve Board's Regulation C, 12 C.F.R. part 203.

The CRA has assumed much greater importance in recent years as a result of the tremendous growth of interstate banking. Because CRA approval is required for bank mergers, attempts by banking organizations to expand interstate operations subject these institutions to community reinvestment scrutiny. Community groups have become adept at protesting merger applications by banks that they believe invest too little in local communities. Even if these protests fail to derail a merger—the usual outcome—they focus adverse publicity on the applicant and may delay the transaction. Banking firms often find it expedient to enhance their community reinvestment policies if they plan to merge or expand. (This, of course, may have been what the framers of the CRA had in mind when they wrote the statute.)

How does a federal banking agency decide whether a financial institution has compiled a sufficient record of serving the needs of low- and moderate-income residents? New regulations adopted in 1995 set forth a complex methodology for assigning ratings. The basic rules applicable to most banks utilize lending, investment, and service tests (the following material paraphrases the Comptroller's regulation, 12 C.F.R. §25).

The *lending test* evaluates a bank's record of helping to meet the credit needs of its assessment area(s) through its lending activities by considering a bank's home mortgage, small business, small farm, and community development lending. If consumer lending constitutes a substantial majority of a bank's business, the OCC evaluates the bank's consumer lending in one or more of the following categories: motor vehicle, credit card, home equity, other secured, and other unsecured loans. The Comptroller also considers originations and purchases of loans, along with any other loan data the bank provides, including data on loans outstanding, commitments, and letters of credit. A bank may ask the OCC to consider loans originated or purchased by consortia in which the bank participates or by third parties in which the bank has invested, but only if the loans meet the definition of community development loans. Loans by a bank's affiliate may also be considered in some circumstances.

In evaluating a bank's lending performance, the Comptroller considers (1) the number and amount of the bank's home mortgage, small business, small farm, and consumer loans in the bank's assessment area(s); (2) the geographic distribution of the bank's home mortgage, small business, small farm, and consumer loans; (3) the characteristics of the borrower, such as income or size of business; (4) income levels; (5) the bank's community development lending, including the number and amount of community development loans and their complexity and innovativeness; and (6) the bank's use of innovative or flexible lending practices to address the credit needs of low- or moderate-income individuals or geographical areas.

The *investment test* evaluates a bank's record of helping to meet the credit needs of its assessment area(s) through qualified investments that benefit its assessment area(s) or a broader statewide or regional area that includes the bank's assessment area(s). Activities considered under the lending or service tests may not be considered under the investment test.

At a bank's option, the Comptroller will consider a qualified investment made by an affiliate of the bank, if the qualified investment is not claimed by any other institution. Donating, selling on favorable terms, or making available on a rent-free basis a branch of the bank that is located in a predominantly minority neighborhood to a minority depository institution or women's depository institution is considered as a qualified investment. In evaluating the investment performance of a bank, the Comptroller considers the dollar amount of qualified investments, the innovativeness or complexity of qualified investments; the responsiveness of qualified investments to credit and community development needs; and the degree to which the qualified investments are not routinely provided by private investors.

The *service test* evaluates a bank's record of helping to meet the credit needs of its assessment area(s) by analyzing both the availability and effectiveness of a bank's systems for delivering retail banking services and the extent and innovativeness of its community development services. Community development services must benefit a bank's assessment area(s) or a broader statewide or regional area that includes the bank's assessment area(s). Community development services provided by an affiliate of the bank may be considered if the community development service is not claimed by any other institution.

In evaluating the availability and effectiveness of a bank's systems for delivering retail banking services, the Comptroller considers the current distribution of the bank's branches among different income areas; the bank's record of opening and closing branches; the availability and effectiveness of alternative systems for delivering banking services such as ATMs, banking by telephone or computer, and loan production offices in low- and moderate-income areas and serving low- and moderate-income individuals; and the range of services provided in different income areas and the degree to which the services are tailored to meet the needs of those areas. The Comptroller evaluates community development services by considering the extent to which the bank provides those services, as well as its innovativeness and responsiveness in providing them.

A special, community development test applies to wholesale and limited-purpose banks. This test is designed to take into account the fact that such specialized institutions are not in the business of making consumer or small business loans and accordingly may find it difficult to comply with the rules generally applicable to depository institutions.

Another special set of performance standards applies to small banks (those with less than $250 million in assets). The Comptroller considers a small bank's loan-to-deposit ratio; its percentage of loans and other lending-related activities in its assessment area(s); its record of lending to and engaging in other lending-related activities for borrowers of different income levels and for businesses and farms of different sizes; the geographic distribution of its loans; and its record of responding to written complaints about its performance in helping to meet credit needs in its assessment area(s).

In addition to this basic methodology using lending, investment, and service tests, the regulations allow a depository institution the option of proposing its own strategy for meeting its CRA obligations. A bank making this election develops a strategic plan in consultation with members of the public and submits it to the Comptroller for approval. The plan must specify measurable goals for helping to meet the credit needs of each assessment area covered by the plan, particularly the needs of low- and moderate-income geographic areas and low- and moderate-income individuals, through lending, investment, and other services, with lending ordinarily being the most important activity. A bank submitting a strategic plan defines its own criteria for "satisfactory" CRA performance and may even define criteria for "outstanding" performance. A bank may elect to be evaluated under the general lending, investment, and service tests if it fails to meet its own action plan goals.

In evaluating a proposed strategic plan, the Comptroller considers the extent and breadth of lending or lending-related activities. These include the distribution of loans among different areas; loans to businesses and farms of different sizes and individuals of different income levels; the extent of community development lending; the use of innovative or flexible lending practices to address credit needs; the amount and innovativeness, complexity, and responsiveness of the bank's qualified investments; the availability and effectiveness of the bank's systems for delivering retail banking services; and the extent and innovativeness of the bank's community development services.

The Comptroller assigns overall CRA ratings based on the bank's performance under the lending, investment, and service tests, the community development test, the small bank performance standards, or an approved strategic plan. In the case of the lending, investment, and service tests, the regulators assign one of five ranks in each category: "outstanding," "high satisfactory," "low satisfactory," "needs to improve," and "substantial noncompliance." The regulations provide some guidance on how these ratings are to be consolidated into a single CRA rating; in general, heavy priority is given to lending over the other two categories. (Why do you suppose this is?)

The community development performance of wholesale and limited-purpose banks, and the performance of small banks under the special standards applicable to those institutions, is evaluated on a four-tier scale: "outstanding," "satisfactory," "needs to improve," and "substantial noncompliance." Banks operating under a strategic plan must show that they meet the criteria defined in the applicable plan for "outstanding" or "satisfactory" performance; otherwise the bank will generally be rated "needs to improve" or "substantial noncompliance," unless it has elected to be treated under the general criteria in the event it fails to meet its own goals.

As might be expected, evidence of discriminatory or other illegal credit practices adversely affects the OCC's evaluation of a bank's CRA performance. In determining the effect on the bank's rating, the OCC considers the nature and extent of the evidence, the policies and procedures that the bank has in place to prevent discriminatory or other illegal credit practices, any corrective action that the bank has taken or has committed to take, particularly voluntary corrective action resulting from self-assessment, and other relevant information.

A matter of obvious interest is how a relevant "community" is defined for purposes of the act. In this matter, the concept of an "assessment area" is key. The depository institution itself defines its assessment area, subject to agency review. (Why were depository institutions given this power, which seems to carry obvious potential for manipulation?) For most depository institutions (other than limited-purpose or wholesale banks) the assessment area must consist generally of one or more Metropolitan Statistical Areas (MSAs) or one or more contiguous political subdivisions, such as counties, cities, or towns. It must also include the areas in which the bank has its main office, its branches, and its deposit-taking ATMs, as well as surrounding areas in which the bank has originated or purchased a substantial portion of its loans. To prevent gerrymandering by depository institutions, the regulations require that an assessment area must consist only of "whole geographies," may not reflect illegal discrimination, may not arbitrarily exclude low- or moderate-income areas, and may not extend substantially beyond an MSA boundary or beyond a state boundary unless the assessment area is located in a multistate MSA.

Importantly, the regulations do *not* allow bank regulators to use their general enforcement powers under 12 U.S.C. §1818 to assess penalties against lending institutions deemed to be in violation of the CRA. This power was proposed during the debate but in the end eliminated, apparently because of opposition from the Federal Reserve. Thus, CRA enforcement can only take the form of actions on applications for depository facilities; the agencies cannot initiate enforcement actions against recalcitrant depository institutions. (Note, however, that enforcement actions *are* allowed under other statutes, such as the Equal Credit Opportunity Act. An agency sufficiently miffed at a depository institution's CRA record could probably use the ECOA as an excuse to bring an enforcement action against the institution even if no application for a depository facility is pending.)

Depository institutions are required to keep CRA information in a public file and to make it available to anyone who asks. If you want to try an interesting experiment, go to your local bank (or any bank for that matter) and ask to see the file (also look for the CRA notice in the lobby). You may find some pretty worried-looking vice presidents looking at you out of the corners of their eyes!

## QUESTIONS AND COMMENTS

1. President Clinton instructed the banking agencies to undertake a detailed review of the CRA and its administration shortly after he took office in 1993. He wanted to enhance enforcement of the CRA while mitigating unnecessary paperwork and other burdens. The regulation summarized above represents the agencies' response, adopted after an extended rulemaking process during which the agencies held numerous public hearings and received over 13,900 comment letters.

2. The rules have the appearance of being precise and scientific. But how precise are they really? For example, the Comptroller promises to give a bank an "outstanding" rating for lending if it meets standards such as the following: "excellent responsiveness to credit needs in its assessment area(s)," "excellent geographic distribution of loans in its assessment area(s)," "excellent distribution, particularly in its assessment area(s), of loans among individuals of different income levels and businesses," "excellent record of serving the credit needs of highly economically disadvantaged areas in its assessment area(s), low-income individuals, or businesses (including farms) with gross annual revenues of $1 million or less, consistent with safe and sound operations," "extensive use of innovative or flexible lending practices in a safe and sound manner to address the credit needs of low- or moderate-income individuals or geographies," and "it is a leader in making community development loans." Other standards are similar but use different adjectives. Despite the apparent precision of the tests, are they any different from the traditional, discretionary, impressionistic use of regulatory judgment that has always characterized bank examinations? Could it be any other way?

3. In any event, what is the rationale behind the CRA? Presumably, in a capitalist system a bank will invest its funds where it can earn the highest return. If banks can earn a high return from local communities, why can't they be relied on to invest there out of self-interest? If, on the other hand, banks cannot earn as high a return from local investments as from investments elsewhere, what is the justification for insisting that the bank make an uneconomical investment?

4. What model of banks and banking implicitly underlies the CRA? Are banks being treated here as quasi-public entities with a mandate to return credit to local communities, even if investments in those communities are not the most profitable use of the bank's funds? Does the CRA reflect attitudes about the virtues of localism in providing bank services? Are these attitudes anachronistic in today's interstate banking environment, or do they still have current force and application?

## The Community Reinvestment Act: Evolution and Current Issues

***79 Federal Reserve Bulletin 251 (1993)***

The Community Reinvestment Act took effect in November 1978. How well is it working? The answer is, probably a lot better than is often recognized. The legislation has had a major influence on reinvestment activity throughout the country and has brought greater attention to local needs, especially in low-income and minority areas. It has also engendered creative strategies and techniques to stimulate lending for community development. In many parts of the country, community groups and financial institutions have moved from adversarial relations to cooperation in pursuit of mutual goals. . . . [The Act] continues to offer each depository institution wide opportunities for meeting its CRA responsibilities creatively, in a manner that best accommodates the institution and the community it serves.

## Macey and Miller, The Community Reinvestment Act: An Economic Analysis

***79 Virginia Law Review 291 (1993)***

We applaud the basic goals of this legislation. The deterioration of inner-city neighborhoods, and the numerous problems that accompany it . . . are possibly the most fundamental domestic issues facing our nation today. . . . The revitalization of decaying neighborhoods is a fundamental challenge for American public life. We conclude, however, that . . . the CRA in its present form does more harm than good. The CRA . . . is premised on a model of credit markets that was questionable at the time the statute was enacted and that has little relationship to contemporary realities, and on the normative ground that credit markets should be local in nature, despite the lack of any coherent justification for that proposition. The CRA impairs the safety and soundness of an already overstrained banking industry: it promotes the concentration of assets in geographically nondiversified locations, encourages banks to make unprofitable and risky investment and product-line decisions, and penalizes banks that seek to reduce costs by consolidating services or closing or relocating branches. The statute, moreover, imposes a significant tax on bank mergers and deters transactions that would otherwise improve the efficiency and solvency of the nation's banking system.

The CRA subjects the banking industry to costs and burdens that are not imposed on lenders otherwise similarly situated, thus placing depository institutions at a competitive disadvantage compared with their nonbank competitors. Within the depository institution industry, the CRA discriminates against wholesale banks and other specialized institutions that are not well-adapted to community investment lending. The CRA imposes significant compliance costs on institutions, especially smaller institutions. It induces socially unproductive expenditures on public relations and documentation that provide no benefit for local communities. Its requirements are vague and self-contradictory, and its enforcement often appears arbitrary.

The CRA has been turned to purposes that it was not intended to serve, and for which it was poorly designed. . . . The CRA has become a potent political tool in the hands of activist political pressure groups. Some of these groups use the statute to magnify their political importance and to gain special favors for themselves and their leaders, either by way of obtaining funding for pet projects or garnering direct logistical or financial support for their operations. It is possible, moreover, that the threat of a CRA challenge is sometimes used by political leaders for purposes less admirable and more self-serving. . . .

Tragically, the CRA poorly furthers the purposes for which it was designed. It penalizes institutions that actually serve low-income and moderate-income neighborhoods, while rewarding those that do not. It drives capital away from poor neighborhoods by imposing a tax on those depository institutions foolhardy enough to do business in such communities. It discourages innovation in the provision of financial services to low-income and moderate-income neighborhoods. It might even impair the market position of existing institutions that serve local community needs.

It is not as if there are no alternatives to meet the ostensible goals of this poorly designed statute. Local organizations can work at the grass roots level to raise capital and to extend credit to community members who are known to the organization and whose credit-worthiness can be monitored. Such a process of capital formation can be driven by a healthy profit motive rather than by the goal of squeezing as much wealth as possible out of the banking industry. Financial services such as lifeline checking can be afforded to low-income and moderate-income consumers by further deregulation in the financial services industry. And if the goal of the CRA is, or has become, that of subsidizing poor or disadvantaged citizens, that goal, we believe, could more adequately be served by direct subsidy programs rather than by treating depository institutions as some form of public utility that can be assessed to serve general social needs.

Although our evaluation of the CRA is largely negative, we recognize that, like most regulatory programs, it has benefits as well as costs. The CRA does induce depository institutions to return more credit to their local communities, although why this should be considered a desideratum of sound banking is unclear to us. The Act encourages depository institutions to explore market opportunities that they might have otherwise overlooked, and thus it might offer marginal efficiency gains in specialized markets. Some of the funds that are redirected by the CRA do eventually find their way into the hands of needy persons in the form of better access to credit, improved housing, and the like. We believe, however, that these benefits are small relative to the costs.

If we are correct in our critique of the CRA, why is it so popular? The answer, we suggest, is that the CRA benefits discrete, well-organized political interest groups. The principal beneficiaries are community activists, who enjoy great power at the local level in many jurisdictions and who are also influential in Congress. Small businesses and charitable institutions also profit from the statute. The federal banking agencies benefit from the CRA because it enhances their regulatory jurisdictions, and because it offers a powerful threat that the agencies can use in order to induce cooperation in their programs. Politicians like the CRA because it allows them to appease special interest groups through a statutory vehicle that keeps the costs of such appeasement off the explicit balance sheets of both the banks and the federal government. This political coalition is powerful enough to insulate the statute from serious attack, notwithstanding the costs that the statute imposes on the banking industry, residents of low-income and moderate-income neighborhoods, and American taxpayers.

## Swire, Safe Harbors and a Proposal to Improve the Community Reinvestment Act

***79 Virginia Law Review 349 (1993)***

The core of the proposal is to form a "safe harbor" for banks and their holding companies within the enforcement provisions of the Act. . . . The safe harbor that I propose would allow banks meeting certain criteria to receive favorable treatment automatically when they make applications that are subject to review under the CRA. The price of this safe harbor would be a bank's commitment to substantial investment in community development banks ("CDBs") and other qualifying investments.

The safe harbor proposal would go far toward easing the disadvantages noted by Macey and Miller, and likely be superior to the current regime from a public policy perspective. . . . A safe harbor could decrease . . . compliance costs while increasing the amount actually spent pursuing the CRA goal of investing in low-income and moderate-income neighborhoods. In political terms, the safe harbor is well-designed to meet the specific and general themes of the [Clinton administration].

Further, the safe harbor is an appropriate regulatory measure in this instance. Generally, a safe harbor is defined as a regime that includes a general standard that restricts activity, such as the CRA requirement that banks invest in their local communities. The safe harbor also includes a more specific rule that can make activity per se legal, such as the proposed safe harbor if banks invest enough in qualifying CRA investments. [T]he factors that in general make a safe harbor more attractive are present in the CRA context.

## Klausner, Market Failure and Community Investment: A Market-Oriented Alternative to the Community Reinvestment Act

*143 U. Pa. L. Rev. 1561 (1995)*

[Professor Klausner argues that there may be efficiency-based arguments in favor of some type of community reinvestment obligation. Specifically, he identifies a number of market imperfections that, in his view, may leave low-income neighborhoods with suboptimally low levels of credit. Banks may ration credit to low-income or minority neighborhoods for economic reasons: they may not want to incur the fixed costs of familiarizing themselves with particular neighborhoods when the creditworthiness of many borrowers in those neighborhoods may be low, even though some borrowers are perfectly creditworthy. Because there is less publicly available information about credit conditions in low-income areas, banks will not be able to take advantage of these "positive externalities." There may also, in Klausner's view, be significant "neighborhood externalities": The deterioration of a home, storefront, or other property can reduce the value of neighboring properties. On a broad scale, physical deterioration can impair property values in an entire neighborhood. As a result, a lender may refuse to lend in a neighborhood that it perceives to be in decline, even if the property offered as collateral provides sufficient security at the time the loan application is made and the lender is confident that the borrower will maintain the property. In combination, Klausner argues, these market imperfections can compound each other, making the whole more—and worse—than the sum of the parts. Klausner suggests that government intervention may be warranted to overcome these various external effects.]

[Klausner proposes a market for tradable CRA obligations. Under this scheme, all banks would be assigned an obligation to lend in low-income and moderate-income neighborhoods. Banks, however, would be permitted to trade their CRA obligations with one another for cash. Klausner argues that establishing marketable CRA obligations would move the program from an inefficient command-and-control paradigm to one that is more efficiency-oriented and market-based. Klausner notes that similar schemes have been used successfully in areas such as pollution control, preservation of historical and environmentally sensitive sites, and provision of low-income and moderate-income housing.]

[In Klausner's system, every bank would have a specific CRA-qualifying loan requirement in low-income and moderate-income neighborhoods. A bank could meet its obligation by making CRA qualifying loans itself, by joining a consortium or on loan participation arrangement, or by purchasing whole loans that other banks originate.]

*QUESTIONS AND COMMENTS*

1. For additional commentary favorable to the CRA, see Allen J. Fishbein, The Community Reinvestment Act After Fifteen Years: It Works, but Strengthened Federal Enforcement Is Needed, 20 Fordham Urban Law Journal 293 (1993). See also Richard Marsico, A Guide to Enforcing the Community Reinvestment Act, 20 Fordham Urban Law Journal 165 (1993). A more philosophical discussion can be found in Anthony D. Taibi, Banking, Finance, and Community Economic Empowerment: Structural Economic Theory, Procedural Civil Rights, and Substantive Racial Justice, 107 Harvard Law Review 1465 (1994).

2. Professor Swire's proposal for safe harbors in the CRA was popular among many bankers but was ultimately rejected in the 1995 regulations, which continue to use a multi-factor test and do not insulate any institution, even ones with good CRA ratings, from regulatory scrutiny.

3. What do you think of the Macey and Miller argument that the CRA fails even its own purposes because it is likely to drive depository institutions away from the very areas where their services are most needed? Does the argument depend on the size of the relevant "community"? Should the CRA be amended to dispense with the idea of localism in favor of a general obligation on the part of depository institutions to make loans to low- and moderate-income borrowers?

4. Would a depository institution face potential exposure under other statutes such as the Equal Credit Opportunity Act if it failed to include within its defined community reasonably contiguous, low-income areas? Consider the consent decree in the *Chevy Chase* case, excerpted above. A part of the decree describes Chevy Chase's actions with respect to its CRA area: "[i]n defining a [CRA] delineated area, the Bank and Mortgage Company's treatment of the District of Columbia has varied. In 1986, Chevy Chase included the District of Columbia in its delineated area although it had no branches in the District and made few loans outside of heavily white residential areas. In 1989, the institution eliminated the District of Columbia in its entirety from its delineated community, even though, by that time, it had a branch in the heavily white upper northwest area of the District. When that decision was criticized by federal regulators, the institution, in 1992, added the heavily white upper northwest corner of the District to the delineated area. At the time the United States began its investigation, Chevy Chase was still operating under this delineation that included only the most heavily white portion

of the District of Columbia." Do you think the government's action against Chevy Chase may have been motivated, in part, by a perception, based on its self-defined CRA area, that it was deliberately avoiding heavily African American areas in favor of heavily European American ones?

5. Why does the CRA apply only to depository institutions (except credit unions)? Don't all sorts of institutions make loans—consumer finance companies, department stores, credit card companies, pension funds, life insurance companies, automobile credit companies, and much more? Doesn't the CRA create an unequal playing field under which only depository institutions are required to make special efforts to serve their local communities? Is there any justification for this special obligation?

6. What do you think of Professor Klausner's argument that there should be a market for CRA obligations? Professor Klausner argues that his proposal would alleviate some of the problematic features of the CRA, such as the apparent requirement that depository institutions make geographically nondiversified loans, and duties on institutions such as wholesale banks that are poorly equipped to engage in retail lending. Can you think of any objections to the proposal?

## NOTE ON COMMUNITY DEVELOPMENT LENDING

In addition to meeting CRA requirements, banks may make community development loans on their own or respond to other sorts of economic incentives. Authority to engage in community development projects can be found, for national banks, in 12 U.S.C. §24 (Eleventh), added to the law in 1992. This statute authorizes national banks to make investments "designed primarily to promote the public welfare, including the welfare of low- and moderate-income communities or families (such as by providing housing, services, or jobs). A national banking association may make such investments directly or by purchasing interests in an entity primarily engaged in making such investments."

The statute contains several precautions against excessive community development activities. A national bank cannot make investments that subject it to unlimited liability (presumably, this means it cannot become a partner or co-venturer in a community development project). In the aggregate, community development investments generally cannot exceed 5 percent of capital and surplus.

What about charitable activities by banks? These are permitted by 12 U.S.C. §24 (Eighth), which authorizes national banks "to contribute to community funds, or to charitable, philanthropic, or benevolent instrumentalities conducive to public welfare, such sums as its board of directors may deem expedient and in the interests of the association, if it is located in a State the laws of which do not expressly prohibit State banking institutions from contributing to such funds or instrumentalities."

Community development lending is unlikely to occur on a large scale, however, simply because of bankers' public-spiritedness. Some policymakers have recommended, accordingly, that so-called "community development banks" be established. These institutions would receive funding from the government or other sources and would specialize in making loans within local communities, especially impoverished inner cities. The model for the community development bank is, in a sense, the South Shore Bank, a private commercial bank located in Chicago's depressed inner city. This institution has operated profitably while making mortgage and other loans in some of the poorest urban areas in the country. Bill Clinton visited the South Shore Bank during the 1980s and used the institution as a model for his campaign promise to establish one hundred community development banks around the country—a promise that was initially shelved as unrealistic but that bore fruit later in the Clinton administration.

In 1994 Congress enacted the Riegle Community Development and Regulatory Improvement Act, which was intended "to promote economic revitalization and community development through investment in and assistance to community development financial institutions. . . ." 12 U.S.C. §4701(b). This statute creates a fund that can support community development financial institutions, defined as nongovernmental entities whose primary mission is to promote community development, serve a low-income area or targeted population, provide development services in conjunction with equity investments or loans, and maintain accountability to residents of its targeted area or population. Community development financial institutions (which may or may not be depository institutions) apply to the fund for grants or technical assistance.

### d. Lender Liability

Borrowers and others are also protected by a generalized obligation of good faith imposed on banks under a variety of disparate legal principles. As a matter of state law, for example, banks may be required to comply with the general obligation of good faith and fair dealing set forth in §205 of the Restatement (Second) of Contracts (1979), which states that "[e]very contract imposes upon each party a duty of good faith and fair dealing in its performance and its enforcement."

If non-real estate financing is involved, the Uniform Commercial Code provisions on good faith are likely to be implicated. Every contract or duty within the U.C.C. is subject to "an obligation of good faith in its performance or enforcement." U.C.C. §1-203. In addition, acceleration clauses in loan contracts may be subject to U.C.C. §1-208, which states in pertinent part that "[a] term providing that one party or his successor in interest may accelerate payment or performance or require collateral or additional collateral 'at will' or 'when he deems himself insecure' or in words of similar import shall be construed to mean that he shall have power to do so only if he in good faith believes that the prospect of payment or performance is impaired." U.C.C. §1-201(19) defines good faith as "honesty in fact in the conduct or transaction concerned." Some problems under the relevant U.C.C. provisions are discussed in the following case.

## Brown v. Avemco Investment Corp.

*603 F.2d 1367 (9th Cir. 1979)*

FERGUSON, District Judge:

Plaintiffs, citizens of Montana, sued defendant, a Maryland corporation, in a diversity action (28 U.S.C. § 1332) alleging a conversion of an airplane. Defendant counterclaimed for interference with contractual rights. . . .

### FACTS

1. On September 22, 1972, Robert Herriford borrowed $6500 from AVEMCO and executed a promissory note for $9607.92 (amount borrowed plus "add-on" interest and credit for insurance).

2. The promissory note was secured by an agreement granting to AVEMCO a security interest in an airplane. The security agreement contained the following language:

> Time is of the essence of this Security Agreement. It is hereby agreed that if default be made in the payment of any part of the principal or interest of the promissory note secured hereby at the time and in the manner therein specified, or if any breach be made of any obligation or promise of debtor herein contained or secured hereby, or *if any or all of the property covered hereby be hereafter sold, leased, transferred, mortgaged, or otherwise encumbered without the written consent of Secured Party first had and obtained,* or in the event of the seizure of the aircraft under execution or other legal process, or if for any reason Secured Party may deem itself insecure, *then the whole principal sum unpaid upon said promissory note, with the interest accrued thereon* or advanced under the terms of this Security Agreement, or secured hereby, and the interest thereon, *shall immediately become due and payable at the option of Secured Party.* (emphasis added)

The security agreement also provided that the laws of Texas would apply with respect to rights under the agreement.

3. On July 4, 1973, Herriford entered into a lease and option agreement with the three plaintiffs whereby plaintiffs would pay hourly rentals for the plane and contribute equally toward Herriford's debt retirement with AVEMCO. Upon full payment of the mortgage on the airplane, the plaintiffs would have an option to purchase one-fourth ownership (each) of the plane for the sum of one dollar.

4. Plaintiffs became co-insureds with Herriford on the airplane in 1973. Copies of this policy were sent to AVEMCO.

5. On July 9, 1975, the plaintiffs advised AVEMCO that they had exercised their option with Herriford and now tendered to AVEMCO the $4,859.93 still owed by Herriford.

6. On July 18, 1975, AVEMCO refused this offer and wrote to Herriford announcing that because of his failure to comply with the note and security agreement, AVEMCO was accelerating the payments and the entire balance of $5,078.97 was due and payable on or before July 28, 1975. AVEMCO later explained that the additional amount was due to reimburse AVEMCO for its purchase of "Vendor's Single Interest Insurance."

7. On July 25, 1975, plaintiff McAlear advised AVEMCO that plaintiffs did not accept AVEMCO's rejection of their tender and that the money to retire the debt was available to AVEMCO at the First Security Bank of Bozeman, Montana, upon presentation of a satisfaction of the mortgage.

8. On July 29 or 30, 1975, an agent of AVEMCO used a passkey to start the plane and flew it to Seattle.

9. On July 30, 1975, AVEMCO notified Herriford of this repossession and demanded payment of $5,578.97 by August 10, 1975 or the aircraft would be sold with proceeds to be applied first to sale expenses and second to Herriford's account.

10. On September 22, 1975, a bill of sale for the plane was filed by AVEMCO with the Federal Aviation Agency. The consideration was $7000 and the bill of sale was dated August 25, 1975.

### Acceleration

The facts as established at trial are as follows: The security agreement between the debtor Herriford and the creditor AVEMCO provided that if Herriford leased the plane without the consent of AVEMCO, AVEMCO could, at its option, accelerate full payment of the loan. Herriford leased the plane to plaintiffs in 1973. In that year, plaintiffs became co-insureds on the airplane and copies of the policy were sent to AVEMCO. For two years payments continued to be regularly made on the note. When on July 9, 1975, the plaintiffs contacted AVEMCO and offered what they believed was full payment of the debt, AVEMCO refused to negotiate with them and did not inquire further of either Herriford or the plaintiffs about their intention to pay the debt in full. While plaintiffs' offer of $4,859.93 may not have met the legal requirements of a valid tender, AVEMCO's complete disregard of the offer and eagerness to accelerate payment, repossess the plane and sell it for $7000 should have invoked the concern of the district court and prompted an examination of the fairness of the acceleration.

Both the Uniform Commercial Code (U.C.C.) and equity impose this duty. Plaintiffs sought this protection and proposed jury instructions on acceleration which incorporated a test of reasonableness and fairness: the U.C.C. requirement of good faith belief of security impairment. The district court rejected these and instructed that there could be an automatic enforcement of the acceleration clause if the jury merely found the technical breach of a lease without consent. This instruction was erroneous and prejudicial. A new trial is required.

Acceleration clauses are designed to protect the creditor from actions by the debtor which jeopardize or impair the creditor's security. They are not to be used offensively, e.g., for the commercial advantage of the creditor. Acceleration is a harsh remedy with draconian consequences for the debtor. Acceleration is a matter of equity and the courts, including those of Texas, have historically been careful to evaluate the fairness of acceleration in the particular facts of a case. As the Texas Court of Civil Appeals stated in Parker v. Mazur, 13 S.W.2d 174, 175 (Tex. Civ. App. 1928), courts of equity "will scan very closely the enforcement of so hard and rigorous a contract."

In performing their equitable duties, Texas courts have long required that acceleration be reasonable in light of the facts. They would not permit enforcement of acceleration clauses when the debtor's default was due to the debtor's accident or mistake or to the creditor's own fraudulent or inequitable conduct. Nor would they permit acceleration when the facts made its use unjust or oppressive.

The provisions of the U.C.C. impose similar requirements on acceleration in the transactions it governs. The U.C.C. requirements are harmonious with the older equitable tests of reasonableness. Section 1-203 of the U.C.C. imposes an obligation of good faith on the performances or enforcement of every contract or duty within the Code. Section 1-208 further defines and applies the good faith obligation to options to accelerate at will and requires that the accelerating party "in good faith believes that the prospect of payment or performance is impaired."

Texas has adopted the U.C.C.; it became effective in 1967. Section 1.208 of the Texas Business and Commercial Code states:

> *§1.208 Option to accelerate at will*
> A term providing that one party or his successor in interest may accelerate payment or performance or require collateral or additional collateral "at will" or "when he deems himself insecure" or in words of similar import

> shall be construed to mean that he shall have power to do so only if he in good faith believes that the prospect of payment or performance is impaired. The burden of establishing lack of good faith is on the party against whom the power has been exercised.

The Fifth Circuit has applied this Texas statute to acceleration based on a clause authorizing acceleration when the creditor "deemed himself insecure." Sheppard Federal Credit Union v. Palmer, 408 F.2d 1369 (5th Cir. 1969). Acceleration on this basis clearly falls within the specific language of §1.208. . . .

The more difficult question presented in this case is whether the statute applies to "default" acceleration clauses as well as to "insecurity" acceleration clauses. When the creditor chooses to accelerate because the debtor violated a specific provision of the security agreement and not because he feels insecure, does §1.208 apply? Here AVEMCO's agreement with Herriford contains both types of clauses. Yet AVEMCO's asserted basis for the acceleration is breach of the consent-for-lease provision of the security agreement and not the "deem itself insecure" language.

The question of application of §1.208 to this situation has not been answered. Several courts have confronted security agreements which, like the one here, authorized acceleration both when a specific provision is breached and when the creditor deems itself insecure. In these cases, without much discussion, the courts have applied both the U.C.C. and equity principles. . . . This court believes that §1.208 does apply. . . .

According to its language, §1.208 applies when a party in interest may accelerate payment "at will" or "when he deems himself insecure" or "in words of similar import." Here the agreement provided that AVEMCO may, *at its option,* accelerate payment when the debtor leases without consent or when AVEMCO deems itself insecure or when various other contingencies occur. The agreement does not require immediate, automatic acceleration upon one of these events but further ties acceleration to the option of AVEMCO. Section 1.208 applies the Code's good faith concept to such acceleration and provides that the creditor has power to exercise the option "only if he in good faith believes that the prospect of payment or performance is impaired."

An option to accelerate when the debtor leases without consent is different, however, than one based on the creditor's feelings of insecurity. The lease is within the control of the debtor; the feelings of insecurity are subject to the whim and caprice of the creditor. As the U.C.C. Comment to §1-208 suggests, the drafters' greatest concern was with abuse due to the uncontrolled will of the creditor. Some may argue that §1-208 therefore addresses only "insecurity" clause acceleration. While this type of clause may be the primary focus of §1-208 this court does not believe it is the only focus. Abuse is possible with "due-on-lease" acceleration as well. The "option" to accelerate based on a lease, like the one based on feelings of insecurity, could be used by AVEMCO as a sword for commercial gain rather than as a shield against security impairment. Section 1.208, growing from and incorporating equitable principles, defines "good faith" in acceleration to provide protection from such abuse. . . .

*QUESTIONS AND COMMENTS*

1. Consider Professor Fischel's analysis of the rationale for the lender's obligation to act in good faith:

> [T]he rationale for imposing a duty of good faith on lenders relates to the impossibility of drafting a contract covering every possible contingency. If contracts could be negotiated and enforced without any cost, the parties could negotiate an agreement which would preclude attempts by the lender to behave opportunistically. Because of the costs of negotiating and enforcing agreements, however, the parties cannot prevent all opportunistic behavior by contract. Thus the duty of good faith acts as an implied contractual term to achieve what the parties themselves cannot given the costs involved.
>
> While this interpretation of the duty of good faith has a certain appeal, it is not without difficulty. The problem is that distinguishing opportunistic from non-opportunistic behavior can be very complicated if not impossible. A lender will never concede that its actions were designed to obtain a benefit not bargained for in the initial agreement. On the contrary, the lender will claim that its refusal to continue funding was based on its assessment of the debtor and the probability of default. Moreover, not only will distinguishing between these two explanations be difficult, but also the attempt to distinguish them will impair the contractual protection given to the lender in the first instance. . . .
>
> Thus there is a trade-off. The more absolute the discretion of the lender, the stronger the bond of the borrower but the greater the incentive of the lender to behave opportunistically. Conversely, the more expansive the interpretation of the duty of good faith to control opportunistic behavior by the lender, the weaker is the bond of the borrower and the less able the borrower is to use the bond to obtain more favorable credit terms.

Fischel, The Economics of Lender Liability, 99 Yale L.J. 131, 141-142 (1989).

2. The borrower in this case agreed, did he not, that if he were to lease any of the property covered by the security interest without the lender's consent, the lender had the right to accelerate the loan? Why not then hold the borrower to the agreement he made?

3. Is there any reason why a lender might want to retain the right to accelerate a note without needing to demonstrate a belief that the prospect of payment or performance is impaired?

4. In this case U.C.C. §1-208 didn't apply by its terms, did it? If

not, wasn't the court reaching far out into judicial activism to reject the creditor's rights under the agreement?

5. Consider the selection from Professor Fischel above. To what extent do you think the result in Brown v. AVEMCO Investment Corp. was driven by the court's perception that the lender was behaving opportunistically? Are the facts clear enough to draw a confident conclusion?

6. What should the creditor have done in this case? Is a creditor generally obligated to try to work out some sort of compromise or other arrangement with the borrower before proceeding against the collateral?

7. Are there any dangers in attempting to work out a compromise? In Alaska Statebank v. Fairco, 674 P.2d 288 (Alaska 1983), a bank engaged in negotiations for restructuring a loan agreement with a borrower in default. When these negotiations were unsuccessful, the bank took possession of the borrower's store, as permitted by the original agreement. The trial court held, in an opinion affirmed by the Alaska Supreme Court, that the bank had implicitly agreed to provide advance notice before proceeding against the collateral by its conduct during the unsuccessful restructuring negotiations. Thus the note was not in default at the time of the takeover, and even if a default existed the bank had waived it and was estopped to rely on it in demanding payment.

8. What elements of damages may be awarded for a bank's bad faith breach of a loan agreement? In general, the damages available for breaches of contract are limited to pecuniary losses. However, over the past decade a number of courts have held that bad faith breaches of contract can give rise to liability in tort. The advantage of a tort theory for plaintiffs is that it can support elements of damages not standardly available in contract actions: emotional distress, certain elements of economic loss that may not have been foreseeable at the time the contract was made, and punitive damages. This tort theory has been applied to support an award of punitive damages against a bank. See, e.g., First National Bank in Libby v. Twombly, 213 Mont. 66, 689 P.2d 1226 (1984).

9. The tort of bad faith breach of contract arose in the insurance setting and was grounded on a perceived special relationship between an insurance company and its client. It is said, for example, that insureds are likely to be in extremely vulnerable positions at the time they call on insurance companies to perform their obligations. The insured may be suffering a catastrophic loss or may face a potentially ruinous lawsuit. As applied to insurance companies, the tort of bad faith breach is said to protect such vulnerable clients against oppression. Do similar considerations apply when a bank seeks repayment of its loan from a defaulting customer?

10. A bank agrees to provide a mortgage loan for the purchase of commercial real estate. No rate is set at the time of the commitment, but the banker's loan officer tells the customer that he is "reasonably confident" that the rate will not exceed 10 percent. At the last minute,

at a time when the bank's customer has no realistic opportunity to secure additional financing, the bank informs the customer that in light of tightened credit conditions it will need to charge 12 percent on the loan. Does the customer have recourse? Under what theory?

11. What do you expect the effect of cases like *First National Bank in Libby* and *Alaska Statebank* will be on banks' willingness to renegotiate loans when borrowers run into financial difficulties?

## State National Bank of El Paso v. Farah Manufacturing Co., Inc.

*678 S.W.2d 661 (Tex. 1984)*

SCHULTE, Justice.

This case centers around a management change clause contained in a $22,000,000.00 loan agreement. The jury found Appellant bank, acting alone or in conspiracy with any of the other lenders, committed acts of fraud, duress and interference, proximately resulting in damages to Appellee, and set damages at $18,947,348.77. We reform and affirm. . . .

At its meeting on July 9, 1976, the [Farah Manufacturing Co.] board demanded that [William] Farah resign as CEO. A resolution, introduced by Farah and naming Leone as new CEO, was passed. Farah retained the title of board chairman, a ceremonial position with no management responsibilities. His resignation as CEO was demanded on the basis that he was the cause of FMC's management problems and poor financial condition. . . .

In the spring of 1976, FMC had begun to seek a $30,000,000.00 loan to survive losses. An interim agreement was arrived at to be followed in October, 1976, by a finalized loan agreement. Both contained management change clauses. On February 14, 1977, a restructured collateralized loan agreement was reached. FMC maintains that the appraised value of the collateral was $72,000,000.00 which amount is disputed by State National. This latest agreement had the strengthened management change clause. . . .

The clause provided that it would be an event of default under the loan agreement if there occurred:

> Any change in the office of President and Chief Executive Officer of Farah [Manufacturing Company, Inc.] or any other change in the executive management of Farah [Manufacturing Company, Inc.] which any two Banks shall consider, for any reason whatsoever, to be adverse to the interests of the Banks.

At a shareholders' meeting on March 7, 1977, Farah sought to have a new board of directors elected to insure his return to management.

Farah proposed to the board that he be elected CEO. Several factors induced him to change his mind and to vote for the incumbent board which he believed would elect him CEO anyway. Because of the management change clause, the board declined absent a statement of position from the lenders. The lenders initially refused to assert a position. The board suggested Farah personally present his management proposal to the lenders. He did so at Republic in Dallas on March 14, 1977, stressing his return as CEO was the only way to save FMC. After his presentation, Farah was asked to leave the meeting so the lenders could discuss the matter. State National voiced opposition to Farah. No decision was reached. Farah was informed of their indecision and that a change in CEO could constitute a violation of the management change clause. FMC Director Conroy, unknown to Farah, let the lenders know of his (Conroy's) interest in becoming CEO. Conroy was also a director of State National. As of March 14, the lenders knew that if Leone resigned, his successor would be either Farah or Conroy. As stated, Republic was the agent bank for the lenders, including Prudential. On March 15, Bunten of Republic, assigned the daily handling of the loan to Tom Foster of Republic. Tom Foster hired attorney Donohoe to assist him.

On March 16, Farah talked to Bunten, the senior loan officer of Republic, on a flight to New York and repeated the proposal he had made to all the lenders in Dallas two days before. Farah testified, "[h]e (Bunten) said he felt that we ought to disregard the covenant as being boiler plate, they had it in all of their agreements, and run the business and get the thing back in shape." Farah began planning his return to management. Leone tendered his resignation as CEO on March 17. On March 18, Lerner resigned from the board. (Frost and Kozmetsky had resigned on March 9.) Farah nominated three new directors. Only Azar accepted. He was elected. Farah demanded he (Farah) be elected CEO. The directors resisted and Director Conroy asked to be named CEO. Conroy stated the management clause was designed to exclude Farah. Gordon Foster noted a potential default in the loan, and the board named him to talk to the lenders. On March 18 and 19, Gordon Foster talked to Tom Foster, in support of Conroy for CEO. Tom Foster testified from his notes of that meeting that Farah had a probable three of the five directors' votes for CEO. Conroy met with Azar conveying his own desire to be CEO. Azar persisted in his support of Farah in talking to Conroy and Houghton of State National. Azar in speaking to Houghton learned that Houghton believed Farah to be incapable, and he expressed to Azar his bitterness and anger toward Farah in a business sense. Notes prepared by Bettina Whyte of Continental reflect the feeling of that bank that if Farah were elected he should be strongly controlled and have life made miserable for him.

Attorney Donohoe met with Tom Foster on March 20 to determine his course at the March 21 lenders' meeting. Tom Foster's notes indicate the alternatives discussed. One note indicated Azar was viewed as the swing vote on the board in probable favor of Farah. The lenders met on March 21. State National opposed Farah. Attorney Smith for State National testified that the bank's initial participation in the loan had been reliant upon Farah's noninvolvement in management and the inclusion of the management change clause. Continental's position was similar.

The lenders analyzed the ramifications of FMC's bankruptcy, should a default be declared, and their exposure to liability for changes in FMC management. According to the testimony of Daugherty, President of State National, the lenders felt that their only legitimate options, should Farah become CEO, were to either call the loan or let Farah hold office unmolested. Daugherty testified that neither choice was acceptable to the banks. They were adverse to the bankruptcy of FMC. As FMC was not otherwise in default on the loan at the time, State National was unwilling to put El Paso's largest private employer into bankruptcy. . . .

Then on March 22, Donohoe drafted a letter conveying the lenders' position to the board. The letter approved by all the lenders was signed by Tom Foster and delivered to Gordon Foster prior to the board meeting to be held that day. Farah testified that at the time of the board meeting he was unaware of the lenders' meeting of the previous day. He anticipated he would be elected CEO and that his election would be approved by Bunten of Republic, to whom he had spoken on the plane trip to New York. The letter of March 22 read in part:

> The Banks wish to advise the Board that a change of executive management which includes the election of Mr. William Farah as chief executive of the Company or results in his being the power to generally supervise and control the operations and affairs of the Company is unacceptable to the Banks, and the Banks will not grant any waiver of default based thereon. The Banks are, however, willing to consider a waiver of the default clause . . . if the Board decides that a change in the office of the Chief Executive of the Company (involving others than Mr. Farah) is in the best interests of the Company. The Banks do not intend hereby and do not waive any default based on the developments in the Company constituting a material adverse change of circumstances. . . . The Banks are still considering their position regarding the events which have and are coming to their attention.

Tom Foster testified that the lenders did not want to call the loan and create a default which would result in FMC's bankruptcy. He admitted that, if Farah were elected, the lenders had a choice of either doing nothing or attempting to call the loan. Although the interpretation of the letter was left to the board, he conceded that the statement of the lenders, that they would not waive a default, could have created an impression that there would be a default if Farah were elected. He admitted that the "clear understandings" set forth in the further portion of the letter which read:

> Mr. Farah has been making serious efforts to take over the operating management of the company, contrary to what we thought were the clear understandings of the Banks and Company. . . .

were not expressed in the loan agreement. He also conceded that the loan agreement did not pertain to the election of directors.

Gordon Foster presented the letter to the board. Farah disregarded it as inconsistent with what Bunten had told him. J. Farah decided to cast his vote for Leone to remain as CEO. Gordon Foster warned the board it could not vote to put FMC in default and that the loan would probably be called if Farah were elected. Azar testified that the letter gave him the impression that the lenders would close the company or call the loan if Farah were elected. Farah nominated Richard Jaeger and Charles Wood as directors hoping that their presence on the board would insure his election as CEO. Gordon Foster and other directors took exception to these nominations. The meeting was recessed without an election of new directors or CEO. . . .

[O]n March 23, the lenders . . . met with Azar, J. Farah, Conroy and others at Azar's own place of business in El Paso. Azar described Donohoe as the spokesman for the lender group and said Donohoe opened the meeting by saying that "Willie [Farah] was not acceptable as a chief executive officer and president." Azar said he told Donohoe that Farah was the only one who could turn the company around. When asked what else Donohoe had said, Azar responded, "[w]ell, it got to the point where if Willie Farah was elected president of the company, why, he would automatically bankrupt the company and he would padlock it the next day." Azar said that after talking to attorney Thomas on the phone he came back and told Donohoe that "he could take his loan agreement and shove it up his ass." Azar explained he did that "trying to determine how serious they were about bankrupting and closing the company, what was his intent. I intended to push him to the very brink and very edge and find out." Azar said Donohoe's response was "[w]e will." Azar said he then believed Donohoe would bankrupt and padlock the company if the board elected Farah. He said as a result of the meeting, "I was fearful of putting the company in bankruptcy. So I agreed to talk to Mr. Farah and ask him to stand down and not stand for election.". . .

Farah testified that . . . prior to the board meeting, Donohoe "started in" on him by telling him that he (Farah) had been a very incompetent person, had lost $37,000,000.00 and that he (Donohoe) was going to put the company into bankruptcy and padlock the doors the next morning. Farah testified Donohoe "pounded on the table right in front of me, right in my face there," and repeated the statement regarding bankrupting the company and padlocking the doors. Farah said he put the papers he was preparing for the meeting in his briefcase and left the room. Farah said he believed what Donohoe told him and "he (Donohoe) scared the devil out of me." Several witnesses testified that neither Donohoe nor any other of the lender representatives told Farah that FMC would be bankrupted or padlocked.

In accordance with his representation that he would talk to Farah, Azar met with Farah prior to the board meeting. Azar testified he told Farah that the lenders wanted Farah to resign as board chairman and to elect in his stead Gordon Foster (an employee of El Paso National Bank) and Conroy (a director of State National) as CEO. Azar asked Farah to stand down and told him of assurances by the lenders that they would bankrupt and padlock the company. Azar said he (Azar) believed there was no other way to save FMC and that the election of Gordon Foster and Conroy was the only way to prevent FMC's bankruptcy. Farah testified he believed what Azar and Donohoe had told him and that after talking to Azar, "I went to the board meeting, nominated Mr. Conroy to be chief executive officer and Mr. Gordon Foster to be Chairman."

Gordon Foster and Conroy were unanimously elected as nominated. Azar testified that his feelings for Conroy had not changed. Gordon Foster testified that in his opinion, in spite of reservations, Conroy was the only one available who could assume the position. The lenders agreed not to deem Conroy's election as an event of default. . . .

On November 10, 1977, the board passed a resolution calling for Farah's resignation as a director. Although Farah and Azar dissented, they both soon resigned. In January, 1978, Farah gave notice of a proxy fight that he was preparing in order to elect a slate of directors at the March board meeting whereby he could be reinstated as CEO. . . .

In January, 1978, FMC's financial condition was critical. At this time, the lenders determined that they were no longer willing to finance FMC's day-to-day operations although they did want to maintain some type of a long-term loan. FMC's short-term debts were soon to be due. Prior to Farah's return, the lenders had decided that the loan would be restructured whereby the management change clause would be deleted if: (1) FMC repaid the short-term debt by the middle of February, 1978; and (2) the long-term debt were substantially reduced and prepaid through third party accounts receivable financing. These conditions were met and the way was paved for Farah's return as CEO. The restructuring document originally contained a release for lender liability. When discovered by FMC, it was deleted. . . .

[Farah returned as CEO and successfully "turned FMC around."] After his return, he reduced selling and administrative costs, disposed of unusable inventory to generate working capital, expanded international sales and regenerated employee, supplier and retailer confidence in FMC and its products. Since Farah's return to management, FMC has consistently experienced an increase in sales and profits and has regained its position as an effective competitor with other manufacturers of apparel. . . .

FMC's cause of action for fraud focuses upon the March 22 letter and the statements made by Donohoe to Farah and other board members on March 23 of bankruptcy and padlocking if Farah were elected as CEO. The evidence is legally and factually sufficient, albeit conflicting, that on March 21 the lenders had either decided not to declare a default which would result in FMC's bankruptcy or reached no decision on the matter. Neither position was conveyed to the board. Regardless of the position taken, the "warnings" (representations) made in the letter and by Donohoe are characterized by FMC as false threats constituting fraud. . . .

FMC is entitled to a claim of fraud for injuries arising from a promise which was not intended to be performed as opposed to a promise which may have been intended to be performed but which was later unperformed. As previously stated, the representations made amounted to more than a mere opinion, judgment, probability or expectation on the part of the lenders. . . .

As a matter of law, FMC has established a cause of action for fraud. The evidence is legally and factually sufficient to support the jury's finding thereon. . . .

FMC's cause of action for duress focuses upon the March 22 letter, the statements made by Donohoe to Farah and other board members on March 23, and the lenders preventing the election of Wood and Jaeger as directors. The most difficult question posed by State National is whether as a matter of law FMC has established a cause of action for duress whereby it may recover damages.

State National advances five reasons why FMC has no legal basis for an actionable claim of duress. First, it asserts that FMC undertook no new obligation to any lender under duress. In this regard, it is asserted none of the lenders received any undue or unjust benefit that can or should be recovered by FMC.

. . . The second reason states that there is no duress from warnings about enforcing or about the consequences of enforcing contractual rights. The third states that there is no duress when there is no imminent harm or when adequate means of protection are available from the courts. . . .

Its fourth reason states that FMC's claim of vulnerability to duress cannot be based upon pre-existing financial difficulties for which FMC was responsible. . . .

Its fifth reason states that the opinions expressed by the lenders as to indirect changes in management, or as to the personal liability of the directors (Azar) for FMC's bankruptcy upon default, do not constitute duress. . . .

[The court rejected each of these arguments. The banks accrued an unjust benefit merely by their efforts to insure that FMC would be managed by those who had been previously approved. The banks' representations were false threats, not mere warnings about enforcing contractual rights. Donohoe's threat to bankrupt and padlock FMC constituted imminent harm. The claim of duress did not rest on FMC's preexisting financial difficulties but rather on the lenders' threats. Opinions about indirect management changes constituted duress because the lenders viewed the management change clause as permitting them to veto the election of board members who would allow Farah to exercise indirect control.]

As a matter of law, FMC has established a cause of action for duress. The evidence is legally and factually sufficient to support the jury's finding thereon. . . .

[The court then addressed the claim of tortious interference with contract.]

Three reasons are asserted by State National in support of its position that FMC has no legal basis for an actionable claim of interference. The first reason states that the lenders were legally justified and privileged to issue warnings based upon the exercise of contractual rights or upon a financial interest. The second states that there is no evidence showing an intent by the lenders to harm FMC. . . .

A justifiable business interest does not grant absolute privilege to interfere with a contractual relationship between others. *Frank Coulson, Inc.-Buick v. General Motors Corporation,* 488 F.2d 202, 206 (5th Cir. 1974). In determining the propriety of interference, the court in *Coulson* noted that various factors must be weighed. It stated:

> Various important factors have been identified, however, which relate to an appraisal of the private interests of the parties involved as well as to a consideration of the social utility of these private interests. The principal issue thus becomes whether the social benefits derived in permitting acts of intervention outweigh the harm to be expected therefrom.

. . . Interference requires only that acts be done willfully and intentionally. This does not require that the acts be shown to have been undertaken with an intent to harm. . . . FMC proved a prima facie case of interference by legally sufficient evidence. There is also legally sufficient evidence that acts of interference were undertaken without just cause or excuse.

As its third reason asserted to support the proposition that FMC has no legal basis for an actionable claim of interference, State National argues that there is no evidence of interference with an existing or reasonably probable future contract or business relation. Admittedly, actionable interference has traditionally been found to fall within one of these two categories.

The central theme of FMC's case is that the lenders interfered with FMC's own business relations and protected rights. Although the lenders may have been acting to exercise legitimate legal rights or to protect justifiable business interests, their conduct failed to comport with the standards of fair play. Upon consideration of the private interests of the parties and of the social utility thereof, the social benefits derived from permitting the lenders' interference are clearly outweighed by the harm to be expected therefrom.

In view of the foregoing principles, the evidence is legally sufficient that the lenders interfered with FMC's business relations, its election of directors and officers and its protected rights. FMC was entitled to have its affairs managed by competent directors and officers who would maintain a high degree of undivided loyalty to the company. . . .

The evidence is factually sufficient that the interference compelled the election of directors and officers whose particular business judgment and inexperience and whose divided loyalty proximately resulted in injury to FMC. The interference by the lenders was done willfully, intentionally and without just cause or excuse. As a matter of law, FMC has established a cause of action for interference. The evidence is legally and factually sufficient to support the jury's finding thereon.

[The court then addressed the issue of whether the lenders' actions proximately caused the damages.]

Contrary to the arguments of State National, the evidence is legally and factually sufficient that the lenders proximately caused the actions of the board both on and after March 23. Azar was recognized as the swing vote. The evidence is legally and factually sufficient that the lenders caused: Azar's alteration of his position which had been to support Farah's return as CEO; Conroy's election as CEO; Farah's removal as board chairman; Gordon Foster's election to such position; and the non-election of Wood and Jaeger as directors. The evidence is legally and factually sufficient that, after March 23, the lenders proximately caused: the election of Williams, Jaynes and Pulley as directors; the hiring of the Grisanti and Galef firm as a consultant to FMC; and the sale of assets at auction.

According to State National, the lenders were not involved in FMC's operations. First, it argues that any damages sustained as result of the events on or after March 23 are attributable solely to the problems generated during FMC's prior management. Second, it maintains that none of the management decisions rendered by the board after March 23 were dictated by the lenders. Thus, it cannot be liable for any damages resulting from such decisions. It concludes that FMC's performance during the year in controversy was the product of various "inseparably entwined" circumstances unrelated to any lender. Despite such contentions, there is evidence that the elements of proximate cause (cause in fact and foreseeability) exist. The acts of the lenders related to the events of March 23 set in motion a chain of foreseeable events from which FMC sustained injury and for which State National may be held accountable. . . .

*QUESTIONS AND COMMENTS*

1. This case applies several different theories, including a tort theory of interference with contract, to establish the liability of the bank to its borrower. Traditional elements of tortious interference with contract include: (1) the existence of a valid contract or prospective contract; (2) defendant's knowledge of the contract or prospective contract; (3) improper interference with the contract by the defendant; and (4) damages proximately caused by the interference. See Restatement (Second) of Torts §§766-766B (1979). As to what constitutes an improper interference, the Restatement has the following advice:

> [i]n determining whether an actor's conduct in intentionally interfering with a contract or a prospective contractual relation of another is improper or not, consideration is given to the following factors: (a) the nature of the actor's conduct, (b) the actor's motive, (c) the interests of the other with which the actor's conduct interferes, (d) the interests sought to be advanced by the actor, (e) the social interests in protecting the freedom of action of the actor and the contractual interests of the other, (f) the proximity or remoteness of the actor's conduct to the interference and (g) the relations between the parties.

Id. §767.

2. All did not go smoothly for Farah Manufacturing Co. in the wake of this decision. After a period of renewed profitability, the company suspended dividend payments and laid off approximately 1,000 El Paso workers in 1986. In 1988 William Farah replaced his son as president, thus becoming chairman, chief executive officer and president. In 1989 Farah retired as president and chief executive officer. By 1990, as the company suffered continuing losses, Farah attempted another comeback, seeking to unseat a majority of the board of directors and resume the duties of chief executive officer. But Farah lost the contest and was himself ousted as a director, a majority of the shareholders apparently believing the claims of incumbent managers that Farah's own mismanagement was a major cause of more than $40 million in losses for the company's domestic operations.

3. Other than the misrepresentation regarding their intention to declare the loan in default if Mr. Farah were reelected, did the banks do anything wrongful? If they had been truthful with the borrower, would the banks have been within their rights to insist that the loan be declared in default if Mr. Farah were reelected?

4. What was the contract or prospective contract with which the banks interfered?

5. This case apparently stands for the proposition that a bank cannot

threaten to exercise rights under a loan agreement unless it actually intends to carry through with the threat if its demands are not met. Is this a realistic duty to impose on banks? Aren't threats to exercise legal rights standard procedure when two parties are at odds?

6. A bank provides a loan to a merchant for the purchase of inventory. The loan agreement contains a provision allowing the bank to accelerate the loan at will if it concludes that its security is diminished. The agreement provides further that the bank's written notification that its security has been diminished "shall be conclusive and unreviewable as between the parties." The bank's president reads in the local business press that the borrower is "poorly managed" and that customers are "losing interest" in the borrower's "old-fashioned approach to retailing." The president, believing that the loan is insecure, directs that the bank exercise its rights under the acceleration clause. It later turns out that the story in the local press was completely untrue and that the borrower was doing better than ever at the time the loan was accelerated, but that because of the acceleration the borrower was forced to undergo significant expenses in obtaining alternative financing. Does the borrower have recourse? Under what theory?

7. What policies is the court serving in this decision? Do you detect a desire to ensure that corporations are served by competent management with undivided loyalties? If so, is that not properly a subject for substantive corporate law rather than for a tort action for interference with contract?

8. Professor Fischel attacks the holding in Farah as "indefensible":

> The lenders were not behaving opportunistically—that is, they were not trying to extract from the borrowers a benefit for which they had not originally bargained. On the contrary, the banks' actions were clearly contemplated by the management change clause, which was designed for precisely the contingency in which it was used.

Fischel, The Economics of Lender Liability, 99 Yale L.J. 131, 145 (1989). Do you agree?

## Kham & Nate's Shoes No. 2, Inc. v. First Bank of Whiting

*908 F.2d 1351 (7th Cir. 1990)*

EASTERBROOK, Circuit Judge.

Kham & Nate's Shoes No. 2, Inc., ran four retail shoe stores in Chicago. It has been in bankruptcy since 1984, operating as a debtor in possession. First Bank of Whiting, one of Kham & Nate's creditors, appeals from the order confirming its plan of reorganization. This order not only reduces the Bank's secured claim to unsecured status but also allows Khamolaw Beard and Nathaniel Parker, the debtor's principals, to retain their equity interests despite the firm's inability to pay its creditors in full. The bankruptcy judge subordinated the Bank's claim after finding that it behaved "inequitably," and he allowed Beard and Parker to retain their interests on the theory that their guarantees of new loans to be made as part of the reorganization are "new value."

### I

[The bank had extended credit to the debtor since 1981. In 1983 the debtor, faced with cash flow problems, asked for additional funds. Because the debtor owed $440,000 in taxes, the bank insisted that any new credit have priority in repayment over the tax liability. Debtor filed a reorganization petition under chapter 11 of the bankruptcy code, and the bankruptcy judge confirmed that new advances from the bank would have priority. The bank then gave the debtor a $300,000 line of credit, under a loan agreement which provided for cancellation on five days' notice and which added that "nothing provided herein shall constitute a waiver of the right of the Bank to terminate financing at any time."]

[The debtor drew $75,000 on the line of credit. The bank mailed the debtor a letter on February 29, 1985, warning that it would make no new advances after March 7, but it continued to honor draws on the letters of credit it had issued to the debtor prior to the bankruptcy petition. In 1985 the debtor paid off $10,000 on the post-bankruptcy line of credit, but it made no further payments.]

[In 1988 the bankruptcy judge confirmed a new plan of reorganization for the debtor that subordinated the bank's claim on the ground that it had acted inequitably to the debtor in terminating the line of credit.]

Subordination matters only for the $65,000 outstanding on advances under the line of credit authorized by the financing order. Section 510(c) lets bankruptcy judges subordinate claims but does not provide criteria for the exercise of this power. Absence of statutory criteria commits the subject to the courts, to be worked out in the common law fashion. Equitable subordination usually is a response to efforts by corporate insiders to convert their equity interests into secured debt in anticipation of bankruptcy. Courts require the insiders to return to their position at the end of the line. . . . Bank is neither an insider nor a person seeking to collect a penalty, and it has not delayed without justification. It contributed new value under a contract, and it wants no more than the priority Judge Toles promised as the lure.

Cases subordinating the claims of creditors that dealt at arm's length with the debtor are few and far between. Benjamin v. Diamond, 563 F.2d 692 (5th Cir. 1977) (*Mobile Steel Co.*), suggests that subordination depends on a combination of inequitable conduct, unfair advantage to the creditor, and injury to other creditors. Debtor submits that conduct may be "unfair" and "inequitable" for this purpose even though the creditor complies with all contractual requirements, but we are not willing to embrace a rule that requires participants in commercial transactions not only to keep their contracts but also do "more"—just how much more resting in the discretion of a bankruptcy judge assessing the situation years later. Contracts specify the duties of the parties to each other, and each may exercise the privileges it obtained. Banks sometimes bind themselves to make loans (commitment letters and letters of credit have this effect) and sometimes reserve the right to terminate further advances. Courts may not convert one form of contract into the other after the fact, without raising the cost of credit or jeopardizing its availability. Unless pacts are enforced according to their terms, the institution of contract, with all the advantages private negotiation and agreement brings, is jeopardized.

"Inequitable conduct" in commercial life means breach *plus* some advantage-taking, such as the star who agrees to act in a motion picture and then, after $20 million has been spent, sulks in his dressing room until the contract has been renegotiated. Firms that have negotiated contracts are entitled to enforce them to the letter, even to the great discomfort of their trading partners, without being mulcted for lack of "good faith." Although courts often refer to the obligation of good faith that exists in every contractual relation, this is not an invitation to the court to decide whether one party ought to have exercised privileges expressly reserved in the document. "Good faith" is a compact reference to an implied undertaking not to take opportunistic advantage in a way that could not have been contemplated at the time of drafting, and which therefore was not resolved explicitly by the parties. When the contract is silent, principles of good faith—such as the UCC's standard of honesty in fact, UCC §1-201(19), and the reasonable expectations of the trade, UCC §2-103(b) (a principle applicable, however, *only* to "merchants," which Bank is not)—fill the gap. They do not block use of terms that actually appear in the contract.

We do not doubt the force of the proverb that the letter killeth, while the spirit giveth life. Literal implementation of unadorned language may destroy the essence of the venture. Few people pass out of childhood without learning fables about genies, whose wickedly literal interpretation of their "masters'" wishes always lead to calamity. Yet knowledge that literal enforcement means some mismatch between the parties' expectation and the outcome does not imply a general duty of "kindness" in performance, or of judicial oversight into whether a party had "good cause" to act as it did. Parties to a contract are not each others' fiduciaries; they are not bound to treat customers with the same consideration reserved for their families. Any attempt to add an overlay of "just cause"—as the bankruptcy judge effectively did—to the exercise of contractual privileges would reduce commercial certainty and breed costly litigation. The UCC's requirement of "honesty in fact" stops well short of the requirements the bankruptcy judge thought incident to contractual performance. . . .

Bank did not break a promise at a time Debtor was especially vulnerable, then use the costs and delay of obtaining legal enforcement of the contract as levers to a better deal. Debtor and Bank signed a contract expressly allowing the Bank to cease making further advances. The $300,000 was the maximum loan, not a guarantee. The Bank exercised its contractual privilege after loaning Debtor $75,000; it made a clean break and did not demand improved terms. It had the right to do this for any reason satisfactory to itself. . . . The principle is identical to that governing a contract for employment at will: the employer may sack its employee for any reason except one forbidden by law, and it need not show "good cause."

Although Bank's decision left Debtor scratching for other sources of credit, Bank did not create Debtor's need for funds, and it was not contractually obliged to satisfy its customer's desires. The Bank was entitled to advance its own interests, and it did not need to put the interests of Debtor and Debtor's other creditors first. To the extent K.M.C., Inc. v. Irving Trust Co., 757 F.2d 752, 759-63 (6th Cir. 1986), holds that a bank must loan more money or give more advance notice of termination than its contract requires, we respectfully disagree. First Bank of Whiting is not an eleemosynary institution. It need not throw good money after bad, even if other persons would catch the lucre.

Debtor stresses, and the bankruptcy judge found, that Bank would have been secure in making additional advances. Perhaps so, but the contract did not oblige Bank to make all advances for which it could be assured of payment. Ex post assessments of a lender's security are no basis on which to deny it the negotiated place in the queue. Risk must be assessed ex ante by lenders, rather than ex post by judges. If a loan seems secure at the time, lenders will put up the money; their own interests are served by making loans bound to be repaid. What is more, the bankruptcy judge's finding that Bank would have been secure in making additional advances is highly questionable. The judgment of the market vindicates Bank. If more credit would have enabled Debtor to flourish, then other lenders should have been willing to supply it. Yet no one else, not even the SBA, would advance additional money to Debtor.

Both the bankruptcy and district judges characterized as inequitable Bank's decision in December 1983 not to extend additional credit unless Kham & Nate's filed a petition in bankruptcy (or obtained a guarantee from the SBA). According to the courts, this forced the firm into bankruptcy; having propelled it there, Bank was obliged to help. This is insufficient on two levels—first because filing for bankruptcy often helps rather than injures the firm (the automatic stay keeps the wolves and tax collectors from the door), and second because linking an offer of extra credit to a bankruptcy petition does not "force" a firm to file one. A bank may insist on security before lending; bankruptcy followed by an order under §364 was one device for providing it. If Kham & Nate's Shoes did not like the option, it was entitled to shop around. Conditioning new money on higher security no more obliges a Bank to "lend a helping hand" (in excess of contractual promises) than does setting a high rate of interest or taking security in receivables, other ways to deal with a lower probability of repayment.

Although Debtor contends, and the bankruptcy judge found, that Bank's termination of advances frustrated Debtor's efforts to secure credit from other sources, and so propelled it down hill, this is legally irrelevant so long as Bank kept its promises. It is factually questionable too. Why would Bank shoot itself in the foot—spurning what the bankruptcy judge thought to be sure repayment while leaving an outstanding balance of $164,000 that it could not expect to collect if Debtor collapsed? At all events, Debtor could have asked for further orders under §364 making potential lenders secure and ensuring a flow of credit; it did not. It could have asked Judge Toles to clarify his financing order, so that other creditors would know that Bank's priority was limited to $75,000; it did not. A straightforward inference is that even high priority would not have induced other institutions to put up money—just as high priority did not make Bank feel sufficiently secure.

The only breach on Bank's part that Debtor has identified is a technical one: the contract calls for five calendar days' telephonic and written notice, while Bank gave only written notice. (An officer of Bank testified that he gave telephonic notice, but the bankruptcy court's contrary finding is not clearly erroneous.) This offense was trivial. Clauses requiring notice by telephone are designed to ensure that the borrower has five *real* days to find a new lender, that delays in the mail do not diminish the time available. So Bank was obliged to extend credit until five days after Debtor received actual notice—that is, five days after the letter arrived. Bank mailed the letter February 29, 1984, terminating advances as of March 7. If the letter took two days to arrive, Debtor still had five days between notice and the cut-off. If Debtor got less, then an award would be in order for the loss attributable to the inadequate notice. It is safe to assume that the damages would be substantially less than the difference between the value of the $65,000 balance with superpriority and the amount that Bank will receive if the loan is lumped with other unsecured credit. Equitable subordination under §510(c) is not a device to magnify the damages available for inconsequential breaches of contract. . . .

*QUESTIONS AND COMMENTS*

1. *Kham & Nate's Shoes* presents another possible danger for lending institutions: that their claims will be subordinated to the claims of other creditors of a bankrupt borrower. The seminal case on equitable subordination is Pepper v. Litton, 308 U.S. 295 (1939). This was a challenge by a preferred stockholder of a bankrupt corporation to a debt claim against the corporation by its dominant shareholder. The preferred stockholder claimed that prior to bankruptcy the controlling shareholder had caused the corporation to confess judgment in a lawsuit brought against it by the controlling shareholder, thus giving the controlling shareholder a judgment lien that stood before the claim of the preferred shareholder. The Supreme Court agreed with the preferred shareholder that the majority shareholder had acted wrongfully, concluded that equitable subordination was proper under the circumstances, and ordered that the claims of the controlling shareholder be subordinated to those of preferred shareholders. See also Taylor v. Standard Gas & Electric Co., 306 U.S. 307 (1939).

2. The equitable powers of the bankruptcy court to subordinate claims are set forth in 11 U.S.C. §510(c):

> [N]otwithstanding [other provisions], after notice and hearing, the court may—(1) under principles of equitable subordination, subordinate for purposes of distribution all or part of an allowed claim to all or part of another allowed claim or all or part of an allowed interest to all or part of another allowed interest. . . .

As Judge Easterbrook observes in the excerpted case, §510(c) allows bankruptcy judges to subordinate claims but provides no standards to guide the exercise of that power. In the absence of statutory guidance, the courts must formulate their own standards in a common law fashion. On the potential application of equitable subordination doctrine to bank claims, see Chaitman, The Equitable Subordination of Bank Claims, 39 Bus. Law. 1561 (1984).

3. Can the approach to the lender's obligation of good faith found in this case be reconciled with the views expressed in cases such as Brown v. AVEMCO, Alaska Statebank v. Fairco, First National Bank in Libby v. Twombly, and State National Bank v. Farah Manufacturing Co.?

4. Assume that a bank provides a loan to O'Dooley & Co., the loan documents expressly providing that the bank can accelerate the loan if for any reason it deems itself insecure. Now the bank asserts that it is insecure and demands that directors loyal to the bank be appointed or it will accelerate the loan. Facing the prospect of bankruptcy the directors of O'Dooley & Co. go along, resigning and electing nominees of the

bank. Unfortunately, the bank's chosen directors prove incompetent and O'Dooley & Co. is forced into bankruptcy after all. The evidence shows that competent directors might have been able to rescue the company and that the former directors probably were competent. Should the bank's claim in bankruptcy be subordinated to those of the common stockholders of O'Dooley & Co.? Would it make a difference if the bank were a secured lender with a mortgage on certain defined O'Dooley & Co. real property?

5. Assume that provisions of a bank loan give the bank the following powers over the borrower: joint control of all the debtor's bank accounts, the right to place its designee on the board of directors, the right to have a bank employee on the premises participating in the day-to-day operations of the borrower with complete veto powers over any items or matters whatsoever, the right to require liquidation of all assets of the borrower, the right to set salaries of officers and directors, and the right to make a final determination of any dispute between borrower and lender. Are these powers sufficient to justify equitable subordination of the bank's claim against the debtor in bankruptcy based on the loan documents alone? See In re T. E. Mercer Trucking Co., 16 Bankr. 176 (Bankr. D. Tex. 1981).

6. Does a bank face any risk if it obtains additional security from a debtor in default, and the debtor goes into bankruptcy? The Bankruptcy Code provides that transfers to creditors may generally be avoided—that is, treated as ineffective—by the bankruptcy trustee if made within a 90-day period prior to the filing for bankruptcy while the debtor was insolvent, and if the consequence of the transfer is to make the transferee better off than it would have been under bankruptcy liquidation proceedings if the transfer had not been made. 11 U.S.C. §547(b)(4)(A). Transfers may also be avoided if made within a year prior to the filing of the petition and if the transferee was an "insider." 11 U.S.C. §547(b)(4)(B). The Bankruptcy Code provides in pertinent part that with respect to corporations and partnerships an "insider" includes a "person in control of the debtor." 11 U.S.C. §101(30). When a creditor comes to exercise such influence as to "control" the debtor is a matter for interpretation.

## Connor v. Great Western Savings & Loan Association

***69 Cal. 2d 850, 447 P.2d 609, 73 Cal. Rptr. 369 (1968)***

TRAYNOR, Chief Justice.

These consolidated appeals are from a judgment of nonsuit in favor of defendant Great Western Savings and Loan Association in two actions consolidated for trial.

Plaintiffs in each action purchased single-family homes in a residential tract development known as Weathersfield, located on tracts 1158,

1159, and 1160 in Ventura County. Thereafter their homes suffered serious damage from cracking caused by ill-designed foundations that could not withstand the expansion and contraction of adobe soil. Plaintiffs accordingly sought rescission or damages from the various parties involved in the tract development.

Holders of promissory notes secured by second deeds of trust on the homes filed cross-complaints, alleging that their security had been impaired by the damage to the homes. They sought to impose liens on any recovery plaintiffs might obtain from other defendants.

There was abundant evidence that defendant Conejo Valley Development Company, which built and sold the homes, negligently constructed them without regard to soil conditions prevalent at the site. Specifically, it laid slab foundations on adobe soil without taking proper precautions recommended to it by soil engineers. When the adobe soil expanded during rainstorms two years later, the foundations cracked and their movement generated further damage.

In addition to seeking damages from Conejo, plaintiffs sought to hold Great Western liable, either on the ground that its participation in the tract development brought it into a joint venture or a joint enterprise with Conejo, which served to make it vicariously liable, or on the ground that it breached an independent duty of care to plaintiffs. . . .

A joint venture exists when there is "an agreement between the parties under which they have a community of interest, that is, a joint interest, in a common business undertaking, and understanding as to the sharing of profits and losses, and a right of joint control." Although the evidence establishes that Great Western and Conejo combined their property, skill, and knowledge to carry out the tract development, that each shared in the control of the development, that each anticipated receiving substantial profits therefrom, and that they cooperated with each other in the development, there is no evidence of a community or joint interest in the undertaking. Great Western participated as a buyer and seller of land and lender of funds, and Conejo participated as a builder and seller of homes. Although the profits of each were dependent on the overall success of the development, neither was to share in the profits or the losses that the other might realize or suffer. Although each received substantial payments as seller, lender, or borrower, neither had an interest in the payments received by the other. Under these circumstances, no joint venture existed. . . .

Even though Great Western is not vicariously liable as a joint venturer for the negligence of Conejo, there remains the question of its liability for its own negligence. Great Western voluntarily undertook business relationships with South Gate and Conejo to develop the Weathersfield tract and to develop a market for the tract houses in which prospective buyers would be directed to Great Western for their financing. In undertaking these relationships, Great Western became much more than a lender content to lend money at interest on the security of real property. It became an active participant in a home construction enterprise. It had the right to exercise extensive control of the enterprise. Its financing, which made the enterprise possible, took on ramifications beyond the domain of the usual money lender. It received not only interest on its construction loans, but also substantial fees for making them, a 20 percent capital gain for "warehousing" the land, and protection from loss of profits in the event individual home buyers sought permanent financing elsewhere.

Since the value of the security for the construction loans and thereafter the security for the permanent financing loans depended on the construction of sound homes, Great Western was clearly under a duty of care to its shareholders to exercise its powers of control over the enterprise to prevent the construction of defective homes. Judged by the standards governing nonsuits, it negligently failed to discharge that duty. It knew or should have known that the developers were inexperienced, undercapitalized, and operating on a dangerously thin capitalization. It therefore knew or should have known that damage from attempts to cut corners in construction was a risk reasonably to be foreseen. It knew or should have known of the expansive soil problems, and yet it failed to require soil tests, to examine foundation plans, to recommend changes in the prepackaged plans and specifications, or to recommend changes in the foundations during construction. It made no attempt to discover gross structural defects that it could have discovered by reasonable inspection and that it would have required Conejo to remedy. It relied for protection solely upon building inspectors with whom it had had no experience to enforce a building code with the provisions of which it was ignorant. The crucial question remains whether Great Western also owed a duty to the home buyers in the Weathersfield tract and was therefore also negligent toward them.

The fact that Great Western was not in privity of contract with any of the plaintiffs except as a lender does not absolve it of liability for its own negligence in creating an unreasonable risk of harm to them. "Privity of contract is not necessary to establish the existence of a duty to exercise ordinary care not to injure another, but such duty may arise out of a voluntarily assumed relationship if public policy dictates the existence of such a duty." The basic tests for determining the existence of such a duty are clearly set forth in Biakanja v. Irving, [1958], 49 Cal. 2d 647, 650, 320 P.2d 16, 19, as follows:

> The determination whether in a specific case the defendant will be held liable to a third person not in privity is a matter of policy and involves the balancing of various factors, among which are [1] the extent to which the transaction was intended to affect the plaintiff, [2] the foreseeability of harm to him, [3] the degree of certainty that the plaintiff suffered injury,

> [4] the closeness of the connection between the defendant's conduct and the injury suffered, [5] the moral blame attached to the defendant's conduct, and [6] the policy of preventing future harm.

In the light of the foregoing tests Great Western was clearly under a duty to the buyers of the homes to exercise reasonable care to protect them from damages caused by major structural defects.

[1] Great Western's transactions were intended to affect the plaintiffs significantly.

The success of Great Western's transactions with South Gate and Conejo depended entirely upon the ability of the parties to induce plaintiffs to buy homes in the Weathersfield tract and to finance the purchases with funds supplied by Great Western. Great Western's agreement to supply funds to Conejo to build homes in return for a 5 percent construction loan fee and 6.6 percent interest, was on condition that a sufficient number of persons first made commitments to buy homes. Great Western agreed to warehouse land for Conejo on the understanding that the land would be used for a residential subdivision. Great Western also stipulated that advances from its construction loans would be used by Conejo to exercise repurchase options, thereby affording Great Western the opportunity for a $30,000 capital gain. Finally, Great Western took steps to have Conejo channel buyers of homes to its doors for loans, extracting a 1 percent loan fee from Conejo in the process.

[2] Great Western could reasonably have foreseen the risk of harm to plaintiffs.

Great Western knew or should have known that neither Goldberg nor Brown had ever developed a tract of similar magnitude. Great Western knew or should have known that Conejo was operating on a dangerously thin capitalization, creating a readily foreseeable risk that it would be driven to cutting corners in construction. That risk was enlarged still further by the additional pressures on Conejo ensuing from its onerous burdens as a borrower from Great Western.

[3] It is certain that plaintiffs suffered injury.

Counsel stipulated that each of the plaintiff homeowners, if called, would testify that their respective homes sustained damage in varying degrees "of the character of which we have been concerned in this action." Sufficient evidence was presented to show by way of example the existence of damage to the homes and therefore injury to plaintiffs. Under the terms of the pretrial order, the extent of each plaintiff's injury is to be litigated in further proceedings after the question of Great Western's liability is determined.

[4] The injury suffered by plaintiffs was closely connected with Great Western's conduct.

Great Western not only financed the development of the Weathersfield tract but controlled the course it would take. Had it exercised reasonable care in the exercise of its control, it would have discovered that the pre-packaged plans purchased by Conejo required correction and would have withheld financing until the plans were corrected.

[5] Substantial moral blame attaches to Great Western's conduct.

The value of the security for Great Western's construction loans as well as the projected security for its long-term loans to plaintiffs depended on the soundness of construction, Great Western failed of its obligation to its own shareholders when it failed to exercise reasonable care to preclude major structural defects in the homes whose construction it financed and controlled. It also failed of its obligation to the buyers, the more so because it was well aware that the usual buyer of a home is ill-equipped with experience or financial means to discern such structural defects. Moreover a home is not only a major investment for the usual buyer but also the only shelter he has. Hence it becomes doubly important to protect him against structural defects that could prove beyond his capacity to remedy.

[6] The admonitory policy of the law of torts calls for the imposition of liability on Great Western for its conduct in this case. Rules that tend to discourage misconduct are particularly appropriate when applied to an established industry.

By all the foregoing tests, Great Western had a duty to exercise reasonable care to prevent the construction and sale of seriously defective homes to plaintiffs. The countervailing considerations invoked by Great Western and amici curiae are that the imposition of the duty in question upon a lender will increase housing costs, drive marginal builders out of business, and decrease total housing at a time of great need. These are conjectural claims. In any event, there is no enduring social utility in fostering the construction of seriously defective homes. If reliable construction is the norm, the recognition of a duty on the part of tract financiers to home buyers should not materially increase the cost of housing or drive small builders out of business. If existing sanctions are inadequate, imposition of a duty at the point of effective financial control of tract building will insure responsible building practices. Moreover, in either event the losses of family savings invested in seriously defective homes would be devastating economic blows if no redress were available.

Defendants contend, however, that the question of their liability is one of policy, and hence should be resolved only by the Legislature after a marshalling of relevant economic and social data. There is no assurance, however, that the Legislature will undertake such a task, even though tract financing grows apace. In the absence of actual or prospective legislative policy, the court is free to resolve the case before it, and indeed must resolve it in terms of common law. . . .

Mosk, Justice (dissenting).

I dissent.

The evidence is overwhelming, and the majority concede, that as between the lender of funds and the tract developer there was no agency, no joint venture, no joint enterprise. It is clear there was merely a lender-borrower relationship. Nevertheless, the majority here hold the lender of funds vicariously liable to third parties for the negligence of the borrower. This result is (a) unsupported by statute or precedent; (b) inconsistent with accepted principles of tort law; (c) likely to be productive of untoward social consequences. . . .

## *QUESTIONS AND COMMENTS*

1. Connor is an important early precedent for the imposition of lender liability in favor of third parties who have no history of dealings with the depository institution. The overarching principle, with respect to liability to third parties, is that of control: Depository institutions may be liable in some circumstances when they move beyond the role of mere lenders and begin to exercise a significant degree of control over the borrower's activities.

2. Despite its importance as a pathbreaking case in the area of lender liability, *Connor* itself has not received a favorable reception in subsequent law. Most later cases have distinguished *Connor* on the ground that the lender in that case engaged in various nonlender activities. See, e.g., Wierzbicki v. Alaska Mutual Savings Bank, 630 P.2d 998 (Alaska 1981). The California legislature limited *Connor* by adopting Cal. Civ. Code Ann. §3434, which provides that

> [a] lender who makes a loan of money, the proceeds of which are used . . . to finance the . . . improvement of real or personal property for sale or lease to others, shall not be held liable to third persons for any loss or damage occasioned by any defect in the real or personal property . . . unless such loss or damage is a result of an act of the lender outside the scope of the activities of a lender of money or unless the lender has been a party to misrepresentations with respect to such real or personal property.

3. What was the basis of Great Western's liability? That it had sought to evade limits on loans on unimproved property by a "warehousing" arrangement? That Great Western "owned" the land under the warehousing arrangement, even if in substance the land stood as security for a loan? That Great Western knew or should have known that Conejo was inexperienced and undercapitalized? That Great Western failed to examine the foundation plans? That it planned to earn fees and interest from loans to purchasers of the properties? That its inspectors visited the property regularly to ensure that the plans were being followed and that money was disbursed only for completed work?

4. A bank advances a $10 million construction loan to Mason, a developer. Does the bank subject itself to liability if its officers visit the site on a regular basis to ensure that plans are being followed and work done properly? If the bank fails to make such inspections, won't this constitute a breach of the duty of care to shareholders by the bank's officers and directors? What if during such an inspection the bank fails to notice a dangerous condition that results in the death of a passerby?

5. Would *Connor* have been decided the same way if the project was for the construction of a large office building and the purchaser was a sophisticated building management firm? Should it?

6. Justice Traynor rejects as "conjectural" the arguments that imposing liability on lenders such as Great Western would increase housing costs, drive marginal builders out of existence, and decrease the total housing stock. What do you think is the likely impact of the ruling on California housing?

7. After rejecting the above arguments as conjectural, Justice Traynor conjectures that "if reliable construction is the norm, the recognition of a duty on the part of tract financiers to home buyers should not materially increase the cost of housing or drive small builders out of business." Do you agree? What about his statement that "[i]f existing sanctions are inadequate, imposition of a duty at the point of effective financial control of tract building will insure responsible building practices." Do you agree? What about the possibility that in order to avoid potential liability banks might disclaim powers of oversight and control over real estate developers, thus increasing the probability of defective housing? Finally, what about Justice Traynor's comment that "there is no enduring social utility in fostering the construction of seriously defective homes." This is incontrovertible, but doesn't Justice Traynor express a somewhat narrow view of the social utility of a rule protecting lenders against liability in these circumstances?

8. Do you think the bank got what it bargained for in this case? Even though it may have participated in some of the business decisions, did the bank's financial interest ever become that of an equity holder (a holder of a residual claim on assets and income from a project) rather than a holder of debt (a holder of a fixed claim that is entitled to be paid first before the residual equity claim is paid)? Should the bank's liability be greater if it expects to receive a share of the profits and losses as opposed to a mere payback of principal and interest?

## United States v. Fleet Factors Corp.

***901 F.2d 1550 (11th Cir. 1990), cert. denied, 111 S. Ct. 752 (1991)***

KRAVITCH, Circuit Judge:

Fleet Factors Corporation ("Fleet") brought an interlocutory appeal from the district court's denial of its motion for summary judgment in this suit by the United States to recover the cost of removing hazardous waste from a bankrupt textile facility. The district court denied summary judgment because it concluded that Fleet's activities at the facility might rise to the level of participation in management sufficient to impose liability under the Comprehensive Environmental Response Compensation and Liability Act ("CERCLA"), 42 U.S.C. §§9601-57 (1982 & West Supp. 1988), despite the statutory exemption from liability for holders of a security interest. We agree with the district court that material questions of fact remain as to the extent of Fleet's participation in the management of the facility; therefore, we affirm the denial of Fleet's summary judgment motion.

## FACTS

In 1976, Swainsboro Print Works ("SPW"), a cloth printing facility, entered into a "factoring" agreement with Fleet in which Fleet agreed to advance funds against the assignment of SPW's accounts receivable. As collateral for these advances, Fleet also obtained a security interest in SPW's textile facility and all of its equipment, inventory, and fixtures. In August, 1979, SPW filed for bankruptcy under Chapter 11. The factoring agreement between SPW and Fleet continued with court approval. In early 1981, Fleet ceased advancing funds to SPW because SPW's debt to Fleet exceeded Fleet's estimate of the value of SPW's accounts receivable. On February 27, 1981, SPW ceased operations and began to liquidate its inventory. Fleet continued to collect on the accounts receivable assigned to it under the Chapter 11 factoring agreement. In December 1981, SPW was adjudicated a bankrupt under Chapter 7 and a trustee assumed title and control of the facility.

In May 1982, Fleet foreclosed on its security interest in some of SPW's inventory and equipment, and contracted with Baldwin Industrial Liquidators ("Baldwin") to conduct an auction of the collateral. Baldwin sold the material "as is" and "in place" on June 22, 1982; the removal of the items was the responsibility of the purchasers. On August 31, 1982, Fleet allegedly contracted with Nix Riggers ("Nix") to remove the unsold equipment in consideration for leaving the premises "broom clean." Nix testified in deposition that he understood that he had been given a "free hand" by Fleet or Baldwin to do whatever was necessary at the facility to remove the machinery and equipment. Nix left the facility by the end of December, 1983.

On January 20, 1984, the Environmental Protection Agency ("EPA") inspected the facility and found 700 fifty-five gallon drums containing toxic chemicals and forty-four truckloads of material containing asbestos. The EPA incurred costs of nearly $400,000 in responding to the environmental threat at SPW. On July 7, 1987, the facility was conveyed to

Emanuel County, Georgia, at a foreclosure sale resulting from SPW's failure to pay state and county taxes.

The government sued Horowitz and Newton, the principal officers and stockholders of SPW, and Fleet to recover the cost of cleaning up the hazardous waste. The district court granted the government's summary judgment motion with respect to the liability of Horowitz and Newton for the cost of removing the hazardous waste in the drums. The government's motion with respect to Fleet's liability, and the liability of Horowitz and Newton for asbestos removal costs was denied. Fleet's motion for summary judgment was also denied. The district court, sua sponte, certified the summary judgment issues for interlocutory appeal and stayed the remaining proceedings in the case. Fleet subsequently brought this appeal challenging the court's denial of its motion for summary judgment. . . .

The Comprehensive Environmental Response Compensation and Liability Act was enacted by Congress in response to the environmental and public health hazards caused by improper disposal of hazardous wastes. The essential policy underlying CERCLA is to place the ultimate responsibility for cleaning up hazardous waste on "those responsible for problems caused by the disposal of chemical poison." Accordingly, CERCLA authorizes the federal government to clean up hazardous waste dump sites and recover the cost of the effort from certain categories of responsible parties.

The parties liable for costs incurred by the government in responding to an environmental hazard are: 1) the present owners and operators of a facility where hazardous wastes were released or are in danger of being released; 2) the owners or operators of a facility at the time the hazardous wastes were disposed; 3) the person or entity that arranged for the treatment or disposal of substances at the facility; and 4) the person or entity that transported the substances to the facility. The government contends that Fleet is liable for the response costs associated with the waste at the SPW facility as either a present owner and operator of the facility, see 42 U.S.C. §9607(a)(1), or the owner or operator of the facility at the time the wastes were disposed, see 42 U.S.C. §9607(a)(2).

The district court, as a matter of law, rejected the government's claim that Fleet was a present owner of the facility. The court, however, found a sufficient issue of fact as to whether Fleet was an owner or operator of the SPW facility at the time the wastes were disposed to warrant the denial of Fleet's motion for summary judgment. On appeal each party contests that portion of the district's court's order adverse to their respective interests. . . .

CERCLA . . . imposes liability on "any person who at the time of disposal of any hazardous substance owned or operated any . . . facility at which such hazardous substances were disposed of. . . ." 42 U.S.C. §9607(a)(2). CERCLA excludes from the definition of "owner or operator" any "person, who, without participating in the management of a . . . facility, holds indicia of ownership primarily to protect his security interest in the . . . facility." 42 U.S.C. §9601(20)(A). Fleet has the burden of establishing its entitlement to this exemption. There is no dispute that Fleet held an "indicia of ownership" in the facility through its deed of trust to SPW, and that this interest was held primarily to protect its security interest in the facility. The critical issue is whether Fleet participated in management sufficiently to incur liability under the statute.

The construction of the secured creditor exemption is an issue of first impression in the federal appellate courts. The government urges us to adopt a narrow and strictly literal interpretation of the exemption that excludes from its protection any secured creditor that participates in any manner in the management of a facility. We decline the government's suggestion because it would largely eviscerate the exemption Congress intended to afford to secured creditors. Secured lenders frequently have some involvement in the financial affairs of their debtors in order to insure that their interests are being adequately protected. To adopt the government's interpretation of the secured creditor exemption could expose all such lenders to CERCLA liability for engaging in their normal course of business.

Fleet, in turn, suggests that we adopt the distinction delineated by some district courts between permissible participation in the financial management of the facility and impermissible participation in the day-to-day or operational management of a facility. In United States v. Mirabile, the first case to suggest this interpretation, the district court granted summary judgment to the defendant creditors because their participation in the affairs of the facility was "limited to participation in financial decisions." No. 84-2280, slip op. at 3 (E.D. Pa. Sept 6, 1985) (available on WESTLAW as 1985 WL 97). The court explained "that the participation which is critical is participation in operational, production, or waste disposal activities. Mere financial ability to control waste disposal practices . . . is not . . . sufficient for the imposition of liability." *Mirabile,* No. 84-2280, slip op. at 4. The court concluded that "before a secured creditor . . . may be held liable, it must, at a minimum, participate in the day-to-day operational aspects of the site. [Here, the creditor] . . . merely foreclosed on the property after all operations had ceased and thereafter took prudent and routine steps to secure the property against further depreciation." Id. at 12.

The court below, relying on *Mirabile,* similarly interpreted the statutory language to permit secured creditors to

> provide financial assistance and general, and even isolated instances of specific, management advice to its debtors without risking CERCLA liability if the secured creditor does not participate in the day-to-day management of the business or facility either before or after the business ceases operation.

*Fleet Factors Corp.,* 724 F. Supp. at 960 (S.D. Ga. 1988). . . . Applying this standard, the trial judge concluded that from the inception of Fleet's relationship with SPW in 1976 to June 22, 1982, when Baldwin entered the facility, Fleet's activity did not rise to the level of participation in management sufficient to impose CERCLA liability. The court, however, determined that the facts alleged by the government with respect to Fleet's involvement after Baldwin entered the facility were sufficient to preclude the granting of summary judgment in favor of Fleet on this issue.

Although we agree with the district court's resolution of the summary judgment motion, we find its construction of the statutory exemption too permissive towards secured creditors who are involved with toxic waste facilities. In order to achieve the "overwhelming remedial" goal of the CERCLA statutory scheme, ambiguous statutory terms should be construed to favor liability for the costs incurred by the government in responding to the hazards at such facilities. The district court's broad interpretation of the exemption would essentially require a secured creditor to be involved in the operations of a facility in order to incur liability. This construction ignores the plain language of the exemption and essentially renders it meaningless. Individuals and entities involved in the operations of a facility are already liable as operators under the express language of section 9607(a)(2). Had Congress intended to absolve secured creditors from ownership liability, it would have done so. Instead, the statutory language chosen by Congress explicitly holds secured creditors liable if they participate in the management of a facility.

Although similar, the phrase "participating in the management" and the term "operator" are not congruent. Under the standard we adopt today, a secured creditor may incur section 9607(a)(2) liability, without being an operator, by participating in the financial management of a facility to a degree indicating a capacity to influence the corporation's treatment of hazardous wastes. It is not necessary for the secured creditor actually to involve itself in the day-to-day operations of the facility in order to be liable—although such conduct will certainly lead to the loss of the protection of the statutory exemption. Nor is it necessary for the secured creditor to participate in management decisions relating to hazardous waste. Rather, a secured creditor will be liable if its involvement with the management of the facility is sufficiently broad to support the inference that it could affect hazardous waste disposal decisions if it so chose. We, therefore, specifically reject the formulation of the secured creditor exemption suggested by the district court in *Mirabile.*

This construction of the secured creditor exemption, while less permissive than that of the trial court, is broader than that urged by the government and, therefore, should give lenders some latitude in their dealings with debtors without exposing themselves to potential liability. Nothing in our discussion should preclude a secured creditor from monitoring any aspect of a debtor's business. Likewise, a secured creditor can become involved in occasional and discrete financial decisions relating to the protection of its security interest without incurring liability.

Our interpretation of the exemption may be challenged as creating disincentives for lenders to extend financial assistance to businesses with potential hazardous waste problems and encouraging secured creditors to distance themselves from the management actions, particularly those related to hazardous wastes, of their debtors. As a result the improper treatment of hazardous wastes could be perpetuated rather than resolved. These concerns are unfounded.

Our ruling today should encourage potential creditors to investigate thoroughly the waste treatment systems and policies of potential debtors. If the treatment systems seem inadequate, the risk of CERCLA liability will be weighed into the terms of the loan agreement. Creditors, therefore, will incur no greater risk than they bargained for and debtors, aware that inadequate hazardous waste treatment will have a significant adverse impact on their loan terms, will have powerful incentives to improve their handling of hazardous wastes.

Similarly, creditors' awareness that they are potentially liable under CERCLA will encourage them to monitor the hazardous waste treatment systems and policies of their debtors and insist upon compliance with acceptable treatment standards as a prerequisite to continued and future financial support. Once a secured creditor's involvement with a facility becomes sufficiently broad that it can anticipate losing its exemption from CERCLA liability, it will have a strong incentive to address hazardous waste problems at the facility rather than studiously avoiding the investigation and amelioration of the hazard.

In *Maryland Bank & Trust Co.*, the court aptly described and weighed the competing policy interests of creditors and the government in interpreting the secured creditor exemption:

> In essence, the defendant's position would convert CERCLA into an insurance scheme for financial institutions, protecting them against possible losses due to the security of loans with polluted properties. Mortgagees, however, already have the means to protect themselves, by making prudent loans. Financial institutions are in a position to investigate and discover potential problems in their secured properties. For many lending institutions, such research is routine. CERCLA will not absolve them from responsibility for their mistakes of judgment.

632 F. Supp. at 580 (citations omitted).

We agree with the court below that the government has alleged sufficient facts to hold Fleet liable under section 9607(a)(2). From 1976 until SPW ceased printing operations on February 27, 1981, Fleet's involvement with the facility was within the parameters of the secured creditor exemption to liability. During this period, Fleet regularly advanced funds to SPW against the assignment of SPW's accounts receivable, paid and arranged for security deposits for SPW's Georgia utility services, and informed SPW that it would not advance any more money when it determined that its advanced sums exceeded the value of SPW's accounts receivable.

Fleet's involvement with SPW, according to the government, increased substantially after SPW ceased printing operations at the Georgia plant on February 27, 1981, and began to wind down its affairs. Fleet required SPW to seek its approval before shipping its goods to customers, established the price for excess inventory, dictated when and to whom the finished goods should be shipped, determined when employees should be laid off, supervised the activity of the office administrator at the site, received and processed SPW's employment and tax forms, controlled access to the facility, and contracted with Baldwin to dispose of the fixtures and equipment at SPW. These facts, if proved, are sufficient to remove Fleet from the protection of the secured creditor exemption. Fleet's involvement in the financial management of the facility was pervasive, if not complete.[13] Furthermore, the government's allegations indicate that Fleet was also involved in the operational management of the facility. Either of these allegations is sufficient as a matter of law to impose CERCLA liability on a secured creditor. The district court's finding to the contrary is erroneous. . . .

With respect to Fleet's involvement at the facility from the time it contracted with Baldwin in May 1982 until Nix left the facility in December 1983, we share the district court's conclusion that Fleet's alleged conduct brought it outside the statutory exemption for secured creditors. Indeed, Fleet's involvement would pass the threshold for operator liability under section 9607(a)(2).[15] Fleet weakly contends that its activity at the facility from the time of the auction was within the secured creditor exemption because it was merely protecting its security interest in the facility and foreclosing its security interest in its equipment, inventory, and fixtures. This assertion, even if true, is immaterial to our analysis. The scope of the secured creditor exemption is not determined by whether the creditor's activity was taken to protect its security interest. What is

13. Generally, the lender's capacity to influence a debtor facility's treatment of hazardous waste will be inferred from the extent of its involvement in the facility's financial management. Here, that inference is not even necessary because there was evidence before the district court that Fleet actively asserted its control over the disposal of hazardous wastes at the site by prohibiting SPW from selling several barrels of chemicals to potential buyers.

15. During oral argument, counsel for Fleet virtually conceded operator liability for its conduct with respect to the facility when he discussed Fleet's potential for liability were it to have fixed a hole in the roof of an SPW building:

JUDGE KRAVITCH: If [Fleet] finds in fixing the roof that there is some asbestos that is being dislodged can it just ignore that? . . .

MR. GOOD: Once it fixes the roof, once it takes over control of fixing the roof, it has opened a potential Pandora's box both as to that asbestos and anything else at the facility underneath it known and unknown.

JUDGE KRAVITCH: Why isn't that analogous to what happened here?

relevant is the nature and extent of the creditor's involvement with the facility, not its motive. To hold otherwise would enable secured creditors to take indifferent and irresponsible actions toward their debtors' hazardous wastes with impunity by incanting that they were protecting their security interests. Congress did not intend CERCLA to sanction such abdication of responsibility. . . .

## In re Bergsoe Metal Corp.

***910 F.2d 668 (9th Cir. 1990)***

KOZINSKI, Circuit Judge:

The Comprehensive Environmental Response, Compensation and Liability Act, 42 U.S.C. §§9601 et seq. (CERCLA), provides that the "owner" of a contaminated facility is liable for the costs of cleanup. It is left for the courts, however, to clean up the mess left behind by complicated financial transactions. . . .

[Bergsoe contacted the Port of St. Helens, Oregon, in 1978 to discuss building a lead recycling plant in St. Helens. As a result, the port issued industrial development revenue bonds and pollution control revenue bonds to provide funds for the acquisition of land and the construction of the lead recycling plant and related pollution control equipment. The port also sold 50 acres of land to Bergsoe and took back a promissory note for $400,000 and a mortgage on the property.]

[As part of the bond issuance, Bergsoe conveyed to the port the land and the recycling plant by warranty deed and leased the property back, with the agreement that it would pay lease rentals to a custodial bank which equaled the principal and interest due on the bonds. The port mortgaged its title to the land and plant to the bank and also assigned to the bank its revenues from the leases.]

[Although the transaction was complicated, it was quite clear, and the Court of Appeals found that the port held the deed to the property primarily to ensure that Bergsoe would meet its obligations under the leases and the bonds; the port had, in other words, a security interest in the property. The question before the court, therefore, was whether the port qualified for the security interest exception under CERCLA or whether it forfeited this protection because it had participated in the management of the facility. Other relevant facts appear in the body of the opinion.]

### II. PARTICIPATION IN MANAGEMENT

The Port may nonetheless be liable under CERCLA if it participated in the management of the Bergsoe plant. Unfortunately, CERCLA does not define the phrase "participating in the management . . . of a facility." The statute thus provides little guidance as to how much control over a facility a secured creditor can exert before it will be liable for cleanup.

To date, only one federal circuit has addressed this question. In *Fleet Factors,* the Eleventh Circuit considered several alternative rules. The government proposed that a secured creditor that participates in any manner in the management of a facility is excluded from the security interest exemption. Id., 901 F.2d at 1554. Fleet Factors proposed a rule adopted by certain district courts, that participation in financial management is allowable, but participation in the day-to-day or operational management of a facility will subject the creditor to liability. Id. The Eleventh Circuit adopted an intermediate rule:

> [A] secured creditor may incur section 9607(a)(2) liability . . . by participating in the financial management of a facility to a degree indicating a capacity to influence the corporation's treatment of hazardous wastes. It is not necessary for the secured creditor actually to involve itself in the day-to-day operations of the facility in order to be liable—although such conduct will certainly lead to the loss of the protection of the statutory exemption. Nor is it necessary for the secured creditor to participate in management decisions related to hazardous waste. Rather, a secured creditor will be liable if its involvement with the management of the facility is sufficiently broad to support the inference that it could affect hazardous waste disposal decisions if it so chose.

Id. at 1557-58.

We leave for another day the establishment of a Ninth Circuit rule on this difficult issue. It is clear from the statute that, whatever the precise parameters of "participation," there must be *some* actual management of the facility before a secured creditor will fall outside the exception. Here there was none, and we therefore need not engage in line drawing.

EAC points to several facts that it claims demonstrate that the Port participated in the management of the Bergsoe plant. First, that the Port "negotiated and encouraged" the building of the Bergsoe plant. Were this sufficient to remove a creditor from the security interest exception, the exception would cease to have any meaning. Creditors do not give their money blindly, particularly the large sums of money needed to build industrial facilities. Lenders normally extend credit only after gathering a great deal of information about the proposed project, and only when they have some degree of confidence that the project will be successful. A secured creditor will always have some input at the planning stages of any large-scale project and, by the extension of financing, will perforce encourage those projects it feels will be successful. If this were "management," no secured creditor would ever be protected.

EAC next points to certain of the Port's rights under the leases, such as the right to inspect the premises and to reenter and take possession upon foreclosure. This argument suffers from the same flaw as the last; nearly all secured creditors have these rights. That a secured creditor reserves certain rights to protect its investment does not put it in a position of management. What is critical is not what rights the Port had, but what it did. The CERCLA security interest exception uses the active "participating in management." Regardless of what rights the Port may have had, it cannot have participated in management if it never exercised them. And there is no evidence that the Port exercised any control over Bergsoe once the two parties signed the leases.

Finally, EAC argues that the Port participated in management through its actions in giving Front Street control at the plant as part of the 1984 workout. There is, however, no evidence that the Port participated in the decision to hire Front Street; those negotiations were entirely between the Bank, Bergsoe and Front Street. The Port's participation was limited to an agreement between itself, the Bank and Bergsoe. The Port's sole obligation under the agreement was to forego exercising any of its default remedies under the leases so that the workout might proceed. There were separate agreements between Bergsoe and Front Street and between the Bank and Bergsoe. The Port never entered into a contract with Front Street, and there is no evidence of any negotiations between the two.

EAC contends, nonetheless, that the Port is responsible for the Bank's actions in placing Front Street in control because the Bank was acting as the Port's agent, enforcing the Port's rights under the leases. This assertion is belied by the terms of the mortgage and indentures of trust between the Port and the Bank, wherein the Port assigns to the Bank "all right, title and interest of the [Port] in the Lease[s]." ER I at 107. Thus, to the extent the Bank was attempting to enforce the lease terms, it did so pursuant to its own rights under the leases. More to the point, it was not the leases that the Bank was worried about, but the bonds. As trustee for the bondholders, the Bank had a duty to try to keep the plant running so that Bergsoe could pay the principal and interest under the bonds. In negotiating the workout, the Bank was acting not as the Port's agent, but as the bondholders'.

### Conclusion

There being no material issue of fact, we conclude that the Port holds indicia of ownership primarily to protect its security interest and that it did not participate in the management of the Bergsoe recycling plant. The Port is therefore not an owner under 42 U.S.C. §9601(20)(A), and not liable for cleanup costs under 42 U.S.C. §9607. The judgment of the district court is affirmed.

*QUESTIONS AND COMMENTS*

1. As *Fleet Factors* and *Bergsoe Metal* demonstrate, depository institution lawyers must consider the possibility of liability under the federal Comprehensive Environmental Response, Compensation, and Liability Act (CERCLA), 42 U.S.C. §§9601-9657, which imposes cleanup costs on owners and operators of hazardous waste sites, in any case in which a depository institution has lent money to a debtor who operates or is subsequently found to operate a hazardous waste site. The statute contains an exemption for a person who "without participating in the management of a . . . facility, holds indicia of ownership primarily to protect his security interest in the . . . facility." 42 U.S.C. §9601(20)(A). But if a depository institution becomes involved in the management of a hazardous waste facility it risks losing the exemption. The depository institution might then face liability under 42 U.S.C. §9607(a)(2) as a "person who at the time of disposal of any hazardous substance owned or operated any . . . facility at which such hazardous substances were disposed of." The consequence could be strict, joint-and-several liability for the cleanup costs, which can run into millions of dollars.

2. What test for when a lender becomes liable for cleanup costs under CERCLA makes the most sense to you as a matter of policy?

3. The court in *Fleet Factors* charges that it would be an "abdication of responsibility" for a lender to take "indifferent and irresponsible actions toward their debtors' hazardous wastes with impunity by incanting that they were protecting their security interests." But doesn't this heated rhetoric beg the question of whether Congress intended to impose this kind of responsibility on lenders?

4. The court in *Fleet Factors* rejects as "unfounded" the concern that its decision would discourage lenders from providing credit to businesses with potential hazardous waste problems. But why is this concern so obviously unfounded? The court suggests that creditors will carefully investigate potential debtors, and that the "risk of CERCLA liability will be weighed into the terms of the loan agreement." Isn't this tantamount to saying that as a result of the decision, credit will indeed be less available to businesses with potential hazardous waste problems? And if credit is less available, isn't there the potential for increased environmental harm as a result of inadequate precautions taken by financially strapped facility operators?

5. The court in *Fleet Factors* also rejects as unfounded the concern that creditors will distance themselves from any involvement in management as a result of the court's ruling. But again, why is this concern so obviously off the mark? The court suggests that creditors will monitor their debtors' hazardous waste activities in order to reduce their own potential liability. But is this at all responsive to the argument that creditors may

avoid liability altogether by relinquishing any rights—and therefore any monitoring role—in connection with a debtor's hazardous waste activities? Environmental compliance might suffer as a result, might it not?

6. Moreover, doesn't the court overlook the argument that even if a creditor faced *some* potential exposure under CERCLA, its decision whether to step up its monitoring of the debtor's hazardous waste activities would surely take into account the expected increase in the probability of liability that would flow from any enhanced monitoring role? Might not a creditor reasonably conclude that the risks of increased monitoring outweighed the benefits, even if the creditor recognized that it already faced some potential CERCLA exposure as a result of actions already taken?

7. Don't creditors have a sufficient incentive to monitor their debtors' environmental compliance, even in the absence of the sweeping liability created under *Fleet Factors?* After all, creditors want to be repaid, and they are unlikely to be repaid in full if the debtor suffers crippling CERCLA liability. And the creditor may not be able to ensure repayment by taking a security interest if the property available to secure the debt is the site itself, which may become worthless (indeed, may come to have a negative value) in the event that the debtor is found to have violated hazardous waste disposal standards. In such circumstances, won't a creditor tend to monitor the debtor's environmental compliance even if the creditor did not itself fear CERCLA liability? Is it significant that even before *Fleet Factors* creditors routinely conducted environmental audits of any proposed debtors with potential environmental liabilities, required continuous monitoring and reporting of environmentally sensitive operations, and made noncompliance with environmental laws and regulations an event of default under the loan agreement entitling the lender to accelerate the loan?

8. Is the Ninth Circuit's decision in *Bergsoe* consistent with the Eleventh Circuit's approach in *Fleet Factors?* The *Bergsoe* court ruled that for a lender to be liable as a participant, "there must be *some* actual management of a facility before a secured creditor will fall outside the exception." This rule may not be inconsistent with the *facts* of *Fleet Factors,* where there were allegations that the defendant had actually been involved with the management of the site. But isn't this statement in *Bergsoe* arguably inconsistent with the rule set forth in *Fleet Factors?* Do you find it significant that the Ninth Circuit pointedly failed to endorse the Eleventh Circuit's approach?

9. In April 1992 the EPA issued a comprehensive rule governing the liability of a secured lender under CERCLA. The EPA denied that its rule effected an administrative overruling of the *Fleet Factors* case, but most commentators viewed the rule as at least pruning back on the broadest implications of that decision. An excerpt from the text of the rule follows.

## Environmental Protection Agency, National Oil and Hazardous Substances Pollution Contingency Plan: Lender Liability Under CERCLA

***57 Federal Register 18,344 (April 29, 1992)***

. . . .

Questions regarding the judicial interpretation of th[e] "security interest" exemption under CERCLA have generated uncertainty within the financial and lending communities, particularly with regard to the extent to which a secured creditor may undertake activities to oversee the affairs of a person whose facility is encumbered by a security interest . . . for the purposes of protecting the security interest, without incurring CERCLA liability. Specifically, there is concern over whether certain actions commonly taken by a secured creditor—such as monitoring facility operations, requiring compliance with legal requirements and compliance-related activities, refinancing or undertaking loan workouts, providing financial advice, and undertaking other similar actions that may affect the financial, management, and operational aspects of a business—can be considered to be evidence that the secured creditor is "participating in the management of a facility." . . .

This uncertainty was heightened by dicta in the opinion in [*Fleet Factors*]. In this opinion, the court suggested that a secured creditor may be liable if it actually participates in the management of a facility "to a degree indicating a capacity to influence the corporation's treatment of hazardous wastes." The *Fleet Factors* court confirmed, however, the holding of prior cases that some level of actual involvement or participation by a holder in the borrower's facility is required to abrogate the exemption. The court went further, however, and suggested that the exemption could be lost if the holder's actual involvement was so extensive as to support the inference that the holder could affect or influence operational decisions concerning a facility's treatment of hazardous wastes. However, the court's discussion of this issue left open the question of the level or the extent of actual participation that would be sufficient to support this inference.

[*In re Bergsoe Metal Corp.*], which was consistent with the holding of *Fleet Factors* and prior cases, held that "there must be some actual management of the facility before a secured creditor will fall outside the exception," and that the mere capacity or unexercised right to control facility operations is insufficient to void the exemption. . . .]

[The final rule, 40 C.F.R. §300.1100, stated, in part:]

*Security interest exemption.* A person who maintains indicia of ownership primarily to protect a security interest in a vessel or facility, and who does not participate in the management of the vessel or facility, is not an "owner or operator" of such vessel or facility under CERCLA §107(a)(1) or §107(a)(2). The plaintiff bears the burden of establishing that the defendant is liable as an owner or operator. . . .

(c) *Participation in Management Defined.* The term participating in the management of a vessel or facility means that the holder is engaging in acts of facility or vessel management, as defined herein.

(1) Actions That Are Participation in Management. Participation in the management of a facility means, for the purpose of §101(20)(A), actual participation in the management or operational affairs of the vessel or facility by the holder, and does not include the mere capacity to influence, or ability to influence, or the unexercised right to control facility operations. A holder is participating in management, while the borrower is still in possession of the vessel or facility encumbered by the security interest, only if the holder either:

(i) Exercises decisionmaking control over the borrower's environmental compliance, such that the holder has undertaken responsibility for the borrower's hazardous substance handling or disposal practices; or

(ii) Exercises control at a level comparable to that of a manager of the borrower's enterprise, such that the holder has assumed or manifested responsibility for the overall management of the enterprise encompassing the day-to-day decisionmaking of the enterprise with the respect to:

(A) Environmental compliance or

(B) All, or substantially all, of the operational (as opposed to financial or administrative) aspects of the enterprise other than environmental compliance. Operational aspects of the enterprise include functions such as that of facility or plant manager, operations manager, chief operating officer, or chief executive officer. Financial or administrative aspects include functions such as that of credit manager, accounts payable/receivable manager, personnel manager, controller, chief financial officer, or similar functions.

(2) Actions That Are Not Participation in Management

(i) Actions at the Inception of the Loan or Other Transaction. No act or omission prior to the time that indicia of ownership are held primarily to protect a security interest constitutes evidence of participation in management within the meaning of §101(20)(A). . . .

(ii) Policing and Workout. Actions that are consistent with holding ownership indicia primarily to protect a security interest do not constitute participation in management for purposes of section 101(20)(A) of CERCLA. The authority for the holder to take such actions may, but need not, be contained in contractual or other documents specifying requirements for financial, environmental, and other warranties, covenants, conditions, representations or promises from the borrower. Loan policing and workout activities cover and include all activities up to foreclosure and its equivalents. . . .

(A) Policing the Security Interest or Loan. A holder who engages in policing activities prior to foreclosure will remain within the exemption provided that the holder does not by such actions participate in the management of the vessel or facility as provided in 40 CFR 300.1100(c)(1). Such actions include, but are not limited to, requiring the borrower to clean up the vessel or facility during the term of the security interest; requiring the borrower to comply or come into compliance with applicable federal, state, and local environmental and other laws, rules and regulations during the term of the security interest; securing or exercising authority to monitor or inspect the vessel or facility (including on-site inspections) in which indicia of ownership are maintained, or the borrower's business or financial condition during the term of the security interest; or taking other actions to adequately police the loan or security interest (such as requiring a borrower to comply with any warranties, covenants, conditions, representations or promises from the borrower).

(B) Work Out. A holder who engages in work out activities prior to foreclosure and its equivalents will remain within the exemption provided that the holder does not by such action participate in the management of the vessel or facility as provided in 40 CFR 300.1100(c)(1). For purposes of this rule, "work out" refers to those actions by which a holder, at any time prior to foreclosure and its equivalents, seeks to prevent, cure, or mitigate a default by the borrower or obligor; or to preserve, or prevent the diminution of, the value of the security. Work out activities include, but are not limited to, restructuring or renegotiating the terms of the security interest; requiring payment of additional rent or interest; exercising forbearance; requiring or exercising rights pursuant to an assignment of accounts or other amounts owing to an obligor; requiring or exercising rights pursuant to an escrow agreement pertaining to amounts owing to an obligor; providing specific or general financial or other advice, suggestions, counseling, or guidance; and exercising any right or remedy the holder is entitled to by law or under any warranties, covenants, conditions, representations or promises from the borrower. . . .

(d) *Foreclosure on Property and Post-Foreclosure Activities*

(1) Foreclosure. Indicia of ownership that are held primarily to protect a security interest include legal or equitable title acquired through or incident to foreclosure and its equivalents. . . .

(2) Holding Foreclosed Property for Disposition and Liquidation. A holder, who did not participate in management prior to foreclosure and its equivalents, may sell, re-lease property held pursuant to a lease financing transaction (whether by a new lease financing transaction or

substitution of the lessee), liquidate, maintain business activities, wind up operations, undertake any response action under section 107(d)(1) of CERCLA or under the direction of an on-scene coordinator, and take measures to preserve, protect or prepare the secured asset prior to sale or other disposition. . . .

---

The EPA's rule seemed to resolve many of the major questions in the area of lender liability. However, in February 1994 the United States Court of Appeals for the District of Columbia Circuit invalidated the rule on the ground that the EPA lacked authority to restrict by regulation the substance of private rights of action under the statute. Kelley v. Environmental Protection Agency, 15 F.3d 1100 (D.C. Cir. 1994), *cert. denied,* 115 S. Ct. 900 (1995). One American Bankers Association lawyer, reacting to the decision, lamented in mixed metaphor, "You're lending in the dark now. One day, everything looks great, and the next day you're dropped in the middle of the desert."

This was not the end of the story, however. Late in 1995, the Environmental Protection Agency and the Department of Justice issued the following memorandum.

## CERCLA Enforcement Against Lenders and Government Entities That Acquire Property Involuntarily

***Environmental Protection Agency and Department of Justice, December 11, 1995***

This memorandum sets forth the Environmental Protection Agency's ("EPA") and the Department of Justice's ("DOJ") policy regarding the government's enforcement of [CERCLA] against lenders and against government entities that acquire property involuntarily. . . .

### I. Background

. . . EPA and DOJ recognize CERCLA's unintended effects on lenders and government entities and the relative concern from these parties regarding the consequences of potential enforcement. In light of these concerns, lenders may refuse to lend money to an owner or developer of a contaminated or potentially contaminated property or they may hesitate in exercising their rights as secured parties if such loans are made. Additionally, government entities that involuntarily acquire property may be reluctant to perform certain actions related to contaminated or potentially contaminated property.

The language of Section 101(20)(A) leaves lenders and other interested parties uncertain as to which types of actions—such as monitoring vessel or facility operations, requiring compliance with applicable laws, and refinancing or undertaking loan workouts—they may take to protect their security interests without risking EPA enforcement under CERCLA. Courts have not always agreed on when a lender's actions are "primarily to protect a security interest," and what degree of "participation in the management" of the property will forfeit the lender's eligibility for the exemption. This uncertainty was heightened by dicta in the *Fleet Factors* opinion, where the circuit court suggested that a lender participating in the management of a vessel or facility "to a degree indicating a capacity to influence the corporation's treatment of hazardous waste" could be considered liable under CERCLA.

The lack of legislative history on and consistent court treatment of the CERCLA Section 101(20)(A) security interest exemption prompted EPA to address potential lender liability for cleanup costs at CERCLA sites in the Lender Liability Rule, which was promulgated in April 1992. . . . However, in Kelley v. EPA, the Circuit Court of Appeals for the District of Columbia vacated the Rule on the ground that EPA lacked authority to issue the Rule as a binding regulation. Nevertheless, the Kelley decision did not preclude EPA and DOJ from following the provisions of the Rule as enforcement policy, and the agencies have generally done so.

## II. Policy Statement

This memorandum reaffirms EPA's and DOJ's intentions to follow the provisions of the Lender Liability Rule as enforcement policy. EPA and DOJ endorse the interpretations and rationales announced in the Rule and its preamble. The purpose of this memorandum is to provide guidance within EPA and DOJ on the exercise of enforcement discretion in determining whether particular lenders and government entities that acquire property involuntarily may be subject to CERCLA enforcement actions. In making such determinations, EPA and DOJ personnel should consult both the regulatory text of the Rule and the accompanying preamble language in exercising their enforcement discretion under CERCLA as to lenders and government entities that acquire property. . . . After the promulgation of the Lender Liability Rule, but prior to its invalidation, several district and circuit courts adhered to the terms of the Rule or interpreted the statute in a manner consistent with the Rule. Moreover, notwithstanding the Rule's invalidation in Kelley, since that decision several courts have also interpreted the statute in a way that is consistent with the Rule. EPA and DOJ believe that this case law is further evidence of the reasonableness of the agencies' interpretation of the statute, as embodied formerly in the Rule and now in this policy statement.

### III. Use of This Policy

The policies and procedures established in this document and any internal procedures adopted for its implementation are intended solely as guidance for employees of EPA and DOJ. They do not constitute rulemaking and may not be relied on to create a right or benefit, substantive or procedural, enforceable at law, or in equity, by any person. EPA and DOJ reserve the right to act at variance with this guidance or its internal implementing procedures.

---

In October 1996, Congress enacted the Asset Conservation, Lender Liability, and Deposit Insurance Protection Act of 1996 as part of the 1997 Department of Defense Appropriations Act. (What, by the way, does lender liability under CERCLA have to do with the Defense Department?) The new statute provides, generally, that the relevant section of the EPA's Final Rule "shall be deemed to have been validly issued under authority of [CERCLA]" and that "[n]o additional judicial proceedings shall be necessary or may be held with respect to 'the rule.' " The statute goes on to preclude any judicial review of the rule and to confirm that the president or a delegatee of the president is not deprived of power to amend the rule. Has this *deus ex machina* resolved the plot, or do you foresee more twists ahead?

## D. REGULATION OF DEPOSIT TAKING

The preceding section discussed various regulations of the *asset* side of a bank's balance sheet. We turn now to the *liability* side of a bank's balance sheet to discuss the following subjects: (1) limitations on deposit interest; (2) issues arising under the Federal Deposit Insurance Act; and (3) policy issues in the federal deposit insurance programs.

### 1. *Limitations on Deposit Interest Rates*

We treat first a matter that today is largely a matter of historical interest, but which until recently was a fundamental pillar of banking regulation: limitations on deposit interest rates. Deposit interest rate controls came into federal law during the Depression. The Banking Act of 1933 prohibited the payment of interest on demand deposits and provided for administrative regulation of interest on time and savings accounts. The Federal

Reserve Board and the Federal Home Loan Bank Board eventually adopted ceilings on deposit interest. The Federal Reserve Board's Regulation Q applied to national and state member banks as well as foreign bank branches. The FHLBB's regulation, applicable to savings institutions under its jurisdiction, permitted these institutions to pay a "thrift differential" of 0.25 percent over the rate permitted to commercial banks.

As recounted in Chapter 1, this regulatory structure proved unstable when interest rates soared to record highs in the late 1970s. In the Depository Institutions Deregulation and Monetary Control Act of 1980, Congress mandated a six-year phase-out of interest rate controls (through the Depository Institutions Deregulation Committee), and authorized nationwide NOW accounts. Congress continued the process in the Garn-St Germain Depository Institutions Act of 1982, which created a bank equivalent of the money market mutual fund and accelerated the elimination of the thrift differential. Today deposit interest rates are effectively deregulated; Regulation Q serves only the vestigial function of regulating advertising of interest rates and penalties for early withdrawal.

## 2. *Issues Under the Federal Deposit Insurance Act*

The pressing current issues regarding the liability side of a bank's balance sheet concern the administration and design of the federal deposit insurance system. This subsection treats a few of the more important issues that have arisen in the administration and interpretation of the deposit insurance system; the next subsection addresses broader policy issues going to the design of the program.

First, some background on the federal deposit insurance programs is in order. The essential structure of these programs is fairly simple. Banking institutions—commercial banks, savings and loans, savings banks, credit unions, and a few other miscellaneous institutions—are eligible for federal deposit insurance. Federally chartered institutions and state member banks are *required* to carry federal deposit insurance. Other state-chartered institutions are *permitted,* but not required, to carry federal deposit insurance. As a practical matter, virtually all banking organizations with the exception of some credit unions find it essential to obtain federal deposit insurance if they are to remain in business at all.

The deposit insurance programs for commercial banks and savings institutions are administered by the FDIC (prior to FIRREA the deposit insurance funds for most savings institutions were administered by the FSLIC). The FDIC administers two separate deposit insurance funds: the Bank Insurance Fund (BIF), which principally insures commercial banks, and the Savings Association Insurance Fund (SAIF), which principally insures savings and loans. Credit unions are insured by the National

Credit Union Share Insurance Fund (NCUSIF). To qualify for insurance an institution must make an application to the FDIC or the NCUA.

Insurance is not a matter of right. It is possible—although uncommon—for an institution to have its insurance coverage suspended or terminated for egregious violations of federal law or principles of sound management. Suspension and termination of insurance are discussed in Chapter 7.

The deposit insurance programs are funded by premiums assessed on program participants. 12 U.S.C. §1817(b). Deposit insurance premiums are now adjusted for risk. The amount of the risk adjustment is fairly slight, however, and in the view of some commentators falls below the differential in premiums that would be required if the system were to be fully risk-adjusted.

Coverage under the federal deposit insurance programs was originally set at $2,500 per account. This figure was increased gradually through time; the current figure is $100,000 per account. Individuals may have as many accounts as they like, and the accounts will be insured up to $100,000 so long as they are at different depository institutions. Thus if a single depositor has three accounts at the same bank each for $75,000, her funds will be protected only up to $100,000. But if the depositor places these funds in three different banks they will be protected in full. The $100,000 figure is evidently quite generous; it is not difficult for depositors to spread considerable wealth across a variety of banks and receive full coverage.

Basic to the administration of the federal deposit insurance system is the definition of a "deposit." Many arrangements with banks can readily be identified as deposits. If you put money in a checking account or a savings account at a commercial bank or thrift, you have made a deposit that will be covered by federal deposit insurance. The same is true if you invest in a certificate of deposit issued by one of these institutions. But banks engage in a variety of other transactions that may or may not be considered "deposits" for purposes of the deposit insurance scheme. The following case considers the definition of "deposit" in an important modern commercial context.

## FDIC v. Philadelphia Gear Corp.

***476 U.S. 426 (1986)***

Justice O'Connor delivered the opinion of the court.

We granted certiorari to consider whether a standby letter of credit backed by a contingent promissory note is insured as a "deposit" under the federal deposit insurance program. We hold that, in light of the longstanding interpretation of petitioner Federal Deposit Insurance Corporation (FDIC) that such a letter does not create a deposit and, in light of the fact that such a letter does not entrust any noncontingent assets to the bank, a standby letter of credit backed by a contingent promissory note does not give rise to an insured deposit.

I

Orion Manufacturing Corporation (Orion) was, at the time of the relevant transactions, a customer of respondent Philadelphia Gear Corporation (Philadelphia Gear). On Orion's application, the Penn Square Bank, N.A. (Penn Square) issued a letter of credit for the benefit of Philadelphia Gear in the amount of $145,200. The letter of credit provided that a draft drawn upon the letter of credit would be honored by Penn Square only if accompanied by Philadelphia Gear's "signed statement that [it had] invoiced Orion Manufacturing Corporation and that said invoices have remained unpaid for at least fifteen (15) days." Because the letter of credit was intended to provide payment to the seller only if the buyer of the invoiced goods failed to make payment, the letter of credit was what is commonly referred to as a "standby" or "guaranty" letter of credit. See, e.g., 12 CFR §337.2(a), and n.1 (1985) (defining standby letters of credit and mentioning that they may "'guaranty' payment of a money obligation"). A conventional "commercial" letter of credit, in contrast, is one in which the seller obtains payment from the issuing bank without looking to the buyer for payment even in the first instance. See ibid. (distinguishing standby letters of credit from commercial letters of credit). . . .

On the same day that Penn Square issued the standby letter of credit, Orion executed an unsecured promissory note for $145,200 in favor of Penn Square. The purpose of the note was listed as "Back up Letter of Credit." Although the face of the note did not so indicate, both Orion and Penn Square understood that nothing would be considered due on the note, and no interest charged by Penn Square, unless Philadelphia Gear presented drafts on the standby letter of credit after nonpayment by Orion.

On July 5, 1982, Penn Square was declared insolvent. Petitioner FDIC was appointed its receiver. Shortly thereafter, Philadelphia Gear presented drafts on the standby letter of credit for payment of over $700,000 for goods delivered before Penn Square's insolvency. The FDIC returned the drafts unpaid.

Philadelphia Gear sued the FDIC in the Western District of Oklahoma. Philadelphia Gear alleged that the standby letter of credit was an insured deposit under the definition of "deposit" set forth at 12 U.S.C. §1813(*l*)(1), and that Philadelphia Gear was therefore entitled to $100,000 in deposit insurance from the FDIC. See 12 U.S.C. §1821(a)(1) (setting forth $100,000 as the maximum amount generally insured by the FDIC for any single depositor at a given bank). In apparent hopes of obtaining additional funds from the FDIC in the latter's capacity as receiver rather than as insurer, respondent also alleged that terms of the standby letter of credit allowing repeated reinstatements of the credit made the letter's total value more than $145,200.

The District Court held that the total value of the standby letter of credit was $145,200; that the letter was an insured deposit on which the FDIC was liable for $100,000 in deposit insurance; and that Philadelphia Gear was entitled to prejudgment interest on that $100,000. The FDIC appealed from the District Court's ruling that the standby letter of credit backed by a contingent promissory note constituted a "deposit" for purposes of 12 U.S.C. §1813(*l*)(1) and its ruling that Philadelphia Gear was entitled to an award of prejudgment interest. Philadelphia Gear cross-appealed from the District Court's ruling on the total value of the letter of credit.

**II**

Title 12 U.S.C. §1813(*l*)(1) provides:

> The term "deposit" means —
>
> (1) the unpaid balance of money or its equivalent received or held by a bank in the usual course of business and for which it has given or is obligated to give credit, either conditionally or unconditionally, to a commercial . . . account, or which is evidenced by . . . a letter of credit or a traveler's check on which the bank is primarily liable: *Provided,* That, without limiting the generality of the term "money or its equivalent," any such account or instrument must be regarded as evidencing the receipt of the equivalent of money when credited or issued in exchange for checks or drafts or for a promissory note upon which the person obtaining any such credit or instrument is primarily or secondarily liable. . . .

Philadelphia Gear successfully argued before the Court of Appeals that the standby letter of credit backed by a contingent promissory note constituted a "deposit" under 12 U.S.C. §1813(*l*)(1) because that letter was one on which the bank was primarily liable, and evidenced the receipt by the bank of "money or its equivalent" in the form of a promissory note upon which the person obtaining the credit was primarily or secondarily liable. The FDIC does not here dispute that the bank was primarily liable on the letter of credit. Nor does the FDIC contest the fact that the backup note executed by Orion is, at least in some sense, a "promissory note." The FDIC argues rather that it has consistently interpreted §1813(*l*)(1) not to include standby letters of credit backed only by a contingent promissory note because such a note represents no hard assets and thus does not constitute "money or its equivalent." Because the alleged "deposit" consists only of a *contingent* liability, asserts the FDIC, a standby letter of credit backed by a contingent promissory note does not give rise to a "deposit" that Congress intended the FDIC to insure. Under this theory, while the note here may have been labeled a promissory note on its face and may have been a promissory note under state law, it was not a promissory note for purposes of the federal law set forth in 12 U.S.C. §1813(*l*)(1). See D'Oench, Duhme & Co. v. FDIC, 315 U.S. 447, 456 (1942) (holding that liability on a promissory note acquired by the FDIC is a federal question); First National Bank v. Dickinson, 396 U.S. 122, 133-134 (1969) (holding that federal law governs the definition of branch banking under the McFadden Act).

The Court of Appeals quite properly looked first to the language of the statute. Finding the language of the proviso in §1813(*l*)(1) sufficiently plain, the Court of Appeals looked no further. But as the FDIC points out, the terms "letter of credit" and "promissory note" as used in the statute have a federal definition, and the FDIC has developed and interpreted those definitions for many years within the framework of the complex statutory scheme that the FDIC administers. The FDIC's interpretation of whether a standby letter of credit backed by a contingent promissory note constitutes a "deposit" is consistent with Congress' desire to protect the hard earnings of individuals by providing for federal deposit insurance. Since the creation of the FDIC, Congress has expressed no dissatisfaction with the FDIC's interpretation of "deposit"; indeed, Congress in 1960 adopted the FDIC's regulatory definition as the statutory language. When we weigh all these factors together, we are constrained to conclude that the term "deposit" does not include a standby letter of credit backed by a contingent promissory note.

### *A*

Justice Holmes stated that, as to discerning the constitutionality of a federal estate tax, "a page of history is worth a volume of logic." New York Trust Co. v. Eisner, 256 U.S. 345, 349 (1921). Although the genesis of the Federal Deposit Insurance Act may not be quite so powerful a substitute for legal analysis, that history is worthy of at least a page of recounting for the light it sheds on Congress' purpose in passing the Act. Cf. Watt v. Alaska, 451 U.S. 259, 266 (1981) ("The circumstances of the enactment of particular legislation may persuade a court that Congress did not intend words of common meaning to have their literal effect").

When Congress created the FDIC, the Nation was in the throes of an extraordinary financial crisis. See generally F. Allen, Since Yesterday: The Nineteen-Thirties in America 98-121 (1940); A. Schlesinger, The Crisis of the Old Order 474-482 (1957). More than one-third of the banks in the United States open in 1929 had shut their doors just four years later. Bureau of the Census, Historical Statistics of the United States: Colonial Times to 1970, pt. 2, pp. 1019, 1038 (1976). In response to this financial crisis, President Roosevelt declared a national banking holiday effective the first business day after he took office. 48 Stat. 1689. Congress in turn responded with extensive legislation on banking, including the laws that gave the FDIC its existence.

Congress' purpose in creating the FDIC was clear. Faced with virtual panic, Congress attempted to safeguard the hard earnings of individuals against the possibility that bank failures would deprive them of their savings. Congress passed the 1933 provisions "[i]n order to provide against a repetition of the present painful experience in which a vast sum of *assets and purchasing power* is 'tied up.'" S. Rep. No. 77, 73d Cong., 1st Sess., 12 (1933) (emphasis added). The focus of Congress was therefore upon ensuring that a deposit of "hard earnings" entrusted by individuals to a bank would not lead to a tangible loss in the event of a bank failure. As the chairman of the relevant Committee in the House of Representatives explained on the floor:

> [T]he purpose of this legislation is to protect the people of the United States in the right to have banks in which their deposits will be safe. They have a right to expect of Congress the establishment and maintenance of a system of banks in the United States where citizens may place their hard earnings with reasonable expectation of being able to get them out again upon demand. . . .
>
> [The purpose of the bill is to ensure that] the community is saved from the shock of a bank failure, and every citizen has been given an opportunity to withdraw his deposits. . . .
>
> The public . . . demand of you and me that we provide a banking system worthy of this great Nation and banks in which citizens may place the fruits of their toil and know that a deposit slip in return for their hard earnings will be as safe as a Government bond.

77 Cong. Rec. 3837, 3838, 3840 (1933) (remarks of Rep. Steagall). See also id., at 3913 (remarks of Rep. Keller) ("[We must make] it absolutely certain that . . . any and every man, woman, or child who puts a dollar in any bank can absolutely know that he will under no circumstances lose a single penny of it"); id., at 3924 (remarks of Rep. Green) ("It is time that we pass a law so secure that when a man puts his money in a bank he will know for sure that when he comes back it will be there"). To prevent bank failure that resulted in the tangible loss of hard assets was therefore the focus of Congress' effort in creating deposit insurance.

Despite the fact Congress revisited the deposit insurance statute in 1935, 1950, and 1960, these comments remain the best indication of Congress' underlying purpose in creating deposit insurance. . . .

Congress' focus in providing for a system of deposit insurance—a system that has been continued to the present without modification to the basic definition of deposits that are "money or its equivalent"—was clearly a focus upon safeguarding the assets and "hard earnings" that businesses and individuals have entrusted to banks. Congress wanted to ensure that someone who put tangible assets into a bank could always get those assets back. The purpose behind the insurance of deposits in general, and especially in the section defining deposits as "money or its equivalent," therefore, is the protection of assets and hard earnings entrusted to a bank.

This purpose is not furthered by extending deposit insurance to cover a standby letter of credit backed by a contingent promissory note, which involves no such surrender of assets or hard earnings to the custody of the bank. Philadelphia Gear, which now seeks to collect deposit insurance, surrendered absolutely nothing to the bank. The letter of credit is for Philadelphia Gear's benefit, but the bank relied upon Orion to meet the obligations of the letter of credit and made no demands upon Philadelphia Gear. Nor, more importantly, did Orion surrender any assets unconditionally to the bank. The bank did not credit any account of Orion's in exchange for the promissory note, and did not treat its own assets as increased by its acceptance of the note. The bank could not have collected on the note from Orion unless Philadelphia Gear presented the unpaid invoices and a draft on the letter of credit. In the absence of a presentation by Philadelphia Gear of the unpaid invoices, the promissory note was a wholly contingent promise, and when Penn Square went into receivership, neither Orion nor Philadelphia Gear had lost anything except the ability to use Penn Square to reduce Philadelphia Gear's risk that Philadelphia Gear would go unpaid for a delivery of goods to Orion. . . .

Although the FDIC's interpretation of the relevant statute has not been reduced to a specific regulation, we conclude nevertheless that the FDIC's practice and belief that a standby letter of credit backed by a contingent promissory note does not create a "deposit" within the meaning of 12 U.S.C. §1813(*l*)(1) are entitled in the circumstances of this case to the "considerable weight [that] should be accorded to an executive department's construction of a statutory scheme it is entrusted to administer." Chevron U.S.A. Inc. v. Natural Resources Defense Council, Inc., 467 U.S. 837, 844 (1984). As we have stated above, the FDIC's interpretation here of a statutory definition adopted wholesale from the FDIC's own regulation is consistent with congressional purpose, and may certainly stand.

### III

Philadelphia Gear essentially seeks to have the FDIC guarantee the contingent credit extended to Orion, not assets entrusted to the bank by Philadelphia Gear or by Orion on Philadelphia Gear's behalf. With a standard "commercial" letter of credit, Orion would typically have unconditionally entrusted Penn Square with funds before Penn Square would have written the letter of credit, and thus Orion would have lost something if Penn Square became unable to honor its obligations. As the FDIC concedes, deposit insurance extends to such a letter of credit backed by an uncontingent promissory note. But here, with a standby letter of credit backed by a contingent promissory note, Penn Square was not in possession of any of Orion's or Philadelphia Gear's assets when it went into receivership. Nothing was ventured, and therefore no insurable deposit was lost. We believe that, whatever the relevant State's definition of "letter of credit" or "promissory note," Congress did not by using those phrases in 12 U.S.C. §1813(*l*)(1) intend to protect with deposit insurance a standby letter of credit backed only by a contingent promissory note. We thus hold that such an arrangement does not give rise to a "deposit" under 12 U.S.C. §1813(*l*)(1).

Accordingly, the judgment of the court below is reversed, and the case is remanded for further proceedings consistent with this opinion.

Reversed and remanded.

Justice MARSHALL, with whom Justice BLACKMUN and Justice REHNQUIST join, dissenting.

There is considerable common sense backing the Court's opinion. The standby letter of credit in this case differs considerably from the savings and checking accounts that come most readily to mind when one speaks of an insured deposit. Nevertheless, to reach this common-sense result, the Court must read qualifications into the statute that do not appear there. We recently recognized that even when the ingenuity of businessmen creates transactions and corporate forms that were perhaps not contemplated by Congress, the courts must enforce the statutes that Congress has enacted. Congress unmistakably provided that letters of credit backed by promissory notes constitute "deposits" for purposes of the federal deposit insurance program, and the Court's attempt to draw distinctions between different types of letter of credit transactions forces it to ignore both the statute and some settled principles of commercial law. Here, the inflexibility of the statute as applied to modern financial transactions is a matter for Congress, not the FDIC or this Court, to remedy.

It cannot be doubted that the standby letter of credit in this case meets the literal definition of a "deposit" contained in 12 U.S.C. §1813(*l*)(1). It is "a letter of credit . . . on which the bank is primarily liable . . . issued in exchange for . . . a promissory note upon which [Orion] is primarily or secondarily liable." The Court, however, holds that the note in this case, whether or not it is a promissory note under the Uniform Commercial Code (UCC) and Oklahoma law, is not a promissory note for purposes of the Federal Deposit Insurance Act. We should assume, absent convincing evidence to the contrary, that Congress intended for the term "promissory note" to derive its meaning from the ordinary sources of commercial law. I believe that there is no such evidence in this case.

The Court justifies its restrictive reading of the term "promissory note" in large part by arguing that Congress would not have wanted to include in that term any obligation that was not the present equivalent of money. The keystone of the FDIC's arguments, and of the Court's decision, is that Orion did not entrust "money or its equivalent" to the bank. The note in this case, however, was the equivalent of money, and the Court's reading of Congress' intent is therefore largely irrelevant. . . .

While the Court purports to examine what Congress meant when it said "promissory note," in fact the Court's opinion does not rest on any special attributes of Orion's note. Rather, the Court rules that when an individual entrusts a negotiable instrument to a bank, that instrument is not "money or its equivalent" for purposes of §1813(*l*)(1) so long as the bank promises not to negotiate it or collect on it until certain conditions are met. That is a proviso that Congress might have been well advised to include in the Act, but did not. I therefore dissent.

## *QUESTIONS AND COMMENTS*

1. This case involves standby letters of credit, a subject treated earlier in this chapter.

2. The issuing bank in this case, Penn Square, is one of the more notorious banks of the modern era. Based in an Oklahoma City shopping center, the Penn Square Bank accumulated a massive portfolio of bad loans to wildcat oil drillers, speculative real estate developers, and other high rollers. William G. Patterson, the officer who made many of the bad loans, was a flamboyant figure who liked to drink liquor out of his cowboy boots and wear Mickey Mouse beanies to work. The comic aspects aside, the failure of Penn Square on July 5, 1982, was a disaster for the huge Continental Illinois National Bank & Trust Co., which had purchased participations in many of Penn Square's bad loans. Continental Illinois failed in 1983 and was saved only by a $4.5 billion federal bailout.

For entertaining accounts of the Penn Square failure, see P. Zweig, Belly Up: The Collapse of the Penn Square Bank (1985), and M. Singer, Funny Money (1985).

3. Wasn't the Philadelphia Gear company dead right about the statutory language? 12 U.S.C. §1813(*l*)(1) provides that "deposit" means "the unpaid balance of money or its equivalent received or held by a bank or savings association in the usual course of business . . . which is evidenced by . . . a letter of credit . . . on which the bank or savings association is primarily liable." There was no doubt that Penn Square had issued a letter of credit on which it was primarily liable, was there?

The case went off instead on the ground that Orion had not given "money or its equivalent" to the bank. But why not? The statute unequivocally states that a letter of credit evidences the receipt of the equivalent of money "when . . . issued in exchange for . . . a promissory note upon which the person obtaining any such credit . . . is primarily or secondarily liable." There was no doubt that Orion had given Penn Square a note, was there? Or that Orion was primarily or secondarily liable on the note? Why isn't the plain language of the statute fully sufficient to dispose of the case?

4. The majority opinion concluded that the statute means something other than what it seems to say by looking to the FDIC's consistent interpretation of standby letters of credit as not being "deposits"—evidenced principally by the fact that the FDIC had never charged insurance premiums on standby letters of credit. The FDIC's interpretation, however, had never been stated in a formal rule. Should a longstanding interpretation of this sort be enough to trump the plain language of the statute? What about the fact that Congress had reenacted and amended the definition of "deposit" on several occasions and had never attempted to reverse the FDIC's position?

5. The majority opinion finds an indication of congressional intent to safeguard the "hard earnings" that businesses and individuals entrust to banks. It then concludes that the congressional intent is not served by insuring standby letters of credit because such instruments do not represent the commitment of hard earnings to the bank. Is this coherent? Assume a bank makes you an unsecured personal loan of $50,000 and credits the funds to your account. Do these funds represent your "hard earnings"? What about the fact that Orion issued a promissory note to Penn Square for $145,200—doesn't this represent Orion's "hard earnings"? After all, if Orion defaults on the debt to Philadelphia Gear, Penn Square Bank can be expected to proceed against Orion on the note and seek to recover the balance from Orion's assets. Did Orion not work hard to obtain these assets?

6. What social policies do you think underlie the majority opinion in this case? What about protecting justified expectations (and not giving windfalls)? Is it significant that despite the fact that standby letters of credit had become a multibillion dollar industry, no holder of such a letter had until this case sought treatment as a depositor under the FDIC fund? Or is this simply a function of the fact that until recently banks—especially large banks that issue standby letters of credit—didn't fail?

7. Are any concerns evident other than not providing an unbargained-for windfall to holders of standby letters? What about protecting the federal deposit insurance fund against potentially devastating liability to holders of standby letters of credit in the event of an economic collapse? On the other hand, isn't there an argument that the FDIC fund

would actually have been strengthened if the Court had ruled the other way? Consider the impact on the assessment base of including hundreds of billions of dollars worth of standby letters of credit in the calculation of deposits. Why didn't the FDIC lay claim to this mother lode?

8. What happens to the claim of Philadelphia Gear as a result of this case? Why did the company apparently believe it might get more than $100,000 out of the FDIC?

## NOTE ON BROKERED DEPOSITS

A deposit is a deposit is a deposit. There are no requirements that individuals make deposits in local banks; they can invest their funds in banks anywhere in the country and get the full benefits of federal deposit insurance. Moreover, as we noted above, if they have more than $100,000 to invest they can easily split their deposits among many institutions and have all their accounts fully insured so long as no one institution has more than $100,000. This legal background creates an obvious opportunity for interstate competition for deposits, assisted by the services of professional deposit brokers. During the early 1980s in fact a very considerable business of deposit brokerage developed, to the dismay of the FDIC.

In 1983 the FDIC and FHLBB attempted to squelch deposit brokerage by promulgating regulations limiting insurance coverage for funds placed by a deposit broker to $100,000 per broker, per depository institution, but the D.C. Circuit struck down the regulations as inconsistent with the applicable statutes. FAIC Securities, Inc. v. United States, 768 F.2d 352 (D.C. Cir. 1985).

Starting in 1989, however, Congress has imposed increasingly stringent regulation of brokered deposits. The law now provides that insured depository institutions that are "not well capitalized" may not "accept funds obtained, directly or indirectly, by or through any deposit broker for deposit into 1 or more deposit accounts." 12 U.S.C. §1831f(a). "Deposit broker" is defined to include, inter alia, "any person engaged in the business of placing deposits, or facilitating the placement of deposits, of third parties with insured depository institutions or the business of placing deposits with insured depository institutions for the purpose of selling interests in those deposits to third parties." 12 U.S.C. §1831f(g)(1). Excluded from the definition of "deposit broker" are, inter alia, the institution itself, its employees, certain fiduciaries, and "an agent or nominee whose primary purpose is not the placement of funds with depository institutions." Perhaps most importantly, an insured depository institution may not, if it uses a deposit broker, pay a rate of interest that significantly exceeds usual market rates. 12 U.S.C. §1831f(e). If the institution is undercapitalized, it may not solicit deposits through means other than deposit brokers if the rates of interest are significantly higher than prevailing market rates. 12 U.S.C. §1831f(h).

*QUESTIONS AND COMMENTS*

1. For criticism of brokered deposits, see Macey & Miller, Bank Failures, Risk Monitoring, and the Market for Bank Control, 88 Colum. L. Rev. 1153, 1199-1202 (1988).

2. Why did the FDIC want to stamp out deposit brokerage? Isn't such brokerage an economically efficient way of directing capital to higher valued uses? Why is it different than other kinds of brokerage?

3. How effective do you think the statutory limits on deposit brokers will be?

4. To the extent to which the statutory limits on deposit brokers are effective, do you think that on balance they will bolster the deposit insurance funds? If a troubled institution is foreclosed from competing effectively in an interstate deposit market that is open to healthy institutions, won't this increase the likelihood that it will become insolvent? Consider the fact that soon after the prohibition on brokered deposits for troubled institutions became effective, the FDIC found it necessary to waive the rule as applied to the hundreds of banks and thrifts operating under government conservatorship.

5. Assume a corporation keeps more than $100,000 in an account at the First National Bank. The bank becomes insolvent, and the corporation is not repaid the excess of its deposits over the insurance maximum. Should the corporate treasurer be liable to shareholders for dereliction of duty? More generally, why would anyone ever keep more than $100,000 on deposit in a single institution?

## 3. Policy Issues in the Federal Deposit Insurance Programs

Underlying the specific issues under the federal deposit insurance program are a variety of weighty questions going to the overall soundness of the deposit insurance system itself. As we observed in Chapter 1, few analysts today dispute the case for *some* system of federal deposit insurance. Even free market theorists like Milton Friedman have endorsed the concept of deposit insurance.

Very much in question, however, is how a federal deposit insurance system should be *structured.* The present system is often criticized as creating perverse incentives for banks and imposing unnecessary costs on the public. Those criticisms, which have been present in the scholarly literature for some time, have attained compelling public policy importance as a result of the dramatic and catastrophic rash of bank and thrift failures in the late 1980s. Many analysts agree that the bank failure problem is largely a function of deep flaws in the design of the existing deposit insurance system.

Congress eschewed any fundamental changes in the basic structure of federal deposit insurance when it rescued the thrift industry in FIRREA. Although this legislation transferred control over the savings and loan insurance fund to the FDIC, the essential elements of the deposit insurance program itself remained intact. But FIRREA mandated a number of comprehensive studies to examine federal deposit insurance, including an important study by the Treasury Department. See U.S. Department of Treasury, Modernizing the Financial System (1991). Congress also made changes in the 1991 FDICIA law, as discussed below.

### a. Analogy to Private Insurance

In understanding the criticisms of federal deposit insurance, it is useful to contrast deposit insurance with risk insurance supplied in private markets. Economists have long understood that the existence of insurance creates what they whimsically call "moral hazard." If actor A obtains complete insurance against a certain risk, she no longer needs to fear harm if the risk insured against comes to pass. So far, so good: As an economic matter it is desirable that there be a market in which risk can be transferred from those who are more risk-adverse to those who are less risk-averse. However, the transfer of the risk has an effect on A's behavior incentives: Because she no longer fears harm, she no longer has an incentive to take precautions to avoid the harm. She might even take affirmative steps to cause the harm to occur if she gets some collateral benefit from doing so. Most of you probably know intuitively what moral hazard is from observing your own driving behavior when behind the wheel of a rented car carrying comprehensive collision coverage.

Private insurance markets have developed a variety of mechanisms to reduce moral hazard. One example is coinsurance: The insured is required to bear a part of the risk insured against, thus reducing the insured's incentives to let the harm occur. Deductibles and policy limits cause risk to remain on the insured.

Another device to control moral hazard is risk-adjusted premiums. Those who have a history of automobiles accidents have to pay more for insurance; insurance companies understand that on a statistical basis people who have had accidents in the past are more likely to have accidents in the future than people who have not had accidents. Regardless of their accident history, young unmarried men may have to pay more for automobile insurance than middle-aged married women, again because of actuarial data indicating that persons in the former category are more likely to have an accident than persons in the latter category.

Insurance companies also reduce moral hazard by writing exclusions into policies for egregious, illegal, or intentional conduct. A's beneficiaries will receive life insurance benefits if she dies in an automobile accident, but not if the crash was a suicide. By excluding suicide, insurance companies reduce the possibility that an insured person will deliberately kill himself in order to confer a benefit on his beneficiaries.

These private market mechanisms are, of course, imperfect: Insureds continue to display moral hazard in their behavior. But markets do not strive for perfection; they seek to minimize costs. It is probable that the risk-reducing devices found in private insurance contracts are relatively good at equating the marginal cost of moral hazard with the marginal cost of imposing an additional increment of risk on the insured party.

When we come to federal deposit insurance, however, the situation appears quite different. The first difference is that the party insured is the depositor, not the bank. If a bank engages in exceedingly risky behavior, it may go broke. If this happens federal deposit insurance will not protect the bank's shareholders; they will be wiped out. This feature of the bank insurance system could be said to mitigate moral hazard as compared with private insurance schemes, which shift risk away from the actor directly rather than from the actor's creditors.

However, a significant element of moral hazard remains in a system where creditors are protected against borrower default. Corporate finance theory sees debtholders as exercising a significant risk-reducing influence on corporate management. Debtholders have a fixed claim on the corporate assets and income; they want to be sure that their investments are not jeopardized by extremely risky management decisions that may or may not pan out. Accordingly, debtholders are commonly understood to exercise a significant monitoring function—for example, by means of bond covenants—to ensure against excessive risk-taking by their borrowers.

Deposit insurance places banks in a different position than typical industrial firms because it shifts insolvency risk away from depositors, who are the principal bank debtholders. These depositors accordingly have little incentive to monitor a bank's behavior to control risk-taking. This is especially true in recent years as a result of the widespread public perception (substantially confirmed by the handling of the Continental Illinois National Bank failure) that certain banks are "too big to fail" and therefore any depository investment in these banks, no matter how large, is effectively 100 percent guaranteed by the federal government.

Without the moderating influence of depositors, bank managers may be inclined to gamble with their bank's assets, theorizing that if the gamble pays off, the bank and its shareholders will win big, and if the gamble does not pay off, most of the costs will be borne by the federal deposit insurance funds. Thus moral hazard is significantly present in the federal deposit insurance system despite the fact that the insured parties are depositors rather than banks themselves.

Aside from the nature of the insured party, the other key difference between federal deposit insurance and private risk insurance is the relative absence in the federal scheme of analogues to the private risk-controlling mechanisms described above. There is very little coinsurance in the federal deposit system. Because there is no deductible, anyone with an account below $100,000 is protected in full. Uninsured depositors—those with accounts over $100,000—do incur some risk of bank failure, but as a practical matter this risk is low. Data show that when handling failed banks the FDIC usually arranges for all depositors to be protected, even those with uninsured balances. Thus as a practical matter depositors do not monitor their bank's managers to make sure that the managers avoid taking excessive risks. Most people who deposit money in a bank do not have the foggiest notion of whether the bank is in good financial health or bad. They have no reason to know because their funds are insured regardless of the bank's fortunes. Contrast this behavior with that of buyers of corporate bonds: They are usually quite careful to check up on the corporation's credit rating before investing their money because they know that they will suffer if the corporation goes broke.

Nor is there much segmentation of banking markets by risk category. The insurance premiums paid by depository institutions are not significantly adjusted for risk. Morgan Guaranty Bank must pay roughly the same premium as the technically insolvent (and fictional) Smith Bank. Banks staffed by officers of the highest qualifications and caliber must pay premiums similar to those staffed by individuals such as those responsible for the downfall of the Penn Square Bank. Moreover, there is little by way of exclusions. Even if bank managers engage in fraudulent or criminal activities, depositors are still paid off in full (although the managers themselves are likely to wind up in prison).

This is not to say that the federal deposit insurance system lacks any devices to control bank risk—au contraire! Virtually the entire structure of banking regulation studied so far, and much of the regulations we will study in later chapters, is ultimately explained as a means of controlling bank risk. Limitations on entry, on activities and investments, on bank/nonbank affiliations, and much more can be understood as attempts to control risk through various proxies deemed to correlate with high levels of riskiness. Further, the regulatory system is backed up by a comprehensive program of bank examination designed to ferret out and deter high-risk behavior. And the FDIC retains the ultimate threat of suspending or terminating deposit insurance if a bank fails to moderate its taste for risk.

It is impossible to say in the abstract whether the medley of risk-reducing devices available to bank supervisory agencies is more or less efficient at reducing bank risk than their counterparts in the private sector. The relatively low incidence of bank failure between 1933 and 1980 suggests that these devices may have been fairly effective. However, since 1980, as we have seen in Chapter 1 and will discuss in greater detail in Chapter 8, the incidence of bank failure has risen dramatically. The deposit insurance fund for savings and loans has been bankrupted several times over, and the bank insurance fund also ran into serious difficulties. These events suggest that whatever may have been the case before 1980, the design of federal deposit insurance may no longer be effective at controlling bank risk. The following discussion considers some of the problems with federal deposit insurance and addresses the major proposals for reform.

### b. Market Discipline

One approach frequently suggested in the literature is to encourage private sector monitoring of the risk-taking behavior of banks by placing their private investors at some risk in the event that the bank fails. Potential candidates for such a monitoring role include shareholders, debtholders, and depositors.

*Shareholders.* Shareholders stand to lose their entire investments in the event of bank failure. To this extent they no doubt encourage conservative bank management. On the other hand, shareholders of banks, like shareholders of other firms, have a built-in incentive to encourage managers to take substantial risks. Shareholders can do well if a firm takes risks because they capture the lion's share of the profits from such risks, while standing to lose only the amount of their investments if the risks pan out badly.

This risk-taking preference for shareholders is, in part, a function of a firm's leverage. Shareholders of highly leveraged firms (that is, firms with a high ratio of debt to equity; recall our discussion of leverage in Chapter 1) prefer that a firm's managers take greater risk than do shareholders of low-leverage firms. The reason is obvious: As leverage goes up, the payoff to shareholders per dollar of investment from profitable activities increases while the total investment that shareholders place at risk is reduced. As we observed in Chapter 1, banks are highly leveraged relative to other industries. Thus, other things equal, we would expect bank shareholders to prefer greater risk-taking than do shareholders of other kinds of firms.

All this suggests that bank shareholders are not particularly reliable monitors of management risk-taking. Interestingly, the framers of the National Bank Act appear to have understood this. As originally adopted, the National Bank Act (like a number of state statutes) imposed double liability on bank shareholders: If the bank became insolvent, shareholders would lose their investments and, in addition, could be assessed (required to pay into the bank) the par value of their stock again. This feature of double liability presumably mitigated shareholders' taste for risk-taking by bank managers. This double liability provision, however, was eliminated from banking law in the 1930s. (Why do you think it was abandoned?)

Today the bank regulators attempt to ensure adequate solvency by means of "capital adequacy" rules that require banks to maintain minimum levels of capital as a cushion against default. These capital adequacy rules are discussed in the following subsection.

*Debtholders.* Another potential source of market discipline are holders of debt securities. For monitoring purposes debt has advantages over equity in that debtholders do not share in the profits if a bank does very well; they receive only their contractual interest payments. Thus they do not share the stockholders' incentives to take excessive risks. On the other hand, debtholders other than depositors do not have the right to withdraw their funds on demand. Thus they cannot cause bank runs by rapidly withdrawing funds. For this reason, too, holders of debt securities might appear well-qualified as private sector monitors.

Among debtholders, the class of investors best suited to imposing market discipline would appear to be holders of subordinated debt. This is so for several reasons. First, holders of senior debt may not be sufficiently risk-averse. They will be repaid even if the bank becomes insolvent, so long as the bank does not go so deeply under water that its assets are not sufficient to cover their claims. Thus, unless checked by other investors, senior debtholders may not discourage bank managers from taking unwise business risks. Second, holders of subordinated debt are the first to lose their investments after the equity is wiped out. Accordingly, they have a strong incentive to monitor the activities of bank managers carefully on a day-to-day basis to make sure that the bank does not take excessive risks. Finally, holders of subordinated debt are typically represented by a trustee who is specifically charged under the trust indenture with monitoring the bank and protecting rights of holders under that document. Thus monitoring by subordinated debtholders under a trust indenture is not eroded by each investor's relying on others to look out for her or his interests.

Largely for historical reasons, banks have not tended to obtain capital by means of subordinated debt issues. Thus despite the theoretical advantages of subordinated debt as a device for market discipline, it was not particularly significant in practice. Recently, however, some of the larger banks have issued significant amounts of subordinated debt, and the use of this device has been encouraged by revised capital adequacy standards, as we discuss below.

*Depositors.* Finally, consider depositors. Depositors have some attractive features as forces for imposing market discipline. Because depositors make up a large proportion of a bank's capitalization, their interests are likely to be influential with bank managers. Moreover, the depositor's claim against the bank is typically that of a general or unsecured creditor (subject however to rules in some states giving depositors priority over other unsecured creditors). Thus in the absence of deposit insurance depositors would usually lose some of their investment if their banks became insolvent. Depositors therefore have an incentive to monitor bank managers to prevent excessive risk.

There are at least three significant problems, however, with relying on depositors to impose market discipline: (1) under the current regulatory regime depositors are usually protected in full and accordingly have no incentive to impose market discipline; (2) depositors may not have easy access to information necessary for them to make an informed judgment about the condition of their banks; and (3) depositor discipline, when it occurs, might take the form of runs that create more problems than they cure.

The first problem is how to place depositors at some risk of bank failure. A number of solutions have been proposed. Even without implementing legislation, the FDIC—instead of paying off even uninsured depositors, as it often does today—could greatly increase its use of resolution procedures in which uninsured depositors are not made whole. This, then, would place uninsured depositors at some risk. We discuss some of these procedures in Chapter 8.

Other mechanisms to accomplish the same result would require legislative as opposed to administrative action. The simplest approach might be to reduce the present $100,000 deposit ceiling to some figure high enough to protect small depositors—say $25,000—but nevertheless low enough to increase the amount of uninsured deposits in the banking system. Although reducing the insurance ceiling would not prevent depositors from splitting their funds into many insured accounts, the transactions costs of dividing funds into accounts of $25,000 or less likely would be so large that an increased number of depositors would be willing to place their funds at some risk by placing deposits over the insurance limit.

Alternatively, consider the merits of some form of coinsurance system, in which depositors would be fully insured up to some relatively low figure—say $25,000—and then only partially insured thereafter. For example, deposits between $25,000 and $50,000 could be 75 percent insured; deposits between $50,000 and $75,000 could be 50 percent insured; deposits between $75,000 and $100,000 could be 25 percent insured; and all deposits over $100,000 could be uninsured. Another form of coinsurance would impose the equivalent of a deductible, under which, for example, depositors would be uninsured for the first $1,000 of losses but fully insured thereafter up to $100,000. This latter proposal is politically unpopular because it would impose the costs of bank failure disproportionately on small depositors who arguably can least afford the losses.

A second problem with using depositors to impose market discipline is that depositors may not have access to information necessary for them to make an informed judgment about their bank's financial condition. In the first place, banking agencies are loath to disclose such information about the banks they supervise, arguing that disclosure is irrelevant for insured depositors and dangerous for uninsured depositors because it could lead to runs. See 12 C.F.R. §4.16 (Comptroller of the Currency regulation prohibiting public dissemination of records "containing or relating to an examination, operating, or condition report . . . relating to the affairs of any bank or affiliate thereof"); 12 C.F.R. §309.5(c)(8) (FDIC regulation exempting from disclosure "[r]ecords contained in or related to examination, operating, or condition reports by or on behalf of, or for the use of, the FDIC or any agency responsible for the regulation or supervision of financial institutions"). Not only is this information kept from the public, in some cases it was kept from the banks themselves. The FDIC only began in 1982 to disclose its ratings of bank condition to banks under its supervision, and the Comptroller of the Currency did not follow suit for national banks until 1987.

Supervisory reports are not the only available sources of information about a bank's condition, however. Bank holding companies subject to federal securities laws must file disclosure documents of various sorts, including registration statements and prospectuses, proxy statements, and annual and quarterly reports. All federally regulated banks are required to file quarterly reports of condition and income ("call reports") with their federal supervisory agencies, which are available to the public soon afterwards. Federally regulated banks are required to prepare and make available annual disclosure statements to security holders. Section 913 of FIRREA requires the publication of final orders issued with respect to any administrative enforcement proceeding, subject to allowance for reasonable delay in the event that the banking agency determines that immediate publication would threaten the safety and soundness of the bank. Banks that wish their debt to be rated by a reputable rating agency must share detailed financial information with the agency, which presumably will be reflected in the agency's published rating. Finally, nothing prohibits a bank from reporting developments to securities markets on a regular basis. Provided that such reporting is fair and accurate, the bank will not be subject to liability and might gain a valuable reputation by convincing market professionals that its securities are a good investment.

Even if full information about a bank's condition were relatively easy to obtain, however, it is not clear that depositors would make a strong effort to seek out and analyze the data. Unlike holders of debt securities, depositors are not protected by a trustee or other individual specifically charged with looking after their interests. Each depositor's incentive is to monitor a bank only up to the point where the investment in monitoring is justified by the returns from doing so. But for the most part depositors have relatively small amounts on the line. The $100,000 deposit insurance ceiling provides a powerful incentive to investors to keep their deposits below this amount. Further, even in the absence of a deposit insurance ceiling it is not clear that banks would attract huge individual investments. Because greater returns are typically available in securities markets than in bank investments (why should this be so?), individuals and corporate money managers often attempt to minimize the amounts they keep on deposit by retaining only as much as is necessary to perform transactions. In recent years this situation has changed somewhat as investors have found bank-issued certificates of deposit to be attractive investment vehicles; but in general banks remain the preferred vehicle for small investments. Thus, because most depositors have small amounts on the line, they would rationally invest relatively few resources in ensuring that the banks in which they invest are safe.

Further, because depositors are disorganized, they are subject to free-rider effects. If depositors believed that other depositors would obtain and analyze the information, they might be unwilling to do so themselves even if doing so might be cost effective for them. They might want to "free ride" on the monitoring services of other depositors. And because all depositors have the same sorts of incentives—that is, low incentives—the free rider effects can be expected to further reduce the incentive of all depositors to perform the necessary analysis and take effective action.

A third problem with depositor discipline is the form that such discipline is likely to take. A number of commentators have argued that depositors do not have an effective "voice" in bank management. In general—partly because of the fact noted above that small depositors do not have much of an incentive to monitor banks on a regular basis—depositors can be expected to exert little influence. When they do hear of a problem with their bank, it is virtually costless for them to take their money out immediately. Accordingly, depositor discipline is likely to take the forms of runs when it does occur, and runs, it is argued, are hardly a desirable means of encouraging managers to avoid risks. Those who favor depositor discipline respond that if adequate information is made available regularly, depositors are not likely to engage in catastrophic runs, and that in any event the costs of runs must be balanced against the benefits depositor discipline might confer in the form of inducing bank managers to behave in a conservative fashion to begin with.

*QUESTIONS AND COMMENTS*

1. There are a few empirical studies of the effectiveness of market discipline. One study examined interest rate data for certificates of deposit

of five different maturities at 300 different banks, and concluded that the market does exact a price for risk-taking. See Hannan & Hanweck, Bank Insolvency Risk and the Market for Large Certificates of Deposit, 20 J. Money, Credit & Banking 1203 (1988). Other studies finding some evidence of market discipline include Baer & Brewer, Uninsured CD Deposits as a Source of Market Discipline: Some New Evidence, Economic Perspectives, Federal Reserve Bank of Chicago, Sept./Oct. 1986 (examining ratio of equity market value to total assets, and variance of returns on bank equity, and concluding that uninsured depositors can exert discipline even when banks are solvent); Scott, Deposit Insurance and Bank Regulation: The Policy Choices, 44 Bus. Law. 907 (1989) (analyzing interest rates on $1 million certificates of deposit offered by 54 banks and finding a spread of 230 basis points); Short, Bank Problems and Financial Safety Nets, Economic Review of the Federal Reserve Bank of Dallas, Mar. 1987 (noting evidence suggesting that depositors, at least depositors in medium- and small-sized banks, demand higher risk premiums from problem banks). For a survey of the evidence, see G. Benston, R. Eisenbeis, P. Horvitz, E. Kane, & G. Kaufman, Perspectives on Safe and Sound Banking 179-186 (1986).

One recent study compared the default risk premium on bank subordinated debt to a variety of other measures of risk, including Moody's and Standard and Poor's bond ratings and an FDIC measure of bank risk. The study found that the risk premiums were only weakly related to the Moody's and Standard and Poor's ratings and uncorrelated with the FDIC's measure of bank risk. The authors conclude that "the impact of the cost of [subordinated debt] on bank risk-taking behavior is unlikely to coincide with the directions desired by bank managers." Avery, Belton, & Goldberg, Market Discipline in Regulating Bank Risk: New Evidence from the Capital Markets, 20 J. Money, Credit & Banking 597 (1988).

2. The FDIC endorsed the concept of market discipline in its 1983 study, Deposit Insurance in a Changing Environment (GPO 1983), which concluded that increased market discipline could be a valuable device for controlling excessive risk-taking incident to bank deregulation. The study suggested that the most desirable means of achieving market discipline may be the "modified payoff" closure strategy, under which insured depositors are paid off in full when a bank is closed and uninsured depositors, along with other creditors, are given an advance representing the FDIC's estimate of their pro rata share of the present value of the bank's remaining assets.

The FDIC experimented with market discipline in handling the failure of the Penn Square Bank (the issuer of the standby letter of credit in the *Philadelphia Gear* case, supra). The results were unfavorable. The disruption caused by the Penn Square failure contributed to the collapse of Continental Illinois National Bank and Trust Company in 1984, which in turn necessitated a costly federal bailout. The failure of a huge institution like Continental, in turn, frightened many in the banking community and caused a reassessment of whether it would be desirable as a matter of policy, or feasible as a matter of politics, to allow a huge money center bank to fail.

In 1987 the FDIC did an about-face on market discipline in its study Mandate for Change: Restructuring the Banking Industry (GPO 1987). The study has this to say about market discipline:

> The near-failure of Continental Illinois National Bank and Trust Company made it clear that the risks to the system are far greater when dealing with a large bank than with small institutions. It became evident that there are reasons that the FDIC or, more generally, the U.S. government, cannot permit a large bank failure to be handled in a way that would result in losses to depositors. It was felt that the chance of a deposit run on other large banks if uninsured funding sources lose confidence probably is too great to effect a modified payoff or similar transaction in this type of situation. Moreover, it is unlikely that any major industrialized country would permit creditors to experience a loss because of a major bank failure. Finally, Continental served to remind everyone banks are "special" in several ways, including funding sources. Banks are one of the few types of institutions that are highly leveraged and rely on short-term instruments redeemable at par as the primary source of funding. Thus, market discipline can be exercised suddenly and without warning and, as occurred in the early 1930s, could spread to an unacceptable proportion of the industry. This is one of the primary reasons why there is a deposit insurance system in the United States. For these reasons, the FDIC does not believe that increased depositor discipline is practical in the current structure of the U.S. banking system.

The FDIC reiterated its opposition to increased use of depositor discipline in its 1989 study, Deposit Insurance for the Nineties: Meeting the Challenge (GPO 1989).

3. One recent study by Professor Helen A. Garten rejects the assumption that depositor discipline will cause banks to control their risk-taking. In order for such a process to occur, according to Professor Garten,

> three preconditions must exist that, although present in the corporate securities market, are not now present in the deposit market. First, there must be a group of investors for whom risk is the primary consideration in choosing an investment. . . . [M]ost bank depositors are not investors in this sense at all, but are concerned with factors other than risk when they select a bank. Those depositors who do meet this definition of an investor are a relatively small group concentrated in only the very largest banks. Second, investors must have access to the information they deem relevant to their investment decisions. . . . [T]he market already generates sufficient information about banks' financial conditions to permit the interested depositor to evaluate the present risk posture of at least the major

> banking institutions. Moreover, there is considerable evidence that investors in bank deposits do in fact use this information. Nevertheless, investors are equally concerned about the final disposition of their bank in the event of unanticipated failure. Determining whether a bank is more likely to be liquidated, resulting in losses for its uninsured depositors, or to be saved through a federally assisted merger or capital injection, insuring protection in full of all depositors, is essential to evaluating the risks associated with an investment. Yet this determination cannot be made solely on the basis of disclosure about a bank's current financial position. . . . Third, market discipline must be severe enough to be felt by bank management and investors but not so severe that there is no opportunity to respond to the market's preferences. If the consequence of any misreading of the market is always immediate failure, market discipline is counterproductive, resulting not in safer banks, but simply in fewer banks. . . . [I]n the market for deposits, sudden and devastating bank runs are the only form of discipline that is likely to occur. Although proponents of market discipline contemplate some bank failure to serve as a warning to other banks of the power of the market, bank runs have precisely the opposite effect, actually discouraging both bank depositors and management from expending any energy in the ongoing management of risk.*

Garten, Banking on the Market: Relying on Depositors to Control Bank Risks, 4 Yale J. on Reg. 129, 131-132 (1986) (footnotes deleted).

For a contrasting viewpoint endorsing the potential utility of market discipline, see Macey & Miller, Bank Failures, Risk Monitoring, and the Market for Bank Control, 88 Colum. L. Rev. 1153 (1988).

4. If deposits were partially uninsured, would depositors remain ignorant about the condition of their banks? What would they be likely to do? What sorts of banks are likely to fight hardest against proposals for coinsurance of deposits?

5. Do you agree that depositor discipline would stimulate runs that might guarantee the failure of banks that otherwise might be able to return to profitability? If depositor discipline had been a reality in the savings and loan industry in the 1980s, do you think the problems of the industry would have been more or less expensive for taxpayers?

6. What about the argument that depositor discipline might encourage too-conservative banking practices? If bankers fear that risk-taking might cause runs, they might be wary of taking even desirable risks, right?

### c. Risk-Adjusted Premiums

An alternative to market discipline, which Congress has now instructed the FDIC to implement, is to charge banks for insurance coverage based on the perceived risk that the bank will fail. This of course is the analog to private insurance markets in which insurers charge higher premiums to individuals deemed to fall into higher risk categories.

A perfectly priced risk-adjusted insurance system would have many benefits over the existing regulatory structure. Such a system could potentially replace a large portion of existing bank regulation. Limitations on bank assets or activities, for example, would arguably be unnecessary if a bank were required to pay a premium for deposit insurance exactly reflecting the risk posed by such activities and investments. In place of categorical restrictions on bank expansion it could be possible for bank managers to make their own assessment of what activities are in the best interests of their institutions. Banks could potentially act as more efficient financial intermediaries and could contribute to social wealth by directing capital to higher valued uses. Further, perfectly risk-adjusted deposit insurance premiums could potentially obviate the need for capital adequacy standards. They could allow bankers to assess for themselves the relative pros and cons of various possible capital structures. Finally, the unwieldy and costly system of examination and enforcement could be considerably reduced under such a system. As the FDIC and others have acknowledged, "[i]t is clear that a properly implemented risk-related insurance system (that is, one in which assessments closely approximate the expected cost of each bank to the deposit insurance fund) would be superior to our current system." FDIC, Deposit Insurance in a Changing Environment A-3 (GPO 1983).

The FDICIA legislation broke new ground in 1991 by requiring the FDIC, by regulation, to "establish a risk-based assessment system for insured depository institutions." 12 U.S.C. §1817(b)(1)(A). A risk-based assessment system is one in which the depository institution's insurance assessments are calculated on the basis of (1) the probability that the deposit insurance fund will incur a loss with respect to the institution, taking into consideration the risks attributable to different categories and concentrations of assets and liabilities, as well as other factors in the FDIC's discretion; (2) the likely amount of the loss if it occurs; and (3) the revenue needs of the deposit insurance funds. 12 U.S.C. §1817(b)(1)(C).

Although Congress has now mandated the use of risk-based deposit premiums, it has provided precious little guidance as to how a program of risk-based premiums should be structured, leaving virtually all decisions on implementation to the FDIC. That agency faces a substantial challenge in devising a workable set of rules in this area.

The brute fact is that no one has yet developed a reliable and administratively feasible means for measuring deposit insurance risk. Part of the problem is that bank risk has many elements. Professor Sherman Maisel identifies the following five types of risk that would need to be estimated in any reasonably accurate risk weighting system: (1) interest rate risk; (2) credit risk; (3) the risk of fraud and insider abuse; (4)

operating risk; and (5) diversification risk. S. Maisel, Risk and Capital Adequacy in Commercial Banks (1981). Exact measurement of these risks would be difficult, although Maisel believes it might be possible to get a sufficient measure to price insurance premiums.

A number of commentators have suggested that the uniform rating system for bank condition used by federal bank regulators (the "CAMEL" system) might be used to measure bank risk. As we will discuss in Chapter 7, examiners use the CAMEL guidelines to grade the quality of capital, assets, management, earnings, and liquidity, and then assign a composite score ranging from 1 (for the most solvent banks) to 5 (for the shakiest banks). The FDIC objects on a number of grounds to using the CAMEL ratings for the purpose of pricing deposit insurance. Such a system, according to the FDIC, would be "relatively expensive to . . . implement" because (1) it would require annual examinations; (2) the ratings are largely based on subjective examiner judgment; (3) banks are examined by different agencies that do not necessarily apply the guidelines consistently; and (4) the linkage between the CAMEL rating and the insurance assessment might create an adversarial relationship between examiner and bank that could undermine the reliability of the ratings. FDIC, Deposit Insurance in a Changing Environment A-5 (GPO 1983).

One intriguing possibility for pricing deposit insurance is to allow a role for the private sector. Assume, for example, that private insurers were allowed to provide some type of reinsurance or supplemental insurance for bank deposits. Because this additional insurance would be limited in extent, it would not subject the private provider to the essentially uninsurable risk of nationwide bank panic. Thus the private sector could offer the insurance and would have the appropriate incentive to price it accurately. See Baer, Private Prices, Public Insurance: The Pricing of Federal Deposit Insurance, 9 Economic Perspectives of the Federal Reserve Bank of Chicago, Sept./Oct. 1985. If such a system were instituted the federal insurance rates could be set on the basis of the private market rates for the bank in question. The potential advantage of private insurance is that the private insurer's self-interest is placed behind the risk evaluation. Among the disadvantages of such a system are that it might involve unnecessary duplication of resources, and it is unclear whether the private sector would be willing to take on the task of evaluating bank risk.

The FDICIA encourages exploration of options for private sector pricing of the risk-based insurance premiums. It provides that in implementing a risk-based system, the FDIC may "obtain private reinsurance covering not more than 10 percent of any loss the [FDIC] incurs with respect to an insured depository institution," and may base the institution's assessment in whole or in part on the costs of the reinsurance so obtained. 12 U.S.C. §1817(b)(1)(B). In furtherance of the same goal, Congress instructed the FDIC to study the feasibility of establishing a private reinsurance system, including a demonstration project of the activities required to establish a private reinsurance system. FDICIA §322.

*QUESTIONS AND COMMENTS*

1. For a review, see Murton, A Survey of the Issues and the Literature Concerning Risk-Related Deposit Insurance, FDIC Banking & Econ. Rev. 11 (Mar. 1986).

2. What do you think about proposals to set federal deposit insurance premiums on the basis of prices charged by private insurers? Do these proposals depend on any assumptions about the structure and incentives of private insurance markets? Would not private insurance create an inefficiency by, in effect, requiring duplicative inspections of bank operations—one by the federal regulators and one by the private insurers in order to price the insurance policies?

3. What about requiring banks to sell subordinated debt on capital markets and pricing insurance on the basis of the default premium that the capital markets exact from the issuing bank as a condition to take on the debt? Would this work for smaller banks as well as larger ones?

4. What does it say about the reliability of bank examinations if the FDIC itself is unwilling to use its CAMEL ratings as a proxy for assessing bank risk in setting deposit insurance premiums?

5. What about heightening the incentives of a bank's nondeposit creditors to exercise discipline by enacting a nationwide depositor preference statute, under which bank depositors would be given statutory priority over other unsecured creditors in the event of bank failure? Congress enacted such a statute in 1995.

6. What other important class of actors have we omitted in this discussion of market discipline? What about a bank's managers? They may be shareholders, but their principal interest in the bank is usually the benefits (including salary, perquisites, bonuses, and reputation) associated with being a bank executive. Those benefits will be lost if the bank fails. Given that managers run the bank and are not subject to perfect shareholder control, why can we not rely on their self-interest as an adequate means of preventing inefficient risk-taking?

7. Obviously, market discipline is only as good as the amount of information available about the institution, and disclosure of the condition of a bank is only as good as the accounting method used to report assets and liabilities. Traditionally, banks have reported on a historical cost (book value) basis. They have not marked their assets to market value. One obvious reason why banks have not marked to market is that it is very difficult to assign a market value to loans in a bank's portfolio—indeed, one of the principal reasons that financing is provided

by banks is that the assets in question are ones for which organized markets have a difficult time assigning a value.

Still, banks could more easily mark to market their holdings of securities regularly traded on organized markets. And even if banks cannot determine the market value of their loan portfolios with perfect certainty, they may be able to provide more information than book value alone.

Section 121 of FDICIA calls on the federal banking agencies to develop a method for insured depository institutions to provide supplemental disclosure of estimated fair market value of assets and liabilities, to the extent feasible and practicable, in certain reports filed with the agencies. In a related development, the Financial Accounting Standards Board (FASB) issued Statement No. 107 (December 1991) requiring entities with $150 million or more in assets to "disclose the fair value of financial instruments, both assets and liabilities recognized and not recognized in the statement of financial position, for which it is practicable to estimate fair value. If estimating fair value is not practicable, this Statement requires disclosure of descriptive information pertinent to estimating the fair value of a financial instrument. . . ."

The Federal Financial Institutions Examination Council (FFIEC) has requested comment on a proposal that insured depository institutions required to file annual reports under §112 of FDICIA should provide supplemental "fair value" disclosures for their assets and liabilities. This would include the disclosures required under FASB Statement 107, along with supplemental unaudited disclosures about fair values of nonfinancial assets and liabilities (such as commercial loans). The FFIEC has also solicited comments on whether insured depository institutions should include supplemental fair value disclosures in their reports of condition to the bank supervisory agencies, which would include information about off-balance sheet assets and liabilities as well as on-balance sheet items. See 58 Fed. Reg. 19257 (April 13, 1993).

### d. Early Regulatory Intervention

Another approach to the deposit insurance dilemma, which was enacted into law in the 1991 FDICIA legislation, is to mandate early regulatory intervention for troubled banks. The idea is deceptively simple. If banks are closed exactly at the point of economic insolvency, there will never be a need to draw down the deposit insurance funds; indeed, in theory deposit insurance per se would be unnecessary because depositors would always be paid off in full. The only costs of federal regulation would be the transactions costs of monitoring a bank's capital and handling the closure when the bank became economically insolvent. Further, bank managers would have more appropriate incentives to avoid taking risks because a far greater proportion of a bank's risk would be placed on shareholders, who no longer would have the ability to "lay off" some of the risk of things going bad on creditors. Shareholder monitoring could therefore be used to reduce risk-taking by bank managers.

This idea has considerable appeal. If even the concept of economic insolvency had been binding on the FHLBB, hundreds of insolvent thrift institutions would have been shut down during the 1980s before they fell hopelessly under water. Savings and loan institutions were often propped up during this period by a variety of "creative" accounting practices that allowed the thrift regulators leeway *not* to close them even though the institutions were clearly insolvent in economic terms. The FSLIC avoided rapid closure in many cases prior to 1989 because its assets fell far short of what would be required to pay off depositors if all insolvent savings and loans were shut down. This form of regulatory forbearance aggravated the losses in the thrift industry and contributed to the costs of the 1989 FIRREA legislation. The crisis in the savings and loan industry probably would have been mitigated if early closure had been utilized during the 1980s.

Implementing this early closure concept, however, presents significant practical difficulties. Most importantly, accurately determining the current market value of a bank's assets is a daunting and possibly impossible task. It is, accordingly, extremely difficult to determine the point of economic insolvency where bank closure should occur in theory.

In the absence of firm information about when a bank becomes insolvent, it might seem appropriate to close the bank at some point *prior* to insolvency at a time when its assets are known to exceed its liabilities. But closing a bank too early imposes costs of its own, including losses of going-concern value and the costs of receivership or conservatorship proceedings themselves. There may also be more subtle costs in the form of higher capital costs for depository institutions: persons looking for good investments may be deterred from investing in a bank out of fear that the bank will be closed prior to the point of economic insolvency and their investments will be wiped out.

The dilemma of when to close a bank may be mitigated—although probably not resolved altogether—through early regulatory intervention prior to closure. Banking agencies have always intervened more forcefully in the affairs of insured depository institutions as their capital levels dropped to the point of near-insolvency, but the early closure concept implies even more vigorous intervention than has been the case heretofore. Advocates of early closure have also suggested that the regulators be effectively forced to intervene promptly to restore capital levels, in order to preclude the possibility that they would respond to political pressures and exercise "forbearance."

These proposals, which had been circulating in the academic literature for several years, bore fruit in the Federal Deposit Insurance Corporation Improvement Act of 1991. Section 131 of the FDICIA, 12 U.S.C. §1831o, requires "prompt corrective action" when depository institutions run into capital adequacy problems. Institutions deemed "undercapitalized" are required to submit capital restoration plans to their supervisory agencies, detailing how they plan to increase their capital to acceptable levels. Unless a capital restoration plan has been approved by the applicable regulator and complied with by the depository institution, an undercapitalized institution is restricted in its asset growth and must receive prior regulatory approval for business expansion plans.

More stringent limitations apply to insured depository institutions that are deemed "significantly undercapitalized," that fail to submit an acceptable capital restoration plan, or that fail to comply with the terms of a plan that has been accepted by the regulator. With respect to such institutions, federal regulators are required to implement one or more of the following actions: (1) requiring that the institution be recapitalized, either through the sale of securities or by merger or acquisition by another firm; (2) restricting transactions with affiliates; (3) restricting the interest rates that the institution pays on deposits; (4) restricting asset growth or requiring a reduction in total assets; (5) restricting activities; (6) improving management, for example by replacing board members, dismissing top managers, or hiring new personnel; (7) requiring prior Federal Reserve approval of any capital distributions by the parent holding company; (8) prohibiting deposits from correspondent banks; (9) requiring that the institution's holding company divest itself of the institution itself or of other, nondepository subsidiaries, or that the depository institution divest itself of shaky subsidiaries; and (10) taking "any other action that the agency determines will better carry out the purpose of this section" than the actions specifically mentioned. Compensation of senior executive officers of such institutions is also severely restricted.

Institutions in even greater trouble—those deemed "critically undercapitalized"—are subject to the most onerous regulatory constraints. Such institutions may not, without poor FDIC approval, enter any material transaction other than in the usual course of business, extend credit for any highly leveraged transaction, make any material change in accounting methods, engage in any transaction covered by §23A(b) of the Federal Reserve Act (governing transactions with affiliates), pay excessive compensation or bonuses, or pay interest at a rate that would increase the institutions' cost of funds to a level significantly exceeding prevailing interest rates on insured deposits. In addition, a critically undercapitalized depository institution is generally prohibited from making principal or interest payments on its subordinated debt.

If prompt corrective action does not succeed in stabilizing a shaky institution and returning it to capital adequacy, the FDICIA encourages the banking agencies to "facilitate early resolution of troubled insured depository institutions whenever feasible if early resolution would have the least possible long-term cost to the deposit insurance fund." FDICIA §143. Consistently with this principle favoring early resolution, Congress "contemplates" that resolution transactions would observe the following principles: (1) the transaction should be negotiated competitively, taking into account the value of expediting the process; (2) the institution resulting from the transaction should meet all applicable minimum capital standards; (3) the transaction should involve substantial private investment; (4) existing security holders should make "substantial concessions"; (5) directors and senior management of the resulting institution should be qualified, and should not include individuals substantially responsible for the troubled institution's problems; (6) the FDIC should have an opportunity to "participate in the success of the resulting institution" (what does this mean?); and (7) the transaction should be structured so that the FDIC does not acquire a significant percentage of the troubled institution's problem assets, succeeds to a share of the preexisting security holders' interests in proportion to the extent of the assistance it provides, and limits the assistance in terms and amount, while at the same time introducing new private investors who share risk with the FDIC. Id.

As we will discuss in Chapter 8, the federal banking agencies now have substantial powers to close a troubled insured depository institution prior to the point of technical insolvency. Early closure is specifically required for critically undercapitalized institutions, in the form of a provision requiring the appropriate federal banking agency, not later than 90 days after the depository institution becomes critically undercapitalized, to appoint a receiver or conservator or to "take such other action as the agency determines . . . would better achieve the purpose of [the prompt corrective action rules] after documenting why the action would better achieve that purpose." Section 38(h) of the Federal Deposit Insurance Act, as added by FDICIA §131. In any event a receiver must ordinarily be appointed if the institution in question remains critically undercapitalized after the expiration of three calendar quarters. Id.

Federal banking agencies also have discretion to close an institution prior to insolvency in other circumstances. They may do so, for example, when a depository institution is found to be in an unsafe or unsound condition, even if not technically insolvent; when the institution has willfully violated a final cease-and-desist order; when the institution is likely to incur losses that will deplete all or substantially all its capital, and there is no reasonable prospect for the institution to become adequately capitalized without federal assistance; when there is a violation of any law or regulation, or any unsafe or unsound practice, that is likely to weaken the institution's condition; and when the institution is undercapitalized (as opposed to critically undercapitalized) and either has no reasonable prospect of returning to capital adequacy or fails to undertake prompt corrective action. 12 U.S.C. §1821(c)(5).

*QUESTIONS AND COMMENTS*

1. For scholarly studies endorsing the early closure concept, see, e.g., G. Benston & G. Kaufman, Risk and Solvency Regulation of Depository Institutions: Past Policies and Current Options (Federal Reserve Bank of Chicago Staff Mem. 88-1 (1988)); E. Kane, The Gathering Crisis in Federal Deposit Insurance (1985).

2. Are there any constitutional problems with the government closing a bank before the point of actual insolvency? See Fahey v. Mallonee, 332 U.S. 245, 254 (1947).

3. Are there any costs of a rapid closure rule? Note that an early closure rule might require closure in some situations where a bank became temporarily insolvent but then quickly returned to profitability. Is this something to worry about? What about the costs of reorganization?

4. Consider the political impacts of an early closure policy. Congressional hearings in 1989 charged that five senators had interceded with federal regulators to urge regulatory forbearance for a thrift institution from which they had received substantial campaign contributions. In a separate matter House Speaker Jim Wright was forced to resign in a swirl of allegations including the charge that he had improperly interceded with federal regulators on behalf of thrifts in his district. As a result of these and other disclosures, stricter closure policies may find a congenial reception on Capitol Hill in the future as a means of deflecting political pressure from constituents seeking regulatory forbearance.

### e. Narrow Banks

A final proposal, attributed to Brookings Institution scholar Robert A. Litan and others, is to separate insured deposits from risky lending and investment. See R. Litan, What Should Banks Do? (1987). The idea is to preserve deposit insurance where it is most useful—in offering depositors an essentially risk-free deposit account—but to eliminate most of the problems with the existing system. Under the narrow bank proposal, bank managers would be prevented from using insured deposits to engage in excessively hazardous activities by severe limits on the assets that could be held against insured deposits. On the other hand, existing restrictions on bank activities and investments would be removed to the extent that the assets involved would be supported by uninsured deposits. The narrow bank proposal is an interesting combination of heightened regulation—for "narrow banks" with insured deposits—and reduced regulation—for other banks without insured deposits.

If properly implemented the narrow bank concept would essentially obviate the need for deposit insurance. As long as the deposits in narrow banks are fully secured by safe and readily marketable assets the bank would be highly unlikely to fail—at least as long as strict limits are placed on activities, off-balance sheet investments, and transactions with affiliates. The principal residual failure risk would appear to be the danger of bank fraud, which while not insubstantial would be greatly mitigated by the prohibition on devoting assets to loans. To be sure, depositors in narrow banks would continue to receive protection from federal deposit insurance, but the cost of the deposit insurance program to the federal government would be minimal.

Although the initial proposals envisaged narrow banks as separately capitalized and independently operated institutions, Professor Scott has pointed out that this degree of segregation would not be necessary: The essence of a narrow bank can be maintained within a broader financial institution by the simple device of ensuring that the insured deposits are fully secured by a lien on the narrow bank's pool of low-risk assets. Scott, Deposit Insurance and Bank Regulation: The Policy Choices, 44 Bus. Law. 907 (1989). Thus the narrow bank might not be subject to severe operating inefficiencies.

What is the chief objection to narrow banks? It is that narrow banks may throw out the baby of preventing runs and panics with the bath water of excessive risk-taking. While undoubtedly many people would place their savings in narrow banks, many others would be attracted to the higher interest paid by unregulated banks that are permitted to invest in higher-risk—and therefore higher-yield—assets. But unregulated institutions face a failure risk essentially no different from that faced by commercial banks prior to the institution of federal deposit insurance in 1933. If enough wealth came to be concentrated in these "fat" banks, the nation would arguably once again become subject to the danger of catastrophic banking panics. In such a case the narrow bank would have accomplished little by way of improving the safety of the nation's banking system while overcoming some of the defects of federal deposit insurance.

## *QUESTIONS AND COMMENTS*

1. Do we already have a form of narrow bank—albeit one without deposit insurance—in the form of the money market mutual fund? These institutions invest in a highly diversified portfolio of safe and liquid instruments, such as government securities and high-grade commercial paper. Some mutual funds, which invest only in U.S. Treasury securities, are virtually as safe as federally insured bank deposits. Open-end funds also typically offer limited checking and other funds transfer privileges. So far there have been no noteworthy failures of open-end funds. What lessons on the narrow bank proposal can we draw from the experience with money market mutual funds?

2. Congress toyed with implementing a version of the narrow bank

concept in 1991, but ultimately backed off the idea. However, it did mandate an FDIC study of the "feasibility of authorizing insured depository institutions to offer both insured and uninsured deposit accounts to customers." FDICIA §321. Do you see any advantages with a "two-window" deposit system? Any problems?

## E. CAPITAL REGULATION

Let us now turn from a focus on the liability side of a bank's balance sheet to a topic that will sometimes require a comparison of the asset *and* the liability sides—namely, capital regulation. As we will see, capital regulation has long been a feature of banking law. In recent years, however, this topic, which had been a somewhat arcane backwater, has exploded into prominence with the enormous rise in importance of capital adequacy within the overall system of bank regulatory policy.

What is the purpose of capital adequacy rules? They guard against excessive riskiness in banking. A bank's capital—roughly speaking, the excess of its assets over its liabilities—is its cushion against insolvency. As long as a bank has positive capital in real economic terms, it is not insolvent. Thus, bank capital protects depositors, and because of federal deposit insurance, the capital of insured banks protects the deposit insurance funds.

So much is simple: One way of protecting the federal deposit insurance funds is to insist that insured banks maintain adequate reserves of capital. But translating the basic principle that bank capital should be "adequate" into an enforceable and administrable regulation is much more difficult. Relevant terms must be carefully defined against a background of rapid financial and legal innovation, and appropriate, objectively verifiable tests for capital adequacy must be formulated. These have proved no easy tasks. In large measure the difficulties stem from the fact that we cannot simply compare a bank's capital per se with its assets per se. There are different types of capital—some more "tangible" or "realer" than others—and different types of assets—some riskier than others—and to clump them all together into a single capital adequacy rule would be unfair and possibly counterproductive. Distinctions must be made, and the distinctions involve the bank regulatory system in an area of considerable complexity and confusion.

We start with a review of the rules that require depository institutions to maintain specified levels of minimum capital. We then move to the problem of capital adequacy as a ratio of capital to assets.

## 1. Traditional Minimum Capital Rules

Depository institutions are generally required to commence business with a specified level of minimum capital. As we have seen, the National Bank Act requires that national banks start with an initial capital the amount of which varies depending on the location of the institution. 12 U.S.C. §51. The Comptroller of the Currency has fleshed out this initial capital rule and generally requires a higher level of initial capitalization than is mandated under the statute. All the capital stock must be paid in before the institution is authorized to commence business. 12 U.S.C. §53.

What happens if the capital stock is not paid in or if capital becomes impaired as a result of losses? The National Bank Act requires that the Comptroller assess the shareholders pro rata to make good the shortfall. If shareholders don't pay on the assessment, their interest in the institution can be sold off and charged against the assessment. If the shortfall is not rectified within three months, the institution can be placed in receivership. 12 U.S.C. §55. These provisions might sound like useful mechanisms for maintaining a bank's capital and thus preventing insolvency and losses to the deposit insurance funds. The truth, however, is that they have been all but moribund for many years, with virtually no enforcement even though hundreds of depository institutions have fallen into capital-impaired positions in recent years.

More currently relevant are the provisions restricting the payment of dividends by depository institutions in capital-impaired condition. The general rule is that a depository institution may not declare a dividend when its capital is impaired or if the dividend would have the effect of impairing capital. See 12 U.S.C. §56 (national banks). Many more teeth were added to the law by the Federal Deposit Insurance Corporation Improvement Act of 1991, which established a system of prompt corrective action for any insured institution that falls below specified capital levels (we have already studied this system earlier in this chapter). This law restricts the ability of the board of directors of an undercapitalized insured depository institution to declare dividends or take any other action that would have the effect of distributing cash or other assets to shareholders. The law requires, generally, that no insured depository institution may make a capital distribution of any kind if, after the distribution, the institution would be undercapitalized. Moreover, undercapitalized insured depository institutions are required to submit an acceptable capital restoration plan to the appropriate federal banking agency. The capital restoration plan must (a) specify the steps the institution plans to take to restore capital adequacy, (b) set goals for capital restoration, and (c) provide further information about the kinds of activity in which the institution plans to engage during the pendency of the capital restoration plan. 12 U.S.C. §1831o. This system of prompt corrective action in effect creates a regime of capital restoration that mimics quite closely the old, superseded rules on minimum capital, discussed above, that still maintain a shadowy existence within the U.S. Code. Minimum capital rules are not dead; they simply live on in another form.

## 2. *Capital Adequacy Ratios*

Traditional regulations of minimum capital have been supplemented by what is today a much more important regulatory system which generally requires that depository institutions maintain a certain *ratio* of capital to assets.

There are currently two separate capital adequacy rules for all depository institutions: leverage ratios and risk-adjusted capital ratios. Thrift institutions are generally required to satisfy an additional, tangible capital ratio. Although the accounting concepts used to calculate these ratios are often quite technical, the basic rules are relatively simple. A brief description follows.

### a. Leverage Ratios

The traditional ratio is the leverage test. This is simply a gross ratio of capital to assets without any adjustment for risk. Determination of the applicable leverage ratios has been a matter of some political controversy; the banking agencies eventually agreed to require "core" capital equal to 3 percent of adjusted total assets for the highest-rated institutions, with somewhat higher ratios for banks with lower ratings. Core capital is defined in accordance with the risk-adjusted capital adequacy guidelines, discussed immediately below.

### b. Risk-Adjusted Capital Guidelines

Until recently the leverage ratios were the only bank capital regulations. Banks were required to keep a minimum amount of capital per dollar of assets. But this measure was quite crude because the assets against which capital had to be maintained varied widely in riskiness. Banks, accordingly, could operate at various levels of risk while complying with the capital adequacy standard.

This regulatory structure became increasingly problematic with the advent of significant foreign competition in banking markets because capital adequacy rules varied among major banking nations. International dialogue on uniform capital standards bore fruit in 1987 when the federal banking agencies reached a risk-based capital agreement with the Bank of England. The U.S./U.K. agreement was expanded in 1988 into a broad-based international framework for capital standards by action of the Committee on Banking Regulations and Supervisory Practices, which meets under the auspices of the Bank for International Settlements in Basel, Switzerland (thus its shortened name, the "Basel Agreement"). Federal banking agencies then proposed and adopted risk-based capital guidelines in conformity with the overall framework of the Basel Agreement.

The risk-adjusted capital adequacy guidelines function as follows. The first step is to sort each institution's assets into one of four different risk categories, each of which carries a different risk weight: (1) 0 percent for assets deemed essentially risk-free (such as cash, claims backed by the full faith and credit of the U.S. government, and balances due from Federal Reserve banks); (2) 20 percent for slightly more risky assets (such as portions of loans conditionally guaranteed by the U.S. government or the governments of other major industrial nations); (3) 50 percent for still more risky assets (including government-issued revenue bonds and first mortgage residential loans); and (4) 100 percent for all other assets (including all private sector loans and bank-owned real estate).

Total assets in each category are multiplied by the applicable risk weight for each category, and the products are summed. For example, if institution A had $100 million in category 1 assets, $100 million in category 2 assets, $100 million in category 3 assets, and $100 million in category 4 assets, the institution's total risk-adjusted capital would be $170 million ($100 million × 0 + $100 million × .2 + $100 million × .5 + $100 million × 1).

The guidelines also account for off-balance sheet items such as letters of credit. Each off-balance sheet item is multiplied by a credit conversion factor to determine the "credit equivalent value" of the particular off-balance sheet activity. Four credit conversion factors are established, ranging from 100 percent for direct credit substitutes such as standby letters of credit to 0 percent for unused portions of commitments with an original maturity of one year or less. This amount is also adjusted for risk based on the identity of the borrower to determine the risk-adjusted credit equivalent value, which is then added to total risk-adjusted capital. If our institution A has $50 million outstanding in standby letters of credit for private commercial enterprises and no other off-balance sheet activities, an additional $50 million will be added to its risk-adjusted assets of $170 million ($50 million × 1 (credit conversion factor) × 1 (risk weight applicable for private borrowers)). The institution's total risk adjusted assets would then be $220 million.

Once the total of risk adjusted assets is calculated, the next step is to determine an institution's capital. The guidelines require that an institution's capital base be first divided into two categories: "tier 1" or "core" capital, and "tier 2" or "supplementary" capital. Tier 1 capital includes common stockholder's equity, qualifying noncumulative perpetual preferred stock, and minority interests in equity accounts of subsidiaries; goodwill is not included. Tier 2 capital includes (subject to various limitations and exclusions) allowances for loan and lease losses, perpetual preferred stock not included in tier 1 capital, subordinated debt, intermediate term preferred stock, and certain other hybrid capital instruments and notes. Tier 2 capital is comprised of debt or equity instruments that are considered to be less permanent or to have less certain value than the components of core capital. Total capital is determined by adding tier 1 and tier 2 capital, subject to the limitation that the total of tier 2 capital may not exceed the amount of tier 1 capital; this sum is then reduced by certain deductions.

The final step is to determine whether an institution's total capital exceeds the minimum regulatory requirements, which are stated as a percentage of total risk-adjusted assets. The guidelines were implemented over a three-year period commencing on December 31, 1990; a ratio of 8 percent total capital to total risk-adjusted assets came into effect on December 31, 1992.

Thus, a bank's minimum total capital will be determined by multiplying its total risk-adjusted assets (including off-balance sheet items) by 8 percent. Further, because the amount of tier 2 capital may not exceed the amount of tier 1 capital, the guidelines in effect impose a separate tier 1 capital to risk-adjusted assets ratio of 4 percent. If institution A in the above example would have total risk-adjusted assets of $220 million, its minimum total capital would be $17.6 million and its minimum tier 1 capital would be $8.8 million. Thus, if institution A had total capital in excess of $17.6 million and tier 1 capital in excess of $8.8 million, it would ordinarily be considered in compliance with the risk-based capital guidelines.

## *QUESTIONS AND COMMENTS*

1. In 1993 the Basel Committee proposed to modify the 1988 capital accord in a number of ways. Several of these proposals dealt with so-called derivative instruments, such as interest-rate swaps, that have become important in financial markets over the past few years.

The Basel Committee defined the conditions under which depository institutions would be permitted to "net" credit risks with a given counterparty to avoid overestimating the risk of a given transaction. Second, the committee proposed to levy specific capital charges against open positions in debt and equity securities on banks' trading books and in foreign exchange. These were not picked up by the counterparty credit risk requirements of the 1988 accord. If a bank has invested heavily in options, for example, it faces the risk of price fluctuations in the underlying security. The committee proposed to take account of this market risk, although the precise mechanism it intended to use was not clearly established.

Finally, the committee proposed to address the interest rate risk run by banks—that is, the risk imposed by the mismatch in the duration of a bank's assets and liabilities. Here, however, the committee indicated that it would not impose substantive regulation but rather seek to establish a common reporting framework for interest rate risk. The committee recognized "that a certain degree of interest rate mismatching is a normal feature of the business of banking," and opined that "the existing capital requirements can be regarded as providing adequate protection against interest rate risk exposure in most situations. The measurement system is designed to identify institutions that may be incurring extraordinarily large amounts of interest rate risk. Within that context, it would be left to national authorities to determine what if anything might be done." Reading between the lines, one suspects that the committee was unable to reach agreement among its own members about the proper treatment of interest rate risk under the capital adequacy regime and decided to punt the matter to each member state's domestic banking supervisors.

2. Section 305 of FDICIA required the federal banking agencies to review their risk-based capital standards to ensure that those standards take adequate account of interest rate risk, concentration of credit risk, and the risks of nontraditional activities. The most important of these factors is surely interest rate risk. The federal banking agencies have advocated two different approaches to measuring and controlling interest rate risk within the framework of the capital adequacy rules. The OTS favored a more conservative rule and a more sophisticated methodology than the other banking regulators; eventually two rules were issued, one by the OTS and one jointly by the Comptroller, the Federal Reserve, and the FDIC. The rules are quite technical and need not be described in detail here.

Something of their flavor can be grasped from the general features of the OTS rule. Under the OTS approach, savings associations with a greater than "normal" level of interest rate exposure are subject to a deduction from total capital for purposes of calculating their risk-based capital requirement. Interest rate exposure, in turn, is measured as the decline in net portfolio value (a measure of the market value of an institution's investment portfolio) that would result from a 200 basis point shock [rise] in market interest rates. The interest rate risk (IRR) component to be deducted from total capital is one-half the difference between an institution's measured exposure and the "normal" level of exposure, which is defined as 2 percent of the estimated economic value of its assets. See Office of Thrift Supervision, Regulatory Capital: Interest Rate Risk Component, 58 Fed. Reg. 45,799, 45,801-02 (August 31, 1993).

The other banking agencies have adopted a less stringent approach that permits a depository institution under their supervision to use either its own internal model of interest rate risk or a supervisory model that requires banks to report their assets, liabilities and off-balance-sheet positions in time bands based on their remaining maturities or nearest repricing dates. Each position would then be multiplied by an interest rate risk weight that represents the estimated sensitivity of the economic value of that position to a specified change in market interest rates. The risk-weighted positions of all balances would be summed to produce a net risk-weighted position that represents the estimated change in the bank's net economic value and is the primary quantitative measure used by the agencies to assess a bank's interest rate risk. See Comptroller of the Currency et al., Risk-Based Capital Standards; Concentration of Credit Risk and Risks of Nontraditional Activities, 59 Fed. Reg. 64,561 (December 15, 1994).

3. Following the recommendations of the Basel Committee, U.S. banking agencies have amended risk-based capital standards to recognize the risk-reducing benefits of bilateral netting in financial contracts. The rules permit depository institutions to net out, for risk-based capital purposes, interest and exchange rate contracts subject to legally enforceable bilateral netting arrangements, subject to specified criteria. See, e.g., Comptroller of the Currency, Risk-Based Capital Standards; Bilateral Netting Requirements, 59 Fed. Reg. 66,645 (1994).

### c. Savings Association Capital Rules

An issue of current importance is the capital rules applicable to savings associations (savings and loans and savings banks). Capital standards for these institutions were the major sticking point in the battles over FIRREA. The savings industry lobbied vigorously against stringent capital guidelines, arguing that overly harsh regulations would force closure of many shaky, but currently solvent, savings institutions. To the surprise of many, Congress resisted most of these pleas and imposed rigorous—some might say draconian—capital adequacy standards on the savings industry.

Section 301(5)(t) of FIRREA subjects federally insured savings associations to three capital standards: (1) a 1.5 percent tangible capital to total assets ratio (tangible capital consists generally of common stock and retained earnings; it excludes "supervisory goodwill," an element of core capital, which is the premium paid by investors who purchased a failed thrift); (2) a 3 percent leverage ratio; and (3) a risk-based capital requirement. In addition, the statute provides that these standards must not be less stringent than the capital standards applicable to national banks. The latter requirement has been particularly controversial because it places the fate of many thrifts in the hands of the Comptroller of the Currency.

The Comptroller has the power to drive many thrifts out of business—or at least to require significant infusions of new capital as a condition of remaining in operation—by adopting stringent capital requirements for national banks.

## *QUESTIONS AND COMMENTS*

1. Do the risk-based guidelines effectively prevent a risk-preferring bank from taking on a great deal of risk? Can a bank comply with the guidelines and still operate in a risky manner? Consider the following:

a. The risk-adjusted capital adequacy guidelines did not originally account for interest rate risk. Is this a major oversight? Why do you think interest rate risk was not included? The 1991 FDICIA legislation requires federal banking agencies to revise their risk-based capital standards to take adequate account of interest-rate risk. FDICIA §305(b)(1)(A)(i).

b. Studies show that many bank failures occur as a result of fraud and self-dealing by bank insiders. Do the capital adequacy guidelines take account of this risk?

c. The guidelines lump all private sector assets in the highest risk category. Does this present opportunities for banks to increase their risk exposure while remaining within the guidelines? FDICIA requires that the revised guidelines take account of the "concentration of credit risk." FDICIA §305(b)(1)(A)(ii). What does this mean?

2. The banking agencies originally contemplated that they might discard leverage ratios once risk-adjusted guidelines were in place. Instead they decided to retain leverage ratios as an additional level of capital adequacy regulation. Was this wise? What sorts of risk are not picked up by the capital adequacy guidelines that are covered by the leverage ratios? Consider in this regard the fact that under the risk-adjusted guidelines a bank that invested solely in category 1 assets—which are assigned a risk weight of zero—could apparently get away with having no capital at all. Is this a problem? Are there private market constraints on a bank's ability to achieve such high levels of leverage?

3. What impact do you think the guidelines will have on off-balance sheet activities by banks? Will the impact be beneficial?

4. Is the whole project of capital adequacy flawed? Note that it forces banks to hold more capital than they might want to hold in a purely competitive, free-market environment. Would it not be more economically efficient to allow banks to hold the level of capital they desire? To the extent that banks tend to be undercapitalized, would a preferable solution be to require them to disclose the nature of the risks

they are undertaking and then let informed capital markets force banks to adjust to optimal capital levels?

5. For an excellent introduction to the subject of capital adequacy, see Camille M. Caesar, Note, Capital-Based Regulation and U.S. Banking Reform, 101 Yale Law Journal 1525 (1992).

## United States v. Winstar Corporation

***Supreme Court of the United States***
***1996 U.S. LEXIS 4266; 64 U.S.L.W. 4739, 1996 WL 359767 (July 1, 1996)***

SOUTER, J. announced the judgment of the Court and delivered an opinion, in which STEVENS, J. and BREYER, J. joined, and in which O'CONNOR, J. joined except as to Parts IV-A and IV-B.

The issue in this case is the enforceability of contracts between the Government and participants in a regulated industry, to accord them particular regulatory treatment in exchange for their assumption of liabilities that threatened to produce claims against the Government as insurer. Although Congress subsequently changed the relevant law, and thereby barred the Government from specifically honoring its agreements, we hold that the terms assigning the risk of regulatory change to the Government are enforceable, and that the Government is therefore liable in damages for breach.

### I

We said in Fahey v. Mallonee, 332 U.S. 245, 250 (1947), that "banking is one of the longest regulated and most closely supervised of public callings." That is particularly true of the savings and loan, or "thrift," industry, which has been described as "a Federally-conceived and assisted system to provide citizens with affordable housing funds." . . . Because the contracts at issue in today's case arise out of the National Government's efforts over the last decade and a half to preserve that system from collapse, we begin with an overview of the history of federal savings and loan regulation.

### *A*

[As the condition of the thrift industry worsened during the 1980s, the Government developed a two-pronged strategy to cope with the crisis: extensive deregulation, which allowed thrift institutions to enter new lines of business, and] new "regulatory accounting principles" (RAP) that in many instances replaced generally accepted accounting principles (GAAP) for purposes of determining compliance with its capital requirements. . . . [The result of these practices was that by 1984 the difference between RAP and GAAP net worth at S&Ls stood at $9 billion, which meant that the industry's capital position, its cushion to absorb losses, was overstated by $9 billion.] The reductions in required capital reserves, moreover, allowed thrifts to grow explosively without increasing their capital base, at the same time deregulation let them expand into new (and often riskier) fields of investment. [The easing of federal regulatory requirements was accompanied by similar initiatives on the state level, especially in California, Florida, and Texas.]

While the regulators tried to mitigate the squeeze on the thrift industry generally through deregulation, the multitude of already-failed savings and loans confronted FSLIC with deposit insurance liabilities that threatened to exhaust its insurance fund. . . . By 1988, the year of the last transaction involved in this case, FSLIC was itself insolvent by over $50 billion. . . . And by early 1989, the GAO estimated that $85 billion would be needed to cover FSLIC's responsibilities and put it back on the road to fiscal health. . . . In the end, we now know, the cost was much more even than that. . . .

Realizing that FSLIC lacked the funds to liquidate all of the failing thrifts, the Bank Board chose to avoid the insurance liability by encouraging healthy thrifts and outside investors to take over ailing institutions in a series of "supervisory mergers." . . . Such transactions, in which the acquiring parties assumed the obligations of thrifts with liabilities that far outstripped their assets, were not intrinsically attractive to healthy institutions; nor did FSLIC have sufficient cash to promote such acquisitions through direct subsidies alone, although cash contributions from FSLIC were often part of a transaction. . . . Instead, the principal inducement for these supervisory mergers was an understanding that the acquisitions would be subject to a particular accounting treatment that would help the acquiring institutions meet their reserve capital requirements imposed by federal regulations. . . . [More than 300 such mergers occurred between 1980 and 1986, as opposed to only 48 liquidations.]

***B***

Under Generally Accepted Accounting Principles (GAAP) there are circumstances in which a business combination may be dealt with by the "purchase method" of accounting. . . . The critical aspect of that method for our purposes is that it permits the acquiring entity to designate the excess of the purchase price over the fair value of all identifiable assets acquired as an intangible asset called "goodwill.". . . In the ordinary case, the recognition of goodwill as an asset makes sense: a rational purchaser in a free market, after all, would not pay a price for a business in excess of the value of that business's assets unless there actually were some intangible "going concern" value that made up the difference. . . .

For that reason, the purchase method is frequently used to account for acquisitions, . . . and GAAP expressly contemplated its application to at least some transactions involving savings and loans. . . . Goodwill recognized under the purchase method as the result of an FSLIC-sponsored supervisory merger was generally referred to as "supervisory goodwill."

Recognition of goodwill under the purchase method was essential to supervisory merger transactions of the type at issue in this case. Because FSLIC had insufficient funds to make up the difference between a failed thrift's liabilities and assets, the Bank Board had to offer a "cash substitute" to induce a healthy thrift to assume a failed thrift's obligations. Former Bank Board Chairman Richard Pratt put it this way in testifying before Congress:

"The Bank Board . . . did not have sufficient resources to close all insolvent institutions, [but] at the same time, it had to consolidate the industry, move weaker institutions into stronger hands, and do everything possible to minimize losses during the transition period. Goodwill was an indispensable tool in performing this task."

Supervisory goodwill was attractive to healthy thrifts for at least two reasons. First, thrift regulators let the acquiring institutions count supervisory goodwill toward their reserve requirements. . . . This treatment was, of course, critical to make the transaction possible in the first place, because in most cases the institution resulting from the transaction would immediately have been insolvent under federal standards if goodwill had not counted toward regulatory net worth. From the acquiring thrift's perspective, however, the treatment of supervisory goodwill as regulatory capital was attractive because it inflated the institution's reserves, thereby allowing the thrift to leverage more loans (and, it hoped, make more profits). . . . A second and more complicated incentive arose from the decision by regulators to let acquiring institutions amortize the goodwill asset over long periods, up to the forty-year maximum permitted by GAAP. . . . Amortization recognizes that intangible assets such as goodwill are useful for just so long; accordingly, a business must "write down" the value of the asset each year to reflect its waning worth. . . . The amount of the write down is reflected on the business's income statement each year as an operating expense. . . . At the same time that it amortizes its goodwill asset, however, an acquiring thrift must also account for changes in the value of its loans, which are its principal assets. The loans acquired as assets of the failed thrift in a supervisory merger were generally worth less than their face value, typically because they were issued at interest rates below the market rate at the time of the acquisition. . . . This differential or "discount," . . . appears on the balance sheet as a "contra-asset" account, or a deduction from the loan's face value to reflect market valuation of the asset. . . . Because loans are ultimately repaid at face value, the magnitude of the discount declines over time as redemption approaches; this process, technically called "accretion of discount," is reflected on a thrift's income statement as a series of capital gains. . . .

The advantage in all this to an acquiring thrift depends upon the fact that accretion of discount is the mirror image of amortization of goodwill. In the typical case, a failed thrift's primary assets were long-term mortgage loans that earned low rates of interest and therefore had declined in value to the point that the thrift's assets no longer exceeded its liabilities to depositors. In such a case, the disparity between assets and liabilities from which the accounting goodwill was derived was virtually equal to the value of the discount from face value of the thrift's outstanding loans. . . . Thrift regulators, however, typically agreed to supervisory merger terms that allowed acquiring thrifts to accrete the discount over the average life of the loans (approximately seven years), . . . while permitting amortization of the goodwill asset over a much longer period. Given that goodwill and discount were substantially equal in overall values, the more rapid accrual of capital gain from accretion resulted in a net paper profit over the initial years following the acquisition. . . . The difference between amortization and accretion schedules thus allowed acquiring thrifts to seem more profitable than they in fact were.

The downside of a faster accretion schedule, of course, was that it exhausted the discount long before the goodwill asset had been fully amortized. As a result, this treatment resulted in a net drag on earnings over the medium and long terms. . . . Many thrift managers were apparently willing to take the short term gain, . . . and others sought to stave off the inevitable losses by pursuing further acquisitions. . . .

Some transactions included yet a further inducement, described as a "capital credit." Such credits arose when FSLIC itself contributed cash to further a supervisory merger and permitted the acquiring institution to count the FSLIC contribution as a permanent credit to regulatory capital. By failing to require the thrift to subtract this FSLIC contribution from the amount of supervisory goodwill generated by the merger, regulators effectively permitted double counting of the cash as both a tangible and an intangible asset. . . . Capital credits thus inflated the acquiring thrift's regulatory capital and permitted leveraging of more and more loans.

. . . [T]he accounting treatment to be accorded supervisory goodwill and capital credits was the subject of express arrangements between the regulators and the acquiring institutions. While the extent to which these arrangements constituted a departure from prior norms is less clear, an acquiring institution would reasonably have wanted to bargain for such treatment. Although GAAP demonstrably permitted the use of the purchase method in acquiring a thrift suffering no distress, the relevant thrift regulations did not explicitly state that intangible goodwill assets created by that method could be counted toward regulatory capital. . . . Indeed, the rationale for recognizing goodwill stands on its head in a supervisory merger: ordinarily, goodwill is recognized as valuable because a rational purchaser would not pay more than assets are worth; here, however, the purchase is rational only because of the accounting treatment for the shortfall. . . . In the end, of course, such reasoning circumvented the whole purpose of the reserve requirements, which was to protect depositors and the deposit insurance fund. As some in Congress later recognized, "goodwill is not cash. It is a concept, and a shadowy one at that. When the Federal Government liquidates a failed thrift, goodwill is simply no good. It is valueless. That means, quite simply, that the taxpayer picks up the tab for the shortfall." 135 Cong. Rec. 11795 (1989) (Rep. Barnard). . . . To those with the basic foresight to appreciate all this, then, it was not obvious that regulators would accept purchase accounting in determining compliance with regulatory criteria, and it was clearly prudent to get agreement on the matter.

The advantageous treatment of amortization schedules and capital credits in supervisory mergers amounted to more clear-cut departures from GAAP and, hence, subjects worthy of agreement by those banking on such treatment. In 1983, the Financial Accounting Standards Board (the font of GAAP) promulgated Statement of Financial Accounting Standards No. 72, which applied specifically to the acquisition of a savings and loan association. SFAS 72 provided that "if, and to the extent that, the fair value of liabilities assumed exceeds the fair value of identifiable assets acquired in the acquisition of a banking or thrift institution, the unidentifiable intangible asset recognized generally shall be amortized to expense by the interest method over a period no longer than the discount on the long-term interest-bearing assets acquired is to be recognized as interest income." . . . In other words, SFAS 72 eliminated any doubt that the differential amortization periods on which acquiring thrifts relied to produce paper profits in supervisory mergers were inconsistent with GAAP. SFAS 72 also barred double-counting of capital credits by requiring that financial assistance from regulatory authorities must be deducted from the cost of the acquisition before the amount of goodwill is determined. . . . Thrift acquirers relying on such credits, then, had every reason for concern as to the continued availability of the RAP in effect at the time of these transactions.

*C*

Although the results of the forbearance policy, including the departures from GAAP, appear to have been mixed, . . . it is relatively clear that the overall regulatory response of the early and mid-1980's was unsuccessful in resolving the crisis in the thrift industry. . . . As a result, Congress enacted [FIRREA] with the objects of preventing the collapse of the industry, attacking the root causes of the crisis, and restoring public confidence.

FIRREA . . . obligated OTS to "prescribe and maintain uniformly applicable capital standards for savings associations" in accord with strict statutory requirements. 12 U.S.C. §1464(t)(1)(A). In particular, the statute required thrifts to "maintain core capital in an amount not less than 3 percent of the savings association's total assets," 12 U.S.C. §1464(t)(2)(A), and defined "core capital" to exclude "unidentifiable intangible assets," 12 U.S.C. §1464(t)(9)(A), such as goodwill. Although the reform provided a "transition rule" permitting thrifts to count "qualifying supervisory goodwill" toward half the core capital requirement, this allowance was phased out by 1995. 12 U.S.C. §1464(t)(3)(A). According to the House Report, these tougher capital requirements reflected a congressional judgment that "to a considerable extent, the size of the thrift crisis resulted from the utilization of capital gimmicks that masked the inadequate capitalization of thrifts."

The impact of FIRREA's new capital requirements upon institutions that had acquired failed thrifts in exchange for supervisory goodwill was swift and severe. OTS promptly issued regulations implementing the new capital standards along with a bulletin noting that FIRREA "eliminates [capital and accounting] forbearances" previously granted to certain thrifts. Office of Thrift Supervision, Capital Adequacy: Guidance on the Status of Capital and Accounting Forbearances and Capital Instruments Held by a Deposit Insurance Fund, Thrift Bulletin No. 38-2, Jan. 9, 1990. OTS accordingly directed that "all savings associations presently operating with these forbearances . . . should eliminate them in determining whether or not they comply with the new minimum regulatory capital standards." Ibid. Despite the statute's limited exception intended to moderate transitional pains, many institutions immediately fell out of compliance with regulatory capital requirements, making them subject to seizure by thrift regulators.

### *D*

This case is about the impact of FIRREA's tightened capital requirements on three thrift institutions created by way of supervisory mergers. Respondents Glendale Federal Bank, FSB, Winstar Corporation, and The Statesman Group, Inc. acquired failed thrifts in 1981, 1984, and 1988, respectively. After the passage of FIRREA, federal regulators seized and liquidated the Winstar and Statesman thrifts for failure to meet the new capital requirements. Although the Glendale thrift also fell out of regulatory capital compliance as a result of the new rules, it managed to avoid seizure through a massive private recapitalization. Believing that the Bank Board and FSLIC had promised them that the supervisory goodwill created in their merger transactions could be counted toward regulatory capital requirements, respondents each filed suit against the United States in the Court of Federal Claims, seeking monetary damages on both contractual and constitutional theories. . . .

## II

We took this case to consider the extent to which special rules, not generally applicable to private contracts, govern enforcement of the governmental contracts at issue here. We decide whether the Government may assert four special defenses to respondents' claims for breach: the canon of contract construction that surrenders of sovereign authority must appear in unmistakable terms . . . ; the rule that an agent's authority to make such surrenders must be delegated in express terms . . . ; the doctrine that a government may not, in any event, contract to surrender certain reserved powers . . . ; and, finally, the principle that a Government's sovereign acts do not give rise to a claim for breach of contract. . . .

[The Court, by a divided vote and without majority opinion, affirmed the judgment of the court below, that the Government had breached its contractual obligations to the acquiring institutions, and that none of the government's special defenses applied to relieve it from liability. The Court remanded the case for further proceedings to determine the appropriate measure and amount of damages.]

### *QUESTIONS AND COMMENTS*

1. This case illustrates a controversy, by now fairly longstanding, as to the extent of the federal government's responsibility for the changes in thrift institution capital standards that Congress enacted into law in the FIRREA statute of 1989. Prior to the enactment of this statute, the FSLIC had attempted to induce investors to recapitalize failed thrifts by promising special accounting treatment for the successor institutions—treatment that would allow these institutions to operate despite the fact that they did not have enough capital as measured by standard GAAP accounting. A principal way in which this could be done was to count supervisory and regulatory goodwill on their books as capital, which could be written off over an extended period of time.

When Congress enacted FIRREA in 1989, it drastically limited the use of such supervisory and regulatory goodwill. The effect was catastrophic for investors who had previously injected capital into failed thrift institutions in reliance on the earlier, more lenient accounting standards. A massive wave of litigation followed, involving tens of billions of dollars in potential damages. The excerpted case resolves the key issue of liability, but leaves many other issues open.

2. After the *Winstar* decision was announced, the market value of several publicly traded thrifts rose dramatically as investors calculated the potential increase in the value of the firms that might flow from the expected damage awards.

3. Now that investors in failed thrift institutions had prevailed on the matter of liability, the next issue became one of damages. It appeared fairly clear that the government would owe restitutionary damages; that is, it would be required to repay the value that the thrift institutions lost as a result of the withdrawal of supervisory goodwill under FIRREA. The government's potential exposure, moreover, could be greatly magnified if it were required to pay consequential damages for the amounts that the thrift institution could have *earned* if the capital which was written down had been put to more productive use—that is, if the institutions in question had made the loans that they would have been permitted to make if they had been allowed to maintain the supervisory or regulatory goodwill on their books as originally promised. Equally uncertain, and potentially large, was the government's potential exposure for consequential damages for losses incurred when an institution was seized and forced out of business as a result of the regulatory change. At this writing, these issues are largely unresolved.

4. Do you think the government should be liable to individual officers or directors (or other employees) of an institution that failed as a result of the government's abrogation of its agreements? Many of these individuals lost their jobs and suffered both economic and emotional harm in consequence. On what theory might the government be liable? Were officers and directors third-party beneficiaries of the supervisory goodwill agreements? Arguably, their only benefit was that they continued to work for the institutions that relied on the efficacy of the agreements, given that otherwise their employers faced potential ruin, correct?

5. What do you think of the OTS's behavior in the principal case? If it did have discretion to make allowances for the fact that the investors had relied on supervisory goodwill, shouldn't it have done so? Weren't the thrift capital rules in FIRREA pretty much an exercise of pure expropriation as applied to investors in failed thrifts who were relying on supervisory goodwill to remain in operation? Or can you think of some other justification (apart from the government's financial exigency) that could support what the agency did in this case?

6. In the wake of the *Winstar* case, goodwill claims could be expected to become even more important in mergers involving thrift institutions. Sellers of thrifts with pending claims against the government would want to receive the full value of their claims in the purchase price. Buyers, however, would probably not want to pay a large premium without knowing more about the case, and in any event would not want to take on the litigation risk. Can you think of a possible way to resolve this

potential impasse? One solution might be to create a litigation trust, under which any recoveries from the supervisory goodwill litigation would be given to the sellers even after closing. Creating an effective litigation trust, however, is a challenging legal task fraught with dangers and difficulties: among other things, a federal statute prohibits assignment of claims against the federal government, so some sort of trust or participating certificate structure might be necessary; there might also be serious and potentially adverse tax consequences if the transaction were not structured with extreme care.

## F. SWAPS AND DERIVATIVES

A full discussion of current trends in the banking industry today should take account of the explosive growth of so-called financial derivative products, a market in which the large commercial banks are major (though not exclusive) players. The issue with respect to bank involvement in these derivatives markets is not whether banks are permitted to engage in such activities. Swaps and other over-the-counter derivative transactions are clearly part of the business of banking, and banks can clearly engage in such transactions, either as "end users" or as dealers. However, the derivatives market has become extremely controversial in recent years, especially with highly publicized financial disasters linked to derivatives trading, such as the bankruptcy of Orange County, California, or the failure of Barings Brothers in England, one of the world's oldest merchant banks, as a result of unauthorized derivatives contracts entered into by a junior trader based in Singapore. A number of bills have been proposed in Congress to place this market under more stringent regulation. If such legislation were to pass, banks, among other major players in the derivatives market, would be among those most affected.

What are these shadowy things called derivatives? Professor Henry Hu describes the derivatives market as follows.

### Hu, Misunderstood Derivatives: The Causes of Informational Failure and the Promise of Regulatory Incrementalism

***102 Yale L.J. 1457 (1993)***

[A] "derivative" is simply a contract that either allows or obligates one of the parties (the "end-user") to buy or sell an asset. Naturally, movements in the value of the underlying asset affect the value of such a contract. Indeed, the contract's defining characteristic is that its value derives from the value of the "underlying [asset]," be it a specific stock, commodity, stock index, interest rate, or exchange rate.

Many derivatives are traded on organized exchanges; an individual can purchase them with a call to a broker. As with the purchase of shares of stock on an exchange, the end-user need not worry about who is on the other side of the transaction. Generally speaking, not only must these exchange-traded derivatives have standardized contractual terms, they also must generate enough trading activity to support a liquid market.

Sophisticated end-users, typically corporations and sovereign entities, can participate in an alternative market. They can negotiate directly with the finance divisions of some industrial corporations, various financial institutions, or, most frequently, money center banks. These contracts comprise the "over-the-counter" or "OTC" derivatives market. Since there are no clearinghouse arrangements in this market, the end-user must be confident that the dealer is creditworthy and will honor its contractual commitments—the price of contractual freedom is a greater risk of default.

From a private perspective, derivatives serve several financial functions. First, lower transaction costs can mean that the derivative is a cheaper alternative to investing in the underlying asset. Second, end-users may be able to arbitrage differences between the price of the derivative and the price of the underlying asset, or between prices in different capital markets. Third, and perhaps most important, derivatives enable end-users to transfer or modulate their market risks—risks that appear to have been particularly high in recent years. For instance, currency exchange rate volatility increased with the breakdown of the Bretton Woods system in 1973 and increased further in the 1980's. Similarly, interest rate volatility has reached unprecedented levels, higher than even the period just before 1929. Commodity price volatility in the late 1970's and 1980's far exceeded the volatility experienced in the 1950's and 1960's.

Derivatives can insulate end-users from exogenous risks—a derivative that rises in value if oil prices fall could protect a sheikdom, while one that rises along with oil prices will insulate an airline. End-users may prefer a world where their market risks have, in effect, gone away. To accomplish this end, they use two basic types of contracts as "building blocks" to create a wide variety of derivatives. "Option-based products" provide price insurance by giving the owner of the contract the right, but not the obligation, to buy an asset at a specified price. The obligation is one-sided and the owner of the option pays a fee—the "option price." "Forward-based products" freeze the price of the underlying asset. One party agrees to sell and the other party agrees to buy an asset at a specified price at a specified future time, and neither party pays any fee.

The type of derivative that has sparked much of the current regulatory concern is a forward-based product called a "swap." In a swap, one party agrees to provide a sequence of cash flows and in return the other party provides a different sequence of cash flows. Careful specification of the nature, timing, and amount of this swap of cash flows can insulate the end-user from an adverse movement in, say, interest rates; in such a case, the contract is called an interest rate swap. Similar exchanges may protect against movements in exchange rates, commodity prices, or stock prices.

[Earlier in the article, Professor Hu notes that the] OTC derivatives market has enjoyed enormous growth. On a crude, "notional amount" basis the market for selected OTC derivatives reached four trillion dollars by year-end 1991, eight times its level five years before. The notional amount of outstanding "swaps," one important genus of derivatives, now exceeds the combined value of all shares listed on the New York and Tokyo stock exchanges. Such activities are concentrated in those large, money center financial institutions central to the world's financial system. The size of these markets and the prominence of the market players mean that the stakes in the derivatives game are high. Moreover, because they are novel, complex, and opaque, derivatives activities look risky, certainly riskier than the real estate lending that contributed to the most recent banking crisis.

Thus, it is not surprising that regulatory concern over OTC derivatives activity has grown along with the OTC derivatives market. Specifically, the pioneering 1988 international capital adequacy standards for commercial banks included provisions for the "credit risks" created by these nontraditional financial products. A second round of international regulatory action appears possible, if not imminent. Some industry leaders and regulators worry that OTC derivatives could cause the next great banking crisis, and major governmental studies on the risks posed by derivatives are now under way on three continents. These studies come during a comprehensive rethinking of the regulation of commercial banks, investment banks, and capital markets in America.

Closer analysis of regulatory concerns leads to a striking puzzle and a corresponding dilemma. Many regulators—as well as some bankers—believe that, too often, bankers know too little about the risks their derivatives pose to the banks themselves. Indeed, the immediate impetus for massive regulatory efforts came when Gerald Corrigan, the president of the Federal Reserve Bank of New York, warned a group of assembled bankers that they had "all better take a very, very hard look at off-balance sheet activities" and that such activities "must be understood by top management, as well as by traders and rocket scientists." This poses the puzzle: how could banks suffer from such systematic informational failures? Banks have put many of their best and brightest to work on these new financial products. How could such knowledgeable sellers, as opposed to investors or consumers, not have adequate information?

Although there is neither consensus nor conclusive evidence regarding the existence of such structural informational failure on the part of banks, there is no such disagreement regarding regulatory informational failure. Observers agree that regulators know less than the bankers and that they know too little. One senior Bank of England official remarked that this knowledge gap is "too great for normal communication." It is difficult for regulators to understand the risks of any individual derivative transaction with certainty, much less the risks of more complex derivative transactions or a bank's entire portfolio of derivative transactions. If the puzzle is why banks know so little, then the dilemma is how can regulators, who know even less, be effective. How can the blind guide the nearsighted? . . .

## Basel Committee on Banking Supervision, Bank for International Settlements, Risk Management Guidelines for Derivatives

***July 27, 1994***

As part of its on-going efforts to address international bank supervisory issues, the Basle Committee on Banking Supervision is currently engaged in several activities to strengthen the prudential supervision of banks' derivatives operations. One of these activities has been a reassessment of the key elements of sound management of the risks involved in derivatives. . . .

Neither derivatives, nor the individual risks inherent in them are, by themselves, new. Institutions have been active for some time in forwards, swaps, and options and have routinely addressed credit, market, liquidity, operation and legal risks in their more traditional activities. However, the growing complexity, diversity and volume of derivatives products, facilitated by rapid advances in technology and communications, pose increasing challenges to managing these risks. Sound risk management practices are an important element in meeting these challenges. . . .

Derivatives instruments have become increasingly important to the overall risk profile and profitability of banking organizations throughout the world. Broadly defined, a derivatives instrument is a financial contract whose value depends on the values of one or more underlying assets or indexes. Derivatives transactions include a wide assortment of financial contracts, including forwards, futures, swaps and options. In addition, other traded instruments incorporate derivatives characteristics, such as those with imbedded options. While some derivatives instruments may have very complex structures, all of them can be divided into the basic building blocks of options, forward contracts or some combination thereof. The use of these basic building blocks in structuring derivatives instruments allows the transfer of various financial risks to parties who are more willing, or better suited, to take or manage them.

Derivatives contracts are entered into throughout the world on organized exchanges and through over-the-counter (OTC) arrangements. Exchange-traded contracts are typically standardized as to maturity, contract size and delivery terms. OTC contracts are custom-tailored to an institution's needs and often specify commodities, instruments and/or maturities that are not offered on any exchange. . . .

Derivatives are used by banking organizations both as risk management tools and as a source of revenue. From a risk management perspective, they allow financial institutions and other participants to identify, isolate and manage separately the market risk in financial instruments and commodities. When used prudently, derivatives can offer managers efficient and effective methods for reducing certain risks through hedging. Derivatives may also be used to reduce financing costs and to increase the yield of certain assets. For a growing number of banking organizations, derivatives activities are becoming a direct source of revenue through "market-making" functions, position taking and risk arbitrage:

- *"market-making"* functions involve entering into derivatives transactions with customers and with other market-makers while maintaining a generally balanced portfolio with the expectation of earning fees generated by a bid/offer spread;
- *position-taking,* on the other hand, represents efforts to profit by accepting the risk that stems from taking outright positions in anticipation of price movements;
- *arbitrageurs* also attempt to take advantage of price movements, but focus their efforts on trying to profit from small discrepancies in price among similar instruments in different markets.

Participants in the derivatives markets are generally grouped into two categories based primarily on their motivations for entering into derivatives contracts.

*End-Users* typically enter into derivatives transactions to achieve specified objectives related to hedging financing or position taking in the normal course of their business operations. A wide variety of business enterprises are end-users. They include, but are not limited to, a broad range of financial institutions such as banks, securities firms and insurance companies; institutional investors such as pension funds, mutual funds and specialized investment partnerships; and corporations, local and state governments, government agencies and international agencies.

*Intermediaries,* which are sometimes referred to as "dealers," cater to the needs of end-users by "making markets" in OTC derivatives instruments. In doing so, they expect to generate income from transaction fees, bid/offer spreads and their own trading positions. Important intermediaries, or derivative dealers, include major banks and securities firms around the world. As intermediaries, banks have traditionally offered foreign exchange and interest rate management products to their customers and generally view derivatives products as a financial risk management service.

The basic risks associated with derivatives transactions are not new to banking organizations. In general, these risks are credit risk, market risk, liquidity risk, operations risk and legal risk. Because they facilitate the specific identification and management of these risks, derivatives have the potential to enhance the safety and soundness of financial institutions and to produce a more efficient allocation of financial risks. However, since derivatives also repackage these basic risks in combinations that can be quite complex, they can also threaten the safety and soundness of institutions if they are not clearly understood and [properly] managed.

Recognizing the importance of sound risk management to the effective use of derivatives instruments, the following guidance is intended to highlight the key elements and basic principles of sound management practice for both dealers and end-users of derivatives instruments. These basic principles include:

1. Appropriate oversight by boards of directors and senior management;
2. Adequate risk management process that integrates prudent risk limits, sound measurement procedures and information systems, continuous risk monitoring and frequent management reporting; and,
3. Comprehensive internal controls and audit procedures. . . .

*QUESTIONS AND COMMENTS*

1. The Basel Committee is a committee of banking supervisory authorities established by the central bank governors of the Group of Ten countries in 1975. It currently consists of senior representatives of bank supervisory authorities and central banks from Belgium, Canada, France, Germany, Italy, Japan, Luxembourg, Netherlands, Sweden, Switzerland, United Kingdom, and the United States. It usually meets at the Bank for International Settlements in Basel, Switzerland.

2. In a part of the report not excerpted above, the Basle Committee recognized that "[o]ne outstanding feature of financial markets is the increasing use of sophisticated models by major institutions as their principal means of measuring and managing risk. As a consequence, supervisory agencies will need to assure that they (and external auditors) have staff with sufficient mathematical knowledge to understand the issues and

that the reliability of models can be independently certified by external experts." How easy do you think it will be for even the most highly qualified outside auditor or bank supervisor to review the computer models used by a major derivatives dealer, assess its reliability, and apply it to the firm's portfolio? And where are the bank regulatory agencies going to find PhDs in finance who are capable of understanding the models yet willing to work on a government salary?

3. For risk-management recommendations to securities firms that parallel in some respects the Basel Committee report excerpted above, see International Organization of Securities Commissions, Operational and Financial Risk Management Control Mechanisms for Over-the-Counter Derivatives Activities of Regulated Securities Firms (1994). The U.S. General Accounting Office weighed in with its report on Financial Derivatives: Actions Needed to Protect the Financial System (1994). A wide variety of technical information on OTC derivatives can be found in various pamphlets and other publications of the International Swaps and Derivatives Association, Inc.

4. For additional background on swaps, one of the most important derivative products, see Henry T.C. Hu, Swaps, the Modern Process of Financial Innovation and the Vulnerability of a Regulatory Paradigm, 138 University of Pennsylvania Law Review 333 (1989).

## G. CORPORATE LAW REGULATION

Banks are corporations and accordingly are subject to many of the principles of corporate law that govern business associations generally. This section discusses some of the corporate issues that have special impact on banking institutions. We first consider issues related to the management and control of depository institutions. Then we explore a specific issue of capital structure—the problems that arise when an institution is organized in "mutual" as opposed to "stock" form.

### *1. Issues of Management and Control*

The question of who manages and controls the affairs of a depository institution is related, as we saw in previous sections of this chapter, to the legal problems of enforcement and bank failure. These topics are examined in greater depth in Chapters 7 and 8, since questions of management and control tend to arise in particularly poignant fashion when a depository institution has run into difficulties. Even when the institution is perfectly solvent, however, the law regulates issues of management and control and provides procedures to deal with conflicts when they arise.

Like other business firms, banks are organized with boards of directors and executive officers. National banks, for example, are specifically empowered to "elect or appoint directors, and by its board of directors, to appoint a president, vice president, cashier, and other officers, define their duties, require bonds of them and fix the penalty thereof, dismiss such officers or any of them at pleasure, and appoint others to fill their places." 12 U.S.C. §24 (Fifth).

As with corporations generally, the business affairs of a depository institution are under the stewardship of a board of directors. In fact, the National Bank Act tracks language often found in state corporation laws when it provides that the "affairs of each [national bank] shall be managed" by a board of directors. 12 U.S.C. §71. The board has overall responsibility for running the institution. In addition, the board is typically authorized to prescribe bylaws regulating the general business of the institution. For national banks, see 12 U.S.C. §24 (Sixth).

Board members for depository institutions are chosen in the same general way as for corporations generally: nearly always, they are elected by the shareholders. See 12 U.S.C. §71 for the rules on national banks. Applicable law typically requires a certain minimum number of directors; national banks must have at least five. 12 U.S.C. §71. The statutes may provide mechanisms for removing directors, with or without cause, and for filling vacancies as they arise prior to an annual meeting. In general, the rules applicable to banks are similar to the rules applying to corporations generally.

Although the board has overall responsibility for managing the affairs of a depository institution, day-to-day decision making will nearly always be delegated to executive officers, only some of whom may serve on the board (some statutes, including the National Bank Act, require that the president be a member of the board, see 12 U.S.C. §76). Where the board's responsibilities end and those of subordinate officers begin is often unclear. Delicate questions arise: How involved should the board be in supervising the bank's officers? What sorts of decisions are so important that they should be made only by the board acting as a whole? Clearly, the board should be informed of fundamental matters affecting the firm and should make basic decisions about corporate policy. If you ever serve as general counsel for a depository institution, you will probably be called on for advice on questions such as these.

Within top management, complex questions of agency arise as to the authority of certain officials to bind the institution as a whole. Banks often support many vice presidents, and it could be perilous for a party dealing with a bank to rely on an individual's status as vice president as a sure indication that he or she is qualified to speak for or contractually bind the institution. If you are representing a potential borrower, for example, it might be advisable to obtain the loan commitment from an officer whom you know to be fully authorized to make the representation in question. Questions of the authority of bank officers will be resolved under the ordinary law of agency.

Management of banking institutions tends to be more heavily regulated than that of other industries. For example, every director of a national bank must, "during his whole term of service, be a citizen of the United States, and at least a majority of the directors must have resided in the State, Territory, or District in which the association is located, or within one hundred miles of the location of the office of the association, for at least one year immediately preceding their election, and must be residents of such State." 12 U.S.C. §72. A limited waiver is available if the national bank is a subsidiary of a foreign institution.

What do you think is the purpose of these citizenship and residency requirements? Do they serve any useful purpose in a world of interstate banking and information superhighways? What would be the harm if a majority of the directors lived outside the charmed circle defined in the statute? We don't find citizenship and residency requirements of this sort for ordinary business corporations; indeed, if a state were to impose such requirements they would be of dubious constitutionality. Why is a national bank different?

Other provisions require that bank directors hold stock in their institutions. In the case of national banks, every director must own at least $1,000 par value stock in the bank or an equivalent interest in the bank's holding company. 12 U.S.C. §72. What is the purpose of this provision? Arguably, it is useful to have directors own stock in the bank because doing so tends to align their financial interests with those of the bank. But is §72 the best way to accomplish this purpose? Is it useful or appropriate to tie the ownership requirement in with par value stock (note that it is not necessary to own par value stock in the holding company). Can you think of any more effective means to align the interests?

Directorship in a bank may impair a bank director's ability to serve on other boards. The Depository Institution Management Interlocks Act of 1978 is a major source of such rules (subject however to waiver by administrative regulation, see 12 U.S.C. §3207). Under this statute, management officials of depository institutions or their holding companies generally may not serve in a similar capacity in an unaffiliated depository institution or holding company if an office of the second institution is located in the same metropolitan statistical area or the same or a contiguous city, town, or village. 12 U.S.C. §3202. What is the purpose of this requirement? To police against conflicts of interest? To discourage anticompetitive behavior? We don't ordinarily find this kind of restriction in general corporation statutes. What is special about banks?

Another provision, 12 U.S.C. §3203, establishes even more stringent rules on management interlocks in banking firms with over $1 billion in assets. Management officials of such firms are generally prohibited from serving as management officials of unaffiliated depository institutions or holding companies with more than $500 million in assets, *regardless of where the second firm is located.* Again, what is the purpose of this rule? Given the scarcity of high-level talent in any field of human endeavor, wouldn't it be desirable for the very best directors to serve on the boards of more than one large banking institution?

Still other restrictions apply to interlocking management of banks and securities firms under the Glass Steagall Act. Section 32 of that statute, 12 U.S.C. §78, provides that no officer, director, or employee of a securities firm (as defined) may serve at the same time as an officer, director, or employee of a national bank or state member bank, unless the Fed has permitted such service by regulation after concluding that the overlap would not unduly influence the investment policies of the bank or the investment advice it provides to its customers. Again, we can detect a congressional purpose to police against conflicts of interest, here between the banking and securities functions. Is a prohibition on management interlocks a good way to serve this policy? What are the social costs of such a regulation?

Another provision added by FIRREA, codified at 12 U.S.C. §1831i, requires that insured depository institutions or depository institution holding companies must give at least 30 days' advance notice to the appropriate federal banking agency of the proposed addition of any individual to the board of directors or the employment of any individual as a senior executive officer—if the company in question is less than two years old, has undergone a change of control within the past two years, or is not in compliance with applicable requirements for minimum capital adequacy. The federal regulators may disapprove the proposal if "the competence, experience, character, or integrity of the individual . . . indicates that it would not be in the best interests of the public to permit the individual to be employed by, or associated with, the depository institution or . . . holding company." Do you think this rule serves a useful purpose? Recall that the fiasco in the savings and loan industry was blamed largely on unethical, incompetent, or even criminal behavior by managers of the failed institutions. Perhaps if this provision had been in place, many of these individuals would have been weeded out at the beginning and the costs associated with their actions avoided. On the other hand, how confident are you that the agency can, after what will necessarily be a fairly summary review, confidently determine whether the person in question is suited for the management of a depository institution? What about the interests of those excluded from participating in a depository institution under this section—their careers are on the line. The statute does not appear to provide excluded individuals with procedural protections such as the right to have a hearing, receive formal notice of charges, present evidence, confront and cross-examine witnesses, and the like. Shouldn't they be entitled to greater safeguards than are available under this provision? Doesn't this statute open up a dangerous possibility that agencies will impair the ability of qualified individuals to serve in their chosen profession, on the basis of inappropriate factors such as favoritism, gossip, or abuse?

Beyond the express qualifications for directors required by these statutes, the law provides banking regulators with plentiful authority to control the makeup of bank boards and management teams by more informal methods. For example, any application to establish a new bank must include detailed decriptions of the background and qualifications of the proposed managers. As we saw in Chapter 2, bank regulators scrutinize the proposed officers and directors closely and do not hesitate to criticize when they believe these persons are poorly qualified. To be sure, this restraint applies only during the initial phases of a depository institution's life; qualified people could drop out and others could come on who lack the same skills or background. Nevertheless, bank regulators continue to monitor an institution's management throughout its life and will bring perceived deficiencies to the attention of the appropriate individuals. If the institution does not rectify the situation, the regulators have powerful weapons for removing unwanted individuals, as we discuss at greater length in Chapter 7.

## *QUESTIONS AND COMMENTS*

1. Consider the extraordinary breadth and scope of the power that banking law and bank regulators exercise over the selection of top managers for depository institutions. Few other businesses impose such stringent requirements on who may serve in management or subject professional managers to the threat of being summarily rejected because of deficiencies perceived by members of the agency's staff. Do you think this pervasive scrutiny of personnel is justified? What arguments can you develop in favor of the regulatory scheme? What arguments can you think of in opposition? Which appear more weighty?

2. If we are going to subject proposed officers and directors to comprehensive oversight, why not expand the controls still further? Perhaps banking regulators should set up a licensing system, much like the system that applies to attorneys, to ensure that bank managers come to the job equipped with high levels of professional competence and excellent moral character. Wouldn't it be a good idea, for example, for the Comptroller of the Currency to mandate a standardized examination for officers and directors of national banks, supplemented by the inquiry of a character and fitness committee? After all, bankers bear a heavy responsibility in managing other people's money, just as lawyers are

responsible for taking care of other people's legal affairs; surely managing a bank is as technically and intellectually challenging as many areas of legal practice. Would you support the creation of such an examination requirement?

3. What if a proposed board member turns out to have a bipolar disease in which periods of extreme activity alternate with deep depression—but the disease is currently under control through medication. Should the regulators consider this as a factor in evaluating the individual?

4. What if the proposed individual has declared bankruptcy in the past two years? Should bankruptcy be considered a disqualifying event?

5. What if the proposed individual has been convicted of driving under the influence of alcohol within the past two years? Or, what if he or she has not been convicted of any crime but admits to having a problem with alcohol?

6. Given the rapidly changing face of banking, as discussed throughout this book, the skills a manager developed in the 1970s are surely out of date in the 1990s. Should bank managers be required to take regular continuing education classes as a condition for retaining their positions?

## 2. *Problems of Mutual Organization*

Traditionally some banking institutions, especially savings and loans, have been held in a "mutual" form of ownership. A mutual institution operates without common stock; ownership rights inhere (in theory) in the depositors. The putative "owners" elect the management team that runs the institution. On the thrift side of the industry, mutuals have traditionally played an important role. Nearly all thrift institutions were held in mutual form at one time, and despite some conversions to stock form, there were 1,471 FSLIC-insured mutual thrift institutions as late as year-end 1989. Their assets were worth $286 billion—no small amount.

Because of the differences in ownership structure, mutual institutions are quite different from those in stock form. Shareholders in stock institutions benefit or lose in proportion to the performance of their firms; accordingly, they tend to monitor the managers to ensure good performance. In contrast, the depositor-owners of mutual institutions have exercised very little effective control over their firms; especially if they are insured, they have little interest in the institution's performance. The boards of directors of mutual institutions tend to be self-perpetuating; existing directors select themselves or their replacements. Moreover, because the stock is held in mutual form by depositors, with no shares traded on the market, it is quite difficult for a raider to launch a takeover bid.

One significant problem with the mutual form of ownership is that the value of the concern often far exceeds the amounts actually held on deposit. This means that if mutual ownership really means what it seems to mean, depositors should have a right to this excess wealth if the mutual form is ever abandoned in favor of a more conventional stock form of ownership. In practice, this has not proven to be the case. Mutual-to-stock conversions have generated large surpluses, but the principal beneficiaries have tended to be the managers of the institution who obtain large numbers of shares in the new stock institution.

The FIRREA law in 1989 sparked a huge wave of mutual-to-stock conversions. In part, these transactions were intended to raise new capital for the converting institution. Because they have no stock, mutual institutions have no easy way to raise capital; they cannot simply issue shares in the market. Often conversion to stock form was the most feasible mechanism for coming into compliance with the new, tougher capital adequacy requirements. But in addition to capital adequacy concerns, it turned out that mutual-to-stock conversions could be enormously profitable for the managers of these institutions, a factor that surely played an important role in the wave of conversions that occurred during the early 1990s.

These conversions proved to be controversial. Typically, they take the form of "subscription" offers in which existing depositors and managers are given prior rights to purchase stock in the new stock institution; the proceeds go to the corporate treasury rather than into the hands of the ostensible "owners." In a number of mutual-to-stock conversions, critics have charged that the insiders profited at the expense of the depositor/owners by underpricing the stock sold as an incident to the conversion or by acquiring more shares than the number to which they were fairly entitled. Managers can do this by causing their institutions to give them options to purchase large amounts of stock at the conversion price, secure in the knowledge that the stock will immediately rise in value after completion of the subscription period because of underpricing. The evidence is fairly strong that, at least during the heyday of mutual-to-stock conversions, the stock was indeed undervalued: the average first-week price appreciation for the shares issued in 130 thrift conversions between January 1, 1992, and April 20, 1994, was 27.7 percent.

In other cases, critics alleged that insiders had arranged for the conversion to be effected as part of a merger transaction in which the shares of the former mutual institution were acquired at bargain prices by an acquiring firm, which then would generously reward the insiders of the mutual firm with lucrative consulting contracts or other benefits.

Despite these problems, the Office of Thrift Supervision adopted a permissive attitude toward mutual-to-stock conversions even when the transaction had the appearance of conferring a significant benefit on the management of the converting institution. For the OTS, the increases in capital and enhanced operating efficiency that the stock form offers apparently outweighed the unfairness, real or perceived, to depositors. Judicial challenges to mutual-to-stock conversions are unlikely to be successful as long as the transaction complies with OTS regulations. See Ordower v. OTS, 999 F.2d 1183 (7th Cir. 1993).

The outcry was taken up in Congress, with legislation being introduced in 1994 to police against the alleged abuses. Senate Banking Committee Chairman Donald Riegle, one of the chief sponsors, warned that "this self-dealing should stop, and stop now. These outrageous conversions are not victimless crimes. To the extent that management and insiders are skimming off the net worth of the institution through a conversion, they are doing so at the expense of the institution and its account holders. Significantly, such transactions also siphon capital that ultimately protects the deposit insurance system."

The OTS and the FDIC responded to the alleged abuses by tightening up their rules on the matter. They significantly toughened appraisal standards, thus policing against egregious mispricing of the stock issued during the conversion. They subjected converting state-chartered institutions to essentially the same rules as those for federal institutions, and they restricted conversions that were structured as mergers with another institution, which had been criticized for allowing "giveaways" to the buyer.

## *QUESTIONS AND COMMENTS*

1. Why would an institution elect to operate in mutual form, given the problems of management discipline that inhere in the absence of common stock? Why do you think such institutions arose in the first place? Do they still have a purpose in today's banking world?

2. The FDIC staff proposed at one time that conversion rights, which have been available only to existing depositors, should be made transferable. If such rights were transferable, a market would develop in which speculators purchased rights to subscribe in any eventual mutual-to-stock subscription. This proposal was vehemently opposed by managers of mutual institutions, who recognized that the consequence would be that speculators would purchase the subscription rights and then pressure the managers to effect a conversion. The proposal was not adopted. Should it have been?

3. Once a conversion has been approved but before it is consummated, third parties might make unsolicited offers to acquire the converting firm by paying depositors additional compensation above and beyond what they expect to receive in the conversion plan. Essentially, these offers represent attempts by the bidder to appropriate some of the value which would otherwise be realized by corporate insiders or others in the conversion. Citing the need to "protect the integrity of the conversion process, lessen the vulnerability of converting associations to attempts

to take unfair advantage of the results of a conversion, and otherwise . . . to avoid injury to a converting association," the Office of Thrift Supervision has adopted a regulation providing in pertinent part that "[p]rior to the completion of a conversion, no person shall make any offer, or any announcement of an offer, for any security of the converting savings association issued in connection with the conversion. . . ." 12 C.F.R. §563b.3(i)(2). Do you agree with this regulation? Doesn't it stop ordinary free-market processes in their tracks? Is the rationale that unless the managers of mutual institutions are protected against unsolicited takeover bids during the conversion process, they are less likely to commence the process in the first place?

4. Who are the real owners of the surplus value of a mutual institution? Why not say that the value belongs to the people as a whole, and appropriate it by imposing a tax on the transaction? Such a proposal, which surfaced at one point in the debate on mutual-to-stock conversions, quickly evoked outraged howls from all involved. Whether or not taxation is a good idea, who do you think should receive the benefit of a conversion?

## 3. *Credit Union Membership*

We saw that credit unions are mutual institutions that have typically been limited to serving people who have some sort of affiliation in common. This common bond requirement is embodied, for federal credit unions, in Section 109 of the Federal Credit Union Act, 12 U.S.C. §1759, which provides that "[f]ederal credit union membership shall be limited to groups having a common bond of occupation or association, or to groups within a well-defined neighborhood, community, or rural district." If applied strictly, the common bond requirement would significantly constrain the growth of federal credit unions.

In 1982 the National Credit Union Administration significantly liberalized its interpretation of the common bond requirement, allowing membership in a federal credit union to be drawn from multiple unrelated occupational groups, each with its own common bond. Federal credit unions were quick to take advantage of the enormous growth possibilities that this interpretation seemed to offer, expanding their membership rapidly—so rapidly, in fact, that the commercial banking industry began to feel concern about competition from these upstarts. The matter came to a head in 1996 with a challenge to the organization of the AT&T Family Federal Credit Union, which had grown into a significant banking presence with 112,000 members in more than 150 disparate occupational groups spread across all 50 states, including employeees of a major tobacco company, an auto supply chain, and a television station. In 1994 it had more than 63,000 loans outstanding totaling over $268 million—not large by commercial banking standards, but far from insignificant.

In 1996, however, the District of Columbia Circuit dealt a serious blow to the federal credit union movement by holding that the "common bond" requirement means that members of a federal credit union must share the *same* common bond. First National Bank & Trust Co. v. National Credit Union Administration, 90 F.3d 525 (D.C. Cir. 1996). Do you think this was the right decision, given the growth of interstate banking and the consolidation in the banking industry discussed elsewhere in this book? Is there anything a credit union can do to avoid the scope of the ruling? Could a credit union attempt to expand on the theory that its members share a common bond of "association" rather than occupation? Presumably, merely being members of the same credit union is not enough of an "association" to satisfy the common bond requirement—otherwise the requirement would mean nothing. But what would be enough?

## H. LIABILITY OF OFFICERS, DIRECTORS, AND THIRD PARTIES

A major area of banking law, at least in the years since the savings and loan crisis struck in earnest in the mid-1980s, is the liability of officers, directors, and third parties for malfeasance committed in connection with a depository institution. Officers and directors are charged with managing an institution competently, honestly, and to the best of their ability. In performing this task, they rely on a wide range of professionals—attorneys, accountants, and appraisers, among others—who provide services to depository institutions. What rights does the institution (or more often the FDIC as stand-in for the institution after failure) have against such officers, directors, and third parties? What should be the proper public policy about the standards of liability in this area?

One might argue that such parties should be held to exacting standards when they perform services for a depository institution. After all, they are in a sense charged with protecting the funds of depositors who have no ability to protect themselves—or, alternatively, of taxpayers whose funds are at potential risk because of federal deposit insurance. No one doubts that millions of dollars in losses from failed depository institutions could have been avoided if these parties had provided more competent service before and during the savings and loan crisis.

However, before concluding that the standard of liability should be extraordinarily stringent, consider the *ex ante* effects of such a rule. Who would want to serve on the board of directors of a depository institution, or perform legal, appraisal, or accounting services for such a firm, if they feared ruinous liability for a single misstep? What kinds of insurance policies would the institution or its service providers have to obtain to protect themselves against this risk of devastating loss? What kinds of premiums would they have to pay if the liability threshold were set at too high a level?

Most of us have had the experience of going through a metal detection device at an airport that has been set at too sensitive a level. The extra sensitivity of such devices might be considered desirable, since it makes it more difficult for a wrongdoer to sneak weapons or other dangerous materials aboard. On the other hand, if the sensitivity is set too high, the harm imposed on passengers in terms of delay and inconvenience can exceed the marginal gains in protection against terrorism. Could something of the sort be going on, in a sense, in depository institution regulation?

At some point, the costs of imposing liability on officers, directors, and third parties may exceed the benefits. Most informed people would agree with this proposition in the abstract: the level of liability can be set too high. But where, in practice, the level *ought* to be set is another matter.

Few areas of banking law have been as contentious in recent years as this matter of officer, director, and third-party liability. We will read in the pages that follow of the *Kaye, Scholer* case, in which the OTS exerted what some regarded as unconscionable pressure on a law firm to settle charges of malfeasance in its representation of an insolvent thrift institution. For every *Kaye, Scholer* there are probably hundreds of smaller cases in which the appropriate standard of officer, director, or third-party liability becomes an important issue. If you practice banking law, it is likely that at some point in your career you will become involved in one or another aspect of these liability issues.

## 1. *Officer and Director Liability*

High-ranking officers and directors of depository institutions are fiduciaries; they owe fiduciary duties of care and loyalty to their institutions. For the most part, these duties are established under common law. But an officer or director also has a duty to exercise reasonable care to ensure that the institution obeys other applicable law.

The officers and directors owe a duty of care to their institutions, but they have available a defense that their actions were taken in the exercise of sound business judgment. Even if they make decisions that do not turn out well, they will not, in theory, face liability for damages as long as their actions are reasonably well-considered and well-informed in light of what is known at the time the decisions are made. Even good decisions can have unfavorable outcomes; the law of banking, like corporate law generally, recognizes this fact by not holding officers and directors liable, without more, for the financial condition of their enterprises. Traditional causes of action against corporate managers include such serious charges as breach of fiduciary duty, gross negligence, negligence, and breach of contract.

Stockholders of banks, like stockholders of other corporations, have rights against directors of their companies in the event that the directors breach the overarching duties of loyalty and care. Thus many banking law principles—for example, the rules against self-dealing loans or those designed to prevent imprudent investments—are potentially enforceable also as a matter of corporate law by means of shareholders derivative litigation, brought either by shareholders of a bank or, in the case of bank subsidiaries in a holding company structure, by shareholders of the parent bank holding company.

Are the fiduciary duties of bank directors the same or different from the duties applicable to other corporations? Consider the Supreme Court's early articulation of the duties of bank directors, still often cited in decisions:

> [D]irectors must exercise ordinary care and prudence in the administration of the affairs of a bank, and this includes something more than officiating as figure heads. They are entitled under the law to commit banking business, as defined, to their duly authorized officers, but this does not absolve them from the duty of reasonable supervision, nor ought they to be permitted to be shielded from liability because of want of knowledge of wrongdoing, if that ignorance is the result of gross inattention. . . .

Briggs v. Spalding, 141 U.S 132, 165-166 (1891).

If the bank in question is state-chartered, the fiduciary duties of its directors will be defined under state law. If the institution is federally chartered, the weight of authority holds that the fiduciary duties of directors are established as a matter of federal common law; in this regard state common law will of course be relevant as persuasive, but not binding, authority. The Supreme Court's decision in O'Melveny & Myers v. FDIC, 114 S. Ct. 2048 (1994), excerpted below, may however cast doubt on the applicability of federal common law in this area.

Bank directors and officers may be liable to their banks for violation of statutes or regulations as well as for breach of common law fiduciary duties. Difficult questions are presented, however, in determining which statutes or regulations may form the basis of liability. If the enactment in question does not expressly create a private right of action in the bank, the issue becomes whether such a private right should be recognized by implication. This question, broadly speaking, turns on whether Congress (or the state legislature) intended to create a private right of action. See Merrill Lynch, Pierce, Fenner & Smith, Inc. v. Curran, 456 U.S. 353, 377-378 (1982); Touche Ross & Co. v. Redington, 442 U.S. 560, 568 (1979). Attempts to establish private rights of action under comprehensive bank regulatory schemes have usually foundered on the argument that since Congress created wide-ranging enforcement rights for bank regulators, its failure to create similar rights for private parties could not have been inadvertent.

Although in general contour the law applicable to officers and directors of solvent institutions is fairly uniform, differences among jursidictions do exist, and these differences can give rise to choice-of-law issues. When the institution is state-chartered, the choice of law is easy: at least in the absence of federal preemption, the applicable law is the law of the chartering state (this is a straightforward application of the "internal affairs" doctrine of corporate law).

But what if the depository institution operates under a *national* charter? Does state law govern, or federal? And if federal law governs, where can it be found? In days past, it was not very important for there to be a federal law applicable to officers and directors of national banks, since all national banks did business within the borders of a single state. No longer. We will see in Chapter 5 that geographical boundaries are breaking down rapidly as banks increasingly do business on an interstate basis. For a national bank doing business on a truly interstate basis, it might not make sense to apply the law of any particular state. These considerations may lead a court to adopt federal rather than state law as the rule of decision when the institution is federally chartered. See RTC v. Chapman, 29 F.3d 1120 (7th Cir. 1994).

What is the applicable standard of fault necessary to establish an officer or director's liability? The starting point of analysis today is a provision of FIRREA, 12 U.S.C. §1821(k), which provides in pertinent part that "a director or officer of an insured depository institution may be held personally liable for monetary damages in any civil action by, on behalf of, or at the request or direction of the [FDIC] . . . for gross negligence, including any similar conduct or conduct that demonstrates a greater disregard of a duty of care . . . including intentional tortious conduct, as such terms are defined and determined under applicable State law. Nothing in this paragraph shall impair or affect any right of the [FDIC] under other applicable law."

While this statute clearly subjects officers and directors of failed depository institutions to liability for conduct that amounts to gross negligence (or worse) in suits brought by the FDIC, see RTC v. Gallagher, 10 F.3d 416 (7th Cir. 1993), it leaves important questions unanswered.

For example, the statute applies in terms to lawsuits brought by the FDIC after an institution has failed. What then is its impact on suits brought against an officer or director of a *solvent* institution?

And what if otherwise applicable law would impose liability for mere *simple* negligence, not gross negligence? Should the new statute be viewed as preemptive, so that the old simple negligence rule is no longer operative, or should the more stringent standard of liability prevail even though it is also older? Courts have split on this important issue in cases where the institution in question was state-chartered, some ruling that the new statute is preemptive, some holding that state negligence claims are preserved. In the case of federally chartered institutions, courts have considered the argument that in addition to the explicit statutory standard of gross negligence, there also exists a federal common law cause of action based on simple negligence. Another question is whether, even if §1821(k) preempts claims based on negligence, it has a similar force with respect to other causes of action such as breach of contract or breach of fiduciary duty. It is fair to say that the cases are all over the map.

In Resolution Trust Corporation v. Cityfed Financial Corp., 57 F.3d 1231 (3d Cir. 1995), *cert. granted sub nom.* Atherton v. Federal Deposit Insurance Corp., 116 S. Ct. 1415 (1996), the Third Circuit issued an exhaustive opinion concluding that the gross negligence provisions of FIRREA did not foreclose the RTC (now superseded by the FDIC) from pursuing claims under state law for simple negligence and breach of fiduciary duty, or federal claims against officers and directors of a federally chartered institution for negligence short of gross negligence. The Supreme Court's decision on this point should clarify the question of the preemptive effect of FIRREA's gross negligence standard.

As you reread the statute, how would you resolve these questions?

## *QUESTIONS AND COMMENTS*

1. Consider the following remarks by Harris Weinstein, chief counsel of the OTS:

> Historically, the first rule for a bank or thrift fiduciary has been to safeguard the depositors' money. Unlike equity investors, depositors neither seek capital gain nor undertake risk of capital loss. When they deposit their money in banks, they expect it still will be there when they present an instrument of withdrawal. Officers and directors of depository institutions therefore have more demanding responsibilities than officers and directors of other corporations in determining the number and magnitude of risks

> that they can cause their institutions to take. It is the obvious obligation of the institution's fiduciaries to take every reasonable step to avoid loss of deposited funds. . . . Because of the importance of safekeeping depositors' funds, directors and officers of a depository institution must be held to "standards of probity and fidelity more lofty than those of the marketplace." Accordingly, officers and directors of depository institutions are held to a strict fiduciary duty to act in the best interest of the institution, its shareholders and its depositors.
>
> Only loose or wishful thinkers would claim that the presence of federal deposit insurance eliminates this historic duty of bankers to depositors. . . . [E]very fiduciary of a federally insured depository institution owes the federal insurer, at the very minimum, the same high fiduciary duties that are owed depositors—and that . . . is the duty not to risk insolvency and the resulting loss of funds deposited with the institution.

Weinstein, Remarks Delivered at Southern Methodist University, Dallas, Tex., Sept. 13, 1990.

2. Do you agree with Mr. Weinstein that officers and directors of depository institutions owe a high level of fiduciary duty to the FDIC? Consider the fact that under standard corporate law principles officers and directors are not generally considered to owe fiduciary duties to debtholders prior to insolvency or near-insolvency. The traditional rationale for recognizing fiduciary duties to debtholders at insolvency is that they are the de facto equity holders at this point (when the equity is wiped out, all the residual risk of the enterprise is borne by debtholders). But Mr. Weinstein's theory goes well beyond this, doesn't it, in that it would recognize a fiduciary duty to the FDIC (and, presumably, damages liability for violation of this duty) for risky decisions taken well *prior* to insolvency, so long as those decisions eventually result in insolvency. Is this a sensible extension of existing theory in the special context of depository institutions?

3. One reason fiduciary duties are not generally owed to debtholders prior to insolvency is that debtholders are considered able to protect themselves by contract. If a debtholder is concerned that a manager of the debtor firm might take excessive risks, the debtholder can insist on a security interest (such as a mortgage) or can make the occurrence of a risky action an "event of default," justifying acceleration and immediate repayment of the debt. Does the federal government, in its role as bank regulator, have similar powers to protect itself by contract? What about the fact that the government enjoys enormous powers (discussed in Chapter 7 of this book) to prevent bank managers from engaging in "unsafe or unsound" activities?

4. Another reason fiduciary duties are not generally owed to debtholders prior to insolvency is that shareholders and debtholders have a conflict of interest over the level of risk that they would prefer a firm to take on. Shareholders are usually thought of as preferring a higher level

of risk because if a risky project pans out well, the shareholders reap all the benefits, whereas if a risky project fails and the firm is bankrupted, the shareholders incur the costs of failure only up to the value of their investments, after which all additional losses are borne by debtholders. Conversely, debtholders are usually thought to prefer a low level of risk because low-risk projects tend to assure that the firm will do well enough to pay off the debt, even if shareholders do not earn much by way of profit. How can a corporate manager resolve this conflict of interest if he or she is held to owe fiduciary duties to *both* shareholders and debtholders?

5. Mr. Weinstein says, at a later point of this speech, that "the government has an unlimited negative equity risk while it has none of the potential for gain that common shareholders enjoy. This type of equity position should call forth the highest conceivable standard of fiduciary conduct." Is this a correct analysis? In the absence of deposit insurance, depositors are not equity holders, are they? Why does the government suddenly become a "negative equity" holder as a result of the fact that it may stand in the shoes of depositors in the event that a depository institution fails and the government is required to pay off insured deposits? And how can the government realistically be called an "equity" holder when it retains significant rights after insolvency to share, along with other creditors, in what remains of the depository institution's assets?

## 2. *Liability of Attorneys, Accountants, and Appraisers*

As in the case of suits against officers and directors, litigation against professionals such as attorneys, accountants, and appraisers who have rendered services to a depository institution can be based on traditional tort causes of action, principally professional negligence. The usual elements of a negligence suit—such as duty, breach of duty, causation, and damage—must ordinarily be present in these professional liability cases as well. At the same time, attorneys, accountants, and appraisers who provide services to depository institutions now face significant additional potential liability exposure as "institution-affiliated parties." The following case deals with claims and defenses asserted under state tort law.

### O'Melveny & Myers v. FDIC

*114 S. Ct. 2048 (1994)*

SCALIA, J.:

The issue in this case is whether, in a suit by the Federal Deposit Insurance Corporation as receiver of a federally insured bank, it is a federal-law or rather a state-law rule of decision that governs the tort liability of attorneys who provided services to the bank.

## I

American Diversified Savings Bank (ADSB or S & L) is a California-chartered and federally insured savings and loan. The following facts have been stipulated to, or are uncontroverted, by the parties to the case, and we assume them to be true for purposes of our decision. ADSB was acquired in 1983 by Ranbir Sahni and Lester Day, who respectively obtained 96% and 4% of its stock, and who respectively served as its chairman/CEO and president. Under their leadership, ADSB engaged in many risky real estate transactions, principally through limited partnerships sponsored by ADSB and its subsidiaries. Together, Sahni and Day also fraudulently overvalued ADSB's assets, engaged in sham sales of assets to create inflated "profits," and generally "cooked the books" to disguise the S & L's dwindling (and eventually negative) net worth.

In September 1985, petitioner O'Melveny & Myers, a Los Angeles-based law firm, represented ADSB in connection with two real estate syndications. At that time, ADSB was under investigation by state and federal regulators, but that fact had not been made public. In completing its work for the S & L, petitioner did not contact the accounting firms that had previously done work for ADSB, nor state and federal regulatory authorities, to inquire about ADSB's financial status. The two real estate offerings on which petitioner worked closed on December 31, 1985. On February 14, 1986, federal regulators concluded that ADSB was insolvent and that it had incurred substantial losses because of violations of law and unsound business practices. Respondent stepped in as receiver for ADSB. . . .

[R]espondent sued petitioner in the United States District Court for the Central District of California, alleging professional negligence and breach of fiduciary duty. The parties stipulated to certain facts and petitioner moved for summary judgment, arguing [inter alia, that knowledge of the conduct of ADSB's controlling officers must be imputed to the S & L, and hence to respondent, which, as receiver, stood in the shoes of the S & L].

## II

It is common ground that the FDIC was asserting in this case causes of action created by California law. Respondent contends that in the adjudication of those causes of action (1) a federal common-law rule and not California law determines whether the knowledge of corporate officers acting against the corporation's interest will be imputed to the corporation; and (2) even if California law determines the former question, federal common law determines the more narrow question whether knowledge by officers so acting will be imputed to the FDIC when it sues as receiver of the corporation.

The first of these contentions need not detain us long, as it is so plainly wrong. "There is no federal general common law," Erie R. Co. v. Tompkins, 304 U.S. 64 (1938) . . .

We turn, then, to the more substantial basis for the decision below, which asserts federal pre-emption not over the law of imputation generally, but only over its application to the FDIC suing as receiver. . . . The issue in the present case is whether the California rule of decision is to be applied to the issue of imputation or displaced. . . .

Section 1821(d)(2)(A)(i) [of FIRREA], which is part of a Title captioned "Powers and duties of [the FDIC] as . . . receiver," states that "the [FDIC] shall . . . by operation of law, succeed to—all rights, titles, powers, and privileges of the insured depository institution. . . ." 12 U.S.C. §1821(d)(2)(A)(i) (1988 ed., Supp. IV). This language appears to indicate that the FDIC as receiver "steps into the shoes" of the failed S & L . . . , obtaining the rights "of the insured depository institution" that existed prior to receivership. Thereafter, in litigation by the FDIC asserting the claims of the S & L—in this case California tort claims potentially defeasible by a showing that the S & L's officers had knowledge—[any defense good against the original party is good against the receiver]. . . .

[T]his is not one of those cases in which judicial creation of a special federal rule would be justified. . . . What is fatal to respondent's position . . . is that it has identified no significant conflict with an identifiable federal policy or interest. There is not even at stake that most generic (and lightly invoked) of alleged federal interests, the interest in uniformity. The rules of decision at issue here do not govern the primary conduct of the United States or any of its agents or contractors, but affect only the FDIC's rights and liabilities, as receiver, with respect to primary conduct on the part of private actors that has already occurred. Uniformity of law might facilitate the FDIC's nationwide litigation of these suits, eliminating state-by-state research and reducing uncertainty—but if the avoidance of those ordinary consequences qualified as an identifiable federal interest, we would be awash in "federal common-law" rules.

The closest respondent comes to identifying a specific, concrete federal policy or interest that is compromised by California law is its contention that state rules regarding the imputation of knowledge might "deplet[e] the deposit insurance fund." But neither FIRREA nor the prior law sets forth any anticipated level for the fund, so what respondent must mean by "depletion" is simply the forgoing of any money which, under any conceivable legal rules, might accrue to the fund. That is a broad principle indeed, which would support not just elimination of the defense at issue here, but judicial creation of new, "federal-common-law" causes of action to enrich the fund. Of course we have no authority to do that, because there is no federal policy that the fund should always win. . . .

Even less persuasive—indeed, positively probative of the dangers of respondent's facile approach to federal-common-law-making—is respondent's contention that it would "disserve the federal program" to permit California to insulate "the attorney's or accountant's malpractice," thereby imposing costs "on the nation's taxpayers, rather than on the negligent wrongdoer." By presuming to judge what constitutes malpractice, this argument demonstrates the runaway tendencies of "federal common law" untethered to a genuinely identifiable (as opposed to judicially constructed) federal policy. What sort of tort liability to impose on lawyers and accountants in general, and on lawyers and accountants who provide services to federally insured financial institutions in particular, [involves a host of considerations that must be weighed and appraised]—including, for example, the creation of incentives for careful work, provision of fair treatment to third parties, assurance of adequate recovery by the federal deposit insurance fund, and enablement of reasonably priced services. Within the federal system, at least, we have decided that that function of weighing and appraising [is more appropriate for those who write the laws than for those who interpret them]. . . .

We conclude that this is not one of those extraordinary cases in which the judicial creation of a federal rule of decision is warranted. As noted earlier, the parties are in agreement that if state law governs it is the law of California; but they vigorously disagree as to what that law provides. We leave it to the Ninth Circuit to resolve that point. The judgment is reversed and the case remanded for proceedings consistent with this opinion.

So ordered.

## *QUESTIONS AND COMMENTS*

1. In this case, we see a discussion of a defense to an FDIC suit against a third-party service provider. In this regard, what does the Court mean by "imputation"? Suppose in an FDIC lawsuit against an accountant for negligently certifying a failed depository institution's financial statements, the defendant argues that the certification would never have been made had the prior officers of the institution not concealed material facts from the auditor at the time the institution was still in operation? Can the misconduct of prior management be imputed to the FDIC-receiver of the failed institution and used as a defense to the negligence action? If so, the imputation might be available as a defense against liability to the FDIC for professional malpractice.

2. Can you see why imputation is such an important issue in litigation after bank failure? The former officers and directors whose actions

are challenged are not in the picture. Moreover, the fact that their institution failed indicates that they may have played fast and loose with the rules—either before or after the institution ran into difficulties. Further, the accountant, attorney or appraiser will often be able to use the FDIC's own words against it in an imputation case, since the FDIC will nearly always be suing the institution's former management and will in that litigation be making allegations of managerial malfeasance that can support a potential defense in litigation against a third-party service provider.

3. What kinds of defenses or pleas might be available against the FDIC if a jurisdiction recognizes the principle of imputation? Contributory negligence? Comparative negligence? Equitable defenses such as waiver, estoppel, or unclean hands? Mitigation of damages based on the FDIC's alleged failure to preserve the receivership estate?

4. What was actually decided in *O'Melveny & Myers*—that the defendant was entitled to the defense of imputation?

5. What social policies underlie the law in this area? Since we assume that the FDIC in no way participated in the wrongdoing of the former officers and directors but rather succeeded to the institution's legal rights by operation of law, does imputation make sense at all? Consider that imputation insulates from liability parties who may also have been at fault for the harms to the institution, and it forces an innocent party—the FDIC—to bear the costs. Consider also that the deposit insurance fund will lose the potential recovery. On the other hand, can anything be said in favor of imputation?

6. What attitude towards the FDIC's litigation posture do you detect in Justice Scalia's opinion? If you were representing the FDIC, would you think twice before again inviting the Court to approve the development of a federal common law of FDIC receiverships?

## Office of Thrift Supervision v. Kaye, Scholer, Fierman, Hayes & Handler

This matter, which never resulted in a formal adjudication, was settled by consent of the parties. The case grew out of Kaye, Scholer's representation of Lincoln Savings & Loan, the infamous Arizona thrift institution headed by Charles Keating of "Keating Five" fame. Kaye, Scholer was retained as litigation counsel for Lincoln after an adversarial relation had grown up between Lincoln and its regulator, the OTS. Lincoln eventually failed, at considerable cost to the government. OTS later instituted an administrative enforcement action against Kaye, Scholer and three of its partners, seeking $275 million in "restitution."

What made the enforcement action extraordinarily powerful is that OTS utilized its authority to freeze Kaye, Scholer's assets and finances. The firm was required to place in escrow a quarter of most partners' shares of firm earnings and to segregate greater percentages for the two attorneys principally involved. OTS demanded five days' written notice of any expenditures greater than $50,000. The firm, its partners, and their families could not dispose of their assets except under specified limitations. Under the terms of the applicable statute, Kaye, Scholer had no opportunity for a hearing on the freeze. Kaye, Scholer claimed that its banks almost immediately shut off its line of credit, placing it in severe financial straits. Arguably, the lack of a prior hearing meant that there would never be a hearing, given the devastating consequences of a freeze order of this dimension.

Faced with potential loss of clients and even bankruptcy, Kaye, Scholer threw in the towel six days after the freeze order was issued and agreed to pay $41 million in fines. The firm also consented to obey a detailed set of prescriptions as to what it could and could not do in representing financial institution clients in the future. The two principal Kaye, Scholer lawyers in the case, Peter Fishbein and Karen Katzman, were barred from representing depository institutions and suspended from practice before the OTS; a lesser sanction was administered to the third attorney.

The facts of the case may never be known, because Kaye, Scholer settled before any formal adjudication. What we have instead is a series of charges by OTS to the effect that Kaye, Scholer engaged in a pattern of illegal conduct that violated the agency's rules and regulations. See In re Fishbein, OTS AP-92-19 (Department of the Treasury, March 1, 1992). Kaye, Scholer never filed an official response, but it did circulate a press release answering the charges. See Stephen Gillers & Roy D. Simon, Jr., Regulation of Lawyers: Statutes and Standards 772-78 (1989). Kaye, Scholer's defense was that it acted as litigation counsel would and should act under the circumstances when an adversarial relationship has developed between the client and a government agency. Kaye, Scholer's position was backed by a written report from Geoffrey Hazard, a professor then at Yale Law School and a leading authority on legal ethics.

Among the points of controversy were the following:

— The OTS charged that Kaye, Scholer had made false and misleading statements and failed to disclose material facts in documents filed with the agency. Kaye, Scholer responded that it was merely acting as a zealous advocate of its client's interests, as it was required to do under the applicable rules of legal ethics, and that it was entitled to present its client's case in the most favorable light and to rely on its client's account of the underlying facts in issue as well as on the reports of other independent professionals.

— The OTS charged that Kaye, Scholer falsely represented that certain investments enjoyed grandfather rights, even though the firm knew that some of the key documents had been backdated. Kaye, Scholer's response was essentially that the backdating was irrelevant: Because the legal outcome was the same, in Kaye, Scholer's view, whether or not the documents had been backdated, the firm had no obligation to disclose this fact to the OTS.

— The OTS charged that Kaye, Scholer had inappropriately failed to disclose material facts in connection with Lincoln's role in financing a personal tax shelter for persons who controlled the institution's parent firm, in violation of the rules on affiliate transactions and the obligation to make safe and sound loans. Kaye, Scholer responded that the government had full notice of the transaction and had in fact raised questions about its legality, so no further disclosure was required from the firm.

— OTS charged that Kaye, Scholer had interposed itself between the agency and personnel at Lincoln, thus impeding the government's investigation. OTS argued that by substituting itself for Lincoln, Kaye, Scholer succeeded to the same reporting and disclosure requirements that applied to its client and that Kaye, Scholer violated those requirements in various ways. Kaye, Scholer responded that by interposing itself between agency and client, it was simply acting as litigation counsel would ordinarily act in like circumstances.

— OTS relied on the presence of backdated documents to charge that Kaye, Scholer had negligently or recklessly failed to provide proper legal advice to Lincoln that some of its direct investments were not, in fact, grandfathered, although the law firm knew that some of the documents had been backdated. Kaye, Scholer denied the allegation.

— OTS charged that Kaye, Scholer had committed an ethical violation by failing to inform the board of directors at Lincoln that certain of its officers were engaging in conduct inimical to the institution. OTS further alleged that Kaye, Scholer had a conflict of interest to which the client had not consented, since it represented simultaneously the savings and loan and its parent company. Kaye, Scholer, backed by its ethics expert, responded that there was no present conflict with the dual representation, since none of the issues involved the two clients in conflicting postures, and that it was reasonable to conclude that the firm had no responsibility to advise Lincoln's board about the alleged legal and fiduciary violations by Lincoln's officers and employees.

## *QUESTIONS AND COMMENTS*

1. On institution-affiliated parties, see Raymund G. Kawasaki, Liability of Attorneys, Accountants, Appraisers and Other Independent Contractors Under the Financial Institutions Reform, Recovery, and Enforcement Act of 1989, 42 Hastings Law Journal 249 (1990).

2. Although the *Kaye, Scholer* case was an earthquake within the depository institution bar, the position taken by the OTS in the *Lincoln* case had been presaged, to a degree, by Judge Sporkin's Shakespearean

oration, in Lincoln Savings & Loan Assn. v. Wall, 743 F. Supp. 901, 920 (D.D.C. 1990), on the failures of the legal profession in coping with the thrift institution crisis: "Where were these professionals, a number of whom are now asserting their rights under the Fifth Amendment, when these clearly improper transactions were being consummated? Why didn't any of them speak up or disassociate themselves from the transactions? Where also were the outside accountants and attorneys when these transactions were effectuated?"

3. The Kaye, Scholer controversy sparked a flood of commentary, most of it highly critical of the OTS. For a sampling, see George H. Brown, Financial Institution Lawyers as Quasi-Public Enforcers, 7 Georgetown Journal on Legal Ethics 637 (1994); Stephen McG. Bundy and Einer Elhauge, Knowledge About Legal Sanctions, 92 Michigan Law Review 261 (1993); Naomi Cahn, Foreword: Responsible Lawyers: George Washington Law Review Symposium on Community, Pluralism and Professional Responsibility, 63 George Washington Law Review 955 (1995); Dennis Curtis, Old Knights and New Champions: Kaye, Scholer, the Office of Thrift Supervision, and the Pursuit of the Dollar, 66 Southern California Law Review 985 (1993); Geoffrey C. Hazard, Jr., Lawyer Liability in Third Party Situations: The Meaning of the Kaye, Scholer Case, 26 Akron L. Rev. 395 (1992); Joyce A. Hughes, Law Firm Kaye, Scholer, Lincoln S&L and the OTS, 7 Notre Dame Journal of Legal Ethics and Public Policy 177 (1993); Howell Jackson, Reflections on Kaye, Scholer: Enlisting Lawyers to Improve the Regulation of Financial Institutions, 66 Southern California Law Review 1019 (1993); James O. Johnston and Daniel S. Schecter, Introduction, Kaye, Scholer and the OTS—Did Anyone Go Too Far?, 66 Southern California Law Review 977 (1993); Peter C. Kostant, When Zeal Boils Over: Disclosure Obligations and the Duty of Candor of Legal Counsel in Regulatory Proceedings after the Kaye Scholer Settlement, 25 Arizona State Law Journal 487 (1993); David Luban, Social Responsibilities of Lawyers: A Green Perspective, 63 George Washington Law Review 955 (1995); Jonathan R. Macey and Geoffrey P. Miller, Kaye, Scholer, FIRREA, and the Desirability of Early Closure: A View of the Kaye, Scholer Case from the Perspective of Bank Regulatory Policy, 66 Southern California Law Review 977 (1993); Harris Weinstein, Attorney Liability in the Savings and Loan Crisis, 1993 U. Ill. L. Rev. 53, 59 (1993); David B. Wilkins, Making Context Count: Regulating Lawyers After Kaye, Scholer, 66 Southern California Law Review 1145 (1993); Charles R. Zubrzycki, Note, The Kaye, Scholer Case: Attorneys' Ethical Duties to Third Parties in Regulatory Situations, 6 Georgetown Journal of Legal Ethics 977 (1993).

4. Press accounts reported that insurance companies imposed significant premium increases and reductions in coverage in the wake of the *Kaye, Scholer* case. Is there anything problematic about this, if true?

5. Although the $41 million fine paid by Kaye, Scholer appears

draconian, some reports indicated that the firm had previously billed Lincoln Savings more than $13 million and that its liability insurance carrier was going to pick up the vast bulk of the remainder. Do you think the OTS let Kaye, Scholer off too cheaply?

6. Why do you think the OTS acted so harshly against Kaye, Scholer? Was the firm's conduct egregious, or was the OTS trying to send a signal to the rest of the world? If the latter, was it proper for the agency to make a scapegoat or example out of one firm, when doing so greatly damaged the firm's reputation and finances? Wasn't it particularly unfair for the OTS to take after Kaye, Scholer without giving formal advance warning that it intended to hold law firms representing thrift institutions to a different standard than the traditional standard of adversary representation in which law firms have traditionally engaged?

7. What about the propriety of the OTS's exercise of its authority to freeze assets? Was there any real risk that Kaye, Scholer would dissipate its assets during the litigation? Isn't there a serious danger that OTS will abuse its freeze authority in order to coerce settlements, knowing that few, if any, firms will be able to hold out for long in the face of a freeze?

8. What do you make of the ethical arguments put forward by the OTS? In any event, why is legal ethics any of OTS's legitimate concern? Note that although breach of a rule of legal ethics is not in itself tantamount to legal malpractice, plaintiffs can generally introduce evidence of ethical lapses in malpractice suits against attorneys.

9. Do you detect in the OTS's view of the case some conflict in the model of the lawyer's obligations when representing a depository institution before a regulatory agency? Didn't the OTS suggest, in its charges, that Kaye, Scholer had some type of obligation to assist the agency in its enforcement efforts? Wouldn't this be exactly contrary to an attorney's traditional role of zealous representation of its client? But perhaps a lawyer's role *should* be different in this context, given the strong government interests involved. What do you think?

10. Note the significant gap between the views of OTS and those of Kaye, Scholer on whether the firm had an obligation to look behind the representations of its clients and, in effect, monitor its own client. If Kaye, Scholer had been told by the client that a certain state of affairs existed, wasn't it entitled to rely on the client's representations? But what if Kaye, Scholer had reason to doubt that the client's representations were fully truthful? Did it have a duty to investigate at that point? How can a law firm investigate its own client and still remain within the bounds of trust and confidence that epitomize the traditional attorney-client relationship? Is the firm's only option at this point to withdraw?

11. If attorneys are obligated to monitor their own clients, isn't there a danger of a chilling effect—that is, clients, knowing that their attorneys may be monitoring them, may become *less* willing to share information with them. In the absence of full information, won't the

attorney be at a significant disadvantage in guiding the client toward legality in structuring its affairs?

12. Is there something about the regulation of depository institutions that justifies more expansive legal obligations for attorneys who represent these entities than for lawyers in other fields? For discussion, see Howell Jackson, Reflections on Kaye, Scholer: Enlisting Lawyers to Improve the Regulation of Financial Institutions, 66 Southern California Law Review 1019 (1993) (suggesting a theoretical case for bank attorney liability rules as a response to the moral hazard problem associated with depository institutions); David B. Wilkins, Making Context Count: Regulating Lawyers After Kaye, Scholer, 66 Southern California Law Review 1145 (1993) (arguing for an analysis of an attorney's ethical obligations based on context and suggesting that bank regulatory attorneys might be treated differently than others).

13. Was part of the problem in the *Kaye, Scholer* case the fact that the lead attorney, Fishbein, was a litigator and not a professional banking lawyer? Perhaps Fishbein simply applied the ethics of a litigator to what was more appropriately seen as a regulatory problem. Note that the settlement agreement required that Kaye, Scholer appoint a banking partner with at least ten years' experience to supervise Kaye, Scholer's representation of insured depository institutions. Is this a sensible condition to impose?

14. Also as part of the settlement, Kaye, Scholer agreed to disclose material facts relating to a banking matter even when Kaye, Scholer has determined that the facts are not relevant to its theory of applicable law, if the banking agency might have a different view. Thus, Kaye, Scholer did not pursue its argument that it was not required to disclose things which it deemed to be legally irrelevant even if the agency would think otherwise. Is this an appropriate condition to impose on a law firm acting as outside counsel to a depository institution? If you were a partner in another firm representing depository institution clients, would you follow the model of the Kaye, Scholer settlement in your practice?

15. Note that Kaye, Scholer was a large and prominent firm and that the amount of damages obtained by the OTS was very large even in settlement. Do you think the enforcement tools possessed by OTS are likely to be equally effective when applied to small law firms? Aren't large firms the most appealing targets because they have the deepest pockets? Might the effect of the OTS action, at the margin, be to drive some large firms out of the business of representing depository institutions and to substitute smaller firms in their place? Would this be a salutary result? Could a law firm that wanted to represent depository institution clients but that did not want to place all of its (and its partners') assets at risk, restructure into several smaller firms with, for example, close professional relationships among the attorneys in the different firms? See Dennis Curtis, Old Knights and New Champions: Kaye, Scholer, the

Office of Thrift Supervision, and the Pursuit of the Dollar, 66 Southern California Law Review 985 (1993).

16. Can you think of other downside effects of imposing a whistleblower obligation on a depository institution's outside counsel? Is it possible that such liability might reduce counsel's ability to influence the institution's managers to comply with legal rules? See David B. Wilkins, Making Context Count: Regulating Lawyers After Kaye, Scholer, 66 Southern California Law Review 1145 (1993).

17. What really caused the disaster at Lincoln Savings? Was it the default by the lawyers, as Judge Sporkin and the OTS claimed? Weren't the root causes perhaps deeper—an ill-designed system of regulation for savings and loans institutions, congressional incompetence and inaction, and a feckless agency unable to stand up to the political pressures manifested by Charles Keating in his desperate—and temporarily successful—effort to keep his institution afloat? See Jonathan R. Macey and Geoffrey P. Miller, Kaye, Scholer, FIRREA, and the Desirability of Early Closure: A View of the Kaye, Scholer Case from the Perspective of Bank Regulatory Policy, 66 Southern California Law Review 977 (1993).

# 4 BANK HOLDING COMPANIES

## A. INTRODUCTION

A bank holding company is simply a company that has control over any bank or over any other company that has control over any bank. 12 U.S.C. §1841(a)(1). Holding companies are popular devices for the conduct of financial services activities because they offer flexibility of operation, relief from certain regulatory constraints, and economies of scale or scope compared with stand-alone banks.

Laws regulating bank holding companies have developed based on a long-standing and widely held belief that the size and scope of banking organizations must be sharply constrained to ensure that they never become a threat to the republic by amassing too much economic or political power vis-à-vis the citizenry at large. The laws regulating bank holding companies attempt to control the economic power of banking conglomerates by prohibiting firms engaged in the banking business from engaging in general commercial business. In recent years, however, the fears of bank dominance of the economic and political system have declined somewhat. Other reasons, however, also exist for singling bank holding companies out for special regulatory treatment. For one, regulators have feared that those controlling bank holding companies might compromise the financial integrity of the banks within the holding company in order to provide resources to other firms within the holding company. Second, a widely shared belief holds that banks need special regulatory protection to prevent them from failing, a belief that the presence of a federally backed deposit insurance scheme substantiates. It is thought that regulation is needed to make sure that the assets of any bank within a holding company will not be used in ways that are inconsistent with the public policy goals of protecting the safety and soundness of the bank and its depositors. A closely related justification for imposing special regulatory treatment is to ensure that bank holding companies will be a "source of strength" for its subsidiary banks.

A final reason for restricting the activities of bank holding companies is to prevent a bank from engaging in favoritism. Specifically, the drafters of the Bank Holding Company Act feared that a holding company might loan money only to customers of their subsidiaries, refraining from making loans to creditworthy customers who did not deal with their subsidiaries.

## B. THE STATUTORY SCHEME

The legal restrictions on bank holding companies are found principally, though not exclusively, in the Bank Holding Company Act of 1956 (BHCA), as amended, which is administered by the Board of Governors of the Federal Reserve System. It is the BHCA that defines a bank holding company (BHC) as "any company which has control over any bank or over any company that is or becomes a bank holding company." 12 U.S.C. §1848(a)(1). The coverage of the act, therefore, turns on three key concepts: "bank," "control," and "company." These coverage questions are addressed in the following material.

### *1. "Bank"*

What is a "bank"? By now, you are several weeks into this topic and may feel you know what a bank is, especially given the extensive discussion in Chapter 1 on exactly that topic. But you would probably be mistaken, because the concept of a "bank" for BHCA purposes differs in some respects from the general understanding of that concept.

The original version of the statute defined a "bank" for BHCA purposes as any institution "which (1) accepts deposits that the depositor has a legal right to withdraw on demand, and (2) engages in the business of making commercial loans." This seems like a perfectly good definition, and it in fact proved serviceable for many years. The early 1980s, however, witnessed the growth of the "nonbank bank." Nonbank banks were "institutions that offer[ed] services similar to those of banks but which [were not subject to the BHCA] because they conduct[ed] their business so as to place themselves arguably outside the narrow definition of 'bank' found in §2(c) of the Act. Many nonbank banks, for example, offer[ed] customers NOW (negotiable order of withdrawal) accounts which function like conventional checking accounts but because of prior notice provisions do not technically give the depositor a 'legal right to withdraw on demand. . . . Others offer[ed] conventional checking accounts, but avoid[ed] classification as 'banks' by limiting their extension of commercial credit to the purchase of money market instruments such as certificates of deposit and commercial paper." Board of Governors of the Federal Reserve System v. Dimension Financial Corp., 474 U.S. 361 (1986).

The nonbank bank was a truly impressive regulatory loophole. An institution had to give up very little to qualify as a nonbank bank. It could retain its national or federal bank charter and could continue to provide FDIC or FSLIC insurance on deposits. All it had to do was give up one or the other of the two prongs of the BHCA definition of "bank." It could be in the business of making commercial loans so long as it did not offer demand deposit accounts; and with the development of the NOW account in the early 1980s, it could offer a deposit instrument that was functionally equivalent to a checking account without losing its status as a nonbank bank. Alternatively, if it wanted to offer checking accounts, it had only to avoid being in the business of making commercial loans. It could continue to make residential mortgage and consumer finance loans, and, with the growth of the commercial paper market, it could purchase short-term debt securities of blue chip corporations that had nearly all the functional features of a commercial loan without being classed as such.

The reason the nonbank bank was such an appealing loophole is that it offered relief from two extremely important regulatory regimes under the BHCA. First, under the BHCA, the only firms that could own or control a *bank* were those engaged in activities "closely related to banking" (more on this anon). But *any* firm—even an automobile manufacturer or software manufacturer—could own or control a *nonbank bank.* Thus, the nonbank bank offered a way for all sorts of ordinary commercial firms to enter the banking business.

Equally important, the nonbank bank loophole offered what appeared to be a tremendous opportunity for interstate banking. As we discuss more fully in Chapter 5, bank holding companies could not until recently acquire or form banks in other states unless the state where the subsidiary was located specifically authorized entry by out-of-state banking organizations. Until the mid-1980s, no states had opened their markets to out-of-state BHCs. But nothing in the law prevented the acquisition of a *nonbank bank* in another state. Accordingly, the concept of the nonbank bank threatened to undermine the whole regulatory structure governing geographic bank expansion.

The Fed attempted to plug the nonbank bank loophole by including NOW accounts within the definition of demand deposits and by including commercial paper and similar money market instruments within the scope of the statutory term "commercial loans." But the Supreme Court would have none of it, concluding that the Fed had exceeded its powers in stretching the statutory language beyond its natural meaning. Board of Governors of the Federal Reserve System v. Dimension Financial Corp., 474 U.S. 361 (1986).

Congress plugged this loophole in 1987 after several years of struggling with the problem. The new definition of bank, which the Competitive Equality Banking Act inserted in the Bank Holding Company Act, defines bank as an institution that is an "insured bank" under the Federal Deposit Insurance Act, or that (i) accepts demand deposits or deposits that the depositor may withdraw by check or similar means for payment to third parties or others; and (ii) is engaged in the business of making commercial loans. 12 U.S.C. §1841(c)(1).

A bank is an insured bank under the Federal Deposit Insurance Act if insured by the FDIC. 12 U.S.C. §1813(h). The FDIC insures all national banks and all members of the Federal Reserve System by law. In addition, state banks may elect to obtain FDIC insurance. Under the current definition of the term "bank," if an institution is insured by the FDIC, it will be a bank for purposes of the Bank Holding Company Act.

Even if not insured by the FDIC, a bank may still be a bank under the second part of the Bank Holding Company Act's new definition. A depository institution cannot avoid being designated as a bank merely by refraining from offering demand deposits. The new act's definition of a bank will include any institution that offers "check-like" deposit accounts. Thus an institution that offers NOW accounts now will be considered a bank if it also makes commercial loans. In addition, the Competitive Equality Banking Act was also intended to include institutions that offer customers the right to transfer money by wire and institutions that allow customers to have excess funds in their accounts automatically transferred among various accounts at certain times (so-called automatic sweep arrangements).

Significantly, this new definition of bank retains the traditional requirement that a bank offer both demand deposits and be engaged in the business of making commercial *loans*. Thus previous case law defining a commercial loan is still important. The critical case on this issue is the opinion just mentioned, Board of Governors of the Federal Reserve v. Dimension Financial Corporation.

## 2. *"Company"*

Quite apart from whether a particular firm is a "bank" for BHCA purposes, the BHCA does not apply if the entity alleged to be a BHC does not qualify as a "company" under the BHCA. Under the Bank Holding Company Act, the term "company" means any "corporation, partnership, business trust, association, or similar organization, or any other trust unless by its terms it must terminate . . . [within 25 years]." 12 U.S.C. §1841(b). Difficulty arises when a group of individuals sharing some common bond or relationship have a controlling interest in a bank. The question then becomes whether the individuals form a "partnership" or "association" that would cause them to be a "company" under the Bank Holding Company Act. Very little law is found on this subject, and the Federal Reserve has been rather understanding in cases where a family group owns a controlling interest of a bank, so long as there is no evidence of domination or control by one member of the family.

Presumably, the relevant partnership law of the state in question will control on the issue of whether a partnership exists. Under the Uniform Partnership Act, a partnership is defined as an association of two or more persons to carry on as co-owners a business for profit. Uniform Partnership Act §6(1). The Act provides that a person's receipt of a share of a business's profits is prima facie evidence that the person is a partner in the business. Id. §7(4).

### 3. *"Control"*

A corporation does not become a bank holding company merely by owning stock in a bank. Rather, the corporation must acquire control of a bank or of another company that controls a bank.

The statute, 12 U.S.C. §1841(a), articulates three conditions constituting control over a bank: (1) owning, controlling, or having the power to vote 25 percent of any class of voting securities of a bank or a bank holding company, (2) controlling the election of a majority of the board of directors of a bank or a bank holding company; and (3) exercising a direct or indirect controlling influence over the institution's management or policies.

The Federal Reserve Board is given a considerable amount of discretion in determining whether a company has "control." The Bank Holding Company Act requires that all companies obtain prior approval of the Federal Reserve for any acquisition that will cause the company to become a bank holding company.

The statute presumes that any company that owns, controls, or votes less than 5 percent of any class of voting securities of a bank or bank holding company does not have control. 12 U.S.C. §1841(a)(3). However, this is merely a rebuttable presumption. Id. If a bank owns less than 5 percent of a class of voting securities it is entitled to a board adjudication on the issue of whether it is in control of a bank. 12 U.S.C. §1843(a)(4); see also 12 C.F.R. §225.2.

The board has firmly resisted attempts to sidestep bank control restrictions. For example, in 1982 the board struck down an agreement by Security Corp. to effectively take over American National Bank (American) of Duncan, Oklahoma, by buying a large block of nonvoting shares. American had been established by five directors and shareholders of

Security (an Oklahoma bank holding company) who planned to act as the directors of American and who along with another director of Security would also hold all of American's outstanding voting shares. Security would own in its own name nonvoting stock representing 99.6 percent of American's total equity.

Security maintained that this ownership structure did not violate a state law that barred holding companies from having "power to vote 15 percent or more of the voting shares of each of two or more banks." The board, however, concluded that the interlocking relationship between the board of Security Corp. and the organizers of the new bank, the nominal investment of the voting stockholders, and the assumption of nearly all financial risk by the holding company made it clear that Security would have control. But such control was illegal without the Federal Reserve Board's prior approval, an approval the board could not grant under the Bank Holding Company Act because it would violate an Oklahoma law prohibiting multibank holding companies. Letter from William W. Wiles, Secretary to the Board, to J. A. Maurer, President, Security Corp. dated June 23, 1982. Had the board not acted as it did, similar intrastate or interstate acquisitions of banks would undoubtedly have arisen patterned on the Security Corp. model.

## C. RESTRICTIONS ON BANK HOLDING COMPANY ACTIVITIES: THE "CLOSELY RELATED TO BANKING" TEST

Companies may want to avoid being designated as a bank holding company so as to avoid Federal Reserve Board regulation of their nonbanking activities. In particular, the general rule is that bank holding companies cannot acquire or retain "direct or indirect ownership or control of any voting shares of any company which is not a bank." 12 U.S.C. §1843(a). If a company acquires a bank, it has two years to rid itself of its nonbanking components. Id.

This general rule, however, is subject to a number of important exceptions. In the present section we consider the most important of these exceptions, under which bank holding companies may acquire nonbank affiliates the activities of which the Federal Reserve Board has concluded are "so closely related to banking or managing or controlling banks as to be a proper incident thereto." 12 U.S.C. §1843(c)(8).

The statute goes on to provide that:

> In determining whether a particular activity is a proper incident to banking or managing or controlling banks the Board shall consider whether its

> performance by an affiliate of a holding company can reasonably be expected to produce benefits to the public such as greater convenience, increased competition, or gains in efficiency, that outweigh possible adverse effects, such as undue concentration of resources, decreased or unfair competition, conflicts of interest, or unsound banking practices.

Id.

The Board's Regulation Y lists activities that the Federal Reserve Board has determined to be closely related to banking. The board adds to the list from time to time. A sample of the items on the Regulation Y list includes the following:

1. Making, acquiring, or servicing loans or other extensions of credit (including issuing letters of credit) for the account of the bank holding company or the account of others. Credit may be extended, for example, via consumer finance, credit cards, mortgages, commercial finance, and factoring.
2. Performing functions of a trust company, including activities of a fiduciary, agency, or custodial nature.
3. Acting as investment or financial adviser to real estate or mortgage trusts or to investment companies registered under the Investment Company Act of 1940, providing portfolio investment advice, and furnishing general economic information.
4. Leasing personal or real property or acting as agent, broker, or adviser where the leases are the functional equivalent of an extension of credit.
5. Making equity and debt investments in corporations or projects designed to promote community welfare.
6. Providing data processing and transmission services (subject to limitations stated in Association of Data Processing Service Organizations v. Board of Governors, 745 F.2d 677 (D.C. Cir. 1984)).
7. Acting as underwriter for credit life insurance and credit accident and health insurance that is directly related to an extension of credit.
8. Providing courier services for checks, commercial papers, documents, and written instruments that are exchanged among banks and financial institutions.
9. Providing management consulting advice to nonaffiliated bank and nonbank depository institutions.
10. Issuing money orders having a face value of not more than $1,000 and selling travelers checks and U.S. savings bonds.
11. Performing appraisals of real estate.
12. Arranging commercial real estate equity financing by acting as intermediary in certain real estate projects.

13. Providing securities brokerage services and incidental activities such as offering custodial services, individual retirement accounts, and cash management services, if the securities brokerage services are restricted to buying and selling securities solely as agent for the account of customers.
14. Underwriting and dealing obligations of the United States, other government bodies, and other obligations that state member banks of the Federal Reserve System may be authorized to underwrite and deal in, including bankers' acceptances and certificates of deposit.
15. Providing foreign exchange and advisory transactional services, including arranging "swaps," through separate subsidiaries complying with board regulations.
16. Acting through a separate subsidiary as a futures commission merchant for nonaffiliated persons in the execution and clearance on major commodity exchanges of future contracts for bullion, foreign exchange, government securities and other money market instruments.
17. Providing investment advice on financial futures and options on futures.
18. Providing consumer financial counselling subject to board conditions.
19. Providing tax planning and preparation services.
20. Offering check guaranty services.
21. Operating an agency for collecting overdue accounts receivable.
22. Operating a credit bureau.

If a bank holding company wishes to engage in a business not already on the list, it must first seek a board determination that the activity is closely related to banking.

## National Courier Association v. Board of Governors of the Federal Reserve System

*516 F.2d 1229 (D.C. Cir. 1975)*

McGowan, J.

[The Federal Reserve Board found that certain courier services and related transportation services should be added to the Regulation Y list. These courier and transportation services were to be used for:]

(i) the internal operations of the holding company and its subsidiaries;
(ii) checks, commercial papers, documents, and written instruments

> (excluding currency or bearer-type negotiable instruments) as are exchanged among banks and banking institutions;
>
> (iii) audit and accounting media of a banking or financial nature and other business records and documents used in processing such media.

12 C.F.R. §225.4(a)(11) (1974).

A fourth category of service that may be provided by bank-affiliated couriers is contained in the following "interpretation," also added to Regulation Y by the contested order:

> [T]he furnishing of courier services for non-financially-related material upon the specific, unsolicited request of a third party when courier services are not otherwise reasonably available may be regarded as an incidental activity of a bank-related courier.

Id. §225.129.

For the reasons stated below, the regulation under attack is upheld in part, and in part held invalid.

### I

We note at the outset the limited nature of the question we have been asked to decide. Section 4(c)(8) of the Bank Holding Company Act provides that the general ban on the ownership by a bank holding company of shares in any company other than a bank shall not apply to

> shares of any company the activities of which the Board after due notice and opportunity for hearing has determined (by order or regulation) to be so closely related to banking or managing or controlling banks as to be a proper incident thereto.

12 U.S.C. §1843(c)(8) (1970). By an amendment of the same section in 1970 the Board has been further instructed as follows:

> In determining whether a particular activity is a proper incident to banking or managing or controlling banks the Board shall consider whether its performance by an affiliate of a holding company can reasonably be expected to produce benefits to the public such as greater convenience, increased competition, or gains in efficiency, that outweigh possible adverse effects, such as undue concentration of resources, decreased or unfair competition, conflicts of interest, or unsound banking practices.

Id.

The parties are agreed that there are two distinct issues raised by a bank holding company's seeking to hold shares in a company engaged in non-banking activities, and that they correspond to the statutory segments set out above. The first is whether those activities are "closely related to banking." This is a question that asks only whether the activities in question are generally of a kind that Congress, having concluded that "banking and commerce should remain separate," forbade bank holding companies to engage in, without regard to the merits of such engagement in a particular case.

The second or so-called "public benefits" issue, derived from the 1970 amendments to the Act, is one which normally must be resolved upon specific facts. It poses the question whether the performance of a non-banking activity by a bank holding company affiliate will achieve a favorable balance of the kinds of benefits and adverse effects enumerated in the statute. Naturally the conclusion that the non-banking activity of one bank holding company would be anticompetitive or threaten "unsound banking practices" may not hold for a different bank holding company under different circumstances.

Recognizing this distinction in the nature of the two issues, the Board had reserved the latter for case-by-case resolution at the time of individual bank holding company applications to engage in courier service. The parties are therefore agreed that no Board determination on the "public benefits" of such engagement is now before this court for review. What is before us is the final resolution of the former or "closely related" issue with respect to the activities that the Board has added to Regulation Y. The Board's determination that these are not activities necessarily forbidden to bank holding companies takes the form of a rule intended to be binding on all future parties to individual application proceedings.

## II

Courier services were described in the statement accompanying the Board's order as the "transportation of any item with a critical time schedule, provided such items are small in bulk, light in weight, and require only ordinary security measures." The items which are carried by courier service in far the greatest volume are financial documents and records—particularly banking instruments—which require speedy transportation from one place of business to another. It thus appears that the nation's banks are by far the largest consumers of courier services, accounting for more than half of that industry's sales. The industry itself is about thirty years old, and has thus far remained largely independent of the banks, though it is dominated by a very few firms.[6]

6. The record contains estimates that the total annual revenues of the courier industry are approximately $76 million, the share of the largest five firms $65 million, and that of the single largest firm (Purolator, Inc.) $46 million.

Of the three categories of courier services that the Board has found to be "closely related" to banking, the first, that of courier services "for the internal operations of the holding company and its subsidiaries," is not in issue. The provision of services by one bank affiliate is expressly allowed by Section 4(c)(1)(C) of the statute. 12 U.S.C. §1843(c)(1)(C) (1970).

The second category is that of courier services "for checks, commercial papers, documents, and written instruments (excluding currency or bearer-type instruments) as are exchanged among banks and banking institutions." What is meant are the so-called "cash letters" in which one bank transmits all the checks, drafts, and money orders that must be cleared or otherwise processed at another bank. . . .

The third category of "closely related" courier services are those "for audit and accounting media of a banking or financial nature and other business records and documents used in processing such media." The term "media" appears simply to refer to the physical form (paper documents, magnetic tapes, etc.) in which the financial data to be processed are conveyed. . . .

The fourth category of authorized courier services, that contained in the Board's separate "interpretation," is largely self-explanatory. Bank-affiliated couriers may carry non-financially related material if requests for such services are unsolicited and it is not otherwise reasonably available. . . .

### III

No challenge is made to the procedure by which the amendments to Regulation Y were adopted, but merely to their substance. In this respect our task is to set aside the Board's findings of fact if they are "arbitrary, capricious, an abuse of discretion, or otherwise not in accordance with law,"[8] while deciding "all relevant questions of law" ourselves. 5 U.S.C. §706 (1970).

Without slighting the difficulties of separating questions of law and fact, but also without rehearsing them at any length, we address what seems to us the single "question of law" in the case, and that is the proper definitions of the statutory phrase "closely related." Is it an intentionally vague phrase by which Congress very largely left it up to the Board to decide what kinds and degrees of relationships are sufficiently close? Or is there some more specific connection that the Board must find exists between banking and the assertedly related activity? . . .

8. In keeping with its view that its findings in this case were not "required by statute to be made on the record after opportunity for an agency hearing," the Board maintains that the proper standard of review of those findings is the "arbitrary and capricious" rather than the "substantial evidence" standard. Petitioners do not appear to contest this conclusion, urging instead that the question decided by the Board was one of law.

. . . [R]eminding ourselves that the matter is one expressly committed by the statute to the Board, we think we owe considerable deference to the Board's judgment that a particular activity is "closely related to banking." Rather than define that term with any precision, therefore, we simply require that the Board go about making its "closely related" decision in a reasoned fashion consistent with the legislative intent.

The Board must, we think, articulate the ways in which banking activities and the proposed activities are assertedly connected, and must determine, not arbitrarily or capriciously, that the connections are close. As to what kinds of connections may qualify, at least the following seem to us within the statutory intent:

1. Banks generally have in fact provided the proposed services.
2. Banks generally provide services that are operationally or functionally so similar to the proposed services as to equip them particularly well to provide the proposed service.
3. Banks generally provide services that are so integrally related to the proposed services as to require their provision in a specialized form.

We turn, then, to the question of whether the Board has rationally found such connections in this case.

### A. *BANKING MATERIAL*

The Board appears to have found all three of the foregoing kinds of connections between banking and courier service for banking material. It made clear, for example, that it did not regard courier service as the exclusive historical province of specialized carriers. It noted that "three bank holding companies, all of which became subject to the Bank Holding Company Act as a result of the 1970 Amendments, are engaged in providing 'for hire' courier service."[16]

As to the second kind of connection, the Board pointed out that the internal operation of a bank often involves it in transportation activities of the kind involved in courier service. According to the Board, "a number of banks, particularly those which operate a significant number of branches, engage in the transportation of such items as checks, internal memoranda and data processing material between branches . . . ." The business of banking, after all, does not consist solely of abstract interest computations and lending and borrowing decisions. It is in an equally important sense the management of the torrential stream of documents and records that

16. We note that banks subject to the National Bank Act are themselves empowered to provide, incidentally to banking, a "messenger service by means of an armored car or otherwise." 12 C.F.R. §7.7490 (1970). See note 21 infra and accompanying text.

are the medium of financial transactions. And if it would be impossible to say that the management of that stream *within* a bank is not "banking," it would also be hard to say that management of that stream between banks is not "closely related" to banking.

The third kind of connection—the dependence of banks on a specialized form of the proposed services—has been the most emphasized in this case. The Board concluded that "courier services for cash letters play a vital role in the check clearing process," and that "the transportation of a cash letter has been so integrated into the process by which checks are collected as to be part of the present payments mechanism." . . . Petitioners do not really dispute the point, but urge that, if the necessity of a service to banking activities may justify the establishment of a bank affiliate to provide the service itself, then the banks may expand into any number of industries whose goods and services they consume. Telephone service is given as an example. Apart from noting that this kind of connection to banking is not the only one present in the case, we can only respond by emphasizing that the service must be required by the bank in a specialized form, as is not true of telephone service or of many others that banks employ.

The Board has thus articulated several ways in which banking and courier services for banking materials may properly be considered related. Record evidence in support of each is ample, and we cannot say that in finding the relation a "close" one the Board was arbitrary or capricious.

### B. FINANCIALLY RELATED DATA PROCESSING MATERIALS

. . . [T]he Board treated the transportation of data processing material as bearing the same relation to data processing itself as the transportation of cash letters bears to banking, and we cannot say that it was arbitrary or capricious in doing so.

The difficult question, of course, is whether the similarity of these two relations was enough. There is no question that courier service for data processing material has been found "closely related to banking" not because of its connection to banking per se but because of its relation to financial data processing, an activity banks are permitted to engage in. We are not so much bothered by the illogic of the reasoning (which could be overcome by simply asserting that the data processing industry as a whole is "closely related to banking") as we are by the danger, pressed on us by petitioners, that if the Board is permitted to string together a chain of close relations, the limitation means nothing.

Certainly the Board will not be permitted to tack one close relation on to another indefinitely, but we cannot forbid it in this case. The relations are of distinctly different kinds. That of financial data processing to banking may be thought of as horizontal, in the sense that these are parallel and kindred financial services. That of banking to the transportation of cash letters, and of financial data processing to the transportation of audit and accounting media, may be thought of as vertical, in the sense that transportation is a non-financial service necessary to the provision of financial services. Rather than threaten infinite repetition, the Board's reasoning seems rather to complete the missing fourth side of a square. More persuasive than its symmetry, however, are the practical realities it reflects. The record suggests that in many cases check processing and financially related data processing are carried on at the same location and by the use of the same equipment. It would seem anomalous to require that similar material, quite possibly generated by a single customer and destined for a single bank computer, be transported by two separate couriers.

We have not overlooked the fact that no restrictions are placed by the challenged regulation upon whom a bank-affiliated courier may serve. The carriage of banking materials authorized in the second part of the Board's order will presumably be between banks, but neither need be an affiliate of the bank-affiliated courier. The carriage of data processing materials under the third part of the Board's order may be between two places of business neither of which is a bank, a bank affiliate, or a customer of either. A bank-affiliated courier may thus carry the financially related records of a firm with which it has no dealings (let us say a department store that does its banking elsewhere), to the independent data processor of that firm's choice. It is at this point that the Board has put its discretion to determine the closeness of relations to banking under the greatest strain.

We do not think it has exceeded that discretion, however. Authorization to provide courier services to banks and bank affiliates must carry with it the authorization to provide the same services generally. The reason is that otherwise the bank-affiliated courier services, which may be of superior quality, would be "tied" by law to the other services which banks and their affiliates provide. The anti-competitive effects of such a tie in respect of banking services would contravene the Act's most basic purposes. Recognizing this, the Board has in fact not only authorized but intends to *require* bank affiliated couriers to provide their services generally and without discrimination.

### *C. GENERAL COURIER SERVICES WHERE UNSOLICITED AND NOT OTHERWISE AVAILABLE*

The Board has apparently not taken the manifestly untenable position that the transportation of non-financially related material becomes "closely related" to banking simply because such service is provided without solicitation and is not otherwise available. Its position appears instead to be that in such circumstances concededly *non*-closely related services may be provided because they are purely "incidental." It suggests, in other words, that in requiring that the "activities" of bank affiliates be closely related to banking, Congress meant only their *ordinary* or *principal* activities, and left them free to engage in other activities certified by the Board to be "incidental."

The notion that bank affiliates may be permitted to engage not only in activities that are "closely related to banking," but also in "incidental" activities was not first introduced by the Board in the context of courier services. It apparently takes the same view with respect to all categories of "closely related" activities, having announced in the first sentence of its Regulation Y:

> . . . [A]ny bank holding company may engage, or retain or acquire an interest in a company that engages solely in one or more of the [closely related] activities specified below, *including such incidental activities as are necessary to carry on the activities so specified.*

12 C.F.R. §225.4(a) (1974) (emphasis supplied). The Board has in fact gone on to specify the activities that may be engaged in as "incidental" to one other "closely related" activity, that of financially related data processing. Nor is the permissibility of activities "incidental" to those that are expressly authorized a notion that originated with the Board. That section of the National Bank Act which circumscribes the activities of nationally chartered banks entitles them "[t]o exercise . . . all such incidental powers as shall be necessary to carry on the business of banking." 12 U.S.C. §24 (1970).[21]

The idea is thus fairly well established that Congress intended some reasonable latitude in the limitations it placed upon the activities of banks and their affiliates. In enumerating the activities that could be carried on, it certainly could not have meant to forbid engagement in such other "incidental" activities as were reasonably necessary to carrying out those that were enumerated.

The justification for the "incidental" courier services at issue here is, however, quite different. It is not, as far as we can tell, that the carriage of non-financially related material is in any way necessary to the successful operation of the courier service affiliates. Rather, it is that the provision of such service would serve "the convenience of the public." We have in effect been asked to approve a doctrine of "incidental" activities under which the Board may permit bank affiliates to engage in such activities because such engagement would be a generally beneficial thing. The Board has made quite an appealing case in this respect. If requests

21. Examples of "incidental" activities that national banks have been permitted to engage in are the maintenance of postal substations on bank premises, the provision of messenger services, and the acquiring of equity interests in community development projects, though such an interest would "clearly not [be] a bankable asset by ordinary standards." 12 C.F.R. §§7.7480, 7.7482, 7.7490 (1974).

for non-financially related courier services must be unsolicited, it may seem unlikely that a bank's courier affiliate would ever get very deeply involved in providing them. If such services must be otherwise unavailable, then those who employ it would appear to gain, while no competitor of the bank loses.[23] It might thus be argued that the provision of general courier services under the conditions the Board has imposed offends none of the policies against economic concentration and conflicts of interest which underlie the statutory separation of commerce and banking.

But Congress did not instruct the Board to allow or disallow bank involvement in non-financial activities as may be required by the policies which counsel a separation of commerce and banking. Having heeded that counsel itself, it decreed the separation, and instructed the Board to enforce it. Its decision hardly seems an unreasonable one, even in the context of this case, for it is not at all clear that the Board's non-solicitation and non-availability conditions would in fact prevent bank-affiliated couriers from becoming substantially involved in general courier service. The problem, of course, is the inexactitude of such terms as "unsolicited" and "not otherwise reasonably available."

The result is that while there may be some warrant in the statute for the Board's permitting as "incidental" those activities that are necessary to the bank affiliate's closely related activities, we can find no such warrant for its determination that non-financially related courier services are "incidental" and therefore permissible if unsolicited and otherwise unavailable. The Board's order, which we have sustained in other respects, we decline to do so in this one. . . .

The petition for review is denied in all respects with the exception that so much of the so-called "interpretation" added to Regulation Y as relates to the furnishing of courier services for non-financially-related material, treated within ¶III. C. of this opinion is set aside.

It is so ordered.

## *QUESTIONS AND COMMENTS*

1. *National Courier* is generally considered the fullest statement on the issue of determining whether nonbanking activities are closely related to banking under the Bank Holding Company Act.

23. In discussing at oral argument the kinds of material transportable under this portion of the Board's order, the parties were careful in their choice of which of the Board's examples to stress. Opponents of the order dwelt on the cut flowers; its defenders, on the human blood, always pictured as being rushed to donees in extremis. In answer to the latter suggestion, we suppose that, if and when there is a true emergency requiring a bank affiliate to carry human blood, no one will object if it does so. If there is no true emergency, any real need will presumably be met in other ways.

2. Compare the incidental powers clause of 12 U.S.C. §24 (Seventh), which gives national banks the power to exercise "all such incidental powers as shall be necessary to carry on the business of banking," with the closely related to banking clause of the Bank Holding Company Act as construed in *National Courier.* Which language appears to grant broader powers?

3. Why are bank holding company affiliates permitted to engage in a broader range of activities than banks themselves?

4. What does it mean to say that a particular activity is a "proper incident to banking or managing or controlling banks"? Does this phraseology really provide the Federal Reserve Board with much guidance, or is it an open-ended invitation to the board to do whatever it wants? Did the court in *National Courier* provide much guidance for the board?

5. The statutory language does, in fact, appear to provide some guidance. The statute says that in determining whether a particular activity is a proper incident to banking or to managing or controlling banks, the board shall consider whether the holding company's performance of the activity can reasonably be expected to produce public benefits, such as greater convenience, competition or efficiency, that outweigh possible adverse effects, such as undue concentration of resources, decreased or unfair competition, conflicts of interest, or unsound banking practices. Read literally, the statute appears to say that if the public derives a net benefit from a particular activity, then that activity is closely related to banking. Does this make sense? How does the court in *National Courier* interpret this language? Is it correct to say, as the court in *National Courier* appears to, that the issue of public benefits is not related to the proper incident test at all, but rather poses a separate hurdle that individual applicants must satisfy once it is determined that the activity in question is closely related to banking?

*National Courier's* two-step approach to interpreting the Bank Holding Company Act was summarized succinctly in Association of Bank Travel Bureaus v. Board of Governors of the Federal Reserve System, 568 F.2d 549 (7th Cir. 1978): "The Board has interpreted Section 4(c)(8) to include two distinct tests. First the Board must determine whether an activity is "closely related" to banking. . . . [I]t then must decide whether the activity is a "proper incident to banking" by weighing the benefits against the possible adverse effects." Id. at 551. In this case the Federal Reserve Board had determined that operating a travel agency was not an activity closely related to banking. The court held that, having made this determination, the board was not required to determine whether the efficiency gains or other public benefits that might accrue from the activity outweighed any possible adverse effects.

6. Does the fact that a particular activity is efficient for a bank holding company to perform mean that the activity is a proper incident to banking? An economist would say that any transaction that increases

value for all affected parties is efficient. R. Posner, Economic Analysis of Law 15 (3d ed. 1986). Gains in efficiency are said to arise whenever a firm can buy or sell a particular product or service at a profit in mutually consensual transactions. How could a court ever say that an activity that a holding company enters voluntarily with an expectation of profit could not be efficient? The obvious reason is that the statute only permits bank holding companies to engage in activities closely related to banking. Courts have concluded that this statutory language operates as the real constraint on the board's discretion. As the Fifth Circuit stated in Alabama Association of Insurance Agents v. Board of Governors of the Federal Reserve System, "[t]he Board's function is not to promote the public interest consistent with the policies of the Bank Holding Company Act, but to determine what activities are closely related to banking." 533 F.2d 224, 242 (5th Cir. 1976), *cert. denied,* 435 U.S. 904 (1978). Thus the statute has not been used to require an efficiency-based cost benefit test. Rather, it seems that the statutory language operates to prevent entry by bank holding companies into certain markets.

7. A 1992 amendment to Regulation Y permits bank holding companies to provide financial advisory services to "financial and non-financial institutions," as well as to "high net worth individuals . . . [and] foreign governments and their agencies." These services may include:

> financial advice in connection with joint ventures, structuring of leveraged buy-outs and capital raising efforts, restructurings, reorganizations, interest-rate collars, and interest-rate floors . . . [as well as financial advice concerning] swaps, caps and similar transactions involving currency exchange rates and prices, as well as economic and financial indices.

In addition, the rule authorizes bank holding companies to provide combined investment advice and security brokerage services. Although the new rule makes it easier for bank holding companies to provide nonbank-related financial advice, two restrictions were retained. First, bank holding companies offering financial advisory services may not "perform routine tasks or operations on a daily or continuous basis." This restriction aims to ensure that bank holding companies are not controlling firms under the guise of providing financial advisory services. Second, financial advisors may not divulge confidential information about a client to affiliates absent that client's permission.

## Association of Data Processing Services Organizations, Inc. v. Board of Governors of the Federal Reserve System

***745 F.2d 677 (D.C. Cir. 1984)***

SCALIA, Circuit Judge:

. . . On February 23, 1979, Citicorp applied for authority to engage, through its subsidiary Citishare, in the processing and transmission of banking, financial, and economic related data through timesharing, electronic funds transfer, home banking and other techniques. It also sought permission to sell its excess computing capacity and some computer hardware. The Board published notice of Citicorp's application, which was protested by ADAPSO, and set it for formal hearing. Before the hearing was held, Citicorp amended its application to add certain activities and to request amendment of Regulation Y to permit the activities it had specified. The Board published an Amended Order for Hearing and invited public comments and participation. A formal hearing was held before an Administrative Law Judge in which the merits of both the application and the proposed rule were considered. In addition, more than sixty companies and individuals submitted written comments on the proposed rule. On March 29, 1982, the ALJ decided that the activities proposed by Citicorp were closely related to banking and would produce benefits to the public which would outweigh their costs. The ALJ also recommended amendments to Regulation Y that would permit those activities contained in the Citicorp application. On July 9, 1982, the Board adopted the ALJ's recommendation to approve the Citicorp application, with certain restrictions. On August 23, 1982, the Board adopted the ALJ's recommended amendments to Regulation Y, again with certain restrictions. ADAPSO, and two of its members, participants in the actions below, filed these petitions for review. . . .

## II. Closely Related to Banking

This appeal requires us . . . to decide whether the Board of Governors acted arbitrarily or capriciously—either because no substantial evidence existed to support its factual premises, or in any other respect—when it concluded, based on the record of the proceedings before it, that the new activities Citicorp proposed were closely related to banking. The test which the Board applied was that developed by this court in *National Courier;* supra, 516 F.2d at 1237:

> As to what kinds of connections may qualify [as closely related to banking], at least the following seem to us within the statutory intent:
>
> 1. Banks generally have in fact provided the proposed services.
> 2. Banks generally provide services that are operationally or functionally so similar to the proposed services as to equip them particularly well to provide the proposed service.
> 3. Banks generally provide services that are so integrally related to the proposed services as to require their provision in a specialized form. . . .

### *The "Data Test"*

Petitioners do not contend that the *National Courier* criteria are in themselves erroneous . . . , but they do contend, preliminarily, that the

Board erroneously applied them to *the kinds of data involved in the proposed services,* rather than to the *services themselves.*

The depth of confusion that surrounds this argument is suggested by the fact that the Board's brief denies that a data test was applied, while the briefs of intervenors supporting the Board acknowledge that, at least as to the Regulation Y order, it was applied but assert that its application was lawful. We must address the Board's contention first.

The Board is quite correct that the Citicorp order specifically examined each of the eight categories of data processing the applicant proposed to provide. But some of those categories were only described with reference to (1) the data processing technology employed and (2) the nature of the data to be provided or processed, and the Board clearly held that the former "is not determinative of whether [the] activity is permissible." The conclusion is therefore inescapable that, even in the Citicorp order, a data test was employed. . . .

It is even clearer that the Regulation Y order employs a data test. No more is needed to establish this than the text of the new regulation which the order adopted. Permissible activities of bank holding companies now include:

> Providing to others data processing and data transmission services, facilities (including data processing and data transmission hardware, software, documentation or operating personnel), data bases, or access to such services, facilities, or data bases by any technological means, if:
>
> (i) The data to be processed or furnished are financial, banking, or economic, and the services are provided pursuant to a written agreement so describing and limiting the services;
>
> (ii) The facilities are designed, marketed, and operated for the processing and transmission of financial, banking, or economic data; and
>
> (iii) The hardware provided in connection therewith is offered only in conjunction with software designed and marketed for the processing and transmission of financial, banking, or economic data, and where the general purpose hardware does not constitute more than 30 percent of the cost of any packaged offering. . . .

We must confront, therefore, the stark question whether the data test, as the determinant of whether data processing services are closely related to banking, is arbitrary or capricious. We think not. It would of course be preferable, from the point of view of accuracy alone, to make every "closely related" determination on a more narrow, specific, case-by-case basis—to ask, as petitioners would have the Board do, whether data processing for budget analysis, for bookkeeping, and for accounting each separately qualifies for the exemption. Indeed, it would be even *more* accurate to get even *more* specific, and to ask whether budget analysis for manufacturing entities, budget analysis for retail sales entities, and budget analysis for personal service entities each separately qualifies. But the whole point of rulemaking as opposed to adjudication (or of statutory law as opposed to case-by-case common law development) is to incur a small possibility of inaccuracy in exchange for a large increase in efficiency and predictability. What the present controversy comes down to is simply whether there is reasonable assurance that the activities embraced within the data test—not all of which have been individually examined or even yet foreseen—will be closely related to banking under one or more of the broad *National Courier* tests. We think that there is.

As a theoretical matter, to begin with, the test is appealing. The record of this proceeding amply demonstrates, if any demonstration is needed, that banks regularly develop and process for their customers large amounts of banking, financial and economic data, and that they do so (and will presumably continue to do so) through the most advanced technological means. Once that is acknowledged, it is difficult to envision how any provision of data processing services dealing with data of that particular type would not meet at least the second of the *National Courier* tests:

> Banks generally provide services that are operationally or functionally so similar to the proposed services as to equip them particularly well to provide the proposed service.

*National Courier,* supra, 516 F.2d at 1237. Perhaps it may not be in the public interest for them to provide one or another of such services, for anticompetitive or other reasons. But that relates to the "public benefits" determination, which is made case-by-case rather than in the amended Regulation Y, and whose resolution in the Citicorp order is not under challenge on this appeal.

In addition to its theoretical reasonableness, there is the fact that the Board, in the course of this proceeding, considered specific applications of the principle to various specific data processing uses proposed by Citicorp—finding all of them to be within one of the *National Courier* criteria, and many to be within the most rudimentary criterion that "[b]anks generally have in fact provided the proposed services," id. We find adequate support in the record for those conclusions. . . .

*Economic Data*

We turn next to an objection of petitioners that relates not to the data test as such, but to the types of data which the data test embraces.

The previous version of Regulation Y permitted bank holding companies to engage in "storing and processing other banking, financial, or *related economic* data, such as performing payroll, accounts receivable or payable or billing services." . . . In the combined adjudication-rulemaking here at issue, the ALJ's Recommended Decision accepted Citicorp's proposal that this be expanded to include the processing and transmission of "banking, financial and *economic related* data." . . . (emphasis added). The Board rejected that recommendation, agreeing with petitioners here that "economic related data" was "too broad a category and includes data that are not closely related to banking." . . . It adopted, however, an expansion of the previous language to "banking, financial and *economic* [as opposed to *economic-related*] data," and permitted Citicorp to engage in such activities. This expansion of prior authority was based upon its conclusion that "the record in this proceeding supports a finding that banks process *economic* data." . . .

We agree. The testimony amply establishes the proposition that banks have long served their customers by developing and making available information regarding the national and international economy, including economic projections useful for investment decisions. The existing Regulation Y itself permitted the provision of "general economic information and advice, general economic statistical forecasting services and industry studies." . . . The current amendment of Regulation Y, which merely enables banks to make such information available in a new and more useful fashion, thus clearly meets the second of the *National Courier* criteria, and perhaps the first as well. Petitioners complain that "[n]owhere in the record has there been any demonstration that banks have historically provided economic services even approaching the sophistication, scale and business mode approved by the Board in its Orders." . . . Perhaps so, but that is progress. It is not the purpose of the Bank Holding Company Act restrictions to confine banks to the same level, or crudeness, or technological simplicity of services previously provided—but merely to services of a closely related nature. . . .

*Hardware*

In both the Citicorp order and the Regulation Y order, the Board approved bank holding company provision of data processing hardware to their customers. . . . The issue boils down, as Citicorp suggests, to almost "a tautology." In effect, to authorize the provision of banking, financial and economic data processing is to authorize the provision of banking, financial and economic hardware and software. Whether it be considered "integrally related" to the authorized service or, perhaps more realistically, simply part of it, the provision of specialized hardware is reasonably included. . . . In any case, we think that the reasoning of [*National Courier*] supports the proposition that the economic necessity of offering a service that is not closely related to banking in order to sell another service that is, justifies the provision of the one as "incidental" to the other.

There is an obvious limitation upon this principle: At some point the tail begins to wag the dog. If it should be found, for example, that data processing services cannot be sold in an economically feasible manner without manufacturing data processing hardware; and if the banks' profits from the latter should exceed their profits from the former, surely the provision of data processing services would be incidental to hardware manufacture rather than vice-versa. But the Board has adequately taken that limitation into account, by specifying, as described above, that the cost of the hardware (including both specialized and general purpose hardware) cannot exceed 30 percent of the cost of the package. . . .

The challenge which the Board faced in the current proceeding was the perennial regulator's problem of adjusting the outlines of regulation to accommodate technological change. Virtually unprecedented difficulties of adjustment are presented by the torrent of recent scientific innovation in the fields of electronics and telecommunications, which possess a peculiar capability to destroy the categories of enterprise upon which regulation is based. Communications merges into data processing and data processing into banking. . . .

The record of the present proceeding displays a careful and conscientious effort by the Board to cope with these difficulties. We are not inclined to complicate its task further by attempting to exercise close and necessarily inexpert supervision of its judgments. That would be particularly inappropriate under a governing statute such as this one, which commits it to the Board to apply a standard of such inherent imprecision ("closely related to banking") that a discretion of almost legislative scope was necessarily contemplated. If there is a problem in such broad delegation, it would assuredly not be solved by effectively taking the delegation from the Board and placing it in our own hands. Having assured ourselves that the Board has acted reasonably, consistently and with procedural regularity in giving content to the statutory standard, our task is at an end.

In addition to the major points discussed above, we have considered the other objections urged by petitioners and find them insubstantial. For these reasons, the petitions are

Denied.

## *QUESTIONS AND COMMENTS*

1. What exactly is the "data test"? In its brief, the board denied that a data test was being used. What sort of test did it think it was using?

2. What is the argument that the data test is arbitrary and capricious as a measure of whether data processing services are closely related to banking?

3. The board found, and the court agreed, that processing "economic related" data is not closely related to banking, while processing "economic" data is closely related. What's the difference? Or put another way, what particular activities are bank holding company affiliates barred

from engaging in as a consequence of the fact that the processing of "economic related" data is not closely related to banking?

4. Judge Scalia opines that "at some point the tail begins to wag the dog" and the provision of data processing services that are closely related to banking becomes incidental to the provision of general purpose hardware. How did the Federal Reserve respond to this possibility? Is this solution likely to solve the problem, or will bank holding companies be able to manipulate these percentages?

5. Can the uses to which the general purpose hardware in *Association of Data Processors* are being put be distinguished from the courier services that the court disapproved in *National Courier?* Is the court in fact relaxing the *National Courier* test just a bit?

## Citicorp, New York, New York

***Fed. Res. Bull. 656-660 (Oct. 1982)***

### Order Approving Acquisition of [an Insolvent] Savings and Loan Association

Citicorp, New York, New York, a bank holding company within the meaning of the Bank Holding Company Act, has applied for the Board's approval . . . to acquire 100 percent of the voting shares of Fidelity Federal Savings and Loan Association of San Francisco, San Francisco, California ("Fidelity"). . . . Fidelity is a federally chartered and insured savings and loan association and is the successor by supervisory conversion of Fidelity Savings and Loan Association, San Francisco, California, a California guarantee stock savings and loan association, that was closed by the State of California on April 13, 1982, and placed under the receivership of the Federal Savings and Loan Insurance Corporation ("FSLIC").

By letters, dated August 13 and September 8, 1982, the Federal Home Loan Bank Board ("FHLBB") requested that the Board act expeditiously upon this application in light of the emergency nature of the situation at Fidelity and its deteriorating financial condition. . . .

Citicorp's application to acquire Fidelity was filed and has been considered by the Board under section 4(c)(8) of the Bank Holding Company Act, which deals with the permissible nonbanking activities of a bank holding company.

Section 4(c)(8) of the act authorizes a bank holding company to acquire a nonbank company if the activities of the nonbank company are determined by the Board to be "so closely related to banking or managing or controlling banks as to be a proper incident thereto." . . .

With respect to the "proper incident" requirement, section 4(c)(8) of the act requires the Board to consider whether the performance of the activity by an affiliate of a bank holding company "can reasonably be expected to produce benefits to the public, such as greater convenience, increased competition, or gains in efficiency that outweigh possible adverse effects, such as undue concentration of resources, decreased or unfair competition, conflicts of interests, or unsound banking practices."

In 1977, the Board considered the general question whether savings and loan association ("S&L") activities are a proper incident to banking. At that time, the Board determined that, as a general matter, S&L activities were not a proper incident to banking because the potential adverse effects of generally allowing affiliations of banks and savings and loan associations were then sufficiently strong to outweigh such public benefits as might result in individual cases. . . .

Fidelity's predecessor was placed in receivership on April 3, 1982, more than five months ago, and Fidelity's condition has steadily deteriorated since that time. Fidelity continues to lose deposits at a rate in excess of $1 million per day and to experience operating losses, estimated at over $200,000 per day. Fidelity has now exhausted its net worth and, as contemplated at the time the FHLBB authorized the FSLIC to transfer the assets and liabilities of Fidelity's predecessor to Fidelity, Fidelity's net worth will be maintained by advances from the FSLIC, absent consummation of Citicorp's proposal.

In view of the determination by the FHLBB, the primary supervisory authority for Fidelity, with respect to the emergency financial condition at Fidelity, the substantial savings to the FSLIC through the Citicorp proposal, the present circumstances of the thrift industry and the financial condition of a large number of its members, and the other favorable public benefit considerations . . . the Board has determined that consummation of the Citicorp proposal, as specifically conditioned in this Order, may reasonably be expected to result in substantial public benefits. These benefits include increased competition and greater convenience to the public through the restoration of Fidelity as an effective competitor and through Citicorp's stated commitments to meet the credit needs of Fidelity's communities. In its evaluation of the public benefits in this case, the Board also has taken into account the beneficial effect on the financial community as a whole of implementing an additional mechanism for the solution of the difficult problems for the thrift industry and the federal insurance funds posed by the poor earnings situation of this industry. . . .

In addition, the Board has considered other possible adverse effects that might be associated with this particular application, including the potential for decreased or unfair competition, conflicts of interests, financial risks, diversion of funds, participation in impermissible activities, evasion of interest rate limitations, unsound banking practices, and undue concentration of resources.

In view of Citicorp's limited presence in the relevant California markets served by Fidelity, the number and size of financial organizations operating in these California markets, the legal prohibitions against Citicorp's expansion of its bank subsidiaries into California, and the fact that Fidelity is a failing institution with limited competitive vigor, the Board concludes that this proposal would not have any significant adverse effects on existing or potential competition in any relevant market. Indeed, the proposed acquisition will have a substantial beneficial impact on competition by ensuring the continued operation of Fidelity as a viable institution through access to the financial and managerial resources of Citicorp.

The affiliation of Citicorp and Fidelity also is not likely to result in unfair competition in view of the various conditions imposed by the Board that require Fidelity to be operated independently and not utilized to further or enhance the activities of Citicorp's other subsidiaries. In addition, Fidelity's activities will be limited to those permissible under the act and its offices will be limited to locations at which banks located in California may establish branches.

To guard against possible adverse effects of affiliation in this case between a banking organization and a savings and loan association, including the potential for unfair competition and diversion of funds, the Board has established the following as conditions for its approval of the application:

1. Citicorp shall operate Fidelity as a federal savings and loan association having as its primary purpose the provision of residential housing credit. Fidelity shall limit its activities to those permitted to federal savings and loan associations currently under the Home Owners' Loan Act and to bank holding companies and their subsidiaries under section 4(c)(8) of the Bank Holding Company Act. . . .

2. Fidelity shall not establish or operate a remote service unit at any location outside California.

3. Fidelity shall not establish or operate branches at locations not permissible for national or state banks located in California.

4. Fidelity shall be operated as a separate, independent, profit-oriented corporate entity and shall not be operated in tandem with any other subsidiary of Citicorp. . . .

5. To the extent necessary to ensure independent operation of Fidelity and prevent the improper diversion of funds, there shall be no transactions between Fidelity and Citicorp or any of its subsidiaries without the prior approval of the Federal Reserve Bank of New York. This limitation encompasses the transfer, purchase, sale or loan of any assets or liabilities, but does not include infusions of capital from Citicorp or the payment of dividends by Fidelity to Citicorp.

6. Citicorp shall not change Fidelity's name to include the word "bank" or any other term that might confuse the public regarding Fidelity's status as a nonbank thrift institution.

7. Fidelity shall not convert its charter to that of a state savings

and loan association or other state chartered thrift institutions or to a national or state commercial bank without the Board's prior approval.

The Board concludes that consummation of the proposal, subject to the conditions set out in this Order . . . , may not reasonably be expected to result in conflicts of interests, unsound banking practices, undue concentration of resources, or other adverse effects. . . .

By Order of the Board of Governors, effective September 28, 1982.

### *QUESTIONS AND COMMENTS*

We learn here that the Federal Reserve Board had previously routinely rejected applications by bank holding companies to acquire savings and loan institutions. How could the board have determined in good faith that operating a savings and loan is not "closely related to banking"? Is this the test the board applies, or is some other test involved here?

## J. P. Morgan & Co., Inc., New York, New York: Federal Reserve Board Order Conditionally Approving Underwriting and Dealing in Certain Securities

*73 Fed. Res. Bull. 810 (1987)*

[The Federal Reserve Board considered applications by bank holding companies for approval under §4(c)(8) for authority to engage, through wholly owned subsidiaries, in underwriting and dealing in the following securities: (1) debt securities, including sovereign debt, corporate debt, convertible debt, and securities issued by a trust or other vehicle secured by or representing an interest in debt obligations; and (2) equity securities, including common stock, preferred stock, American Depository Receipts, and other direct and indirect equity ownership interests in corporations and other entities.]

[As will be seen in Chapter 6, these applications represented a major change in the understanding of the lines of business in which commercial banks could engage. It had long been thought that the Glass-Steagall Act erected a wall between the commercial and investment banking industries, subject only to narrow exceptions such as the power of commercial banks to underwrite and deal in government securities. The idea that a commercial bank would underwrite corporate debt, even through its holding company, would have been seen as extraordinary; that such an institution could underwrite corporate stock, nothing short of outlandish. Yet with the changing financial environment of the 1980s and the blurring of the distinction between commercial and investment banking that accompanied it, this is exactly what happened. In the aspect of the controversy discussed here, the bank holding companies received approval under the BHCA to engage in the proposed activities.]

[The Federal Reserve Board approved the applications under the *National Courier* test. In doing so, it addressed the broader marketplace dynamics that were sweeping over the financial services industry. Essentially, the board found that the proposed securities powers were closely related to banking because of the technological convergence that was occurring between the two industries.]

These applications are before the Board in a financial environment in which the business of banking itself is undergoing fundamental changes. Traditionally, banks served a unique role as financial intermediaries. Because of their cumulative knowledge about the financial condition of borrowers, banks were able to make more informed credit decisions than most other market participants. However, recent dramatic developments in the facilities for storing, analyzing, and transmitting data through increasingly improving computer and telecommunications technology has enabled potential investors to obtain needed financial information with less reliance on intermediaries such as banks.

In short, the traditional core function of a bank of financing the most creditworthy businesses has been reduced, as these businesses, which formed the foundation of the banks' commercial lending base, have looked increasingly to the capital markets to finance their operations.

In response to this technological revolution, banks have sought to continue to service their traditional customer base, within the boundaries of current statutory restrictions, by providing certain types of investment banking or functionally similar services, such as providing loan guarantees and other similar off-balance sheet financial support, privately placing securities, securitizing loan assets, syndicating and selling bank loans, and engaging in interest rate and currency swaps.

These activities are a natural extension of the fundamental business of commercial banking of financial intermediation, representing the same basic function conducted in a different manner.

The movement of banks into securities underwriting and related activities is reflected in the active participation by foreign offices of U.S. banks and bank holding companies in securities markets overseas—as underwriters and dealers in debt and equity securities—where they are not under the regulatory constraints of the Glass-Steagall Act. U.S. banks maintain securities affiliates in London, Tokyo and other international financial centers and were among the leading underwriters of Eurosecurities in 1986 and 1987. In recognition of these fundamental changes in the structure of the financial markets, the Board has urged Congress to repeal the Glass-Steagall Act limitations and authorize bank holding companies, subject to appropriate safeguards, to engage in securities underwriting and dealing activities.

### 2. *Close Functional and Operational Similarity . . .*

. . . [Banks may currently underwrite certain securities called "eligible" securities such as U.S. government bonds. The underwriter performs the same basic function when underwriting these sorts of securities as when underwriting the securities that are the subject of this application. First the underwriter] identifies the issuer's financing needs and advises the issuer concerning the terms, amount and timing of the securities to be issued. The underwriter then sets a price at which it believes the securities can be sold to investors at a profit to the underwriter.[20] This function involves both an analysis of factors affecting the price of securities of the particular issuer as well as factors affecting the general level of prices in the market and the demand for that type of security. The underwriter distributes the securities to investors and also generally deals in the issuer's securities, that is, maintains a secondary market in the issuer's securities by purchasing and selling them for the underwriter's own account.

In the Board's judgment, the functions involved in underwriting debt and equity securities in general are very similar to those involved in the underwriting of eligible debt securities as well as in other credit, advisory and financial intermediation services performed by banks.

#### Origination and Structuring Function

With respect to the underwriter's function of originating and structuring the new issue of securities, banks now perform these operations as a part of their ordinary banking activities and their eligible debt securities underwriting activities. Banks have developed special expertise in advising businesses about structuring securities underwritings as a result of their conventional functions of commercial lending, providing corporate financial advice generally, and in placing debt and equity securities with investors in private transactions.

20. In a firm commitment underwriting, the issuer sells the entire issue of securities to an underwriter or underwriting syndicate at a pre-determined public offering price, net of underwriting discounts and commissions. The underwriter or underwriting syndicate then reoffers, either directly or through a selling group, the securities to the public at the public offering price. The underwriter or underwriting syndicate, thus, assumes the risk that the securities cannot be resold at a price in excess of their net purchase price. In "best efforts" underwriting, instead of buying the new securities from the issuer and reselling them, the underwriter sells the securities as the agent of the issuer in return for an agent's commission.

### Risk Assessment Function

In the case of underwriting debt securities, the underwriter's pricing and risk assessment function requires an analysis of the creditworthiness of the particular issuer. As part of the proposed debt securities underwriting activity, the underwriting subsidiaries would be required to evaluate the creditworthiness of corporate as well as governmental issuers. Banking organizations have the required expertise to carry out this function as a result of the traditional banking activities of extending credit to corporate and governmental borrowers, managing their own assets and liabilities, purchasing debt securities for their own account and performing investment advisory and trust activities. Moreover, in regularly issuing letters of credit and other credit enhancements for issues of debt securities, banks engage in activities that require credit evaluation and analysis functions that are the same as or substantially similar to, those of an underwriter.

The Board also believes that banks have unique expertise in performing this credit analysis function because of the role of banks in underwriting and dealing in money market instruments, establishing pools of assets for securitization and evaluating the underlying risks of the constituent elements in a pool, advising issuers and assisting them in the private placement of their debt securities, and generally assessing credit and interest rate risk. Indeed, banks are among the largest firms that act as agent in the private placement of corporate securities.[23] . . .

### Distribution Function

Banks currently establish distribution networks for the securities being underwritten and contact potential purchasers of the securities when they underwrite eligible securities. Banks also perform very similar operations when they arrange syndications of loans[26] and privately place debt and equity securities.

### Dealer Functions

Acting as dealer in debt and equity securities fundamentally involves judging anticipated movements in the market price of the securities held in inventory. Banks perform these functions currently when acting as dealers in eligible securities as well as in their investment and advisory

23. The Board previously recognized the substantial involvement of commercial banks in private placements. Federal Reserve Board Staff Study, Commercial Bank Private Placement Activities (1977). See also Comptroller of the Currency, Federal Deposit Insurance Corporation, Federal Reserve Board, Commercial Bank Private Placement Activities (1978). In 1987, seven commercial banks privately placed $15.9 billion of debt securities. Investment Dealers Digest, March 21, 1988, at 19.

26. In 1987, banks arranged loan syndications of over $100 billion. . . .

activities.[27] As explained above, banking organizations are particularly well equipped to evaluate the credit and market risks associated with pricing securities being underwritten and, accordingly, have the special expertise to make analogous judgments in conducting a dealer operation.

Finally, the Board notes that the entire securities underwriting activity is one aspect of serving as a financial intermediary, because in essence underwriters serve to channel funds of investors to businesses in need of capital. Thus, underwriting ineligible corporate securities, as noted above, has a very close functional and operational similarity to the established role of banks in lending funds of bank depositors to businesses for working capital and other purposes. . . .

### *B. PROPER INCIDENT TO BANKING ANALYSIS*

[The Federal Reserve Board found that the proposed activities offered significant public benefits, including increased competition in securities underwriting and distribution markets. They also helped to maintain domestic and international competitiveness in a global marketplace in which foreign firms did not operate under the same constraints as to their securities powers.

[These benefits outweighed the adverse effects of the proposal, which the board had determined in prior orders to include the potential for unfair competition, undue concentration of resources, and loss of public confidence in bank and thrift affiliates in which bank holding companies underwrite and deal in certain types of ineligible securities. However, the board confirmed earlier orders that imposed a series of "prudential" limitations on securities activities by bank holding companies.]

To minimize the potential for securities underwriting and dealing risk to be passed to federally insured bank or thrift affiliates, the structural framework established in the earlier Orders requires that the new activities be conducted in a corporation over which the affiliated banks or thrifts have no ownership, financial, management or operational control. Thus, the new activities would be conducted through a company that is controlled by the parent holding company and not by the affiliated bank or thrift institution, that does not have any officer, director, or employee in common with the bank or thrift affiliate, and that has separate offices from any affiliate bank or thrift. The underwriting subsidiaries are required to maintain capitalization in accordance with industry norms. This capitalization must be provided by the holding company from its funds and not from the resources of its bank or thrift subsidiaries or, indeed, from the resources of the parent holding company needed to support these bank or thrift subsidiaries.

27. Fourteen of the 46 primary dealers in U.S. government securities are banks.

The Orders also established operating limitations to regulate transactions by an affiliate bank or thrift with, or for the benefit of, an underwriting subsidiary in order to prevent the transfer of risk to federally insured affiliates, conflicts of interest and other adverse effects. In general, these limitations:

—preclude the holding company and any affiliate from purchasing ineligible securities from the underwriting subsidiary during the underwriting and for 60 days thereafter or while the underwriting subsidiary is making a market in the security;

—prevent a bank or thrift from lending to issuers to enhance the creditworthiness of securities underwritten by the underwriting subsidiary, or to pay off the principal and interest on such securities;

—prohibit a bank or thrift from knowingly lending to customers secured by or for the purpose of purchasing securities underwritten by the underwriting subsidiary during the underwriting or in which it makes a market;

—require disclosure by the underwriting subsidiary to ensure that the public will not confuse the underwriting subsidiary with its federally insured affiliates and will know that the instruments purchased from the underwriting affiliate are not federally insured deposits or guaranteed or otherwise backed by a bank or thrift affiliate (unless such is the case);

—prohibit an affiliated bank and thrift from acting as agent for, or engaging in marketing activities on behalf of, the underwriting subsidiary;

—limit self-dealing transactions between the underwriting subsidiary and its bank and thrift affiliates acting in a fiduciary capacity; and

—prohibit the transfer of confidential customer information between the bank or thrift and underwriting subsidiary without customer consent. . . .

Reservation of Authority to Modify Operating Limitations Based Upon Experience

Because these proposals represent the first major entry of banking organizations into the field of underwriting and dealing in corporate debt and equity securities, the Board believes it appropriate to proceed cautiously and has established an extensive framework of prudential limitations to address conflicts of interest, unsound banking practices, and other adverse effects. After the underwriting subsidiaries have established a record of experience in the proposed activities, the Board may review the continued appropriateness of particular limitations.

Similarly, the Board may from time to time, based upon the supervisory process and experience with the activities, establish additional limitations on the conduct of the activities to ensure that the subsidiaries' activities are consistent with safety and soundness, conflict of interest and other considerations relevant under the BHC Act. . . .

*QUESTIONS AND COMMENTS*

1. Does the Federal Reserve Board here adopt an "evolving" standard for the term "closely related to banking," one that accommodates changes in markets and technology? Recall the jurisprudential problem faced by the courts in interpreting the incidental powers of national banks under 12 U.S.C. §24 (Seventh), which we considered in Chapter 3. Is the problem here similar? Are there any differences from the standpoint of political legitimacy arising out of the fact that the statute is here being interpreted by an administrative agency with authority to enforce the statute in question? Is the discretion of such an agency to adopt an "evolving" standard greater or less than that of a court?

2. Where does the Fed get the power to impose prudential restrictions and operating limitations of the sort described in the order? Isn't the behavior either consistent with the statute or not? Even if the Fed has power to impose discretionary constraints of this sort, do you see any dangers in this approach? Are there any realistic limits to the Fed's authority in this regard? Should there be?

3. Other aspects of bank holding company entry into debt and equity securities underwriting are treated in Chapter 6.

## D. OTHER EXEMPTIONS FROM THE BANK HOLDING COMPANY ACT'S GENERAL PROHIBITION

The Bank Holding Company Act prohibits bank holding companies from acquiring any firm that is not a bank and then proceeds to make exceptions to this general rule. The most important exception—for activities that are closely related to banking—was discussed in the preceding section.

In addition, a bank holding company may control a company whose business is solely involved in "holding or operating properties used wholly or substantially by any banking subsidiary of [the] bank holding company." 12 U.S.C. §1843(c)(1). The same statute permits bank holding companies to own shares in companies that conduct a safe deposit business, or furnish and perform services for the bank holding company and its banking subsidiaries, or that were organized to liquidate the assets acquired from a bank holding company or from any other source if acquired before May 9, 1956. These are all activities in which the bank within the holding company structure could engage directly, and the exemption simply permits the bank holding company to deal in the activity itself if it so chooses. See 12 C.F.R. §225.104.

A grandfather clause contained in the Bank Holding Company Act permits bank holding companies to retain shares in nonbanking subsidiaries owned when the statute took effect. In particular, the Bank Holding Company Act was amended in 1970 to include holding companies that owned only one bank. These one-bank holding companies were allowed to keep any nonbank subsidiaries owned as of June 30, 1968. The Federal Reserve, however, retains the power to force these bank holding companies to abandon these protected activities if they would result in an "undue concentration of resources, decreased or unfair competition, or unsound banking practices." 12 U.S.C. §1843(a)(2). In addition, the Federal Reserve simply can impose regulations that curtail the operations of the holding company affiliates. See Minnesota Small Loan Co., 38 Fed. Reg. 1308 (1973).

## E. ACTIVITIES RESTRICTIONS ON BANKS AND BANK SUBSIDIARIES WITHIN A HOLDING COMPANY STRUCTURE

So far we have discussed the activities restrictions that 12 U.S.C. §1843(c)(8) applies to nonbanking subsidiaries of bank holding companies. Essentially the same restrictions apply to the activities of bank holding companies themselves under 12 U.S.C. §1843(a)(2), although bank holding companies enjoy limited additional authority to manage and provide services to their affiliates. We now consider whether a *bank* or a *subsidiary of a bank* within a holding company structure may engage in activities that would not be permissible either for the bank holding company itself or for its nonbanking subsidiaries.

The answer to this question might seem obvious. Congress clearly imagined that bank holding companies would be allowed to engage in activities *broader* than the activities permitted to their subsidiary banks. While how *much* broader may be a matter of debate, it is evident that few, if any, in the Congresses that passed and amended the Bank Holding Company Act believed that banks would enjoy activities powers *greater* than the powers of their parent holding companies.

The question addressed in this section has caused a surprising amount of confusion for the courts and for the Fed, even though the basic issue is quite straightforward. The following case establishes the framework of the law in this area.

## Independent Insurance Agents of America, Inc. v. Board of Governors of the Federal Reserve System

***890 F.2d 1275 (2d Cir. 1989), cert. denied, 111 S. Ct. 44 (1990)***

Jon O. Newman, Circuit Judge:

The extent to which banks should be permitted to engage in nonbanking activities is a major controversy in this country, attracting the increasing attention of Congress, administrative agencies, and courts. This petition for review of an order of the Board of Governors of the Federal Reserve System ("the Board" or "the Fed") brings before us one facet of that controversy. The issue is whether the Fed was entitled to conclude that section 4 of the Bank Holding Company Act of 1956 ("the Act" or "BHCA") does not restrict bank subsidiaries of a bank holding company from selling insurance. The issue arises on a petition filed by the Independent Insurance Agents of America ("IIAA") challenging the Board's March 3, 1989, order, which permitted two Indiana state banks acquired by the Merchants National Corporation, a bank holding company, to resume specified insurance activities permitted under Indiana law. Merchants National Corp., 75 Fed. Res. Bull. 388 (1989) (*"Merchants II"*). The Board's order rested upon a determination that the nonbanking prohibitions of section 4 of the Act, as amended, 12 U.S.C. §1843 (1988), do not apply to the activities of the bank subsidiaries of a bank holding company. Concluding that this construction of section 4 is within the range of reasonable interpretation that the pertinent administrative agency is entitled to make, we deny the petition for review and leave this long-simmering controversy for such further consideration as Congress cares to give it.

### Background . . .

*The statutory framework.* Before introducing the facts, it will be helpful to outline briefly the pertinent statutory provisions of the Bank Holding Company Act. The principal regulatory powers of the Fed concerning bank holding companies are set forth in sections 3 and 4 of the Act. 12 U.S.C. §§1842, 1843. Section 3 requires Board approval of the acquisition of ownership or control of any bank by a bank holding company, with narrow exceptions not here relevant. Section 3 sets forth factors governing acquisition approval, focusing on the competitive effect of the proposed acquisition, the financial and managerial resources of both the holding company and the acquired bank, and the convenience and needs of the community served. 12 U.S.C. §1842(c).

Section 4 of the Act, the focal point of the Board's order in this case, contains two sets of prohibitions. First, it specifies, in what might be called the "ownership clause," that a bank holding company may not "retain direct or indirect ownership or control of any voting shares of any company which is not a bank or bank holding company." 12 U.S.C. §1843(a)(2). Second, it provides, in what might be called the "activities clause," that a bank holding company may not "engage in any activities other than (A) those of banking or of managing or controlling banks . . . and (B) those permitted under [section 4(c)(8) of the Act]. . . ." Id. Section 4(c)(8) sets forth the so-called "closely related to banking" exception to the nonbanking provision. Id. §1843(c)(8). In relevant part, section 4(c)(8) states that the section 4(a) nonbanking prohibitions shall not bar ownership by a bank holding company of:

> shares of any company the activities of which the Board after due notice and opportunity for hearing has determined (by order or regulation) to be so closely related to banking or managing or controlling banks as to be a proper incident thereto, but for purposes of this subsection it is not closely related to banking or managing or controlling banks for a bank holding company to provide insurance as a principal, agent or broker. . . .

Id.

*Facts.* A number of states, including Indiana, historically have authorized state-chartered banks to provide insurance services to their customers. On July 1, 1986, Merchants National Corporation, a bank holding company within the meaning of the BHCA, 12 U.S.C. §1841(a), sought permission from the Fed to acquire the stock of two banks chartered under the laws of the State of Indiana, the Anderson Banking Company ("Anderson Bank") and the Mid State Bank of Hendricks County ("Mid State Bank"). Both of these state banks had engaged in general insurance activities prior to the date of Merchants National's applications, Anderson Bank directly since its incorporation in 1916, and Mid State Bank since its purchase of an insurance agency in 1985. Merchants National subsequently made a commitment that Mid State Bank would transfer to itself all insurance activities from its insurance agency subsidiary and thereafter conduct all such activities directly in the bank.

The initial Merchants National applications were protested by various insurance industry trade groups, including the IIAA, on the ground that the provisions of section 4 of the Act apply to the insurance activities of state banks owned by bank holding companies and therefore that the acquisitions of Anderson Bank and Mid State Bank could not be approved without termination of their insurance activities to the extent required under section 4. In response to the protests, Merchants National committed that it would cause the banks to divest their insurance agency activities within two years unless, within that time, it received Board approval for the banks to retain their insurance activities. Merchants National agreed that, prior to such approval, the banks would limit their insurance activities to the renewal of existing policies. In light of these commitments, the Board approved the applications on October 29, 1986. 72 Fed. Res. Bull. 838 (1986).

On February 5, 1987, Merchants National filed an application seeking Board approval for Anderson Bank and Mid State Bank to resume the insurance activities that had just been suspended pursuant to the acquisition commitments. Merchants National sought permission on two alternative grounds. First, it contended that Anderson Bank and Mid State Bank were exempt from the insurance provisions of section 4 of the Act pursuant to the "grandfather" provision of section 4(c)(8)(D), as amended, 12 U.S.C. §1843(c)(8)(D), under which a bank holding company or any of its subsidiaries is permitted to engage in insurance agency activity in which the holding company or the subsidiary was engaged on May 1, 1982, subject to certain geographical and functional limitations. Second, Merchants National sought more broadly a determination that the nonbanking prohibitions of section 4 of the Act do not apply to activities conducted directly by banking subsidiaries of a bank holding company. In *Merchants I,* the Board rejected the first contention but agreed with the second one. After the prior appeal to this Court and the expiration of the moratorium, the Board issued the decision challenged on this petition for review. *Merchants II.*

## The Board's Decision

The core of the Board's decision in *Merchants II* was its conclusion, previously expressed in *Merchants I,* that the provisions of section 4 limiting the nonbanking activities of bank holding companies do not apply to bank subsidiaries of a bank holding company. Consistent with this view, the Board also ruled, as it had in *Merchants I,* that section 4's prohibition upon a bank holding company's acquisition of a nonbanking entity (unless that entity engages only in activities "closely related to banking") does not apply to a holding company's acquisition of a bank. The Board recognized an exception to this latter conclusion in those instances, illustrated by the *Citicorp (South Dakota)* case, 71 Fed. Res. Bull. 789 (1985), where the Board finds an evasion arising from a holding company's acquisition of an entity that purports to be a "bank" but engages in insignificant banking activities, indicating that the acquisition is "primarily, if not solely" for the purpose of enabling the holding company to engage in the target's nonbanking activities. *Merchants II,* Fed. Res. slip op. at 8 n. 11.

The Board grounded its conclusions on several considerations. First, the Board pointed out that the limitations of section 4(a)(2) apply in express terms to "bank holding companies," not to "banks." Id. at 11. Second, the Board relied on what it considered a structural argument: the "ownership clause" of section 4 restricts the entities that a bank holding company may acquire or retain, and the "activities clause" restricts the activities that the bank holding company itself may engage in. In the Board's view, if the restriction on activities applied to the activities of subsidiaries of a bank holding company, the restriction on acquisition or retention of nonbank entities would be superfluous. Id. at 11-13. Third, the Board emphasized that the restriction on acquisition or retention was broadly phrased to prohibit "direct or indirect" ownership, whereas the restriction on engaging in activities omitted the comparable adverbs "directly or indirectly," words the Board appears to acknowledge would have made the restrictions of section 4 applicable to activities of a bank holding company's subsidiaries. Id. at 12-13. Fourth, the Board asserted that since the enactment of the Bank Holding Company Act, it has consistently declined to read the activities restriction of section 4 as applicable to bank subsidiaries of a bank holding company. Id. at 15-16. Fifth, the Board found in the legislative history of the Bank Holding Company Act and its subsequent amendments a congressional purpose to leave the scope of permissible activities of bank subsidiaries of a bank holding company subject only to the authority that issued the banks' charter, without any further restriction from the Act itself. Id. at 17-20. . . .

Finally, the Board noted that its decision leaving the activities of bank subsidiaries to regulation by the chartering authority applied only to activities carried on directly by those banks and did not insulate from section 4 the activities of subsidiaries of the bank subsidiaries. This application of section 4 to third generation entities, those owned by the subsidiaries of a bank holding company, was based on section 2(g)(1) of the Act, 12 U.S.C. §1841(g)(1), which provides that shares of such third generation entities are deemed to be held indirectly by the bank holding company; as a result, whether such entities may be owned by a subsidiary of a bank holding company is governed, in the Board's view, by section 4's limitation on entities that may be owned by a bank holding company. *Merchants II,* Fed. Res. slip op. at 25.

### DISCUSSION

There can be no doubt that the Bank Holding Company Act is "intended to implement a congressional policy against control of banking and nonbanking enterprises by a single business entity." See Lewis v. BT Investment Managers, Inc., 447 U.S. 27, 46, 100 S. Ct. 2009, 2020, 64

L. Ed. 2d 702 (1980). What is less clear is the extent to which Congress has decided to implement that policy. IIAA contends that Congress has required a nearly complete separation of banking and nonbanking activities, precluding bank holding companies and all entities within their systems from engaging in nonbanking activities other than the "closely related to banking" activities specifically identified in section 4(c)(8) of the Act. The Board believes that Congress has not gone so far. In its view, Congress required a significant degree of separation with respect to bank holding companies themselves, but did not wish to displace the traditional authority of state and national bank chartering authorities to determine what nonbanking activities could appropriately be engaged in by banks that are subject to their jurisdiction, even though such banks were owned by a bank holding company under the jurisdiction of the Fed.

In resolving this dispute, we must keep in mind that we are not making an initial construction of a statute, but rather reviewing a construction made by an expert regulatory agency. In that context, our task is to determine whether Congress has "directly spoken to the precise question at issue," and, if so, to give effect to any "unambiguously expressed intent of Congress," or, if not, to determine "whether the agency's answer is based on a permissible construction of the statute." Chevron U.S.A., Inc. v. Natural Resources Defense Council, Inc., 467 U.S. 837, 842-43, 104 S. Ct. 2778, 2781, 81 L. Ed. 2d 694 (1984). Though both sides support their views of the statute by relying on some of the statutory language, we cannot say that the provisions of the Act reveal an unambiguous congressional intent concerning the precise question at issue. We find no provision that says, in substance, "The Board may not regulate the activities of bank subsidiaries of bank holding companies," or "Bank subsidiaries of bank holding companies may engage in nonbank activities to the extent permitted by their chartering authorities." The Board reads the Act as if it contained such language. On the other hand, we find no provision that says, in substance, "Bank subsidiaries of bank holding companies may not engage in nonbank activities." The IIAA reads the Act as if it contained this wording. The question for us is whether the Board's interpretation of the language that does appear in the Act is reasonable, an inquiry we undertake by examining all relevant sources, including such clues as the statutory language may provide.

Both sides claim that the text of the Act supports their interpretations, and each can find some, but not overwhelming, support in various words and phrases. As the Board noted in its decision, the limitations of section 4(a)(2) apply in terms to "bank holding companies," not to "banks." However, that observation somewhat begs the question, which is whether the limitations upon bank holding companies should be interpreted to restrict the activities those entities may engage in *indirectly* through their banking subsidiaries. Of similarly little, if any weight, is the argument that because the "ownership clause" of section 4(a)(2) does not bar a bank holding company from owning subsidiary banks, the "activities clause" should be interpreted not to apply to activities of subsidiary banks. The argument is a non sequitur. It would be entirely sensible for Congress, if it wished, to bar a bank holding company from owning nonbanks and also prohibit a bank holding company from engaging indirectly in nonbank activities conducted by its bank subsidiaries. For its part, the IIAA points to the language prohibiting bank holding companies from engaging in nonbank activities and assumes that this language means "engage in directly or through subsidiaries."

Somewhat more supportive of the Board's position are textual arguments arising from comparisons of the "activities clause" with other language in section 4(a)(2). First, the grandfather proviso of section 4(a)(2) permits a bank holding company to engage in those activities "in which directly or through a subsidiary" it was engaged in at designated times and under designated circumstances. The Board points out that no similar phrase modifies the "activities clause." Second, the "ownership clause" prohibits the retention of "direct or indirect" ownership of nonbanks, and no similar phrase modifies the prohibition on engaging in nonbank activities. The use of these phrases in section 4(a)(2) and their absence from the "activities clause" might imply a deliberate congressional choice not to restrict the activities of bank subsidiaries, but might also result from drafting different clauses at different times and assembling them without intending differences in phrasing to have significance.

The Board derives a somewhat stronger argument for its interpretation from the structure of the Act. It points out that if the "activities clause" applied to subsidiaries of a bank holding company, the "ownership clause" would be virtually superfluous, since, under that reading, the "activities clause" alone would preclude a bank holding company from owning a nonbank. Moreover, as the Board further points out, such a reading would appear to create some internal inconsistencies. For example, section 4(c)(14) permits a bank holding company, under specified circumstances, to own an export trading company; however, this would be prohibited if the "activities clause" applied to subsidiaries of a bank holding company since that clause exempts only the "closely related to banking" activities set forth in section 4(c)(8), which do not include export trading. IIAA's only response is that the (c)(14) exemption would control over the (a)(2) "activities clause" since it comes later in the statute. That canon of construction may sometimes be helpful in resolving irreconcilable inconsistencies, but it need not be invoked where the statute may be interpreted to avoid the inconsistency in the first place.

However, IIAA also finds support for its interpretation in the structure of section 4. As IIAA points out, section 4(c)(8), establishing the circumstances for exempting various entities from the restrictions of section 4, including the "activities clause" of section 4(a)(2), uses the term "company" to describe those entities, and "company" is defined by section

2(b) broadly enough to include a bank. See 12 U.S.C. §1841(b). Moreover, section 4(c)(8) instructs the Board, in deciding whether a particular activity is "a proper incident to banking," to assess whether the performance of that activity "by an affiliate of a holding company" will produce public benefits, and "affiliate" is defined by section 2(k) to include a "company" and, hence, a bank. See 12 U.S.C. §1841(k). The available inference is that subsidiary banks are subject to the "activities clause" because they are within the category of entities exempted from that clause by section 4(c)(8).

Perhaps the most perplexing aspect of the structural arguments concerns the Board's contention that though it has no authority to preclude bank subsidiaries of a bank holding company from engaging in nonbank activities, it does have authority to preclude the subsidiaries of a bank subsidiary from engaging in nonbank activities. Thus, the Board adopts a generation-skipping approach: It may prohibit nonbank activities by bank holding companies and by their "grandchildren," i.e., the subsidiaries of their bank subsidiaries, but not by their bank "children," i.e., the holding companies' immediate bank subsidiaries. The Board's rationale is that the prohibition in the "ownership clause" on "direct or indirect" ownership of nonbank entities precludes a bank holding company from indirectly owning the nonbank subsidiary of its own bank subsidiary.

This contention elicits conflicting responses from IIAA and Merchants National. IIAA contends that the Fed can prohibit nonbanking activities at all three levels and cites the apparent awkwardness and perhaps illogic of the Board's generation-skipping approach as evidence that the Board's interpretation of the "activities clause" is incorrect. As IIAA points out, under the Board's reading of section 4(a)(2), a holding company's bank subsidiary that owns a nonbank subsidiary can escape the prohibition of the "ownership clause" by merging the "grandchild" into the bank subsidiary and operating the nonbank activities itself. That is precisely what Mid-State Bank did in this proceeding. For its part, Merchants National argues that the Fed may bar nonbanking activities only of a holding company itself and may not preclude those of either second generation bank subsidiaries or their third generation subsidiaries.

IIAA's position has the virtue of consistency in reading the Act to preclude nonbank activities throughout a bank holding company's system. Moreover, if the Board is correct that Congress wished to leave the activities of bank subsidiaries subject to the regulation of only their chartering authorities, one is left to wonder why those authorities were not relied on to control all of a bank subsidiary's activities, whether conducted directly by the bank subsidiary itself or indirectly through its own subsidiary. On the other hand, if the Board is right that the Act leaves the nonbank activities of bank subsidiaries within the control of bank chartering authorities but precludes nonbank activities by holding companies and by the subsidiaries of their bank subsidiaries, this would not be the first time that Congress has adjusted the competing positions of strong forces with a compromise of imperfect symmetry. We think it prudent not to resolve the issue of the Board's authority over the nonbank activities of subsidiaries of bank subsidiaries until that issue is squarely presented. . . .

After assessing all of the relevant considerations, we are satisfied that the Board, acting within its sphere of competence, has made a reasonable interpretation of section 4(a)(2), one that confides decisions concerning the scope of insurance and other nonbank activities of bank subsidiaries to their national and state chartering authorities. If that interpretation is to be altered, Congress will have to enact suitable legislation.

The petition for review is denied.

## *QUESTIONS AND COMMENTS*

1. Why did the Fed disclaim regulatory authority over the operations of a bank, as opposed to its subsidiaries? Isn't this behavior inconsistent with the board's general propensity to not only protect but expand its bureaucratic turf?

2. After *Merchants National,* are all bets off if a state chooses to allow its state-chartered banks to engage in activities not permitted to a bank holding company's nonbanking subsidiaries under 12 U.S.C. §1843(c)(8)? Does the Federal Reserve or any other agency retain authority to rein in state banks that go too far? Consider the fact (discussed at greater length in Chapter 2) that a bank holding company must obtain the Federal Reserve's approval to acquire a state-chartered bank, 12 U.S.C. §1842(c), and that the Board may reject such an application if in its opinion the financial and managerial resources or future prospects of the concerned institutions are unfavorable. Consider also the fact (discussed at greater length in Chapter 7) that the FDIC has authority to suspend or terminate deposit insurance of any depository institution found to be operating in an unsafe or unsound manner. Given these protections, is there still reason to view *Merchants National* as a potential threat to the scheme of federal banking regulation?

3. The Federal Deposit Insurance Corporation Improvement Act of 1991, which was enacted in late 1991, amended 12 U.S.C. §§1811 et seq. by adding the following new section:

> *Section 24. Activities of insured state banks*
>
> (a) In general. After the end of the 1-year period beginning on the date of the enactment of the Federal Deposit Insurance Corporation Act of 1991, an insured State bank may not engage as principal in any type of activity that is not permissible for a subsidiary of a national bank unless—

(1) the Corporation has determined that the activity poses no significant risk to the appropriate deposit insurance fund; and

(2) the bank is, and continues to be, in compliance with applicable capital standards prescribed by the appropriate Federal banking agency.

(b) Insurance underwriting.

(1) In general. Notwithstanding subsection (a), an insured State bank may not engage in insurance underwriting except to the extent such activities are permissible for national banks.

4. The *Michigan National* case leaves open several important questions. The one that caused the court the greatest perplexity was the Federal Reserve Board's odd position that, although it had no authority to regulate the activities of a BHC's bank subsidiary, it retained the authority to regulate the activities of a *subsidiary* of the bank subsidiary. Why do you think the Fed asserted this authority while giving up the larger power of regulating the bank itself—especially given the fact, as the court observes, that a banking firm can usually fold the activities of a bank's subsidiary into the bank and then conduct them directly without restriction under the BHCA's "activities" clause. This issue is addressed in the following case.

## Citicorp v. Board of Governors of the Federal Reserve System

***936 F.2d 66 (2d Cir. 1991)***

. . . .

In *Merchants II* [890 F.2d 1275 (2d Cir. 1989), *cert. denied,* 111 S. Ct. 44 (1990)] we noted the Board's additional position that, although the Act denied the Board authority to preclude bank subsidiaries of a bank holding company from engaging in nonbank activities, it nonetheless empowered the Board to preclude the subsidiaries of bank subsidiaries from engaging in nonbank activities. Though the insurance interests pressed upon us the "apparent awkwardness and perhaps illogic," id. at 1282, of the Board's generation-skipping approach, we confined our ruling to approval of the Board's construction of the Act to permit nonbank activities by bank subsidiaries (the first generation after the holding company), and left for another day the issue of whether the Act could simultaneously be construed to bar nonbank activities by a subsidiary's subsidiaries (the second generation). That day has now arrived.

*The Board's Operating Subsidiary Rule.* Long before the administrative and judicial rulings in *Merchants II,* the Board had issued Regulation Y, the so-called "operating subsidiary rule," which purports to govern the activities of subsidiaries of a bank holding company. See 12 C.F.R. Pt. 225 (1990) (current version). In general, such subsidiaries must limit their activities to those banking and "closely related to banking" activities permitted by section 4 of the Act. However, one provision of Regulation Y permits state-chartered banks, without the Board's prior approval, to acquire

> all . . . of the securities of a company that engages solely in activities in which the parent bank may engage, at locations at which the bank may engage in the activity, and subject to the same limitations *as if the bank were engaging in the activity directly.*

Id. §225.22(d)(2)(ii) (emphasis added). Thus, under Regulation Y and the Board's construction of section 4, as endorsed in *Merchants II,* a subsidiary of a state-chartered bank subsidiary of a holding company may engage in nonbank activities permitted to the bank under state law, provided that the activities are conducted under the same limitations that would apply if the bank were engaging in the activities "directly."[1]

*The Delaware Regulatory Framework.* In May 1990, Delaware enacted the Bank and Trust Company Insurance Powers Act of 1989, 67 Del. Laws, c.223 (1990) ("the Delaware statute"). The Delaware statute permits Delaware banks, under certain conditions, to engage in insurance activities (other than title insurance). The statute affords the banks the option of conducting insurance activities through a "department" or "division" of the bank or through a subsidiary of the bank.

Whichever option is chosen, the statute requires substantial structural barriers between the bank's insurance activities and its banking activities.

For example, the statute requires that the assets of the bank may be applied only to satisfy the non-insurance liabilities of the bank and not those of the bank's insurance "division"; id. §8, and the assets of the insurance "division" may be applied only to satisfy the liabilities of that "division" and not the other liabilities of the bank, id. §22. The statute places a 25 percent limit on the amount of the bank's total capital, surplus, and undivided profits that may be allocated to its insurance "division," id. §10, and the minimum capital that the bank is required to maintain under Delaware banking law may not be used to meet the separate capital requirements of the "division" imposed by state insurance law, id. §3. The statute provides that for purposes of the Delaware Insurance Code an insurance "division" of a bank is treated as an insurance company "in the same manner and to the same extent as if it were its separately incorporated subsidiary . . . with separate capital accounts, assets and liabilities." Id. §17.

In general, Delaware authorizes its bank commissioner to regulate

1. A comparable regulation applies to operating subsidiaries of national banks. 12 C.F.R. §225.22(d)(1) (1990).

the banking activities of state-chartered banks and authorizes its insurance commissioner to regulate the insurance activities of a bank's insurance "division." Id. §§5, 38. However, the statute permits the bank commissioner to supervise the insurance "division" whenever he determines that the "division's" activities are "likely to have a materially adverse effect on the safety and soundness of the bank." Id. §5.

*Citicorp's Banking and Insurance Activities in Delaware.* Citicorp is a bank holding company with assets of more than $200 billion. In 1982, Citicorp obtained a charter from Delaware for Citibank Delaware, a commercial bank wholly owned by Citicorp. Citibank Delaware has assets of more than $2 billion and serves customers in 35 states.

In 1986, with the approval of the Fed, Citicorp established Family Guardian as a wholly owned subsidiary to underwrite and sell certain credit-related insurance expressly authorized for bank holding companies by section 4(c)(8)(A) of the BHCA, 12 U.S.C. §1843(c)(8)(A). The day after the Delaware statute was enacted, Citicorp transferred all of the voting shares of Family Guardian to Citibank Delaware in order to permit Family Guardian to transact the broader range of insurance activities authorized under the Delaware statute for insurance "divisions" and subsidiaries of Delaware banks. Family Guardian then began to expand its operations to include insurance underwriting and other insurance activities within the scope of Delaware law, though beyond the scope of the "closely related to banking" activities specified in section 4(c)(8) of the BHCA.

*The Pending Litigation.* Soon after the expansion of Family Guardian's insurance activities, various insurance industry trade associations filed a petition with the Board, contending that Family Guardian's activities were not permitted under the operating subsidiary rule of Regulation Y. The complainants argued that the barriers required by the Delaware statute between the banking and insurance activities of a Delaware-chartered bank were so substantial that a Delaware bank, such as Citicorp Delaware, could not engage in insurance activities "directly" within the meaning of Regulation Y. Since Citicorp Delaware could not engage in these insurance activities "directly," the argument continued, its subsidiary, Family Guardian, was not operating within the limitations of Regulation Y.

The Fed accepted the contentions of the complainants, ruled that the activities of Family Guardian were not authorized by Regulation Y, and concluded that these activities, if not exempted by Regulation Y, were impermissible under the BHCA for an entity owned by a subsidiary of a subsidiary of a bank holding company. Citicorp, 76 Fed. Res. Bull. 977 (1990). The Board ordered Citicorp to cause Family Guardian to cease providing any insurance activities beyond those authorized and approved by the Board under section 4(c)(8)(A). Citicorp then brought this petition for review to challenge the Board's ruling.

## Discussion

Citicorp makes two arguments. First, it contends that the insurance activities of Family Guardian are permitted for the bank subsidiary of Citicorp by virtue of the Board's operating subsidiary rule. Second, it contends that, if the operating subsidiary rule does not permit insurance activities by Family Guardian, the Board lacks statutory authority under the BHCA to proscribe the activities of a subsidiary of a holding company's bank subsidiary.

[The court first considered whether the board's operating subsidiary rule applied to the facts of the case. The rule authorizes subsidiaries of state-chartered banks to engage in activities "subject to the same limitations as if the bank were engaging in the activity directly." The board argued that Family Guardian's activities were not authorized by the rule, since Citibank Delaware could not engage in these activities directly. Under the Delaware statute, if Citibank Delaware were to engage in insurance activities itself, as opposed to doing so through a subsidiary, it would have to do so through a department or division of the bank which would be financially segregated from the rest of the bank and subject to regulation by the Delaware commissioner of insurance. The board argued that these limitations were so stringent that Citibank Delaware would not be engaged "directly" in the insurance business if it operated such a division. The court expressed "wonderment," "unease," and "concern" about the board's "troublesome" position. Nevertheless, it was willing to assume, without deciding the issue, that the board's interpretation of its rule was sufficiently reasonable to withstand judicial scrutiny. This left the question whether the board in fact possessed the power to regulate the activities of the state bank's subsidiary, the issue to which the court now turned.]

Citicorp contends that the BHCA does not permit the Fed to regulate the activities of the subsidiary of a bank subsidiary of a holding company. Before the *Merchants II* litigation, that contention would have posed a substantial issue because a major controversy then existed as to whether the BHCA permitted non-banking activities (other than those specifically authorized by section 4(c)(8)) to be conducted anywhere in a system controlled by a bank holding company. The insurance interests in Merchants II contended that neither a holding company, nor a bank subsidiary, nor the subsidiary of a bank subsidiary could engage in nonbanking activities. However, the Fed disagreed with that interpretation of the Act and argued that the bank subsidiaries of a holding company were beyond the Board's regulatory authority. In the Fed's view, Congress intended to leave unimpaired the primary regulatory authority of state and national bank chartering agencies to determine the activities of institutions under their jurisdiction. We agree with that construction of the statute.

Thus, in the aftermath of *Merchants II,* we take the Act as if it said in terms, "The Board is without authority to limit the activities of a bank subsidiary of a bank holding company." Now the question is whether the Board may nonetheless regulate the activities of a bank subsidiary's subsidiary. The rationale of the position that the Board successfully urged upon us in Merchants II requires an answer consistent with the interpretation the Board there urged us to adopt. The Board urged, and we agreed, that Congress wanted bank chartering agencies to regulate the activities of banks within their jurisdiction. By virtue of their authority over the banks that they charter, those agencies have ample authority to determine the permissible activities of the subsidiaries owned by the banks. We have been given no reason to believe that Congress wanted the jurisdiction of bank chartering authorities to end at the corporate structure of the bank itself, rather than extend throughout the chain of companies owned by the bank. Surely a bank chartering agency, charged with the responsibility to maintain the soundness of a bank, is vitally interested in the assets owned by a bank, including shares of wholly owned subsidiaries. In the pending case, Delaware has demonstrated that its regulatory authority over Delaware-chartered banks is not confined to activities occurring within the bank, but extends to insurance activities whether conducted within the bank (albeit in a separate "division") or in a subsidiary of the bank.

Moreover, the Board has provided no basis for believing that Congress wished to create two classes of state-chartered banks—those owned and not owned by bank holding companies. Before *Merchants II,* such an argument was plausible; Congress might have wanted those state-chartered banks owned by holding companies to be confined to banking activities, leaving banks not so owned to have broader activity. But once the Board persuaded us to read the statute to leave all state-chartered banks free to sell insurance, subject to state, not Board, regulation, there is no basis for believing that Congress simultaneously adopted a generation-skipping approach and authorized the Board to bar the subsidiaries of state-chartered banks from selling insurance whenever those banks were in turn the subsidiaries of a holding company. . . .

The Fed reminds us that in *Merchants II* we contemplated the possibility that the Fed might be correct both in its view that the BHCA permitted a state-chartered bank subsidiary of a holding company to be immune from coverage of the BHCA and in its view that the Act nevertheless reached the subsidiary's subsidiary. We there observed that "*if* the Board is right [in both views], this would not be the first time that Congress has adjusted the competing positions of strong forces with a compromise of imperfect symmetry." 890 F.2d at 1282 (emphasis added) (citation omitted). But in *Merchants II,* we were required to decide only whether the Board was entitled to read the Act to leave the regulation of the nonbank activities of holding company banks to chartering authorities. We were not obliged to endorse the Board's additional (and "perplexing," id.) view that the Act reached the subsidiary's subsidiary. The fact that we peered into the abyss of conflicting statutory constructions that occur in federal law and noted that in some instances they reflect political realities does not mean that we accepted both aspects of the Fed's views. In *Merchants II* we had to decide whether the possibility of an asymetrical [sic] construction of the BHCA precluded the view advanced by the Fed with respect to coverage of holding company banks, and we agreed with the Fed that it did not. Now we face the issue whether the Fed's view concerning BHCA coverage of the subsidiary's subsidiary is only a tolerable inconsistency or an entirely untenable construction, and we conclude it is the latter.

The conclusion we reach enjoys the support of the other two of the three bank regulating authorities of the nation, the Federal Deposit Insurance Corporation ("FDIC") and the Office of the Comptroller of the Currency ("OCC"). The Chairman of the FDIC advised the Fed in 1989, "In our view, subsidiaries of state banks are beyond the scope of the Bank Holding Act. . . ." Letter of L. William Seidman to Alan Greenspan, April 28, 1989. Similarly, the OCC informed the Fed, "The Office of the Comptroller of the Currency (OCC) does not believe that the BHCA gives the FRB the authority to regulate or define permissible activities of state banks, whether conducted directly or through subsidiaries." Letter of Dean S. Marriott to William W. Wiles, April 28, 1989. In neither instance were the views of these national bank regulators grudging disclaimers of desirable authority; on the contrary, both the FDIC and the OCC expressed the belief that leaving operating subsidiaries of state chartered banks subject to the regulating authority of state banking regulators, whether or not such banks were owned by bank holding companies, was both a sound construction of the BHCA and a desirable policy of bank regulation.

We recognize that courts are not obliged to defer to interpretations of a statute made by agencies not responsible for its administration. It is the Fed, not the FDIC or the OCC, that administers the BHCA. Nevertheless, having reached the conclusion that the BHCA, in light of the construction previously urged upon us by the Fed, must be understood to leave the subsidiaries of state-chartered banks to state regulating authorities, we take some comfort in knowing that those with significant national responsibilities for maintaining a sound banking system share our view of the statute. We would surely be reluctant to read the Act to preclude coverage of subsidiaries of holding company banks in the face of unanimous views by national bank regulators that such a construction is bad law and bad policy. The disagreement among national banking regulators does not leave us free to adopt whatever construction seems best in our judgment. We are still obliged to begin our task by according deference to the view of the agency directly responsible for administering the Act. But when that view clashes with the construction of the statute that the same agency has urged us to adopt, we need not elevate deference to blind obeisance, and we can notice the contrary view of significant banking regulators.

In *Merchants II,* it is likely that we would have upheld the Board had it chosen to interpret the BHCA to bar nonbanking activities throughout a bank holding company's system, even though we ultimately agreed with the Board's interpretation that the Act permitted bank subsidiaries of holding companies to engage in nonbanking activities. As we acknowledged in *Merchants II,* the BHCA is not clear as to whether it requires bank holding companies and all subsidiaries within their systems to observe a total separation from nonbanking activities. But however that issue is resolved, the Act must be interpreted as a whole and must retain some internal coherence. The Board ruled that whether bank subsidiaries may engage in nonbanking activities is a matter for the chartering authorities of those banks, and not for the Board. Once that decision was made, we cannot agree that the Act can sensibly be construed to permit the Board to displace bank-chartering authorities in determining what activities are permitted for the subsidiaries of bank subsidiaries.

The petition for review is granted, and the order of the Board is vacated.

## *QUESTIONS AND COMMENTS*

1. What is the apparent purpose behind the operating subsidiary rule?

2. Was the Fed construing Regulation Y in a manner consistent with its arguments in earlier decisions?

3. The Federal Deposit Insurance Corporation Improvement Act of 1991, which was enacted in late 1991, amended 12 U.S.C. §§1811 et seq. by adding the following new §24 on the activities of insured state banks:

> (d) Subsidiaries of Insured State Banks.
>
> (1) In general. After the end of the 1-year period beginning on the date of the enactment of the Federal Deposit Insurance Corporation Act of 1991, a subsidiary of an insured State bank may not engage as principal in any type of activity that is not permissible for a subsidiary of a National bank unless—
>
> (A) The Corporation has determined that the activity poses no significant risk to the appropriate deposit insurance fund; and
>
> (B) the bank is, and continues to be, in compliance with applicable capital standards prescribed by the appropriate Federal banking agency.
>
> (2) Insurance underwriting prohibited.
>
> (A) Prohibition. Notwithstanding paragraph (1), no subsidiary

> of an insured State bank may engage in insurance underwriting except to the extent such activities are permissible for national banks.
>
> (B) Continuation of existing activities. Notwithstanding subparagraph (A), a well-capitalized insured State bank or any of its subsidiaries that was lawfully providing insurance as principal in a State on November 21, 1991, may continue to provide as principal, insurance of the same type to residents of the state . . . individuals employed in the State, and any other person to whom the bank or subsidiary has provided insurance as principal, without interruption. . . .

What does this new statute say about the lobbying power of the insurance industry?

4. In your opinion, is insurance underwriting "closely related to banking"? Is it banking? If not, how is it different from banking?

5. The Board expressed concern that initiatives such as Delaware's "could promote potentially destructive competition among the states with adverse consequences for the national interest in safeguarding the safety and soundness of the nation's financial system and the federal deposit insurance funds." 76 Fed. Res. Bull. 977 (1990). Do you agree? Isn't the Delaware statute what the dual banking system is all about?

6. Why do you think Delaware might have made it so difficult to conduct an insurance business out of a bank itself as opposed to an operating subsidiary? Why did Delaware allow the business to be conducted out of a bank at all?

7. The excerpted case dealt only with subsidiaries of *state*-chartered banks. Would the same reasoning apply to subsidiaries of *national* banks? Can you think of any reason why national banks might receive different treatment?

## F. REGULATION OF TRANSACTIONS AMONG BANK HOLDING COMPANY AFFILIATES

As noted at the outset of this chapter, one of the primary justifications offered for regulating the activities of bank holding companies was a desire to eliminate the problems that arise when banks extend credit or otherwise transfer valuable goods, services, or other consideration to their affiliates. Such transactions cause concern for the following reasons: First, the holding company might be tempted to extend credit to an insolvent or financially shaky subsidiary in order to transfer wealth from depositors (ultimately the FDIC) to the holding company. Second, if a bank engages in such transactions with a nonbanking subsidiary, the bank might be tempted to decline similar transactions with competitors of the subsidiary. Finally, to the extent that banks have a lower cost of funds than other firms, their holding companies might be able to obtain an unfair competitive advantage over nonbanking firms by obtaining access to these low-cost funds.

A classic example illustrating the potential for trouble in making such transactions is the sad story of the Hamilton National Bank in Chattanooga, Tennessee. Hamilton National bought low-quality mortgages from a nonbanking subsidiary of its holding company. When the mortgages failed to perform, the bank became insolvent and the FDIC was required to make good the insured deposits. It appeared that the subsidiary bank may have been operated for the benefit of its holding company affiliate. See Rose & Talley, Bank Transactions with Affiliates: The New Section 23A, 100 Banking L.J. 423 (1983).

A number of discrete bank regulations control the abuse of a bank by its holding company or affiliates within the holding company. The capital adequacy guidelines discussed in Chapter 3 limit the ability of a holding company to take capital out of a subsidiary bank in the form of dividends. Conflicts of interest are subject to the lending limits and rules against insider loans also treated in Chapter 3. Conflicts of interest in securities activities are addressed in Chapter 6. Rules on bank insolvency, discussed in Chapter 8, impose restrictions on the ability of a holding company to remove wealth from a subsidiary bank. For example, the FDIC has a prior claim on the assets of other banks in a holding company structure in the event of bank insolvency. Also, the Federal Reserve Board has asserted that a holding company should operate as a "source of strength" to its subsidiary banks, infusing capital into bank subsidiaries that run into financial trouble. Even though the board's "source of strength" policy has been questioned in court, MCorp Financial v. Board of Governors of the Federal Reserve System, 900 F.2d 852 (5th Cir. 1990), *rev'd in part sub nom.* Board of Governors of the Federal Reserve System v. MCorp Financial, 502 U.S. 32 (1991), it remains a matter of importance in the ongoing debate about the proper regulation of intercorporate transactions.

The present section concerns two statutory provisions that restrict intercorporate transactions within a bank holding company structure, namely §§23A and 23B of the Federal Reserve Act. Although these statutes were adopted at different times, they operate as a unified statutory scheme and, accordingly, are best treated together.

Although §23A is rich in technical detail, its basic structure is simple: It prohibits "covered transactions" between a bank and an "affiliate" that violate certain quantitative or qualitative limits. The key concepts, therefore, are "covered transaction," "affiliate," and the nature of the qualitative and quantitative prohibitions.

The term "covered transaction" in §23A includes: (1) any loan or extension or credit to an affiliate; (2) any purchase of or investment in securities owned by the affiliate; (3) any purchase of assets from an affiliate except where specifically exempted by the board; (4) any acceptance of securities issued by the affiliate as collateral for a loan to any person or firm; and (5) any issuance of a guarantee, acceptance, or letter of credit, including a standby letter of credit, on behalf of the affiliate. 12 U.S.C. §371c(b)(7).

The term "affiliate" in §23A is defined to include, inter alia: (1) a company that controls a bank or is controlled by a company that controls a bank; (2) a bank subsidiary of a bank; (3) a company that is controlled by or for the benefit of people who control a bank or a company that controls a bank; (4) a company whose board of directors constitute a majority of the board of directors of a bank; (5) a company that is sponsored or advised on a contractual basis by a bank or its affiliate or subsidiary; (6) an investment company for which the bank acts as investment advisor; or (7) any company that the board determines to have a relationship with a bank that "may" affect the nature of the transactions between the company and the bank.

Covered transactions with an affiliate are subject to two quantitative limitations under §23A. 12 U.S.C. §371c(b)(1). First, the section prohibits individual covered transactions with an affiliate exceeding 10 percent of a bank's capital and surplus. 12 U.S.C. §371c(a)(1)(A). Second, no bank may have more than 20 percent of its capital and surplus tied up in all of its covered transactions with affiliates at any one time. 12 U.S.C. §371c(a)(1)(B).

Covered transactions are also subject to a number of qualitative limitations under §23A. Thus banks may not purchase "low-quality assets" from affiliates unless the bank had committed itself to purchase the asset, pursuant to an independent credit evaluation, prior to the time that the asset was acquired by the affiliate. 12 U.S.C. §371c(a)(3). A "low-quality asset" is one classified as substandard, doubtful, or loss, singled out for special mention in the most recent report of a federal or state regulator, or in default or renegotiation due to deteriorating condition. 12 U.S.C. §371c(b)(10). Covered transactions between a bank and its affiliates must be "on terms and conditions that are consistent with safe and sound banking practices." 12 U.S.C. §371c(a)(4). And loans and other extensions of credit between a bank and an affiliate must be secured by collateral having a value (depending on the nature of the collateral) of at least 100 percent of the amount loaned. 12 U.S.C. §371c(b)(10).

Section 23A contains some important exceptions to these restrictions. Notwithstanding other provisions of §23A, banks may (1) give immediate credit to an affiliate for uncollected items received in the ordinary course of business; (2) make loans to affiliates that are fully secured by obligations of the United States or by a segregated, earmarked account at the lending bank; (3) purchase assets from an affiliate for which a readily identifiable public market quotation is available, where the assets are purchased at the market price; and (4) purchase services from a nonbank affiliate, 12 U.S.C. §371c(d)(1). The restrictions of §23A are also significantly less severe when the transaction is with a *bank* affiliate. Banks are free to make deposits in an affiliated bank in the ordinary course of a correspondent business, 12 U.S.C. §371c(d)(2). Indeed, a bank may engage in transactions that would otherwise be prohibited under §23A so long as the transactions are made with other bank subsidiaries of the same bank holding company and do not involve low-quality assets.[1]

Section 23B, added to the Federal Reserve Act by the Competitive Equality Banking Act of 1987, supplements the basic prohibitions of §23A. 12 U.S.C. §371c-1. Section 23B applies to (1) the sale of securities or other assets to an affiliate; (2) the payment of money or the furnishing of services to an affiliate; (3) any transaction in which an affiliate acts as an agent or broker or receives a fee for its services to the bank; and (4) any transaction with a third party in which an affiliate has a financial interest. All of these transactions are subject to a general requirement that they be on terms and conditions that are at least as favorable to the bank or its subsidiary as those that apply or would apply to comparable arm's length transactions.

Section 23B also contains a number of outright prohibitions on transactions. A bank or its subsidiary may not knowingly purchase or acquire securities from an underwriting or selling syndicate in which an affiliate of the bank is a principal underwriter, unless the purchase is approved by a majority of the bank's disinterested directors prior to the public offering. And no member bank, bank subsidiary, or affiliate may publish any advertisement or enter any agreement suggesting that the bank is responsible for the obligations of its affiliates.

Do the prohibitions and limitations in §§23A and 23B make sense to you? Consider the following excerpt from an influential, but controversial, law review article.

## Fischel, Rosenfield, & Stillman, The Regulation of Banks and Bank Holding Companies

*73 Va. L. Rev. 301, 326-327 (1987)*

. . . If a nonbanking subsidiary of a bank holding company is losing money, a decision must be made whether to support that business, in

1. 12 U.S.C. §371c(d)(1). A bank qualifies for this exemption if it owns 80 percent or more of the voting shares of the bank with which the transaction is to be consumated, or if the same company controls 80 percent or more of the voting shares of the two banks involved.

the hope that its fortunes will improve, or to abandon it. This calculus, which is recurrently required of many businesses, is unaffected by the presence of an affiliated bank. No incentive exists for the bank to "subsidize" its financially troubled affiliate by extending credit at below the market rate of interest. It is important to recognize that the profits of banks are not constrained by regulation to any particular level—banks are not subject to rate-of-return regulation. Consequently, there is no incentive for a bank to shift profits to an unregulated affiliate.[77] An example illustrates the lack of incentive for a bank to cross-subsidize an affiliate.

If the "troubled" affiliate can obtain debt financing at arm's length from an independent bank at an annual interest rate of, say, fifteen percent, that cost of credit reflects an independent and realistic assessment of the risks attendant to the loan. A related bank has no incentive to lend at less than fifteen percent. The bank could have made a loan to a third party of identical risk at fifteen percent. The difference between fifteen percent and the lower rate charged the affiliate (say, ten percent) is the opportunity cost of transferring credit at less than the market rate. The forgone interest (five percent in this case) represents an income stream the bank could have realized and, consequently, is a cost of the below-market loan to the affiliate. The total cost of credit to the holding company is the cost the affiliate pays (ten percent) plus the lost earnings of the bank (five percent), which is equal to the cost of borrowing in the market (fifteen percent). Put simply, although a troubled business might appear to pay less than market rate for its loan, the related bank suffers a corresponding loss in income. The firm as a whole cannot reduce the cost of borrowing by charging an uneconomical transfer price.[78] Thus, the fear of cross-subsidization is groundless because nothing can be gained by causing a below-market transfer of credit from the bank to a troubled affiliate.

The concept of opportunity cost likewise demonstrates the fallacy of the argument that banks would make loans at below-market rates to purchasers of securities from a related underwriter or would purchase the securities themselves at prices in excess of the market price. Such decisions would simply transfer a loss from the underwriter to the bank but would do nothing to reduce the size of the loss itself. The bank would therefore have no incentive to engage in these practices.

77. Obviously, if loans between affiliates are made at the market rate of interest (i.e., at the same rate an independent third-party bank would charge the troubled affiliate), no cross-subsidy or conflict of interest occurs. Indeed, such loans may illustrate efficiencies wherein transaction costs are less for an intrafirm transfer than an arm's-length transaction.

78. See Hirshleifer, On the Economics of Transfer Pricing, 29 J. Bus. 172 (1956).

*QUESTIONS AND COMMENTS*

1. What explains the exceptions from the coverage of §23A for (1) loans secured by securities of the United States or by earmarked accounts at the lending bank; (2) credits for uncollected items received in the ordinary course of business; (3) purchases of assets with a readily identifiable market price; and (4) purchases of services from a nonbank affiliate? Is there one unifying theme to these exceptions, or are several rationales at work?

2. What explains the markedly more lenient treatment under §23A for transactions between banks within a single holding company structure? Is the theory that all banks in a holding company will be stringently controlled by some bank regulator, so that transactions between two highly regulated banks are not as dangerous as transactions between a bank and a less stringently regulated nonbank affiliate? If so, is the theory valid given the possibility that a bank holding company might attempt to avoid regulatory scrutiny by transferring doubtful assets between banks under the jurisdiction of different regulators? Is the theory, rather, that transactions between banks pose fewer dangers of low-cost insured depositor funds being used for the benefit of nondepository affiliates? Does this rationale make sense? Or is the theory that the regulatory system should allow bank holding companies to achieve economies of scale by operating their subsidiary banks, if not as branches, at least as integrated parts of a unitary banking institution? What do you think of this rationale?

3. As a result of the lenient regulatory treatment for transactions between affiliated banks, as compared to transactions between a bank and a nonbank affiliate, do banking organizations have an incentive to operate new businesses within bank subsidiaries as opposed to nonbank subsidiaries? To what extent do the activities and geographic restrictions on banks (discussed in Chapters 3 and 5) limit the value of this option?

4. Recall that purchases of assets with readily available and publicly identifiable market quotations are exempted from the coverage of §23A. This exemption allows banks to "purchase" securities from affiliates subject to agreements to resell, free of the quantitative limits and collateral requirements otherwise applicable under the statute. Yet a securities purchase with an agreement to resell (a "repo" in popular parlance) is in every functional term a loan rather than a securities purchase. Is this a loophole in the statute? If so, should it be closed?

5. How easy is it for the regulators to enforce the prohibitions of §§23A and 23B? In some respects, attempts to detect and punish violations of these statutes resemble attempts to control insider trading under the securities laws. It is relatively easy to disguise transactions through the use of proxies and intermediaries. For example, a bank holding company could cause a bank to make a loan to a corporation that is not an affiliate

of the bank. On its face this would be perfectly permissible under §§23A and 23B. In exchange for the loan, however, the borrower may agree to provide a line of credit to a nonbank affiliate of the bank's holding company. This roundabout means of evading the prohibition on extensions of credit to affiliates would probably be unsuccessful if detected but may be exceedingly hard to detect, particularly since the bank and the holding company subsidiary are likely to be under the jurisdiction of different regulators, and the borrower may not be under the control of any banking official. Perhaps for this reason, there are few cases enforcing §§23A and 23B. For one case in which penalties were assessed, see Fitzpatrick v. FDIC, 765 F.2d 569 (6th Cir. 1985). There, however, the violations were blatant and readily observable by the regulators because the bank involved in the transactions had become insolvent.

Can you think of ways to make §§23A and 23B more easily enforceable? Would these be desirable as a matter of public policy?

6. What is your opinion of the argument made by Fischel, Rosenfield, and Stillman? Are transactions among bank affiliates really like taking money from one pocket and putting it in another, or are there significant externalities involved in the form of low-cost, federally insured deposits on which affiliates of an insured bank may draw?

## G. SAVINGS AND LOAN HOLDING COMPANIES

### 1. *The Regulatory Scheme*

Unlike bank holding companies, savings and loan holding companies are not subject to the regulatory oversight of the Federal Reserve Board. Instead, the Office of Thrift Supervision (OTS) has primary regulatory responsibility. The FDIC also has significant regulatory authority over savings and loan holding companies. As with the statutory scheme governing bank holding companies, a savings and loan holding company is "any company which directly or indirectly controls a savings association or controls any other company which is a savings and loan holding company." 12 U.S.C. §1467a(a)(1)(D).

The focal point of the statutory scheme governing savings and loan holding companies is 12 U.S.C. §1467a(c)(1). This provision prohibits savings and loan holding companies and their savings and loan subsidiaries from engaging in any activity or rendering any services "for the purpose or with the effect of evading any law or regulation applicable to such savings association." 12 U.S.C. §1467a(c)(1)(A). The restrictions on the activities of savings and loan holding companies are more strict than the restriction on bank holding companies. While a bank holding company can engage in any activity that is closely related and a proper incident to banking, a savings and loan holding company is restricted to activities permissible to the savings and loan affiliate of the holding company.

Savings and loan holding companies' nonbank subsidiaries do, however, have express statutory authority to engage in a certain range of activities, including providing management services for a savings and loan affiliate, managing property used by a savings and loan affiliate, conducting an insurance agency business, and engaging in other activities approved by the Board of Governors of the Federal Reserve System as permissible for bank holding companies, unless the director of the OTS has prohibited the activity for savings and loan holding companies.

Thus where the OTS gives its approval, a savings and loan holding company and its non-savings and loan affiliates may engage in any activity that the Federal Reserve Board has permitted banks to engage in. 12 U.S.C. §1467a(c)(2)(F). But the OTS is free to impose limitations on savings and loan holding company activities that go beyond the limitations imposed by the Federal Reserve Board on bank holding companies. The OTS considers the following factors when considering a proposal by a savings and loan holding corporation to engage in a new activity:

> (i) whether the performance of the activity described in such application by the company or the subsidiary can reasonably be expected to produce benefits to the public (such as greater convenience, increased competition or gains in efficiency) that outweigh possible adverse effects of such activity (such as undue concentration of resources, decreased or unfair competition, conflicts of interest, or unsound financial practices);
>
> (ii) the managerial resources of the companies involved; and
>
> (iii) the adequacy of the financial resources, including capital, of the companies involved.

12 U.S.C. §1467a(c)(4)(B).

In addition, the FDIC must give prior written approval to any company that wishes to acquire a savings and loan association. 12 U.S.C. §1467a(e)(1)(B). FIRREA confers on the OTS oversight authority for all holding company affiliates, not just FDIC-insured savings associations within the holding company structure. Whenever the director of the OTS determines that reasonable cause exists to believe that the continuation by a savings and loan holding company of any activity constitutes a serious risk to the safety, soundness, or stability of a SLHC's subsidiary savings association, he may "impose such restriction as the Director determines to be necessary to address such risk." 12 U.S.C. §1467a(p)(1). When the director determines that a savings and loan holding company is engaged in an activity that imposes a serious risk to the financial health of a savings association within the holding company, the director is empowered to issue a "directive" to the holding company that: (1) limits the payment of dividends by the savings association; (2) limits transactions between the savings association, the holding company, and the subsidiaries or affiliates of either; and (3) limits any activities of the savings association that might create a serious risk that the liabilities of the holding company and its affiliates may be imposed on the savings association. Id.

In addition, FIRREA applies the restrictions on affiliate transactions contained in §§23A and 23B of the Federal Reserve Act to all savings associations in the same manner and to the same extent as they apply to member banks. As with BIF-insured banks, exemptions from §23A or 23B may be granted only by the Federal Reserve Board.

## 2. *The Qualified Thrift Lender Test*

Historically, the most important difference between the regulation of savings and loan holding companies and the regulation of bank holding companies concerns the treatment of single savings and loan holding companies—companies that control only one savings and loan—and multiple savings and loan holding companies—companies that control more than one savings and loan. Until the Competitive Equality Banking Act was passed in August 1987, there were essentially no legal restrictions on the scope of activities of single savings and loan holding companies. As a result, some very large financial and general industrial corporations have been able to acquire savings and loan associations.

The Competitive Equality Banking Act retained a regulatory exemption for single savings and loan holding companies, but introduced a new test called the "qualified thrift lender" test (QTL) to determine which single savings and loan holding companies qualify to be exempt from the general restrictions on the activities of savings and loan holding companies. A single savings and loan association holding company faces no activity restrictions whatsoever as long as the savings association that it controls satisfies the QTL test. As already noted in Chapter 3, the exemption for qualified thrift lenders was designed to reward those thrift lenders who demonstrate a commitment to housing finance.

# 5 GEOGRAPHIC LIMITATIONS

We saw in Chapter 1 that the American banking system was traditionally a system of *unit banks*: Banks were required to operate out of a single office and could not open branch offices of any sort. Nor, traditionally, did banking organizations enter new markets by means of bank subsidiaries of a common holding company. Bank mergers were also rare, either at the holding company level or by means of consolidation of banks. What you saw was what you got: The bank building *was* the bank; there was no other.

Unit banking in its pure form is an anachronism today. Every state permits multi-office banking. And although many banks are still independent, the movement towards consolidation and geographic expansion continues to gain force. Bank expansion has even jumped across state lines with a vengeance in the form of bank holding companies acquiring subsidiary commercial banks and thrifts in other states. Interstate branching is now a reality and, as a consequence of important legislation enacted in 1994, it is certain to develop over the coming years.

Moreover, geographic expansion through branches or bank holding companies represents only part of a broader marketplace trend towards geographically extended banking. Banks are expanding within states and nationwide by means of all sorts of devices, including interstate loan promotion offices, credit card operations, deposit solicitation, and much more.

Despite these developments that have eroded the force of independent unit banking, limitations on geographic bank expansion remain at both the state and federal level, at least for now.

Some states retain limitations on branching by state-chartered institutions. At the federal level, the authorization for interstate branching is subject to state override, and even holding company expansion is subject to some limitation. Moreover, geographic bank expansion is subject to significant control under the antitrust laws and other statutes that limit a bank's ability to gain market share.

## A. RATIONALE FOR GEOGRAPHIC RESTRICTIONS

Why should a government want to restrict the geographic scope of a bank's activities? After all, geographic restrictions on business expansion are highly anomalous in the American system. We do not prohibit pencil manufacturers from opening plants at new locations, and we certainly do not prohibit them from conducting their business across state lines. What, then, is special about banks that requires such unusual regulatory treatment? Let us consider the arguments for and against geographic restrictions on banking.

Consider first the case *against* geographic restrictions. The argument is easy to state: Bank expansion benefits consumers of bank services. Elimination of geographic restrictions would increase competition in banking, enhancing the quality of banking services and lowering the price. Geographic bank expansion would permit banks to offer full-service banking at remote locations, enhance the efficiency of the check-clearing system, facilitate the flow of capital to efficient uses, and reduce operating costs due to economies of scale. Because banks would operate more efficiently if allowed to expand freely interstate, they would be less prone to failure; accordingly, the safety and soundness of the banking system would be enhanced. In short, according to this view of the matter, elimination of geographic restrictions on bank expansion would increase social wealth and economic efficiency.

Now consider the case in *favor* of geographic restrictions. Those who support geographic restrictions claim, first, that such restrictions do not reduce efficiency or service quality. Second, proponents of geographic restrictions claim that such rules prevent undue concentration in banking markets. Concentration, in turn, is said to create a number of discrete hazards: It reduces competition, thus lowering service quality and increasing price; it reduces local control over banking; it unfairly disadvantages rural areas; it gives inordinate economic power to a few private entities; it drives local firms from the market; and it jeopardizes the safety and soundness of the banking system as a whole. Concentrated banking systems are subject to political domination in a way that diverse banking systems are not. Moreover, the danger of bank panics makes it imperative that the regulatory system not allow very large banks to fail, thus necessitating costly federal bailouts and unfairly disadvantaging small banks.

In addition to the economic considerations for and against geographic bank expansion, a variety of "political" arguments are advanced in favor of geographic restrictions on bank expansion. These arguments, advanced vigorously by groups such as the Conference of State Bank Supervisors, include the value of local ownership and control and the danger that massive financial institutions may come to exercise undue influence over government.

## *QUESTIONS AND COMMENTS*

1. Many of these political arguments are epitomized in the nation's longstanding suspicion of "bigness" in financial institutions. Suspicion of bigness in banking traces back to the Progressive Movement and especially the writings of Louis D. Brandeis. In Other People's Money and How the Bankers Use It (1914), Brandeis warned about a "curse of bigness" in the nation's financial institutions. Size alone was a threat to the public welfare, Brandeis argued, because those in charge of the public's money were liable to abuse the power entrusted to them. Brandeis' solution was to decentralize: reduce the "inefficiencies of excessive size" and establish an economy of smaller organizations that would not have to "bend[] the knee to the money lords." The Brandeis tradition is alive and well today. See, e.g., D. Leinsdorf, Citibank (1973).

2. The argument that a diversified banking system is necessary to achieve the goal of local control has found voice in judicial decisions. In Lewis v. BT Investment Managers, Inc., 447 U.S. 27, 38 (1979), the Supreme Court stated "[w]e readily accept the submission that, both as a matter of history and as a matter of present commercial reality, banking and related activities are of profound local concern. . . . [S]ound financial institutions and honest financial practices are essential to the health of any State's economy and to the well-being of its people. Thus, it is not surprising that ever since the early days of our Republic, the States have chartered banks and have actively regulated their activities." And in Northeast Bancorp. Inc. v. Board of Governors of the Federal Reserve System, 472 U.S. 159, 177 (1985), the Court noted the "historical fact that our country traditionally has favored widely dispersed control of banking. While many other western nations are dominated by a handful of centralized banks, we have some 15,000 commercial banks attached to a greater or lesser degree to the communities in which they are located."

3. Consider the American system in comparison with that of our "peer group" countries, none of which imposes geographic restrictions of the sort that have typified American banking. Japan's mammoth economy is dominated by a small number of "city banks," operating over

3,000 branches nationwide and controlling about half of the nation's total bank deposits. Large institutions also dominate domestic markets in Canada, Great Britain, France, and West Germany.

4. The fact that in other industrialized countries banks have grown very large in the absence of geographic restrictions suggests that there must be significant economies of scale in banking. Oddly, however, studies of American banking markets have demonstrated only relatively weak economies of scale in commercial banking. Moreover, in a number of markets small unit banks have been able to succeed quite well in head-to-head competition with big-city rivals. Researchers have not offered any particularly satisfactory explanation of the seeming conflict between the evidence from other countries and that obtained through studies of the U.S. system.

5. Do you agree that allowing domestic banks to grow very large would place undue political power in the hands of private parties? What dangers to the public interest might flow from allowing any one institution to control a large proportion of the nation's bank deposits?

6. As far as political influence is concerned, is it clear that big banks exercise disproportionate leverage on Capital Hill and in statehouses? What about the political muscle of small banks as exercised through the Independent Bankers Association of America and the Conference of State Bank Supervisors?

7. What do you think of the argument that local control of banking helps insulate the banking system from political domination? What does "local control" mean *other* than political domination?

8. Do you see any tension between the argument that big banks exercise undue political influence and the contention that they are subject to potential political domination?

9. Apart from the political domination argument, the Conference of State Bank Supervisors supports local control of banking institutions on the ground that "the influence financial institutions exercise over the monetary activities of American businesses and individuals [should] be controlled essentially within the territories served." Isn't this justification perfectly circular? Can you think of any other policy reasons why it might be in the public interest to maintain local control over banks?

10. The Conference of State Bank Supervisors is the leading national lobby in support of the dual banking system. Can you see the linkage between the concept of a dual banking system and the control of geographic bank expansion?

11. Studies have found that banks tended to operate more branches before the deregulation of deposit interest rates than they did after deposit interest rates were deregulated. Why might this be so?

12. For analysis of the economic arguments that bear on the question of bank expansion and consolidation, compare Geoffrey P. Miller, Legal Restrictions on Bank Consolidation: An Economic Analysis, 77 Iowa Law Review 1083 (1992) with Arthur E. Wilmarth, Too Big to Fail,

Too Few To Serve? The Potential Risks of Nationwide Banks, 77 Iowa Law Review 957 (1992) and Arthur E. Wilmarth, The Potential Risks of Nationwide Consolidation in the Banking Industry: A Reply to Professor Miller, 77 Iowa Law Review 1133 (1992). See also Arthur E. Wilmarth, Too Good to Be True? The Unfulfilled Promises Behind Big Bank Mergers, 2 Stanford Journal of Law, Business and Finance 1 (1996).

## B. BRANCHING RESTRICTIONS

### *1. The McFadden Act and "Competitive Equality"*

A number of states still restrict the power of state-chartered commercial banks to branch intrastate. Those restrictions raise two general types of legal issues. First, there are all sorts of interpretative questions arising under particular state statutes. We pass these by because their significance is limited to the borders of the state where they arise. Second, state branching restrictions raise questions under the McFadden Act, which applies state branching restrictions to national banks. The cases that follow consider issues under the McFadden Act.

### First National Bank of Logan v. Walker Bank & Trust Co.

***385 U.S. 252 (1966)***

Justice CLARK delivered the opinion of the Court.

These cases involve the construction of those portions of the National Bank Act, 44 Stat. 1228, 12 U.S.C. §36(c), which authorize a national banking association, with the approval of the Comptroller of the Currency, to establish and operate new branches within the limits of the municipality in which the bank is located, if such operation is "at the time expressly authorized to State banks by the law of the State in question."[1] Two national banks with their main banking houses in Logan

1. The National Bank Act, 44 Stat. 1228, 12 U.S.C. §§36(c)(1) and (2) provides in pertinent part:

> (c) A national banking association may, with the approval of the Comptroller of the Currency, establish and operate new branches: (1) Within the limits of the city, town or village in which said association is situated, if such establishment and operation are at the time expressly authorized to State banks by the law of the State in question; and (2) at any point within the State in which said association is situated, if such establishment and operation are at the time authorized to State banks by the statute law of the State in question by language specifically granting such authority affirmatively and not merely by implication or recognition, and subject to the restrictions as to location imposed by the law of the State on State banks. . . .

and Ogden, Utah, respectively, seek to open branches in those municipalities. The Utah statute prohibits Utah banks, with certain exceptions not here relevant, from establishing branches except by taking over an existing bank which has been in operation for not less than five years. Utah Code Ann., Tit. 7, c.3, §6 (1965 Supp.).[2] . . .

### 1. The Facts

In No. 51, the petitioner maintains its principal banking house in Logan, Utah, which is a second class city under Utah law (Utah Code Ann., Tit. 10, c.1, §1 (1953, as amended)), and is therefore subject to §7-3-6 of the Utah Code, supra. It applied to the Comptroller of the Currency for a certificate to establish an "inside" branch office in Logan. At the time of the application there were no other banks with their main banking offices in Logan. However, there were two branches of banks whose home offices were situated outside of Logan, one of which belonged to respondent, Walker Bank & Trust Co., whose home office was located in Salt Lake City. . . .

In Nos. 73 and 88, the First Security Bank of Utah, a national bank, applied for a certificate from the Comptroller to establish a branch bank in Ogden, where it maintained its principal banking house. Its proposal was to open a new branch and not to take over an existing bank in Ogden. Under Utah law, Ogden is also a second class city and the "take over" provision of §7-3-6, supra, was therefore applicable. Two other banks have their main offices in Ogden. . . .

### 2. The National Bank Act: Its Background

There has long been opposition to the exercise of federal power in the banking field. Indeed, President Jefferson was opposed to the creation of the first Bank of the United States and President Jackson vetoed the

2. Utah Code Ann., Tit. 7, c.3, §6 (1965 Supp.), provides:

*7-3-6. Business conducted at banking house—Branching of offices—Violation of section a misdemeanor.*

The business of every bank shall be conducted only at its banking house and every bank shall receive deposits and pay checks only at its banking house except as hereinafter provided.

Except in cities of the first class, or within unincorporated areas of a county in which a city of the first class is located, no branch bank shall be established in any city or town in which is located a bank or banks, state or national, regularly transacting a customary banking business, unless the bank seeking to establish such branch shall take over an existing bank. No unit bank organized and operating at a point where there are other operating banks, state or national, shall be permitted to be acquired by another bank for the purpose of establishing a branch until such bank shall have been in operation as such for a period of five years.

Act of Congress extending the charter of the second Bank of the United States. However, the authority of Congress to act in the field was resolved in the landmark case of McCulloch v. Maryland, 4 Wheat. 316 (1819). There Chief Justice Marshall, while admitting that it does not appear that a bank was in the contemplation of the Framers of the Constitution, held that a national bank could be chartered under the implied powers of the Congress as an instrumentality of the Federal Government to implement its fiscal powers. The paramount power of the Congress over national banks has, therefore, been settled for almost a century and a half.

Nevertheless, no national banking act was adopted until 1863, . . . and it was not until 1927 that Congress dealt with the problem before us in these cases. This inaction was possibly due to the fact that at the turn of the century, there were very few branch banks in the country. At that time only five national and 82 state banks were operating branches with a total of 119 branches. By the end of 1923, however, there were 91 national and 580 state banks with a total of 2,054 branches. The Comptroller of the Currency, in his Annual Report of 1923, recommended congressional action on branch banking. The report stated that if state banks continue to engage "in unlimited branch banking it will mean the eventual destruction of the national banking system. . . ." Soon thereafter legislation was introduced to equalize national and state branch banking. The House Report on the measure, H.R. Rep. No. 83, 69th Cong., 1st Sess., 7 (1926), stated among other things:

> The bill recognizes the absolute necessity of taking legislative action with reference to the branch banking controversy. The present situation is intolerable to the national banking system. The bill proposes the only practicable solution by stopping the further extension of state-wide branch banking in the Federal reserve system by State member banks and by permitting national banks to have branches in those cities where State banks are allowed to have them under State laws.

This bill failed to pass in the Senate and, although Congress continued to study the problem, it was not until 1927 that the McFadden Act was adopted. The bill originated in the House and, in substance, proposed that both national and state banks be permitted to establish "inside" branches within the municipality of their main banking facilities in those States that permitted branch banking at the time of the enactment of the bill. The intent of the Congress to leave the question of the desirability of branch banking up to the States is indicated by the fact that the Senate struck from the House bill the time limitation, thus permitting a subsequent change in state law to have a corresponding effect on the authority of national banks to engage in branching. The Senate Report concluded that the Act should permit "national banks to have branches in those cities where State banks are allowed to have them under State laws." S. Rep. No. 473, 69th Cong., 1st Sess., 14 (1926). In the subsequent Conference Committee, the Senate position was adopted. State banks which were members of the Federal Reserve System were also limited to "inside" branches. A grandfather clause permitted retention of branches operated at the date of enactment. H.R. Rep. No. 1481, 69th Cong., 1st Sess., 6 (1926). The Act was finally passed on February 25, 1927, and became known as the McFadden Act of 1927, taking its name from its sponsor, Representative McFadden. At the time of its enactment he characterized it in this language:

> As a result of the passage of this act, the national bank act has been so amended that national banks are able to meet the needs of modern industry and commerce and *competitive equality* has been established among all member banks of the Federal reserve system.

(Emphasis added.) 68 Cong. Rec. 5815 (1927).

During the economic depression there was much agitation that bank failures were due to small undercapitalized rural banks and that these banks should be supplanted by branches of larger and stronger banks. The Comptroller of the Currency advocated that national banks be permitted to branch regardless of state law. Hearings before a Subcommittee of the Senate Committee on Banking and Currency pursuant to S. Res. No. 71, 71st Cong., 3d Sess., 7-10 (1931). Senator Carter Glass held a similar belief and introduced a bill that would authorize national banks to organize branches irrespective of state law beyond and "outside" the municipality of its principal banking house. His proposal was strenuously opposed and was eventually defeated. It was not until the Seventy-third Congress that the Banking Act of 1933 was adopted. Senator Glass, the ranking member of the Senate Committee on Banking and Currency and the dominant banking figure in the Congress, was sponsor of the Act. In reporting it to the Senate for passage, he said, the Act "required that the establishment of branch banks by national banks in States which by law permit branch banking should be under the regulations required by State law of State banks." 77 Cong. Rec. 3726 (1933). In a colloquy on the floor of the Senate with Senator Copeland as to the purpose of the Act (with reference to branch banking by national banks), Senator Glass said that it would be permissible "in only those States the laws of which permit branch banking, and only to the extent that the State laws permit branch banking." Moreover, to make it crystal clear, when Senator Copeland replied that "it permits branch banking only in those States where the State laws permit branch banking by State banks," Senator Glass was careful to repeat: *"Only in those States and to the extent that the State laws permit branch banking."* (Emphasis added.) 76 Cong. Rec. 2511 (1933). Remarks of other members of Congress also indicate that they shared the understanding of Senator Glass. . . . As finally passed, the Act permitted national banks to establish outside branches if such branches could be established by state banks under state law. It is well to note that the same Act also removed the restriction on outside branch banking by state member banks previously imposed by the McFadden Act.

### 3. The Policy of Competitive Equality

It appears clear from this résumé of the legislative history of §36(c)(1) and (2) that Congress intended to place national and state banks on a basis of "competitive equality" insofar as branch banking was concerned. Both sponsors of the applicable banking Acts, Representative McFadden and Senator Glass, so characterized the legislation. It is not for us to so construe the Acts as to frustrate this clear-cut purpose so forcefully expressed by both friend and foe of the legislation at the time of its adoption. To us it appears beyond question that the Congress was continuing its policy of equalization first adopted in the National Bank Act of 1864.

The Comptroller argues that Utah's statute "expressly authorizes" state banks to have branches in their home municipalities. He maintains that the restriction, in the subsequent paragraph of the statute limiting branching solely to the taking over of an existing bank, is not applicable to national banks. It is a strange argument that permits one to pick and choose what portion of the law binds him. Indeed, it would fly in the face of the legislative history not to hold that national branch banking is limited to those States the laws of which permit it, and even there "only to the extent that the State laws permit branch banking." Utah clearly permits it "only to the extent" that the proposed branch takes over an existing bank.

The Comptroller also contends that the Act supersedes state law only as to "whether" and "where" branches may be located and not the "method" by which this is effected. We believe that where a State allows branching only by taking over an existing bank, it expresses as much "whether" and "where" a branch may be located as does a prohibition or a limitation to the home office municipality. As to the restriction being a "method," we have concluded that since it is part and parcel of Utah's policy, it was absorbed by the provisions of §§36(c)(1) and (2), regardless of the tag placed upon it.

Affirmed.

## *QUESTIONS AND COMMENTS*

1. Underlying the *Walker Bank* case was an early experiment in deregulation by Comptroller of the Currency James J. Saxon. Appointed

in 1961, Saxon attempted to limit the McFadden Act by administrative regulation, stating publicly (and perhaps less than tactfully) that "[t]he branching powers of National Banks should, in my judgment, not be limited according to those policies which the individual States find appropriate to meet their local needs through State-chartered banks." Saxon, Branching Powers and the Dual Banking System, 101 Comptroller of the Currency Annual Report 316, 318 (1963). Saxon's efforts generated a firestorm of litigation, most of it decided unfavorably to the Comptroller. Even after Saxon's departure from office, however, the Comptroller's Office continued to take a narrow view of the McFadden Act.

2. Utah has since repealed the branching restriction at issue in *Walker Bank.*

3. Why do you think the Utah statute at issue in *Walker Bank* required that in cities where a bank was already in operation a branch bank could be established only by taking over an existing bank? Why were large cities exempted from this rule? What about the provision requiring that certain banks be in operation for five years before they could be taken over and converted into branches?

4. How plausible was the Comptroller's position that the McFadden Act subjects national banks only to the initial state determination of whether a branch can be established, and not to any conditions that a state might impose on the creation of such branches?

5. The Comptroller's reading of the McFadden Act might be seen as an attempt to increase competition in the banking industry and enhance banking services. Could you infer any additional motivations?

6. Justice Clark draws a "policy" of "competitive equality" out of the legislative history of the McFadden Act and applies that policy to conclude that the McFadden Act would be violated by the acquisitions in question. How clear-cut is this policy in the legislative history? The McFadden Act was passed to help out national banks, which were operating at a competitive disadvantage because state banks enjoyed broader branching privileges. Is it so clear that Congress also intended to protect state banks?

7. How reliable is the legislative history cited by the Court, anyway? Can one infer from the fact that Representative McFadden sponsored the legislation that he is an authoritative guide to its meaning? The Court relies heavily on a statement by Representative McFadden to the effect that the bill established a principle of "competitive equality" among all member banks. Although the Court declares this statement to have been made "at the time of [the McFadden Act's] enactment," Representative McFadden actually placed it in the Congressional Record ten days after the Act had passed, while Congress was in recess. The Supreme Court reinterpreted the legislative history in *Clarke v. SIA,* 479 U.S. 388 (1987), which is excerpted below.

8. Note that the statute at issue in *Walker Bank* prohibited banks

from establishing de novo branches in a city "in which is located a bank." At the time of the First National Bank of Logan's application to establish a branch, there were no other banks with their principal offices in Logan, although the Walker Bank and one other bank had branches there. The Supreme Court assumes that the statute would prohibit a state-chartered bank in Logan from establishing a branch there, but is this completely clear? Couldn't the word "located" in the state statute refer only to the principal offices of a bank? How would the case have come out if the Comptroller had approved the branch application on this ground? What if there was an authoritative determination by the state banking agency or the state supreme court to the effect that a bank is "located" where it has branches: Would the Comptroller be free to interpret the statute differently? See Marshall & Ilsley Corp. v. Heimann, 652 F.2d 685, 697 n.20 (7th Cir. 1981), *cert. denied,* 455 U.S. 981 (1982).

9. Is it perfectly clear that the Comptroller's policy would have permanently upset the competitive balance between state and national banks? What do you think state legislatures would have done if the Supreme Court had ruled the other way in *Walker Bank?*

10. After *Walker Bank* a national bank client asks your advice. A statute of the state where your client is located provides that banks in cities of over 100,000 may establish an unlimited number of branches in their home cities, but that they may not branch at all outside their home cities. Your client, which is located in a city of more than 100,000, wants to establish branches in suburban areas outside the city limits in order to serve customers who are moving away from the inner city. Can it do so? Consider 12 U.S.C. §36(e): "No branch of any national banking association shall be established or moved from one location to another without first obtaining the consent and approval of the Comptroller of the Currency." In Mutschler v. Peoples National Bank of Washington, 607 F.2d 274 (9th Cir. 1979), the court held that the Comptroller did not have the power to authorize a national bank to "move" into areas where under state law neither state banks nor similarly situated national banks could have established and operated a new branch in the first place. Can you see why a contrary decision might have opened an enormous loophole in the McFadden Act?

## First National Bank in Plant City, Florida v. Dickinson

***396 U.S. 122 (1969)***

Chief Justice BURGER delivered the opinion of the Court.

In this case we are called upon to construe §7 of the McFadden Act of 1927, 44 Stat. 1228, as amended, 12 U.S.C. §36, as it relates to the definition of a branch bank for the purpose of determining the scope of branch banking available to a national bank in a State that prohibits branches for state banks.

12 U.S.C. [§36(j)] provides in pertinent part:

> [(j)] The term "branch" as used in this section shall be held to include any branch bank, branch office, branch agency, additional office, or any branch place of business . . . at which deposits are received, or checks paid, or money lent.

Florida prohibits all branch banking by state chartered banks; by statute a Florida bank may "have only one place of doing business," and all the business of the bank is to be carried on at that place "and not elsewhere." The issue must be resolved by determining what constitutes a "branch" or "additional office"; there is a threshold question of the extent to which this is governed by federal law.

The First National Bank in Plant City, Florida, is a national banking association organized and operated pursuant to the National Bank Act, 12 U.S.C. §21 et seq.; it sought and received from the United States Comptroller of the Currency permission to operate . . . an armored car messenger service. . . . The Comptroller's letter authorizing the armored car messenger service relied upon paragraph 7490 of the Comptroller's Manual for National Banks,[2] a relatively recent ruling which specifically authorizes such a service. . . . [The letter] contained explicit instructions to First National designed to insure that deposits so received would not become bank liabilities until actually in the hands of the bank teller at the chartered office or regular "banking house"; and that checks cashed for customers would be deemed paid at the bank when the cash was handed to the messenger, not when the cash was delivered to the customer by the armored car teller. . . .

. . . [C]ustomers having an account with First National could, upon signing a "comprehensive Dual Control Contract," arrange to have the armored car call at their place of business to pick up cash and checks for deposit, or to bring cash to them in exchange for checks delivered to the armored car teller. The contract provided that in each situation the bank's armored car messenger would be the agent of the customer. Additionally, proffered deposits were accompanied by a transmittal slip upon which

2. Comptroller's Manual for National Banks ¶7490.

> *Messenger service*
> To meet the requirements of its customers, a national bank may provide messenger service by means of an armored car or otherwise, pursuant to an agreement wherein it is specified that the messenger is the agent of the customer rather than of the bank. Deposits collected under this arrangement are not considered as having been received by the bank until they are actually delivered to the teller at the bank's premises. Similarly, a check is considered as having been paid at the bank when the money is handed to the messenger as agent for the customer.

the customer itemized the funds being deposited in the same manner as with deposits made at the chartered office of the bank. The transmittal slip contained a "Contract" which provided that in this off-premises transaction the bank was the agent of the customer, and that "the transmittal of said currency, coin and checks, shall not be deemed to be a deposit until delivered into the hands of the bank's tellers at the said banking house." Sums of cash for transmission to the customer were accompanied by a charge slip indicating that the customer's account had been charged for the amount of the order.

The armored car was owned and controlled by the bank; the teller and driver-guard in the car were bank employees. The bank paid the cost of armored car operations and assumed complete responsibility for the monies, checks, and deposits during transit by means of an insurance policy bought and paid for by it to protect the customer and the bank. The armored car service operated six days per week in Plant City and the surrounding trade area in Hillsborough and Polk Counties. The armored car had a plate glass window, a sliding drawer, and a counter on one side where customers might be served. The truck bore the name of the bank and had two-way radiophone communication with the bank. All movements and routing of the armored car were directed by the bank. First National handled about $1,000,000 per week through the armored car. . . .

### Federal Statute and Policy

The conditions under which national banks may establish branches are embodied in §7 of the McFadden Act, 44 Stat. 1228, as amended, codified in 12 U.S.C. §36. One such condition is that a "branch" may be established only when, where, and how state law would authorize a state bank to establish and operate such a branch, 12 U.S.C. §36(c). First National Bank of Logan, Utah v. Walker Bank & Trust Co., 385 U.S. 252, 87 S. Ct. 492, 17 L. Ed. 2d 343 (1966).

We have noted that the State of Florida permits no branch banking under a statute providing that banks are to "have only one place of doing business"; the business of the bank may be transacted at that place "and not elsewhere." The parties agree generally that the McFadden Act permits national banks to branch if and only if the host States permit one of its own banks to branch; the Florida Bank Comptroller insists that the State of Florida unequivocally forbids off-premises banking of any kind. Thus the lines are clearly drawn; the question presented is whether the activities of First National authorized by the United States Comptroller are branch banking.

At the outset we note that, while Congress has absolute authority over national banks, the federal statute has incorporated by reference the limitations which state law places on branch banking activities by state banks. Congress has deliberately settled upon a policy intended to foster "competitive equality." *Walker Bank,* 385 U.S., at 261, 87 S. Ct., at 497, 17 L. Ed. 2d 343. State law has been utilized by Congress to provide certain guidelines to implement its legislative policy.

We need not review the legislative history of the McFadden Act and prior national bank legislation as it relates to this problem; that task was performed by Mr. Justice Clark in *Walker Bank,* supra, where a unanimous Court noted that the McFadden Act was a response to the competitive tensions inherent in a dual banking structure where state and national banks coexist in the same area. That Act reflects the congressional concern that neither system have advantages over the other in the use of branch banking. . . . The policy of competitive equality is therefore firmly embedded in the statutes governing the national banking system. The mechanism of referring to state law is simply one designed to implement that congressional intent and build into the federal statute a self-executing provision to accommodate to changes in state regulation.

We reject the contention made by amicus curiae National Association of Supervisors of State Banks to the effect that state law definitions of what constitutes "branch banking" must control the content of the federal definition of [§36(j)]. Admittedly, state law comes into play in deciding how, where, and when branch banks may be operated, *Walker Bank,* supra, for in §36(c) Congress entrusted to the States the regulation of branching as Congress then conceived it. But to allow the States to define the content of the term "branch" would make them the sole judges of their own powers. Congress did not intend such an improbable result, as appears from the inclusion in §36 of a general definition of "branch." On this point the language of the Court of Appeals perhaps overstated the relation of state law to the problem, since the threshold question is to be determined as a matter of federal law, having in mind the congressional intent that so far as branch banking is concerned "the two ideas shall compete on equal terms and only where the States make the competition possible by [allowing] their own institutions [to] have branches." In short, the definition of "branch" in [§36(j)] must not be given a restrictive meaning which frustrate [sic] the congressional intent this Court found to be plain in *Walker Bank,* supra.

### FEDERAL DEFINITION OF BRANCH BANK

Against this background, we turn to the question whether the off-premises business activities conducted by First National amounted to "branch" banking within the meaning of the McFadden Act. Since national banks are "necessarily subject to the paramount authority of the United States," First National Bank in St. Louis v. Missouri, 263 U.S. 640, 656, 44 S. Ct. 213, 215, 68 L. Ed. 486 (1924), we consult that part of the McFadden Act that defines the term "branch." 12 U.S.C. [§36(j)] provides:

> [(j)] The term "branch" as used in this section shall be held to include any branch bank, branch office, branch agency, additional office, or any branch place of business . . . at which deposits are received, or checks paid, or money lent.

Although the definition may not be a model of precision, in part due to its circular aspect, it defines the minimum content of the term "branch"; by use of the word "include" the definition suggests a calculated indefiniteness with respect to the outer limits of the term. However, the term "branch bank" at the very least includes *any* place for receiving deposits or paying checks or lending money apart from the chartered premises; it may include more. It should be emphasized that, since [§36(j)] is phrased in the disjunctive, the offering of any one of the three services mentioned in that definition will provide the basis for finding that "branch" banking is taking place. Thus not only the taking of deposits but also the paying of checks or the lending of money could equally well provide the basis for such a finding. Although the District Court briefly discussed the possibility that checks were being paid, we confine ourselves to the question of whether deposits were received. . . .

First National and the Comptroller of the Currency urge that the challenged activity does not amount to branch banking under [§36(j)]. First National relies heavily, if indeed not entirely, upon carefully drawn contracts with its customers who use armored car or deposit receptacle services. The bank urges that, "deposit" being a word of art, the determination of when a deposit is made is not a casual one inasmuch as that determination fixes important legal relationships of the parties.

The bank also urges that creation of a deposit being purely a matter of intent, the issue is governed exclusively by the private contract. Since these contracts must be interpreted under state law, the argument runs, no "deposit" is actually received as such until monies delivered to the armored car or the receptacle are physically delivered into the hands of a bank teller at the chartered premises. Until such time the bank may not, under the contracts, be held to account for the customer's funds.

We have no difficulty accepting the bank's argument that the debtor-creditor relationship is a creature of contract and that the parties can agree that until monies are physically delivered to the bank no deposit will be credited to the customer's account. We are satisfied, however, that the contracts have no significant purpose other than to remove the possibility that the monies received will become "deposits" in the technical and legal sense until actually delivered to the chartered premises of the bank.

We do not challenge the right of the contracting parties to fix rights and risks as between themselves; nothing in the law precludes the parties from agreeing, for example, that the bank does not assume the status of bailee, with liability for loss of money in transit. But while the contracting parties are free to arrange their private rights and liabilities as they see fit, it does not follow that private contractual arrangements, binding on the parties under state law, determine the meaning of the language or the reach of [§36(j)].

Because the purpose of the statute is to maintain competitive equality, it is relevant in construing "branch" to consider, not merely the contractual rights and liabilities created by the transaction, but all those aspects of the transaction that might give the bank an advantage in its competition for customers. Unquestionably, a competitive advantage accrues to a bank that provides the service of receiving money for deposit at a place away from its main office; the convenience to the customer is unrelated to whether the relationship of debtor and creditor is established at the moment of receipt or somewhat later.

We need not characterize the contracts as a sham or subterfuge in order to conclude that the conduct of the parties and the nature of their relations bring First National's challenged activities within the federal definition of branch banking. Here, penetrating the form of the contracts to the underlying substance of the transaction, we are satisfied that . . . the bank has, for all purposes contemplated by Congress in [§36(j)], received a deposit. The money is given and received for deposit even though the parties have agreed that its technical status as a "deposit" which may be drawn on is to remain inchoate for the brief period of time it is in transit to the chartered bank premises. The intended deposits are delivered and received as part of a large-scale continuing mode of conducting the banking business designed to bring basic bank services to the customers.

Since the putative deposits are in fact "received" by a bank facility apart from its chartered place of business, we are compelled, in construing [§36(j)], to view the place of delivery of the customer's cash and checks accompanied by a deposit slip as an "additional office, or . . . branch place of business . . . at which deposits are received."

Here we are confronted by a systematic attempt to secure for national banks branching privileges which Florida denied to competing state banks. The utility of the armored car service [is] obvious; many States permit state chartered banks to use this eminently sensible mode of operations, but Florida's policy is not open to judicial review any more than is the congressional policy of "competitive equality." Nor is the congressional policy of competitive equality with its deference to state standards open to modification by the Comptroller of the Currency.

Affirmed.

## *QUESTIONS AND COMMENTS*

1. In 1987 a district counsel in the Comptroller's office declared that a deposit pick-up service operated by a national bank was not a "branch." The action was a direct challenge to the Supreme Court's opinion in *Plant City.* A federal district court declared the service illegal, and on appeal the Comptroller, represented by the Department of Justice, renounced the district counsel's views and conceded that the service violated the McFadden Act. The Second Circuit agreed. Brown v. Clarke, 878 F.2d 627 (2d Cir. 1989).

2. The bank was right, was it not, that its contracts with customers brought the armored car services outside the term "branch" as a matter of form? If the armored car acts strictly as an agent of the customer, deposits are not received, checks are not paid, and money is not lent until the armored car arrives back at the bank's brick-and-mortar office. Wouldn't it have been perfectly consistent with the statutory language for the Court to conclude that this service was not, in fact, a branch?

3. The Court relies on the principle of "competitive equality" that the Court in *Walker Bank* drew out of the legislative history. But there was no evidence in the legislative history that the Congress that passed the McFadden Act gave any consideration to the possibility that banking services would be offered by means of armored cars. Was the Court correct in considering the abstract principle of "competitive equality" so binding as to control the decision?

4. The Court readily acknowledges the utility of armored car services, calling them an "eminently sensible mode of operations," but claims that the utility of the service is not a matter for judicial review. Do you think the Court is really impervious to public policy considerations of this sort? Should it be? If the statute is sufficiently open-textured to permit a particular interpretation, even if it is not the only possible interpretation, why can't the utility of a particular practice or activity be a legitimate subject for judicial consideration?

5. Why didn't the majority defer to the Comptroller's interpretation of the McFadden Act? What theory of administrative functioning might be implicit in the majority's decision not to defer?

6. If you were advising the First National Bank in Plant City while it was considering whether to offer the armored car service, what risks would you identify in the plan? Why would any bank, especially a small one, be willing to act as a test case?

7. A national bank sets up an office to perform routine trust services at a place where it could not open a branch under the McFadden Act. At this office the bank consults with customers and prospective customers about the proposed services; discusses accounts with trust beneficiaries; reviews proposed trust instruments; provides a location for customers to

execute wills and trusts; reviews wills and trusts for customers; and researches trust and estate problems. No deposits are taken, no checks paid, and no money lent. A federal statute, 12 U.S.C. §92a, authorizes the Comptroller to approve trust activities for national banks whenever the laws of the state authorize or permit the exercise of trust powers by state banks and other companies that compete with national banks. The Comptroller approves the activities in question on the ground that state banks are permitted to perform trust services. Is the national bank's activity legal? See St. Louis County National Bank v. Mercantile Trust Co. National Association, 548 F.2d 716 (8th Cir. 1976), *cert. denied,* 433 U.S. 909 (1977) (concluding that the activities in question violated 12 U.S.C. §92a).

8. How far does the principle of competitive equality extend? Does it mean that state and national banks must compete on equal terms in all respects? It couldn't possibly mean this; otherwise there would be no differences between the regulatory regimes for state and federal banks. See Langevoort, Interpreting the McFadden Act: The Politics and Economics of Shared ATMs and Discount Brokerage Houses, 41 Bus. Law. 1265, 1269 (1986) (competitive equality doctrine proves too much because virtually anything a bank does to expand its geographic or product base is designed to achieve a competitive advantage).

9. A national bank establishes and operates an automatic teller machine (ATM) at a location where it could not open a branch under the McFadden Act. Under the terms of the contract with customers, communications between customers and the bank through the ATM are considered as "instructions to consummate" transactions rather than transactions per se. Can this arrangement be distinguished from *Plant City?* See Independent Bankers Association of America v. Smith, 175 U.S. App. D.C. 184, 534 F.2d 921, *cert. denied,* 429 U.S. 862 (1976) (invalidating a Comptroller's regulation permitting such arrangements on the ground that they could not be distinguished from the arrangement struck down in *Plant City*).

10. State A enacts a statute providing that state-chartered banks can utilize ATMs "to the same extent that other financial institutions chartered and regulated by any agency of the federal government are permitted to provide such services within this state." Does this create a preposterous circle in which federal law refers to state law and the state refers right back to federal law? How would you cut the Gordian knot? See State Bank of Fargo v. Merchants National Bank & Trust Co. of Fargo, 593 F.2d 341 (8th Cir. 1979) (looking to rules governing ATM use by federal savings and loans and credit unions).

11. In the wake of the *Independent Bankers Association* case described above, the Comptroller revised his regulation to permit a national bank to take deposits and disburse cash to customers through an ATM placed at a location where it could not establish a branch, so long as the bank

does not "own or rent" the ATM. Can this arrangement be distinguished from the scheme struck down in *Independent Bankers Association* on the ground that the national bank has not "established" or "operated" a branch under 12 U.S.C. §36(c)? See Independent Bankers Association of New York State v. Marine Midland Bank, 757 F.2d 453 (2d Cir. 1985), *cert. denied,* 476 U.S. 1186 (1986) (distinguishing *Independent Bankers Association* and concluding that the ATM facility was permissible if not owned or rented by the national bank).

12. A client asks for your advice about a scheme under which several national banks will form a joint venture, which in turn will purchase and operate ATMs to be used by the banks for customer services at various locations that would be prohibited to branches of the banks under the McFadden Act. What would you say?

13. A national bank establishes a loan production office at which potential loan customers are solicited and loan applications are accepted subject to "approval" from the home office. The office is located at a place where the bank could not establish a branch under the McFadden Act. Is the loan production office permissible under the Act? Cf. Independent Bankers Association v. Heimann, 201 U.S. App. D.C. 27, 627 F.2d 486 (D.C. Cir. 1980) (dismissing a challenge to a Comptroller's regulation authorizing such loan production offices on the ground that the party challenging the regulation had waited too long (12 years) before bringing its grievance to the attention of the court).

## Clarke v. Securities Industry Association

***479 U.S. 388 (1987)***

WHITE, J., delivered the opinion of the Court. . . .

In these cases, we . . . review, and reverse, a judgment that the Comptroller of the Currency exceeded his authority in approving the applications of two national banks for the establishment or purchase of discount brokerage subsidiaries.

### I

In 1982, two national banks, Union Planters National Bank of Memphis (Union Planters) and petitioner Security Pacific National Bank of Los Angeles (Security Pacific), applied to the Comptroller of Currency for permission to open offices that would offer discount brokerage services to the public.[1] Union Planters proposed to acquire an existing discount

1. Discount brokers execute trades on behalf of their customers but do not offer investment advice. As a result, the commissions they charge are substantially lower than those charged by full-service brokers. See Securities Industries Assn. v. Board of Governors, 468 U.S. 207, 209, n.2 (1984).

brokerage operation, and Security Pacific sought to establish an affiliate named Discount Brokerage. Both banks proposed to offer discount brokerage services not only at their branch offices but at other locations inside and outside of their home States.

In passing on Security Pacific's application, the Comptroller was faced with the question whether the operation of Discount Brokerage would violate the National Bank Act's branching provisions. Those limitations, enacted as §§7 and 8 of the McFadden Act, 44 Stat. 1228, as amended, are codified at 12 U.S.C. §36 and 12 U.S.C. §81. Section 81 limits "the general business" of a national bank to its headquarters and any "branches" permitted by §36. Section 36(c) provides that a national bank is permitted to branch only in its home State and only to the extent that a bank of the same State is permitted to branch under state law. The term "branch" is defined at 12 U.S.C. [§36(j)] "to include any branch bank, branch office, branch agency, additional office, or any branch place of business . . . at which deposits are received, or checks paid, or money lent."

The Comptroller concluded that "the non-chartered offices at which Discount Brokerage will offer its services will not constitute branches under the McFadden Act because none of the statutory branching functions will be performed there." Pet. for Cert. in No. 85-971, p.39a. He explained that although Discount Brokerage would serve as an intermediary for margin lending, loan approval would take place at chartered Security Pacific offices, so that Discount Brokerage offices would not be lending money within the meaning of [§36(j)]. Likewise, although Discount Brokerage would maintain, and pay interest on, customer balances created as an incident of its brokerage business, the Comptroller concluded that these accounts differ sufficiently in nature from ordinary bank accounts that Discount Brokerage would not be engaged in receiving deposits.[2] He further observed that treating offices conducting brokerage activities as branches under [§36(j)] would be inconsistent with the "long-

2. The Comptroller relied primarily on the fact that banks publicly solicit deposits and use deposited funds in lending, while credit balances maintained by brokers are not, as such, directly solicited from the public, and are subject to regulatory restrictions regarding use by brokers. See the Securities Investor Protection Act, 15 U.S.C. §78aaa et seq. (restricting advertising, promotional, and selling practices of brokers regarding interest-bearing free credit balances); 17 CFR §240.15c3-2 (1986) (regulating the use of credit balances by brokers).

Although the Comptroller believed that [§36(j)] should be read narrowly to define "branch" only with reference to receiving deposits, making loans, and cashing checks, he recognized that there is authority supporting a broader reading. In St. Louis County National Bank v. Mercantile Trust Company National Assn., 548 F.2d 716 (CA8 1976), *cert. denied,* 433 U.S. 909 (1977), a trust office operated by a national bank was held to be a branch. While disagreeing with this holding, the Comptroller took the position that it "should at the very least be limited to those dealings with the public requiring a specialized banking or similar license." . . .

standing and widespread" practice of banks' operating nonbranch offices dealing in United States Government or municipal securities. Id., at 44a. Accordingly, the Comptroller approved Security Pacific's application.

Respondent, a trade association representing securities brokers, underwriters, and investment bankers, brought this action in the United States District Court for the District of Columbia. Among other things, respondent contended that bank discount brokerage offices are branches within the meaning of [§36(j)] and thus are subject to the geographical restrictions imposed by §36(c).[4] . . .

### III

"It is settled that courts should give great weight to any reasonable construction of a regulatory statute adopted by the agency charged with the enforcement of that statute. The Comptroller of the Currency is charged with the enforcement of banking laws to an extent that warrants the invocation of this principle with respect to his deliberative conclusions as to the meaning of these laws. See First National Bank v. Missouri, 263 U.S. 640, 658." Investment Company Institute v. Camp, 401 U.S., at 626-627.

Respondent contends that the Comptroller's interpretation of the Bank Act is not entitled to deference because it contradicts the plain language of the statute. Respondent relies on 12 U.S.C. §81, which provides that:

> The general business of each national banking association shall be transacted in the place specified in its organization certificate and in the branch or branches, if any, established or maintained by it in accordance with the provisions of section 36 of this title.

In respondent's view, the unambiguous meaning of §81 is that "national banks may locate their business only at their headquarters or licensed branches within the same state." Brief for Respondent 11. However, §81 is considerably more ambiguous than respondent allows. The phrase "[t]he general business of each national banking association" in §81 need not be read to encompass all the business in which the bank engages, but, as we shall explain, can plausibly be read to cover only those activities that are part of the bank's core banking functions. . . .

Respondent also relies on the following statement, which Representative McFadden placed in the Congressional Record 10 days after the passage of the McFadden Act, while Congress was in recess:

4. Respondent also contended that national banks are entirely prohibited from offering discount brokerage services by the Glass-Steagall Act, 12 U.S.C. §24 (1982 ed. and Supp. III); 12 U.S.C. §§78, 377, 378. This contention was rejected by the District Court, a holding that is not before us.

> [Section 36(j)] defines the term "branch." Any place outside of or away from the main office where the bank carries on its business of receiving deposits, paying checks, lending money, or transacting any business carried on at the main office, is a branch if it is legally established under the provisions of this act.

68 Cong. Rec. 5816 (1927). We do not attach substantial weight to this statement, which Congress did not have before it in passing the McFadden Act. As the Comptroller persuasively argues, Representative McFadden cannot be considered an impartial interpreter of the bill that bears his name, since he was not favorably disposed toward branch banking. If we took literally Representative McFadden's view of [§36(j)], we would have to conclude that Congress intended to overturn the Attorney General's opinion in *Lowry National Bank,* 29 Op. Atty. Gen. 81 (1891), which this Court had previously approved in First National Bank v. Missouri, 263 U.S., at 658. Congress never specifically indicated such an intention, and we find it hard to imagine that it would have made such a change without comment.

It is significant that in passing the McFadden Act, Congress recognized and for the first time specifically authorized the practice of national banks' engaging in the buying and selling of investment securities. See Act of Feb. 25, 1927, ch. 191, §2, 44 Stat. 1226. Prior to 1927, banks had conducted such securities transactions on a widespread and often interstate basis, without regard to the locational restriction imposed by §5190 on "the usual business of each national banking association." We find it unlikely that Congress, in recognizing and explicitly authorizing this practice, would have undertaken to limit its geographic scope through the branching law without specifically noting the restriction on the prior practice.

For the foregoing reasons, we conclude that Congress did not intend to subject a bank's conduct of a securities business to the branching restrictions imposed by 12 U.S.C. [§36(j)]. We do not view our decision today as inconsistent with our prior decisions interpreting 12 U.S.C. [§36(j)] as embodying a policy of "competitive equality" between state and national banks. See, e.g., First National Bank in Plant City v. Dickinson, 396 U.S. 122 (1969). The Comptroller reasonably interprets the statute as requiring "competitive equality" only in core banking functions, and not in all incidental services in which national banks are authorized to engage.[23] We are not faced today with the need to decide whether

23. If the "competitive equality" principle were carried to its logical extreme, the ability of a national bank to carry on an incidental activity such as the safe-deposit business would be limited to the same extent as a state bank's ability to do so under state law. However, . . . the legislative history of the McFadden Act rather clearly indicates that Congress intended national banks to be able to carry on a safe-deposit business without locational restrictions.

there are core banking functions beyond those explicitly enumerated in [§36(j)]; it suffices, to decide this case, to hold that the operation of a discount brokerage service is not a core banking function.

Accordingly, the judgment of the Court of Appeals is affirmed, insofar as it held that respondent has standing, and reversed on the merits.

It is so ordered.

## *QUESTIONS AND COMMENTS*

1. In Chapter 1 we described the 1980s as a period of "revolution" in banking. *Clarke* is part of the legal fallout of that revolution. The Glass-Steagall Act had long been thought to bar virtually all bank involvement in equity securities. In the 1980s, however, bank holding companies sought—and won—authority to offer discount stock brokerage services through nonbanking subsidiaries. See SIA v. Board of Governors of the Federal Reserve System, 468 U.S. 207 (1984). The *Clarke* case involved discount brokerage offered through a bank itself; the SIA challenged this activity under the Glass-Steagall Act but the Supreme Court did not address the question (see note 4 of the opinion). We discuss the breakdown of the Glass-Steagall wall between commercial and investment banking at length in Chapter 6. For the moment we deal with the *Clarke* case for its bearing on the interpretation of the McFadden Act.

2. In the other McFadden Act cases we have read, the national bank's business expansion was challenged by state banks or their representatives. Why weren't state banks challenging the activity in question here?

3. Is the analysis in *Clarke* consistent with that in *Walker Bank* and *Plant City?* Isn't a requirement that margin loans advanced by a securities brokerage subsidiary be subject to "approval" at the home office simply a matter of form, not substance? Can this arrangement be distinguished in a principled way from the arrangement in *Plant City* under which the armored car service acted only as agent of the customer in depositing checks or making withdrawals from the home office?

4. What do you think the Court in *Clarke* might mean by "core banking functions"?

5. After the *Clarke* decision a national bank client comes to you for advice about the following proposal. The bank wants its discount brokerage to offer customers the right to open "sweep" accounts in a money market fund operated by the brokerage in which proceeds from securities sales can be deposited. As with many money market funds, the customer would have the right to draw checks on this account payable to third parties. The client informs you that its discount brokerage has offices in

several different states. Advise the client as to whether this proposal would be permissible under the McFadden Act.

6. A national bank in State A establishes a branch at a location that would not be permissible under state law for a similarly situated state-chartered bank, but that would be permissible under state law for a similarly situated state-chartered savings institution. Is the national bank branch permissible under the McFadden Act? See Department of Banking & Consumer Finance of the State of Mississippi v. Clarke, 809 F.2d 266 (5th Cir.), *cert. denied,* 483 U.S. 1010 (1987) (the *"Deposit Guaranty"* case) (concluding that in light of changes in powers granted to thrift institutions, state savings associations were "state banks" within the meaning of 12 U.S.C. §36(j)).

7. Federal savings and loans and savings banks are currently allowed to branch statewide even if a state has more restrictive branching policies for its state-chartered thrifts. See Independent Bankers Association of America v. FHLBB, 557 F. Supp. 23 (D.D.C. 1982) (upholding FHLBB's authority to authorize statewide branching by federally chartered thrifts). Coupled with the result in *Deposit Guaranty,* does this suggest the eventual demise of all remaining McFadden Act limitations on branching within a state?

## 2. *Interstate Branching*

So far we have talked only about branching *within* a state. What if a bank attempts to open a branch in *another* state? Interstate branching, as we have noted, is the rule for most industries. But until recently it was extremely uncommon in the banking industry, largely because of legal restrictions. Although those restrictions are now rapidly breaking down, they are still important.

The basic restrictions are found under the federal McFadden Act and under state law. The McFadden Act generally prohibits any interstate branching by national banks, 12 U.S.C. §36(c), and this prohibition is carried over for state-chartered member banks by 12 U.S.C. §321. Federal law does not expressly prohibit interstate branching by state-chartered banks that are not members of the Federal Reserve System, but many states prohibit banks from other states from opening branches within their borders. Such a prohibition might once have faced constitutional challenge under the Dormant Commerce Clause, see Miller, Interstate Branching and the Constitution, 41 Bus. Law. 337 (1986). Now, however, the Riegle-Neal Interstate Banking and Branching Efficiency Act of 1994 (Riegle-Neal Act) has given at least implicit congressional recognition to the authority of a state to bar out-of-state banks that try to enter by opening a branch.

Since the 1980s, these restrictions have begun to break down. Section 334 of the Garn-St Germain Act of 1982, 12 U.S.C. §1464(r)(1), expressly authorizes the OTS to approve interstate branching by federal thrifts. The statute generally requires, however, that thrift institutions branching across state lines must have a specified high percentage of assets devoted to residential home mortgages. States also got into the act. A number of states—New York being the most prominent—enacted enabling legislation authorizing banks chartered in other states to expand into the enacting state's market by means of branches rather than through separately incorporated subsidiaries of a common holding company. Typically, these state initiatives include reciprocity provisions that base approval for entry into the state through branching on the condition that the entering bank's state offer similar privileges to banks chartered in the state where the new branch is to be established.

Another route to interstate branching draws on the authority to relocate a principal office under 12 U.S.C. §30(b), which provides in pertinent part that "[a]ny national banking association, upon [approval by two-thirds of the shareholders and the Comptroller] may change the location of its main office . . . to any . . . location within or outside the limits of the city, town, or village where it is located, but not more than thirty miles beyond such limits." Cast yourself in the role of an attorney for a national bank wishing to expand into a contiguous state. How would you structure a transaction using the §30(b) relocation authority?

In First Fidelity Bank, N.A., Comptroller of the Currency Corporate Decisions 94-04, the Comptroller addressed the following fact pattern. A bank holding company owned national banks in Pennsylvania and New Jersey. The Pennsylvania bank subsidiary applied for permission under §30(b) to relocate its main office from Philadelphia to Salem, New Jersey, a town less than thirty miles away. It also sought to retain its existing branches in Pennsylvania and to convert its former main office in Philadelphia into a branch. The Pennsylvania and New Jersey banks then sought to consolidate into a single national bank with main offices in Salem, New Jersey, and to convert the former main office of the New Jersey bank into a branch of the consolidated institution. The applicants argued that under 12 U.S.C. §30(b), the Pennsylvania bank did not have to divest its Pennsylvania branches when it moved its principal office to New Jersey. They argued further that the consolidated bank, which would have its principal office in New Jersey, could maintain all its branches in New Jersey under 12 U.S.C. §36(b)(2), which provides in pertinent part that a consolidated national bank may retain and operate as a branch any office which immediately prior to the consolidation was in operation as a main office or a branch and if such office "might be established as a new branch of the resulting bank. . . ." Since under New Jersey law the consolidated bank, headquartered in New Jersey, could establish new branches in New Jersey, the applicants claimed that all the preexisting branches in New Jersey, as well as the former head office in New Jersey that was being converted into a branch, were permissible for the consolidated institution. The Comptroller approved the applications in the decision cited above.

Presto! Ersatz interstate branching! Two separate banks in different states were converted into a single bank operating branches in two states. And the process would not necessarily end there. Suppose now that the consolidated national bank wishes to expand into New York? The holding company establishes a subsidiary national bank in New York with its principal office close to the New Jersey border (if the holding company has an existing New York bank, it can use this if the main office is close to New Jersey, or it can effect a merger of the existing institution with the new New York bank in which the resulting bank has its main offices close to the New Jersey border). The New York bank then seeks to move its main office into New Jersey under §30(b), retaining all its branches in New York and converting its former main office into a branch. It then consolidates with the existing bank that is already doing business in New Jersey and Pennsylvania. The effect would be a creeping expansion in which a bank would end up operating branches in as many states as it wished.

This strategy of interstate banking by means of home office relocation across a state line and conversion of the former headquarters into a branch has stumbled in at least one jurisdiction, Ghiglieri v. Ludwig, 64 USLW 2779, 1996 WL 315947 (N.D. Tex. 1996), but it has been used by a substantial number of banks to finesse their way into interstate branching operations.

In the Riegle-Neal Act of 1994 (on which we will have more to say later), Congress addressed the relocation question. It implicitly acknowledged the legality of interstate relocations of the sort described above, but it provided in revised 12 U.S.C. §30(c) that "[i]n the case of a national bank which relocates the main office of such bank from 1 State to another State after May 31, 1997, the bank may retain and operate branches within the State from which the bank relocated such office only to the extent authorized in [12 U.S.C. §36(e)(2)]." The corresponding provision in §36(e)(2) provides, subject to minor exceptions, that "[i]n the case of a national bank which relocates the main office of such bank from 1 State to another State after May 31, 1997, the bank may retain and operate branches within [the State of its former main office] only to the extent the bank would be authorized . . . to acquire, establish, or commence to operate a branch in [the State of its former home office] if . . . the bank had no branches in such State. . . ." The Conference Committee stated that "after June 1, 1997, a national bank relocating its main office to another state may maintain its branches in the first state only if those branches could have been established by a bank with its home State in the new State." H.R. Conf. Rep. No. 651, 103d Cong., 2d

Sess. 57 (August 2, 1994). Thus, it appears that, absent further congressional action, the authority to establish interstate branches through home office relocations will terminate in 1997.

The Riegle-Neal Interstate Banking and Branching Efficiency Act of 1994 is a fundamental piece of legislation that appears likely to constitute the basic charter for interstate bank expansion in future years. The Riegle-Neal Act authorizes interstate branching through two devices. The first device is direct branching across state lines if permitted by state law. The second method is interstate branching incident to an interstate merger.

The statute provides (12 U.S.C. §36(g)) that a national bank may, with the Comptroller's permission, establish and operate a branch in another state in which it does not maintain a branch if the host state has adopted a law that applies equally to all banks and that expressly permits all out-of-state banks to establish de novo branches within its borders. Effectively, the law allows states to "opt-in" to interstate branching. Similar rules apply to state-chartered banks, 12 U.S.C. §1828(d)(4) and to foreign banks (subject to additional requirements), 12 U.S.C. §3103(a).

Section 102 of the Riegle-Neal Act provides an alternative and probably more effective method for interstate branching. Beginning in 1997, or earlier if a state so provides, federal banking agencies may approve mergers between insured banks with different home states without regard to whether such transactions are prohibited under the laws of any state. To block such mergers, states must opt-out by passing legislation before June 1, 1997, that applies equally to all out-of-state banks and that expressly prohibits merger transactions involving out-of-state banks. In the absence of an opt-out, the branches of the merging partner in one state can be converted into branches of the surviving bank, which may be chartered or have its principal offices in another state. The resulting bank may establish, acquire, and operate additional branches at any location where any bank involved in the transaction could have established, acquired, or operated a branch under applicable federal or state law if the bank had not been a party to the merger transation. In other words, the successor institution acquires the branching rights previously enjoyed by the merging partners.

The authorization for interstate mergers explicitly preserves state age laws—laws that require that the bank being acquired in a merger must have been in existence for a specified period of time. However, the maximum extent of state age laws is set at five years. The new law also preserves state taxation authority and state and federal antitrust laws. In addition, Congress specifically declared its intention not to disturb the authority of states to set branching policy for banks they charter, or to supervise, regulate, and examine these banks.

*QUESTIONS AND COMMENTS*

1. Do you think Congress had interstate branching in mind when it authorized national banks to relocate their home offices within a thirty-mile radius? Wasn't this statute enacted for a simpler time when a bank's purpose was simply to move its home office a few miles away in order to conduct its business with somewhat greater efficiency?

2. How likely is it that states will allow out-of-state or foreign banks to establish de novo branches within their borders? What political interests are likely to fight proposed opt-in legislation?

3. Clearly, Congress granted much greater leeway for interstate branching via mergers than via the establishment of de novo branches. Why do you think it made this distinction? What interest groups might have supported one provision but opposed the other?

4. What is the public policy behind state age laws that prohibit bank mergers unless the bank to be acquired has been in existence for a specified, relatively lengthy period of time? Why did Congress preserve these laws? What political interests do you detect at work here?

## C. GEOGRAPHIC EXPANSION BY BANK HOLDING COMPANIES

While interstate *branching* is still in its toddlerhood (as we saw in the previous section), interstate *banking* by means of holding companies is well established. The Riegle-Neal Act of 1994 administered the *quietus* to all remaining state legislation barring such expansion and opened up the national market to full-scale interstate banking. We begin our discussion with a brief reprise of the McFadden Act, follow with a discussion of state limitations on bank holding company acquisitions of non-bank subsidiaries, and conclude by outlining current law on interstate bank acquisitions.

### 1. *The McFadden Act: A Reprise*

Expansion by bank holding companies is a substitute for branching, albeit an imperfect one. A banking holding company must maintain the separate corporate existence of its subsidiary banks, even if it owns all the stock of each subsidiary. Financial transactions between a bank holding company and its subsidiaries are limited in important respects by §§23A and 23B of the Federal Reserve Act, 12 U.S.C. §§371c, 371c-1. These limitations have already been discussed in Chapter 4.

In addition, there is a danger that if a holding company operates its subsidiary banks too much like branch banks, the whole arrangement will be declared a sham and brought within the restrictions of the McFadden Act. In Michigan National Corporation, 64 Fed. Res. Bull. 127 (1978), the Fed considered a holding company's use of an "accommodation transaction services" program among its subsidiary banks. Under this program, a customer of a subsidiary bank could, at the location of any other subsidiary bank, effect a deposit to, or withdrawal from, any account maintained at the customer's bank of record, or effect payments on any mortgage or installment loan extended to the customer by the customer's bank of record. Legally, the program was implemented through the creation of temporary "accommodation accounts" at the second bank, which would exist only long enough to effect clearance of the transaction between the two banks. Each customer was informed that the accommodating bank was not the customer's bank of record and that the transaction would not be effective until the accommodating bank settled its accounts with the customer's bank of record.

The Fed lauded the arrangement as "an innovative means of providing services to retail banking customers that produces substantial public benefits, both in terms of increased convenience to the individual consumer and enhanced competition in the banking industry." But it held that the program violated the McFadden Act as interpreted in *Plant City.* In substance, "the receipt of funds by an accommodating bank for transfer to a bank of record effects a deposit at the bank of record and is indistinguishable from a deposit at a branch, particularly as perceived by the customer. The separate corporate status of each . . . bank and the technically conditional nature of the ATS transactions have little or no effect on the convenience afforded to the banking customer or the competitive advantage thereby accruing to [the participating] banks." The Fed concluded, further, that the accommodating banks would, in substance, be operating as branches "established and operated" by the bank of record within the meaning of §36(c). Ergo, the McFadden Act barred the application.

## *QUESTIONS AND COMMENTS*

1. Was the board right in concluding that the accommodating bank was operating as a branch "established" and "operated" by the bank of record? If anyone established and operated the bank of record, it was the parent bank holding company, was it not? And last we checked, bank holding companies are not subject to the McFadden Act. Given the fact that the arrangement was good for consumers, didn't the board stretch too far in outlawing it?

2. Many banks are willing to assist customers of other banks in

effecting wire transfers of funds to and from the customer's account in another bank. The board in *Michigan National* stressed that this type of accommodation transaction is not subject to the McFadden Act. Given the reasoning of the decision, why not?

3. Is *Michigan National* still good law in light of *Clarke v. SIA?* What would you counsel a client that wanted to embark on a similar program today?

## 2. *Interstate Holding Company Acquisitions: Nondepository Institutions*

The legal problems in the area of interstate holding company acquisitions chiefly arise as a result of the influence of in-state banks that seek protection from competition from out-of-state institutions. Protectionist legislation inevitably raises issues under the Commerce Clause of the U.S. Constitution. Two subquestions are involved: (1) whether in the absence of congressional authorization the state action in question discriminates against or otherwise places an undue burden on interstate commerce in violation of the dormant Commerce Clause; and (2) if the state action standing by itself would violate the Commerce Clause, whether Congress has authorized the state to regulate commerce as it did (if so, there is no Commerce Clause violation).

### Lewis v. BT Investment Managers, Inc.

*447 U.S. 27 (1980)*

Justice BLACKMUN delivered the opinion of the Court.

This case concerns the constitutionality of two Florida statutes regulating the conduct of investment advisory and trust services within that State. . . .

#### I

Appellee Bankers Trust New York Corporation (Bankers Trust) is a corporation organized under the laws of the State of New York. It maintains its principal place of business in that State. It is a bank holding company within the meaning of §2(a) of the Bank Holding Company Act of 1956, 70 Stat. 133, as amended, 12 U.S.C. §1841(a) (1976 ed. and Supp. II) (Act). Accordingly, it is subject to federal restrictions on the kinds of subsidiaries it may own or control. Upon authorization from the Board of Governors of the Federal Reserve System, however, it is permitted to own or control shares of any company the business of which is "so closely related to banking or managing or controlling banks as to be a proper incident thereto." §4(c)(8) of the Act, 12 U.S.C. §1843(c)(8). By regulation, the Board has designated both the provision of investment or financial advice and the performance of certain trust functions as "closely related" business within the meaning of this statute. See 12 CFR §§225.4(a)(4) and (5) (1979).

In 1972, the management of Bankers Trust decided to seek the Board's approval for an investment management subsidiary to operate in Florida. On October 3 of that year, Bankers Trust filed a formal proposal for such a subsidiary, which it planned to operate from offices in Palm Beach. Appellee BT Investment Managers, Inc. (BTIM), was Bankers Trust's intended vehicle for entry into the Florida market. It was incorporated under the laws of the State of Delaware as a wholly owned subsidiary on November 24, 1972. Three days later it qualified to do business in Florida. The application to the Board proposed that BTIM would provide "portfolio investment advice," as well as "general economic information and advice, general economic statistical forecasting services and industry studies" to persons other than banks. . . .

The reaction of the Florida financial community to Bankers Trust's proposed investment subsidiary was decidedly negative. The State Comptroller, the Florida Bankers Association, and the Palm Beach County Bankers Association, Inc., all filed comments with the Board objecting to the Bankers Trust proposal. More importantly for present purposes, the state legislature was persuaded to take action. On November 30, 1972, shortly after BTIM had qualified to do business in the State, a special session of the legislature amended Fla. Stat. §659.141 (1). That statute, which had been on the books only since March 28 of that year, was expanded to prohibit an out-of-state bank holding company from owning or controlling a business within the State that sells investment advisory services to any customer, rather than just to "trust companies or banks" in Florida, as the statute theretofore had read.[2] This amendment took effect, without the Governor's approval, on December 21, 1972. There is evidence that the amendment was a direct response to Bankers

2. See 1972 Fla. Laws, ch. 72-726, §§1-7. As so amended, §659.141 (1) read in pertinent part:

> [N]o bank, trust company, or holding company, the operations of which are principally conducted outside this state, shall acquire, [or] retain, *or own,* directly or indirectly, all, or substantially all the assets of, or control over, any *bank or* trust company having a place of business in this state where the *business of banking or* trust business or functions are conducted, or acquire, [or] retain, *or own* all, or substantially all, of the assets of, or control over, any business organization having a place of business in this state where or from which it furnishes investment advisory services [to trust companies or banks] in this state.

The italicized words were added, and the bracketed words were deleted, by the December 1972 amendment.

Trust's pending application, and that it had the strong backing of the local financial community.

On April 26, 1973, the Board rejected Bankers Trust's proposal on the ground that it would conflict with state law. Bankers Trust New York Corp., 59 Fed. Res. Bull. 364. The Board observed that the proposal contemplated de novo entry into the Florida investment management market rather than acquisition of an existing concern, and it noted that de novo entry ordinarily has a desirable procompetitive impact. Absent evidence of a contrary effect in this case, the Board intimated that it would have been favorably inclined toward the proposal. But it found that the December amendment to Fla. Stat. §659.14 (1) "was intended to, and does, prohibit the performance of investment advisory services in Florida by non-Florida bank holding companies." 59 Fed. Res. Bull., at 365. In view of its obligation to respect the dictates of state law, the Board found itself constrained to reject the proposal. See 12 U.S.C. §1846; Whitney Nat. Bank v. Bank of New Orleans, 379 U.S. 411, 424-425 (1965).

Within six months of the Board's decision, the two appellees filed this action seeking declaratory and injunctive relief.

**II**

This appeal presents two distinct but related questions with respect to the validity of the challenged Florida statutes. The first is whether the statutes, viewed independently of federal legislation regulating the banking industry, burden interstate commerce in a manner contrary to the Commerce Clause. The second is whether Congress, by its own legislation in this area, has created an area in which the States may regulate free from Commerce Clause restraints. Since there is no contention that federal legislation pre-empts the state laws in question, federal law becomes important only if it appears that the Florida statutes cannot survive without federal authorization. Thus, the second question becomes pertinent only if we reach an affirmative answer to the first.

These questions arise against a backdrop of familiar principles. The Commerce Clause grants to Congress the power "[t]o regulate Commerce . . . among the several States." U.S. Const., Art. 1, §8, cl. 3. Although the Clause thus speaks in terms of powers bestowed upon Congress, the Court long has recognized that it also limits the power of the States to erect barriers against interstate trade. This limitation upon state power, of course, is by no means absolute. In the absence of conflicting federal legislation, the States retain authority under their general police powers to regulate matters of "legitimate local concern," even though interstate commerce may be affected. Where such legitimate local interests are implicated, defining the appropriate scope for state regulation is often a matter of "delicate adjustment." Yet even in regulating to protect local interests, the States generally must act in a manner consistent with the "ultimate . . . principle that one state in its dealings with another may not place itself in a position of economic isolation." Baldwin v. G. A. F. Seelig, Inc., 294 U.S. 511, 527 (1935). However important the state interest at hand, "it may not be accomplished by discriminating against articles of commerce coming from outside the State unless there is some reason, apart from their origin, to treat them differently." Philadelphia v. New Jersey, 437 U.S., at 626-627.

Over the years, the court has used a variety of formulations for the Commerce Clause limitation upon the States, but it consistently has distinguished between outright protectionism and more indirect burdens on the free flow of trade. The Court has observed that "where simple economic protectionism is effected by state legislation, a virtually *per se* rule of invalidity has been erected." Id., at 624. In contrast, legislation that visits its effects equally upon both interstate and local business may survive constitutional scrutiny if it is narrowly drawn. The Court stated in Pike v. Bruce Church, Inc., 397 U.S. 137 (1970):

> Where the statute regulates evenhandedly to effectuate a legitimate local public interest, and its effects on interstate commerce are only incidental, it will be upheld unless the burden imposed on such commerce is clearly excessive in relation to the putative local benefits. . . . If a legitimate local purpose is found, then the question becomes one of degree. And the extent of the burden that will be tolerated will of course depend on the nature of the local interest involved, and on whether it could be promoted as well with a lesser impact on interstate activities.

Id., at 142.

The principal focus of inquiry must be the practical operation of the statute, since the validity of state laws must be judged chiefly in terms of their probable effects.

### III

With these principles in mind, we first turn to §659.141 (1). This statute has been the chief object of controversy, since it is the statute that prevents appellees from setting up their projected investment advisory business within Florida. The statute prohibits ownership of local investment or trust businesses by firms possessing two characteristics: a certain kind of business organization and purpose, whether it be as a bank, trust company, or a bank holding company; and location of principal operations outside Florida.

Appellant and the amici supporting his position argue that the District Court's analysis of §659.141 (1) is flawed in three respects: First, the statute assertedly affects only matters of local character that have insufficient interstate attributes to bring federal constitutional limitations into play. Second, the District Court erroneously labeled the statute protectionist legislation and thus incorrectly relied upon the "per se rule of invalidity" identified in Philadelphia v. New Jersey, 437 U.S., at 624. Appellant argues that the statute should be treated as neutral legislation subject to the less stringent standards of Pike v. Bruce Church, Inc., supra, and he argues that it meets this test. Third, the District Court failed to accord proper significance, in appellant's view, to the Bank Holding Company Act of 1956. Appellant argues that the Act grants authority to the States to prohibit out-of-state bank holding companies from owning local subsidiaries that provide bank-related services.

### *A*

The first of these arguments needs only brief mention. We readily accept the submission that, both as a matter of history and as a matter of present commercial reality, banking and related financial activities are of profound local concern. As appellees freely concede, sound financial institutions and honest financial practices are essential to the health of any State's economy and to the well-being of its people. Thus, it is not surprising that ever since the early days of our Republic, the States have chartered banks and have actively regulated their activities.

Nonetheless, it does not follow that these same activities lack important interstate attributes. An impressive array of federal statutes regulating not only the provision of banking services but also the formation of banking organizations, the rendering of investment advice, and the conduct of national investment markets, is substantial evidence to the contrary. We do not understand appellant to dispute the validity of these enactments, all of which rest primarily on Congress' powers under the Commerce Clause. Indeed, appellant's arguments under the Bank Holding Company Act assume the validity of federal regulation in this sphere. This Court has observed that the same interstate attributes that establish Congress' power to regulate commerce also support constitutional limitations on the powers of the States. Philadelphia v. New Jersey, 437 U.S., at 622-623. For present purposes, it is clear that those limitations apply.

### *B*

The contentions that the District Court erred by applying too stringent a standard in defining the limits of Florida's regulatory authority, and that §659.141 (1) is evenhanded local regulation, are more substantial. We nonetheless agree with the District Court's conclusion that this statute is "parochial" in the sense that it overtly prevents foreign enterprises from competing in local markets.

The statute makes the out-of-state location of a bank holding company's principal operations an explicit barrier to the presence of an investment subsidiary within the State. As Bankers Trust's application before the Board itself indicates, it thus prevents competition in local markets by out-of-state firms with the kinds of resources and business interests that make them likely to attempt de novo entry. Appellant virtually concedes this effect, and the circumstances of enactment suggest that it was the legislature's principal objective. . . .

. . . In the District Court and to some extent on this appeal, appellant and supporting amici have argued that the Florida legislation advances several important state policies. Among those that have been specifically identified are an interest in discouraging undue economic concentration in the arena of high finance; an interest in regulating financial practices, presumably to protect local residents from fraud; and an interest in maximizing local control over locally based financial activities. We think that these alleged purposes fail to justify the extent of the burden placed upon out-of-state bank holding companies.

Discouraging economic concentration and protecting the citizenry against fraud are undoubtedly legitimate state interests. But we are not persuaded that these interests justify the heavily disproportionate burden this statute places on bank holding companies that operate principally outside the State. Appellant has demonstrated no basis for an inference that all out-of-state bank holding companies are likely to possess the evils of monopoly power, that they are more likely to do so than their homegrown counterparts, or that they are any more inclined to engage in sharp practices than bank holding companies that are locally based. Nor is there any reason to conclude that outright prohibition of entry, rather than some intermediate form of regulation, is the only effective method of protecting against the presumed evils, particularly when other out-of-state businesses that may be just as large or far-flung are permitted to compete in the local market. We conclude that these asserted state interests simply do not suffice to eliminate §659.141(1)'s apparent constitutional defect.

With regard to the asserted interest in promoting local control over financial institutions, we doubt that the interest itself is entirely clear of any tinge of local parochialism. In almost any Commerce Clause case it would be possible for a State to argue that it has an interest in bolstering local ownership, or wealth, or control of business enterprise. Yet these arguments are at odds with the general principle that the Commerce Clause prohibits a State from using its regulatory power to protect its own citizens from outside competition. In any event, the interest is not well served by the present legislation. The statute, for example, does not restrict out-of-state ownership of local bank holding companies. Nor, as appellant concedes, does it prevent entry by out-of-state entities other than those having the prohibited organizational forms. There is thus no reason to believe that the State's interest in local control, to the extent it legitimately exists, has been significantly or evenhandedly advanced by the statutory means that have been employed.

For these reasons, we conclude that the District Court did not err in holding that §659.141 (1) directly burdens interstate commerce in a manner that contravenes the Commerce Clause's implicit limitation on state power. . . .

*QUESTIONS AND COMMENTS*

What if a state adopted a law prohibiting any bank or bank holding company from offering investment advice in the state if the institution in question controls more than 2.5 percent of nationwide banking assets? The legislature asserts an interest in preventing undue concentration of financial power. Would this pass muster under *BT Investment Managers?* Would the answer depend in part on the structure of the state's banking industry?

## 3. *Interstate Holding Company Acquisitions: Depository Institutions*

Virtually all bank holding companies once operated subsidiary banks only in the state where the bank holding company had its principal place of business. Today, however, most big bank holding companies own banks located in other states. The trend is accelerating: In another decade, chances are that all large bank holding companies will operate subsidiary banks in many states.

Some brief history: The Bank Holding Company Act contained a provision, labeled the "Douglas Amendment," that prohibited the board from approving an application by a banking holding company of a bank located in one state to acquire a bank located in a different state unless the acquisition "was specifically authorized by the statute laws of the State in which such bank is located, by language to that effect and not merely by implication." For many years, no state authorized holding companies from other states to enter their markets. In the early 1980s, however, interstate banking compacts began to form—agreements among states in a region to open their banking markets to each other's bank holding companies. The appeal of these regional compacts was that states could, and did, exclude the states which were home to the big "money center" banks—states such as New York, Illinois, and California. In Northeast Bancorp v. Board of Governors, 472 U.S. 159 (1985), the Supreme Court upheld one of these compacts against a statutory and constitutional challenge, on the ground that it was authorized by the Douglas Amendment.

This decision sparked a massive consolidation of the banking industry into interstate compacts. Over time, the strictures on interstate acquisitions relaxed. States with money center banks were invited into some of the compacts, and many states authorized acquisition of their banks by bank holding companies from any state. Although a few states held out against full-scale interstate banking, the movement towards free bank acquisition throughout the country gathered momentum through the 1980s and early 1990s.

In 1994 Congress essentially recognized the inevitability of interstate banking and junked the old system entirely by repealing the Douglas Amendment. The Riegle-Neal Act provided that the Federal Reserve Board may approve an application of an adequately capitalized and managed bank holding company "to acquire control of, or acquire all or substantially all of the assets of, a bank located in a State other than the home State of such bank holding company, without regard to whether such transaction is prohibited under the law of any State." 12 U.S.C. §1842(d). State age laws are preserved as long as they do not exceed five years. In addition, the Act imposes national and statewide concentration limits and expressly preserves state deposit cap legislation (we discuss these provisions in the following section).

Accordingly, the law now permits full-scale interstate banking by bank holding company acquisitions, subject only to limited impediments. Over time—and probably very quickly—the largest banking firms are going to expand to every state. The pace of change in the U.S. banking industry will accelerate even beyond the torrid velocity of the 1980s and early 1990s. Within a few years, we are likely to see an industry in which the old days of unit or geographically limited banking are nothing but a nostalgic memory.

## 4. *Concentration Rules Under the Riegle-Neal Act*

In the section that follows, we will consider the impact of antitrust law on bank expansion. Before addressing the antitrust law directly, however, we treat a set of concentration rules found in the Riegle-Neal Act of 1994, rules that are intended to limit consolidation in the banking industry. At least one purpose behind these rules is identical to the purpose behind the antitrust law: to ensure vigorous competition and to prevent firms from cooperating with one another to raise prices or restrict output. The structure-performance hypothesis in economics posits that anticompetitive behavior is much easier for firms in highly concentrated industries, since (among other things) the costs of organizing a cartel are much lower when only a few firms dominate the market. The antitrust laws police against excessive concentration, but they do so only with a finding that the firm that results from the merger will have a degree of market power—that is, the power to impose at least a small but significant and nontransitory increase in price above prevailing or likely future levels. Arguably, an alternative way to protect the competitive process is simply to impose aggregate caps on concentration levels, without regard to any need to establish that the resulting firm will be able to exercise market power.

The Riegle-Neal Act of 1994 adopts this approach with respect to interstate bank expansion. The law prohibits any such interstate expansion when the applicant controls, or would control upon consummation of the proposed transaction, more than 10 percent of the total amount in deposits of insured depository institutions in the United States. Essentially, once a banking firm (comprised of all insured depository institutions held by a single holding company) reaches a 10 percent deposit share nationwide, it is no longer allowed to expand through interstate acquisitions or branching but may do so only through intrastate acquisitions or internal growth.

The law imposes statewide limits as well. A banking firm (including all depository institution subsidiaries of a common holding company) may not expand into a state where it already operates a depository institution or a branch if the effect of the acquisition would be to give the firm 30 percent or more of the total deposits of depository institutions in that state. States may by legislation or regulatory action increase the level of permissible deposit concentration beyond the 30 percent specified in the federal law.

In addition, the law expressly disclaims any effect on state deposit caps which limit the amount of statewide deposits that can be controlled by a single entity. States are thus free to impose nondiscriminatory limits on aggregate deposits that are more stringent than the 30 percent statewide limit for interstate acquisitions established by federal law.

## *QUESTIONS AND COMMENTS*

1. Can you analyze the politics behind the various deposit concentration rules described above?

2. Are these concentration limits really justified by antitrust principles? Under conventional antitrust analysis, a market in which no one firm controls more than 10 percent of the action would be viewed as highly unconcentrated, and there would be no thought of regulation. If conventional market power analysis would not support such a stringent limitation on aggregate concentration, what does?

3. Perhaps the 10 percent limitation on aggregate national deposits can be seen not as a device to promote competition but rather as a means for preventing the undue concentration of financial power in a single

hand. Are there dangers to the political system from this kind of concentration of economic power that would not be presented, say, by a relatively concentrated market for petroleum, automobiles, or defense production?

4. If a banking firm is approaching the 10 percent national deposit limit, can it implement any strategies for continuing to expand despite the law? What if it began to cut back on funding itself through deposits in favor of alternative funding devices—say, by issuing commercial paper or other securities on the market? Would this be problematic?

5. The previous question raises a broader issue. Why should the law focus exclusively on measures of concentration in the market for bank deposits? Banks serve other markets, such as those for commercial loans, home mortgage loans, investment advisory services, and so on. The legislation takes no account of concentration levels in these other markets. Should it have done so?

6. Even if the 10 percent national concentration limit is not clearly justifiable as a means to protect competition, can the 30 percent statewide limit be supported on grounds of antitrust policy? Can you see a reason why it might be more efficient to impose a deposit cap than to base the antitrust analysis on the existence of market power in a state?

7. On the other hand, where do you think Congress found the 30 percent figure for statewide concentration? Is there anything talismanic about 30 percent? What about the argument that, under the new law, a bank that obtains a large market share in a state and begins to raise prices will be vulnerable to banking firms from other states that may enter and compete away its profits?

8. Can't the 30 percent statewide cap operate as a form of overt favoritism toward large in-state banks? It appears that nothing in federal law prevents a bank from acquiring more than 30 percent of statewide deposits so long as it does not operate branches or maintain affiliations with out-of-state banks. Is this scenario at all worrisome?

## D. ANTITRUST CONSIDERATIONS

### 1. *Introduction*

Geographic bank expansion inevitably affects the competitive structure of the industry. In large measure the effect is to increase competition. When a bank opens a new branch or a bank holding company establishes a subsidiary bank in a new area, these new institutions enter into competition with existing firms in the market. Consumers benefit because the increased competition enhances service quality and reduces price.

Some forms of geographic bank expansion, however, threaten to reduce competition. A merger of two existing institutions reduces the number of competing or potentially competing firms. The increased concentration in banking, in turn, could cause the resulting firm to possess monopoly power—the ability to affect price by unilateral action—or to possess the ability to form a cartel through explicit or implicit agreements with other firms in the market. Thus if a bank or bank holding company expands through acquisition of, or merger with, an established institution, the transaction is subject to scrutiny under antitrust principles. In this section we consider how these antitrust principles apply to the case of mergers or acquisitions by banks and bank holding companies.

Things would be simple if the banking industry were subject to the same scheme of antitrust regulation that applies to other industries. But this is not quite the case. And although the substantive legal principles enforced by the bank regulatory system are nearly identical to those enforced under the general antitrust system, the unique characteristics of the banking industry gives a special "twist" to these principles as applied to bank and bank holding company mergers.

Banking is subject to a set of special provisions that authorize federal banking agencies to scrutinize proposed transactions on antitrust (and other) grounds. These special antitrust provisions are contained in the Bank Merger Act, 12 U.S.C. §1828(c) (governing mergers between federally insured commercial banks), the Bank Holding Company Act, 12 U.S.C. §1842(c) (governing mergers, consolidations, or acquisitions of banks or bank holding companies by institutions that are or will become bank holding companies), the Change in Bank Control Act, 12 U.S.C. §1817(j) (governing acquisitions of commercial banks or thrifts by individuals or groups of individuals), and the Savings and Loan Holding Company Act, 12 U.S.C. §1730a(e)(1) (governing acquisitions, mergers, or consolidations involving savings and loan holding companies). Mergers of insured savings institutions are governed by an administrative regulation that provides, inter alia, that satisfaction of the Clayton and Sherman antitrust acts is a precondition to approval of the merger.

Although these schemes differ in some respects, they are alike both in overall approach and in many specific provisions. Each provision requires that banking firms wishing to consummate a merger or similar transaction must apply in writing to a designated federal banking agency, which, depending on the type of transaction, may be the Comptroller of the Currency, the Federal Reserve Board, the FDIC, or the OTS. In evaluating applications the designated agency is typically required to consult with other interested state or federal agencies, including the Department of Justice, and to consider, inter alia, the financial and managerial resources and future prospects of the existing and proposed institutions, as well as the convenience and needs of the community to be served.

The Change in Bank Control Act requires the appropriate federal banking agency to consider the financial condition and the "competence, experience, or integrity" of the acquirer. 12 U.S.C. §1817(j)(7)(C) and (D).

Each provision adopts essentially identical substantive antitrust standards. The responsible federal banking agencies are instructed to disapprove applications if they find that the proposed transaction would (1) result in a monopoly, or be in furtherance of any combination or conspiracy to monopolize or to attempt to monopolize the business of banking in any part of the United States, or (2) have an effect in any section of the country that may be substantially to lessen competition or to tend to create a monopoly, or which in any other manner would be in restraint of trade, unless the responsible agency finds that the anticompetitive effects of the proposed transaction are clearly outweighed in the public interest by the probable effect of the transaction in meeting the convenience and needs of the community to be served.

These banking antitrust provisions are borrowed from the two principal antitrust statutes. The first banking law provision closely tracks §2 of the Sherman Act, 15 U.S.C. §2, which provides that "[e]very person who shall monopolize, or attempt to monopolize, or combine or conspire with any other person or persons, to monopolize any part of the trade or commerce among the several States" is guilty of a criminal offense. The second banking law provision contains language from both §7 of the Clayton Act, which prohibits transactions "where in any line of commerce in any section of the country, the effect . . . may be substantially to lessen competition, or to tend to create a monopoly," and §1 of the Sherman Act, which prohibits contracts, combinations or conspiracies "in restraint of trade." Thus in important respects the antitrust standards applicable under the banking laws appear identical to those applicable under the general antitrust laws.

There are differences, however, between the banking law and the general antitrust law. First, the general antitrust law does not require prior regulatory approval for mergers (although prior notification may be required); the depository institution statutes do require such approval (except for the Change in Bank Control Act, which permits transactions to go forward unless disapproved). Thus depository institution mergers are subject to an additional layer of complexity, delay, and expense as compared with nondepository institution acquisitions.

Second, the depository institution statutes contain an explicit "public interest" defense to charges of antitrust violations under those statutes, under which an otherwise anticompetitive merger might be allowed if shown to serve the public interest in other respects; there is no explicit public interest defense to the general antitrust laws.

Third, the Bank Merger Act and the Bank Holding Company Act impose a 30-day stay of the transaction even after agency approval is obtained.

Fourth, the Bank Merger Act and the Bank Holding Company Act provide a "safe harbor" for mergers that have not been challenged within the 30-day stay; such mergers are thereafter immune from antitrust attack by the Justice Department and probably also are immune from challenge by private parties.

*QUESTIONS AND COMMENTS*

1. This Byzantine legal fabric raises obvious policy questions. Why should we have three distinct bodies of law (the McFadden Act, the depository institution merger statutes, and the general antitrust laws) designed to achieve the same regulatory purpose? If we are concerned with preserving competition, why not have just one system of laws designed to prevent undue financial power? And, if we were to pick one system over another, aren't the general antitrust laws better? In short, given that we have a developed body of antitrust law, what is the purpose of the McFadden Act and the depository institution merger statutes?

2. Consider whether there might be public policy principles applicable to bank mergers other than the concern for protecting competition. If so, then perhaps special treatment for banks might be warranted as serving other regulatory goals. Among other special banking policies that might influence the strictness of antitrust scrutiny for bank mergers, consider the following.

a. We have already seen that the restrictions on geographic bank expansion may be based, in part, on a perceived need to preserve "local control" over banking institutions. Perhaps the bank merger statutes should be interpreted to serve a policy of local control also. Can such a policy be interpolated into the general requirement of these statutes that proposed bank mergers be evaluated to determine whether they serve the public "convenience and needs"?

b. We have also seen that the geographical restrictions are often defended as necessary to prevent banks in the United States from growing too large. The concern about bank size undoubtedly reflects a concern for preserving competition, but it has another element as well. Regardless of the effect on competition, size and size alone is often said to be undesirable in the case of banks. Federal Reserve Board Chairman Paul Volcker proposed in 1985, for example, that the nation's 25 largest bank holding companies be prohibited from merging with each other. This proposal clearly was not warranted by competitive concerns alone: Even a merger of the nation's two largest bank holding companies would create a successor corporation controlling only a relatively small percentage of the nation's total banking assets. Chairman Volcker implicitly acknowledged that the national banking market is not highly concentrated when he observed that antitrust laws "do not appear fully responsive" to the need to "encourage continuing diversification of banking resources." See 71 Fed. Res. Bull. 430 (1985).

c. Finally, consider the policy goal of preserving bank safety and soundness. One view of traditional federal banking regulation is that it represented an elaborate cartel to fix prices and divide markets, all perfectly legal and highly effective because administered and enforced by the government. See Scott, The Uncertain Course of Bank Deregulation, 5 Reg. 40 (May/June 1981). Although the validity of the phrase "cartel" may be open to question, few would dispute that the traditional structure of federal banking regulation suppressed some competition in the banking business. The public policy justification for suppressing competition was that some sacrifice in competition was necessary to insulate the banking system from devastating failures and panics. Does this concern for safety and soundness suggest that the antitrust laws might not be applied as strictly to banking as to other industries?

3. Consider the following attack on the special regulatory treatment of bank mergers:

> [i]n the banking industry, deregulation of geographic location, interest rates on deposits, and permissible business activities is progressively removing special protections and subjecting commercial banking to the rigorous discipline imposed by competition. Deregulation should be extended to bank merger law by abolishing the special public interest defense, correcting the judicial fixation on commercial banking as a distinct line of commerce, eliminating the Cerberus-like agency jurisdiction, and removing the thirty-day statute of limitations for antitrust attacks. Although the transition is likely to be painful to the industry, the result will be a stronger financial system that truly serves the financial convenience and needs of the community.

Note, Commercial Bank Mergers: The Case of Procedural and Substantive Deregulation, 95 Harv. L. Rev. 1914 (1982).

4. As part of its overall review of federal bank regulatory structure, the Bush Task Group recommended that

> [t]he Bank Merger Act . . . should be repealed, with all anti-competitive analysis performed by the Department of Justice, utilizing normal antitrust standards. . . . The appropriate supervisory agencies should review merger/acquisition notifications solely for safety and soundness considerations. Notwithstanding the application of normal antitrust standards, [mergers of failed or failing institutions] should continue to be exempt from prior Department of Justice review. The automatic stay and limited period for the Department of Justice to sue under current law should also be retained.

Blueprint for Reform: The Report of the Task Group on Regulation of Financial Services 91 (1984).

5. Even though the substantive standards applicable under the various bank antitrust statutes are identical, or nearly so, the fact that these standards are applied by three separate banking agencies and the Antitrust Division of the Department of Justice creates a danger of conflicting interpretations. In fact the Comptroller of the Currency is commonly thought to adopt a more lenient attitude towards bank mergers than the Federal Reserve Board. See, e.g., United States v. First City National Bank, 386 U.S. 361, 364-365 (1967) (merger application approved by Comptroller but disapproved by Federal Reserve Board). A study of bank merger procedures conducted by the General Accounting Office found as follows:

> Our review of the Federal bank regulators' evaluations of the competitive effects of proposed mergers showed [that] there was no uniformity to the evaluations nor had specific criteria been developed for making the evaluations. This lack of uniformity is most evident in the methods used by regulators to define the relevant market to be used in evaluating the competitive effects of proposed bank mergers. In addition, Federal bank regulators lack uniformity in their application of the line of commerce and potential competition concepts. This overall lack of uniformity has resulted in conflicting decisions by Federal regulators and subsequent "agency shopping" by financial institutions. Agency shopping occurs when parties to a merger seek out the Federal banking regulator possessing the most lenient standards for approving mergers.

General Accounting Office, Report to the Congress: Bank Merger Process Should Be Modernized and Simplified 10 (1982).

6. Can you see a connection between regulations that might impede banking institution mergers (by making them complex, expensive, and protracted) and bank failure policies? Would it be desirable to facilitate the process by which banking assets are transferred through the private sector rather than by means of government intervention after insolvency? Streamlining of the merger process in order to reduce failure costs is recommended in Macey and Miller, Bank Failures, Risk-Monitoring, and the Market for Bank Control, 88 Colum. L. Rev. 1153 (1988). Congress mandated expedited regulatory approval of bank mergers and acquisitions in 1991. Federal Deposit Insurance Corporation Improvement Act §502 (1991).

## 2. *Market Definition*

We now turn to the mechanics of antitrust analysis. The first step in applying antitrust principles to bank mergers and acquisitions is to identify the relevant markets in which competition is or may be impaired. This is standard procedure in antitrust analysis of any sort. As the following selection explains, the goal is to assess whether the merger will facilitate or enhance the exercise of "market power."

## Overview: U.S. Department of Justice and Federal Trade Commission 1992 Horizontal Merger Guidelines

*57 Fed. Reg. 41,552 (1992)*

### Purpose, Underlying Policy Assumptions and Overview

These Guidelines outline the present enforcement policy of the Department of Justice and the Federal Trade Commission (the "Agency") concerning horizontal acquisition and mergers ("mergers"). . . . They describe the analytical framework and specific standards normally used by the Agency in analyzing mergers. By stating its policy as simply and clearly as possible, the Agency hopes to reduce the uncertainty associated with enforcement of the antitrust laws in this area.

Although the Guidelines should improve the predictability of the Agency's merger enforcement policy, it is not possible to remove the exercise of judgment from the evaluation of mergers under the antitrust laws. . . .

### *Purpose and Underlying Policy Assumptions of the Guidelines*

. . . . The unifying theme of the Guidelines is that mergers should not be permitted to create or enhance market power or to facilitate its exercise. Market power to a seller is the ability profitably to maintain prices above competitive levels for a significant period of time. In some circumstances, a sole seller (a "monopolist") of a product with no good substitutes can maintain a selling price that is above the level that would prevail if the market were competitive. Similarly, in some circumstances, where only a few firms account for most of the sales of a product, those firms can exercise market power, perhaps even approximating the performance of a monopolist, by either explicitly or implicitly coordinating their actions. Circumstances also may permit a single firm, not a monopolist, to exercise market power through unilateral or non-coordinated conduct—conduct the success of which does not rely on the concurrence of other firms in the market or on coordinated responses by those firms. In any case, the result of the exercise of market power is a transfer of wealth from buyers to sellers or a misallocation of resources.

Market power also encompasses the ability of a [buyer or buyers] to depress the price paid for a product to a level that is below the competitive price and thereby depress output. The exercise of market power by buyers ("monopsony power") has adverse effects comparable to those associated with the exercise of market power by sellers. In order to assess potential monopsony concerns, the Agency will apply an analytical framework analogous to the framework of these Guidelines.

While challenging competitively harmful mergers, the Agency seeks to avoid unnecessary interference with the larger universe of mergers that are either competitively beneficial or neutral. In implementing this objective, however, the Guidelines reflect the congressional intent that merger enforcement should interdict competitive problems in their incipiency.

### *OVERVIEW*

The Guidelines describe the analytical process that the Agency will employ in determining whether to challenge a horizontal merger. First, the Agency assesses whether the merger would significantly increase concentration and result in a concentrated market, properly defined and measured. Second, the Agency assesses whether the merger, in light of market concentration and other factors that characterize the market, raises concern about potential adverse competitive effects. Third, the Agency assesses whether entry would be timely, likely and sufficient either to deter or to counteract the competitive effects of concern. Fourth, the Agency assesses any efficiency gains that reasonably cannot be achieved by the parties through other means. Finally the Agency assesses whether, but for the merger, either party to the transaction would be likely to fail, causing its assets to exit the market. The process of assessing market concentration, potential adverse competitive effects, entry, efficiency and failure is a tool that allows the Agency to answer the ultimate inquiry in merger analysis: whether the merger is likely to create or enhance market power or to facilitate its exercise.

## MARKET DEFINITION, MEASUREMENT AND CONCENTRATION

### *OVERVIEW*

A merger is unlikely to create or enhance market power or to facilitate its exercise unless it significantly increases concentration and results in a concentrated market, properly defined and measured. Mergers that either do not significantly increase concentration or do not result in a concentrated market ordinarily require no further analysis.

The analytic process described in this section ensures that the Agency evaluates the likely competitive impact of a merger within the context of economically meaningful markets—i.e., markets that could be subject to the exercise of market power. Accordingly, for each product or service (hereafter "product") of each merger firm, the Agency seeks to define a market in which firms could effectively exercise market power if they were able to coordinate their actions.

. . . . A market is defined as a product or group of products and a geographic area in which it is produced or sold such that a hypothetical profit-maximizing firm, not subject to price regulation, that was the only present and future producer or seller of those products in that area likely would impose at least a "small but significant and nontransitory" increase in price, assuming the terms of sale of all other products are held constant. A relevant market is a group of products and a geographic area that is no bigger than necessary to satisfy this test. . . .

Absent price discrimination, a relevant market is described by a product or group of products and a geographic area. In determining whether a hypothetical monopolist would be in a position to exercise market power, it is necessary to evaluate the likely demand responses of consumers to a price increase. A price increase could be made unprofitable by consumers either switching to other products or switching to the same product produced by firms at other locations. The nature and magnitude of these two types of demand responses respectively determine the scope of the product market and the geographic market. . . .

Once defined, a relevant market must be measured in terms of its participants and concentration. Participants include firms currently producing or selling the market's products in the market's geographic area. In addition, participants may include other firms depending on their likely supply responses to a "small but significant and nontransitory" price increase. A firm is viewed as a participant if, in response to a "small but significant and nontransitory" price increase, it likely would enter rapidly into production or sale of a market product in the market's area, without incurring significant sunk costs of entry and exit. Firms likely to make any of these supply responses are considered to be "uncommitted" entrants because their supply response would create new production or sale in the relevant market and because that production or sale could be quickly terminated without significant loss. Uncommitted entrants are capable of making such quick and uncommitted supply responses that they likely influenced the market premerger, would influence it postmerger, and accordingly are considered as market participants at both times. This analysis of market definition and market measurement applies equally to foreign and domestic firms.

## *QUESTIONS AND COMMENTS*

What sorts of evidence would be relevant to determining whether or not a given firm would be able to exercise market power after a merger?

## United States v. Philadelphia National Bank

***374 U.S. 321 (1963)***

Justice BRENNAN delivered the opinion of the Court.

The United States, appellant here, brought this civil action in the

United States District Court for the Eastern District of Pennsylvania under §4 of the Sherman Act, 15 U.S.C. §4, and §15 of the Clayton Act, 15 U.S.C. §25, to enjoin a proposed merger of The Philadelphia National Bank (PNB) and Girard Trust Corn Exchange Bank (Girard), appellees here. The complaint charged violations of §1 of the Sherman Act, 15 U.S.C. §1, and §7 of the Clayton Act, 15 U.S.C. §18. From a judgment for appellees after trial, see 201 F. Supp. 348, the United States appealed to this Court under §2 of the Expediting Act, 15 U.S.C. §29. Probable jurisdiction was noted. 369 U.S. 883. We reverse the judgment of the District Court. We hold that the merger of appellees is forbidden by §7 of the Clayton Act and so must be enjoined; we need not, and therefore do not, reach the further question of alleged violation of §1 of the Sherman Act.

## I. The Facts and Proceedings Below

### A. *THE BACKGROUND: COMMERCIAL BANKING IN THE UNITED STATES*

Because this is the first case which has required this Court to consider the application of the antitrust laws to the commercial banking industry, and because aspects of the industry and of the degree of governmental regulation of it will recur throughout our discussion, we deem it appropriate to begin with a brief background description.

Commercial banking in this country is primarily unit banking. That is, control of commercial banking is diffused throughout a very large number of independent, local banks—13,460 of them in 1960—rather than concentrated in a handful of nationwide banks, as, for example, in England and Germany. There are, to be sure, in addition to the independent banks, some 10,000 branch banks; but branching, which is controlled largely by state law—and prohibited altogether by some States—enables a bank to extend itself only to state lines and often not that far. It is also the case, of course, that many banks place loans and solicit deposits outside their home area. But with these qualifications, it remains true that ours is essentially a decentralized system of community banks. Recent years, however, have witnessed a definite trend toward concentration. Thus, during the decade ending in 1960 the number of commercial banks in the United States declined by 714, despite the chartering of 887 new banks and a very substantial increase in the Nation's credit needs during the period. Of the 1,601 independent banks which thus disappeared, 1,503, with combined total resources of well over $25,000,000,000, disappeared as the result of mergers.

Commercial banks are unique among financial institutions in that they alone are permitted by law to accept demand deposits. This distinctive power gives commercial banking a key role in the national economy.

For banks do not merely deal in, but are actually a source of, money and credit; when a bank makes a loan by crediting the borrower's demand deposit account, it augments the Nation's credit supply. Furthermore, the power to accept demand deposits makes banks the intermediaries in most financial transactions (since transfers of substantial moneys are almost always by check rather than by cash) and, concomitantly, the repositories of very substantial individual and corporate funds. The banks' use of these funds is conditioned by the fact that their working capital consists very largely of demand deposits, which makes liquidity the guiding principle of bank lending and investing policies; thus it is that banks are the chief source of the country's short-term business credit.

Banking operations are varied and complex; "commercial banking" describes a congeries of services and credit devices.[5] But among them the creation of additional money and credit, the management of the checking-account system, and the furnishing of short-term business loans would appear to be the most important. For the proper discharge of these functions is indispensable to a healthy national economy, as the role of bank failures in depression periods attests. It is therefore not surprising that commercial banking in the United States is subject to a variety of governmental controls, state and federal. Federal regulation is the more extensive, and our focus will be upon it. It extends not only to the national banks, i.e., banks chartered under federal law and supervised by the Comptroller of the Currency. For many state banks, as well as virtually all the national banks, are members of the Federal Reserve System (FRS), and more than 95% of all banks are insured by the Federal Deposit Insurance Corporation (FDIC). State member and nonmember insured banks are subject to a federal regulatory scheme almost as elaborate as that which governs the national banks.

The governmental controls of American banking are manifold. First, the Federal Reserve System, through its open-market operations, control of the rediscount rate, and modifications of reserve requirements, regulates the supply of money and credit in the economy and thereby indi-

5. The principal banking "products" are of course various types of credit, for example: unsecured personal and business loans, mortgage loans, loans secured by securities or accounts receivable, automobile installment and consumer goods installment loans, tuition financing, bank credit cards, revolving credit funds. Banking services include: acceptance of demand deposits from individuals, corporations, governmental agencies, and other banks; acceptance of time and savings deposits; estate and trust planning and trusteeship services; lock boxes and safety-deposit boxes; account reconciliation services; foreign department services (acceptances and letters of credit); correspondent services; investment advice. It should be noted that many other institutions are in the business of supplying credit, and so more or less in competition with commercial banks, for example: mutual savings banks, savings and loan associations, credit unions, personal-finance companies, sales-finance companies, private businessmen (through the furnishing of trade credit), factors, direct-lending government agencies, the Post Office, Small Business Investment Organizations, life insurance companies.

rectly regulates the interest rates of bank loans. This is not, however, rate regulation. The Reserve System's activities are only designed to influence the prime, i.e., minimum, bank interest rate. There is no federal control of the maximum, although all banks, state and national, are subject to state usury laws where applicable. See 12 U.S.C. §85. In the range between the maximum fixed by state usury laws and the practical minimum set by federal fiscal policies (there is no law against undercutting the prime rate but bankers seldom do), bankers are free to price their loans as they choose. Moreover, charges for other banking services, such as service charges for checking privileges, are free of governmental regulation, state or federal.

Entry, branching, and acquisitions are covered by a network of state and federal statutes. A charter for a new bank, state or national, will not be granted unless the invested capital and management of the applicant, and its prospects for doing sufficient business to operate at a reasonable profit, give adequate protection against undue competition and possible failure. Failure to meet these standards may cause the FDIC to refuse an application for insurance, and may cause the FDIC, Federal Reserve Board (FRB), and Comptroller to refuse permission to branch to insured, member, and national banks, respectively. Permission to merge, consolidate, acquire assets, or assume liabilities may be refused by the agencies on the same grounds. Furthermore, national banks appear to be subject to state geographical limitations on branching.

Banks are also subject to a number of specific provisions aimed at ensuring sound banking practices. For example, member banks of the Federal Reserve System may not pay interest on demand deposits, may not invest in common stocks or hold for their own account investment securities of any one obligor in excess of 10% of the bank's unimpaired capital and surplus, and may not pay interest on time or savings deposits above the rate fixed by the FRB. The payment of interest on deposits by nonmember insured banks is also federally regulated. In the case of national banks, the 10% limit on the obligations of a single obligor includes loans as well as investment securities. Pennsylvania imposes the same limitations upon banks chartered under its laws, such as Girard.

But perhaps the most effective weapon of federal regulation of banking is the broad visitatorial power of federal bank examiners. Whenever the agencies deem it necessary, they may order "a thorough examination of all the affairs of the bank," whether it be a member of the FRS or a nonmember insured bank. Such examinations are frequent and intensive. In addition, the banks are required to furnish detailed periodic reports of their operations to the supervisory agencies. In this way the agencies maintain virtually a day-to-day surveillance of the American banking system. And should they discover unsound banking practices, they are equipped with a formidable array of sanctions. If in the judgment of the FRB a member bank is making "undue use of bank credit," the

Board may suspend the bank from the use of the credit facilities of the FRS. The FDIC has an even more formidable power. If it finds "unsafe or unsound practices" in the conduct of the business of any insured bank, it may terminate the bank's insured status. Such involuntary termination severs the bank's membership in the FRS, if it is a state bank, and throws it into receivership if it is a national bank. Lesser, but nevertheless drastic, sanctions include publication of the results of bank examinations. As a result of the existence of this panoply of sanctions, recommendations by the agencies concerning banking practices tend to be followed by bankers without the necessity of formal compliance proceedings.

Federal supervision of banking has been called "[p]robably the outstanding example in the federal government of regulation of an entire industry through methods of supervision. . . . The system may be one of the most successful [systems of economic regulation], if not the most successful." [1 Davis, Administrative Law (1958), §4.04, at 247.] To the efficacy of this system we may owe, in part, the virtual disappearance of bank failures from the American economic scene.

### *B. THE PROPOSED MERGER OF PNB AND GIRARD*

The Philadelphia National Bank and Girard Trust Corn Exchange Bank are, respectively, the second and third largest of the 42 commercial banks with head offices in the Philadelphia metropolitan area, which consists of the City of Philadelphia and its three contiguous counties in Pennsylvania. The home country of both banks is the city itself; Pennsylvania law, however, permits branching into the counties contiguous to the home county, and both banks have offices throughout the four-county area. PNB, a national bank, has assets of over $1,000,000,000, making it (as of 1959) the twenty-first largest bank in the Nation. Girard, a state bank, is a member of the FRS and is insured by the FDIC; it has assets of about $750,000,000. Were the proposed merger to be consummated, the resulting bank would be the largest in the four-county area, with (approximately) 36% of the area banks' total assets, 36% of deposits, and 34% of net loans. It and the second largest (First Pennsylvania Bank and Trust Company, now the largest) would have between them 59% of the total assets, 58% of deposits, and 58% of the net loans, while after the merger the four largest banks in the area would have 78% of total assets, 77% of deposits, and 78% of net loans.

The present size of both PNB and Girard is in part the result of mergers. Indeed, the trend toward concentration is noticeable in the Philadelphia area generally, in which the number of commercial banks has declined from 108 in 1947 to the present 42. Since 1950, PNB has acquired nine formerly independent banks and Girard six; and these acquisitions have accounted for 59% and 85% of the respective banks' asset growth during the period, 63% and 91% of their deposit growth, and 12% and 37% of their loan growth. During this period, the seven largest banks in the area increased their combined share of the area's total commercial bank resources from about 61% to about 90%.

In November 1960 the boards of directors of the two banks approved a proposed agreement for their consolidation under the PNB charter. By the terms of the agreement, PNB's stockholders were to retain their share certificates, which would be deemed to represent an equal number of shares in the consolidated bank, while Girard's stockholders would surrender their shares in exchange for shares in the consolidated bank, receiving 1.2875 such shares for each Girard share. Such a consolidation is authorized, subject to the approval of the Comptroller of the Currency, by 12 U.S.C. (1958 ed., Supp. IV) §215. But under the Bank Merger Act of 1960, 12 U.S.C. (1963 ed., Supp. IV) §1828 (c), the Comptroller may not give his approval until he has received reports from the other two banking agencies and the Attorney General respecting the probable effects of the proposed transaction on competition. All three reports advised that the proposed merger would have substantial anticompetitive effects in the Philadelphia metropolitan area. However, on February 24, 1961, the Comptroller approved the merger. No opinion was rendered at that time. But as required by §1828(c), the Comptroller explained the basis for his decision to approve the merger in a statement to be included in his annual report to Congress. As to effect upon competition, he reasoned that "[s]ince there will remain an adequate number of alternative sources of banking service in Philadelphia, and in view of the beneficial effects of this consolidation upon international and national competition it was concluded that the over-all effect upon competition would not be unfavorable." He also stated that the consolidated bank "would be far better able to serve the convenience and needs of its community by being of material assistance to its city and state in their efforts to attract new industry and to retain existing industry." The day after the Comptroller approved the merger, the United States commenced the present action. No steps have been taken to consummate the merger pending the outcome of this litigation.

### *C. THE TRIAL AND THE DISTRICT COURT'S DECISION*

The Government's case in the District Court relied chiefly on statistical evidence bearing upon market structure and on testimony by economists and bankers to the effect that, notwithstanding the intensive governmental regulation of banking, there was a substantial area for the free play of competitive forces; that concentration of commercial banking, which the proposed merger would increase, was inimical to that free play; that the principal anticompetitive effect of the merger would be felt in the area in which the banks had their offices, thus making the four-county metropolitan area the relevant geographical market; and that commercial banking was the relevant product market. The defendants, in addition to offering contrary evidence on these points, attempted to show business justifications for the merger. They conceded that both banks were economically strong and had sound management, but offered the testimony of bankers to show that the resulting bank, with its greater prestige and increased lending limit,[9] would be better able to compete with large out-of-state (particularly New York) banks, would attract new business to Philadelphia, and in general would promote the economic development of the metropolitan area.[10] . . .

[The Court concluded that §7 of the Clayton Act applies to bank mergers.]

### III. The Lawfulness of the Proposed Merger Under Section 7

The statutory test is whether the effect of the merger "may be substantially to lessen competition" "in any line of commerce in any section of the country." We analyzed the test in detail in Brown Shoe Co. v. United States, 370 U.S. 294, and that analysis need not be repeated or extended here, for the instant case presents only a straightforward problem of application to particular facts.

We have no difficulty in determining the "line of commerce" (relevant product or services market) and "section of the country" (relevant geographical market) in which to appraise the probable competitive effects of appellees' proposed merger. We agree with the District Court that the cluster of products (various kinds of credit) and services (such as checking accounts and trust administration) denoted by the term "commercial banking," see note 5, supra, composes a distinct line of commerce. Some commercial banking products or services are so distinctive that they are entirely free of effective competition from products or services of other financial institutions; the checking account is in this category.

9. See 12 U.S.C. §84. The resulting bank would have a lending limit of $15,000,000, of which $1,000,000 would not be attributable to the merger but to unrelated accounting factors.

10. There was evidence that Philadelphia, although it ranks fourth or fifth among the Nation's urban areas in terms of general commercial activity, ranks only ninth in terms of the size of its largest bank, and that some large business firms which have their head offices in Philadelphia must seek elsewhere to satisfy their banking needs because of the inadequate lending limits of Philadelphia's banks; First Pennsylvania and PNB, currently the two largest banks in Philadelphia, each have a lending limit of $8,000,000. Girard's is $6,000,000.

Appellees offered testimony that the merger would enable certain economies of scale, specifically, that it would enable the formation of a more elaborate foreign department that either bank is presently able to maintain. But this attempted justification, which was not mentioned by the District Court in its opinion and has not been developed with any fullness before this Court, we consider abandoned.

Others enjoy such cost advantages as to be insulated within a broad range from substitutes furnished by other institutions. For example, commercial banks compete with small-loan companies in the personal-loan market; but the small-loan companies' rates are invariably much higher than the banks', in part, it seems, because the companies' working capital consists in substantial part of bank loans. Finally, there are banking facilities which, although in terms of cost and price they are freely competitive with the facilities provided by other financial institutions, nevertheless enjoy a settled consumer preference, insulating them, to a marked degree, from competition; this seems to be the case with savings deposits. In sum, it is clear that commercial banking is a market "sufficiently inclusive to be meaningful in terms of trade realities." Crown Zellerbach Corp. v. Federal Trade Comm'n, 296 F.2d 800, 811 (C.A. 9th Cir. 1961).

We part company with the District Court on the determination of the appropriate "section of the country." The proper question to be asked in this case is not where the parties to the merger do business or even where they compete, but where, within the area of competitive overlap, the effect of the merger on competition will be direct and immediate. This depends upon "the geographic structure of supplier-customer relations." Kaysen and Turner, Antitrust Policy (1959), 102. In banking, as in most service industries, convenience of location is essential to effective competition. Individuals and corporations typically confer the bulk of their patronage on banks in their local community; they find it impractical to conduct their banking business at a distance. The factor of inconvenience localizes banking competition as effectively as high transportation costs in other industries. Therefore, since, as we recently said in a related context, the "area of effective competition in the known line of commerce must be charted by careful selection of the market area in which the seller operates, *and to which the purchaser can practicably turn for supplies,*" Tampa Elec. Co. v. Nashville Coal Co., 365 U.S. 320, 327 (emphasis supplied), the four-county area in which appellees' offices are located would seem to be the relevant geographical market. In fact, the vast bulk of appellees' business originates in the four-county area.[36] Theoretically,

36. The figures for PNB and Girard respectively are: 54% and 63% of the dollar volume of their commercial and industrial loans originate in the four-county area; 75% and 70%, personal loans; 74% and 84%, real estate loans; 41% and 62%, lines of credit; 94% and 72%, personal trusts; 81% and 94%, time and savings deposits; 56% and 77%, demand deposits; 93% and 87%, demand deposits of individuals. Actually, these figures may be too low. The evidence discloses that most of the business done outside the area is with large borrowers and large depositors; appellees do not, by and large, deal with small businessmen and average individuals not located in the four-county area. For example, of appellees' combined total business demand deposits under $10,000, 94% originate in the four-county area. This reinforces the thesis that the smaller the customer; the smaller is his banking market geographically.

The appellees concede that the four-county area has sufficient commercial importance to qualify as a "section of the country" within the meaning of §7.

we should be concerned with the possibility that bank offices on the perimeter of the area may be in effective competition with bank offices within; actually, this seems to be a factor of little significance.[37]

We recognize that the area in which appellees have their offices does not delineate with perfect accuracy an appropriate "section of the country" in which to appraise the effect of the merger upon competition. Large borrowers and large depositors, the record shows, may find it practical to do a large part of their banking business outside their home community; very small borrowers and depositors may, as a practical matter, be confined to bank offices in their immediate neighborhood; and customers of intermediate size, it would appear, deal with banks within an area intermediate between these extremes. So also, some banking services are evidently more local in nature than others. But that in banking the relevant geographical market is a function of each separate customer's economic scale means simply that a workable compromise must be found: some fair intermediate delineation which avoids the indefensible extremes of drawing the market either so expansively as to make the effect of the merger upon competition seem insignificant, because only the very largest bank customers are taken into account in defining the market, or so narrowly as to place appellees in different markets, because only the smallest customers are considered. We think that the four-county Philadelphia metropolitan area, which state law apparently recognizes as a meaningful banking community in allowing Philadelphia banks to branch within it, and which would seem roughly to delineate the area in which bank customers that are neither very large nor very small find it practical to do their banking business, is a more appropriate "section of the country" in which to appraise the instant merger than any larger or smaller or different area. We are helped to

37. Appellees suggest not that bank offices skirting the four-county area provide meaningful alternatives to bank customers within the area, but that such alternatives are provided by large banks, from New York and elsewhere, which solicit business in the Philadelphia area. There is no evidence of the amount of business done in the area by banks with offices outside the area; it may be that such figures are unobtainable. In any event, it would seem from the local orientation of banking insofar as smaller customers are concerned that competition from outside the area would only be important to the larger borrowers and depositors. If so, the four-county area remains a valid geographical market in which to assess the anticompetitive effect of the proposed merger upon the banking facilities available to the smaller customer—a perfectly good "line of commerce," in light of Congress' evident concern, in enacting the 1950 amendments to §7, with preserving small business. As a practical matter the small businessman can only satisfy his credit needs at local banks. To be sure, there is still some artificiality in deeming the four-county area the relevant "section of the country" so far as businessmen located near the perimeter are concerned. But such fuzziness would seem inherent in any attempt to delineate the relevant geographical market. And it is notable that outside the four-county area, appellees' business rapidly thins out. Thus, the other six counties of the Delaware Valley account for only 2% of appellees' combined individual demand deposits; 4%, demand deposits of partnerships and corporations; 7%, loans; 2%, savings deposits; 4%, business time deposits.

this conclusion by the fact that the three federal banking agencies regard the area in which banks have their offices as an "area of effective competition." Not only did the FDIC and FRB, in the reports they submitted to the Comptroller of the Currency in connection with appellees' application for permission to merge, so hold, but the Comptroller, in his statement approving the merger, agreed: "With respect to the effect upon competition, there are three separate levels and effective areas of competition involved. These are the national level for national accounts, the regional or sectional area, and the local area of the City of Philadelphia and the immediately surrounding area."

Having determined the relevant market, we come to the ultimate question under §7: whether the effect of the merger "may be substantially to lessen competition" in the relevant market. Clearly, this is not the kind of question which is susceptible of a ready and precise answer in most cases. It requires not merely an appraisal of the immediate impact of the merger upon competition, but a prediction of its impact upon competitive conditions in the future; this is what is meant when it is said that the amended §7 was intended to arrest anticompetitive tendencies in their "incipiency." Such a prediction is sound only if it is based upon a firm understanding of the structure of the relevant market; yet the relevant economic data are both complex and elusive. And unless businessmen can assess the legal consequences of a merger with some confidence, sound business planning is retarded. So also, we must be alert to the danger of subverting congressional intent by permitting a too-broad economic investigation. And so in any case in which it is possible, without doing violence to the congressional objective embodied in §7, to simplify the test of illegality, the courts ought to do so in the interest of sound and practical judicial administration. This is such a case.

We noted in Brown Shoe Co., supra, at 315, that "[t]he dominant theme pervading congressional consideration of the 1950 amendments [to §7] was a fear of what was considered to be a rising tide of economic concentration in the American economy." This intense congressional concern with the trend toward concentration warrants dispensing, in certain cases, with elaborate proof of market structure, market behavior, or probable anticompetitive effects. Specifically, we think that a merger which produces a firm controlling an undue percentage share of the relevant market, and results in a significant increase in the concentration of firms in that market, is so inherently likely to lessen competition substantially that it must be enjoined in the absence of evidence clearly showing that the merger is not likely to have such anticompetitive effects.

Such a test lightens the burden of proving illegality only with respect to mergers whose size makes them inherently suspect in light of Congress' design in §7 to prevent undue concentration. Furthermore, the test is fully consonant with economic theory. That "[c]ompetition is likely to be greatest when there are many sellers, none of which has any significant market share," is common ground among most economists, and was undoubtedly a premise of congressional reasoning about the antimerger statute.

The merger of appellees will result in a single bank's controlling at least 30% of the commercial banking business in the four-county Philadelphia metropolitan area. Without attempting to specify the smallest market share which would still be considered to threaten undue concentration, we are clear that 30% presents that threat. Further, whereas presently the two largest banks in the area (First Pennsylvania and PNB) control between them approximately 44% of the area's commercial banking business, the two largest after the merger (PNB-Girard and First Pennsylvania) will control 59%. Plainly, we think, this increase of more than 33% in concentration must be regarded as significant.

Our conclusion that these percentages raise an inference that the effect of the contemplated merger of appellees may be substantially to lessen competition is not an arbitrary one, although neither the terms of §7 nor the legislative history suggests that any particular percentage share was deemed critical. The House Report states that the tests of illegality under amended §7 "are intended to be similar to those which the courts have applied in interpreting the same language as used in other sections of the Clayton Act." H.R. Rep. No. 1191, 81st Cong., 1st Sess. 8. Accordingly, we have relied upon decisions under these other sections in applying §7. . . .

There is nothing in the record of this case to rebut the inherently anticompetitive tendency manifested by these percentages. There was, to be sure, testimony by bank officers to the effect that competition among banks in Philadelphia was vigorous and would continue to be vigorous after the merger. We think, however, that the District Court's reliance on such evidence was misplaced. This lay evidence on so complex an economic-legal problem as the substantiality of the effect of this merger upon competition was entitled to little weight, in view of the witnesses' failure to give concrete reasons for their conclusions.

Of equally little value, we think, are the assurances offered by appellees' witnesses that customers dissatisfied with the services of the resulting bank may readily turn to the 40 other banks in the Philadelphia area. In every case short of outright monopoly, the disgruntled customer has alternatives; even in tightly oligopolistic markets, there may be small firms operating. A fundamental purpose of amending §7 was to arrest the trend toward concentration, the *tendency* to monopoly, before the customer's alternatives disappeared through merger, and that purpose would be ill-served if the law stayed its hand until 10, or 20, or 30 more Philadelphia banks were absorbed. This is not a fanciful eventuality, in view of the strong trend toward mergers evident in the area; and we might note also that entry of new competitors into the banking field is far from easy.

So also, we reject the position that commercial banking, because it is subject to a high degree of governmental regulation, or because it deals in the intangibles of credit and services rather than in the manufacture or sale of tangible commodities, is somehow immune from the anticompetitive effects of undue concentration. Competition among banks exists at every level—price, variety of credit arrangements, convenience of location, attractiveness of physical surroundings, credit information, investment advice, service charges, personal accommodations, advertising, miscellaneous special and extra services—and it is keen; on this appellees' own witnesses were emphatic. There is no reason to think that concentration is less inimical to the free play of competition in banking than in other service industries. On the contrary, it is in all probability more inimical. For example, banks compete to fill the credit needs of businessmen. Small businessmen especially are, as a practical matter, confined to their locality for the satisfaction of their credit needs. If the number of banks in the locality is reduced, the vigor of competition for filling the marginal small business borrower's needs is likely to diminish. At the same time, his concomitantly greater difficulty in obtaining credit is likely to put him at a disadvantage vis-à-vis larger businesses with which he competes. In this fashion, concentration in banking accelerates concentration generally.

We turn now to three affirmative justifications which appellees offer for the proposed merger. The first is that only through mergers can banks follow their customers to the suburbs and retain their business. This justification does not seem particularly related to the instant merger, but in any event it has no merit. There is an alternative to the merger route: the opening of new branches in the areas to which the customers have moved—so-called de novo branching. Appellees do not contend that they are unable to expand thus, by opening new offices rather than acquiring existing ones, and surely one premise of an antimerger statute such as §7 is that corporate growth by internal expansion is socially preferable to growth by acquisition.

Second, it is suggested that the increased lending limit of the resulting bank will enable it to compete with the large out-of-state banks, particularly the New York banks, for very large loans. We reject this application of the concept of "countervailing power." If anticompetitive effects in one market could be justified by procompetitive consequences in another, the logical upshot would be that every firm in an industry could, without violating §7, embark on a series of mergers that would make it in the end as large as the industry lender. For if all the commercial banks in the Philadelphia area merged into one, it would be smaller than the largest bank in New York City. This is not a case, plainly, where two small firms in a market propose to merge in order to be able to compete more successfully with the leading firms in that market. Nor is it a case in which lack of adequate banking facilities is causing hardships to individuals or businesses in the community. The present two largest banks in Philadelphia have lending limits of $8,000,000 each. The only businesses located in the Philadelphia area which find such limits inadequate are large enough readily to obtain bank credit in other cities.

This brings us to appellees' final contention, that Philadelphia needs a bank larger than it now has in order to bring business to the area and stimulate its economic development. We are clear, however, that a merger the effect of which "may be substantially to lessen competition" is not saved because, on some ultimate reckoning of social or economic debits and credits, it may be deemed beneficial. A value choice of such magnitude is beyond the ordinary limits of judicial competence, and in any event has been made for us already, by Congress when it enacted the amended §7. Congress determined to preserve our traditionally competitive economy. It therefore proscribed anticompetitive mergers, the benign and the malignant alike, fully aware, we must assume, that some price might have to be paid.

In holding as we do that the merger of appellees would violate §7 and must therefore be enjoined, we reject appellees' pervasive suggestion that application of the procompetitive policy of §7 to the banking industry will have dire, although unspecified, consequences for the national economy. Concededly, PNB and Girard are healthy and strong; they are not undercapitalized or overloaned; they have no management problems; the Philadelphia area is not overbanked; ruinous competition is not in the offing. Section 7 does not mandate cut-throat competition in the banking industry, and does not exclude defenses based on dangers to liquidity or solvency, if to avert them a merger is necessary. It does require, however, that the forces of competition be allowed to operate within the broad framework of governmental regulation of the industry. The fact that banking is a highly regulated industry critical to the Nation's welfare makes the play of competition not less important but more so. At the price of some repetition, we note that if the businessman is denied credit because his banking alternatives have been eliminated by mergers, the whole edifice of an entrepreneurial system is threatened; if the costs of banking services and credit are allowed to become excessive by the absence of competitive pressures, virtually all costs, in our credit economy, will be affected; and unless competition is allowed to fulfill its role as an economic regulator in the banking industry, the result may well be even more governmental regulation. Subject to narrow qualifications, it is surely the case that competition is our fundamental national economic policy, offering as it does the only alternative to the cartelization or governmental regimentation of large portions of the economy. There is no warrant for declining to enforce it in the instant case.

The judgment of the District Court is reversed and the case remanded with direction to enter judgment enjoining the proposed merger.

It is so ordered.

Justice WHITE took no part in the consideration or decision of this case.

[Justices Harlan, Stewart, and Goldburg dissented on the ground that §7 of the Clayton Act did not apply to bank mergers.]

*QUESTIONS AND COMMENTS*

Is Justice Brennan's model of the banking market valid today? Consider the following statements in the majority opinion: (1) "[c]ommercial banking in this country is primarily unit banking," (2) "[c]ommercial banks are unique among financial institutions in that they alone are permitted by law to accept demand deposits," (3) "[t]o the efficacy of [the system of federal banking regulation] we may owe, in part, the virtual disappearance of bank failures from the American scene," (4) "[s]ome commercial banking products or services are so distinctive that they are entirely free of effective competition from products or services of other financial institutions; the checking account is in this category," and (5) "entry of new competitors into the banking field is far from easy." If these statements are not consistent with present-day realities, how should this affect the interpretation of the antitrust laws?

### a. Product Market Definition

The *Philadelphia Bank* case determined that the relevant "line of commerce," or product market, for commercial banking is "the cluster of products (various kinds of credit) and services (such as checking accounts and trust administration) denoted by the term 'commercial banking.'" How workable is this "cluster" approach, especially today when the differences between banks and other institutions are rapidly breaking down? Consider in this regard whether it makes sense today to restrict the line of commerce to commercial banks only, or whether competition from thrift institutions should be included as well.

## United States v. Connecticut National Bank

***418 U.S. 656 (1974)***

Justice POWELL delivered the opinion of the Court.

This case concerns the legality of a proposed consolidation of two nationally chartered commercial banks operating in adjoining regions of Connecticut. The United States brought a civil antitrust action challenging the consolidation under §7 of the Clayton Act, 38 Stat. 731, as amended,

15 U.S.C. § 18. Following a lengthy trial and on the basis of extensive findings and conclusions, the United States District Court for the District of Connecticut dismissed the Government's complaint. 362 F. Supp. 240 (1973). The Government brought a direct appeal pursuant to the Expediting Act, 32 Stat. 823, as amended, 15 U.S.C. §29, and the Court noted probable jurisdiction, 414 U.S. 1127 (1974).

The banks desiring to consolidate, Connecticut National Bank (CNB) and First New Haven National Bank (FNH), have offices in contiguous areas in the south-western portion of Connecticut. CNB maintains its headquarters in the town of Bridgeport, which is situated on the Long Island Sound approximately 60 miles from New York City. CNB is the fourth largest commercial bank in the State. At year-end 1972, it held 6.2% of the deposits in commercial banks in Connecticut. CNB operates 51 offices located in Bridgeport and nearby towns in the extreme southwest section of Connecticut.

FNH has its headquarters in the town of New Haven, approximately 19 miles to the northeast of Bridgeport along the Long Island Sound. FNH is the eighth largest commercial bank in Connecticut. At the end of 1972, it held 4.1% of commercial bank deposits in the State. FNH operates 22 bank offices in New Haven and surrounding towns.

In Connecticut as a whole at the end of 1971, the five largest commercial banks held 61% and the 10 largest commercial banks held 83% of the deposits in such banks in the State. Two large commercial banks based in Hartford, Connecticut Bank & Trust Co. of Hartford and Hartford National Bank, operate essentially statewide. At year-end 1972, they had 41% of the total commercial bank deposits held by Connecticut banks.

CNB and FNH both have offices and are in direct competition in a so-called "four-town area" located between Bridgeport and New Haven. The banks assured the District Court, however, that in implementing the consolidation they would divest themselves of a sufficient number of offices in the four-town area to render insignificant the degree of overlap of their areas of actual operation. The District Court held that this divestiture plan eliminated any antitrust difficulties presented by the merger of direct competitors. 362 F. Supp., at 268-270, 286. The United States has not pursued the point on appeal. Accordingly, the case has been presented to us strictly as a geographic market extension merger on the part of both banks. The proposed consolidation would join the banks under FNH's national charter (with headquarters in Bridgeport). It would have no effect on the number of banks operating in either the Bridgeport or New Haven area. . . .

### I

The District Court concluded that the appropriate "line of commerce" within the meaning of §7 included both commercial banks and savings banks. 362 F. Supp., at 281. The court recognized that its conclusion departed from this Court's holdings in, e.g., United States v. Phillipsburg National Bank, 399 U.S. 350, 359-362 (1970), and United States v. Philadelphia National Bank, 374 U.S. 321, 356-357 (1963). But in the District Court's view the pronouncements in *Phillipsburg National Bank* and *Philadelphia National Bank* "were not intended to be ironclad, hard and fast rules which require a court to don blinders to block out the true competitive situation existing in every set of circumstances." 362 F. Supp., at 280.

Several factors led the District Court to the conclusions that "savings banks are in direct and substantial competition with commercial banks in providing product-services to the banking consumers in Connecticut . . . ," and that "[t]he cold, hard realities of the situation are that savings and commercial banks are fierce competitors in this state." Ibid. The court noted that under state law savings banks in the near future will be permitted to offer one of the traditional indicia of commercial banks, personal checking accounts. It pointed out that savings banks in Connecticut compete with commercial banks for real estate mortgages, personal loans, IPC (individual, partnership, and corporate) deposits, and, the court found, commercial loans. 362 F. Supp., at 280. It cited United States v. Continental Can Co., 378 U.S. 441 (1964), for the proposition that "complete industry overlap" is not required to establish a relevant line of commerce under §7. 362 F. Supp., at 281. It also relied on the omission of the "in any line of commerce" phrase from the Bank Merger Act of 1966, 12 U.S.C. §1828(c)(5)(B), an Act which in other essential respects tracks the language of §7 of the Clayton Act. Finally, it distinguished *Philadelphia National Bank,* supra, and *Phillipsburg National Bank,* supra, by pointing to the absence of significant competition by savings banks in the relevant geographic markets in those cases. 362 F. Supp., at 281. The District Court's conclusion on the appropriate line of commerce caused it to "shade" (i.e., to reduce) the Government's concentration ratios to take into account the presence of savings banks. Id., at 285.

We are in complete agreement with the District Court that *Phillipsburg National Bank* and *Philadelphia National Bank* do not require a court to blind itself to economic realities. Similarly, we have no doubt on this record that savings banks and commercial banks in Connecticut are "fierce competitors," see 362 F. Supp., at 280, to the degree that they offer identical or essentially fungible services. The District Court was also correct that "complete inter-industry competitive overlap need not be shown." *Continental Can Co.,* supra, at 457. As the Court declared in *Continental Can,* "we must recognize meaningful competition where it is found to exist." 378 U.S., at 449. Nonetheless, we hold for several reasons that the District Court was mistaken in including both savings and commercial banks in the same product market for purposes of this case.

Two of the District Court's reasons may be dealt with briefly. The court erred as a matter of law in concluding that the absence of a "line of commerce" phrase in the Bank Merger Act of 1966 alters traditional standards under §7 of the Clayton Act for defining the relevant product market in a bank merger case. United States v. Third National Bank, 390 U.S. 171, 182 n. 15 (1968). See *Phillipsburg National Bank,* 399 U.S., at 359-362. Moreover, the absence of significant competition from savings banks in *Philadelphia National Bank, supra,* and *Phillipsburg National Bank, supra,* is not determinative. The commercial banks in both of those cases faced significant competition from savings and loan associations and other credit institutions. See, e.g., 374 U.S., at 357 n. 34; United States v. Phillipsburg National Bank, 306 F. Supp. 645, 649 (NJ 1969). The Court in both instances nevertheless viewed the business of commercial banking as sufficiently distinct from other credit institutions to merit treatment as a separate "line of commerce" under §7. Analogous distinctions, although perhaps not as sharply defined, are controlling here.

We believe that the District Court overestimated the degree of competitive overlap that in fact exists between savings banks and commercial banks in Connecticut. To be sure, there is a large measure of similarity between the services marketed by the two categories of banks.[3] In our view, however, the overlap is not sufficient at this stage in the development of savings banks in Connecticut to treat them together with commercial banks in the instant case. Despite the strides that savings banks in that State have made toward parity with commercial banks, the latter continue to be able to provide a cluster of services that the former cannot, particularly with regard to commercial customers, and this Court has repeatedly held that it is the unique cluster of services provided by commercial banks that sets them apart for purposes of §7.

The Court declared in *Phillipsburg National Bank,* supra, at 360:

> *Philadelphia Bank* emphasized that it is the cluster of products and services that full-service banks offer that as a matter of trade reality makes commercial banking a distinct line of commerce. Commercial banks are the only financial institutions in which a wide variety of financial products

3. As we have noted, the District Court identified some of the services offered by both savings and commercial banks, including real estate mortgages, personal loans, and time deposits. As the District Court put it in another context, it would be "ostrich-like," 362 F. Supp., at 254, to assume that the two types of banks are not in direct and vigorous competition with regard to the services they share or are not viewed by many bank customers as more or less fungible for purposes of those services. That savings and commercial banks are direct competitors in some submarkets, however, is not the end of the inquiry, as *Phillipsburg* makes clear. Ibid.

> and services—some unique to commercial banking and others not—are gathered together in one place. The clustering of financial products and services in banks facilitates convenient access to them for all banking customers. . . .

(Emphasis in original.) From the vantage point of at least one significant consumer of bank services—the commercial enterprise—commercial banks in Connecticut offer a "cluster of products and services" that their savings bank counterparts do not. The facts of this case indicate that the differences in what commercial banks in the State can offer to that important category of bank customers are sufficient to establish commercial banking as a distinct line of commerce.

The District Court concluded that "meaningful competition" existed between commercial and savings banks for commercial loans. 362 F. Supp., at 280. This conclusion is not supported by the record. Commercial loans, generally speaking, are relatively short-term loans to business enterprises of all sizes, usually for purposes of inventory or working capital. At the end of 1971 commercial banks in Connecticut had outstanding $1.03 billion in commercial loans. Savings banks, by comparison, had $26 million in such loans at that time. The disparity in these figures demonstrates that the commercial bank-loan business in Connecticut is controlled almost exclusively by commercial banks. Moreover, commercial banks in the State offer credit-card plans, loans for securities purchases, trust services, investment services, computer and account services, and letters of credit. Savings banks do not.

It is true that under state law savings banks soon will be able to provide some checking account services. Conn. Pub. Act No. 73-195 (May 14, 1973). This will increase the degree of direct competition between savings banks and commercial banks, because demand deposits have traditionally been a unique attribute of the latter institutions. But even this new authority for savings banks will not allow them to serve commercial customers, who constitute a significant percentage of the clientele of commercial banks. The state statute empowering savings banks to offer demand deposits forbids those banks from marketing the service to anyone "for the purpose of, or in connection with, the carrying on of any business, trade, occupation or profession." Id. §§1(a), 5. Thus, under the new Act, savings banks will be restricted to offering personal checking accounts. Id., §2.

We do not say, and *Phillipsburg National Bank*, supra, and *Philadelphia National Bank*, supra, do not say, that in a case involving a merger of commercial banks a court may never consider savings banks and commercial banks as operating in the same line of commerce, no matter how similar their services and economic behavior. At some stage in the development of savings banks it will be unrealistic to distinguish them from commercial banks for purposes of the Clayton Act. In Connecticut, that point may well be reached when and if savings banks become significant participants in the marketing of bank services to commercial enterprises. But, in adherence to the tests set forth in our earlier bank merger cases, which we are constrained to follow, we hold that such a point has not yet been reached. Accordingly, on remand the District Court should treat commercial banking as the relevant product market. . . .

*QUESTIONS AND COMMENTS*

1. Observe that the Court did not rule out any possibility that thrifts might someday be included in the line of commerce; it only said "not now." But if not now, when? The evidence in *Connecticut National Bank* showed that thrifts were already vigorous competitors in many banking services. How much more vigorous do they need to be before thrift competition can be considered in the antitrust analysis?

Consider in this regard the Garn-St Germain Act of 1982, which authorized thrifts to offer NOW accounts, super-NOW accounts, money market deposit accounts, and overdraft loans, and permitted them to engage in limited, but still significant, commercial lending, nonresidential real estate lending, and service corporation activities. Is the Garn-St Germain Act enough to boost thrifts over the *Connecticut National Bank* threshold for the banking line of commerce?

2. Consider also the changes wrought by the Competitive Equality Banking Act of 1987, which is specifically intended to establish "competitive equality" between banks and thrifts. This statute, as we have already seen, permits thrift holding companies to operate interstate on essentially the same terms as those applying to commercial bank holding companies. Moreover, it authorizes multiple savings and loan holding companies (companies controlling more than one thrift institution) to engage in the same activities permitted to commercial bank holding companies by the Federal Reserve Board. 12 U.S.C. §1730a(c)(2). Are these changes enough to bring thrifts within the commercial banking line of commerce?

3. Consider finally FIRREA, which in some respects continues the trend of consolidating thrift regulation with banking regulation. As we have seen, FIRREA abolished the FHLBB and the FSLIC and vested the responsibilities of these agencies in the FDIC and the OTS (which, like the Office of the Comptroller of the Currency, is located in the Treasury Department). FIRREA brings savings institutions within the purview of the Bank Merger Act and the Change in Bank Control Act. And it permits bank holding companies to acquire healthy thrifts, thus opening the way for large holding companies to operate with a mixture of thrift and commercial bank subsidiaries. Is this enough to establish thrifts as part of the same line of commerce as commercial banks?

4. These questions must be addressed, in the first instance, by the

banking agencies—especially the Federal Reserve Board—that make the initial determinations on bank merger applications. Consider in this regard the Federal Reserve Board's approach to thrift competition. The board initially refused to take thrift competition into account, but in a series of decisions since 1983 has stated that "thrift institutions have become, or have the potential to become, major competitors of commercial banks." E.g., AmSouth Bancorporation, 73 Fed. Res. Bull. 351, 352 n.4 (1987). Typically, the board assesses the impact of thrift competition by recomputing market share statistics on the assumption that 50 percent of the deposits held by thrift institutions are included in the relevant market.

5. The FDIC's policy statement on bank merger transactions provides that

> [t]he FDIC will view the relevant product market as consisting of those particular banking services offered by the merging institutions or to be offered by the combined institution and the functional equivalent of such services offered by other types of competitors, including, as the case may be, other depository institutions, securities firms, finance companies, etc. For example, [NOW accounts] offered by savings institutions are in many respects the functional equivalent of demand deposit checking accounts. Similarly, captive finance companies of automobile manufacturers may compete directly with banks for automobile loans and mortgage bankers may compete directly for real estate loans.

54 Fed. Reg. 39043 (Sept. 22, 1989).

6. If competition from thrift institutions can be considered, what about money market mutual funds? After all, for many people the Merrill-Lynch cash management account is a practical substitute for a checking account at a commercial bank. The ready substitutability of money market mutual funds and commercial checking accounts is demonstrated by the fact that when interest rates reached record levels in the early 1980s, bank customers took billions of dollars out of checking accounts and invested them in money funds.

7. So far we have considered only nonbank entry into the banking field. What about *bank* entry into traditional *nonbanking* fields, particularly securities activities? As will be seen in Chapter 6, over the past decade depository institutions and their holding companies have entered many traditional securities lines, including advising mutual funds, securities brokering, placing commercial paper, and even underwriting and distributing corporate debt and equities. These activities, presumably, must now be included in the "cluster" of activities defining the commercial bank line of commerce. Then should competition from securities firms be considered in the line of commerce analysis?

## Definition of a Product Market: U.S. Department of Justice and Federal Trade Commission 1992 Horizontal Merger Guidelines

*57 Fed. Reg. 41,552 (1992)*

### Product Market Definition

The Agency will first define the relevant product market with respect to each of the products of each of the merging firms.

#### *GENERAL STANDARDS*

Absent price discrimination, the Agency will delineate the product market to be a product or group of products such that a hypothetical profit-maximizing firm that was the only present and future seller of those products ("monopolist") likely would impose at least a "small but significant and nontransitory" increase in price. That is, assuming that buyers likely would respond to an increase in price for a tentatively identified product group only by shifting to other products, what would happen? If the alternatives were, in the aggregate, sufficiently attractive at their existing terms of sale, an attempt to raise prices would result in a reduction of sales large enough that the price increase would not prove profitable, and the tentatively identified product group would prove to be too narrow.

Specifically, the Agency will begin with each product (narrowly defined) produced or sold by each merging firm and ask what would happen if a hypothetical monopolist of that product imposed at least a "small but significant and nontransitory" increase in price, but the terms of sale of all other products remained constant. If, in response to the price increase, the reduction in sales of the product would be large enough that a hypothetical monopolist would not find it profitable to impose such an increase in price, then the Agency will add to the product group the product that is the next-best substitute for the merging firm's product. In considering the likely reaction of buyers to a price increase, the Agency will take into account all relevant evidence, including, but not limited to, the following:

(1) Evidence that buyers have shifted or have considered shifting purchases between products in response to relative changes in price or other competitive variables;
(2) Evidence that sellers base business decisions on the prospect of buyer substitution between products in response to relative changes in price or other competitive variables;

(3) The influence of downstream competition faced by buyers in their output markets; and
(4) The timing and costs of switching products.

The price increase question is then asked for a hypothetical monopolist controlling the expanded product group. In performing successive iterations of the price increase test, the hypothetical monopolist will be assumed to pursue maximum profits in deciding whether to raise the prices of any or all of the additional products under its control. This process will continue until a group of products is identified such that a hypothetical monopolist over that group of products would profitably impose at least a "small but significant and nontransitory" increase, including the price of a product of one of the merging firms. The Agency generally will consider the relevant product market to be the smallest group of products that satisfies this test. . . .

*QUESTIONS AND COMMENTS*

1. The Department of Justice has attempted to use a submarket or product-oriented approach to line-of-commerce analysis for commercial banking. In particular, the Justice Department has focused on transaction accounts and nonmortgage commercial lending to small and medium-sized businesses. This submarket approach tends to define product markets as being more concentrated than those generated by the cluster approach—and thus to increase the stringency of antitrust scrutiny over some bank mergers.

The Federal Reserve Board, on the other hand, has repeatedly affirmed its support for the cluster approach, both in congressional testimony and in its orders approving bank acquisitions, including acquisitions later challenged by the Justice Department under its submarket approach. There have been reports that the Fed may be willing to reconsider its support for the cluster idea, but to date there has been no formal change on the Fed's part.

2. Consider the approach advocated in Note, The Line of Commerce for Commercial Bank Mergers: A Product-Oriented Redefinition, 96 Harv. L. Rev. 907 (1983). The author identifies four "customer segments" each with its own product markets: (1) the household segment, including markets for real estate loans, other secured loans, unsecured consumer credit, transaction accounts, nonnegotiable deposits, and investment services; (2) the local business segment, involving long-term credit, short-term credit, transaction accounts, and long-term investments; (3) the regional business segment, involving these same basic business services plus short-term investment services for idle cash; and (4) the national business segment, involving the same basic services as the regional busi-

ness segment, with the possible exception of short-term investment services that national firms may be able to perform directly.

3. Aren't there serious problems with the administrability of a product-oriented approach? How should the banking submarkets be defined? If banking is disaggregated into four, five, or more distinct lines of commerce, won't this greatly multiply problems of proof in bank merger cases? Instead of one economic analysis of the relevant product markets there would have to be several analyses. And the complexity would extend to geographic markets, would it not, since different submarkets undoubtedly have markedly different geographic features? Consider also problems of remedy: Would a court have to order selective divestiture of different activities depending on competitive conditions in particular submarkets?

Perhaps these problems are what the Supreme Court sought to avoid in *Philadelphia National Bank,* when it noted that

> large borrowers and large depositors . . . may find it practical to do a large part of their banking business outside their home community; very small borrowers and depositors may, as a practical matter, be confined to bank offices in their immediate neighborhood; and customers of intermediate size, it would appear, deal with banks within an area intermediate between these extremes. . . . So also, some banking services are evidently more local in nature than others. But that in banking the relevant geographical market is a function of each separate customer's economic scale means simply that a workable compromise must be found. . . .

374 U.S. at 360-361.

4. Is a product-oriented approach likely to lead to more stringent or more lenient antitrust enforcement?

### b. Geographic Market Definition

The *Philadelphia National Bank* case stated that "the proper question to be asked [in identifying the relevant geographic market] is not where the parties to the merger do business or even where they compete, but where, within the area of competitive overlap, the effect of the merger on competition will be direct and immediate." Id. at 357. The Court concluded that because "[i]ndividuals and corporations typically conduct the bulk of their patronage on banks in their local community," the "area in which [the merging firms'] offices are located would seem to be the relevant market." Id. at 359.

The opinion thus established a presumption that the relevant market is the area or areas in which either of the merging firms actually maintains offices. Typically, if a bank maintains an office within a city, the city will be one of the markets in which the effect on competition is assessed. Alternatively, if a bank maintains offices outside the city limits, the relevant market is likely to be determined on the basis of county lines (as in *Philadelphia National Bank*).

*Philadelphia National Bank* was decided on the assumption of geographically limited banking. The dramatic increases in branch banking, bank holding company expansion, and interstate banking, coupled with the panoply of other devices by which banks can compete in extended geographic areas (ATMs, bank-by-mail, loan production offices, and other nonbank subsidiaries of bank holding companies, interstate credit card activities, national money markets, and much more) indicate that the *Philadelphia National Bank* approach may not be entirely satisfactory today. These marketplace changes suggest that the market might usefully be defined as somewhat broader than the cities or counties in which the merging firms operate offices. Such broader market definitions, however, have not to date received a favorable response from the Supreme Court.

## United States v. Connecticut National Bank

***418 U.S. 656 (1975)***

[The first part of this opinion is reproduced earlier in this chapter.]

### II

The District Court ruled that the relevant geographic market, or "section of the country," under §7, is the State as a whole. 362 F. Supp., at 283. We think the District Court erred on this point for several reasons. If the State were the relevant geographic market, it would then be appropriate to analyze this not as a potential-competition case but as a direct-competition case involving the consolidation of two firms holding an aggregate market share of approximately 10%. Even if this figure is "shaded" by a factor of 10% to account for the influence of banks in New York, see id., at 260; *Philadelphia National Bank,* 374 U.S., at 364 n.40, the consolidation of CNB and FNH would create a firm holding a 9% share of statewide commercial-bank deposits. Mergers between direct competitors producing smaller shares of less concentrated markets have been held illegal under §7.

The State cannot be the relevant geographic market, however, because CNB and FNH are not direct competitors on that basis (or for that matter on any other basis pertinent to this appeal). The two banks do not operate statewide, nor do their customers as a general rule utilize commercial banks on that basis. The offices of the two banks are restricted to adjoining sections of the southwest segment of Connecticut. Although the two banks presumably market a small percentage of their loans to large customers on a statewide or broader basis, it is undoubtedly true that almost all of their business originates locally. For example, "about 88% of CNB's total deposit business derive[s] from the towns in which CNB has offices." 362 F. Supp., at 250. As the District Court noted in a finding that is inconsistent with its conclusion on the appropriate section of the country, "[c]ommon sense . . . would indicate that the relevant market areas of CNB and FNH generally coincide with where each has established branch offices." Ibid.

As indicated by our opinion today in [*United States v.*] *Marine Bancorporation,* [484 U.S. 602, (1974)], the relevant geographic market of the acquired bank is the localized area in which that bank is in significant, direct competition with other banks, albeit not the acquiring bank. This area must be defined in accordance with this Court's precedents in prior bank-merger cases. Yet the District Court's conclusion on this issue conflicts with *Philadelphia National Bank,* supra. The Court emphasized in that case:

> In banking, as in most service industries, convenience of location is essential to effective competition. Individuals and corporations typically confer the bulk of their patronage on banks in their local community; they find it impractical to conduct their banking business at a distance. . . . The factor of inconvenience localizes banking competition as effectively as high transportation costs in other industries.

374 U.S., at 358 (footnote and citations omitted). In recognition of the local character of the great majority of commercial bank activities, *Philadelphia National Bank* indicated that the relevant geographic market in bank-merger cases must be drawn narrowly to encompass the area where "the effect of the merger on competition will be direct and immediate." Id., at 357. Moreover, the geographic market must be delineated in a way that takes into account the local nature of the demand for most bank services. It "must be charted by careful selection of the market area in which the seller operates, and to which the purchaser can practicably turn for [alternatives]. . . ." Id., at 359 (citations, internal quotations, and italics omitted). Because the economic scale of separate categories of consumers of bank services will vary, a workable compromise must be struck "to delineate the area in which bank customers that are neither very large nor very small find it practical to do their banking business. . . ." Id., at 361.

On remand the District Court must determine pursuant to the localized approach denoted above the geographic market in which CNB operates and to which the bulk of its customers may turn for alternative commercial bank services. It must do the same with regard to FNH, for this case presents the unusual fact situation of a consolidation of two banks, each with a history of de novo geographic expansion, rather than the acquisitions of a geographically stable bank as in *Marine Bancorporation.* The task is important, because the definition of the respective geographic markets determines the number of alternative avenues of entry theoretically open to CNB in piercing FNH's area of significant competitive influence and vice versa.

We are not unaware of the difficulty of the assignment confronting the District Court. An element of "fuzziness would seem inherent in any attempt to delineate the relevant geographical market." *Philadelphia National Bank,* supra, at 360 n.37. The task is made especially taxing here by the fragmented character of the distribution of the banking offices of the two banks, especially CNB. Apparently because the Connecticut branching statute has created a checkerboard of "open" and "closed" towns, CNB and FNH have expanded in the past in a manner that produced readily definable, completely covered areas around the towns where they have their home offices. There is, for example, a gap consisting of four towns in the extreme southwest section of Connecticut in which CNB has no offices, although it has established offices in almost all of the surrounding towns in that part of the State. That gap presumably will have to be excluded from consideration on remand.

The difficulty of the responsibility imposed on the District Court with regard to defining the geographic markets of the two banks is ameliorated by several considerations. First, the burden of producing evidence on this subject is on the Government. The Government repeatedly notes that it is not required to define geographic markets by "metes and bounds," citing United States v. Pabst Brewing Co., 384 U.S. 546, 549 (1966). To the extent that this means that such markets need not—indeed cannot—be defined with scientific precision, it is accurate. But it is nevertheless the Government's role to come forward with evidence delineating the rough approximation of localized banking markets mandated by *Philadelphia National Bank,* supra, and *Phillipsburg National Bank,* supra.

Second, we affirm that portion of the District Court's judgment holding that the Government cannot rely, without more, on Standard Metropolitan Statistical Areas (SMSA's) as defining the geographic markets of the two banks. See 362 F. Supp., at 249-250, 281-282. SMSA's are prepared by the Office of Management and Budget to determine areas of economic and social integration, principally on the basis of the commuting patterns of residents. They are not defined in terms of banking criteria, and they were not developed as a tool for analyzing banking markets. Id., at 249. Exclusive reliance on SMSA's here may lead to inaccuracies. For example, as the District Court noted, only 57% of CNB's deposits originate from the Bridgeport SMSA. Id., at 250, 282. This is because CNB's offices extend to several areas outside the Bridgeport SMSA. The Bridgeport SMSA is relevant, if at all, only to the CNB offices located in Bridgeport, and even then it is at best a crude indicator. The same is true of the New Haven SMSA and the FNH offices located in the town of New Haven. In sum, although the Bridgeport and New Haven SMSA's may be helpful in defining the general metropolitan characteristics of southwest Connecticut, they are not sufficiently refined in terms of realistic commercial banking markets to satisfy the Government's burden. The Government must demonstrate more accurately than is possible solely with SMSA's the localized banking markets, or areas of significant competitive influence, surrounding the sites where CNB and FNH maintain their banking offices.

Third, the District Court may not, as the banks would have it, rely solely on towns as the relevant geographic markets. The towns served by the two banks are highly significant geographic units, because state law restraints on de novo branching are defined in terms of towns. But not all towns are closed to de novo branching by one or the other bank, and it seems fair to assume that the area of significant competitive influence of some bank offices may extend beyond town boundaries.

On remand, the District Court must delineate the localized banking markets surrounding the sites where CNB and FNH maintain their bank offices. It must then evaluate the economically and legally feasible alternative methods of entry, if any, into those areas available to one bank or the other.

## III

In conformity with its approach in *Marine Bancorporation*, the Government argues that the State as a whole, although not a banking market, is nonetheless a "section of the country" within the meaning of §7 of the Clayton Act. The Government repeats the concern expressed in *Marine Bancorporation* that a statewide linkage of oligopolies "may" arise and that large banks across the state "may engage" in more standardized behavior as a result. Moreover, the Government contends that a statewide approach is appropriate because the challenged consolidation would eliminate one of eight banks in Connecticut with the potential for statewide operation. "Thus the effect of a merger which eliminates even one of these banks will be felt statewide, for it will have an impact in every local market in the state where that bank does not currently operate but which it *might* otherwise enter."

We reject the Government's statewide approach here, as we did in *Marine Bancorporation*. The Government's argument that "a geographic area need not be a banking market to be a section of the country . . ." is foreclosed by the precedents. Its theory of linked oligopolies appears to be as devoid of evidentiary support here as it was in *Marine Bancorporation*. Finally, its concern for any area of the State in which CNB or FNH "might" enter independently of the consolidation is too speculative to establish a case under the Clayton Act. In advancing the latter argument, the

Government borders on espousing a per se rule against geographic market extension mergers by Connecticut commercial banks so long as any town in the State remains open to de novo branching. On remand the District Court will address itself to the geographic markets in which CNB and FNH presently operate.

The judgment is vacated and the case is remanded for further consideration consistent with this opinion.

It is so ordered.

*QUESTIONS AND COMMENTS*

1. Was the Court correct in excluding from the geographic market areas of potential competition where the merging partners were not presently engaged in actual competition?

2. Why was the Court so keen on maintaining the "localized approach" of *Philadelphia National Bank?* Might concerns for administrability have played a role?

3. Consider the impact on geographic market definition of a "product-oriented" approach to product markets. Presumably, once banking services are divided into distinct product submarkets, it would then be necessary to define separate geographic markets for each product submarket. Thus, the market for small deposits would be the immediate local area surrounding the bank's offices; the market for large certificates of deposits might be nationwide; and the market for various other products and services might fall somewhere in between. But would this not add even further complexity to an already complicated task?

## Definition of a Geographic Market: U.S. Department of Justice and Federal Trade Commission 1992 Horizontal Merger Guidelines

***57 Fed. Reg. 41,552 (1992)***

### Geographic Market Definition

For each product market in which both merging firms participate, the Agency will determine the geographic market or markets in which the firms produce or sell. A single firm may operate in a number of different geographic markets.

#### *GENERAL STANDARDS*

Absent price discrimination, the Agency will delineate the geographic market to be a region such that a hypothetical monopolist that was the only present or future producer of the relevant product at locations in that region would profitably impose at least a "small but significant and nontransitory" increase in price, holding constant the terms of sale for all products produced elsewhere. That is, assuming that buyers likely would respond to a price increase on products produced within the tentatively identified region only by shifting to products produced at locations of production outside the region, what would happen? If those locations of production outside the region were, in the aggregate, sufficiently attractive at their existing terms of sale, an attempt to raise price would result in a reduction in sales large enough that the price increase would not prove profitable, and the tentatively identified geographic area would prove to be too narrow.

In defining the geographic market or markets affected by a merger, the Agency will begin with the location of each merging firm (or each plant of a multiplant firm) and ask what would happen if a hypothetical monopolist of the relevant product at that point imposed at least a "small but significant and nontransitory" increase in price, but the terms of sale at all other locations remained constant. If, in response to the price increase, the reduction in sales of the product at that location would be large enough that a hypothetical monopolist producing or selling the relevant product at the merging firm's location would not find it profitable to impose such an increase in price, then the Agency will add the location from which production is the next-best substitute for production at the merging firm's location.

In considering the likely reaction of buyers to a price increase, the Agency will take into account all relevant evidence, including, but not limited to, the following:

(1) Evidence that buyers have shifted or have considered shifting to relative changes in price or other competitive variables;
(2) Evidence that sellers base business decisions on the prospect of buyer substitution between geographic locations in response to relative changes in price or other competitive variables;
(3) The influence of downstream competition faced by buyers in their output markets; and
(4) The timing and costs of switching suppliers.

The price increase question is then asked for a hypothetical monopolist controlling the expanded group of locations. In performing successive iterations of the price increase test, the hypothetical monopolist will be assumed to pursue maximum profits in deciding whether to raise the price at any or all of the additional locations under its control. This process will continue until a group of locations is identified such that a hypothetical monopolist over that group of locations would profitably impose at least a "small but significant and nontransitory" increase, including the price charged at a location of one of the merging firms.

The "smallest market" principle will be applied as it is in product market definition. The price for which an increase will be postulated, what constitutes a "small but significant and nontransitory" increase in price, and the substitution decisions of consumers all will be determined in the same way in which they are determined in product market definition.

*QUESTIONS AND COMMENTS*

The FDIC's policy statement on bank merger transactions states that

> [t]he FDIC will view the relevant geographic market as consisting of those areas in which offices of the merging institutions are located and from which the institutions derive the predominant portion of their loan, deposit or other business and where existing and potential customers of the merging and resulting institutions may reasonably be expected to find alternative sources of banking services. Where practical, the geographic market will be defined in terms of political subdivision to facilitate statistical analysis.

54 Fed. Reg. 39,043 (1989).

## 3. *Market Share Analysis*

Once the product and geographic markets are specified, the analysis turns to an assessment of the degree of concentration in the relevant market or markets before and after the proposed transaction. At one time the degree of concentration was typically measured by assessing the total share of the market held by the top four or five firms before and after the proposed transaction. More recently antitrust analysis has turned to the "Herfindahl-Hirschman Index," described in the following selection.

### Calculation of Market Shares: U.S. Department of Justice and Federal Trade Commission 1992 Horizontal Merger Guidelines

***57 Fed. Reg. 41,552 (1992)***

#### Calculating Market Shares

*GENERAL APPROACH*

The Agency normally will calculate market shares for all firms (or plants) identified as market participants . . . based on the total sales or capacity currently devoted to the relevant market together with that which likely would be devoted to the relevant market in response to a "small but significant and nontransitory" price increase. Market shares can be expressed either in dollar terms through measurement of sales, shipments, or production or in physical terms through measurement of sales, shipments, production, capacity, or reserves. . . .

### CONCENTRATION AND MARKET SHARES

Market concentration is a function of the number of firms in a market and their respective market shares. As an aid to the interpretation of market data, the Agency will use the Herfindahl-Hirschman Index (HHI) of market concentration. The HHI is calculated by summing the squares of the individual market shares of all the participants.[17] Unlike the four-firm concentration ratio, the HHI reflects both the distribution of the market shares of the top four firms and the composition of the market outside the top four firms. It also gives proportionately greater weight to the market shares of the larger firms, in accord with their relative importance in competitive interactions.

The Agency divides the spectrum of market concentration as measured by the HHI into three regions that can be broadly characterized as unconcentrated (HHI below 1000), moderately concentrated (HHI between 1000 and 1800), and highly concentrated (HHI above 1800). Although the resulting regions provide a useful framework for merger analysis, the numerical divisions suggest greater precision than is possible with the available economic tools and information. Other things being equal, cases falling just above and just below a threshold present comparable competitive issues.

### *GENERAL STANDARDS*

In evaluating horizontal mergers, the Agency will consider both the post-merger market concentration and the increase in concentration resulting from the merger.[18] Market concentration is a useful indicator

17. For example, a market consisting of four firms with market shares of 30 percent, 30 percent, 20 percent and 20 percent has an HHI of 2600 ($30^2 + 30^2 + 20^2 + 20^2 = 2600$). The HHI ranges from 10,000 (in the case of a pure monopoly) to a number approaching zero (in the case of an atomistic market). Although it is desirable to include all firms in the calculation, lack of information about small firms is not critical because such firms do not affect the HHI significantly.

18. The increase in concentration as measured by the HHI can be calculated independently of the overall market concentration by doubling the product of the market shares of the merging firms. For example, the merger of firms with shares of 5 percent and 10 percent of the market would increase the HHI by 100 ($5 \times 10 \times 2 = 100$). The explanation for this technique is as follows: In calculating the HHI before the merger, the market shares of the merging firms are squared individually: $(a)^2 + (b)^2$. After the merger, the sum of those shares would be squared: $(a + b)^2$, which equals $a^2 + 2ab + b^2$. The increase in the HHI therefore is represented by 2ab.

of the likely potential competitive effect of a merger. The general standards for horizontal mergers are as follows:

(a) Post-Merger HHI Below 1000. The Agency regards markets in this region to be unconcentrated. Mergers resulting in unconcentrated markets are unlikely to have adverse competitive effects and ordinarily require no further analysis.

(b) Post-Merger HHI Between 1000 and 1800. The Agency regards markets in this region to be moderately concentrated. Mergers producing an increase in the HHI of less than 100 points in moderately concentrated markets post-merger are unlikely to have adverse competitive consequences and ordinarily require no further analysis. Mergers producing an increase in the HHI of more than 100 points in moderately concentrated markets post-merger potentially raise significant competitive concerns. . . .

(c) Post-Merger HHI Above 1800. The Agency regards markets in this region to be highly concentrated. Mergers producing an increase in the HHI of less than 50 points, even in highly concentrated markets post-merger, are unlikely to have adverse competitive consequences and ordinarily require no further analysis. Mergers producing an increase in the HHI of more than 50 points in highly concentrated markets post-merger potentially raise significant competitive concerns. . . . Where the post-merger HHI exceeds 1800, it will be presumed that mergers producing an increase in the HHI of more than 100 points are likely to create or enhance market power or facilitate its exercise. The presumption may be overcome by a showing that . . . it [is] unlikely that the merger will create or enhance market power or facilitate its exercise, in light of market concentration and market shares. . . .

## *QUESTIONS AND COMMENTS*

1. The FDIC's policy statement provides that [f]or purposes of assessing the degree of concentration in a market, a proposed merger transaction will normally be approved (absent objection from the Department of Justice) where the post merger [HHI] in a relevant geographic market is 1,800 points or less or, if more than 1,800, would increase less than 200 points as a result of the merger. 54 Fed. Reg. 39,043 (Sept. 22, 1989).

2. Why is the HHI index considered a more accurate measure of industry concentration than leading firm concentration ratios?

3. In 1988 the Department of Justice issued guidelines for international merger cases that contained a general section restating the Department's views on mergers generally. The guidelines state in pertinent part that "[t]he HHI concentration thresholds set forth in the Department's Merger Guidelines are, however, not bright line tests except to the extent that they define 'safe harbors.' Where a merger does not fall within HHI

'safe harbor,' the Department proceeds to consider the merger's effect on concentration along with all other relevant factors bearing on whether the merger would likely create, enhance, or facilitate the exercise of market power." Do the 1988 guidelines merely recapitulate the department's views as expressed in the 1984 guidelines, or do they perhaps reinterpret the 1984 guidelines in some relatively significant way?

4. Keep in mind that the Riegle-Neal Act of 1994 imposes national and statewide deposit caps for interstate acquisitions and also expressly preserves deposit caps under state law.

5. In 1996 the Department of Justice and the federal banking agencies issued additional, informal guidelines for bank mergers. The guidelines create two screens, Screen A and Screen B. The banking agencies rely primarily on Screen A, which looks at competition in predefined markets as determined by the Federal Reserve. If the calculation specified in Screen A does not result in a postmerger HHI over 1800 and an increase of more than 200, the banking agencies are "unlikely to further review the competitive effects of the merger." However, the Federal Reserve is "likely to review the transaction further" if, in such a case, the proposed merger would result in a postmerger market share in excess of 35 percent. If the merger exceeds the 1800/200 threshold, applicants are encouraged to "consider providing additional information." Such information may include evidence that the merging parties do not significantly compete with one another, evidence that rapid economic change has resulted in an outdated geographic market definition and an alternative market is more appropriate, evidence that market shares are not an adequate indicator of the extent of competition in the market, and evidence concerning entry conditions, including evidence of entry by institutions within the past two years and the growth of those institutions since entry.

The Department of Justice, which also reviews bank mergers, announced that it would initially review transactions using data from the banking agencies' Screen A. If a proposed merger exceeds the 1800/200 threshold in Screen A, the Department of Justice encourages applicants to "consider submitting the calculations set forth in Screen B." Screen B differs from Screen A in several respects: it looks only to offices of the merging institutions that make commercial loans in the relevant market, and it defines the geographic markets differently than does the Fed.

The Justice Department also warns that in some cases it may further review proposed mergers even if they do not exceed the 1800/200 threshold in Screen A. This is most likely "when Screen A does not reflect fully the competitive effects of the transaction in all relevant markets, in particular lending to small and medium-sized businesses." For example, the department announced that it is "more likely to review a transaction if the predefined market in which the applicants compete is significantly larger than the area in which small business lending competition may exist. . . ."

The Justice Department also encouraged applicants to include evidence of competition from sources not included in Screen B. A thrift institution, for example, may be able to show that it is actively engaged in providing services to commercial customers, particularly loans for business startups or working capital purposes and cash management services. A credit union may have such membership restrictions, or lack of restrictions, and offer such services to commercial customers that it should be considered to be in the market. Parties to the proposed merger may be able to show evidence of competition by out-of-market institutions for commercial customers, particularly competition for loans for business startups or working capital purposes. Finally, there may be "evidence of actual competition by nonbank institutions for commercial customers, especially competition for loans for business startup or working capital purposes."

The new guidelines are evidently intended to simplify the sometimes arcane process of obtaining bank merger approval from two sets of agencies (the Department of Justice and the banking agencies) that often applied somewhat different standards of antitrust analysis. Reading between the lines, the guidelines do not appear to represent any sort of interagency compromise, but they do at least provide a uniform framework for preparing the merger application papers and analysis.

## AmSouth Bancorporation, Birmingham, Alabama

***73 Fed. Res. Bull. 351 (1987)***

### ORDER APPROVING ACQUISITION OF A BANK HOLDING COMPANY

AmSouth Bancorporation, Birmingham, Alabama, a bank holding company within the meaning of the Bank Holding Company Act (12 U.S.C. §1841 et seq. ("Act")), has applied for the Board's approval under section 3 of the Act to acquire the successor by merger to First Tuskaloosa Corporation, Tuscaloosa, Alabama ("Company"), and thereby indirectly to acquire The First National Bank of Tuskaloosa, Tuscaloosa, Alabama ("Bank").

Notice of the application, affording an opportunity for interested persons to submit comments, has been given in accordance with section 3(b) of the Act (51 Federal Register 40,515 (1986)). The time for filing comments has expired, and the Board has considered the application and all comments received in light of the factors set forth in section 3(c) of the Act (12 U.S.C. §1842(c)).

Applicant, the largest commercial banking organization in Alabama, controls two subsidiary banks with total deposits of $3.7 billion, representing approximately 18.1 percent of the total deposits in commercial banks in the state. Bank is the sixth largest commercial banking organization in the state, with total deposits of $295.6 million, representing 1.4 percent of the total deposits in commercial banks in the state. Upon consummation of the proposed transaction, Applicant would remain the largest banking organization in Alabama, with total deposits of $4.0 billion, representing 19.5 percent of the total deposits in commercial banks in the state. The Board does not believe consummation of this proposal would have any significant effect on the concentration of banking resources in Alabama.

Both Applicant and Bank compete directly in the Tuscaloosa banking market. Applicant operates two branches in the market and is the smallest of the six commercial banking organizations operating in the market. Applicant controls total deposits of $13.3 million, representing 2.5 percent of the deposits in commercial banks in the market. Bank is the largest commercial banking organization in the market, with total deposits of $277.2 million, representing 52.7 percent of the deposits in commercial banks in the market. Upon consummation of the proposal, Applicant's share of the deposits in commercial banks in the market would increase to 55.2 percent. The Tuscaloosa banking market is considered to be highly concentrated, with the four largest commercial banks controlling 97 percent of the deposits in commercial banks in the market. The Herfindahl-Hirschman Index ("HHI") for the market is 4,046 and would increase by 265 points to 4,311 upon consummation of the proposal.[3]

In reviewing the effect of this proposal on existing competition in the Tuscaloosa market, the Board has considered in particular Applicant's small absolute and relative size in the market and the modest increase in market concentration in the context of the market's overall competitive structure. As noted, Applicant is the smallest depository institution in the market, controlling only 2.5 percent of deposits in commercial banking organizations in the market. In this regard, the Board has considered that since Applicant entered the market in 1976, its market share has remained unchanged, despite a substantial increase in the markets deposits. Moreover, four other commercial banking organizations would remain as competitors in the market upon consummation. These include

3. Under the revised Department of Justice Merger Guidelines (49 Federal Register 26,823 (June 29, 1984)), a market in which the post-merger HHI is above 1800 is considered highly concentrated. In such markets, the Department is likely to challenge a merger that increases the HHI by more than 50 points. The Department has informed the Board that a bank merger or acquisition generally will not be challenged (in the absence of other factors indicating anticompetitive effects) unless the post-merger HHI is at least 1800 and the merger increases the HHI by at least 200 points. The Justice Department has stated that the higher than normal HHI thresholds for screening bank mergers for anticompetitive effects implicitly recognizes the competitive effect of limited-purpose lenders and other non-depository financial entities. The Department of Justice has informed the Board that it will not challenge this acquisition.

the largest banking organizations in the state, which have the financial and managerial resources to compete effectively in the market.

The Board also notes that Alabama's largest and second largest thrift institutions with large branch networks in numerous Alabama markets, have a significant competitive presence in the Tuscaloosa market. They, together with another thrift institution, control approximately 37 percent of the market's total deposits.[4] These thrift institutions exert a considerable competitive influence in the market as providers of NOW accounts and commercial and consumer loans. In the Board's view, the competition afforded by these thrift institutions is a substantial mitigating factor in this case.[5] Finally, the Board notes that there are a number of credit unions, offices of large national consumer and commercial finance companies, as well as offices of other non-depository providers of financial services in the Tuscaloosa market, that offer a broad range of competitive services.

Based upon the above considerations, the Board concludes that consummation of the proposal is not likely substantially to lessen competition in the Tuscaloosa banking market.

The financial and managerial resources of Applicant, its subsidiary banks, and Bank are consistent with approval. Considerations relating to the convenience and needs of the communities to be served are also consistent with approval, especially in light of Applicant's willingness to increase its efforts to better ascertain and meet the credit needs of the communities it serves. Based on the foregoing and other facts of record, the Board has determined that consummation of the proposed transaction would be in the public interest and that the application should be approved.

On the basis of the record, the application is approved for the reasons summarized above. The transaction shall not be consummated before the thirteenth calendar day following the effective date of this Order, or later than three months after the effective date of this Order, unless such period is extended for good cause by the Board or by the Federal Reserve Bank of Atlanta pursuant to delegated authority.

By order of the Board of Governors, effective March 17, 1987.

### Dissenting Statement of Chairman Volcker and Governor Angell

We would also approve the proposed acquisition by AmSouth of First Tuskaloosa, but unlike the majority of the Board, we would require

4. The Board has previously indicated that thrift institutions have become, or have the potential to become, major competitors of commercial banks.

5. If 50 percent of deposits held by thrift institutions in the Tuscaloosa banking market were included in the calculation of market concentration, the share of total deposits held by the four largest organizations in the market would be 94.4 percent. Applicant would control 2.0 percent of the market's deposits and Bank would control 40.8 percent of the market's deposits. The HHI would increase by 159 points to 2833.

AmSouth, as a condition of approval, to divest an office or offices equivalent to its current position in the market. We would do so because, in our view, given the already highly concentrated nature of the Tuscaloosa banking market, the proposal without a divestiture would unduly reduce the competitive forces at work in the area.

We agree with the majority that the increase in concentration in the market consequent upon the merger is small. The question posed, however, is whether, in a market already so highly concentrated, a merger involving the dominant bank in the market with another viable competitor should be approved without a divestiture designed to maintain existing competitive options. In this case of a highly concentrated market, we believe that an acquisition that will eliminate an effective and forceful competitor from the market and further concentrate the market share of the dominant institution in that market should not go forward.

*QUESTIONS AND COMMENTS*

1. The Federal Reserve Board reports at n.3 of this decision that

> the Department [of Justice] has informed the Board that a bank merger or acquisition generally will not be challenged . . . unless the post-merger HHI is at least 1800 and the merger increases the HHI by at least 200 points. The Justice Department has stated that the higher than normal HHI thresholds for screening bank mergers for anticompetitive effects implicitly recognizes the competitive effect of limited-purpose lenders and other non-depository financial entities.

Do you see why this policy might be a response to the *Philadelphia National Bank* decision?

2. The merger proposed in this case involved the Tuscaloosa banking market, which had a pre merger HHI of 4,046 and a proposed increase of the HHI of 265 points to 4,311. Even under the lenient Justice Department policy noted above, isn't this merger obviously objectionable on antitrust grounds? Why didn't the Department of Justice or the Federal Reserve Board require divestment of AmSouth's Tuscaloosa branches as a condition to approving the merger?

## 4. *Entry Analysis and Potential Competition*

The effect of a merger on competition must be determined with reference not only to its effect on firms already in the market but also to its impact on firms not presently active in the market that might be induced to enter if prices were raised above competitive levels as a result of the merger. If a large number of firms are waiting in the wings and poised to enter the market quickly if prices rise, this "potential competition" can mitigate the apparent anticompetitive effects of a merger.

The 1992 Merger Guidelines deal with potential entry through the use of two concepts. An "uncommitted potential entrant" is a firm that, in response to even a small but significant and nontransitory price increase, would likely enter the market quickly without incurring significant sunk costs of entry and exit. Because these uncommitted potential entrants would influence the market both before and after the merger in question, they are considered full-scale market participants at both times and treated as if they were already present in the relevant market.

If, on the other hand, a firm would have to incur significant sunk costs to enter a market, it is classified as a "committed" entrant under the Guidelines. The likelihood that such firms would enter the market must be evaluated with regard to the long-term profitability of entry to such firms in light of the irreversible costs that must be incurred in the short term in order to enter. The following selection from the 1992 Merger Guidelines deals with such "committed" entrants.

## The Committed Entry: U.S. Department of Justice and Federal Trade Commission 1992 Horizontal Merger Guidelines

*57 Fed. Reg. 41,552 (1992)*

### Entry Analysis

#### *OVERVIEW*

A merger is not likely to create or enhance market power or to facilitate its exercise, if entry into the market is so easy that market participants, after the merger, either collectively or unilaterally could not profitably maintain a price increase above premerger levels. Such entry likely will deter an anticompetitive merger in its incipiency, or deter or counteract the competitive effects of concern.

Entry is that easy if entry would be timely, likely, and sufficient in its magnitude, character and scope to deter or counteract the competitive effects of concern. In markets where entry is that easy (i.e., where entry passes these tests of timeliness, likelihood, and sufficiency), the merger raises no antitrust concern and ordinarily requires no further analysis.

The committed entry treated in this section is defined as new competition that requires expenditure of significant sunk costs of entry and exit. The Agency employs a three-step methodology to assess whether committed entry would deter or counteract a competitive effect of concern.

The first step assesses whether entry can achieve significant market impact within a timely period. If significant market impact would require a longer period, entry will not deter or counteract the competitive effect of concern.

The second step assesses whether committed entry would be a profitable and, hence, a likely response to a merger having competitive effects of concern. Firms considering entry that requires significant sunk costs must evaluate the profitability of the entry on the basis of long-term participation in the market, because the underlying assets will be committed to the market until they are economically depreciated. Entry that is suffient to counteract the competitive effects of concern will cause prices to fall to their premerger levels or lower. Thus, the profitability of such committed entry must be determined on the basis of premerger market prices over the long term.

A merger having anticompetitive effects can attract committed entry, profitable at premerger prices, that would not have occurred premerger at these same prices. But following the merger, the reduction in industry output and increase in prices associated with the competitive effect of concern may allow the same entry to occur without driving market prices below premerger levels. After a merger that results in decreased output and increased prices, the likely sales opportunities available to entrants at premerger prices will be larger than they were premerger, larger by the output reduction caused by the merger. If entry could be profitable at premerger prices without exceeding the likely sales opportunities—opportunities that include pre-existing pertinent factors as well as the merger-induced output reduction—then such entry is likely in response to the merger.

The third step assesses whether timely and likely entry would be sufficient to return market prices to their premerger levels. This end may be accomplished either through multiple entry or individual entry at a sufficient scale. Entry may not be sufficient, even though timely and likely, where the constraints on availability of essential assets, due to incumbent control, makes it impossible for entry profitably to achieve the necessary level of sales. Also, the character and scope of entrants' products might not be fully responsive to the localized sales opportunities created by the removal of direct competition among sellers of differentiated products. . . .

## NOTE ON THE POTENTIAL COMPETITION DOCTRINE

The Department of Justice once devoted considerable attention to the potential competition doctrine, a device for challenging mergers. The basis for the challenge was the belief that the combination of a firm from outside the market with a substantial firm in the market impermissibly reduced the beneficial effects which the outside firm previously exercised over in-market competition by waiting in the wings, poised to enter if firms in the relevant market engaged in anticompetitive behavior.

The potential competition doctrine comes in two variants. First, the merger might remove "perceived potential competition" by eliminating a significant present competitive threat that constrains the behavior of firms already in the market. Second, the merger might eliminate "actual potential competition" by preventing an opportunity for improvement in market performance resulting from the entrance of the new firm de novo or by means of a toehold acquisition, rather than through merger with a major firm in the relevant market. The difference between these variants can be subtle and is often of little practical significance.

At one time, the potential competition doctrine had some importance as a means of challenging bank mergers. There were two reasons for this special importance.

First, as we have seen, geographic banking markets have traditionally been quite narrowly constrained for purposes of antitrust analysis. Nevertheless, a merger between two banking firms that eliminates a substantial amount of actual competition might be immune from standard antitrust challenges because, under *Philadelphia Bank,* no overlap between markets is recognized. In a case like this, the potential competition doctrine may be the only avenue for challenging the merger on anticompetitive grounds.

Second, the potential competition doctrine applies only when there are a limited number of potential de novo entrants (if the number of potential entrants is large, the elimination of one potential de novo entrant will not substantially lessen the amount of potential competition). In many industries de novo entry is possible from anywhere in the country (or abroad), so the number of potential entrants is large. In the banking industry, however, geographic restrictions on bank expansion have historically limited the number of potential de novo entrants to only a few firms, thus satisfying one of the preconditions for applying the potential competition doctrine.

Despite these considerations, the potential competition doctrine is increasingly seen as posing only a minor obstacle, at most, to bank mergers. The leading judicial precedent in the area, Mercantile Texas Corp. v. Board of Governors, 638 F.2d 1255 (5th Cir. 1981), is viewed by many bank lawyers as greatly reducing the effectiveness of potential competition challenges to bank mergers by setting forth a difficult burden of proof for parties challenging a merger. Perhaps more importantly, the massive trend toward interstate banking that has been under way since the mid-1980s and that has been further accelerated by the Riegle-Neal Act of 1994 has greatly increased the number of potential entrants in most banking markets, thus reducing the probability that entry into the market by a merging firm would significantly reduce the amount of potential competition in the market.

Despite its currently dormant status, the potential competition doctrine has not been repudiated by the Department of Justice (the 1992 Merger Guidelines do not deal with the doctrine). The Justice Department's views on potential competition are set forth—but in this respect not superseded—in the earlier 1984 Merger Guidelines §4.11.

# 6 SECURITIES POWERS OF BANKING INSTITUTIONS

## A. INTRODUCTION

Chapter 3 examined congressional attempts to regulate the commingling of banking and commerce. In this chapter we focus on the relationship between banking and investment banking. Just as it is often believed that banking and commerce ought not be mixed, so too, many have argued, mixing the business of banking and the business of dealing in securities is a dangerous proposition.

Indeed, for years the perceived need to separate banking and investment banking was even more firmly entrenched among regulators than the need to separate banking and commerce, due to the widespread belief that the securities affiliates of the nation's commercial banks were responsible for the Great Depression.

Throughout their history, U.S. banks have had a keen interest in the securities business. Part of the reason that the federal government allowed banks to obtain national charters as well as state charters was to provide a convenient method by which the government could sell its bonds to banks to finance the Civil War. Similarly, commercial banks played a large part in financing the United States' participation in World War I through the sale of Liberty Bonds. During the early twentieth century, banks were major participants in securities markets. They dominated the underwriting and distribution of corporate debt securities and participated, to a lesser but still significant extent, in underwriting corporate equities. The typical pattern was for a commercial bank to establish a securities "affiliate" that would undertake these tasks with some degree of separation from the traditional commercial bank. Banks could, however, and did underwrite securities operations directly as well. Investment banks competed with commercial banks for business, but the distinction between investment and commercial banking was not nearly so clear-cut during the early years of the century as it became later on—especially after the Glass-Steagall Act was enacted in 1933. This statute forms the basis of the present chapter.

We have already examined, in Chapter 3, certain securities powers of depository institutions, with special reference to their authority to own and hold securities for an institution's own account. In that context, we also touched on other concepts important for this chapter: brokerage, dealing, and underwriting. These concepts do not always have a precise meaning, but the essential ideas are these. *Brokerage* is the process of bringing together a buyer and a seller of a security for a commission, without taking a position in the transaction. This is what 12 U.S.C. §24 (Seventh) means when it refers to "purchasing and selling . . . securities and stock without recourse, solely upon the order, and for the account of, customers. . . ." *Dealing* is the business of holding securities in inventory, and buying and selling them on the market in order to make a profit on the spread between the sales price and the purchase price. *Underwriting,* broadly understood, is the process of distributing securities to the public. There are two main types of underwritings. In a "firm commitment" underwriting, the underwriter guarantees the price that the issuing firm will receive; the transaction can be conceptualized as being similar to a wholesaling arrangement in which the securities firm purchases the securities in bulk from the issuer and then "retails" them to the public at a higher price. Most major public offerings today take the form of firm commitment underwritings. In a "best efforts" underwriting, the underwriter does not guarantee that the issuing firm will receive the asking price; it merely agrees to use its best efforts to market the securities at that price. Obviously the underwriter takes on more risk in a firm commitment underwriting than in a best efforts underwriting. These distinctions should be kept in mind in the pages that follow.

## B. GLASS-STEAGALL: THE LEGAL MAGINOT LINE BETWEEN COMMERCIAL AND INVESTMENT BANKING

Despite the many similarities between commercial banking and investment banking, the banking laws of the United States attempt to separate the two businesses. The Glass-Steagall Act, part of the Banking Act of 1933, is the statute concerned with the overlap between commercial and investment banking. There are four important provisions:

First, §16 of the Act, 12 U.S.C. §24 (Seventh), prohibits national banks from underwriting, selling, and dealing in specified securities. Section 5(c) of Glass-Steagall makes the restrictions imposed by §16 applicable to state-chartered banks that are members of the Federal Reserve System. 12 U.S.C. §335.

Second, §20 of the Act forbids affiliations between banks and firms "engaged principally in the issue, flotation, underwriting, public sale, or distribution . . . of stocks, bonds, debentures, notes or other securities." 12 U.S.C. §377. Section 20 applies only to national banks and banks that are members of the Federal Reserve System.

Third, §21 forbids investment banks from taking deposits and thereby engaging in commercial banking. Thus under §21, any person "engaged in the business of issuing, underwriting, selling, or distributing . . . stocks, bonds, debentures, notes, or other securities" is prohibited from engaging "to any extent whatever" in the business of deposit banking. 12 U.S.C. §378(a)(1).

Finally, §32 prohibits an individual involved in any aspect of the investment banking business from serving as an officer, director, or employee of a national or state-chartered member bank. 12 U.S.C. §78.

These provisions might be thought of as follows. Two sections control the power of commercial and investment banks to enter onto one another's turf: §16 limits the power of commercial banks to enter the securities business; §21 limits the power of securities firms to engage in commercial banking. Although the two sections are phrased in somewhat different terms, the courts tend to view them as drawing essentially the same line from two different perspectives. The other two sections limit connections between commercial and investment banks. Section 32 governs the sharing of staff or management across the banking-securities divide, and §20 controls affiliations between firms in the two industries. Taken as a whole, these four sections of the Glass-Steagall Act have been thought of as erecting a high wall between investment and commercial banking. As we shall see, that wall is now breaking down.

A chairman of the Board of Governors of the Federal Reserve System described the separation of commercial and investment banking as "perhaps the single most important anomaly that now plagues our financial system." Statement by Alan Greenspan before the Senate Comm. on Banking, Housing and Urban Affairs, December 1, 1987, 74 Fed. Res. Bull. 91 (1988). As we will see, confusion about what defines these two types of banking has forced the courts and regulatory agencies to spend a great deal of time construing the Glass-Steagall Act. It has also led to a strong demand for the services of banking lawyers.

Perhaps the leading opinion interpreting §16 of the Glass-Steagall Act was rendered by the Supreme Court in *Investment Co. Institute v. Camp*. This case represents the most complete attempt by any court to justify Glass-Steagall's separation of commercial and investment banking.

## Investment Co. Institute v. Camp

*401 U.S. 617 (1971)*

Justice STEWART delivered the opinion of the Court.

These companion cases involve a double-barreled assault upon the efforts of a national bank to go into the business of operating a mutual investment fund. The petitioners . . . are an association of open-end investment companies and several individual such companies. . . .

The issue before us is whether the Comptroller of the Currency may, consistently with the banking laws, authorize a national bank to offer its customers the opportunity to invest in a stock fund created and maintained by the bank. Before 1963 national banks were prohibited by administrative regulation from offering this service. The Board of Governors of the Federal Reserve System, which until 1962 had regulatory jurisdiction over all the trust activities of national banks, allowed the collective investment of trust assets only for "the investment of funds held for true fiduciary purposes." The applicable regulation, Regulation F, specified that "the operation of such Common Trust Funds as investment trusts for other than strictly fiduciary purposes is hereby prohibited." The Board consistently ruled that it was improper for a bank to use "a Common Trust Fund as an investment trust attracting money seeking investment alone and to embark upon what would be in effect the sale of participations in a Common Trust Fund to the public as investments." 26 Fed. Reserve Bull. 393 (1940).

In 1962 Congress transferred jurisdiction over most of the trust activities of national banks from the Board of Governors of the Federal Reserve System to the Comptroller of the Currency, without modifying any provision of substantive law. The Comptroller thereupon solicited suggestions for improving the regulations applicable to trust activities. Subsequently, new regulations were proposed which expressly authorized the collective investment of monies delivered to the bank for investment management, so-called managing agency accounts. These proposed regulations were officially promulgated in 1963 with changes not material here. In 1965 the First National City Bank of New York submitted for the Comptroller's approval a plan for the collective investment of managing agency accounts. The Comptroller promptly approved the plan, and it is now in operation. This plan, which departs in some respects from the plan envisaged by the Comptroller's Regulation, is expected, the briefs tell us, to be a model for other banks which decide to offer their customers a collective investment service.

Under the plan the bank customer tenders between $10,000 and $500,000 to the bank, together with an authorization making the bank the customer's managing agent. The customer's investment is added to the fund, and a written evidence of participation is issued which expresses in "units of participation" the customer's proportionate interest in fund assets. Units of participation are freely redeemable, and transferable to anyone who has executed a managing agency agreement with the bank. The fund is registered as an investment company under the Investment Company Act of 1940. The bank is the underwriter of the fund's units of participation within the meaning of that Act. The fund has filed a registration statement pursuant to the Securities Act of 1933. The fund is supervised by a five-member committee elected annually by the participants pursuant to the Investment Company Act of 1940. The Securities and Exchange Commission has exempted the fund from the Investment Company Act to the extent that a majority of this committee may be affiliated with the bank, and it is expected that a majority always will be officers in the bank's trust and investment division. The actual custody and investment of fund assets is carried out by the bank as investment advisor pursuant to a management agreement. Although the Investment Company Act requires that this management agreement be approved annually by the committee, including a majority of the unaffiliated members, or by the participants, it is expected that the bank will continue to be investment advisor.

**III**

Section 16 of the Glass-Steagall Act as amended, 12 U.S.C. §24, Seventh, provides that the

> business of dealing in securities and stock [by a national bank] shall be limited to purchasing and selling such securities and stock without recourse, solely upon the order, and for the account of, customers, and in no case for its own account. . . . Except as hereinafter provided or otherwise permitted by law, nothing herein contained shall authorize the purchase by [a national bank] for its own account of any shares of stock of any corporation.

The petitioners contend that a purchase of stock by a bank's investment fund is a purchase of stock by a bank for its own account in violation of this section.

Section 16 also provides that a national bank "shall not underwrite any issue of securities or stock." And §21 of the same Act, 12 U.S.C. §378(a), provides that "it shall be unlawful—(1) For any person, firm, corporation, association, business trust, or other similar organization, engaged in the business of issuing, underwriting, selling, or distributing, at wholesale or retail, or through syndicate participation, stocks, bonds, debentures, notes, or other securities, to engage at the same time to any extent whatever in the business of [deposit banking]." The petitioners contend that the creation and operation of an investment fund by a bank which offers to its customers the opportunity to purchase an interest in the fund's assets constitutes the issuing, underwriting, selling, or distributing of securities or stocks in violation of these sections.

The questions raised by the petitioners are novel and substantial. National banks were granted trust powers in 1913. Federal Reserve Act, §11, 38 Stat. 261. The first common trust fund was organized in 1927, and such funds were expressly authorized by the Federal Reserve Board by Regulation F promulgated in 1937. Report on Commingled or Common Trust Funds Administered by Banks and Trust Companies, H.R. Doc. No. 476, 76th Cong., 2d Sess., 4-5 (1939). For at least a generation, therefore, there has been no reason to doubt that a national bank can, consistently with the banking laws, commingle trust funds on the one hand, and act as a managing agent on the other. No provision of the banking law suggests that it is improper for a national bank to pool trust assets, or to act as a managing agent for individual customers, or to purchase stock for the account of its customers. But the union of these powers gives birth to an investment fund whose activities are of a different character. The differences between the investment fund that the Comptroller has authorized and a conventional open-end mutual fund are subtle at best, and it is undisputed that this bank investment fund finds itself in direct competition with the mutual fund industry. One would suppose that the business of a mutual fund consists of buying stock "for its own account" and of "issuing" and "selling" "stock" or "other securities" evidencing an undivided and redeemable interest in the assets of the fund. On their face, §§16 and 21 of the Glass-Steagall Act appear clearly to prohibit this activity by national banks.

But we cannot come lightly to the conclusion that the Comptroller has authorized activity that violates the banking laws. It is settled that courts should give great weight to any reasonable construction of a regulatory statute adopted by the agency charged with the enforcement of that statute. . . .

The difficulty here is that the Comptroller adopted no expressly articulated position at the administrative level as to the meaning and impact of the provisions of §§16 and 21 as they affect bank investment funds. . . .

## IV

There is no dispute that one of the objectives of the Glass-Steagall Act was to prohibit commercial banks, banks that receive deposits subject to repayment, lend money, discount and negotiate promissory notes and the like, from going into the investment banking business. Many commercial banks were indirectly engaged in the investment banking business when the Act was passed in 1933. Even before the passage of the Act it was generally believed that it was improper for a commercial bank to engage in investment banking directly. But in 1908 banks began the practice of establishing security affiliates that engaged in, inter alia, the business of floating bond issues and, less frequently, underwriting stock issues. The Glass-Steagall Act confirmed that national banks could not engage in investment banking directly, and in addition made affiliation with an organization so engaged illegal. One effect of the Act was to abolish the security affiliates of commercial banks.

It is apparent from the legislative history of the Act why Congress felt that this drastic step was necessary. The failure of the Bank of United States in 1930 was widely attributed to that bank's activities with respect to its numerous securities affiliates. Moreover, Congress was concerned that commercial banks in general and member banks of the Federal Reserve System in particular had both aggravated and been damaged by stock market decline partly because of their direct and indirect involvement in the trading and ownership of speculative securities. The Glass-Steagall Act reflected a determination that policies of competition, convenience, or expertise which might otherwise support the entry of commercial banks into the investment banking business were outweighed by the "hazards" and "financial dangers" that arise when commercial banks engage in the activities proscribed by the Act.

The hazards that Congress had in mind were not limited to the obvious danger that a bank might invest its own assets in frozen or otherwise imprudent stock or security investments. For often securities affiliates had operated without direct access to the assets of the bank. This was because securities affiliates had frequently been established with capital paid in by the bank's stockholders, or by the public, or through the allocation of a legal dividend on bank stock for this purpose. The legislative history of the Glass-Steagall Act shows that Congress also had in mind and repeatedly focused on the more subtle hazards that arise when a commercial bank goes beyond the business of acting as fiduciary or managing agent and enters the investment banking business either directly or by establishing an affiliate to hold and sell particular investments. This course places new promotional and other pressures on the bank which in turn create new temptations. For example, pressures are created because the bank and the affiliate are closely associated in the public mind, and should the affiliate fare badly, public confidence in the bank might be impaired. And since public confidence is essential to the solvency of a bank, there might exist a natural temptation to shore up the affiliate through unsound loans or other aid. Moreover, the pressure to sell a particular investment and to make the affiliate successful might create a risk that the bank would make its credit facilities more freely available to those companies in whose stock or securities the affiliate has invested or become otherwise involved. Congress feared that banks might even go so far as to make unsound loans to such companies. In any event, it was thought that the bank's salesman's interest might impair its ability to function as an impartial source of credit.

Congress was also concerned that bank depositors might suffer losses on investments that they purchased in reliance on the relationship between the bank and its affiliate. This loss of customer good will might "become an important handicap to a bank during a major period of security market deflation." More broadly, Congress feared that the promotional needs of investment banking might lead commercial banks to lend their reputation for prudence and restraint to the enterprise of selling particular stocks and securities, and that this could not be done without that reputation being undercut by the risks necessarily incident to the investment banking business. There was also perceived the danger that when commercial banks were subject to the promotional demands of investment banking, they might be tempted to make loans to customers with the expectation that the loan would facilitate the purchase of stocks and securities. There was evidence before Congress that loans for investment written by commercial banks had done much to feed the speculative fever of the late 1920's. Senator Glass made it plain that it was "the fixed purpose of Congress" not to see the facilities of commercial banking diverted into speculative operations by the aggressive and promotional character of the investment banking business.

Another potential hazard that very much concerned Congress arose from the plain conflict between the promotional interest of the investment banker and the obligation of the commercial banker to render disinterested investment advice. . . .

In sum, Congress acted to keep commercial banks out of the investment banking business largely because it believed that the promotional incentives of investment banking and the investment banker's pecuniary stake in the success of particular investment opportunities was destructive of prudent and disinterested commercial banking and of public confidence in the commercial banking system. As Senator Bulkley put it:

> If we want banking service to be strictly banking service, without the expectation of additional profits in selling something to customers, we must keep the banks out of the investment security business.

## V

The language that Congress chose to achieve this purpose includes the prohibitions of §16 that a national bank "shall not underwrite any issue of securities or stock" and shall not purchase "for its own account . . . any shares of stock of any corporation," and the prohibition of §21 against engaging in "the business of issuing, underwriting, selling, or distributing . . . stocks, bonds, debentures, notes, or other securities." In this litigation the Comptroller takes the position that the operation of a bank investment fund is consistent with these provisions, because participating interests in such a fund are not "securities" within the meaning of the Act. It is argued that a bank investment fund simply makes available to the small investor the benefit of investment management by a bank trust department which would otherwise be available only to large investors, and that the operation of an investment fund creates no problems that are not present whenever a bank invests in securities for the account of customers.

But there is nothing in the phrasing of either §16 or §21 that suggests a narrow reading of the word "securities." To the contrary, the breadth of the term is implicit in the fact that the antecedent statutory language encompasses not only equity securities but also securities representing debt. And certainly there is nothing in the language of these provisions to suggest that the sale of an interest in the business of buying, holding, and selling stocks for investment is to be distinguished from the sale of an interest in a commercial or industrial enterprise.

. . . [W]e are persuaded that the purposes for which Congress enacted the Glass-Steagall Act leave no room for the conclusion that a participation in a bank investment fund is not a "security" within the meaning of the Act. From the perspective of competition, convenience, and expertise, there are arguments to be made in support of allowing commercial banks to enter the investment banking business. But Congress determined that the hazards outlined above made it necessary to prohibit this activity to commercial banks. Those same hazards are clearly present when a bank undertakes to operate an investment fund.

A bank that operates an investment fund has a particular investment to sell. It is not a matter of indifference to the bank whether the customer buys an interest in the fund or makes some other investment. If its customers cannot be persuaded to invest in the bank's investment fund, the bank will lose their investment business and the fee which that business would have brought in. . . .

Promotional incentives might also be created by the circumstance that the bank's fund would be in direct competition with mutual funds that, from the point of view of the investor, offered an investment opportunity comparable to that offered by the bank. The bank would want to be in a position to show to the prospective customer that its fund was more attractive than the mutual funds offered by others. The bank would have a salesman's stake in the performance of the fund, for if the fund were less successful than the competition the bank would lose business and the resulting fees.

A bank that operated an investment fund would necessarily put its reputation and facilities squarely behind that fund and the investment opportunity that the fund offered. The investments of the fund might be conservative or speculative, but in any event the success or failure of the fund would be a matter of public record. Imprudent or unsuccessful management of the bank's investment fund could bring about a perhaps unjustified loss of public confidence in the bank itself. If imprudent management should place the fund in distress, a bank might find itself under pressure to rescue the fund through measures inconsistent with sound banking.

The promotional and other pressures incidental to the operation of an investment fund, in other words, involve the same kinds of potential abuses that Congress intended to guard against when it legislated against bank security affiliates. It is not the slightest reflection on the integrity of the mutual fund industry to say that the traditions of that industry are not necessarily the conservative traditions of commercial banking. The needs and interests of a mutual fund enterprise more nearly approximate those of securities underwriting, the activity in which bank security affiliates were primarily engaged. When a bank puts itself in competition with mutual funds, the bank must make an accommodation to the kind of ground rules that Congress firmly concluded could not be prudently mixed with the business of commercial banking.

And there are other potential hazards of the kind Congress sought to eliminate with the passage of the Glass-Steagall Act. The bank's stake in the investment fund might distort its credit decisions or lead to unsound loans to the companies in which the fund had invested. The bank might exploit its confidential relationship with its commercial and industrial creditors for the benefit of the fund. The bank might undertake, directly or indirectly, to make its credit facilities available to the fund or to render other aid to the fund inconsistent with the best interests of the bank's depositors. The bank might make loans to facilitate the purchase of interests in the fund. The bank might divert talent and resources from its commercial banking operation to the promotion of the fund. Moreover, because the bank would have a stake in a customer's making a particular investment decision—the decision to invest in the bank's investment fund—the customer might doubt the motivation behind the bank's recommendation that he make such an investment. If the fund investment should turn out badly there would be a danger that the bank would lose the good will of those customers who had invested in the fund. It might be unlikely that disenchantment would go so far as to threaten the solvency of the bank. But because banks are dependent on the confidence of their customers, the risk would not be unreal.

These are all hazards that are not present when a bank undertakes to purchase stock for the account of its individual customers or to commingle assets which it has received for a true fiduciary purpose rather than for investment. These activities, unlike the operation of an investment fund, do not give rise to a promotional or salesman's stake in a particular investment; they do not involve an enterprise in direct competition with aggressively promoted funds offered by other investment companies; they do not entail a threat to public confidence in the bank itself; and they do not impair the bank's ability to give disinterested service as a fiduciary or managing agent. In short, there is a plain difference between the sale of fiduciary services and the sale of investments.

**VI**

The Glass-Steagall Act was a prophylactic measure directed against conditions that the experience of the 1920's showed to be great potentials for abuse. The literal terms of that Act clearly prevent what the Comptroller has sought to authorize here. Because the potential hazards and abuses that flow from a bank's entry into the mutual investment business are the same basic hazards and abuses that Congress intended to eliminate almost 40 years ago, we cannot but apply the terms of the federal statute as they were written. We conclude that the operation of an investment fund of the kind approved by the Comptroller involves a bank in the underwriting, issuing, selling, and distributing of securities in violation of §§16 and 21 of the Glass-Steagall Act. . . .

It is so ordered.

## *QUESTIONS AND COMMENTS*

1. What do you think of the idea that the distinction between commercial banking and investment banking that the Glass-Steagall Act seeks to create may be, in essence, a false dichotomy? After all, the businesses of commercial banking and investment banking are essentially the same—each provides capital to firms in need of financing. A firm in need of capital may borrow it from a commercial bank, or it may obtain the money by selling stock or other securities. Firms will select the financing method with the lowest net cost. How convincing do you find this analysis in light of Investment Co. Institute v. Camp?

2. The Glass-Steagall Act does not contain a definition of the term "security." Both the Securities Act of 1933,[1] and the Securities Exchange

1. Section 2 of the 1933 Act, 15 U.S.C. §77b, states in part:

> When used in this subchapter, unless the context otherwise requires—
>
> (1) the term "security" means any note, stock, treasury stock, bond, debenture, evidence of indebtedness, certificate of interest or participation in any profit-sharing agreement, collateral-trust certificate, preorganization certificate or subscription, transferable share, investment contract, voting-trust certificate, certificate of deposit for a security, fractional undivided interest in oil, gas, or other mineral rights, . . . or, in general, any interest or instrument commonly known as a "security," or any certificate of interest or participation in, temporary or interim certificate for, receipt for, guarantee of, or warrant or right to subscribe to or purchase, any of the foregoing.

Act of 1934[2] contain definitions of the term "security" that take into account the different purposes of those Acts. It might seem plausible that these definitions of "security" would shed some light on how "security" should be defined in the Glass-Steagall Act. However, the definition cannot simply be borrowed from these statutes and adopted for Glass-Steagall because the congressional purposes underlying the securities acts differs from the congressionally articulated goals of Glass-Steagall. See A. G. Becker v. Board of Governors of the Federal Reserve System, 693 F.2d 136, 146 (D.C. Cir. 1982) (no reason to assume that Congress intended the term "security" to bear the same meaning in these different statutes); Note, A Conduct-Oriented Approach to the Glass-Steagall Act, 91 Yale L.J. 102 (1981).

3. What sort of guide does the Court in *Investment Co. Institute (ICI)* provide to future courts attempting to determine whether a particular financial instrument is a security?

4. *ICI* is unquestionably the Supreme Court's most influential opinion construing Glass-Steagall. *ICI* contains a lavish presentation of Glass-Steagall's legislative history that identifies a number of financial "hazards" and "dangers" that Congress feared if commercial banks were to engage in the investment banking business. One commentator has observed that each of the hazards and dangers

> constitute either (1) a legislative intention to ensure that commercial banks are held to a higher standard of care when making investments than investment banks (so-called safety concerns) or (2) a legislative intention that banks be held to a higher standard of care than other financial institutions when dealing with customers (so-called conflicts of interest concerns).

Macey, Special Interest Groups Legislation and the Judicial Function: The Dilemma of Glass-Steagall, 33 Emory L.J. 1, 11 (1983).

Do you agree with this characterization of the Court's reading of the legislative history? If so, what do you think is the justification for

2. Section 3 of the Securities Exchange Act of 1934, 15 U.S.C. §78c(a), states in part:

> (10) The term "security" means any note, stock, treasury stock, bond, debenture, certificate of interest or participation in any profit-sharing agreement or in any oil, gas, or other mineral royalty or lease, any collateral-trust certificate, preorganization certificate or subscription, transferable share, investment contract, voting-trust certificate, certificate of deposit, or in general, any instrument commonly known as a "security;" or any certificate of interest or participation in, temporary or interim certificate for, receipt for, or warrant or right to subscribe to or purchase, any of the foregoing; but shall not include currency or any note, draft, bill of exchange, or banker's acceptance which has a maturity at the time of issuance of not exceeding nine months, exclusive of days of grace, or any renewal thereof the maturity of which is likewise limited.

holding banks to a higher standard of care than other sorts of financial institutions?

Professor Macey continues his article below.

## Macey, Special Interest Groups Legislation and the Judicial Function: The Dilemma of Glass-Steagall

***33 Emory L.J. 1 (1983)***

### . . . 1. Banks' Standard of Care When Making Investments

The first hazard described [by the court] was considered "obvious": that a bank might invest its own assets in . . . imprudent stock or security investments. It is hard to fathom how Glass-Steagall reduces the risks of banks making imprudent investment decisions. Perhaps Congress actually believed *all* investments in stock or securities to be inherently more risky than *all* other commercial banking activities. Actually, what is "obvious" is the fact that bank ownership of high grade, blue chip stock, which is prohibited by the Act, is inherently far less risky than many bank loans such as those to third world countries or to real estate investment trusts, to use modern day examples. A possible defense of the separation prescribed by the Act could be that *most* stock or security purchases are more risky than *most* personal or commercial loans. But the incoherence of this defense is apparent. It is just as likely that the opposite is true, i.e., that most stock or securities are *less* risky than most bank loans.

Risk levels are reflected by risk premiums incorporated into interest rates. The higher the risk premium and rate of interest, the greater the risk of the investment, all other factors being equal. The relevant characteristics of a portfolio are its expected return and its riskiness. Rates of return on stocks should be higher on average than rates of return on commercial loans if such lending activity is somehow inherently "safer." There is no evidence that this is so. And, while commercial lenders—since they hold debt as opposed to equity instruments—are often in a better position in case of default, the greater liquidity of stock is a significant safety feature. Furthermore, the proscriptions of Glass-Steagall do not apply merely to banks' acquisitions, but to all securities—debt as well as equity. Clearly, if the relevant indicia of safety is the rate of return, by forbidding banks from diversifying their asset portfolios by holding stock, the Glass-Steagall Act makes commercial banking a riskier endeavor, not a safer one.

Besides this "obvious" danger to bank safety, the Court determined that the legislative history of the Glass-Steagall Act evinces a congressional concern with the "subtle hazards that arise when a commercial bank goes beyond the business of acting as fiduciary or managing agent and enters the investment banking business." Several of these dangers can be described generally as a concern that banks will exacerbate bad lending decisions by "throwing good money after bad." *Camp* evinces a concern that a commercial bank would either invest in a particular company's stock or participate in the underwriting or promotion of such stock and then "make its credit facilities more freely available to those companies in whose stock or securities the affiliate has invested or become otherwise involved." In addition to lines of credit, Congress "feared that banks might even go so far as to make unsound loans to such companies." Moreover, just as banks might loan money to a corporation in order to bolster the value of the corporation's stock, so too might banks make loans to bank customers that customers would use to buy stock, thereby puffing up the price of the security. If the loans were made with the "expectation that (the proceeds) would facilitate the purchase of stocks and securities," then a bank's efforts to manipulate stock prices would influence the bank to make bad commercial loans.

Each of these "bank stability" arguments is incoherent. Unless a bank is *trying* to bankrupt itself there is no reason to believe it would engage in any of these activities. A congressional attempt to ensure bank stability for the reasons articulated in *Camp* and described above is analogous to a hypothetical rule that would restrict bank loans to one per customer. This rule might be justified on the grounds that it prevents banks from suffering losses on subsequent loans in order to insure being repaid on the first loan. Such a rule would clearly do more harm than good since frequently second loans are fully justified. Banks have more than ample market incentives to restrict their lending in such a way as to maximize net revenue for the bank.

In sum, any notion that Glass-Steagall can be justified on grounds that commercial banks are somehow made safer by the Act's prohibitions is clearly misguided, since the law, if anything, accomplishes precisely the opposite result. If allowed to buy and sell stocks, commercial banks could diversify their portfolio of assets, thereby reducing risk. Similarly, by entering the investment banking business, banks could achieve cost savings in numerous ways. As a firm's costs of operation are reduced, the firm necessarily becomes less risky since such a firm can earn a concomitantly lower gross return on investment without risking insolvency.

### 2. Conflicts of Interest

The Supreme Court in *Camp* articulated a separate though closely related set of congressional motives behind the Glass-Steagall Act. The legislature was said to have acted under the premise that public confidence and customer good will are essential to bank solvency. Based on this premise, the Court seemed to believe that terrible things might happen if a bank depositor lost money on a securities investment bought from a bank. For example, the customer might withdraw his money from the bank, thereby threatening the bank's stability. Similarly, if the bank's securities department proved unprofitable, public confidence in the bank would erode.

None of these public confidence concerns, however, provides a persuasive justification for Glass-Steagall. There is no reason whatsoever why public confidence in a bank will be threatened more if the bank loses money in its securities operations than in its lending operations. It is even more far fetched to presume that the stability of the banking system generally is threatened by irate deposit customers making withdrawals because of losses suffered in stock purchases. Actually, the effect will be that deposits will simply flow to those banks that give sound investment advice. These banks, and a fortiori the banking system, will be strengthened by their securities activities. Any residual problems will be solved by deposit insurance. . . .

## *QUESTIONS AND COMMENTS*

1. While agreeing with Professor Macey's basic point that commercial banking activities are not inherently safer than investment banking activities, an important article by Professors Fischel, Rosenfield, and Stillman has extended Macey's analysis of the *ICI* decision in two ways. Their first point concerns the conflicts of interest that banks face when they assume the promotional role of an investment banker. The Supreme Court feared that allowing banks and their affiliates to enter the securities business would cause commercial bankers to become "promoters" rather than "bankers," and that as a result they would be unable to "function as an impartial source of credit" for their customers. Investment Co. Institute v. Camp, 401 U.S. 617, 630-631 (1971) Fischel, Rosenfield, and Stillman argue that this concern does not square with economic theory:

> Virtually all firms—and certainly all financial service firms, including investment banks—provide information as well as products and services. Businesses and individuals routinely turn to investment bankers, fund managers, accountants, lawyers, and the like for investment and financial advice. There is nothing special about the financial counsel offered by banks. That banks could conceivably offer their customers misleading investment advice that could, at least in the short run, be profitable to the bank does not distinguish banks from any other provider of information. . . .
>
> The incentive to provide misleading information is minimized because a firm's reputation is a critical asset that controls the firm's long-term viability and business prospects. . . . [A] bank that manipulates customers

> by offering poor investment services or financial advice in an effort to enrich itself and its affiliates may well be driven out of the market by banks offering superior performance and service.
>
> Finally, a strong argument can be made that the advice provided by banks would be more, not less, disinterested if banks and their affiliates could offer other financial products. For example, because banks cannot offer many types of investments, they have an incentive to promote debt financing instead of a mix of debt and equity financing. Consider as an analogy a rule prohibiting law firms from offering services to both partnerships and corporations. One class of law firm would market and promote the partnership form, while others would market and promote the corporate form. Although clients would not necessarily make the wrong choice, the cost of making the correct choice would increase—visits to both types of law firm might be required. These costs could be avoided if businesses could turn to a single law firm for "disinterested" counsel. . . . The same would be true if customers could turn to a single financial firm for "disinterested" advice concerning different financial products.

Fischel, Rosenfield & Stillman, The Regulation of Banks and Bank Holding Companies, 73 Va. L. Rev. 301, 324-325 (1987).

2. The second point made by Fischel, Rosenfield, and Stillman concerns the question of whether keeping commercial banks out of investment banking promotes the safety of the commercial banking industry. These authors observe that combining commercial and investment banking may *reduce* rather than increase the overall riskiness of the firm that is engaged in both activities. Id. at 320. The argument is that the Glass-Steagall Act may increase commercial bank riskiness by preventing such banks from attaining a low-cost means to diversify their portfolios. Fischel, Rosenfield, and Stillman's argument is based on modern portfolio theory, which has demonstrated that the riskiness of a particular asset—such as a security—cannot be viewed in isolation because regardless of how risky one particular asset may be, the risk may be offset by combining that asset with other assets in a portfolio. For example, holding stock in an amusement park may be very risky because a long rainy period during the summer months could wipe out the park's projected earnings. But a portfolio that contained not only amusement park stock, but stock in an umbrella company as well, may eliminate much of the risk associated with holding only the individual amusement park stock. Based on modern portfolio theory, Fischel, Rosenfield and Stillman conclude that "there are unexploited opportunities for reducing the risk of banks' assets by combining banking with nonbanking activities" such as investment banking. Id. at 321.

3. Justice Harlan dissented in *ICI* on standing grounds. He would have denied standing to the special interest group petitioning for relief on the grounds that whatever the Glass-Steagall Act was intended to accomplish, it was not simply designed "to protect petitioner's class against

competitive injury." 401 U.S. at 640. Justice Harlan found it "reasonably plain that, if anything, the Act was adopted despite its anticompetitive effects rather than because of them." Id.

This observation by Justice Harlan essentially is predicated on a particular view of the legislative process. A number of commentators have taken a much different view of the legislative process that generated Glass-Steagall and have concluded that the act as passed precisely *because* of its anticompetitive effects. Professor Macey has written that "Glass-Steagall was passed because a special interest group, namely investment bankers (perhaps along with some commercial bankers who wanted to leave the field), was able to persuade Congress to prohibit commercial banks from competing with the group. . . . Glass-Steagall clearly represents an agreement between a special interest group and the legislature." Macey, Special Interest Groups Legislation and the Judicial Function: The Dilemma of Glass-Steagall, 33 Emory L.J. 1, 17-20 (1983). Professor George Benston has concluded that "the evidence supports the belief that the investment bankers and underwriters were concerned about severe competition from banks and bank affiliates and sought (successfully in 1933) to eliminate these competitors." Benston, Federal Regulation of Banking, Analysis and Policy Recommendations, 13 J. Bank Res. 216, 222 (1983). Judge Frank Easterbrook has reached a similar conclusion, see Easterbrook, Foreword: The Court and the Economic System, 98 Harvard L. Rev. 4, 57 (1984), as has William Shugart II, A Public Choice Perspective of the 1933 Banking Act, in The Financial Services Revolution (C. England & T. Huertas, eds. 1988).

Professor Donald Langevoort, however, replies that "[t]he claims made by Benston, Easterbrook and Macey are based on deduction rather than discovered fact: convinced that there is no *rational* economic policy to support a wall of separation between banking and the securities industry . . . , they conclude that the only possible alternative explanation is a skewing of the political process by those who later turned out to be immense beneficiaries of the statute." Langevoort, Statutory Obsolescence and the Judicial Process: The Revisionist Role of the Courts in Federal Banking Regulation, 85 Mich. L. Rev. 672, 692 (1987). Langevoort supplies an "explanation for the separation of investment and commercial banking that does not involve special-interest pressure from the private investment bankers." Id. at 697. Thus he finds a public interest-oriented justification for the Glass-Steagall Act. Specifically he claims that Glass-Steagall was intended to achieve the goal of "influencing the use of funds in the financial system." Id. at 683.

Professor Langevoort contends that Congress was troubled by the fact that during the 1920s, banks often loaned money to individuals and firms to help them finance securities purchases. Langevoort argues that Glass-Steagall was designed to prevent banks from using their funds in this way:

> [T]he principal motivation [for passage of Glass-Steagall] was pursuit, perhaps more emotional than rational, of the channeling objective—an attempt to force banks to redirect their resources, efforts, and energies to the traditional business of commercial lending by foreclosing the securities temptation. If any special interest group was instrumental in this regard, it was probably the smaller businesses and farmers . . . who considered the unavailability of credit at least partially responsible for their current woes. Many in Congress . . . also viewed separation as a politically attractive way of appearing to respond punitively to the bankers' recently exposed excesses.

Id. at 697. Thus Langevoort argues that the discovery that 41 percent of all commercial bank assets were invested in securities or securities-related loans was "the most significant statistic leading to eventual passage of the Glass-Steagall Act." Id. at 694.

4. Does the fact that the Glass-Steagall Act does nothing to prohibit commercial banks from making loans to individuals or to securities firms for the purpose of buying securities make you doubt Langevoort's analysis? Professor Macey writes that "Langevoort's analysis is rather ironic in light of the fact that during the stock market crash of October 1987, the hesitancy of commercial banks to extend credit to securities firms was a source of great concern to regulators, particularly the Federal Reserve Board, which exerted significant pressure on commercial banks to extend funds to brokerage houses in need of cash." Macey, The Political Science of Regulating Bank Risk, 49 Ohio State L.J. 1277, 1291 n.75 (1989).

5. Macey argues that the "major flaw" in Langevoort's argument is that "bank lending and securities underwriting, which Glass-Steagall attempts to separate, are substitutes for one another." Thus, in Professor Macey's view, Langevoort's argument that lending by commercial banks to individuals and firms involved in the securities business deprived other businesses of capital is untenable, because the securities firms that received money from commercial banks were using it to supply these other businesses with capital by purchasing and underwriting corporate debt and equity. Id.

## C. DISCOUNT BROKERAGE SERVICES

A discount broker is a financial intermediary that executes trades for clients for low commissions. The principal difference between traditional stockbrokers and discount brokers is that traditional brokers provide investment advice to their clients while discount brokers merely enter orders for clients who wish to buy or sell. Discount brokers, however, do offer their customers margin accounts, which are brokerage accounts in which the broker loans the customer money to purchase securities. The securities purchased serve as collateral for the loan. The Federal Reserve Board regulates margin accounts, and the board's Regulation T controls the amount of credit that can be extended to margin account customers.

The offering of discount brokerage accounts by commercial banks raises a number of interesting legal questions. The first question we will consider is whether a national bank can offer discount brokerage services.

## Securities Industry Association v. Comptroller of the Currency

***577 F. Supp. 252 (D.D.C. 1983), aff'd per curiam, 758 F.2d 739 (D.C. Cir. 1985), rev'd on other grounds sub nom. Clarke v. Securities Industry Association, 479 U.S. 388 (1987)***

FLANNERY, District Judge.

This matter is before the court on cross-motions for summary judgment. Plaintiff Securities Industry Association ("SIA"), a national trade association representing more than five hundred securities brokers, dealers and underwriters, challenges the actions of the Comptroller of the Currency, C. T. Conover, in approving the applications of two national banks for the establishment or purchase of discount securities brokerage subsidiaries. . . .

### Facts

On June 23, 1982 Union Planters National Bank of Memphis applied to the Comptroller for approval of the acquisition by Union Planters of Brenner Steed and Associates, Inc., a discount brokerage business in Memphis, Tennessee. In its application Union Planters said it intended to offer securities brokerage services through Brenner Steed at certain branch offices of Union Planters in Tennessee, at affiliated banks in Tennessee, and at correspondent banks in Tennessee and six other states.

On July 2, 1982 Security Pacific National Bank applied to the Comptroller for approval of its proposed establishment of a new operating subsidiary to provide discount brokerage services. In its application Security Pacific said the new subsidiary would offer brokerage services at certain Security Pacific branch offices and might in the future offer those services at non-branch offices in California and other states. The new subsidiary will process and extend margin loans.

Brenner Steed is, and the Security Pacific subsidiary will be, "discount" brokerages, which will buy and sell securities solely as agent, on the order and for the account of customers. Neither will purchase or sell securities for its own account, nor engage in underwriting, nor give investment advice. "Discount" brokers are so characterized because their commissions are significantly lower than those charged by full-service brokers who, in addition to trading on behalf of customers, offer investment advice.

On August 26, 1982 the Comptroller approved the Security Pacific application. On September 20, 1982 the Comptroller approved the Union Planters application, and in September, 1982 Union Planters acquired Brenner Steed. This action followed.

### DISCUSSION

SIA argues that the Comptroller's decisions should be set aside as in excess of his statutory authority [because] the operation of a brokerage business by a national bank or its affiliate violates Sections 16 and 21 of the Glass-Steagall Act of 1933, 12 U.S.C. §§24 Seventh, 378. . . .

### *B. THE GLASS-STEAGALL ACT*

*1. The Act does not limit bank affiliates to securities transactions solely for pre-existing customers.* SIA argues that Glass-Steagall permits banks to provide brokerage services only to pre-existing, bona fide bank customers. Glass-Steagall, says SIA, intended to erect impenetrable barriers between commercial banks and investment banks in order to avoid the kind of rampant speculation of the 1920's which brought the banking system to the brink of collapse, when banks would use depositors' money to push speculative securities out on the market. In support of its argument SIA points to two provisions of Glass-Steagall. Section 21, 12 U.S.C. §378, prohibits any organization "engaged in the business of issuing, underwriting, selling or distributing, at wholesale or retail . . . securities . . ." from engaging at the same time in the banking business. Discount brokers engage in the retail purchase and sale of securities and so, argues the SIA, are prohibited from being part of a banking business at the same time.

Section 16, 12 U.S.C. §24 Seventh, limits bank brokerage activity to that "upon the order, and for the account of, customers . . . ." This section, says SIA, is a very limited exception to the otherwise unyielding barrier between commercial and investment banking established by Glass-Steagall, and exists only in order to accommodate existing bank customers. In support of its position, SIA cites several early Comptroller opinions holding that Section 16 limits bank brokerage transactions to those performed for customers of the bank whose relationship with the bank exists independently of the securities transaction. . . . The SIA concedes that the Comptroller modified his position in 1974 when, in approving an application to provide Automatic Investment Services, a ruling upheld by this court, . . . the Comptroller reversed his prior interpretations to say that "accommodation" did not mean that banks could not charge customers for the brokerage service. But the Comptroller left untouched, says SIA, the requirement that the customer relationship exist independent of the securities transaction conducted as part of the brokerage services.

The court is not persuaded by SIA. The language of Section 16 limiting bank securities to those "for the account of customers" does not limit bank brokerage activity, but serves to distinguish such activity from buying and selling of securities by the bank for its own account. Despite the exhaustive cataloging in the legislative history of Glass-Steagall of the ills arising out of the previous intermingling of investment and commercial banking, there is no mention of limiting bank brokerage activity. On the contrary, the one mention appearing in the legislative history says that Glass-Steagall will permit national banks to sell and buy securities for their customers "to the same extent as heretofore." And as the Comptroller demonstrates, through citation both to earlier case law and secondary sources, prior to the passage of Glass-Steagall banks offered brokerage services to members of the general public, and not just to existing customers.

The early opinions of the Comptroller relied on by SIA embody "an overcautious approach to bank regulation reflecting the atmosphere of the years immediately after the 1929 market crash," . . . and have gradually been disavowed by the Comptroller in the intervening decades. . . .

In accordance with the foregoing, the court holds that the Glass-Steagall Act does not prohibit the ownership and operation by national banks of subsidiaries engaged in the brokerage business. . . .

### *QUESTIONS AND COMMENTS*

1. The Supreme Court affirmed that aspect of the court's decision allowing commercial banks to offer discount brokerage services. Clarke v. Securities Industry Association, 479 U.S. at 409.

2. May nonbank subsidiaries of bank holding companies serve as discount brokers consistent with the Bank Holding Company Act? Consider the following case.

## Securities Industry Association v. Board of Governors of the Federal Reserve System

***468 U.S. 207 (1984)***

Justice Powell delivered the opinion of the Court. . . .

BankAmerica Corp. (BAC) is a bank holding company within the meaning of the Bank Holding Company Act. In March 1982, BAC applied to the Federal Reserve Board (Board) for approval under §4(c)(8) of the Act to acquire 100 percent of the voting shares of The Charles Schwab Corp., a company that engages through its wholly owned subsidiary, Charles Schwab & Co. (Schwab), in retail discount brokerage. The Board ordered that formal public hearings be held before an Administrative Law Judge (ALJ) to consider the application. The Securities Industry Association (SIA), a national trade association of securities brokers, and petitioner here, opposed BAC's application. . . .

[The court concluded that the proposed activity was permissible under §4(c)(8) of the Bank Holding Company Act.]

### *B*

The Board expressly considered and rejected SIA's argument that BAC's acquisition of Schwab violates the Glass-Steagall Act. That Act comprises four sections of the Banking Act of 1933. Only one of those four sections is applicable here. That provision, §20, as set forth in 12 U.S.C. §377, provides in relevant part:

> [N]o member bank shall be affiliated in any manner described in subsection (b) of section 221a of this title with any corporation, association, business trust, or other similar organization *engaged principally in the issue, flotation, underwriting, public sale, or distribution* at wholesale or retail or through syndicate participation of stocks, bonds, debentures, notes, or other securities. . . .

(Emphasis added.) A bank holding company's subsidiaries are bank affiliates within the meaning of §20. 12 U.S.C. §221a(b). Section 20, therefore, prohibits BAC's proposed acquisition if Schwab is "engaged principally" in any of the activities listed therein.

SIA concedes that Schwab is not engaged in the "issue, flotation, underwriting, . . . or distribution" of securities. It argues, however, that the term "public sale" of securities as used in §20 applies to Schwab's brokerage business. The Board rejected this argument, holding that "Schwab is not engaged principally in any of the activities prohibited to member bank affiliates by the Glass-Steagall Act." 69 Fed. Res. Bull., at 114. The Board has broad power to regulate and supervise bank holding companies and banks that are members of the Federal Reserve System. In this respect, the Board has primary responsibility for implementing the Glass-Steagall Act, and we accord substantial deference to the Board's interpretation of that Act whenever its interpretation provides a reasonable construction of the statutory language and is consistent with legislative intent. . . .

"Public sale" is used in conjunction with the terms "issue," "flotation," "underwriting," and "distribution" of securities. None of these terms has any relevance to the brokerage business at issue in this case. Schwab does not engage in issuing or floating the sale of securities, and the terms "underwriting" and "distribution" traditionally apply to a function distinctly different from that of a securities broker. An underwriter normally acts as principal whereas a broker executes orders for the purchase or sale of securities solely as agent. Under the "familiar principle of statutory construction that words grouped in a list should be given related meaning," Third National Bank v. Impac, Ltd., 432 U.S. 312, 322, 97 S. Ct. 2807, 2313, 58 L. Ed. 2d 368 (1977) (footnote omitted), the term "public sale" in §20 should be read to refer to the underwriting activity described by the terms that surround it, and to exclude the type of retail brokerage business in which Schwab principally is engaged.

This reading of the statute is further supported by the Board's longstanding interpretation of identical language found in §32 of the Glass-Steagall Act, 12 U.S.C. §78. That section prohibits interlocking management or employment between banks and any entity "primarily engaged in the *issue, flotation, underwriting, public sale, or distribution,* at wholesale or retail, or through syndicate participation" of securities. 12 U.S.C. §78 (emphasis added). In January 1936, the Board interpreted the list of prohibited activities described in §32 to exclude the kind of brokerage activities at issue here. Specifically, the Board ruled that

> [a] broker who is engaged solely in executing orders for the purchase and sale of securities on behalf of others in the open market is not engaged in the business referred to in section 32.

22 Fed. Res. Bull. 51, n.1 (1936). Because §§32 and 20 contain identical language, were enacted for similar purposes, and are part of the same statute, the long-accepted interpretation of the term "public sale" to exclude brokerage services such as those offered by Schwab should apply as well to §20. The Board's interpretation of the disputed term is supported by the plain language of the statute. It is also entirely consistent with legislative intent.

The legislative history demonstrates that Congress enacted §20 to prohibit the affiliation of commercial banks with entities that were engaged principally in "activities such as underwriting." [Board of Governors v. Investment Co. Institute,] 450 U.S., at 64, 101 S.Ct., at 985; see [Investment Co. Institute v. Camp,] 401 U.S., at 630-634, 91 S.Ct., at 1098-1100. In 1933, Congress believed that the heavy involvement of commercial banks in underwriting and securities speculation had precipitated "the widespread bank closings that occurred during the Great Depression." *ICI,* 450 U.S., at 61, 101 S.Ct., at 984. One of the most serious threats to sound commercial banking perceived by Congress was the existence of "bank affiliates" that "devote themselves in many cases to perilous underwriting operations, stock speculation, and maintaining a market for the banks' own stock often largely with the resources of the parent bank." . . .

Congressional concern over the underwriting activities of bank affiliates included both the fear that bank funds would be lost in speculative investments and the suspicion that the more "subtle hazards" associated with underwriting would encourage unsound banking practices. See *Camp*, 401 U.S., at 630, 91 S.Ct., at 1099. None of the more "subtle hazards" of underwriting identified in *Camp* is implicated by the brokerage activities at issue here.[23] Because Schwab trades only as agent, its assets are not subject to the vagaries of the securities markets. Moreover, Schwab's profits depend solely on the volume of shares it trades and not on the purchase or sale of particular securities. Thus, BAC has no "salesman's stake" in the securities Schwab trades. It cannot increase Schwab's profitability by having its bank affiliate extend credit to issuers of particular securities, nor by encouraging the bank affiliate improperly to favor particular securities in the management of depositors' assets. Finally, the fact that §16 of the Glass-Steagall Act allows banks to engage directly in the kind of brokerage services at issue here, to accommodate its customers, suggests that the activity was not the sort that concerned Congress in its effort to secure the Nation's banks from the risks of the securities market.

In sum, we see no reason to disturb the Board's determination that "the business of purchasing or selling securities upon the unsolicited order of, and as agent for, a particular customer does not constitute the 'public sale' of securities for purposes of section 20." 69 Fed. Res. Bull., at 114. This interpretation of the Glass-Steagall Act is reasonable, consistent with the plain language of the statute and its legislative history, and deserves the deference normally accorded the Board's construction of the banking laws.

## IV

The Board determined in this case that a securities brokerage business that is essentially limited to the purchase and sale of securities for the account of customers, and without provision of investment advice to purchaser or seller, is "closely related" to banking. We hold that the Board's determination is consistent with the language and policies of the BHC Act. We also hold that the Board's determination that the Glass-Steagall Act permits bank holding companies to acquire firms engaged

23. See *Camp*, 401 U.S., at 631-634, 91 S.Ct., at 1099-1100 (identifying the "subtle hazards" of affiliation with underwriting firms). All these "subtle hazards" are attributable to the promotional pressures that arise from affiliation with entities that purchase and sell particular investments on their own account.

in such a brokerage business is reasonable and supported by the plain language and legislative history of the Act. We therefore affirm the judgment of the Court of Appeals.

It is so ordered.

*QUESTIONS AND COMMENTS*

1. In light of the discussion earlier in this chapter, is this decision really a surprise insofar as it concludes that securities brokerage is "closely-related to banking" under the Bank Holding Company Act? What could be more "closely related" to commercial banking than a business such as securities sales that is a close substitute for commercial banking?

2. Brokerage firms buy and sell securities for customers and give investment advice. At times they also serve as underwriters and dealers, buying and selling securities for their own accounts. After Securities Industry Association v. Comptroller and Securities Industry Association v. Board of Governors of the Federal Reserve System ("Schwab"), it was clear that commercial banks and bank holding companies could offer discount brokerage services. The next hurdle was an express ruling that they could offer investment advice in conjunction with the offering of discount brokerage services.

In Securities Industry Association v. Board of Governors of the Federal Reserve System (NatWest), 821 F.2d 810 (D.C. Cir. 1987), the D.C. Circuit upheld the Federal Reserve's ruling that National Westminster Bank PLC (NatWest) and its subsidiary NatWest Holdings, Inc., could provide both investment advice and securities brokerage to institutional customers through a newly formed subsidiary called County Services Corporation. Crucial to the resolution of the case was the court's conclusion that the subsidiary was not involved in a public sale of securities. 821 F.2d at 813-814. If County Services was involved in a public sale, it would have been in violation of §20 of Glass-Steagall, which prohibits member banks from affiliating with any corporation "engaged principally in the issue, flotation, underwriting, public sale, or distribution of securities." 12 U.S.C. §377.

The D.C. Circuit concluded that combining brokerage services and investment advice does not involve underwriting because underwriting involves purchasing securities as principal, whereas a broker normally executes orders for the purchase or sale of securities solely as agent. 821 F.2d at 813. Similarly, the court concluded that combining brokerage services and investment advice is not a "public sale" of securities. *NatWest* represented another defeat for the securities industry in its efforts to stave off competition from the commercial banking sector.

3. In Banking Circular 274 (1993), the Comptroller established policy on the retail sale of securities by national banks. The circular warns

that banks might be found to have engaged in unsafe and unsound practices if they contract with a party that violates the securities laws. Thus, if a bank refers customers to a third-party broker-dealer and receives a benefit for making the referral, the bank may be held responsible for legal and regulatory compliance by the third-party broker-dealer. Moreover, the OCC claims examination authority over the securities sales operations of unaffiliated third parties with whom banks contract for securities sales.

The circular establishes guidelines to ensure that customers will not confuse securities products with deposit products. These guidelines encourage physical separation between deposit-taking and securities activities, and they specifically discourage securities sales by tellers. National banks must disclose that the securities products they are selling are not FDIC-insured, are not guaranteed by the bank, and involve investment risk, including the loss of principal. National banks may not offer investment products with names similar to that of the bank. Any relationship between the bank and the securities affiliate, any relationship between the bank and other securities entities, and any fees, sales charges, and penalties associated with securities and mutual fund shares must be disclosed. Not only must disclosures be made in all written and oral presentations as well as on advertising and promotional materials, but national banks are advised by the OCC to obtain a statement signed by the customer acknowledging that the disclosures have been made in a timely fashion.

Banks selling securities must also comply with the National Association of Securities Dealers' suitability rules. These rules require that banks selling securities must determine that the securities are appropriate investments for the particular customers making the purchase; the banks must obtain information about the customer's financial position, tax status, and investment objectives before making a recommendation. The OCC circular expresses concern that compensation for bank employees not be structured in such a way as to provide employees with incentives to sell securities products over other "more suitable" products.

## D. INVESTMENT COMPANY ACTIVITIES

In Investment Co. Institute v. Camp, 401 U.S. 617 (1971)(*ICI I*), the case excerpted above, the Court struck down a national bank's attempt to operate an open-end investment company. Recall that open-end investment companies are mutual funds that continuously issue new shares and stand ready to redeem the investor's interest at any time. It might have been reasonable, especially given the broad language in the *ICI I* opinion about "subtle hazards," to assume that the Glass-Steagall Act prohibits banks from having any part in the organization or operation of investment companies of any sort.

As things have turned out, this expectation would have been entirely misguided. Banking organizations are now heavily involved in the investment company business. Indeed, investments in bank-affiliated funds became one of the fastest growing parts of the banking business. How did the banking industry enter the mutual fund business, despite the apparent blanket prohibition in *ICI I?*

An important early step was the Supreme Court's decision in Board of Governors v. Investment Co. Institute, 450 U.S. 46 (1981)(*ICI II*). The Federal Reserve Board had issued a regulation permitting a bank holding company and its nonbank subsidiaries to organize, sponsor, and advise a *closed-end* investment company so long as they did not extend credit to the investment company and played no role in the sale or distribution of its shares. Unlike an open-end investment company, a closed-end investment company does not stand ready to redeem customer investments and rarely issues shares after its initial organization. Customers wishing to cash out of a closed-end company must sell their shares on a secondary market such as a stock exchange, much as stockholders in ordinary industrial firms must do to liquidate a position. Because of this feature, closed-end companies do not allow customers to write checks on their accounts.

The Investment Company Institute challenged the Fed's regulation permitting bank holding companies to organize, sponsor, and advise closed-end funds, on the ground that the regulation violated the Glass-Steagall Act and the intent of Congress to separate commercial and investment banking. The Supreme Court rejected these arguments.

How was *ICI II* consistent with *ICI I,* which seemed to hold that interests in an open-end investment company were securities that the bank was underwriting in violation of the Glass-Steagall Act? The Court explained:

> [T]he decision by an investment adviser to purchase or sell securities on behalf of a closed-end investment company is critically different from the comparable decision by the operator of the mutual fund reviewed in *Camp.* When an adviser makes a change in the securities portfolio of a closed-end company, the adviser is acting for the account of its customer—not for its own account. In *Camp,* however, the securities in the portfolio of the mutual fund were at least arguably the property of the bank itself and therefore the bank was arguably acting for its own account within the meaning of §16.

450 U.S. 66.

With respect to the "subtle hazards" identified by the Court in *ICI I,* the Court further explained:

> The Court in *Camp* recognized that in enacting the Glass-Steagall Act, Congress contemplated other hazards in addition to the danger of banks using bank assets in imprudent securities investments. But none of these "more subtle hazards" would be present were a bank to act as an investment adviser to a closed-end investment company subject to the restrictions imposed by the Board. Those restrictions would prevent the bank from extending credit to the investment company and would also preclude the promotional pressures that are inherent in the investment banking business.

Id.

## *QUESTIONS AND COMMENTS*

1. How convincing is the *ICI II* Court's distinction from *ICI I?* Why did the Court twice use the word "arguably" in the first passage quoted above? Doesn't the later decision implicitly undermine the earlier case?

2. What do you think of the argument that many of the same dangers and subtle hazards that the Court recognized in *ICI I* were also present in *ICI II?* Was the only difference the fact that the Court was in a *proregulatory* frame of mind in *ICI I* but a *deregulatory* frame of mind when it decided *ICI II?* A banking firm, on this analysis, is just as likely to invest in imprudent investments through a closed-end fund as through an open-end fund. Similarly, banking firms might make loans to customers to facilitate the purchase of closed-end shares just as they might to facilitate the purchase of open-end shares. A banking firm is just as likely to make unsound loans to companies in which the closed-end fund has invested as it is to make unsound loans to companies in which the open-end fund has invested. Bank customers might suffer losses on their investments in either kind of investment company—indeed, customers who have invested in closed-end companies might suffer greater losses because they cannot liquidate their positions through direct redemption of shares.

3. In *ICI I,* the Court viewed the Glass-Steagall Act as an outright prohibition on commercial bank involvement in the securities business. 401 U.S. 629-30. Does the opinion in *ICI II* indicate that, as a practical matter, it is impossible to effectuate Congress's wish to separate commercial and investment banking?

4. The Court in *ICI II* stated that none of the subtle hazards identified in *ICI I* would be present if a bank holding company were to act as an investment adviser to a closed-end investment company. 450 U.S. 67. The Court based this conclusion, in part, on the fact that the Federal Reserve Board had imposed certain restrictions on the activities of bank-

affiliated investment advisers. The Court stated that "if the restrictions imposed by the Board's interpretive ruling are followed, investment advisory services—even if performed by a bank—would not violate the requirements of section 16." Id. 62. Why should the restrictions imposed by the Board be relevant? Would the *ICI I* Court have been satisfied if the Comptroller had similarly restricted the activities of the national bank in that case?

5. The Board's rule permitting bank holding companies to sponsor, organize, and manage closed-end funds is codified in Regulation Y. 12 C.F.R. §225.25(b)(4); see also 12 C.F.R. §225.125.

6. The holding in *ICI II* applied to nonbanks in a bank holding structure. Does the same rule extend to banks themselves? Given that shares in a closed-end company are securities, may national and state member banks sponsor such securities consistent with §16 of the Glass-Steagall Act?

## NOTE ON BANK INVOLVEMENT IN THE INVESTMENT COMPANY BUSINESS

Banking firms have continued to make inroads into the investment company business in the years since *ICI II*. For example, it is clear that banking firms can act as investment advisers to both open-end and closed-end funds. Thus, a bank or bank holding company can manage a fund's portfolio subject to the direction of the fund's board of directors.

The power to act as investment advisor, however, may be subject to prudential limitations. Under the Federal Reserve Board's regulation, for example, bank holding companies should not advise a fund with a name similar to that of the bank holding company, purchase the shares of a fund for its own account, purchase fund shares in a ficudiary capacity, extend credit to the fund, or distribute the fund's shares. In addition, the board requires that a customer who purchases or sells securities of the fund through the holding company or who is advised by the holding company to purchase shares of the fund must be informed in writing of the holding company's involvement with the fund and must also be informed that the shares of the fund are not federally insured and are not guaranteed by, or obligations of, any bank.

Besides allowing bank holding companies to offer investment advice, the board authorizes them to act as custodians, transfer agents, and registrars to both open-end and closed-end funds. In Mellon Bank Corporation, 79 Federal Reserve Bulletin 626 (1993), the board authorized a bank holding company to provide administrative services to mutual funds as well. The board decided that allowing a bank holding company that serves as investment advisor to a mutual fund to also provide the essential ministerial or supporting functions as administrator of that fund would not significantly increase the ability of the bank holding company to control the fund.

It is not yet clear whether a bank holding company has the power to sponsor and underwrite open-end funds through a nonbank subsidiary. As discussed below, so-called "section 20" subsidiaries of bank holding companies now engage in full-scale securities underwriting of stocks and bonds. It would seem that such a subsidiary might have similar powers to distribute open-end fund shares. The board, however, has discouraged such activities. State-chartered banks that are not members of the Federal Reserve System are not prohibited by the Glass-Steagall Act from sponsoring and underwriting open-end funds (or engaging in other underwriting activities, for that matter), but the FDIC requires that such activities be conducted through a subsidiary of the bank, and it places certain other limitations on the activity.

## E. COMMERCIAL PAPER CASES: THE ULTIMATE BREACH OF THE MAGINOT LINE

The foregoing opinions allow banks and bank holding companies to engage in discount brokerage and permit affiliates of bank holding companies, as well as banks themselves, to provide investment advisory services in conjunction with securities brokerage. The principal remaining bastion of investment banking was the underwriting of securities. The battles on this front in the war between commercial and investment banks have centered around a series of cases that involved the commercial banks' entry into the commercial paper business.

Commercial paper has become an increasingly important source of short-term financing for publicly held corporations. At the time of the litigation in *Bankers Trust I,* which follows, commercial paper accounted for one quarter of all of the short-term corporate debt outstanding. J. P. Judd, Competition Between Commercial Paper Markets and Commercial Banks 39, 48 (Staff paper, Federal Reserve Bank of San Francisco). The rise of the commercial paper market had encroached considerably on the traditional lending operations of major U.S. banks with many large corporate clients. Such blue-chip customers found that they could save interest expense by issuing short-term commercial paper rather than by taking out bank loans. If commercial paper was not a "security" under Glass-Steagall, then commercial banks would be free to underwrite and trade in the instrument.

## Securities Industry Association v. Board of Governors of the Federal Reserve System (Bankers Trust I)

***468 U.S. 137 (1984)***

Justice BLACKMUN delivered the opinion of the Court.

This case involves a challenge to the efforts of a state commercial bank to enter the business of selling third-party commercial paper. The Board of Governors of the Federal Reserve System (Board) concluded that such activity by state member banks is not prohibited by the Banking Act of 1933, ch. 89, 48 Stat. 162 (commonly known as the Glass-Steagall Act) because commercial paper is neither a "security" nor a "note" within the meaning of that Act and therefore falls outside the Act's proscriptions. The District Court disagreed with the Board, but the Court of Appeals deferred to the Board's interpretation and reversed the judgment of the District Court. . . .

### I

During 1978 Bankers Trust Company (Bankers Trust), a New York-chartered member bank of the Federal Reserve System, began serving as agent for several of its corporate customers in placing their commercial paper[1] in the commercial-paper market. Petitioners, the Securities Industry Association (SIA), a national securities-industry trade association, and A.G. Becker Inc. (Becker), a dealer in commercial paper, informally expressed concern to the Board about Bankers Trust's commercial-paper activities. SIA and Becker subsequently petitioned the Board for, among other things, a ruling that Bankers Trust's activities are unlawful under §§16 and 21 of the Act, 12 U.S.C. §§24 Seventh and 378(a)(1). Section 16 prohibits commercial banks from underwriting "securities or stocks," while §21 prohibits them from marketing "stocks, bonds, debentures, notes, or other securities." Petitioners asserted that Bankers Trust's activities violated both §16 and §21.

On September 26, 1980, the Board responded to petitioners' request for enforcement of §§16 and 21 against Bankers Trust. See Federal Reserve System, Statement Regarding Petitions to Initiate Enforcement Action (1980), App. 122A (Board Statement). The Board acknowledged that Congress enacted the Act to prevent commercial banks from engaging in certain investment-banking activities, but explained that Congress did not intend the Act's prohibitions to cover every instrument that could

1. "Commercial paper" refers generally to unsecured, short-term promissory notes issued by commercial entities. Such a note is payable to the bearer on a stated maturity date. Maturities vary considerably, but typically are less than nine months.

be characterized as a "note" or "security." The Board expressed concern that such a broad interpretation might preclude commercial banks from maintaining many of their traditional activities. Accordingly, the Board took the position that "if a particular kind of financial instrument evidences a transaction that is more functionally similar to a traditional commercial banking operation than to an investment transaction, then fidelity to the purposes of the Act would dictate that the instrument should not be viewed as a security." Id., at 135A. Applying this "functional analysis" to commercial paper, the Board concluded that such paper more closely resembles a commercial bank loan than an investment transaction and that it is not a "security" for purposes of the Glass-Steagall Act. Because of this determination, the Board did not consider whether Bankers Trust's involvement with commercial paper constitutes "underwriting," within the meaning of the Act. . . .

. . . At the administrative level, the Board took the position that commercial paper was not a "security" within the meaning of the Act, and that, therefore, it did "not appear necessary to examine the dangers that the Act was intended to eliminate." . . . Before this Court, however, the Board appears to have changed somewhat the nature of its argument. The Board's counsel now insists that the activities of Bankers Trust "involv[e] none of the 'hazards' that this Court identified" as the concerns at which the Act is aimed. We previously have stated that post hoc rationalizations by counsel for agency action are entitled to little deference: "It is the administrative official and not appellate counsel who possesses the expertise that can enlighten and rationalize the search for the meaning and intent of Congress." Investment Company Institute v. Camp, 401 U.S. 617, 628, 91 S. Ct. 1091, 1097, 28 L. Ed. 2d 367 (1971). As a result, the Board's presentation here of the policies behind the Act as they apply to this case is of less significance than it would be if it had occurred at the administrative level. Because of this apparent shift, moreover, the contours of the Board's present position are somewhat unclear; much of the Board's argument now addresses the particular characteristics of the commercial paper in this case, apparently leaving open the possibility that commercial paper with different characteristics would qualify as a "security" and be subject to the Glass-Steagall Act's proscriptions. To the extent that the Board has changed its position from that adopted at the administrative level, its interpretation is entitled to less weight.

## III

### *A*

In *Camp* this Court explored at some length the congressional concerns that produced the Glass-Steagall Act. Congress passed the Act in the aftermath of the banking collapse that produced the Great Depression of the 1930's. The Act responded to the opinion, widely expressed at the time, that much of the financial difficulty experienced by banks could be traced to their involvement in investment-banking activities both directly and through security affiliates. At the very least, Congress held the view that the extensive involvement by commercial banks had been unwise; some in Congress concluded that it had been illegal. Senator Glass stated bluntly that commercial-bank involvement in securities had made "one of the greatest contributions to the unprecedented disaster which has caused this almost incurable depression." 75 Cong. Rec. 9887 (1932).

Congressional worries about commercial-bank involvement in investment-bank activities reflected two general concerns. The first was the inherent risks of the securities business. Speculation in securities by banks and their affiliates during the speculative fever of the 1920's produced tremendous bank losses when the securities markets went sour. In addition to the palpable effect that such losses had on the assets of affected banks, they also eroded the confidence of depositors in the safety of banks as depository institutions. This crisis of confidence contributed to the runs on the banks that proved so devastating to the solvency of many commercial banks.

But the dangers that Congress sought to eliminate through the Act were considerably more than the obvious risk that a bank could lose money by imprudent investment of its funds in speculative securities. The legislative history of the Act shows that Congress also focused on "the more subtle hazards that arise when a commercial bank goes beyond the business of acting as fiduciary or managing agent and enters the investment banking business." *Camp,* 401 U.S., at 630, 91 S. Ct., at 1099. The Glass-Steagall Act reflects the 1933 Congress' conclusion that certain investment-banking activities conflicted in fundamental ways with the institutional role of commercial banks. . . .

The Act's design reflects the congressional perception that certain investment-banking activities are fundamentally incompatible with commercial banking. . . . Congress rejected the view of those who preferred legislation that simply would regulate the underwriting activities of commercial banks. Congress chose instead a broad structural approach that would "surround the banking business with sound rules which recognize the imperfection of human nature that our bankers may not be led into temptation, the evil effect of which is sometimes so subtle as not to be easily recognized by the most honorable man." 75 Cong. Rec. 9912 (1932) (remarks of Sen. Bulkley). Through flat prohibitions, the Act sought to "separat[e] as completely as possible commercial from investment banking." Board of Governors of Federal Reserve System v. Investment Company Institute, 450 U.S. 46, 70, 101 S. Ct. 973, 989, 67 L. Ed. 2d 36 (1981) *(ICI).* Such an approach was not without costs in terms of efficiency and competition, but the Act reflects the view that the subtle risks created by mixing the two activities justified a strong prophylaxis. *Camp,* 401 U.S., at 630, 91 S. Ct., at 1098.

### *B*

Sections 16 and 21 of the Act are the principal provisions that demarcate the line separating commercial and investment banking. . . . Because §16 and §21 seek to draw the same line, the parties agree that the underwriting prohibitions described in the two sections are coextensive, and we shall assume that to be the case. In any event, because both §16 and §21 apply to Bankers Trust, its activities in this case are unlawful if prohibited by either section. The language of §21 is perhaps the more helpful, however, because that section describes in greater detail the particular activities of investment banking that Congress found inconsistent with the activity of commercial banks.

It is common ground that the terms "stocks," "bonds," and "debentures" do not encompass commercial paper. The dispute in this case focuses instead on petitioners' claims that commercial paper constitutes a "note" within the meaning of §21, and, if not, that it is nevertheless encompassed within the inclusive term "other securities." Thus, petitioners claim that the plain language of the Act makes untenable the Board's conclusion that commercial paper is not a "security" within the meaning of the Act. Petitioners contend further that the role played by Bankers Trust in placing the commercial paper of third parties is precisely what the Glass-Steagall Act sought to prohibit.

### *C*

Neither the term "notes" nor the term "other securities" is defined by the statute. "This silence compels us to 'start with the assumption that the legislative purpose is expressed by the ordinary meaning of the words used.' " Russello v. United States, 464 U.S. 16, 21, 104 S. Ct. 296, 299, 78 L. Ed. 2d 17 (1983), quoting Richards v. United States, 369 U.S. 1, 9, 82 S. Ct. 585, 591, 7 L. Ed. 2d 492 (1962). Respondents do not dispute that commercial paper consists of unsecured promissory notes and falls within the general meaning of the term "notes." Respondents assert, however, that the context in which the term is used suggests that Congress intended a narrower definition. Because the term appears in a phrase that includes "stocks, bonds, [and] debentures," the Board insists that the Act's prohibitions apply only to "notes [and] other securities" that resemble the enumerated financial instruments. The Board's position seems to be that because "stocks, bonds, [and] debentures" normally are considered "investments," the Act is meant to prohibit the underwriting of only those notes that "shar[e] that characteristic of an investment that is the common feature of each of the other enumerated instruments." Brief for Respondents 23. Applying that criterion to commercial paper, the Board maintains that commercial paper more closely resembles a commercial loan and that it is therefore not an investment of the kind that qualifies as a "security" under the Act.

For a variety of reasons, we find unpersuasive the notion that Congress used the terms "notes . . . or other securities" in the narrow sense that respondents suggest. First, the Court noted in *Camp* that "there is nothing in the phrasing of either §16 or §21 that suggests a narrow reading of the word 'securities.' To the contrary, the breadth of the term is implicit in the fact that the antecedent statutory language encompasses not only equity securities but also securities representing debt." 401 U.S., at 635, 91 S. Ct., at 1101.

There is, moreover, considerable evidence to indicate that the ordinary meaning of the terms "security" and "note" as used by the 1933 Congress encompasses commercial paper. Congress enacted the Glass-Steagall Act as one of several pieces of legislation collectively designed to restore public confidence in financial markets. See the Banking Act of 1933, ch. 89, 48 Stat. 162 (codified as amended in scattered sections of 12 U.S.C.); the Securities Act of 1933, 48 Stat. 74, 15 U.S.C. §77a et seq.; the Securities Exchange Act of 1934, 48 Stat. 881, 15 U.S.C. §78a et seq.; and the Public Utility Holding Company Act of 1935, 49 Stat. 803, 15 U.S.C. §79a et seq. In each of these other statutes, the definition of the term "security" includes commercial paper, and each statute contains explicit exceptions where Congress meant for the provisions of an Act not to apply to commercial paper. These explicit exceptions demonstrate congressional cognizance of commercial paper and Congress' understanding that, unless modified, the use of the term "security" encompasses it. . . .

The difficulty with the Board's attempt to narrow the ordinary meaning of the statutory language is evidenced by the Board's unsuccessful efforts to articulate a meaningful distinction between notes that the Act purportedly covers and those it does not. In other statutes in which commercial paper is exempted from securities regulation, Congress either has identified a particular feature, such as maturity period, that defines the exempted class of "notes," or it has authorized a federal agency to define it through regulation. The Glass-Steagall Act does neither, and the efforts by the Board and the Court of Appeals to provide a workable definition that excludes commercial paper have been fraught with uncertainty and inconsistency. The Court of Appeals concluded that the Act applies only to notes that are issued "to raise money available for an extended period of time as part of the corporation's capital structure." 693 F.2d, at 143. It is not clear that such a distinction finds support even with reference to the statutory language from which it purportedly derives. There is no requirement, for example, that stocks, bonds, and debentures be used only to meet the capital requirements of a corporation, and, even if there were, the legislative history provides little evidence to suggest that such a distinction was one that Congress found significant.

The Board, in contrast, seems to have concluded that a note is covered by the Act only if the note is properly viewed as an "investment." The Board contends that this approach requires it to consider a "cluster" of the note's features, such as its maturity period, its risk features, and its prospective purchasers. Stocks, bonds, and debentures display a wide range of each of these characteristics, however, and the Act's underwriting prohibition does not demonstrate any sensitivity to the characteristics of a particular issue; the Act simply prohibits commercial banks from underwriting them all. Without some clearer directive from Congress that it intended the statutory terms to involve the nebulous inquiry described by the Board, we cannot endorse the Board's departure from the literal meaning of the Act. . . .

### *D*

By focusing entirely on the nature of the financial instrument and ignoring the role of the bank in the transaction, moreover, the Board's "functional analysis" misapprehends Congress' concerns with commercial bank involvement in marketing securities. Both the Board and the Court of Appeals emphasized that Congress designed the Act to prevent future bank losses arising out of investments in speculative, long-term investments. This description of the Act's underlying concerns is perhaps accurate but somewhat incomplete. "[I]n enacting the Glass-Steagall Act, Congress contemplated other hazards in addition to the danger of banks using bank assets in imprudent securities investments." *ICI,* 450 U.S., at 66, 101 S. Ct., at 986. The concern about commercial-bank underwriting activities derived from the perception that the role of a bank as a promoter of securities was fundamentally incompatible with its role as a disinterested lender and adviser. This Court explained in *Camp:*

> In sum, Congress acted to keep commercial banks out of the investment banking business largely because it believed that the promotional incentives of investment banking and the investment banker's pecuniary stake in the success of particular investment opportunities was destructive of prudent and disinterested commercial banking and of public confidence in the commercial banking system.

401 U.S., at 634, 91 S. Ct., at 1100.

At the administrative level, the Board expressly chose not to consider whether these concerns are present when a commercial bank has a pecuniary interest in promoting commercial paper. Although the Board indicates before this Court that such activities do not implicate the concerns of the Act, we are unpersuaded by this belated assertion. In adopting the Act, for example, Congress concluded that a bank's "salesman's interest" in an offering "might impair its ability to function as an impartial source of credit." *Camp,* 401 U.S., at 631, 91 S.Ct., at 1099. In the commercial-paper market, where the distribution of an issue depends heavily on the creditworthiness of the issuer, a bank presumably can enhance the marketability of an issue by extending backup credit to the issuer. Similarly, as a commercial bank finds itself in direct competition with other commercial-paper dealers, it may feel pressure to purchase unsold notes in order to demonstrate the reliability of its distribution system, even if the paper does not meet the bank's normal credit standards. Recognizing these pressures, this Court stated in *Camp:* "When a bank puts itself in competition with [securities dealers], the bank must make an accommodation to the kind of ground rules that Congress firmly concluded could not be prudently mixed with the business of commercial banking." Id., at 637, 91 S. Ct., at 1102.

The 1933 Congress also was concerned that banks might use their relationships with depositors to facilitate the distribution of securities in which the bank has an interest, and that the bank's depositors might lose confidence in the bank if the issuer should default on its obligations. This concern would appear fully applicable to commercial-paper sales, because banks presumably will use their depositor lists as a prime source of customers for such sales. To the extent that a bank sells commercial paper to large bank depositors, the result of a loss of confidence in the bank would be especially severe.

By giving banks a pecuniary incentive in the marketing of a particular security, commercial-bank dealing in commercial paper also seems to produce precisely the conflict of interest that Congress feared would impair a commercial bank's ability to act as a source of disinterested financial advice. . . . This conflict of interest becomes especially acute if a bank decides to distribute commercial paper on behalf of an issuer who intends to use the proceeds of the offering to retire a debt that the issuer owes the bank.

In addressing these concerns before this Court, the Board focuses primarily on the extremely low rate of default on prime-quality commercial paper. We do not doubt that the risk of default with commercial paper is relatively low—lower perhaps than with many bank loans. For several reasons, however, we find reliance on this characteristic misplaced. First, it is not clear that the Board's exemption of commercial paper from the proscriptions of the Act is limited to commercial paper that is "prime." The statutory language admits of no distinction in this respect, and the logic of the Board's opinion must exempt all commercial paper from the prohibition on underwriting by commercial banks. Second, as described above, it appears that a bank can make a particular issue "prime" simply by extending backup credit to the issuer. Such a practice would seem to fit squarely within Congress' concern that banks would use their credit facilities to aid in the distribution of securities.

More importantly, however, there is little evidence to suggest that Congress intended the Act's prohibitions on underwriting to depend on the safety of particular securities. Stocks, bonds, and debentures exhibit the full range of risk; some are less risky than many of the loans made by a bank. And while the risk features of a security presumably affect whether it qualifies as an "investment security" that a commercial bank may purchase for its own account, the Act's underwriting prohibition displays no appreciation for the features of a particular issue; the Act just prohibits commercial banks from underwriting any of them, with an exception for certain enumerated governmental obligations that Congress specifically has chosen to favor. See 12 U.S.C. §24 Seventh. The Act's prophylactic prohibition on underwriting reflects Congress' conclusion that the mere existence of a securities operation, "'no matter how carefully and conservatively run, is inconsistent with the best interests'" of the bank as a whole. 75 Cong. Rec. 9913 (1932) (remarks of Sen. Bulkley, quoting a statement issued by the Bank of Manhattan Trust Co.).

In this regard, the Board's focus on the fact that commercial banks traditionally have acquired commercial paper for their own accounts is beside the point. It is clearly true, as the Board asserts before this Court, that Congress designed the Glass-Steagall Act to cause banks to invest more of their funds in short-term obligations like commercial paper instead of in longer term and more speculative securities. By so doing, Congress hoped to enhance the liquidity of funds and protect bank solvency. But the authority to discount commercial paper is very different from the authority to underwrite it. The former places banks in their traditional role as a prudent lender. The latter places a commercial bank in the role of an investment banker, which is precisely what Congress sought to prohibit in the Act.[11]

11. The Board makes an additional argument based on §16's restrictions on securities purchases by commercial banks. Section 16 prohibits commercial banks from "dealing in securities" on their own account altogether, and permits them to "purchase for [their] own account" only "investment securities." The Board argues that commercial paper does not constitute an "investment security" within the meaning of that term in §16, and hence that §16 would not permit commercial banks to purchase commercial paper for their own account if commercial paper were classified as a "security." Because commercial banks traditionally *have* acquired commercial paper for their own account, and because that practice universally has been assumed not to run afoul of the Glass-Steagall Act, the Board argues that the practice cannot be reconciled with §16 unless commercial paper is not deemed a "security."

Even if the Board is correct that commercial paper is not an "investment security" under §16, something that we need not decide, we find the Board's argument unpersuasive because it rests on the faulty premise that the process of acquiring commercial paper necessarily constitutes "the business of dealing" in securities. The underlying source of authority for

The Board also seeks comfort in the fact that commercial paper is sold largely to "sophisticated" investors. Once again, however, the Act leaves little room for such an ad hoc analysis. In its prohibition on commercial-bank underwriting, the Act admits of no exception according to the particular investment expertise of the customer. The Act's prohibition on underwriting is a flat prohibition that applies to sales to both the knowledgeable and the naive. Congress expressed concern that commercial-bank involvement in securities operations threatened the ability of commercial banks to act as "financial confidant and mentor" for both "the poor widow" and "the great corporation." 75 Cong. Rec. 9912 (1932) (remarks of Sen. Bulkley). . . .

Finally, it is certainly not without some significance that Bankers Trust's commercial-paper placement activities appear to be the first of that kind since the passage of the Act. The history of commercial-bank involvement in commercial paper prior to the Act is not well documented; evidently, commercial banks occasionally dealt in commercial paper, but their involvement was overwhelmingly in the role of discounter rather than dealer. Since enactment of the Act, however, there is no evidence of commercial-bank participation in the commercial-paper market as a dealer. The Board has not offered any explanation as to why commercial banks in the past have not ventured to test the limits of the Act's prohibitions on underwriting activities. Although such behavior is far from conclusive, it does support the view that when Congress sought to "separat[e] as completely as possible commercial from investment banking," *ICI*, 450 U.S., at 70, 101 S. Ct., at 989, the banks regulated by the Act universally recognized that underwriting[12] commercial paper falls on the investment-banking side of the line.

---

national banks to conduct business is the first sentence of §16, which originated as §8 of the National Bank Act of 1864, ch. 106, 13 Stat. 101. That provision grants national banks the authority to exercise "all such incidental powers as shall be necessary to carry on the business of banking" and enumerates five constituent powers that constitute "the business of banking." One of those powers is "discounting and negotiating promissory notes." 12 U.S.C. §24 Seventh. The Board appears to concede that the authority for national banks to acquire commercial paper is grounded in this authorization to discount promissory notes. The subsequent prohibition on engaging in "[t]he business of dealing in securities" does not affect this authority; while the Glass-Steagall Act does not define the term "business of dealing" in securities, the term clearly does not include the activity of "discounting" promissory notes because that activity is defined to be a part of the "business of banking." In short, the fact that commercial banks properly are free to acquire commercial paper for their own account implies not that commercial paper is not a "security," but simply that the process of extending credit by "discounting" commercial paper is not part of the "business of dealing" in securities.

12. Because of its conclusion that the commercial paper in this case was not a "security" under the Act, the Court of Appeals did not consider whether the activity of Bankers Trust constitutes "underwriting" within the meaning of §16, or "the business of issuing, underwriting, selling, or distributing" within the meaning of §21. We express no opinion on these matters, leaving them to be decided on remand.

### IV

For the foregoing reasons, the judgment of the Court of Appeals is reversed, and the case is remanded for further proceedings consistent with this opinion.

It is so ordered.

## *QUESTIONS AND COMMENTS*

1. The Federal Reserve Board expressed concern in *Bankers Trust I* that adoption of a definition of "security" broad enough to include commercial paper would lead to the prohibition of legitimate commercial banking activity. The board's concern was particularly directed at certificates of deposit, bankers' acceptances, and loan participations. A certificate of deposit is a bank's written acknowledgment of the receipt of a sum of money on deposit that the bank agrees to pay back (with interest) to the bearer at a later date. A bankers' acceptance is a guarantee by a commercial bank that its customer will pay for goods purchased on credit. Bankers' acceptances expedite transactions in which the parties are unfamiliar with each other, but have confidence in the bank's credits. Loan participations involve the sale of one or more interests in a large loan by a bank to other lenders. Is there any merit to the Federal Reserve's contention? Note that issuing certificates of deposit and discounting them are activities specifically authorized by Glass-Steagall. See 12 U.S.C. §24 (Seventh).

2. *Bankers Trust I* dealt solely with the narrow question of whether commercial paper is a "security" for purposes of Glass-Steagall. As footnote 12 of the majority opinion makes clear, the issue of whether Bankers Trust was "underwriting, issuing, selling, or distributing" securities was left for another day. That day was not far off.

In a letter to Bankers Trust Company after *Bankers Trust I,* the Federal Reserve Board said that Bankers Trust would not violate Glass-Steagall if it placed certain restrictions on its commercial paper activities. In particular, the board indicated that if the bank's sale of commercial paper resembled private placements of securities—making sales as agent to a small number of sophisticated investors, rather than as a firm commitment underwriting to the general public—then such sales would not be prohibited by Glass-Steagall. The district court for the District of Columbia overturned the Federal Reserve's ruling on the grounds that bank sales of commercial paper, even as restricted by the Federal Reserve, involved the subtle hazards that the Supreme Court described in *ICI.* Securities Industry Association v. Board of Governors of the Federal Reserve System, 627 F. Supp. 695 (D.D.C. 1986). The court of appeals' reaction to the district court is contained below. As the decision in *Bankers Trust I* is of interest because it contains the Supreme Court's most complete discussion of the definition of a "security" under Glass-Steagall, the following case is of interest because it contains the fullest statement of the meaning of "issuing," "underwriting," and "distributing" under the Act.

## Securities Industry Association v. Board of Governors of the Federal Reserve System (Bankers Trust II)

***807 F.2d 1052 (D.C. Cir. 1986), cert. denied, 483 U.S. 1005 (1987)***

BORK, Circuit Judge. . . .

We must determine, first, if the Board has reasonably concluded that the commercial paper placement activities of Bankers Trust fall within the permissive language of section 16. To determine this, we must look at the question of what the statute means by "underwrite," for underwriting not only triggers section 21's prohibitions but also defeats section 16's permissive effect. We must, in contrast, address the meaning of section 21's terms "issuing, . . . selling, or distributing" only if section 16 is inapplicable. . . . Therefore, if we find that the Board acted reasonably in concluding that section 16 permits Bankers Trust's activities, that is the end of our analysis. . . .

We find that the Board reasonably concluded that an "underwriting" defeats the section 16 exemption only if it includes a public offering; private placements therefore do not for this purpose constitute statutory "underwriting." The Board's reliance on the distinction between public offerings and private placements is reasonable because the distinction derives support from congressional intent embodied in contemporaneous securities legislation and reasonably relates to concerns that the Glass-Steagall Act sought to meet.

### *1. CONTEMPORANEOUS SECURITIES LEGISLATION*

. . . [Unlike the Glass-Steagall Act], the Securities Act of 1933 defines the term "underwriter" (although the Securities Exchange Act of 1934 provides useful evidence on the meaning of that term as used in the Securities Act). While the evidence of the ordinary congressional cognizance of the term "underwrite" or "underwriter" thus comes from only one piece of similar legislation, that legislation, the Securities Act of 1933, is the closest to Glass-Steagall in time and purpose of the various statutes relied on in *SIA*. The Securities Act and the Glass-Steagall Act were signed into law within three weeks of each other and both statutes were among the legislative reforms that marked President Roosevelt's first hundred days in office. Thus, while the precise purposes of the Securities Act and the Glass-Steagall Act may differ, both emerged from the same effort to restructure the American financial markets; absent any contrary indication, we must consider Congress' understanding of the financial terms it used in one statute highly relevant to discovering the meaning attached to similar but ambiguous terms in the other. With that rule in mind, we turn to the Securities Act of 1933.

SIA contends that the significance of the Securities Act for this case is that it provides an express exemption from registration for "transactions by an issuer not involving any public offering." 15 U.S.C. §77d(2) (1982). SIA asserts that this exemption demonstrates Congress' ability knowingly to provide an exemption from statutory requirements for private offerings; Congress' failure so to provide in section 16 of the Glass-Steagall Act means that the Board acted unreasonably when by interpreting the term "underwrite" it effectively read such a private offering into the Act. This point would have considerable force, except that the history of the Securities Act's exemption betrays SIA's argument and, in fact, establishes the converse—that Congress did understand the concept of underwriting to connote involvement in a public offering of securities.

The Securities Act in section 2(11) defines an "underwriter" as "any person who has purchased from an issuer with a view to, or offers or sells for an issuer in connection with, the distribution of any security, or participates or has a direct or indirect participation in any such undertaking, or participates or has a direct participation in the direct or indirect underwriting of any such undertaking." 15 U.S.C. §77b(11) (1982). An "underwriter" thus cannot exist unless a "distribution" exists. . . .

The Board's responsibility in this case was to arrive at a reasonable determination of what should constitute a private offering under the Glass-Steagall Act. The Board found Bankers Trust's activities to constitute a private offering because (1) the bank "places commercial paper by separately contacting large financial and non-financial institutions," (2) the bank "does not place commercial paper with any individuals," (3) "the maximum number of offerees and purchasers of commercial paper placed by the bank in any given case is relatively limited," (4) the bank "makes no general solicitation or advertisement to the public" with respect to the placement of particular paper (though it does advertise its activities in business publications to publicize its availability as an agent to issuers), and (5) "the commercial paper placed with the bank's assistance is issued in very large average minimum denominations, which are not a likely investment of the general public." Such considerations properly determine what distinguishes a private from a public offering of securities; we shall shortly see that they also have a strong relationship to one of the principal concerns that animated the Glass-Steagall Act.

### *2. LEGISLATIVE PURPOSES*

As the Supreme Court has amply documented, the legislative history of the Glass-Steagall Act shows that, besides "the obvious risk that a bank could lose money by imprudent investment of its funds in speculative securities," Congress sought to address "'the more subtle hazards that arise when a commercial bank goes beyond the business of acting as fiduciary or managing agent and enters the investment banking business.'" *SIA,* 468 U.S. at 145, 104 S. Ct. at 2984 (quoting *Camp,* 401 U.S. at 630, 91 S. Ct. at 1098). . . .

Congress recognized that these pressures largely resulted from the heavy fixed costs incurred by commercial banks in running investment banking operations. In the period immediately preceding the financial collapse that precipitated the enactment of Glass-Steagall, the distribution of an issue of securities took place through an elaborate syndication involving various tiers of purchase, banking, and selling groups managed by an originating banker who handled the negotiations with the issuer. See 1 L. Loss, Securities Regulation 164-66 (2d ed. 1961). The precise details of the distribution process, as it then existed, are not important for our purposes. What is important is that "a large number of the leading originators of securities, particularly the security affiliates of commercial banks," developed "large selling organizations" in this period. Gourrich, Investment Banking Methods Prior to and Since the Securities Act of 1933, 4 Law & Contemp. Probs. 44, 49 (1937). Indeed, the "bank affiliates were particularly active in constructing substantial retail organizations" to distribute the securities to which they had committed themselves as originators or members of a purchase group. Id. at 48 n. 8.

Congress was well aware of these developments. The heavy overhead incurred by banks to carry these large retail operations caused much of the congressional concern about "subtle hazards" that animated the sponsors of the Glass-Steagall Act. As one of the principal sponsors stated:

> In order to be efficient a securities department had to be developed; it had to have salesmen; and it had to have correspondent connections with smaller banks throughout the territory tributary to the great bank. Organizations were developed with great enthusiasm and efficiency. The distribution of the great security issues needed for the development of the country was facilitated, and the country developed. But the sales departments were subject to fixed expenses which could not be reduced without the danger of so disrupting the organization as to put the institution at a disadvantage in competition with rival institutions. These expenses would turn the operation very quickly from a profit to a loss if there were not sufficient organizations and underwritings to keep the sales departments busy.
>
> It was necessary in some cases to seek for customers to become makers of issues of securities when the needs of those customers for long-

> term money were not very pressing. Can any banker, imbued with the consciousness that his bond-sales department is, because of lack of securities for sale, losing money and at the same time losing its morale, be a fair and impartial judge as to the necessity and soundness for a new security issue which he knows he can readily distribute through channels which have been expensive to develop but which presently stand ready to absorb the proposed security issue and yield a handsome profit on the transaction?
>
> It is easy to see why the security business was overdeveloped and why the bankers' clients and country bank correspondents were overloaded with a mass of investments many of which have proved most unfortunate.

75 Cong. Rec. 9911 (1932) (remarks of Sen. Bulkley).

The distinction between public and private offerings meshes well with the congressional goal of eliminating the "subtle hazards" of conflicts of interest and abuse of fiduciary relationships in banking. Senator Bulkley's remarks show a concern with the development of a vast selling apparatus necessary to participate in the distribution of "great security issues needed for the development of the country" and mirror the unchallenged evidence in the literature that banks in the early twentieth century were building that type of large selling organization.

In light of the specific congressional focus on the large fixed costs that accompanied retail participation in public distributions, it seems highly plausible that one line Congress might have drawn in adopting the permissive language of section 16 of the Glass-Steagall Act was at the point of public offering, a line which could well explain the prohibition against underwriting. While regular involvement in private offerings of securities undoubtedly produces some fixed costs and some attendant pressures, it seems reasonable to think that Congress might have found these relatively minor expenses acceptable when compared with the much heavier fixed burden of having a far-flung retail network to distribute securities to the public. Although implementation of this distinction through the prohibition of commercial-bank underwriting would not address all the "subtle hazards" with which Congress was concerned (for example, it would do nothing to meet the fear that a bank would sell securities for an issuer to help the issuer repay loans to the bank), the prohibition of underwriting is only one of the limitations that section 16 imposes on banks that desire to deal in securities. We believe that the distinction between public and private offerings as drawn by the Board reasonably interprets the prohibition of underwriting and reasonably relates to the elimination of some of those hazards. . . .

. . . We think, in short, that the Board reasonably concluded not only that Bankers Trust's placements of commercial paper meet the literal requirements of section 16, but also that those placements are consistent with the panoply of the Act's purposes.

We therefore reverse the district court's order and reinstate the Board's decision.

It is so ordered.

*QUESTIONS AND COMMENTS*

1. In light of the restrictions imposed on Bankers Trust Company's commercial paper activities, was the firm able to compete for business on an equal footing with investment banks who faced no such constraints? What in particular about the restrictions imposed on Bankers Trust would cause an issuing firm to prefer to deal with an investment bank?

2. It seems clear that the commercial banks did not think the "compromise" reached in *Bankers Trust II* was ideal. While the case was being litigated, the banks were trying a new strategy for entering the commercial paper business. This new strategy centered around §20 of Glass-Steagall. Section 20 prohibits banks from affiliating with any organization "engaged principally in the issue, flotation, underwriting, public sale, or distribution at wholesale or retail or through syndicate participation of stocks, bonds, notes or other securities." 12 U.S.C. §377.

3. Events in this area moved very quickly: The decision of the D.C. Circuit in *Bankers Trust II* was issued on December 23, 1986. On the very next day, the Federal Reserve Board approved an application for Bankers Trust Company to sell securities through a *nonbank affiliate* of the holding company. The board issued a detailed order in support of its conclusion that a bank affiliate's commercial paper sales would not involve conflicts of interest and "subtle hazards" that concerned the Court in *ICI.* In light of the Supreme Court opinion in *Bankers Trust I,* the board could not avoid the conclusion that Bankers Trust's commercial paper activity involved it in the securities business. To permit the bank to engage in underwriting this instrument, the board developed a framework for determining when a bank holding company affiliate is "principally engaged" in the securities business pursuant to §20. The terms of the board's order specified that the subsidiary could place only prime quality commercial paper in minimum denominations of $250,000 with sophisticated investors. Revenues from commercial paper activities were restricted to no more than 5 percent of the subsidiary's total revenues. Bankers Trust was also required to limit its commercial paper placement to no more than 5 percent of all dealer-placed paper. The bank could not back via letters of credit the paper that it placed, nor purchase such paper for its own account. Other constraints included prohibitions on joint marketing and shared officers and directors between the subsidiary and the holding company's subsidiary banks.

4. In the wake of this Federal Reserve Board Order, other major money center bank holding companies obtained board approval to engage, through wholly owned subsidiaries, in securities activities including underwriting and dealing in commercial paper, municipal revenue bonds, and mortgage-related securities. Federal Reserve Board, Order Approving Applications to Engage in Limited Underwriting and Dealing in Certain Securities, 73 Fed. Res. Bull. 473 (1987); Federal Reserve Board, Order Conditionally Approving Application to Underwrite and Deal in Certain Securities to a Limited Extent, 73 Fed. Res. Bull. 607 (1987).

In the midst of this flurry of activity, Congress imposed a moratorium that prohibited the board from approving affiliate involvement in securities activities. Competitive Equality Banking Act of 1987, Pub. L. No. 100-86, 101 Stat. 552. The moratorium did not prevent the board from approving affiliate securities activities so long as the effective date of such approvals was after the expiration date of the moratorium, which occurred on March 1, 1988. The moratorium was enacted to give Congress the opportunity to implement sweeping legislative reform of Glass-Steagall.

The bank holding companies that sought authorizations to conduct securities activities through affiliates under §20 contemplated combining underwriting activities with the activities of an existing subsidiary that would also underwrite and deal in U.S. government securities and general obligation municipal bonds. Some of these bank holding company subsidiaries were involved almost exclusively in the securities business. Why wouldn't a securities affiliate that has 80 percent of its business in U.S. government securities distribution and 20 percent of its business in commercial paper be "engaged principally" in the securities business under §20? As the following case illustrates, the answer to this question is by no means clear-cut.

## Securities Industry Association v. Board of Governors of the Federal Reserve System (Bankers Trust III)

***839 F.2d 47 (2d Cir.), cert. denied, 486 U.S. 1059 (1988)***

CARDAMONE, Circuit Judge:

We review on this appeal those provisions of the Banking Act of 1933 that separated the commercial and investment banking industries and are known as the Glass-Steagall Act. Demand for divorcing banking and securities activities followed in the wake of the stock market crash of 1929, which occurred, it was said, because a mountain of credit rested on only a molehill of cash. The actions of the Federal Reserve Board that we review today allow commercial and investment banking to compete in a narrow market, and to that extent dismantle the wall of separation installed between them by the Glass-Steagall Act. Whether Santayana's notion that those who will not learn from the past are condemned to repeat it fairly characterizes the consequences of the Board's action is not for us to say. Our task is to review the Glass-Steagall Act, the legislative history that surrounded its enactment, and its prior judicial construction to determine whether the Board reasonably interpreted the Act's often ambiguous terms.

The Securities Industry Association (SIA) and seven bank holding companies petition for review of six related orders of the Board of Governors of the Federal Reserve System (Board). The orders approved the bank holding companies' applications to utilize subsidiaries as the vehicle by which they can underwrite and deal in certain securities. The Board determined that the approved activities would not run afoul of §20 of the Glass-Steagall Act, which proscribes affiliations of banks—here, the holding companies' member bank subsidiaries—with entities that are "engaged principally" in underwriting and dealing in securities. At the same time, the Board limited the scope of the approved activities. The decisions allowing bank subsidiaries to engage in securities transactions and the limitations that were imposed are the focus of the petitions seeking review. . . .

**THE BOARD'S ANALYSIS . . .**

Section 20 of the Glass-Steagall Act forbids a member bank of the Federal Reserve System from affiliating with an organization "engaged principally" in, inter alia, underwriting or dealing in securities. 12 U.S.C. §377 (1982). Bank holding companies have been allowed since 1978—without a court challenge by SIA—to acquire or form subsidiaries that underwrite and deal in securities representing obligations of the United States and of states and their political subdivisions. Section 16 of the Glass-Steagall Act expressly permits banks themselves to underwrite and deal in these governmental securities, known as "bank-eligible securities." 12 U.S.C. §24 (Seventh) (1982 & Supp. IV 1986).

Given the authorization in §16 for banks to engage in bank-eligible securities activities, the Board concluded that Congress did not aim in §20 to proscribe bank affiliates from engaging in the same activities. 73 Fed. Reserve Bull. at 478-81. It reasoned that it would be anomalous not to permit the bank's subsidiary to engage in the activities lawfully permitted the bank. That illogical result necessarily follows if bank-eligible securities are defined as "securities" under §20 because that section prohibits a member bank from being affiliated with an organization "engaged principally" in securities dealing. Hence, according to the Board, "securities" cannot logically mean bank-eligible securities. "Securities" in §20 must therefore only refer to those types of securities that under §16 banks cannot themselves deal in or underwrite, known as "bank-ineligible securities." The activities approved in the orders at issue on this appeal—underwriting and dealing in municipal revenue bonds, mortgage related securities, and commercial paper—cannot be conducted by a member bank and are therefore bank-ineligible securities activities.

Establishing as a predicate that the proscription in §20 extends only to bank-ineligible securities, the Board turned to the question of when an affiliate is "engaged principally" in such activity. Relying on its order in Bankers Trust New York Corp., 73 Fed. Reserve Bull. 138 (1987), the Board held that the term "engaged principally" means any substantial activity. 73 Fed. Reserve Bull. at 482. It then concluded that subsidiaries would not be engaged substantially in bank-ineligible activities if no more than five to ten percent of their total gross revenues was derived from such activities over a two-year period, and if the activities in connection with *each* type of bank-ineligible security did not constitute more than five to ten percent of the market for that particular security. Id. at 485-86. The Board then proceeded to approve gross revenue and market share levels at five percent—the low end of the acceptable range—but stated that it would review the five percent limitations within a year after the implementation of its orders. The applicants wanted, of course, to engage in higher levels of activity.

On review, SIA argues that the Board erroneously construed the Glass-Steagall Act by construing the word "securities" in §20 not to include bank-eligible securities. In other words, SIA contends that §20 limits both bank-eligible *and* bank-ineligible security activities by a member bank affiliate. SIA also objects to the Board's construction of "engaged principally." The bank holding companies urge us to adopt the Board's construction of §20 with regard to "securities," but argue, at the same time, that the Glass-Steagall Act mandates that the Board allow a higher level of bank-ineligible activity than that approved. . . .

### DISCUSSION

The two principal issues presented to this court are the Board's constructions of the terms "securities" and "engaged principally" under §20 of the Glass-Steagall Act. . . .

### *II. THE MEANING OF "SECURITIES" IN §20*

. . . Congress' concern was primarily with bank affiliate activities in bank-ineligible securities. Bank affiliates often "devote[d] themselves . . . to perilous underwriting operations, stock speculation, and maintaining a market for the banks' own stock often largely with the resources of the parent bank." . . . According to Senator Glass, "[w]hat the committee had foremost in its thought was to exclude from commercial banking all investment securities except those of an undoubted character that would be surely liquidated; and for that reason we made an exception [in §16] of United States securities and of the general liabilities of States and subdivisions of States." 76 Cong. Rec. 2092 (1933). Given that Glass-Steagall was a means to sever commercial banking only from more speculative, "perilous" investment activities, in which bank-eligible activities were not included, an interpretation of "securities" in §20 that excludes bank-eligible securities from its reach is entirely consistent with Congress' aim. . . .

. . . The evil that Congress intended to attack was bank involvement in speculative securities, that is, bank-ineligible securities. We cannot attribute to Congress a purpose to limit *all* securities activities when it consistently made clear that it was only concerned with *one* type. . . .

### *III. "ENGAGED PRINCIPALLY"*

We now turn to the Board's determination of when a security affiliate is "engaged principally" in activities covered by §20. In their applications the bank holding companies sought to comply with the "engaged principally" standard of §20 by proposing limitations on their underwriting and dealing in bank-ineligible securities. J. P. Morgan & Co., for example, proposed that its bank-ineligible securities activities would not exceed during any rolling two-year period 15 percent of its total business. J. P. Morgan & Co. Proposal, 50 Fed. Reg. 41,025 (1985). It proposed a combination of accounting tests to measure its compliance with the 15 percent limitation. The other companies proposed total volume limits of ten to 15 percent of their total business.

The Board rejected these proposals. Following the analysis set forth in its *Bankers Trust* order, 73 Fed. Reserve Bull. 138 (1987), the Board concluded that "engaged principally" in §20 denotes any "substantial" bank-ineligible activity. See 73 Fed. Reserve Bull. at 482. Measured quantitatively, the Board stated that an affiliate would not be principally or substantially engaged in bank-ineligible activities if: (1) the gross revenue from §20 activities did not exceed five to ten percent of the affiliate's total gross revenues (gross revenue limitation or gross revenue test); and (2) the affiliate's activities in connection with *each* particular type of ineligible security did not account for more than five to ten percent of the total amount of that type of security underwritten domestically by all firms (or, with commercial paper, the average amount of dealer-placed commercial paper outstanding) during the previous calendar year (market share limitation or market share test). Applying this measure to the applications before it, the Board selected the lower five percent figure for both gross revenue and market share limitations. It recognized that this was a "conservative approach," but stated that it would review the limitations within one year of the implementation of its orders. 73 Fed. Reserve Bull. at 485.

The bank holding companies petition for review of this interpretation of "engaged principally." First, they argue that the Board's view contravenes Supreme Court precedent. Second, they contend that the limitation is inconsistent with the language, structure, and legislative intent of the Glass-Steagall Act. Finally, cross-petitioner Security Pacific Corporation argues that the Board erred in adopting an inflexible percentage test instead of approaching each affiliate's application on a case-by-case basis.

The term "engaged principally" is intrinsically ambiguous. As discussed above, we must uphold the Board's interpretation if it is reasonable. Unlike the facts presented on the issue of the scope of §20, the Board's position here does not contradict its prior interpretations. Accordingly, we defer to the Board's construction of §20. . . .

The Board's construction of "engaged principally" as denoting any substantial activity is reasonable. . . . Substantiality is an amorphous qualitative concept that has many quantitative definitional manifestations, which vary with the context in which the term is used. . . . The worries envisioned by bank affiliation with securities firms do not disappear simply because the activity is less than 50 percent of a firm's business.

An example illuminates how equating "principally" in §20 with "chief" or "first" begets the dangers foreseen by Congress. Such an interpretation would allow a member bank to become affiliated with any large integrated securities firm. One commentator has pointed out that reading "principally" as "chief" would allow a bank to be affiliated with Merrill Lynch & Co., Inc., one of the nation's largest investment bankers. See Plotkin, What Meaning Does Glass-Steagall Have for Today's Financial World?, 95 Banking L.J. 404, 414-16 (1977). It cannot be supposed that the Congress that enacted Glass-Steagall would have intended that §20 not prohibit such affiliations. This is not to say that "principally" cannot in some contexts mean "chief" or "first," but rather that in §20 the term must be given a definition that is both sensible *and* in harmony with legislative purpose. . . .

SIA and ICI advance several arguments against the Board's interpretation of "principally." They assert that "engaged principally" in §20 at least covers any firm "formed for the purpose of" underwriting securities, relying on the Supreme Court's statement in *ICI* regarding repealed 19(e) that "[a]ll companies formed for the purpose of issuing or underwriting securities would surely meet the 'engaged principally' test." 450 U.S. at 70 n.43, 101 S. Ct. at 988-89 n.43. Concededly, the subsidiaries here were formed for the purpose of engaging in securities activities.

Yet, this argument is unpersuasive too. The Court's statement in *ICI* is dicta and seems to indicate nothing more remarkable than that a company formed for the purpose of underwriting securities most likely would be expected to be engaged principally in that activity. Further, since §20 does not restrict bank-eligible securities activities, SIA and ICI arguably miss the point. Companies formed for the purpose of dealing in bank-eligible securities would not fall within the prohibitions of §20. . . .

Alternatively, SIA claims that Congress intended that §20 bar underwriting or dealing activities that constitute a "regular" or "integral" part of the affiliate's business, as opposed to "incidental" or "occasional" activities. The activities that concerned Congress did not necessarily arise only with the frequency of their repetition. In any event, the Board's interpretation of "principally" as any "substantial" activity adequately addresses any apprehension arising from the frequency or integral nature of an activity.

The final argument raised by SIA is that because the Board's interpretation of "engaged principally" necessitates regulation, it a fortiori contravenes the Glass-Steagall Act. It is true that "Congress rejected a regulatory approach when it drafted the statute." *Bankers Trust I,* 468 U.S. at 153, 104 S. Ct. at 2988. The Board's interpretation is one that attempts to walk the line that Congress laid down. The mere necessity of "regulation" in carrying out Glass-Steagall's "prohibitions" is insufficient to justify rejection of an otherwise reasonable interpretation of the Act. Cf. *Bankers Trust II,* 807 F.2d at 1067 ("The Glass-Steagall Act does impose a system of flat 'prohibitions' and 'prophylactic' measures, but this cannot obviate the need to examine particular factual situations to determine on which side of the prohibitory line they fall.").

Consequently, the Board's view of "engaged principally" as meaning any substantial activity is reasonable and consistent with Congressional purpose.

### C. *Gross Revenue Limitation*

The Board determined that substantial activity, measured quantitatively, constituted five to ten percent of an affiliate's gross revenues over a two-year period. 73 Fed. Reserve Bull. at 485. It set the approved level of activity at the five percent end of this range, but stated its intent to review this level within a year after the order's effective date. Id.

One troublesome facet of the Board's ruling is that "engaged principally" in §20 is equally restrictive as—if not *more* restrictive than— "primarily engaged" in §32. The Board has stated that if a firm's prohibited activities constitute less than ten percent of its gross business or amount to less than ten million dollars regardless of the percentage figure, the firm is not "primarily engaged" in such activities under §32. By placing the permissible level of §20 activity currently at only five percent of gross revenues—and never more than ten percent—the Board is employing, at least for the present, a more restrictive gross revenue test for §20 than for §32.

This initially seems to contradict the Supreme Court's indication that §§32 and 20 should be interpreted consistently. But with regard to "engaged principally" versus "primarily engaged," §§20 and 32 differ, accordingly, there is justification for interpreting them slightly differently.

The legislative history also supports the conclusion that the Board's stringent quantitative interpretation of §20 is reasonable. . . .

Further support for a stricter interpretation of §20 than of §32 is derived from the fact that the dangers resulting from affiliation are arguably greater than those resulting only from personnel interlocks. The public associates a member bank and its affiliate because of their common ownership and often similar names. The potential for the public to associate the misfortunes of the affiliate with the bank is far greater than the association of firms with personnel interlocks, which are generally unknown to the public.

Given these considerations, we defer to the Board's determination that §20 allows an affiliate to engage in bank-ineligible securities activities so long as those activities do not exceed five to ten percent of the affiliate's gross revenue. This range is both reasonable and consistent with the statute. Because of the Board's expertise we also defer to its decision to set the gross revenue limitation at five percent.

### *D. Market Share Limitation*

The Board's second limitation on the subsidiaries' bank-ineligible securities activities provides that the subsidiaries' involvement in *each* activity may not exceed a five percent share of the total market for that activity. It reasoned that it has employed a market share limitation in determining whether a firm is "primarily engaged" in securities activities within the meaning of §32. 73 Fed. Reserve Bull. at 484. The Board stated that "the fact that an affiliate would be a major force in a particular securities market would be an evidentiary factor suggesting that the affiliate is 'engaged principally' in underwriting securities." Id. It also concluded that a sales volume test—currently employed under its interpretation of §32—would be subject to manipulation and that a market share test "would provide a useful and objective proxy for sales volume." Id. It was concerned that sales volume could be easily inflated by use of repurchase and reverse repurchase agreements for government securities—a common practice among government securities dealers—or by "churning." Id.

The bank holding companies argue that neither §20 nor the legislative history of the Glass-Steagall Act provides a basis for the Board's market share test. They assert that §20 mandates an inquiry only into activities *within* a subsidiary rather than one into the size of the subsidiary's activity in relation to the market as a whole. A market share test, they claim, is intended sub silentio to promote competition rather than to protect against the hazards of affiliation envisioned by Congress. . . .

We discern no support in §20 for the Board's market share limitation. In the legislative history there is evidence that before the enactment of Glass-Steagall, banks and bank affiliates had acquired an increasingly large share of securities activity in relation to investment banks. For example, between 1927 and 1930 the percentage share of commercial banks in origination of bond issues more than doubled. This increasing market share of commercial banks in traditional investment banking activities was not unknown to Congress. But, the fact that this was brought to Congress's attention and that Congress did not directly address it is, if anything, a strong indication that Congress was not concerned about market share. Rather, by using the term "engaged principally," Congress indicated that its principal anxiety was over the perceived risk to bank solvency resulting from their over-involvement in securities activity. A market share limitation simply does not further reduce this congressional worry. . . .

**CONCLUSION**

In sum §20 of the Glass-Steagall Act forbids member bank affiliation with firms that are "engaged principally" in underwriting or dealing in "securities." It was not Congress' plan to forbid affiliates from those activities that banks themselves could engage in without limitation. The Board's interpretation of §20 under which government securities—those that banks may without limitation underwrite and deal in—are excluded from the prohibition contained in §20 is therefore consistent with the Congressional scheme. The Board's qualitative and quantitative constructions of the term "engaged principally" are reasonable, with the exception of the market share limitation. Accordingly, we deny the petitions and cross-petitions for review except with respect to the market share limitation.

Petitions and cross-petitions for review are denied save for the cross-petition for review that seeks to eliminate the market share limitation, which cross-petition is granted.

## *QUESTIONS AND COMMENTS*

1. How persuasive do you find the court's reasoning regarding the meaning of the term "security" in §20 of the Act? Does the court's reasoning comport with a commonsense definition of the term?

2. What difference did it make what definition the court adopted? If it had defined security under §20 to mean all securities, wouldn't bank holding companies still have been allowed to deal in commercial paper and other securities through affiliates?

3. In a January 1989 order, the Federal Reserve Board gave condi-

tional approval to five large holding companies—J. P. Morgan, Chase Manhattan, Bankers Trust, Citicorp, and Security Pacific—to underwrite and deal in fixed debt securities provided they limited such activities to 5 percent of their relevant subsidiary's gross revenues. At the same time the Federal Reserve deferred for a year a decision on whether a bank holding company could underwrite corporate equities.

Before being allowed to start up operations the bank holding companies were required to prove that their capital was adequate, that operating expertise to engage in underwriting debt securities was in place, and that adequate internal controls had been implemented. The subsidiary was also required to register with the Securities and Exchange Commission as a broker-dealer.

The Federal Reserve also imposed a number of stringent "fire walls"—measures designed to separate the operations of the securities subsidiary from those of the bank holding company and its affiliates. The order barred all loans from a holding company bank or thrift subsidiary to the securities unit, except as incidental to clearing of U.S. government securities. It also required that a holding company deduct from its primary capital any loan made to the securities unit for such purposes, unless fully secured by marketable securities. Moreover, the holding company was prevented from transferring capital to its securities subsidiary unless its own capital exceeded the 8 percent minimum stipulated in the Federal Reserve's risk-based capital guidelines. Other controls restricted holding company officers from serving as officers of a securities affiliate and a subsidiary bank and limited the transfer of information between the bank and its securities subsidiary.

4. By the end of 1989 the Federal Reserve had raised the limit on revenues that a securities subsidiary may derive from ineligible activities to 10 percent. In July 1996 the Fed proposed a further liberalization of the revenue limit by raising it to 25 percent. It also lifted three firewalls: It permitted banks and their securities affiliates to share employees and directors, it authorized banks to sell assets to one another, and it allowed some cross-marketing of one another's products.

5. The Federal Reserve also authorized securities subsidiaries of bank holding companies to underwrite and deal in rated securities issued by their affiliates. It further ruled that private placement and riskless principal transactions of a securities affiliate of a bank holding company would qualify as dealings in eligible securities and would not count against the 10-percent (or 25-percent) limitation.

6. One possible advantage to permitting commercial banks to enter the investment banking business was that the banks would enjoy the benefits of diversification of risk by being able to engage in both commercial banking and investment banking. In the case of §20 affiliates, however, banks are not engaging in securities activities themselves. Rather, the nonbank affiliates of bank holding companies are conducting these

securities operations. In fact, the regulatory trend has led bank holding companies to remove permissible securities activities from their banks in order to place those activities in nonbank securities affiliates. Why is this the case? From the standpoint of risk diversification, why does it matter whether a bank's securities activities are conducted within the bank itself or within a separate securities affiliate?

## F. PROSPECTS FOR REFORM OF GLASS-STEAGALL

No less a figure than Federal Reserve Board Chairman Alan Greenspan has argued that Glass-Steagall should be repealed, but that strict divisions between the commercial banking affiliates and the investment banking affiliates within a holding company be maintained. He detailed his position during testimony endorsing S. 1886, the Financial Modernization Act of 1987, which would have erected "fire walls" between commercial banks and their securities affiliates. Greenspan has continued to advocate repeal of the Glass-Steagall Act in the years since then. His reasons for pursuing this approach are worth considering.

### Statement by Alan Greenspan, Chairman Board of Governors of the Federal Reserve System, Before the Committee on Banking, Housing, and Urban Affairs, U.S. Senate, Dec. 1, 1987

*74 Fed. Res. Bull. 91 (1988)*

. . . REASONS FOR REPEAL OF THE GLASS-STEAGALL ACT

A very persuasive case has been made for adoption of the repeal proposal. It would allow lower costs and expanded services for consumers through enhanced competition in an area in which additional competition would be highly desirable. It would strengthen banking institutions, permitting them to compete more effectively at home and abroad in their natural markets for credit that have been transformed by revolutionary developments in computer and communications technology. It could be expected to result in attracting more equity capital to the banking industry when more capital is needed. In sum, the securities activities of banking organizations can provide important public benefits without impairing the safety and soundness of banks if they are conducted by experienced managers, in adequately capitalized companies, and in a framework that insulates the bank from its securities affiliates. . . .

*PUBLIC BENEFITS*

The major public benefit of Glass-Steagall modification would be lower customer costs and increased availability of investment banking services, both resulting from increased competition and the realization of possible economies of scale and scope from coordinated provision of commercial and investment banking services. We believe that the entry of bank holding companies into securities underwriting would, in fact, reduce underwriting spreads and, in the process, lower financing costs to businesses large and small as well as to state and local governments. In addition, participation by bank holding company subsidiaries in dealing in currently ineligible securities is likely to enhance secondary market liquidity to the benefit of both issuers and investors. These, we believe, are important public benefits that will assist in making our economy more efficient and competitive. . . .

It is also important to emphasize that the changes in the Glass-Steagall Act that we support would be likely to yield cost savings in local and regional corporate underwriting and dealing markets. At a minimum, local and regional firms would acquire access to capital markets that is similar not only to the access now available to large corporations but also to that currently available to municipalities whose general obligation bonds are underwritten by local banks.

Another area of substantial expected public benefit is the encouragement of the free flow of investment capital. Both we at the Board and the Congress have stressed the importance of improving the capital ratios of banking organizations, and it can reasonably be assumed that expansion of banking organizations into securities markets should make them more attractive investments. Equally important, banks and securities firms would be free to deploy their capital over a wider range of activities designed to serve the public better.

*EFFECT OF COMPUTER AND COMMUNICATION TECHNOLOGY*

There is another important reason why the Glass-Steagall Act should be changed. Developments in computer and communications technology have reduced the economic role of commercial banks and enhanced the function of investment banking. These permanent and fundamental changes in the environment for conducting financial business cannot be halted by statutory prohibitions, and the longer the law refuses to recognize that fundamental and permanent changes have occurred, the less relevant it will be as a force for stability and competitive fairness in our financial markets. Attempts to hold the present structure in place will be defeated through the inevitable loopholes that innovation forced by competitive necessity will develop, although there will be heavy costs in terms of competitive fairness and respect for law that are so critical to a safe and sound financial system.

The significance of these technological developments is that the key role of banks as financial intermediaries has been undermined. The heart of financial intermediation is the ability to obtain and use information. The high cost of gathering and using facts in the past meant that banks and other intermediaries could profit from their cumulative store of knowledge about borrowers by making significantly more informed credit decisions than most other market participants. These other market participants were thus obliged to permit depository intermediaries to make credit decisions in financial markets and therefore allow bank credit to substitute for what would otherwise be their own direct acquisition of credit market instruments. . . .

### *BANKS' RESPONSE TO NEW COMPETITIVE CONDITIONS AT HOME AND OVERSEAS*

Banks, of course, have not stood still while these vast changes were taking place around them. Indeed, they have responded to the technological revolution by participating in it. Loan guarantees and other off-balance-sheet arrangements, private placement of corporate debt, commercial paper placement, loan participations and sales, and interest rate and currency swaps are examples. Similarly, the foreign offices of U.S. banks and their foreign subsidiaries and affiliates have been actively engaging abroad in a wide variety of securities activities. These include securities, such as corporate debt and equity, that are ineligible in the United States for banks to underwrite and deal, such as corporate debt and equity. In the corporate debt market, for example, U.S. banks' foreign subsidiaries served lead roles in underwritings approaching $17 billion in 1986, or about 10 percent of the volume of such debt managed by the 50 firms most active in the Eurosecurities market last year. These and other essentially investment banking activities have permitted banks to continue to service those customers seeking to rely increasingly on securities markets—provided that the securities are issued abroad. In their home market, banks continue to be sharply limited by the Glass-Steagall Act in competing for the business of acting as intermediaries in the process of investors providing credit to corporations, just at the time that the new financial environment transformed by technological change has made such intermediation a natural extension of the banking business.

### *THE NEED FOR REFORM*

In short, the Congress should modify the financial structure to conform to these changes. If the Congress does not act, but rather maintains the existing barriers of the Glass-Steagall Act, banking organizations will continue to seek ways to service customers who have increasingly direct access to capital markets. But banking organizations are nearing the limits of their ability to act within existing law; and spending real resources to interpret outmoded law creatively is hardly wise. Without the repeal of Glass-Steagall, banks' share of credit markets is likely to decline—as it already has in our measures of short- and intermediate-term business credit. Society would lose the existing expertise and infrastructure of banking and would bear the cost of the redeployment of bank resources as personnel and capital move to nonbanking organizations. Instead, a soundly structured change in the law will allow financial markets to serve us better by lowering costs to users while strengthening financial institutions within a framework that will protect the financial integrity of banks.

### Evaluation of Possible Adverse Effects

The basic principles that I outlined . . . require us to take into account not only public benefits but also possible adverse effects including unsound banking practices, which clearly include the concept of excessive risk, conflicts of interest, impairment of competition, and undue concentration of resources. These concerns have been heightened by the unprecedented decline in the stock market that occurred on October 19, 1987, and the subsequent market volatility. . . .

### *ASSESSMENT OF RISK*

Bank holding company examinations indicate that U.S. banking organizations have generally shown an ability to manage the inherent risks of both their domestic and foreign securities activities in a prudent and responsible manner. Of all the domestic bank failures in the 1980s, to our knowledge none has been attributed to underwriting losses. Indeed, we are unaware of any significant losses in recent years owing to underwriting of domestically eligible securities. For that matter, research over the past 50 years concludes, contrary to the view of the Congress at the time, that bank securities activities were not a cause of the Great Depression and that banks with securities affiliates did not fail in proportionately greater numbers than banks more generally. . . .

Finally, I would note that empirical studies invariably find that underwriting and dealing are riskier than the total portfolio of other banking functions in the sense that the variability of returns to securities activities exceeds that of the returns to the combination of other banking functions. It is also important to note, however, that the average return to securities activities is also usually found to exceed the average return to the combination of other banking functions. In addition, there is evidence of some potential for limited diversification gains, or overall risk reduction, for banks being allowed increased securities powers.

The Congress adopted the Glass-Steagall Act more than 50 years earlier because it believed that banks had suffered serious losses as a result of their participation in investment banking. The Congress also thought that bank involvement in the promotional aspects of the investment banking business would produce a variety of "subtle hazards" to the banking system such as conflicts of interest and loss of public confidence. In answer to these concerns, we believe that the risks of investment banking to depository institutions are containable, that the regulatory framework established in the securities laws minimizes the impact of conflicts of interest, that the federal safety net implemented through deposit insurance and access to Federal Reserve credit will avoid the potential for panic withdrawals from banks if affiliated securities firms experience losses, and that banks can be effectively insulated from their securities affiliates through an appropriate structural framework.

As I have stressed, such an insulating framework can be established. I would now like to turn to what we see as its major elements.

### Need for Fire Walls

Fundamental to our recommendation on repeal of Glass-Steagall, and to our assessment that potential adverse effects of securities activities are clearly manageable, is the view that securities activities can be conducted behind walls designed to separate, insofar as possible, the bank from the risks associated with the securities activities. We see two major elements to an approach toward developing a practical insulating structure:

1. The holding company structure should be used to institutionalize separation between a bank and a securities affiliate.
2. The resulting institutional fire walls should be strengthened by limiting transactions, particularly credit transactions, between the bank and a securities affiliate.

At the same time, and without impairing the necessary separation, the structure should not be so rigid as to prevent affiliated organizations from providing the users of financial products with the improved service and reductions in cost that can come from the joint ownership of securities and banking organizations. We believe that it is both possible and desirable to accomplish both goals—establishing fully adequate fire walls in a context that achieves the economic benefits of joint ownership. . . .

Thus, we believe that the advantages of the holding company structure are both self-evident and overwhelming. Larger banking companies that are most likely to be heavily involved in securities activities should have no serious organizational problems with implementing this approach.

## *QUESTIONS AND COMMENTS*

1. As you know, the Federal Reserve Board has regulatory authority over bank holding companies. Would Chairman Greenspan's recommendations enhance or diminish the board's regulatory authority?

2. Greenspan states that it is "difficult, if not impossible from a practical standpoint for a bank to avoid assuming responsibility and liability for the obligations of its direct subsidiaries." Do you agree with this observation?

3. What public benefits does Greenspan identify? To whom would these benefits flow? Is the chairman of the Federal Reserve primarily concerned with the safety and soundness of the banking system, or with the overall state of the economy?

Chairman Greenspan notes that "there is evidence of some potential for limited diversification gains, or overall risk reduction, for banks being allowed increased securities powers." Would his plan enable banks to take advantage of those powers, or would all of the benefits of diversification accrue to the holding company?

# 7 EXAMINATION AND ENFORCEMENT

In previous chapters we considered a wide variety of regulations restricting the business activities of banks, thrifts, and bank holding companies. Obviously, these elaborate restrictions on bank activities would not prove very effective if violations could not be detected or, once detected, could not be effectively punished. In the present chapter we consider the means by which the regulatory system supervises banking institutions and deals with violations of law and unsound practices. We discuss, first, the supervision system designed to detect illegality and unsound practices and provide early warning of potential failure. Second, we examine the array of enforcement techniques available to bank regulators to rectify problems that have been identified.

## A. BANK SUPERVISION: THE MONITORING SYSTEM

### 1. *Background*

Banking institutions are among the most closely scrutinized businesses in the United States. They are required to report massive amounts of information to their supervisory agencies. They must disclose the results of their operations, the shape of their balance sheets, the general makeup of their assets, their capital structures, their records of investment in local communities, and much more. The most intimate details of their operations are subject to probing analysis by bank examiners whose sole responsibility is to detect illegality and unsafe practices.

Moreover, this regulatory scrutiny is anything but toothless. Institutions that engage in practices that the examiners deem questionable may be subjected to vigorous and ever-increasing regulatory review—some bankers might choose the word "harassment"—until the offending practices are terminated. If the regulators become convinced that an institution is engaged in illegal behavior or unsound practices, they may threaten a cease-and-desist action against the institution or its officers and directors. The officers and directors may be required to obtain additional capital for a financially shaky institution. They may be assessed ruinous civil money penalties for continued violations. They may be sued for civil damages. They may even be removed—fired—from the institutions where they have spent their entire professional lives and, indeed, may be barred from all federally insured institutions. The institution itself may suffer onerous penalties, including suspension or termination of federal deposit insurance. As we will see, the agencies are allowed very broad powers to impose these sanctions.

Not surprisingly, the bank examiner has enjoyed a formidable image in American folklore. Movie cognoscenti will recall that it was a bank examination that sent Jimmy Stewart off the bridge in *It's A Wonderful Life*. Stewart's character, the owner of a building and loan association, had sent his incompetent Uncle Billy, whom he employed as a teller, to the local commercial bank to make a large cash deposit. Uncle Billy lost the money just before Mr. Carter, the humorless horn-rimmed bank examiner, appeared on the scene. Our sympathies are all with Stewart, but it's not hard to see that from the examiner's perspective the situation smacked of incompetence, nepotism, and fraud. Although Stewart's character was rescued by a guardian angel, not all bankers have been so blessed when the flinty-eyed examiner noted discrepancies in the balance sheet. We shall meet some of these unfortunate bankers in the pages that follow.

One would suspect that given these awesome powers, the supervision system would be extraordinarily effective at preventing illegal or unsound practices. For many years this appeared to be the case. Yet the success of the system must be reevaluated in light of the experience during the 1980s and early 1990s. Fraudulent practices have apparently run rampant in the banking industry. A 1988 report issued by a House subcommittee concluded that one-third of all bank insolvencies and three-quarters of all savings and loan insolvencies were linked to insider abuse, fraud, or misconduct. The report criticized banking regulators for failing to detect the problems by more frequent examinations. In addition to fraud and insider abuse, many banks and thrifts engaged in an orgy of unsound banking practices, extending billions of dollars to shaky foreign countries, dubious real estate speculators, and wildcat oilmen. These practices are documented in a study released by the Comptroller of the Currency, which found that poor bank management was a leading cause of the failure of nearly 60 percent of national banks between 1979 and 1987.

The staggering losses incurred by the banking and thrift industries during the 1980s and beyond could have been avoided in every instance had the institution in question been prevented from engaging in unsound practices, or been required to shut its doors prior to or at the point of economic insolvency. Obviously, many institutions were allowed to fall deeply into insolvency before the supervisory authority closed their doors. The collapses of the 1980s and '90s might have been prevented—or at least greatly mitigated—if supervision had functioned as intended.

What happened to allow such an extraordinary breakdown? There is no indication that examiners today are any less competent or more lenient than in years past. And, in general, bank examiners have displayed admirable integrity. Even though bank examinations would appear to provide excellent settings for illegal gratuities in exchange for lenient regulatory treatment, there is little evidence of any widespread breaches of trust.

What, then, accounts for the apparent regulatory failure? A number of theories have been proposed, perhaps none of them fully satisfactory. First, it may well be that bank examiners do not possess a fully adequate methodology for assessing the safety and soundness of the institutions they supervise. No matter how stringent the examination procedure, it will have little effect if the data generated do not accurately identify institutions in need of regulatory attention.

Second, bank examinations may have become less effective as a result of structural changes in the banking industry. As some institutions have become nationwide and even worldwide in scope, conducting a broad range of complex activities, it is increasingly difficult for the examination process to uncover a full picture of the institution's overall financial status. The days when a Mr. Carter could arrive at a bank's doorstep and conduct a reliable audit of the bank's activities from a single location are long past, at least for the nation's larger depository institutions.

Third, the examination force, while adequate in normal times, proved incapable of effectively monitoring an industry in crisis. It was simply impossible for the regulatory system to cope with the large numbers of institutions that became insolvent during the 1980s.

Finally, regulators may sometimes have delayed closing insolvent institutions in hopes that an economic rebound would return the institution to financial health without the need for a costly federal bailout.

Although each of these theories may have merit—and taken together may explain more than any one individually—there is no firm consensus as to what, in fact, caused the regulatory breakdown of the 1980s.

Whatever may have caused this breakdown, it is clear that enforcement for the foreseeable future will be stricter than it has been heretofore. The 1989 thrift bailout legislation, the Financial Institutions Reform, Recovery, and Enforcement Act (FIRREA), greatly increased the authority of federal regulators to punish persons deemed to have engaged in illegal or unsound banking practices. The Department of Justice established an elite task force to prosecute criminal activities by bank officers. Bank examination staffs have been expanded, and compensation for bank examiners has been increased. Members of Congress have pressured federal regulators to seek out and punish those responsible for the banking debacle of the 1980s. The regulators themselves were clearly hearing the message; bank examinations became so stringent by the turn of the decade that top federal officials worried that banks would choke off credit unnecessarily in fear of being criticized if loans soured.

Is this enhanced regulatory enforcement desirable? A simple, and possibly correct, answer is that beefing up bank supervision cannot help but be beneficial. If the problems in the banking system stemmed from excessive leniency and poor judgment in the extension of credit to unsound enterprises, then a solution would appear to be a regulatory system that discourages undue speculation and rewards prudence.

Yet the question may not be quite so simple. Bank supervision is itself quite expensive, employing thousands of people and requiring the expenditure of millions of dollars of social resources. More importantly, the undoubted benefits of stricter regulation—in the form of fewer uneconomical projects being undertaken—must be assessed against the possible costs. When regulation of credit becomes overly strict, then banks may cease providing loans for good projects as well as bad ones. The result could be a credit "crunch," coupled with an undesirable economic slowdown. Moreover, restricting credit to only the safest and most secure borrowers can stifle innovation and entrepreneurship, and may reduce the amount of funds available for economic development in low-income communities. And high-quality personnel may be deterred from entering the banking industry if regulatory oversight becomes too stringent. These costs must be assessed in the balance when one assesses the appropriate level of regulatory scrutiny.

The public policy implications of bank supervision cannot be fully assessed without some consideration of possible regulatory and marketplace alternatives to supervision. Recall the discussion in Chapter 3, where we noted that, at present, federal deposit insurance is characterized by significant moral hazard in the sense that many of the deterrents to excessive risk-taking observed in private insurance markets—deductibles, liability limits, exclusions, and risk-adjusted premiums, among others—are weak or missing in the deposit insurance system. We noted that in place of these private contractual devices the bank regulatory system has traditionally substituted an elaborate monitoring system—bank supervision. Many of the arguments in favor of deposit insurance reform—risk-adjusted premiums, enhanced capital adequacy rules, early closure devices, market discipline, the narrow bank concept—implicitly turn on an assumption that bank supervision, without more, is an insufficient safeguard against risk-taking and moral hazard. As you read the following materials you may want to consider whether that assumption seems correct.

## 2. *The Supervisory System*

The first step in the supervisory process is to gather data in order to assess the institution's current condition and make judgments about its future prospects. There are two crucial elements to this process. First, all banking institutions are required to regularly report extensive data to their supervising agency. They must file quarterly Reports of Condition ("call reports") containing detailed balance sheet data. They must also file Reports of Income either quarterly (for larger banks) or twice a year (for smaller banks). These reports are analyzed by computer. If the computer analysis shows unusual conditions or potentially dangerous deterioration in performance, the supervising agency is likely to schedule an examination, often providing the examiners with detailed instructions on particular problem areas to investigate.

The second element of the data-gathering process is the on-site bank examination. The on-site examination, in theory at least, provides much information that mere self-reporting by banks cannot. It allows examiners to delve into files to detect evidence of fraud or insider abuse that might be effectively disguised in written reports of condition. Examiners may also question officers and directors about the nature of the institution's business.

The on-site examination is highly labor-intensive. A substantial number of examiners may be required to assess the condition of any large institution. Accordingly, it has been difficult, as a practical matter, for banking authorities to conduct frequent examinations of all depository institutions. Instead, the regulatory authorities have conducted a form of "triage" in which institutions previously identified (from call reports or prior examinations) as being in questionable financial condition are examined more frequently than those deemed in sound financial health. The FDIC's goal as of 1990, for example, was to conduct full-scope on-site examinations of problem or near-problem banks at least once a year, and to examine all insured banks at least once every two years. In the 1991 Federal Deposit Insurance Corporation Improvement Act, however, Congress mandated a stepped-up pace for bank examinations as of 1993, with a full-scope, on-site examination for every insured depository institution being required at least once a year, except for certain smaller institutions which must be examined at least every 18 months.

In addition to full-scale on-site examinations, the agencies may conduct "visitations" at more frequent intervals. A "visitation" in this context is without religious significance (although it may induce some bankers to engage in prayer); it is simply a small-scale examination for specific or limited purposes.

Responsibility for examining banking institutions is divided among the various agencies. The FDIC has authority to examine FDIC-insured depository institutions, including savings institutions insured by the FSLIC prior to 1989; its primary authority is over insured state-chartered banks that are not members of the Federal Reserve System. The Comptroller of the Currency has authority to examine national banks. The Federal Reserve Board has power to examine state-chartered institutions that are members of the Federal Reserve System, as well as certain specialized institutions (Edge Act and agreement corporations) devoted to foreign trade, and to inspect bank holding companies. The OTS has authority to examine thrift institutions and their affiliates. The National Credit Union Administration examines federally insured credit unions. And state banking, savings institution, and credit union agencies have authority to examine institutions operating under state charter.

Obviously this balkanized regulatory scheme is subject to numerous potential overlaps and inefficiencies. Congress provided a mechanism for clarifying regulatory responsibilities in the Federal Financial Institutions Examination Council Act of 1978, 12 U.S.C. §§3301-3308. This statute created a new umbrella body, the Federal Financial Institutions Examination Council (FFIEC), comprised of all federal banking agencies with supervisory responsibilities. Working through the FFIEC, the federal banking agencies have established a rough allocation of examination responsibility, virtually eliminating duplicative and wasteful examinations by federal agencies. Congress added teeth to the requirement of cooperation among supervisory agencies in 1994, when it required that federal banking agencies work jointly to eliminate duplicative information requests, coordinate examinations among themselves, and work with state bank supervisors to coordinate examinations and requests for information. 12 U.S.C. §§1820(d)(6), 4804.

The FFIEC does not include representatives of state banking regulators, which have independent examination authority over state-chartered institutions. In general, federal supervisory agencies appear to rely most heavily on state bank examinations in those states where the examination force enjoys a good reputation among their federal peers.

The FFIEC statute required the federal banking agencies to "establish uniform principles and standards and report forms for the examination of financial institutions." 12 U.S.C. §3305(a). Pursuant to this mandate, the agencies have devised a composite rating system for financial institutions under federal supervision. The rating system is known by the acronym CAMEL for the five areas of operation that are individually rated by bank examiners: *C*apital adequacy, *A*sset quality, *M*anagement, *E*arnings, and *L*iquidity.

## FDIC, Manual of Examination Policies, Basic Examination Concepts and Guidelines (1990)

### I. Rationale of Bank Examinations

What are the purposes of bank examinations? Although many answers to this question could be given, several fundamental reasons can be identified. The first relates to the maintenance of public confidence in the integrity of the banking system and in individual banks. Such confidence is clearly essential because the system's customers serve as the source of funding, without which banks would be unable to meet their most fundamental objective of providing financial services. The existence of unhealthy or deteriorating conditions, which may threaten this integrity, should be disclosed through the examiner's evaluation of the bank's capital adequacy, asset quality, management, liquidity position, and earnings capacity. Second, the periodic on-premise examination provides the best means of determining the bank's adherence to laws and regulations. Compliance with statutory and regulatory requirements has traditionally been given high priority by bank supervisors, and this posture has frequently been reaffirmed by Congress. A third response to the question concerns the role examinations play in protecting the financial integrity of the deposit insurance fund. That is, the examination process can help prevent problem situations from remaining uncorrected and deteriorating to the point where costly financial assistance by the FDIC, or even a payoff of depositors, becomes unavoidable. Finally, the examination supplies the supervisor with an understanding of the nature, relative seriousness and ultimate cause of a bank's problems, and thus provides a factual foundation to soundly base corrective measures, recommendations and instructions. The examination thus plays a very key role in the supervisory process itself.

### II. The Uniform Financial Institutions Rating System

#### *INTRODUCTION*

Upon the recommendation of the Federal Financial Institutions Examination Council, the Corporation's Board of Directors adopted a policy statement on November 26, 1979 entitled "Uniform Financial Institutions Rating System" (UFIRS). This statement was similarly adopted by the National Credit Union Administration, Federal Home Loan Bank Board, Board of Governors of the Federal Reserve System and Office of the Comptroller of Currency. The rating system reflects in a comprehensive and uniform fashion an institution's financial condition, compliance with laws and regulations and overall operating soundness. Its primary purpose is to help identify those institutions whose weaknesses in the three aforementioned areas require special supervisory attention and/or warrant a higher than normal degree of supervisory concern. The effective surveillance and supervision of such banks has been and continues to be the first priority of the FDIC.

In accordance with the UFIRS, each bank is assigned a uniform composite rating based on an evaluation of pertinent financial and operational standards, criteria and principles. This overall rating is expressed through use of a numerical scale of "1" through "5" in ascending order of supervisory concern; "1" indicates the highest rating and least degree or concern, while "5" is the lowest rating and therefore the highest degree of supervisory concern.

To aid in implementing the uniform rating system, the Corporation utilizes a similar scale of one to five to assess the five key performance dimensions upon which the composite rating is principally based. These performance dimensions are commonly identified by the acronym "CAMEL": *C*apital adequacy, *A*sset quality, *M*anagement, *E*arnings and *L*iquidity. The balance of this section is devoted to a discussion of the guidelines and standards to be applied when assigning performance ratings and the composite rating.

### *PERFORMANCE EVALUATION*

A description on the graduations utilized in conjunction with the performance ratings is as follows:

*Rating "1"*—Indicates strong performance, significantly higher than average.

*Rating "2"*—Reflects satisfactory performance, performance which is average or above; this includes performance that adequately provides for the safe and sound operation of the bank.

*Rating "3"*—Represents performance that is flawed to some degree and as such is considered fair. It is neither satisfactory nor unsatisfactory but is characterized by performance that is [sic] or below-average quality.

*Rating "4"*—Refers to marginal performance, significantly below average. If left unchecked, such performance might evolve into weaknesses or conditions that could threaten the viability of the institution.

*Rating "5"*—Considered unsatisfactory; performance that is critically deficient and in need of immediate remedial attention. Such performance, by itself or in combination with other weaknesses, threatens the viability of the institution.

The above ratings are to be utilized to measure the five crucial performance dimensions commented on below.

*Capital Adequacy*—Rated in relation to the volume of risk assets; the volume of marginal and inferior quality assets; bank growth experience, plans and prospects; and the strength of management. Consideration should also be given to a bank's capital ratios relative to its peer group, its earnings retention and its access to capital markets or other appropriate sources of financial assistance. The Corporation's policy statement and regulation on capital adequacy must also be taken into account. . . .

*Asset Quality*—Rated in relation to the level, distribution and severity of classified assets; the level and distribution of nonaccrual and reduced rate assets; the adequacy of valuation reserves; and management's demonstrated ability to administer and collect problem credits. Adequate valuation reserves and a proven capacity to police and collect problem loans clearly mitigate to some degree the weaknesses inherent in a given level of classified assets. Asset quality evaluation should also take into consideration any undue degree of concentration of credits or investments, the nature and volume of special mention classifications, and the adequacy of lending policies and credit administration procedures. . . .

*Management*—Must be evaluated against virtually all factors considered necessary to operate the bank within accepted banking practices and in a safe and sound manner. Thus, management is rated in relation to technical competence; leadership and administrative ability; compliance with banking regulation and statutes; ability to plan and respond to changing circumstances; adequacy of and compliance with internal policies; and depth and succession. The assessment of management also takes into account the quality of internal controls, operating procedures and all lending, investment and operating policies; and the involvement of the directors and shareholders. . . .

*Earnings*—Rated with respect to the ability to cover losses and provide for adequate capital; earnings trends; peer group comparisons; the quality and composition of net income; and the degree of reliance on interest-sensitive funds. Consideration should also be given to the interrelationships between and dividend payout ratio, the rate of growth of retained earnings and the adequacy of bank capital. The adequacy of transfers to the valuation reserve, and the extent to which extraordinary items, securities transactions and tax effects contribute to net income, should also be assessed. . . .

*Liquidity*—Rated in relation to the volatility of deposits; the frequency and level of borrowings; technical competence relative to structure of liabilities; availability of assets readily convertible into cash; and access to money markets or other ready sources of funds. The bank's liquidity position should be appraised over a period of time as well as on a particular date. The overall effectiveness of asset-liability management strategies should be considered, as well as the adequacy of and compliance with established liquidity policies. The nature, volume and anticipated usage of credit commitments are also factors to be weighed. . . .

### *COMPOSITE RATINGS*

Assessment of the CAMEL performance dimensions and their interrelationships represents the essential foundation upon which the composite rating is based. Although the rankings of the individual CAMEL components should normally bear a fairly close relationship to the composite rating assigned, the latter is not to be derived merely by computing an arithmetic average of the former. Such a simplistic, mechanical approach may not necessarily reflect the extent of supervisory oversight of the institution that the circumstances demand. For example, it is quite conceivable for a bank to be operating with acceptable management, earnings and liquidity and yet have an excessive volume of adversely classified assets. A remedial program to address these asset weaknesses, as might be incorporated into an informal administrative action, . . . could be an effective supervisory response. Consequently, a composite rating of "3" might be appropriate for such a bank, notwithstanding the fact that higher numerical assessments were assigned to a majority of the other CAMEL elements. Examiners or reviewers are not precluded from considering factors other than the CAMEL components themselves if, in their judgment, these other factors are deemed relevant to an accurate assessment of the overall condition and soundness of a particular bank. The important point to reiterate is that the principal purpose of the UFIRS is to identify, via the composite rating, those institutions which merit special supervisory attention and/or warrant a higher than normal degree of supervisory concern.

Composite ratings are defined and distinguished as follows:

*Composite "1"*—Institutions in this group are basically sound in every respect; any adverse findings or comments are of a minor nature and can be handled in a routine manner. Such institutions are resistant to external economic and financial disturbances and more capable of withstanding the vagaries of business conditions than institutions with lower ratings. As a result, such institutions give no cause for supervisory concern.

*Composite "2"*—Institutions in this group are fundamentally sound, but may reflect modest weaknesses correctable in the normal course of business. The nature and severity of deficiencies, however, are not considered material and, therefore, such institutions are stable and able to withstand business fluctuations quite well. While areas of weakness could develop into conditions of greater concern, the supervisory response is limited to the extent that minor adjustments are resolved in the normal course and operations continue satisfactory.

*Composite "3"*—Institutions in this category exhibit financial, operational or compliance weaknesses ranging from moderately severe to unsatisfactory. When weaknesses relate to financial condition, such institutions may be vulnerable to the onset of adverse business conditions and could easily deteriorate if concerted action is not effective in correcting the areas of weakness. Institutions which are in significant noncompliance with laws and regulations may also be accorded this rating. Generally, these institutions give cause for supervisory concern and require more than normal supervision to address deficiencies. Overall strength and financial capacity, however, are still such as to make failure only a remote possibility.

*Composite "4"*—Institutions in this group have an immoderate volume of serious financial weaknesses or a combination of other conditions that are unsatisfactory. Major and serious problems or unsafe and unsound conditions may exist which are not being satisfactorily addressed or resolved. Unless effective action is taken to correct these conditions, they could reasonably develop into a situation that could impair future viability, constitute a threat to the interests of depositors and/or pose a potential for disbursement of funds by the insuring agency. A higher potential for failure is present but is not yet imminent or pronounced. Institutions in this category require close supervisory attention and financial surveillance and a definitive plan for corrective action.

*Composite "5"*—This category is reserved for institutions with an extremely high immediate or near term probability of failure. The volume and severity of weaknesses or unsafe and unsound conditions are so critical as to require urgent aid from stockholders or other public or private sources of financial assistance. In the absence of urgent and decisive corrective measures, these situations will likely result in failure and involve the disbursement of insurance funds to insured depositors, or some form of emergency assistance, merger or acquisition.

It is the Corporation's view that disclosure of the composite rating to bank management is appropriate. Therefore, the examiner must conclude the Examiner's Comments and Conclusions Schedule with the composite rating assigned. To enable the institution's directorate to better understand and appreciate the significance of this rating, the definition of the particular rating accorded must also be disclosed. It is important to note that only the composite rating and not the individual CAMEL performance rankings is to be indicated. Moreover, the examiner is not to disclose the rating to bank management at the time of the examination, since the Regional Office must concur with the rating and may, in some instances, wish to change it before the examination report is sent to the bank. The rating continues to be subject to the confidentiality restrictions imposed by Part 309 of the FDIC's Rules and Regulations.

## *QUESTIONS AND COMMENTS*

1. Bank examiners at federal agencies, then, are instructed to assign individual ratings on a 1-5 scale (5 being the worst) for each CAMEL category. A composite CAMEL rating is then assigned, again on a 1-5 scale, based on the five factor ratings as well as any other factors that the examiner deems to be material. The composite CAMEL rating is intended as a measure of the bank's performance.

The bank examiner is expected to discuss any unsatisfactory conditions with the bank management. In general, a bank's management is well-advised to adopt a receptive and cooperative tone in response to whatever criticisms—justified or not—the examiner might present. If management appears cooperative, the examiner may delete the criticisms from the final report; if management is obstructive or argumentative, the report is likely to be even more critical than it might have been otherwise. The best opportunity to influence the report is at the initial on-site examination stage.

Once the site examination is complete, the examiner submits a final Report of Examination to his or her supervisors. The Report of Examination includes the CAMEL rating together with extensive supporting documentation and analysis. If the Report of Examination contains adverse findings, higher-level officials at the examining agency may bring the matter up with top bank management. If the agency does not receive a satisfactory explanation or a commitment to rectify the problem, the bank will thereafter certainly be subject to more intensive regulatory scrutiny. In addition, if the bank is assigned a CAMEL rating of 3 or worse, the supervisory agency is likely to institute one or another of the arsenal of enforcement procedures that we discuss in the following section.

2. The perceived purposes of bank supervision have evolved over the years. In the days before federal deposit insurance, bank supervision was thought necessary to prevent bank runs that could turn into large-scale banking panics. In this regard, the perception of supervision was often as important as the reality. If the public believed that banks were strictly supervised, they would be less likely to lose confidence the first time they heard some rumor that the bank was not in good financial condition. Undoubtedly the forbidding image of the bank supervisor in traditional folklore stems in part from the value that bank regulators and bankers alike saw in portraying the supervisory system as diligent, efficient, and unyielding. After the implementation of federal deposit insurance in 1933, however, the value of supervision at stopping bank

runs became attenuated. As we saw in Chapter 1, bank runs are principally controlled these days by federal deposit insurance, coupled with emergency liquidity assistance from the Federal Reserve Board. A new rationale for federal supervision became apparent, however: protecting the assets of the federal insurance funds, which have assumed primary liability for the risk of bank failure. In a real sense, therefore, the bank supervisor today acts as an agent for the federal deposit insurance programs. Can you think of any potential problems, in this regard, with relying on state supervisors of federally insured institutions?

3. How scientific do the CAMEL ratings seem to you? Given that the bank examiner can give variable weighting to the five factors in determining the composite rating, and may consider factors other than the five specifically mentioned, isn't there a high level of subjectivity in the examination process? Are the ratings even logical? How can a bank's performance be "neither satisfactory nor unsatisfactory"?

4. There are few empirical studies of how much bank examinations contribute to failure prediction, perhaps because examination reports are not ordinarily available to economists outside the government. One study by three government economists came up with the following results: First, the only data in examination reports with any statistical significance beyond data available in call reports were the examiners' loan classifications. A credit risk variable based on these loan classifications, when coupled with call report data, did slightly better at predicting failure than call report data alone, especially when the bank examination had occurred a relatively short time before the failure.

This study also examined the predictive quality of the examiners' CAMEL ratings. CAMEL ratings were about equivalent to a model using call data alone when the failure occurred within one year of the examination. When the failure occurred more than a year after the examination, the CAMEL ratings were significantly worse at predicting failure than a model based on call data alone. See Bovenzi, Marino, & McFadden, Commercial Bank Failure Prediction Models, 11 Econ. Rev. of the Fed. Res. Bank of Atlanta 14 (Nov. 1983).

What inferences can you draw from this study regarding the frequency with which examinations should be undertaken? What about the utility of CAMEL ratings as a failure prediction device?

5. Can bank examinations be said to have a function apart from rating the bank and taking steps to prevent failure? What positive results might flow from the repeated personal contacts between agency officials and bank officers that the bank examination procedure facilitates? From the knowledge on the part of bank management that their decisions will be scrutinized by an outside authority?

6. To what extent should the results of bank supervision be made public? What arguments can you develop in favor of public disclosure of supervision data? A bank's creditors—purchasers of its commercial

paper, holders of its bonds and other securities, and so forth—will attend to information about its solvency and operations, will they not? Would providing them with such information serve a valid public policy purpose?

Can you think of arguments against the disclosure of all available information in the government's hands about the condition of a bank? How would disclosure of bank examination reports affect depositors, customers, and bank examiners themselves?

7. A fairly wide range of information about depository institutions is publicly available. Each insured depository institution must prepare and file an annual report of financial condition and management, and such reports are available for public inspection. The relevant banking agency will ordinarily provide call report data on any institution under its supervision. Moreover, banks with outstanding public securities are required to engage in regular securities act reporting. The national rating agencies publish assessments of the default risk for larger banks' debt securities. And a bank itself may voluntarily disclose information about its performance.

Examination reports and workpapers, however, are not publicly available. Such papers are protected against compelled disclosure under an exception to the Freedom of Information Act. See Denny v. Carey, 78 F.R.D. 370, 373 (E.D. Pa. 1978). Whether and to what extent they are also protected against discovery in litigation is as yet unclear. One court held that a Comptroller of the Currency examination report was not protected by a governmental privilege because it contained only facts or interpretations of fact rather than expressions of opinion or professional judgment. Seafirst Corp. v. Jenkins, 644 F. Supp. 1160, 1163-1164 (W.D. Wash. 1986). Another court held that the FHLBB's examination workpapers were protected only by a qualified official information privilege but not by any absolute bank examination privilege. In Re Sunrise Securities Litigation, 109 Bankr. 658 (E.D. Pa. 1990) (requiring production of subpoenaed workpapers to a special master for review as to relevance). Because accountants and other defendants in civil damages actions brought by federal agencies after bank failure are likely to request production of examination reports as a matter of course (why?), there is likely to be more litigation over these issues before the matter is finally settled. How would you weigh the costs and benefits of disclosing reports of examination of the examiner's underlying workpapers? Would the analysis be different if only the CAMEL rating were disclosed?

Would you require public disclosure of final administrative orders? For many years such orders were not disclosed. However, Congress has required that federal banking agencies publish final administrative orders, including written agreements, and any modifications or terminations of such orders. 12 U.S.C. §1818(u). What benefit do you think Congress sought to achieve by this requirement? Note that the requirement does not apply to informal dispositions or agreements. How does this affect the bargaining position of agencies and bank officials charged with violations?

8. Is there any avenue for redress in a court of law if a bank is dissatisfied with its examination report? Until recently, the examination per se was virtually immune from judicial challenge. Since 1987, however, institutions formerly supervised by the FHLBB (now OTS) are entitled to informal review of some of the most important examiner decisions, including loan classifications, with the right to a recommended decision by an independent arbiter. 12 U.S.C. §1442(a). The value of this informal procedure is not clear since the ultimate decision is made by an agency official and is entirely immune from judicial review.

9. The examiner's conclusions and analysis may be challenged in a petition for judicial review of a final agency enforcement order. The probability of success in such a challenge, however, is usually low because reviewing courts are loath to substitute their judgment for that of the expert examiner on the scene. A good object lesson for banks seeking to challenge examination reports is Sunshine State Bank v. FDIC, 783 F.2d 1580, 1583-1584 (11th Cir. 1986). Based on a bank examiner's report, which had classified many loans as loss, doubtful, or substandard, the FDIC brought an enforcement proceeding to remove bank officers and directors from office. An Administrative Law Judge (ALJ), however, rejected most of the examiner's classifications. The FDIC reinstated most of the examiner's classifications, and on petition for review the court of appeals affirmed:

> The expertise of the bank examiners was unique. . . . The examination team spent over 3000 hours in a detailed analysis of the Bank's assets. The examiner-in-charge . . . had participated in over 500 bank examinations, over 150 as examiner-in-charge. The other five examiners had participated collectively in over 1650 examinations. . . . In reaching conclusions about the likelihood of a particular loan being repaid, the examiner applies his expertise, training and experience to the facts and makes inferences and judgments. To properly predict the chances of a given loan being repaid, a person needs this kind of expertise. Unless shown to be arbitrary or capricious or outside a zone of reasonableness, the ALJ, the Board, and the courts must give significant deference to these experts.

Do you think that the court of appeals in this case should have paid greater deference to the findings of the ALJ? Doesn't the result undermine the role of ALJs in this context? What should the court's stance have been if the FDIC had affirmed the ALJ and rejected the bank examiner's classifications?

10. As a supplement (alternative?) to bank examination, should bank financial reports be audited by an independent accounting firm?

Until recently, the bank supervisory agencies did not require independent audits, even though most bank failures in recent years have involved banks that were not independently audited. In the 1991 FDICIA legislation, Congress required all insured depository institutions to file independently audited annual reports with the appropriate federal or state regulators. The FDIC may require that large institutions obtain independent audits on their quarterly financial statements as well. Small depository institutions (generally, those with less than $150 million in assets) are exempted.

11. If a bank uses an independent auditor, should the auditor receive examination data or information as to informal enforcement actions to assist its investigation? Despite congressional pressure, the banking agencies resisted requiring depository institutions to turn this information over to their outside auditors. Why? Congress required them to do so in the FIRREA. See 12 U.S.C. §1817(a)(8) (FDIC-insured institutions); 12 U.S.C. §1782(a)(7) (federally insured credit unions).

12. Often the existence of ongoing frauds is known to bank employees or others outside of the government. Should these individuals be encouraged to become "whistle-blowers" by the prospect of a cash reward? Section 933 of FIRREA authorizes the federal banking agencies to pay rewards for information leading to the recovery of more than $50,000. Is this a good idea? The American Bankers Association opposed the provision on the ground that it could be abused by disgruntled employees and might lead to the agencies' being overburdened by a flood of unsupported hunches. Do you agree?

13. What if a banking agency negligently supervises an institution, and accordingly fails to detect unsafe or unsound practices that eventually harm the bank or cause its failure. Should the bank or anyone else have a cause of action against the agency for money damages based on the negligent supervision? Cases uniformly hold that no such cause of action exists. See, e.g., Harmsen v. Smith, 542 F.2d 496 (9th Cir. 1976); In re Franklin National Bank, 381 F. Supp. 1390 (F.D.N.Y. 1974). Do you concur?

## B. ENFORCEMENT ACTIONS

We move now from the procedures for gathering information to the arsenal of weapons available to federal banking authorities to enforce the banking laws and to punish violations once detected. In distinguishing between information-gathering and enforcement, however, we must add the caveat that in practice the differences between the two functions are not clear-cut. The bank examiner who raises eyebrows at a particular practice is engaged in enforcement, even if his or her only formal role is to prepare a Report of Examination. Thus, while bank supervision performs an information-gathering function, it is also the first—and often the only—step in an enforcement process that moves through a variety of approaches ranging from informal and cooperative procedures to formal and contested ones.

Aside from the informal sanction (or "moral suasion") exerted during the supervision process, the most important enforcement procedures are these: informal agreements and conditions; cease-and-desist orders; suspension or removal of bank officers; civil monetary penalties; suspension or termination of federal deposit insurance; civil litigation; and criminal prosecutions.

Many of these enforcement tools were dramatically strengthened in the 1989 FIRREA legislation. As President Bush said on signing the legislation, "[b]eginning today, penalties for wrongdoing by officers and directors of insured institutions will be increased up to $1 million per day. And criminal penalties will be toughened from yesterday's slap on the wrist to the clang of a prison door. Those who try and loot the savings of their fellow citizens deserve, and will receive, swift and severe punishment." 25 Weekly Comp. Pres. Doc. 1226 (Aug. 9, 1989). Partly as a result of FIRREA, and partly in consequence of the enormous wave of bank failures that swept the country during the 1980s and beyond, we can expect enforcement of the banking laws to be far stricter in the future than it has been heretofore. Many of the issues discussed in this chapter, accordingly, are likely to be highly controversial in the years to come.

Before addressing the different enforcement mechanisms, however, we focus on a cross-cutting issue, namely the question of *who* can be liable under the various enforcement provisions.

## 1. *"Institution-Affiliated Parties"*

Prior to 1989 the enforcement provisions applied to "officers," "directors," and "other person[s] participating in the conduct of the affairs" of depository institutions. The FIRREA scrapped this provision and substituted an expanded definition that sweeps within its scope many persons who formerly had little to fear from bank enforcement actions. The current law sets forth three categories of persons, referred to as "institution-affiliated parties," who are potentially subject to enforcement actions. See 12 U.S.C. §1813(u) (FDIC-insured institutions); 12 U.S.C. §1786(r) (federally insured credit unions).

First, the term "institution-affiliated party" includes "any director, officer, employee, or controlling stockholder (other than a bank holding company) of, or agent for" a federally insured depository institution and any other person who is required to file a change-in-control notice with an appropriate federal banking agency under the Change in Bank Control Act. These persons are assumed to have significant participation in the conduct of the institution, and accordingly no further showing is required in order to subject them to enforcement proceedings.

Second, the term includes "any shareholder (other than a bank holding company), consultant, joint venture partner, and any other person as determined by the appropriate Federal banking agency (by regulation or case-by-case) who participated in the conduct of the affairs" of the institution.

Third, the term includes "any independent contractor (including any attorney, appraiser, or accountant) who knowingly or recklessly participates in—(A) any violation of any law or regulation; (B) any breach of fiduciary duty; or (C) any unsafe or unsound practice, which caused or is likely to cause more than a minimal financial loss to, or a significant adverse effect on" the institution.

The real kicker in this new definition is the third category, which sweeps within the ambit of potential enforcement liability a broad spectrum of independent contractors who deal with the bank. Not surprisingly, the legal, accounting, and appraisal industries were enormously concerned about their potential liability. Through vigorous lobbying, they were able to obtain two key limitations on their exposure, which are embodied in the ultimate definition. First, unlike other persons subject to enforcement actions, independent contractors are liable only if they act "knowingly or recklessly." Mere negligence is not enough, nor, probably, is even gross negligence that falls short of recklessness. Thus the attorney who simply gives bad advice to a bank client probably can escape sanction under this provision. The line between bad advice and recklessness, however, may be a thin one in practice. Second, again unlike other persons subject to enforcement actions, independent contractors are liable only if their actions caused or were likely to cause more than a "minimal" financial loss. It is unclear whether this second requirement will screen out many actions against independent contractors, given the ease with which a regulatory agency may allege that a person's actions caused more than a minimal loss.

## *QUESTIONS AND COMMENTS*

1. What if a bank officer or director has resigned her or his position by the time enforcement proceedings are initiated? Is he or she still subject to potential liability? The D.C. Circuit held in 1989 that an individual who resigns from or otherwise leaves an institution is beyond the enforcement jurisdiction of the banking agencies. Stoddard v. Board of Governors of the Federal Reserve System, 868 F.2d 1308 (D.C. Cir. 1989). Congress

overruled the *Stoddard* case in FIRREA, declaring that banking agencies may initiate enforcement actions against institution-affiliated parties within six years after they leave an institution. 12 U.S.C. §1818(i)(3) (FDIC-insured institutions); 12 U.S.C. §1786(k)(3) (federally insured credit unions). The legislative history indicates a congressional intent that the provision operate retroactively. Can you think of any constitutional problems with this?

2. Assume an attorney is actively involved in counseling a bank and guiding its actions. As a result of the attorney's negligence, the bank suffers losses. The attorney may be subject to suit by the bank. Could she also be brought into a federal enforcement proceeding as an "institution-affiliated party"?

3. Attorney Mann, a third-year associate at the 500-attorney megafirm Dewey, Cheatham & Howe, provides reckless advice to a bank, resulting in several million dollars in losses. The appropriate bank supervisory agency brings an action for a civil money penalty against Mann personally and against Dewey, Cheatham & Howe as a firm. Mann, who is still paying off student loans, is impecunious. Can the law firm be liable for Mann's misconduct? What if the agency sought permanently to bar Dewey, Cheatham & Howe from providing legal services to any insured depository institution? See 12 U.S.C. §1818(e)(7)(F) (an industry-wide order "shall only apply to a person who is an individual, unless the appropriate Federal banking agency specifically finds that it should apply to a corporation, firm, or other business enterprise").

## 2. *Conditional Approvals*

One possible step for banking agencies, either after informal suasion has proved unsuccessful or in cases where an institution seeks to engage in an unusual and potentially risky activity, is to insist that the institution comply with certain agency requirements as a condition of approval of some action that the institution wishes to undertake.

Regulation by such conditional approvals can be a potent enforcement technique. As we have seen, depository institutions must obtain the formal approval of their agencies to engage in a variety of activities. The approval requirement extends to even such apparently routine actions as opening a new branch or (for bank holding companies) entering into a line of business generally approved for bank holding companies by the Federal Reserve Board.

Typically, approvals for routine matters such as this are granted as a matter of course. Power to approve such applications is usually delegated to an agency's regional offices and handled at a relatively modest administrative level. However, an institution that has engaged in activities displeasing to the supervisory agency cannot always be sure that its applications will be granted, even in routine cases. Banking agencies can, and do, use their approval powers to punish banks that have flouted the agencies' wishes. They do so either by denying the approval altogether or, more commonly, by granting it subject to conditions. Violation of conditions imposed in writing may be grounds for a cease-and-desist order, and may even subject bank officers to removal. See 12 U.S.C. §1818(e).

### *QUESTIONS AND COMMENTS*

1. How much bargaining leverage does an institution typically have when a banking agency seeks to impose conditions on approval of regulatory applications? Consider the following quotation from Aman, Bargaining for Justice: An Examination of the Use and Limits of Conditions by the Federal Reserve Board, 74 Iowa L. Rev. 837, 872 (1989): "A party eager to close a deal may not feel it has much negotiating room. In such cases, the Board has superior, indeed coercive, bargaining power."

2. What sorts of conditions may the appropriate regulatory agency impose in connection with its approvals? Many conditions, such as requirements that an institution adhere to clearly established statutory requirements, are entirely unproblematic. But, as Professor Aman observes in the article cited above, the Federal Reserve Board has sometimes obtained conditions in situations where its substantive authority to impose the condition as a matter of administrative regulation is seriously in doubt. For example, the board may condition its approval of a bank holding company's application to acquire a state-chartered bank on the assurance that the newly acquired bank will not engage in activities that the board considers excessively risky, such as real estate development. And this occurs even though the board arguably lacks the legal authority to regulate the activities of state-chartered banks directly, even when the banks are subsidiaries of bank holding companies.

3. Conditions imposed by the banking agencies may be the subject of judicial review. Federal courts have occasionally struck down conditions as in excess of regulatory authority. See, e.g., Securities Industry Association v. Board of Governors of the Federal Reserve System, 839 F.2d 47, 67-68 (2d Cir.), *cert. denied,* 486 U.S. 1059 (1988) (striking down market share limitation in approval for securities activities by bank holding company subsidiaries); First Bancorporation v. Board of Governors of the Federal Reserve System, 728 F.2d 434, 437-438 (10th Cir. 1984) (condition held to be ultra vires and based on incorrect interpretation of the law). If, however, a party has voluntarily agreed to a condition, judicial review may thereafter be unavailable on the theory that the party has waived any objection. This is true despite the fact that a party

as a practical matter may have no choice but to agree or see the entire application rejected.

4. Do you find it a matter of concern that the Federal Reserve Board or other banking agencies might effectively coerce banking institutions to accept conditions voluntarily in situations where the agency would not have statutory authority to impose the condition directly? If this is a matter of concern, what regulatory approach would you suggest to deal with the problem?

### 3. *Written Agreements*

If written conditions are not feasible (because, for example, the institution in question has not made any applications), or if the supervisory agency wants to increase the pressure on the institution to rectify the problems quickly, the agency may seek to negotiate an informal written agreement. From the bank agencies' standpoint, a written agreement has two advantages over informal contacts with bank examiners as a means of inducing regulatory compliance.

First, the written agreement is intended to, and does, attract the attention of top bank management. The banking agencies will usually insist that top management attend the meetings in which the written agreement is negotiated. Relatively high-level officials from the agency's regional office may attend. Moreover, the institution's shortcomings, and its agreement to remedy the defects, are reduced to writing, a step that lends gravity and importance to the matter. And a written agreement, at least if it is well drafted, will clearly define the nature of the obligations that the institution is undertaking—something that may have been left ambiguous in informal discussions with bank examiners.

Second, written agreements provide an independent basis for cease-and-desist proceedings. In theory, a cease-and-desist order would be available even if the institution has violated no law or regulation, and even if the practice in question does not represent a threat to the safety and soundness of the institution, so long as the party against whom proceedings are brought is in violation of a prior written agreement. Thus, with a written agreement in hand, the agency is saved the time and expense of proving substantive charges in the event that the practices in question continue. The agency, however, cannot enforce a written agreement directly in court, nor can it seek civil monetary penalties for violations. The agency's remedy for violation of written agreements is to bring cease-and-desist proceedings. Accordingly, if the agency believes that the problems are not going to be remedied by a written agreement, it may decide to skip the written agreement step and proceed directly to a cease-and-desist action in order to save time.

A written agreement also has several advantages from the standpoint of an institution or institution-affiliated party. It is cheap to negotiate compared with expensive cease-and-desist proceedings. And a written agreement, because it is informal, need not be made public. The parties will be spared damage to their reputations.

## QUESTIONS AND COMMENTS

1. A written agreement takes the form of a contract between the agency and the institution or institution-affiliated party. Is consideration in the common law sense required for such contracts to be enforceable? See Groos National Bank v. Comptroller of the Currency, 573 F.2d 889, 896 (5th Cir. 1978):

> [t]he statute provides that a cease and desist order may issue upon any violation of an agreement between the agency and a bank and says nothing of consideration. Nor is there any reason to import the common law of consideration, proper to private contractual relations, into the relationships between a regulatory agency and the entity it regulates. The Comptroller is authorized by statute to exercise extensive controls upon banks; the statute clearly contemplates that agreements may occur between the Comptroller and banks; and if the Comptroller does enter such an agreement by way of attaining voluntary compliance, we will not introduce the trappings of common-law contractual consideration to question that agreement. To do so would deeply intrude upon the regulatory agency's legitimate efforts to substitute voluntary agreement for formal cease and desist proceedings.

2. How much bargaining leverage does the institution or institution-affiliated party have in negotiating a written agreement? Typically, the agency will let it be known that if the written agreement is not signed, more draconian measures are sure to follow, up to and including closure of the institution. The agency may even have issued a temporary cease-and-desist order (discussed below) to spur the negotiating process forward. Should the common law contractual defense of duress apply?

3. Note that, as in the case of conditional approvals, written agreements may go beyond what the agency would be able to command by formal enforcement proceedings. The agency may insist on an active role in the day-to-day management of depository institutions, acting in some cases as a de facto management committee of an institution's board of directors. A bank's management may be quite willing to sign a written agreement giving the agency these kinds of powers—or to give these powers by oral or implicit understanding in the absence of a written agreement—in order to stave off closure or other severe regulatory sanction. Do you perceive any dangers in giving the agencies this kind of power?

4. What if an agency assumes de facto control over an institution's operations and proceeds to run it into the ground? Does anyone have a cause of action against the agency for money damages? If such an action exists, it would most likely arise under the Federal Tort Claims Act, 28 U.S.C. §1346(b), providing for suits against the United States for "loss of property . . . caused by the negligent or wrongful act or omission of any employee or the Government while acting within the scope of his office or employment, under circumstances where the United States, if a private person, would be liable to the claimant in accordance with the law of the place where the act or omission occurred." But there is an exception to this statute for claims "based upon the exercise . . . of a discretionary function or duty . . . whether or not the discretion involved be abused." 28 U.S.C. §2680(a). In United States v. Gaubert, 111 S. Ct. 1267 (1991), the Supreme Court held that the discretionary function exception shielded the government from damages liability to shareholders based on allegedly negligent behavior of banking officials in carrying out their duties. The discretionary function exception applied even though the complaint charged that the government officials had controlled the day-to-day management of the depository institution. In light of *Gaubert,* it appears that damages claims against federal banking agencies based on alleged mismanagement have little, if any, prospect for success.

5. Are there any dangers to the agency, other than the danger of delay, in using written agreements? A party to a written agreement might claim that part of the quid pro quo for signing the agreement is the agency's promise *not* to institute closure proceedings or formal enforcement actions as long as the signatory is complying with the terms of the agreement. So far these claims have been unsuccessful. See, e.g., Santopadre v. Pelican Homestead & Savings Association, 741 F. Supp. 1252 (E.D. La. 1990). Language in some opinions, however, indicates that agencies will be held to promises, express or implied, in written agreements, including promises not to pursue further regulatory action.

6. Are there constitutional problems if an agency violates a promise made in a regulatory capacity? If the agreement involves parties dealing voluntarily with the agency, and regulatory forbearance is involved, there may be. In Far West Federal Bank v. Director, Office of Thrift Supervision, 746 F. Supp. 1042 (D. Or. 1990), the FHLBB had negotiated a "conversion agreement" under which private parties injected capital into a failing thrift in exchange for loans and regulatory forbearance. Congress later enacted FIRREA. The OTS insisted that the thrift comply with the new, stricter FIRREA capital standards, as well as other regulations that had been waived or not included in the conversion agreement. The district court held that the conversion agreement had created a valid, binding contract, and that the OTS's attempt to alter its terms represented a violation of the Fifth Amendment. The Supreme Court ruled in United States v. Winstar Corp., 64 U.S.L.W. 4739 (1996), that agency promises

to provide favorable accounting treatment in the context of a supervisory merger were enforceable against the government notwithstanding purported nullification by FIRREA.

## 4. *Cease-and-Desist Orders*

If informal mechanisms such as conditions to regulatory approvals or written agreements do not prove efficacious, the agency is likely to institute more formal proceedings. Perhaps the most important—and most frequently utilized—formal supervisory mechanism is the cease-and-desist order. Many cease-and-desist orders are negotiated by consent, obviating the need for extended proceedings. If the respondent (the defendant in a cease-and-desist proceeding) refuses to consent, then formal proceedings will be instituted. Banking agencies are required to file notice of charges, and respondents have the right to a hearing within the agency. See, e.g., 12 U.S.C. §1818(b).

Once the agency has issued its final decision, the respondent may seek judicial review by a petition to an appropriate court of appeals. The appeals court reviews the agency's action under the standards of the Administrative Procedure Act, under which agency action may be set aside on the following grounds: (1) it is found to be arbitrary, capricious, an abuse of discretion, or otherwise not in accordance with law; (2) it represents a violation of constitutional rights; (3) the agency has exceeded its statutory jurisdiction; (4) the agency has failed to observe procedures required by law; or (5) the order is not supported by substantial evidence on the record of the agency hearing. See 5 U.S.C. §706.

Cease-and-desist orders can cover a wide range of practices. Virtually every aspect of an institution's business can be affected to the extent that it impacts on safety and soundness. Thus an institution may be prohibited from extending further credit to insiders in violation of law; may be required to charge off assets classified as loss or doubtful in an examination report; may be required to adopt written loan policies in a form acceptable to the agency; may be forced to raise new capital; may be prohibited from further violations of consumer protection laws; and may even be required to boot out the incumbent management and install a regime acceptable to the agency. Any other requirements reasonably designed to remedy violations of law, to provide a sanction for violations of written agreements or conditions, or to rectify unsafe and unsound practices, can be included in a cease-and-desist order. See 12 U.S.C. §1818(b)(6)-(8) (FDIC-insured institutions); 12 U.S.C. §1786(e)(3)-(4) (federally insured credit unions).

Two main legal issues arise in connection with cease-and-desist orders. First, there is the question of whether the agency has established a basis for the order. Cease-and-desist proceedings may be instituted if the agency believes that the institution or an institution-affiliated party is engaging, has engaged, or is about to engage in (1) an unsafe or unsound practice; (2) a violation of law, rule, or regulation; (3) a violation of a condition imposed in writing by the agency in connection with the granting of any application or request; or (4) a violation of any written agreement between the individual and the agency. The problematic item on this list is the first one. When is a practice or activity "unsafe or unsound"? The term is quite vague; and although the banking agencies have broad discretion to define it, their freedom of action in this regard is not unlimited.

## NOTE ON RESTITUTION

A major problem arising under the cease-and-desist power concerns the scope of restitution remedies in cease-and-desist proceedings. These have been controversial, among other reasons, because they seem much more akin to an action for money damages than an order that the respondent cease and desist from doing something.

Prior to the FIRREA, it was unclear whether the agencies could use cease-and-desist proceedings to force directors to pay indemnity for losses stemming from their wrongful conduct. In Larimore v. Comptroller of the Currency, 789 F.2d 1244 (7th Cir. 1986), the Seventh Circuit held that the Comptroller of the Currency could not use cease-and-desist proceedings to require directors to indemnify a bank against losses on loans that exceeded the bank's lending limit. In FIRREA, however, Congress authorized "affirmative action[s]" to correct conditions resulting from legal violations or unsound banking practices; these include orders requiring the party to

> make restitution or provide reimbursement, indemnification, or guarantee against loss if (i) such depository institution or such party was unjustly enriched in connection with such violation or practice; or (ii) the violation or practice involved a reckless disregard for the law or any applicable regulations or prior order of the appropriate Federal banking agency.

12 U.S.C. §1818(b)(6)(A).

## *QUESTIONS AND COMMENTS*

What if a bank has violated federal equal employment opportunity rules and is thereby subject to a suit for back pay under Title VII of the Civil Rights Act? Could the appropriate banking agency seek reimbursement for injured persons by means of a cease-and-desist order?

## NOTE ON TEMPORARY CEASE-AND-DESIST ORDERS

We have seen that an agency must hold a hearing before issuing a cease-and-desist order. As a practical matter, this means that obtaining a permanent cease-and-desist order can be quite time-consuming. What happens if an institution or institution-affiliated party is engaging in dangerous conduct that could cause irreparable harm to the institution before a hearing could be arranged? The remedy here is a *temporary* cease-and-desist order, analogous in many respects to a temporary restraining order or preliminary injunction in civil litigation.

Agencies may issue temporary cease-and-desist orders when they determine that the activities in question are likely to cause insolvency or significant dissipation of assets or earnings, or are likely to weaken the condition of the bank or otherwise prejudice the interests of depositors prior to completion of permanent cease-and-desist proceedings. 12 U.S.C. §1818(c) (FDIC-insured institutions); 12 U.S.C. §1786(f) (federally insured credit unions). A temporary cease-and-desist order is issued without a prior hearing and becomes effective upon service. It remains effective until the completion of permanent cease-and-desist proceedings, or until a court sets aside the order. Parties subject to temporary cease-and-desist proceedings may go into district court for an injunction against the effectiveness of the temporary cease-and-desist order.

## 5. *Control over Personnel*

Next to the cease-and-desist power, perhaps the most significant formal power employed by federal banking agencies is their power to determine who serves in an institution's top management. This power may be exercised to exclude an individual at a bank's formation simply by refusing to grant a charter unless the individual in question is left off the management team. It may be exercised to prevent the hiring of individuals in some cases. Once an individual has been hired or otherwise participates in the affairs of an institution, he or she can be suspended, removed from office, or prohibited from further affiliation with the institution for conduct that the agency deems sufficiently deleterious. Even more draconian, he or she may be barred from employment at *any* insured institution. And the removal need not be for a short period of time; it can, indeed, be for life.

What is the rationale for vesting these comprehensive employment powers in the federal banking agencies? Clearly, it is based on the belief that the safety and soundness of a bank heavily depends on the character and quality of top bank management. Given the studies we cited earlier, which conclude that fraud, insider abuse, and mismanagement are factors in a high percentage of bank failures, this belief appears eminently justified.

Yet the justification for employment powers implicitly rests on another proposition as well: that the agencies are capable of assessing with a reasonable degree of accuracy whether a particular individual does or does not possess the necessary character and qualifications to be entrusted with important responsibilities in the management of the bank. Here the argument for employment powers becomes somewhat more problematic. It is impossible, just from looking at someone, to determine whether his or her moral character is high or low. Moral character is itself unobservable, except in how a person acts; and the banking agencies are required to make a prediction of how a person is likely to act in the future.

What proxies or evidence would tend to bear on this unobservable quality of moral character? Clearly, if an individual has engaged in bad acts in the past, especially acts of fraud or dishonesty, one can infer that he or she is more likely to engage in such acts in the future than, say, someone whose past career has been spotless. Also, it is often possible to gauge a person's reputation by making discreet inquiries among colleagues and peers. If his or her reputation turns out to be dubious, then, other things equal, it is more likely that he or she will behave badly if entrusted with responsibilities at the bank. In practice, these are the two principal factors—prior bad acts and reputation in the banking community—that the regulators examine in deciding whether to allow a person to serve in a position of responsibility at a banking institution.

Yet these factors are not completely reliable predictors of future conduct. Banking agencies will inevitably make errors in their evaluation of an individual's propensity to bad behavior. Note that the errors come in two varieties. First, the agency may *allow* an individual to become associated with a bank, and the individual may subsequently engage in fraud, illegality, or unsound practices. Second, the agency may *deny* an individual the right to work at a bank, when he or she would have performed in perfectly appropriate fashion had they been allowed in. In either case, the errors can occur for one of two reasons: either because the agency failed to perform an adequate investigation, which would have turned up (or refuted) evidence of prior bad acts or reputation; or because the evidence of prior bad acts or reputation did not accurately predict the individual's propensity to engage in future harmful conduct.

The costs of these errors are large. Given the widespread consensus that improper conduct has contributed to a high percentage of recent failures, it is evident that had the banking agencies excluded the wrongdoers at the outset, much of the harm would not have occurred. Literally tens of billions of dollars in losses to the insurance funds might have been avoided if the banking agencies had only barred the sharp operators or evicted them more rapidly from their perches. Less well recognized, but also potentially important, are the real economic losses associated with the *exclusion* of individuals from the industry who, if allowed to participate, would perform in a lawful and prudent fashion. The costs to a bank officer from being excluded from the industry may be high. The individual may have few realistic job prospects outside the industry; to bar that person altogether from his or her chosen field seems harsh indeed. Moreover, excluding qualified individuals from participating in bank management deprives the banking system of presumably competent personnel.

The regulatory system might be adjusted to control the ratio of the two types of errors to each other. Procedural and substantive safeguards for persons subject to exclusion proceedings would reduce the probability that an honest and qualified individual would be ousted, but increase the probability that dishonest and unqualified people would be allowed to participate in bank management. The greater the safeguards, the fewer the errors of excluding a person who should be included, but the greater the errors of allowing an individual to serve who should be excluded. Other things being equal, the level of safeguards should be set at a level that minimizes the sum of both errors. Determining what that level is, however, is necessarily a matter of conjecture and judgment.

The investigatory system can also be adjusted to control the ratio of correct to incorrect outcomes. The more thoroughly an agency investigates a subject, the more likely it is that the agency will reliably determine character and competence. This is not to say that even the most exacting investigation will identify all bad characters or permit all good characters to serve. Errors will occur even with the most thorough investigations. Moreover, investigations themselves are costly. The ideal, holding other things equal, may be for the agencies to perform investigations up to the point where the value from an additional unit of investigation equals the costs of that unit of investigation. Where this point lies, however, is again a matter of conjecture and surmise. As a practical matter, agencies' investigatory zeal is often more a matter of budget and politics than of error costs and economic analysis.

To bring this discussion down to earth, let us ask the practical question: What procedural protections are available to someone whom a banking agency seeks to exclude from participation in the affairs of a depository institution, or from depository institutions generally? The question has a statutory and a constitutional dimension.

The relevant statutes do provide protections to persons whom a banking agency seeks to bar from an institution or the industry. Under the law as amended by the FIRREA, an individual may not be suspended, removed from office, or prohibited from participating in an institution's affairs unless the agency determines that three substantive conditions are met. First, the individual must be found to have violated (1) any law or regulation; (2) any final cease-and-desist order; (3) any written condition imposed in connection with the grant of an application, or any written agreement "between such depository institution and such agency" (what if the signatory to the written agreement is an individual rather than the institution?). Second, the violation or breach must have resulted in one of these consequences: (1) damage or probable damage to the institution; (2) prejudice or potential prejudice to the depositors; or (3) financial gain or other benefit to the party charged. Third, the violation or breach must either involve personal dishonesty or demonstrate a willful or continuing disregard for the institution's safety and soundness. 12 U.S.C. §1818(e)(1).

Note that a suspension, removal, or prohibition order under §1818(e) has consequences beyond the particular institution in question. FIRREA provides that any individual who is suspended or removed from office or prohibited from participating in the affairs of an institution may not, while the order is in effect, hold any office or participate in the conduct of the affairs of *any* insured depository institution. 12 U.S.C. §1818(e)(7). The agency may waive this condition in writing, but the Conference Committee Report stated dourly that "[t]he Conferees intend that the agencies closely scrutinize any request and review the persons' activity from the time the original order was issued. The Conferees intend that consent should be given only when there is no doubt that such an approval is justified by the complete rehabilitation of an individual."

Persons against whom removal or prohibition orders are issued enjoy certain procedural rights. They have the right to notice of charges and to a hearing on the charges (in practice such hearings are conducted before Administrative Law Judges). The burden of proof is apparently on the agency: The statute provides that the agency may issue a removal or prohibition order only "if upon the record made at any such hearing the agency shall find that any of the grounds specified in such notice have been established." 12 U.S.C. §1818(c)(4). An individual (or the agency's prosecution staff) may appeal an adverse determination by the ALJ to the full agency. Thereafter, an aggrieved individual may seek review in a federal court of appeals under the standards of the Administrative Procedure Act. 12 U.S.C. §1818(h)(2). The individual may also seek a stay of the effectiveness of the agency's order by petitioning a federal district court. 12 U.S.C. §1818(f).

When are the three substantive prerequisites of §1818(e) satisfied? Consider the following case, involving a classic "check-kiting" scheme, in which a depositor fraudulently "manufactured" money by keeping fictitious funds in the process of transfer among different financial institutions.

## Van Dyke v. Board of Governors of the Federal Reserve System

*876 F.2d 1377 (8th Cir. 1989)*

FAGG, Circuit Judge.

John W. Van Dyke, Jr., petitions for review of a final order issued by the Board of Governors of the Federal Reserve System (the Board). See 12 U.S.C. §1818(h)(2) (1982). The order removed Van Dyke from his positions as president and director of the Toy National Bank of Sioux City, Iowa (Toy Bank or the Bank) and prohibited him from participating in certain banking affairs. See id. §1818(e)(4)-(5) (1982). We affirm the Board's order.

Van Dyke maintained personal checking accounts at Toy Bank and another local bank, Norwest Bank of Sioux City, N.A. (Norwest). In early 1987, a Norwest officer told Van Dyke the Norwest Board of Directors insisted steps be taken to correct an unacceptably large overdraft balance in Van Dyke's Norwest account. Van Dyke as president could not be overdrawn at Toy Bank, see 12 C.F.R. §215.4(d) (1987), and his credit there was at its maximum under federal regulations for bank officers, see id. §215.5(c)(3) (1987). Van Dyke thus sought to arrange a loan from a third bank.

Even before completing the preliminary documentation for the loan, however, Van Dyke wrote a $50,000 Toy Bank check against a balance of approximately $355. He deposited this check at Norwest to cover a check written on his account there, which already showed a six-figure overdraft balance. The next business day, Van Dyke conducted the same procedure in reverse by depositing a $51,000 Norwest check at Toy Bank to cover the $50,000 check written the day before. This manipulation gave the appearance of adding to Van Dyke's account in each bank. He repeated the exchange of checks during the following week; at that time, the checks were for $181,000 drawn on a $1340 balance at Toy Bank, followed by a $190,000 check drawn at Norwest. Van Dyke drew all of the checks without sufficient funds to cover the withdrawals from either account, and the bank loan he was in the process of seeking would have been insufficient on its own to cover the total overdrafts.

After a first bank declined to do so, Van Dyke eventually obtained the loan from another bank. The loan proceeds, along with funds from other private sources, cleared the Norwest overdrafts nearly two weeks after Van Dyke wrote the first insufficient funds check. The chairman of Toy Bank's audit committee asked Van Dyke to explain the transactions, and the committee reported the matter to the Toy Bank Board of Directors. The Toy Bank board promptly terminated Van Dyke's account privileges and notified the appropriate banking authorities of its action.

The Office of the Comptroller of the Currency (Comptroller) then initiated this administrative action to remove Van Dyke. See 12 U.S.C. §§1818(e)(1), 1813(q)(1) (1982). The removal notice charged Van Dyke with, among other things, engaging in a "check-kiting scheme" that justified his removal under section 1818(e)(1).

Following an evidentiary hearing, an administrative law judge (ALJ) issued a recommended decision. The ALJ concluded the first of three prerequisites for removal under section 1818(e)(1) had been met because Van Dyke's check-kiting scheme constituted: a violation of law (in this instance, 18 U.S.C. §1344 (Supp. V 1987)); an unsafe and unsound banking practice; and a breach of his fiduciary duty as a bank officer and director. Joint App. at 60. The ALJ also concluded section 1818(e)(1)'s second removal requirement was met because Van Dyke received financial gain when the Bank paid his overdrafts. *Id.* at 61. Indeed, the ALJ sagely observed that "Van Dyke used his position as the chief executive officer of Toy [Bank] to buy time to get out of a pressing financial bind." Id. at 38-39.

Turning to the third statutory requirement for removal, the ALJ described Van Dyke's actions in allowing his personal checking account to become overdrawn as "inexcusable," id. at 48. Despite having concluded Van Dyke's activity "contained all the elements of a violation of 18 U.S.C. §1344," id. at 60, the ALJ determined those actions did not "demonstrate personal dishonesty nor [did] they seem to be of such a nature as to involve a disregard for the safety or soundness of the Bank," id. at 48. On this basis, the ALJ concluded the Comptroller had not satisfied section 1818(e)(1)'s third requirement and recommended the Board dismiss the removal action. The ALJ certified appropriate findings and conclusions to the Board for a determination whether the removal order should issue. See 12 U.S.C. §1818(e)(5) (1982).

The Board on review adopted the ALJ's factual findings and agreed with the recommended decision in all but one respect. The Board, however, determined Van Dyke's conduct in perpetuating the check-kiting scheme demonstrated all three section 1818(e)(1) requirements, including personal dishonesty and willful disregard for the safety or soundness of the Bank. Accordingly, the Board issued its final decision ordering Van Dyke's removal.

On appeal, Van Dyke does not challenge any of the Board's determinations regarding the first and second requirements for removal under section 1818(e)(1). Instead, Van Dyke challenges only the Board's determination that his conduct violated the third statutory removal requirement. Specifically, Van Dyke contends: (1) the Board applied erroneous standards for determining personal dishonesty and willful disregard for the Bank's safety or soundness; and (2) the Board's decision that Van Dyke's conduct involving the insufficient funds checks showed personal dishonesty and willful disregard for the Bank's safety or soundness is not supported by substantial evidence on the record as a whole. *See* 12 U.S.C. §1818(h)(2) (1982); 5 U.S.C. §706(2)(E) (1982). We reject each of Van Dyke's contentions.

The Board determined the ALJ employed an unduly narrow standard for evaluating Van Dyke's culpability because the ALJ equated personal dishonesty with "an intent to gain at the expense of others," Addendum at 21. The Board took the view that while personal dishonesty (which is not defined in the statute) must be evaluated on a case-by-case basis, it need not amount to civil fraud and could encompass a broad range of conduct. According to the Board, this conduct may include: a " 'disposition to lie, cheat[,] or defraud; untrustworthiness; lack of integrity[;] * * * misrepresentation of facts and deliberate deception by pretense and stealth[;] * * * [or] want of fairness and [straightforwardness].' " Id. at 23 (quoted citations omitted); see also id. at 23-24 (discussing legislative history pertaining to personal dishonesty standard).

In light of the ALJ's finding that Van Dyke's check-kiting activity between his accounts at Toy Bank and Norwest "clearly fit[] within the prescription of [section] 1344," Joint App. at 38, the Board necessarily concluded Van Dyke's actions for purposes of this administrative proceeding "involve[d] fraud and a lack of integrity," Addendum at 24. Thus, the Board determined the Comptroller had shown Van Dyke engaged in acts of personal dishonesty within the meaning of section 1818(e)(1). We believe the Board's determination "is based on a permissible construction of the statute." Chevron U.S.A. Inc. v. Natural Resources Defense Council, Inc., 467 U.S. 837, 843, 104 S. Ct. 2778, 2781-82, 81 L. Ed. 2d 694 (1984); see also Stoddard v. Board of Governors, 868 F.2d 1308, 1310 (D.C. Cir. 1989).

Concerning the willful disregard for safety or soundness component of the third removal requirement, the Board noted it had previously accepted the ALJ's conclusion that the check-kiting scheme was an unsafe or unsound banking practice. Addendum at 25. To evaluate Van Dyke's culpability for those actions, the Board adopted a standard that incorporated the general method for identifying unsafe or unsound practices in the first instance. See id. at 26. The standard considers whether Van Dyke's conduct potentially exposed the Bank to an abnormal risk of loss or harm contrary to prudent banking practices. See id.; see also First Nat'l Bank of Eden v. Department of the Treasury, 568 F.2d 610, 611 n.2 (8th Cir. 1978) (per curiam). Applying this standard, the Board concluded Van Dyke's participation in the check-kiting scheme demonstrated "a willful disregard for the safety and soundness of the Bank." Addendum at 25 (footnote omitted). We do not disagree with the Board's conclusion. See Chevron U.S.A. Inc., 467 U.S. at 843-44, 104 S. Ct. at 2781-82.

Turning to Van Dyke's remaining contention, he argues that even applying the Board's articulated standards, the record does not support a determination that his conduct was personally dishonest or showed a willful disregard for the Bank's safety or soundness. This contention is based on Van Dyke's assertion that because "Norwest . . . was always prepared to honor checks drawn by Van Dyke on his account at Norwest[,] . . . Van Dyke can hardly be found to have participated in a scheme or artifice to defraud . . . Toy Bank." Basically, Van Dyke argues that because he expected the loan proceeds immediately and because Norwest in the past permitted him significant overdraft privileges, his conduct in drawing admittedly insufficient funds checks at Toy Bank to advance his personal interests should be excused. Van Dyke also claims his personal dishonesty, if any, was directed only at Norwest and, thus, is irrelevant to his removal from Toy Bank.

Van Dyke's argument is unimpressive. He wrote the first insufficient funds check even before completing the necessary paperwork for the outside bank loan. He continued the scheme while seeking a bank loan that would not cover all the overdrafts the scheme produced. Van Dyke does not suggest he attempted to alert the board of directors (or anyone else at Toy Bank) to any extenuating circumstances surrounding his insufficient funds checks. Indeed, Van Dyke's scheme almost certainly would have collapsed if the bank loan and other private funds had failed to materialize or if Norwest had reversed its stance honoring Van Dyke's insufficient funds checks. In addition, to suggest that we focus exclusively on Van Dyke's dealings with Norwest in evaluating his conduct as a Toy Bank officer and director ignores the inherent multiple-bank characteristics of a check-kiting scheme. See United States v. Taylor, 789 F.2d 618, 621 (8th Cir. 1986).

Van Dyke's substantial evidence argument also appears to ignore the Board's unchallenged determinations that: (1) his conduct toward Toy Bank embraced all the elements of a statutory violation that is premised on fraudulent conduct; and (2) by undertaking the check-kiting scheme, Van Dyke engaged in an unsafe and unsound banking practice connected directly to Toy Bank in accordance with section 1818(e)(1). Under these circumstances, we think it unrealistic for Van Dyke to suggest the Board is powerless to respond to an officer's manipulative, self-dealing activity until actual harm to the Bank occurs. We conclude the Board's decision that Van Dyke's conduct showed personal dishonesty and willful disregard for the Bank's safety and soundness is supported by substantial evidence on the record as a whole.

Accordingly, we affirm the Board's removal and prohibition order.

## *QUESTIONS AND COMMENTS*

1. Observe that although this administrative action was commenced by the Comptroller of the Currency, the final decision was made

by the Federal Reserve Board. This is mandated by statute, see 12 U.S.C. §1818(e)(4). Why this odd allocation of regulatory responsibility?

2. Mr. Van Dyke seems to have run into some personal financial difficulties, but did these rise to a level that would justify his exclusion from participation in the affairs of the bank? After all, he seemed to have been buying time while arranging a loan; does this suggest an intent to harm the bank? And all the funds were apparently repaid, right?

3. Shouldn't the board have deferred to the ALJ's conclusions, based on the evidentiary hearing, that Mr. Van Dyke had not displayed personal dishonesty or disregard for the safety and soundness of the bank?

4. Based on the facts of this case, would you have thrown Mr. Van Dyke out?

5. What would you have counseled Mr. Van Dyke to do if he had come to you in early 1987 immediately after Norwest Bank had insisted that he correct his overdrafts?

## FDIC v. Meyer

*114 S. Ct. 996 (1994)*

THOMAS, J: . . .

### I

On April 13, 1982, the California Savings and Loan Commissioner seized Fidelity Savings and Loan Association (Fidelity), a California-chartered thrift institution, and appointed the Federal Savings and Loan Insurance Corporation (FSLIC) to serve as Fidelity's receiver under state law. That same day, the Federal Home Loan Bank Board appointed FSLIC to serve as Fidelity's receiver under federal law. In its capacity as receiver, FSLIC had broad authority to "take such action as may be necessary to put [the thrift] in a sound solvent condition." . . . Pursuant to its general policy of terminating the employment of a failed thrift's senior management, FSLIC, through its special representative Robert L. Pattullo, terminated respondent John H. Meyer, a senior Fidelity officer.

Approximately one year later, Meyer filed this lawsuit against a number of defendants, including FSLIC and Pattullo, in the United States District Court for the Northern District of California. At the time of trial, Meyer's sole claim against FSLIC and Pattullo was that his summary discharge deprived him of a property right (his right to continued employment under California law) without due process of law in violation of the Fifth Amendment. In making this claim, Meyer relied upon Bivens v. Six Unknown Fed. Narcotics Agents, 403 U.S. 388, which implied a cause of action for damages against federal agents who allegedly violated the Fourth Amendment. The jury returned a $130,000 verdict against FSLIC, but found in favor of Pattullo on qualified immunity grounds.

Petitioner Federal Deposit Insurance Corporation (FDIC), FSLIC's statutory successor, appealed to the Court of Appeals for the Ninth Circuit, which affirmed. . . . [The court concluded that the "sue and be sued" clause in the FSLIC's governing statute constituted a waiver of sovereign immunity, subjecting the agency to suit in federal court. O]n the merits, the court affirmed the jury's conclusion that Meyer had been deprived of due process when he was summarily discharged without notice and a hearing. We granted certiorari to consider the validity of the damages award against FSLIC.

**II**

[The Supreme Court agreed that the "sue and be sued" clause of the governing statute effected a waiver of sovereign immunity, and that the Federal Tort Claims Act did not eliminate this waiver.]

**III**

Although we have determined that Meyer's claim falls within the sue-and-be-sued waiver, our inquiry does not end at this point. Here we part ways with the Ninth Circuit, which determined that Meyer had a cause of action for damages against FSLIC because there had been a waiver of sovereign immunity. The Ninth Circuit's reasoning conflates two "analytically distinct" inquiries. The first inquiry is whether there has been a waiver of sovereign immunity. If there has been such a waiver, as in this case, the second inquiry comes into play—that is, whether the source of substantive law upon which the claimant relies provides an avenue for relief. It is to this second inquiry that we now turn.

Meyer bases his due process claim on our decision in Bivens, which held that an individual injured by a federal agent's alleged violation of the Fourth Amendment may bring an action for damages against the agent. In our most recent decisions, we have "responded cautiously to suggestions that Bivens remedies be extended into new contexts." Schweiker v. Chilicky, 487 U.S. 412, 421 (1988). In this case, Meyer seeks a significant extension of Bivens: he asks us to expand the category of defendants against whom Bivens-type actions may be brought to include not only federal agents, but federal agencies as well.

We know of no Court of Appeals decision, other than the Ninth Circuit's below, that has implied a Bivens-type cause of action directly against a federal agency. Meyer recognizes the absence of authority supporting his position, but argues that the "logic" of Bivens would support such a remedy. We disagree. In Bivens, the petitioner sued the agents of the Federal Bureau of Narcotics who allegedly violated his rights, not the Bureau itself. Here, Meyer brought precisely the claim that the logic of Bivens supports—a Bivens claim for damages against Pattullo, the FSLIC employee who terminated him.[10]

An additional problem with Meyer's "logic" argument is the fact that we implied a cause of action against federal officials in Bivens in part because a direct action against the Government was not available. . . . In essence, Meyer asks us to imply a damages action based on a decision that presumed the absence of that very action.

Meyer's real complaint is that Pattullo, like many Bivens defendants, invoked the protection of qualified immunity. But Bivens clearly contemplated that official immunity would be raised. Id., at 397 (noting that "the District Court [had] ruled that . . . respondents were immune from liability by virtue of their official position"). More importantly, Meyer's proposed "solution"—essentially the circumvention of qualified immunity—would mean the evisceration of the Bivens remedy, rather than its extension. It must be remembered that the purpose of Bivens is to deter the officer. . . . If we were to imply a damages action directly against federal agencies, thereby permitting claimants to bypass qualified immunity, there would be no reason for aggrieved parties to bring damages actions against individual officers. Under Meyer's regime, the deterrent effects of the Bivens remedy would be lost.

Finally, a damages remedy against federal agencies would be inappropriate even if such a remedy were consistent with Bivens. Here, unlike in Bivens, there are "special factors counselling hesitation" in the creation of a damages remedy. Bivens, 403 U.S., at 396. If we were to recognize a direct action for damages against federal agencies, we would be creating a potentially enormous financial burden for the Federal Government. Meyer disputes this reasoning and argues that the Federal Government already expends significant resources indemnifying its employees who are sued under Bivens. Meyer's argument implicitly suggests that the funds used for indemnification could be shifted to cover the direct liability of federal agencies. That may or may not be true, but decisions involving " 'federal fiscal policy' " are not ours to make. . . . We leave it to Congress to weigh the implications of such a significant expansion of Government liability.

## IV

An extension of Bivens to agencies of the Federal Government is not supported by the logic of Bivens itself. We therefore hold that Meyer

10. Although not critical to our analysis, we note that in addition to the Bivens claim against Pattullo, Meyer initially brought a contractual claim against FSLIC, which he later dropped. Meyer also could have filed a claim with FSLIC as receiver for the value of any

had no Bivens cause of action for damages against FSLIC. Accordingly, the judgment below is reversed.[12]

*QUESTIONS AND COMMENTS*

1. Why did Meyer lose, in the end? Was it because he had no constitutional rights protected by the Fifth Amendment?

2. Technically, why wasn't Meyer able to prevail against the United States? What was the defect in his suit against the federal agent Pattullo?

3. Is the court saying that even if Meyer was deprived of his constitutional rights by the FSLIC and its representative, by being fired summarily without notice or hearing, there is absolutely nothing he can do about it? What kind of government would deprive its citizens of constitutional rights and give them no recourse for the losses?

4. Is it true that people in Meyer's position have no recourse? What does the court suggest? Are these measures likely to be adequate?

5. The statute governing FDIC contains a nearly identical sue-and-be-sued clause. See 12 U.S.C. §1819(a) (Fourth) (FDIC "shall have power . . . to sue and be sued, and complain and defend, in any court of law or equity, State or Federal"). Thus, the decision in this case finding that jurisdiction exists that applies technically to the now-abolished FSLIC would appear to be fully applicable to the alive-and-kicking FDIC. How important this precedent will be is not clear, however, since the court in *Meyer* went on to find that there was no remedy under the *Bivens* case against the federal government or its agencies.

## NOTE ON CONTROL OVER HIRING DECISIONS

The *Van Dyke* case concerns the standards for removal or prohibition of persons who are currently participating in the affairs of a depository institution. What about when someone is about to be *hired* by the institution—can the agencies intercede at this point to prevent the affiliation?

FIRREA §914 provides such authority for institutions that have been chartered less than two years, have undergone a change in control within two years, or are not in compliance with minimum capital standards or are "otherwise in a troubled condition." Such institutions must give their bank agencies 30-days' notice before adding any individual to the board of directors or employing any individual as a senior executive

---

contractual rights he believed were violated. See . . . Coit Independence Joint Venture v. FSLIC, 489 U.S. 561, 580-581 (1989).

12. Because we find that Meyer had no Bivens action against FSLIC, we do not reach the merits of his due process claim.

officer. The banking agency may then disapprove the arrangement if "the competence, experience, character, or integrity of the individual with respect to whom such notice is submitted indicates that it would not be in the best interests of the depositors . . . or in the best interests of the public to permit the individual to be employed by, or associated with, the . . . institution. . . ." (Similar rules apply to federally insured credit unions.)

## *QUESTIONS AND COMMENTS*

1. Given the statutory language, are there any real constraints on the power of federal banking agencies to blackball individuals whom they distrust, even if the individuals in question have not been the subject of any formal suspension, removal, or prohibition order? How difficult will it be for an agency to conclude that it would not be in the best interests of the public to allow the employment?

2. What procedural safeguards are there for an individual who has been excluded under this provision? Unlike most enforcement provisions in federal banking law, FIRREA §914 does not provide for a hearing. Nor is there any express provision for judicial review, as there is in almost every other enforcement provision. On the other hand, neither does the statute say expressly that judicial review is *un*available, as it does, for example, in the "whistle-blower" authority FIRREA. See FIRREA §933, providing that "[a]ny agency decision under this section is final and not reviewable by any court." If you represented someone barred from employment under this section, what would you do in order to seek judicial review?

3. Is this section constitutional? The Due Process Clause of the Fifth Amendment protects against deprivations of life, liberty, or property without due process of law. Isn't an employment contract a "property" interest that may not be taken away under this statute without the minimal procedural protections of a notice of charges, some kind of a hearing, and a right to judicial review? Alternatively, couldn't the right to practice one's profession at an institution of one's choice be considered a "liberty" interest protected by the Fifth Amendment? See Connelly v. Comptroller of the Currency, 876 F.2d 1209 (5th Cir. 1989) (court held that the defendant officers of the Comptroller of the Currency were entitled to qualified immunity against a claim that they violated plaintiff's Fifth Amendment rights when they excluded him from the presidency of a proposed national bank; court acknowledged that the defendants' investigation had been "rather shoddy" but found that no clearly established property or liberty interests were at stake).

## NOTE ON EMERGENCY SUSPENSION AND PROHIBITION ORDERS

What if continued participation by an individual in a depository institution's affairs threatens imminent harm to the institution's safety and soundness? The agency may suspend or prohibit any institution-affiliated party on an emergency basis under the standards in 12 U.S.C. §1818(e)(3) (FDIC-insured institutions) and 12 U.S.C. §1786(g)(3) (federally insured credit unions). The grounds for temporary suspension are that the agency determines that "such action is necessary for the protection of the depository institution or the interests of the . . . depositors." The suspension or prohibition is effective immediately upon service of written notice to the affected party and lasts until the agency disposes of the underlying charges, unless a district court stays the order earlier.

A related provision, 12 U.S.C. §1818(g), provides banking agencies with the power to suspend persons charged with federal felonies involving "dishonesty or breach of trust," in cases where "continued service or participation by [the individual] may pose a threat to the interests of the depository institution's depositors or may threaten to impair public confidence in the depository institution." An individual so suspended from office has the right to a hearing within 30 days, at which he or she may present written testimony and oral argument (and oral testimony at the agency's discretion); the agency must render its decision within 60 days after the hearing.

Are these procedures in 12 U.S.C. §1818(g) constitutionally sufficient? The Supreme Court addressed this issue in FDIC v. Mallen, 486 U.S. 230 (1988). The Court recognized as "undisputed" that the suspended bank officer had a property interest, protected by the Fifth Amendment, in continuing his employment with the bank, and that the suspension had deprived him of that interest. The only question was whether the procedural protections afforded under §1818(g) satisfied the requirements of due process. The Court held that the statutory requirements for prompt hearing and decision passed constitutional muster, given the importance of the governmental interest involved and the low likelihood that the suspension was baseless. The Court hinted, but did not decide, that an opportunity to present oral testimony was not constitutionally required.

### *QUESTIONS AND COMMENTS*

1. Given the opinion in *Mallen,* do you think that the temporary suspension power of 12 U.S.C. §1818(e)(3) would survive judicial scrutiny? Note that the agency must go ahead with permanent suspension,

removal, or prohibition proceedings while the temporary suspension is in effect, and that the affected party has the right to a hearing within 60 days of the notice of charges and may petition for review of the final agency decision to a federal court of appeals. The affected party also has the right to seek a stay of the suspension order in federal district court. Are these procedures sufficient? Is the problem the procedures, or the substantive standard at issue: How likely is it that the affected party will be able to establish that the banking agency acted erroneously in concluding that his or her temporary suspension was necessary for the protection of the institution or the interests of depositors?

2. In 1990 Congress enhanced regulatory control over personnel by prohibiting the sale of failed bank assets to certain debtors who have been convicted of bank-related offenses. 12 U.S.C. §1821(p).

## 6. *Civil Monetary Penalties*

The next weapon in the regulatory arsenal is one much feared by bankers: the civil monetary penalty (often known by the acronym "CMP"). Civil monetary penalties should be distinguished from civil damages in litigation. Putting aside punitive damages, civil damages are intended to compensate persons who have been harmed by wrongful conduct. Accordingly, they are (in theory at least) limited to the amount of the harm. Not so for civil monetary penalties. These are *penalties,* not damages, and as penalties they need not bear any particular relationship to the amount of harm inflicted.

The civil monetary penalties were drastically revised and strengthened by FIRREA. In current form, the law provides for civil monetary penalties, generally up to a maximum of $1 million per day, for violations of a wide variety of federal banking statutes. In almost every case, the penalty structure is divided into three "tiers," ranging from the least serious to the most serious offenses.

*First Tier* penalties are for minor violations. Persons who violate laws, regulations, or orders of federal banking agencies may be liable under this tier for not more than $5,000 per day.

*Second Tier* penalties are generally for more serious misconduct. Actions subject to second tier penalties include violations of laws and regulations, as in the case of first tier penalties, but include two other forms of wrongful behavior: (1) recklessly engaging in an unsafe or unsound practice in conducting the affairs of a depository institution, or (2) breaching a fiduciary duty. In all cases, for second tier penalties to apply, the violation, practice, or breach must be part of a pattern of misconduct, cause or be likely to cause more than a minimal loss to the institution, or result in pecuniary gain or other benefit to the person charged. Second tier civil penalties can be as high as $25,000 per day.

*Third Tier* penalties are for very serious misconduct. They include the forms of conduct described for second tier penalties. In addition, the individual must knowingly or recklessly cause a substantial loss to the institution or a substantial pecuniary gain or other benefit to himself or herself by reason of the violation, practice, or breach. Penalties can be as high as $1 million per day.

The individual against whom a civil monetary penalty is sought has the right to a hearing before the agency, and to judicial review in a court of appeals following the hearing.

## *QUESTIONS AND COMMENTS*

1. How should an agency decide what penalty to impose? Note that the agencies possess enormous discretion as to what level of penalty to impose, apparently limited only by the cap on daily penalties within each "tier." What standards should the agency use to determine the level of penalty within this broad limitation? The statute requires the agency to consider mitigating factors, including the appropriateness of the penalty with respect to the size of financial resources and good faith of the institution or person charged, the gravity of the violation, the history of previous violations, and "such other matters as justice may require." E.g., 12 U.S.C. §1818(i)(2)(G). The House Banking Committee's Report stated the following:

> [t]he Committee expects the banking agencies to take into account the mitigating, as well as any aggravating factors, in determining CMP amounts. In that regard, the Committee strongly encourages the regulators to adopt and utilize the interagency policy concerning the assessment of civil money penalties, issued by the Federal Financial Institutions Examination Council in 1980. The 13 guidelines contained in that policy statement should be considered whenever a regulatory agency is assessing the CMP. The FFIEC guidelines specifically do not preclude any regulatory agency from considering other matters relevant to the consideration of a CMP assessment.

Among the other factors listed in the FFIEC Policy Statement are the following: (1) evidence that the violation or pattern of violations was intentional or committed with disregard to the law or the consequences to the institution; (2) the frequency of occurrence of the violations and the length of time the violation has been outstanding; (3) continuation of the violation after the respondent becomes aware of it, or its immediate cessation or correction; (4) failure to cooperate with the agency in effecting the early resolution of the problem; (5) evidence of concealment of the violation, or its voluntary disclosure; (6) any threat of or actual loss or harm to the institution, including harm to public confidence in the institution, and the degree of any such harm; and (7) evidence that participants or their associates received financial or other gain or benefit or preferential treatment as a result of or from the violation. Federal Financial Institutions Examination Council, Press Release, July 23, 1980.

2. Your client, Smith, is served with a Notice of Assessment by the Comptroller of the Currency and informed that the agency will seek civil money penalties. The client believes that the Comptroller is engaged in a vendetta against her. She convinces you that certain officials at the Comptroller's office are, indeed, treating her with excessive harshness. Can you preempt the civil money penalty proceedings by an action in federal court? There is no provision in 12 U.S.C. §1818 for judicial review prior to exhaustion of administrative remedies. However, courts have crafted a limited exception for cases "where the agency has exceeded a plain and unambiguous statutory command or prohibition, or a command or prohibition made clear by 'authoritative judicial determination' . . . —that is, the agency takes 'blatantly lawless' action—in circumstances where no adequate alternative judicial remedy exists for the unlawful activity's victims." Abercrombie v. OCC, 833 F.2d 672, 675 (7th Cir. 1987). What would you advise your client about the probability of success in an action to enjoin the agency from continuing with its administrative proceedings?

3. Say your client Smith exhausted her administrative remedies and then sought review of a civil money penalty in a U.S. court of appeals. What, in general, is the likelihood of success in such a proceeding? See Bullion v. FDIC, 881 F.2d 1368, 1372-1373 (5th Cir. 1989) (noting that remedies or penalties imposed by the agency are "not to be disturbed unless they constitute an abuse of discretion or are otherwise arbitrary and capricious," and observing that "[t]he assessment of a penalty is particularly delegated to the administrative agency").

4. Suppose that after your client has been assessed a substantial civil money penalty, the Department of Justice institutes a criminal prosecution based on the same conduct. Can your client claim that the prosecution is barred by the Double Jeopardy Clause of the Constitution? In United States v. Halper, 493 U.S. 342 (1989), the Supreme Court held that the Double Jeopardy Clause would be violated if a defendant who had been convicted in a criminal proceeding of filing false claims against the government was later assessed civil penalties for the same act, when the amount of the civil penalties bore no rational relationship to the harm caused.

Although not a banking case, *Halper* has obvious implications for the enforcement of the federal banking laws. Note, in analyzing this question, that there is no apparent requirement under the civil money penalties provisions that the amount of the penalties bear any relationship to the amount of the harm actually inflicted by a defendant's conduct. Moreover, the legislative history of FIRREA might plausibly be interpreted as evidencing a punitive intent on the part of Congress. In *Halper,* however, the criminal prosecution *preceded* the civil penalty; should a case be different if the criminal litigation comes *after?* Consider the collateral estoppel effects of the first decision in the two cases. See United States v. Mayers, 897 F.2d 1126 (11th Cir.), *cert. denied,* 111 S. Ct. 178 (1990) (in light of *Halper,* remanding for reconsideration a case where civil money penalties had preceded the criminal indictment).

5. If you conclude that *Halper* would bar subsequent prosecution in the example immediately above, would other constitutional protections for criminal defendants apply as well in civil money penalty proceedings? Is a defendant in a civil money penalty proceeding entitled to confront and cross-examine adverse witnesses? To a presumption of innocence unless the government can establish guilt beyond a reasonable doubt? To indictment by a grand jury? To the protections of the Eighth Amendment's prohibition on excessive fines? Cf. Browning-Ferris Industries v. Kelco Disposal, Inc., 492 U.S. 257 (1989) (excessive fines clause does not apply to limit punitive damages in civil cases).

## 7. *Suspension or Withdrawal of Deposit Insurance*

The final general administrative enforcement mechanism—one rarely used, although potentially enormously powerful—is the termination or suspension of an institution's federal deposit insurance. The FDIC may bring an action to terminate an institution's insurance if it determines that an institution or its directors have engaged or are engaging in unsafe or unsound practices in conducting the business of the institution, the institution itself is in an unsafe or unsound condition, or the institution or its directors have violated any law, regulation, order, or condition imposed in writing, or violated any written agreement. 12 U.S.C. §1818(a)(2). The institution is entitled to notice of charges, a hearing, and judicial review of an adverse determination.

Obviously an order terminating deposit insurance would guarantee a run on the bank if it were made effective immediately. To prevent disruptive runs, deposits remain temporarily insured after the termination of insurance for between six months and two years. However, no new deposits, and no additions to existing accounts, are insured; and once funds are withdrawn they are not thereafter insured if the depositor replenishes the account.

Thus a depositor need not withdraw his or her money immediately after termination of deposit insurance. On the other hand, it would obviously be extremely inconvenient to hold transactions accounts at such an institution. Although depositors may not run the institution in a classical sense, they are certain to withdraw their funds quickly.

Termination of deposit insurance is, in short, the practical equivalent of a death sentence of a banking institution.

For this reason, the termination of deposit insurance is the ultimate civil sanction against an institution. On the other hand, it is a sanction that the FDIC (or NCUA, in the case of credit unions) is loath to use. If a bank is to close, the insurance agencies want to maximize the "going concern" value in order to minimize the losses to the insurance funds. A significant part of going concern value is the value of the deposit accounts held by an institution. Terminating deposit insurance is calculated to reduce or eliminate that going-concern value and, accordingly, is unlikely to be the least-cost method for resolving a bank failure. Hence the infrequency with which the remedy is applied.

As of 1989, the appropriate banking agency may also temporarily suspend deposit insurance—an action less severe than termination. Such an action will suspend FDIC insurance coverage on all deposits received after the order, thus allowing the FDIC to limit its exposure while formal termination proceedings are under way. See 12 U.S.C. §1818(a)(8).

## 8. *Civil Litigation*

In addition to the various formal and informal administrative proceedings we have discussed, federal banking agencies, as well as private parties, may institute civil litigation against institutions or their officers. This civil litigation may be conceptualized as a form of "enforcement," although as we will see, the legal rules being enforced are not typically those relating to safety and soundness under federal banking law. Instead, civil litigation implicates a hodgepodge of different legal rules including state common law, federal securities law, and sometimes, "civil RICO" (the civil analog of the federal criminal racketeering statute).

However, there is a sufficient overlap between the purposes of these other legal regimes and the goals of federal banking law to justify classifying civil litigation against banks or bank officers and directors as a form of regulatory enforcement. This is especially so in the case of lawsuits claiming breaches of fiduciary duty since the damage caused by the alleged breach of duty is often simply financial harm to the institution.

Before an institution has failed, such civil litigation is ordinarily brought by "entrepreneurial" plaintiffs' attorneys. Typically, such suits take the form either of shareholders derivative actions against bank directors, alleging mismanagement and breach of fiduciary duty, or of class actions against an institution or its officers or directors alleging securities fraud. These securities lawsuits are typically filed in bulk whenever—as has happened frequently in recent years—an institution is forced to restate earnings or otherwise revise its financial disclosures as a result on the write-down of bad loans.

Although there has been a substantial amount of private litigation in the bank field, two legal factors have tended to keep the level below what it might have been otherwise. First, the courts have, for the most part, been unwilling to create "private causes of actions" to remedy violations of banking statutes. Because these statutes are parts of comprehensive enforcement schemes administered by government agencies, courts have generally refused to recognize a congressional intent to establish a supplemental and parallel system of private enforcement through litigation under the banking statutes.

Second, the possibility of bank failure adds significantly to the risk of private bank litigation by plaintiffs' attorneys. If a bank fails, existing derivative lawsuits are usually taken over by the FDIC in its capacity as receiver of the defunct institution. The derivative lawsuit is an action in the name of the corporation; and when the FDIC enters the picture it becomes charged with responsibility for enforcing all outstanding claims of the institution. Plaintiffs' attorneys may get elbowed out in the process, thus losing the potential for a lucrative fee at the end. Existing securities act lawsuits are not taken over because these are typically in the form of direct actions against the institution; but these may be stayed pending disposition of the FDIC's suits against officers and directors. Further, the ultimate value of such private suits may be low unless there is an insurance policy in place to cover the liability, since the defendants themselves will often be insolvent.

The most significant civil litigation these days is brought by the FDIC after a depository institution fails. As we discuss in the following chapter, the FDIC, acting as receiver of a failed institution, typically "sells" an institution's legal claims to itself in its "corporate" capacity (that is, an insurer of deposits). The FDIC in its corporate capacity then prosecutes the institution's claims. The FDIC may file multimillion dollar lawsuits against the institution's former officers and directors, or others (such as law firms, accountants, and appraisers) claiming mismanagement, breach of fiduciary duty, fraud, breach of contract, and other causes of action.

Often such litigation generates collateral disputes with insurance companies. Insurers usually provide "bankers blanket bonds" against wrongdoing or fraud by bank officers and directors and officers liability insurance policies for the institution's top management. Some insurance companies face major potential liability in this area, and may vigorously resist paying out on their policies. Thus, issues may arise under the bankers bond as to whether the FDIC has made timely notice and proof of claims. The insurance company may also disclaim directors and officers liability coverage on the ground that the policy excludes criminal misconduct, and the defendants are charged with wrongdoing of a sufficiently serious tenor to fall within the exclusion. Many insurance policies contain a "regulatory" exception, excluding from coverage actions by regulators; these, however, may be challenged as against public policy.

Defendants in civil litigation brought by the FDIC typically respond with a congeries of affirmative defenses. The most significant contemporary issue, in this regard, is whether the defendants can avail themselves of some defense based on the actions of the FDIC or other regulators. Defendants may argue, for example, that the FDIC was contributorily negligent, failed to mitigate damages, assumed the risk, was guilty of "unclean hands," was estopped from complaining of the defendant's behavior, intruded itself as an independent intervening cause in the downfall of the institution, and so on. All of these defenses are quite similar in that they seek to avoid liability by laying off some or all of the blame onto the federal government.

At present the federal courts are in general consensus that the scheme of federal banking regulation does not impose any general duty on the banking agencies towards the institutions they regulate. On the other hand, there is some authority for the proposition that an agency may owe duties towards regulated institutions in either of two situations: (1) conduct undertaken in a *proprietary,* as opposed to a *regulatory,* capacity, or (2) conduct that goes well beyond normal regulatory activities and amounts to a substitution by the agency of its judgment and decisions for those of the institution's officers and directors. Even in such cases, it seems clear after United States v. Gaubert, 499 U.S. 315 (1991), that federal banking agencies and their officials will not be liable for money damages based on actions undertaken in a discretionary capacity, even if the actions involved day-to-day micromanagement of the institution. But *Gaubert* may not be so broad as to extinguish affirmative defenses to claims for money damages by FDIC. Compare FDIC v. Carter, 701 F. Supp. 730 (C.D. Cal. 1987) (FDIC's actions in disposing of the assets of a bank are the proper subject of affirmative defense if they are purely ministerial and not grounded in social or economic policy) with FDIC v. Baker, 739 F. Supp. 1401 (C.D. Cal. 1990) (striking affirmative defenses and concluding that in light of the massive statutory overhaul effected by FIRREA, "no duty devolves onto the FDIC in favor of officers and directors of a failed banking institution when the FDIC's role is either regulator or receiver of that institution").

## *QUESTIONS AND COMMENTS*

1. What would be so terrible about allowing defendants in these cases to claim affirmative defenses based on regulatory miscues by the government? After all, if the government contributes to the damages by its own conduct, why should this not at least mitigate the damages that

the private defendants might otherwise have to pay? Is it fair to make private parties pay for the government's mistakes?

2. On the other hand, what policy arguments support the result in *Baker* over that in *Carter?* Do you think the interest in preserving the assets of the deposit insurance funds is compelling here? What about the concern about repeatedly forcing bank regulators to justify their conduct in the cold light of hindsight? Are there other policies at work here?

3. Consider whether the "no duty" rule (the rule that banking agencies generally owe no legally enforceable duty to the institutions that they regulate) survives the Supreme Court's opinion in O'Melveny & Myers v. FDIC, 114 S. Ct. 2048 (1994). As you (no doubt) recall from Chapter 3, this case held that there is no general federal common law governing litigation by the FDIC against defendants who allegedly committed torts against depository institutions that later went into receivership. When the institution at issue is state-chartered, can it not be argued that the no-duty rule is in fact a form of general common law, which is rejected in the *O'Melveny* case?

## 9. *Criminal Penalties*

The ultimate sanction for wrongdoing by institution-related parties is the criminal law. Although prior to the 1980s bankers were rarely prosecuted criminally for violations of banking and other statutes, that situation began to change late in the decade. By the turn of the decade the Department of Justice was vigorously pursuing thousands of criminal investigations, and prosecutions were beginning to appear more and more frequently in the reported decisions.

The Justice Department's prosecutorial zeal was much enhanced by congressional pressure and by the authorization for appropriation, in FIRREA, of $65 million per year to the department for the purpose of investigating and prosecuting financial institutions crimes between 1990 and 1992. The pressure for enhanced criminal prosecution continued with the Crime Control Act of 1990, Pub. L. No. 101-647, which, in addition to increasing penalties and creating new criminal prohibitions (some of which are described below), established a special Financial Institutions Fraud Unit within the Department of Justice. The Crime Control Act also more than doubled the authorization for appropriation for Justice Department banking enforcement activities, to $162.5 million per year from 1991 to 1993. And it encouraged "whistle-blowers" by authorizing rewards to informants who provide information leading to criminal convictions.

These days, if your client has engaged in serious violations of the banking laws, or in conduct that might amount to fraud, you must always consider the possibility of criminal prosecution. Banking law firms would probably do well to affiliate with attorneys specializing in white-collar criminal defense work.

The range of federal criminal laws potentially applicable to banking transactions is quite broad. The place to start is the bank-specific laws. Federal law prohibits bribing bank examiners, 18 U.S.C. §212, taking kickbacks for loans, 18 U.S.C. §215, acting as a "financial kingpin" by operating a continuing financial crimes enterprise, 18 U.S.C. §225, embezzling or misapplying funds from federally insured institutions, 18 U.S.C. §§656-657, falsifying bank financial statements or reports, 18 U.S.C. §§1005-1007, making false statements in loan applications, 18 U.S.C. §1014, concealing assets from the FDIC, 18 U.S.C. §1032, defrauding or attempting to defraud financial institutions, 18 U.S.C. §1344, obstructing a criminal investigation of a banking institution or its customers, 18 U.S.C. §1510(b), obstructing the examination of a financial institution, 18 U.S.C. §1517, violating removal or suspension orders, 12 U.S.C. §1818(j) (FDIC insured institutions), 12 U.S.C. §1786(*l*) (federally insured credit unions) and participation in bank affairs by persons previously convicted of crimes involving dishonesty or breach of trust, 12 U.S.C. §1829.

FIRREA increased the penalties for most of these violations to up to $1 million in fines and 20 years in prison for each violation, and the Crime Control Act further increased many of these penalties to 30 years (or life in the case of the financial kingpin statute). Violations may also subject the defendant to forfeiture of any property constituting or derived from the proceeds of the crimes. 18 U.S.C. §982(a)(2).

Criminal penalties are also provided for knowing violations of various bank regulatory statutes, such as the Bank Holding Company Act, 12 U.S.C. §1847(a), and the Savings and Loan Holding Company Act, 12 U.S.C. §1467a(i).

In addition to these bank-specific crimes, prosecutors are likely to charge a variety of general federal crimes. These include conspiracy, 18 U.S.C. §371, making false statements to federal officials, 18 U.S.C. §1001, mail fraud, 18 U.S.C. §1341, wire fraud, 18 U.S.C. §1343, and criminal RICO violations, 18 U.S.C. §§1962-1963.

Typically, federal prosecutors will charge numerous offenses in any given indictment, which can then be used by the prosecutors for purposes of plea bargaining. Moreover, an individual found to have violated one or more of these prohibitions cannot expect much leniency in sentencing. Even if sentencing judges wanted to be lenient, despite the public outcry against the "savings and loan crooks," they have very limited discretion in sentencing these days as a result of the guidelines promulgated by the U.S. Sentencing Commission that apply to financial institutions offenses. Particularly severe sentences are mandated under the guidelines for crimes that earn a defendant more than $1 million in receipts.

Bank prosecutions are certain to generate a substantial number of important issues of federal criminal law and procedure. The issues are beyond the scope of the present book; we leave them for specialized courses in federal criminal law. What is evident, however, even from our cursory look at the area, is that this is a field that is certain to burgeon in the coming years.

*QUESTIONS AND COMMENTS*

1. Note that criminal enforcement is in the hands of the Department of Justice, whereas civil enforcement is largely committed to the discretion of the appropriate banking agencies. Can you see any problems with this allocation of responsibility?

2. Is beefed-up criminal enforcement worth the candle? Unlike much civil enforcement, criminal enforcement is retrospective—it punishes people for crimes already committed. Those crimes cannot be undone. To the extent that the wrongdoer can be forced to pay restitution, that remedy is available—and easier to obtain—in a civil action rather than a criminal one. And the goal of removing bad actors from the banking system can be achieved by civil removal or prohibition actions. To be sure, criminal enforcement deters future conduct, but given the enhanced vigor of civil penalties, is the additional deterrence offered by criminal enforcement sufficiently important to warrant a major commitment of regulatory and judicial resources? Do you accept the need for retribution for the harm done to the national economy by the "savings and loan crooks"?

3. Can you think of any conflicts between the goals of criminal enforcement and the protection of the federal insurance funds? Consider the fact that directors and officers liability insurance policies typically exclude criminal conduct from the scope of their coverage.

# 8 BANK FAILURE

We now turn to the event against which the scheme of regulatory enforcement is directed: bank failure. As we saw in Chapter 1, the failure of a bank is often thought to present a severe public policy danger, not only because it imposes losses, anxiety, and inconvenience on depositors and others, but—more importantly—because the failure of one bank may spread to others, creating the danger of generalized banking panics. But what happens when, despite the best efforts of regulators, a banking institution *does* fail? What public policy goals do the regulators seek to accomplish in this circumstance? What goals *should* they seek? What powers are available to regulators to achieve these goals? What remedies are available to the various claimants on a bank's assets after failure: depositors, the FDIC as deposit insurer, holders of the institution's notes or bonds, trade creditors, persons holding legal claims against the institution, and others? What protections are available to those against whom the institution itself had claims prior to failure? The present chapter analyzes these problems, which arise under a special bank failure regime separate and independent from the general federal bankruptcy code.

The United States has recently passed through a catastrophe of virtually unimaginable scale as a result of the failure of many insured banks and thrift institutions.

The problems first manifested themselves in the savings and loan industry in the early 1980s. In 1979 the Federal Reserve adopted a tight monetary policy to control inflation, which had the effect of driving nominal interest rates up to very high levels—the prime rate rose to over 20 percent in 1980. These high rates caused huge operating losses for many thrift institutions, which had to pay high current rates for deposits while earning lower, historical rates on their portfolios of home mortgage loans. By 1981 the thrift industry as a whole was insolvent.

In response to this problem, the government adopted a policy of forbearance—allowing insolvent institutions to continue operating in hopes that the problem would be short-lived and the institutions would return to financial health once interest rates stabilized. No one wanted to face the fact that the Federal Savings and Loan Insurance Corporation (FSLIC) did not have nearly enough money to pay off the depositors. The forbearance policy continued even after interest rates fell in 1981, when it became apparent that the industry was not returning to health.

Meanwhile, a variety of regulatory changes aggravated the problem. For many years the law had prohibited depository institutions from paying any interest on checking accounts, and it had restricted the amounts they could pay on savings and time deposits. These restrictions had long been beneficial to these institutions, since they limited price competition. The high-interest environment of 1979-81, however, resulted in massive disintermediation as bank and thrift customers withdrew their funds and invested them in other assets that paid higher rates, such as Treasury bills and money market mutual funds. Faced with a massive hemorrhage of funds, banks and thrifts prevailed on Congress to deregulate deposit interest rates beginning in 1980.

Further deregulation occurred on the asset side of depository institution balance sheets. Thrifts in particular were granted broad new powers, ostensibly to help them to return to financial health by competing in new markets. In fact, personnel at many thrifts were poorly trained to exercise these new powers, and they committed their institutions to tremendous amounts of bad investments. Individuals of a new kind entered the industry, people who were willing to cut corners and who were none too ethical in their use of depositors' funds. Massive frauds occurred in a number of thrifts.

Meanwhile, Congress did nothing to limit the federal deposit insurance program, which protected depositors up to $100,000 per depositor per institution, and which, de facto, offered infinite coverage because the federal agencies typically paid off all depositors in a failed institution, even those with more than $100,000. Depository institutions that had become insolvent or were operating on very thin capital found that, as a result of deposit interest rate deregulation, they could attract a virtually unlimited supply of money from depositors simply by offering high interest rates. Deposit brokers operating nationwide fueled billions of dollars in certificates of deposit into these high-flying firms. Some thrifts grew like supernovas, doubling or tripling in size in a year or two. Predictably, the firms offering the highest interest rates also tended to be the riskiest or worst-managed firms. Many of these institutions invested a substantial portion of the deposited funds in portfolios of high-yield, high-risk junk bond securities.

As a result of the interaction between deposit insurance and interest rate deregulation, the price system, which is supposed to operate in a capitalist economy to send social resources to their highest and best use, perversely directed depositor funds to the lowest and worst uses. It was the badly managed, poorly capitalized, high-risk institutions that obtained the lion's share of depositor funds. The vast majority of these institutions became insolvent and required costly intervention by the deposit insurance system.

The worst problems occurred in Texas, California, and Florida, where thrift institutions held very broad investment powers and where state regulators failed to police against imprudent or abusive practices. More than forty percent of all taxpayer losses from the savings and loan debacle occurred in Texas alone. The situation in these states was substantially aggravated by a depression in the energy industry in Texas and by a collapse in real estate prices in all three states, California and Florida as well as Texas.

While the worst problems occurred in the savings and loan industry, the commercial banking sector experienced a crisis of its own during the late 1980s. Many commercial banks had invested heavily in commercial real estate lending, which turned out badly when the real estate market crashed. In addition, some of the larger institutions lent money to Latin American and other foreign countries that defaulted during the decade. And nearly all commercial banks were exposed to the interest rate risk that originally bankrupted the savings and loan industry, although the commercial banking sector had less exposure than the thrift sector.

The problem of bank failures eventually forced the FDIC, long considered virtually impervious to failure, to the brink of disaster. Despite increases in premiums and the termination of rebates to banks that once were a matter of course, the FDIC continued to lose money until, by 1991, it too was close to insolvency.

These problems eventually resulted in enormous costs to the American taxpayer. Congress bailed out the savings and loan industry in 1989; and in 1991 it authorized $70 billion in loans to replenish the bank insurance fund. The actual cost of the bailouts is hotly debated, but no one doubts that it is astronomical. Many observers put the tag for the savings and loan cleanup at about $150 billion in present-value terms (and much more if interest payments on the debt needed to fund the bailout are included).

The problems in the industry placed enormous stress on the statutory and administrative system for resolving depository institution failures, an area that had been a lazy backwater in the law since the 1930s. It is a backwater no longer. There have been more court decisions and statutory amendments to this system since 1985 than during the entire period between 1933 and 1985. New legislation has created all sorts of thorny interpretive questions and, sometimes, has raised difficult constitutional issues. See Peter P. Swire, Bank Insolvency Law Now That It Matters Again, 42 Duke Law Journal 469 (1992).

In the pages that follow we describe the current bank failure regime and identify important legal issues that it poses.

## A. A SIMPLIFIED MODEL OF BANK FAILURE

Let's consider a highly simplified model of a bank failure proceeding. The purpose of this exercise is not to describe how bank failures are *actually* handled—although in some respects the model below bears a resemblance to actual practices—but rather to clarify the student's conceptual picture of how bank failures are handled *in theory.* Once the basic concepts are understood, it is easier to grasp some of the complexities—and the problems—associated with the resolution of failed or failing institutions.

We can divide failure procedures into three basic steps: First, a fiduciary of some sort must be appointed to handle the resolution process upon a finding that the institution has become insolvent or otherwise run into serious difficulties. In practice, a government fiduciary is always involved in depository institution failures, even though under Chapter 11 of the Bankruptcy Code—outside the banking context—the debtor-in-possession and the creditor's committees often play the most important roles.

Second, the fiduciary must marshal the assets of the failed institution. In the course of this step the fiduciary must identify all items of potential value owned by the institution—buildings and equipment, business goodwill, outstanding loans and other investments, below market leases and long-term contracts, inchoate claims such as unfiled tort or contract actions, and so on—and must seek to collect on the fair value of these assets.

Third, the fiduciary must deal with claims against the bank—claims of uninsured depositors (those with over $100,000 on deposit at the bank), the FDIC, tort and contract claimants, bondholders, trade creditors, lessors and other entities with contractual relationships with the institution, and so on. In performing this task, the fiduciary's responsibility is to distribute the institution's assets (as marshaled and realized pursuant to the second step) to claimants in their order of priority. This does not mean that the institution will necessarily be physically closed; indeed, in the typical depository institution failure the institution itself remains open, although under different ownership and often under a different name.

Once these steps are complete, the failure is resolved. The former institution has disappeared, its assets sold to solvent entities, and its liabilities paid out to claimants according to their order of priority. The fiduciary declares the task completed and moves on to the next job.

This simple model of bank failure proceedings resembles one well-recognized method for resolving depository institution insolvencies: the so-called deposit payoff or straight liquidation. Most depository institution insolvencies are not resolved with straight liquidations, however, but through more complex transactions, for reasons that we discuss below. Even in the case of straight liquidations, our model is highly schematic.

Nevertheless, the goal of all bank insolvency proceedings, in theory at least, is no different from that presented in our simplified model: appointing a fiduciary, marshaling the assets, and distributing the value of the assets to bona fide claimants in their order of priority. Thus our model identifies the basic structure that underlies many complexities of real world transactions. Further, it provides a normative standard against which actual practices can be measured. We can ask whether the bank failure procedures we observe in practice actually perform the three fundamental tasks—appointment of a fiduciary, marshaling of assets, and distribution in order of priority—in an efficient and reliable fashion. As we will see, this question is not always easy to answer. Let us proceed to examine how each of the steps works in actual practice.

## B. APPOINTMENT OF A FIDUCIARY

In general, the first step to resolving a bank failure is the appointment of a fiduciary to handle the institution's affairs. We must immediately add the caveat that appointment of a fiduciary is not always necessary; in unusual situations a bank may fail de facto and be rescued through the device of "open-bank assistance" without any third-party fiduciary being appointed. For the moment, however, we will put aside the analysis of open-bank assistance transactions and examine the more usual case in which a fiduciary is, in fact, appointed to handle the resolution proceedings.

### 1. *Who May Close an Institution?*

Who has the power to cause the appointment of a fiduciary—in popular (although sometimes inexact) parlance, to "close" a bank? Traditionally, closure power has been vested in the chartering agency. Thus the Comptroller of the Currency closes national banks, 12 U.S.C. §§191, 203.

State banking agencies close state-chartered banks. The Federal Deposit Insurance Corporation Improvement Act of 1991 (FDICIA) also authorized the appropriate federal regulator to close state-chartered banks. 12 U.S.C. §1821(c)(9). The Office of Thrift Supervision has the power to close thrift institutions, including state-chartered institutions. 12 U.S.C. §1464(d)(2)(A). State thrift regulators also close state-chartered institutions. Federally chartered credit unions are closed by the NCUA, 12 U.S.C. §1766, and state credit unions are closed by state credit union regulators or (if insured) by the NCUA.

Until 1991 the FDIC did not have direct closure powers. The FDICIA changed that, allowing the FDIC to close state-chartered insured nonmember banks, 12 U.S.C. §1821(c)(9), and to close any insured depository institution if the grounds for appointment of a conservator or receiver otherwise exist and the appointment is necessary to avoid or mitigate losses to the deposit insurance fund. 12 U.S.C. §1821(d)(10). Even if it does not close an institution directly, the FDIC can effectively force closure by suspending or permanently terminating deposit insurance. See 12 U.S.C. §1821(c)(5)(J).

Although in practice it is almost always a government agency that closes a bank or thrift, closure may be effected by private means as well. A depository institution's charter will ordinarily have provisions governing voluntary dissolution that are similar to provisions contained in the charters of other firms. Thus, in theory at least, shareholders can cause the dissolution of a bank or thrift, and the winding up of its affairs, even if the institution has not been declared insolvent by any government agency (indeed, even if the institution is currently solvent). Moreover, an institution's directors may have authority to effect a de facto liquidation by transferring assets and liabilities to another institution, although such a transaction, if effected voluntarily, may need the consent of the appropriate regulatory agency and/or the shareholders.

## 2. *Standards for Closure*

More controversial than *who* closes an institution are the *grounds* under which an institution may be closed.

A fiduciary may be appointed to take over the affairs of a federally insured depository institution if (1) its assets are insufficient to meet its obligations; (2) the institution has engaged in substantial dissipation of assets due to any violation of statute or regulation or any unsafe or unsound practice; (3) the institution is in an unsafe or unsound condition; (4) the institution has engaged in a willful violation of a final cease-and-desist order; (5) there has been a concealment of the institution's books, records, papers, or assets; (6) the institution is likely to be unable to pay its obligations or meet its depositors' demands in the normal course of business; (7) the institution has incurred or is likely to incur losses that will deplete all or substantially all of its capital, and there is no reasonable prospect for the institution to become adequately capitalized without federal assistance; (8) there is a violation of any law or regulation, or an unsafe or unsound practice that is likely to cause insolvency or substantial dissipation of assets or earnings, weaken the institution's condition, or otherwise seriously prejudice the interests of the institution's depositors or the deposit insurance fund; (9) the institution consents to the appointment; (10) the institution ceases to be an insured institution; (11) the institution is undercapitalized and either has no reasonable prospect of returning to capital adequacy or fails to undertake prompt corrective action; or (12) the institution is critically undercapitalized or otherwise has subtantially insufficient capital. 12 U.S.C. §1821(c)(5).

Depository institutions are typically closed without prior notice or hearing. See 12 U.S.C. §§191, 203(a) (national banks); 12 U.S.C. §1464(d)(2)(B) (savings institutions). Such ex parte regulatory seizures raise obvious due process concerns. The government, however, asserts at least two reasons for acting swiftly. First, when banks are closed they are almost always either insolvent or in imminent danger of becoming insolvent. Thus, almost by definition, an emergency exists that may warrant rapid action (because, among other things, managers of a depository institution that is insolvent or nearly so may have an incentive to take inappropriate risks, knowing that any losses will fall on the deposit insurance funds). Second, if a banking agency had to institute judicial proceedings for closing a depository institution, word of its action could spread to depositors and other creditors, further aggravating the institution's problems and probably triggering a run (even insured depositors might participate in the run out of concern that their funds would be tied up in insolvency proceedings). The value of the institution as a going concern could thereby be depleted.

Courts have long recognized that these compelling interests justify ex parte seizures under the Due Process Clause. See Fahey v. Mallonee, 332 U.S. 245, 253-254 (1947):

> It is complained that [a hearing is available only] after the conservator takes possession instead of before. This is a drastic procedure. But the delicate nature of the institution and the impossibility of preserving credit during an investigation has [sic] made it an almost invariable custom to apply supervisory authority in this summary manner. It is a heavy responsibility to be exercised with disinterestedness and restraint, but in light of the history and customs of banking we cannot say it is unconstitutional.

Although due process does not require a prior hearing for the appointment of a conservator or receiver, it seems clear that a prompt *post*-seizure hearing is required. The banking statutes provide a mechanism for post-seizure judicial challenges in most cases. Thus, a national bank may challenge the appointment of a conservator by action in federal district court, which is instructed to rule "upon the merits." 12 U.S.C. §203(b)(1). A court is instructed to set aside the conservatorship only if the Comptroller's decision is found to be "arbitrary, capricious, an abuse of discretion, or otherwise not in accordance with law" (the familiar standard for review of informal agency action under the Administrative Procedure Act).

Similarly, savings associations may challenge the appointment of a conservator or receiver by the OTS by action in federal district court, which again is directed to rule "upon the merits." 12 U.S.C. §1464(d)(2)(B). The standard of review in savings association cases is not spelled out, but several courts have concluded that the "arbitrary or capricious" standard applies. See, e.g., Guaranty Savings & Loan Association v. FHLBB, 794 F.2d 1339 (8th Cir. 1986).

How stringent, in practice, is judicial review "upon the merits" of whether the agency has acted arbitrarily or capriciously in appointing a receiver or conservator? In the usual case, the courts are not likely to second-guess an administrative agency about such decisions. But in a few cases, attorneys for an institution's former managers have been able to persuade federal district court judges that a seizure was unjustified. They have been less successful on appeal, as the following case illustrates.

## Franklin Savings Association v. Director, Office of Thrift Supervision

*934 F.2d 1127 (10th Cir. 1991)*

Brorby, J.:

The Director of the Office of Thrift Supervision (Director) appeals the decision of the trial court ordering the removal of the director appointed conservator of Franklin Savings Association (Franklin). . . .

Franklin is a state chartered, stock savings and loan association that has been doing business since 1889 in Ottawa, Kansas. Franklin has functioned during most of its existence as a traditional savings and loan association, accepting its depositors' money and in turn loaning these funds to borrowers. Loans were usually secured by a first mortgage on residential real estate. Franklin's profits were derived from the difference in interest paid to depositors and that collected from its borrowers.

In 1973, Franklin was acquired by new ownership who set it upon an expansion course. Franklin now has eight branches, all located in eastern Kansas. In addition, Franklin went "public" with approximately six per cent of its stock being publicly traded on NASDAQ.

In 1981, Franklin decided to adopt "innovative operating strategies" and "nontraditional" pursuits. Over the next eight years its deposits grew from $200 million to over $11 billion, bringing marked changes to the institution.

Franklin's asset base changed as it had acquired numerous forms of mortgage-backed securities. This resulted in a volatile income stream. Franklin attempted both to predict the swings in its income stream with computer modeling, and to hedge its risks using additional and various forms of mortgage-backed securities. The securities bought and sold by Franklin included deep discounted securities, reverse repurchase agreements, long call and put options and strips (both interest only and principal only). Derivative securities (referred to by the district court as "TB 12 assets") entitle the holder to receive only part of the mortgage payments. Such securities are both higher risk and complex, and have only a thin secondary market. Franklin also began acquiring high-yield, noninvestment grade bonds, commonly known as junk bonds. Ultimately, mortgage-backed derivative securities and junk bonds comprised over thirty-five per cent of Franklin's total assets. In addition, Franklin had entered into several off-balance sheet transactions of the same type. Director identified these and other concerns in the form of a supervisory directive issued to Franklin. The underlying basis for Director's concern was the fact these assets were extremely sensitive to both interest rates and principal repayments. Director was also concerned about the liquidity (the ability to immediately turn the assets into cash), as necessary to pay depositors. Director's primary concern was the level of concentration of these assets, i.e., over thirty-five per cent of Franklin's total asset base.

Franklin's liabilities likewise underwent significant changes. Franklin began soliciting deposits nationwide through the use of brokered deposits. These deposits were typically short term and of high cost to Franklin. By the end of 1989, over seventy per cent of Franklin's deposits were brokered. To attract these deposits Franklin had to pay a higher than normal interest rate for a typical savings and loan and, as the deposits were short term, it had to be in a position to turn assets quickly into cash in order to pay depositors as their deposits matured. Director repeatedly expressed his concerns in regard to the extensive use of and significant reliance upon brokered deposits. In November 1989, Director specifically expressed his concern that Franklin's use of brokered deposits had increased significantly over the last six months, both in dollar amount and in relation to total deposits, again Director's primary concern being the level of concentration of these brokered deposits, i.e., over seventy per cent of Franklin's deposits were brokered.

Franklin's position in regard to its concentration of depositors' funds in these high-risk securities was simple. It maintained that it was accurately predicting the performance of these assets; that a market did exist for these assets; and that it had been shrinking the amount of these assets. Concerning its reliance upon brokered deposits, Franklin maintained that the costs of funds had nothing to do with the investments it acquired and that the cost of these funds was actually less than the cost of normal deposits.

Franklin's earnings were declining. . . . Earnings are an important source of capital, and Franklin's prospects of future profit appeared bleak. Director . . . again expressed his concerns to Franklin in November 1989, additionally pointing out that in the fiscal year ended June 30, 1989, Franklin paid its eight executive officers $3.5 million ($1.8 million of which was in bonuses) and paid dividends of approximately $15 million. This was done notwithstanding the fact Franklin itself reported a $9 million loss in that same fiscal year. These expenditures further impaired Franklin's earnings.

By mid-1989, Franklin's metamorphosis was complete. It had been transformed from a traditional savings and loan into something totally different. . . . Franklin began to resemble a securities trading firm rather than a traditional savings and loan association. . . .

On February 15, 1990, Director, apparently deciding the failure to address his concerns must be remedied, made specific findings. These findings were based upon three volumes of documents that included reports of examinations, monthly, quarterly and annual financial reports filed by Franklin, supervisory directives, other required annual reports, and the results of an independent audit. These findings included the following:

> [Franklin] is in an unsafe and unsound condition to transact business in that, among other things, (a) [Franklin] has a significant level of high risk assets, and has placed undue reliance on brokered deposits, (b) [Franklin] has incurred and is likely to incur losses that will deplete all or substantially all of its capital, and there is no reasonable prospect for [Franklin]'s capital to be replenished without Federal assistance, and (c) there is a violation or violations of laws or regulations, or an unsafe or unsound practice or condition which is likely to cause insolvency or substantial dissipation of assets or earnings or is likely to weaken the condition of [Franklin] or otherwise seriously prejudice the interests of its depositors. . . .

Director thereupon proceeded to appoint "not for the purpose of liquidation" the Resolution Trust Corporation as conservator for Franklin.

### Proceedings in District Court

Franklin promptly filed an action pursuant to 12 U.S.C. [§1464(d)(2)(B)] asking that Director be required to remove the conservator. . . . The trial court . . . decided Franklin should have the opportunity to submit evidence outside the administrative record as to "whether or not that evidence was considered" by Director, and "to develop any facts bearing on the question of whether any of the statutory grounds existed." . . . After reviewing the administrative record and the evidence presented to it by both Franklin and Director during an eighteen-day bench trial, the district court . . . ordered Director to remove the conservator, an order which this court stayed and from which this appeal ensues.

### I. Scope of Review

Director contends the trial court should have reviewed Director's decision to appoint a conservator upon the basis of the administrative record and in accordance with the Administrative Procedure Act ("APA"). Franklin contends, however, [that] the expanded hybrid scope of review, as fashioned by the trial court, was correct. Whether the trial court properly limited the scope of review is a question of law, which we review de novo. . . .

We must first define the proper scope of review. . . . The pertinent portions of [the statute] provide:

> The Director shall have exclusive power and jurisdiction to appoint a conservator. . . . If, in the opinion of the Director, a ground for the appointment of a conservator . . . exists, the Director is authorized to appoint ex parte and without notice a conservator. . . . In the event of such appointment, the association may . . . bring an action . . . for an order requiring the Director to remove such conservator. . . , and the court shall upon the merits dismiss such action or direct the Director to remove such conservator. . . .

The plain language of this statute reveals: (1) the director has the exclusive power to appoint a conservator; (2) the director may appoint a conservator if, in his opinion, a statutory ground for the appointment exists; (3) assuming the director has opined the ground for the appointment of a conservator does exist, his decision whether to appoint a conservator is discretionary; and (4) the statute, while clearly authorizing judicial review of the director's decision, fails to specifically define the scope of that review.

We first emphasize . . . that the . . . close supervision, broad discretion, and quick response directed by FIRREA dictates [sic] a narrow and limited scope of review that gives deference to the director's judgment, knowledge, and expertise. . . .

Review "upon the merits" simply means the district court's decision to either dismiss the action or remove the conservator should be based upon the merits of the action (i.e., whether statutory grounds for the appointment of a conservator exist), rather than on procedural or policy oriented grounds. . . . [T]he proper scope of review for appointment decisions . . . is that review be confined to the administrative record in accordance with the APA. . . .

In the case before us, Director did make formal findings and produced and certified a voluminous and detailed agency record for review that would enable the reviewing court to conduct a substantial and meaningful review from the agency record. The trial court, however, determined the three-volume administrative record, as designated by Director, was not the "whole administrative record" since it believed there were missing documents upon which Director relied. . . . The appropriate remedy for this alleged defect would have been for the trial court to call for any missing documents or require Director to testify or provide further explanation. Instead, the district court crafted and conducted a hybrid scope of de novo review. While the director has an obligation to produce for judicial review a designated administrative record, such record does not have to be needlessly elaborate, nor as detailed as the district court here required. . . .

To require that the director has reviewed and relied on all working papers, synopses of all conversations, and other minutiae, would defeat FIRREA's objective requirement of prompt supervisory action. The director need review only such information as he deems necessary or desirable to enable him to arrive at an informed and fair opinion. Absent extraordinary circumstances, the decision of the director as to what information he must review to make an appointment decision should be left to his discretion. The director, in the case of judicial review of his appointment decision, has the obligation to produce and certify the record upon which he relied at the time of the decision. This record must contain sufficient data to allow the reviewing court to determine whether the director had a rational basis for the appointment decision. [The record in] the case before us . . . was adequate to permit meaningful judicial review.

. . . A reading of the administrative record clearly shows [that] the substance of Franklin's positions were before Director when the appointment decision was made. The director is not required to review every document arguably related to the troubled institution in question, nor is a reviewing court. . . .

In summary, we conclude the district court, in reviewing the director's decision to appoint a conservator, should confine its review to that information before the director at the time the appointment decision was made. When the director learns the appointment decision has been challenged, the director has the obligation to produce the information that he relied upon in making his decision to the district court and to certify such information is accurate and complete. Thus, the director's obligation does not extend to all information contained in his files. Should the savings and loan association challenging the appointment decision desire additional information from the agency record than that presented by the director to the district court, it may request such information in accordance with the applicable rules of discovery and evidence. . . .

The focus of the judicial review is to determine whether there exists sufficient evidence in the administrative record to form a reasoned opinion that the statutory grounds for the appointment of a conservator exist. In this case, the district court heard live testimony from twenty-five witnesses; accepted deposition testimony from eighteen witnesses; received over 650 trial exhibits; engaged in credibility determinations regarding competing experts; and basically made its own findings, compared those to the findings of Director, and decided the conservator was wrongly appointed. Such a review was far beyond the court's permissible scope of review. We therefore find the district court erred in improperly expanding the scope of its review. . . .

### III. Review of Director's Decision

. . . In the instant case, Director found three of the [statutory] grounds [for the appointment of a conservator] exist. We will examine each of these three grounds separately, although a determination that Director correctly found the existence of any one of the three statutory grounds is sufficient to uphold Director's appointment decision. [The Court held that the Director had acted properly under all three grounds.]

. . . Accordingly, the decision of the district court is reversed and vacated. This matter is remanded to the district court with instructions to dismiss the action.

## *QUESTIONS AND COMMENTS*

1. Seizures of depository institutions can be exciting and dramatic, with features of a police raid. The details of one operation are recounted in Fidelity Savings & Loan Association v. FHLBB, 540 F. Supp. 1374, 1380 (N.D. Cal.), *reversed,* 689 F.2d 803 (9th Cir. 1982), *cert. denied,* 461 U.S. 914 (1983):

> The only remaining step in the well-orchestrated federal takeover of the state savings and loan association was the physical seizure of the association. Over the weekend, the federal regulators dispatched hundreds of federal bank examiners from all over the country to California to serve in their appointed outposts in individual branches. On Tuesday, April 13, 1982, a handful of federal and state officials entered the Fidelity offices in Oakland, California at precisely 4:40 p.m., twenty minutes before closing. With watches synchronized, the officials entered Fidelity's executive offices and served the papers "closing" the association at 4:47 p.m. According to the

> testimony of . . . an attorney for the FHLBB who was part of the operation in Oakland, different members of the takeover team fanned out to tell other employees in the building of the association's seizure. [The official] also testified that there was some question as to whether the regulators should bar all doors but such was not done because some Fidelity employees needed to go home. There is a dispute in the record as to whether all doors in all Fidelity offices actually were closed; however there is no dispute that the entire operation took less than thirty minutes.

2. The principal ground for closing an institution has always been that it is insolvent. But what does it mean to be "insolvent"? In 1989 the Comptroller formalized two criteria for determining when a national bank is insolvent. Under 12 C.F.R. §5.49, a bank is considered insolvent on a "net worth" basis when it has no remaining equity capital—that is, when its liabilities exceed its assets. This may seem like an obvious definition, but it deviates from prior practice in which the allowance for loan losses was added to the assets for purposes of determining the institution's net worth. The new rule, which conforms to generally accepted accounting principles, is stricter because the allowance for loan losses cannot be used to keep an institution afloat. In addition, an institution may be considered insolvent on a "liquidity" basis when "it is unable to meet its obligations as they mature." An institution may be insolvent on a liquidity basis even if it has a positive net worth if it is unable to sell off assets quickly enough to meet the demands of depositors and other creditors in a timely fashion.

3. Do you think that the "arbitrary or capricious" standard of review provides sufficient due process protections, given the fact that appointment of a fiduciary almost always causes top management to lose their jobs and extinguishes any practical hope an institution's shareholders might have of recovering even a fraction of their investments? Can you think of any standards or procedures that might provide greater protections? What problems would follow from strengthening the protections?

4. What do you make of the requirement that judicial review be "upon the merits?" Do you think Congress actually meant anything out of the ordinary by this phrase? The legislative history sheds little light on the issue. If Congress had intended an unusual procedure for administrative review, wouldn't the legislative history have explicitly noted this fact?

5. At least three constructions appear possible for the phrase "upon the merits."

First, it could mean simply that the reviewing court should examine, not only the procedures used by the agency, but also the substance of its decision. This interpretation suggests that judicial review of closure decisions should be no different in substance than review of all sorts of other agency actions under the arbitrary or capricious standard. In particular, judicial review might be limited, under this interpretation, to the administrative record compiled by the agency. What do you think of this interpretation? Can you identify any flaws in the argument? What is the content of the administrative record if the agency has not held a hearing?

Second, the phrase could instruct the courts to conduct de novo review of facts and law. All evidence that is relevant and not privileged could presumably be introduced into such proceedings. What do you think of this analysis? Is it consistent with the arbitrary or capricious standard for judicial review?

Third, the phrase "upon the merits" might mean something in between standard judicial review on the administrative record and de novo review of facts and law, based on an expanded administrative record. The district court in *Franklin Savings* opted for this third approach, but the appeals panel rejected this interpretation. What is your view?

6. At least in *Franklin Savings* there was an institution—albeit one operating under conservatorship—for the prior management to return to after prevailing in their legal challenge. What about the more common case, in which a receiver is appointed and the assets and deposit liabilities are transferred to another institution? Here a subsequent judicial order terminating a receivership might provide no meaningful relief since the receivership is likely to be devoid of assets by the time the opinion comes down. In this circumstance, should the shareholders or former management have a right to an injunction against the sale of assets?

Note that the relevant statutes seem to make an action to terminate the appointment of a conservator or receiver the exclusive avenue for judicial review, and provide that a court may not otherwise "restrain, or affect the exercise of powers or functions of a conservator." 12 U.S.C. §§203(b)(3), 1464(d)(2)(D). Does this mean that a court may not issue a temporary restraining order or preliminary injunction against the sale of assets? See Haralson v. FHLBB, 267 U.S. App. D.C. 120, 837 F.2d 1123 (D.C. Cir. 1988) (concluding that an action for removal of the receiver is the exclusive remedy). What position do you take on this issue? Are the shareholders sufficiently protected by the fact that the proceeds of the asset sale will redound to the benefit of the receivership?

7. What if an agency engages in improper conduct prior to closing an institution? Is such conduct, in itself, grounds for challenging the receivership? In Biscayne Federal Savings & Loan v. FHLBB, 720 F.2d 1499 (11th Cir. 1983), *cert. denied,* 467 U.S. 1215 (1984), the trial court removed the FSLIC as receiver on the ground that the FHLBB (which had regulated the institution prior to insolvency) had engaged in behavior that the court characterized as "outrageous," "outlandish," "egregious," and "wrapped in a shroud of deception." The appeals court reversed. Without questioning the accuracy of the trial court's factual findings, the appeals court held that these findings were irrelevant. The plaintiff had

stipulated that it was insolvent at the time the receiver was appointed; and since this statutory ground for receivership existed, "judicial inquiry ends!" Does this leave the institution or its shareholders without a remedy?

## 3. *Nature and Powers of the Fiduciary*

So far we have examined the *grounds* for appointment of a fiduciary, and have investigated the available means to challenge that appointment. We turn now to the nature and powers of the fiduciary. What institutions may act as the fiduciary, and what are the scope and limits of their powers when so acting?

Initially, we must distinguish two different fiduciary roles. The traditional method for closing an institution is to shut it down and appoint a *receiver* to marshal its assets and distribute them to creditors. Alternatively, however, the banking agencies may choose to appoint a *conservator* to operate the institution with a view towards maintaining going-concern value in the disposition of its assets. There are differences in powers and legal function between receivers and conservators, although the roles are closely related. We discussed differences in the grounds for appointing these two types of fiduciaries in the previous section.

In practice, the FDIC is nearly always appointed as receiver or conservator for all institutions except for thrift institutions during a limited period, now ended, in which the RTC filled the role of receiver and could act as conservator. What are the FDIC's powers as conservator or receiver? In general, under 12 U.S.C. §1821(d), a conservator or receiver exercises the traditional functions of a common law conservator or receiver. Thus, a fiduciary of either sort succeeds to all the rights, titles, and privileges of the institution. It may collect obligations owing to the institution and pay out the institution's valid obligations. It may cause the institution to merge into another institution or may transfer any assets or liabilities to another institution. It may adjudicate claims against the institution and must distribute assets in the order of priority. It may obtain a stay of any litigation against the institution, may repudiate leases and other executory contracts, and may file lawsuits against the institution's former officers and directors or others who may be liable to the institution. As conservator, the fiduciary may operate the institution in an attempt to return it to solvency. As receiver, it may take any reasonable steps incident to liquidating the institution's affairs. We will discuss some of these functions in more detail in later sections of this chapter.

How does an agency decide whether to appoint a conservator or a receiver? In practice, the decision usually turns on whether or not the institution can be sold quickly. If a sale can be arranged quickly, even in advance of the appointment, then a receivership will be established. If a quick sale is not possible, then a conservatorship may be the preferred route since a conservator's job is to preserve going-concern value.

*QUESTIONS AND COMMENTS*

1. Until recently, receiverships were more common than conservatorships because willing buyers of failed institutions could almost always be found. By 1990, however, the situation had changed dramatically, at least in the thrift industry. Often qualified buyers could not be found for failed institutions, and the only practical alternative was conservatorship. In March 1990, the RTC was managing roughly 350 thrifts in conservatorships. By the mid 1990s, however, the heyday of conservatorships appeared to be waning as banks returned to profitability.

2. What benefit is there to placing a failed institution in a conservatorship if it cannot be sold quickly? The FDIC must provide top managers for each conservatorship it handles. How likely is it that managers hired by the FDIC to run a failed institution are going to do a better job than the institution's former officers who have been displaced? Who would want to take such a job?

3. The FDIC is appointed conservator of First Federal Savings. Later, while the First Federal conservatorship is under way, the FDIC is appointed conservator of Guaranty Savings. First Federal Savings has a breach of contract lawsuit on file against Guaranty Savings for $10 million. Assume that the lawsuit is not frivolous, but that Guaranty Savings has potential defenses. May the FDIC accept both conservatorships?

4. Assume that the FDIC is appointed conservator of Hometown Savings. It bungles the job, causing a substantial dissipation of assets and harming the interests of creditors. Does the agency face any potential liability? See 12 U.S.C. §209(a) (where conservator is a federal agency, provisions of Federal Tort Claims Act apply with respect to conservator's liability for acts or omissions pursuant to conservatorship); United States v. Gaubert, 111 S. Ct. 1267 (1991) (discretionary function exception to the Federal Tort Claims Act bars damages claims against the United States for mismanagement).

## C. RESOLUTION PROCEDURES

At the beginning of this chapter we presented a simplified model of a resolution procedure, under which the fiduciary marshaled the assets and distributed them to claimants in the order of their priority. The actual practice is rarely that simple. To understand the nature of the legal issues that arise in conservatorship or receivership proceedings for depository institutions, it is essential to grasp the basic structure of the principal resolution mechanisms utilized by the FDIC.

Four basic models are available to the FTC for resolving depository institution failures. These four models are open bank assistance, liquidations, purchase and assumption transactions, and bridge bank or new bank facilities.

## *1. Open Bank Assistance*

Open bank assistance is a procedure not much used these days, but one with important theoretical implications. Unlike the other procedures, an open bank assistance transaction does not require the appointment of a receiver or conservator. The institution is never closed; rather, it is rescued on an "open bank" basis through the infusion of new funds.

The principal legal authority for open bank assistance is 12 U.S.C. §1823(c)(8). This statute provides that the FDIC may consider providing direct financial assistance to depository institutions before the appointment of a fiduciary, but only under the following circumstances: (1) grounds for appointment of a fiduciary exist or likely will exist in the future unless capital levels are increased; (2) it is unlikely that the institution can meet its current capital adequacy standards without assistance; (3) the institution's management has been competent and has complied with applicable laws and regulations; and (4) the institution's management has not engaged in insider dealings, speculative practices, or other abusive activities. Assistance can take a variety of forms, including loans, deposits, asset or securities purchases, assumption of liabilities, and capital infusions. No open bank assistance may be provided, however, unless the FDIC's Board of Directors determines that the procedure represents the least costly approach to the problem. 12 U.S.C. §1823(c)(4).

Open bank assistance has drawn considerable political fire because, among other things, it holds the promise that shareholders of an insolvent institution may emerge from the reorganization with valuable equity interests due to federal assistance. The most noteworthy example of open bank assistance to date was the massive federal rescue of Continental Illinois National Bank and Trust Co., a major "money center" bank located in Chicago. Partly as a result of bad loans acquired from the notorious Penn Square Bank, Continental ran into serious financial difficulties in 1984, which precipitated a run by uninsured depositors (mostly foreign governments and foreign corporations). The federal banking agencies feared that closure of a bank as large as Continental might destabilize the entire banking system. They viewed it as "too big to fail" and, accordingly, rescued it with massive infusions of federal money. The eventual resolution was a complex package that provided, among other things, for $4.5

billion in permanent financial assistance to the bank, in exchange for which the bank transferred $4.5 billion in nonperforming loans to the Federal Reserve Bank of Chicago. The FDIC also infused $1 billion in new capital into the bank in exchange for various assets.

*QUESTIONS AND COMMENTS*

1. What is the policy rationale for open bank assistance? We don't ordinarily rescue open firms (other than Chrysler and Lockheed) in other industries. Why should the government act otherwise in the case of banks?

2. What political interests might favor the implementation of open bank assistance?

3. What types of institutions are most likely to benefit from open bank assistance?

## 2. *Liquidations*

The deposit payoff is the banking law equivalent of a simple liquidation. When an institution fails, the FDIC as insurer (in its "corporate capacity") pays off all the insured depositors immediately in cash or by transferring the deposits to another insured institution (it may also pay off the uninsured depositors if it believes that doing so will minimize the costs of the resolution). The FDIC in its corporate capacity is then "subrogated" to—stands in the shoes of—the former depositors and has a claim against the receivership along with other creditors. Meanwhile the FDIC as receiver marshals the assets and distributes them ratably to all creditors (including itself) according to their order of priority. At the conclusion of the process the former institution has disappeared completely, although its assets and liabilities remain in the economy in other hands.

The deposit payoff is the simplest resolution procedure of all and was once quite favored by the FDIC. In recent years, however, the FDIC has used this procedure infrequently, for a number of reasons. First, and most importantly, the deposit payoff dissipates any "going concern value" of the institution. Because the deposits are paid out in cash, any value of the former institution's customer base is eliminated. This is not a serious concern if the institution has already experienced such a serious run that its customer base is worthless. In most cases, however, the failed institution retains a valuable depositor base that would be lost in a deposit payoff. A second problem with deposit payoffs is the FDIC's bad experience with Penn Square liquidation in the early 1980s, when a deposit payoff at a medium-sized Oklahoma bank arguably triggered a massive run at Continental Illinois National Bank.

Today, instead of a straight deposit payoff, the FDIC prefers to use an "insured deposit transfer." This is simply the transfer of insured deposits to another institution, which is willing to compensate the FDIC for the value of the deposit base. Instead of a check from the federal government, customers of the failed bank are informed that their deposits have been transferred to a different institution. They are free, of course, to withdraw these deposits and place them elsewhere, but most customers find that a combination of inertia and convenience keeps them at the new institution.

A third variation on the deposit payoff, with which the FDIC experimented for a time, is the "modified" deposit payoff. In a modified deposit payoff, the FDIC makes full payments to insured depositors and partial payments to uninsured depositors based on the FDIC's estimate of the proceeds of the liquidation of the failed institution's assets. If recoveries on the assets exceed the FDIC's initial estimate, an additional payment is made to the uninsured depositors. If recoveries on the assets fall short of the estimate, the FDIC eats the loss. Although the FDIC used modified deposit payoffs for a number of smaller banks between 1983 and 1985, it has apparently abandoned the technique in more recent years.

*QUESTIONS AND COMMENTS*

1. What are the disadvantages of deposit payoffs? What happens to banking services in the community? Why does the FDIC or RTC rarely consider the deposit payoff the "least cost" resolution procedure?

2. What are the potential advantages of deposit payoff or insured deposit transfers? Should depositors with over $100,000 in an institution be made to worry about whether they will be reimbursed in the event of bank failure?

3. Although the FDIC rarely uses deposit payoffs, and only infrequently uses insured deposit transfers, the RTC, which under FIRREA is charged with administering thrift institution failures, has utilized these techniques with some frequency during its lifetime as an agency. Why might this be so?

## 3. *Purchase and Assumption Transactions*

By far the most favored method for resolving failures of depository institutions is the "purchase and assumption" transaction. In purchase and assumption transactions, a solvent depository institution purchases assets and assumes liabilities of the failed institution. In some respects the purchase and assumption transaction resembles a merger of the failed institution into a solvent one, with the solvent institution paying something for the goodwill of the failed institution as well as for any regulatory advantages (such as relaxation of restraints on geographic expansion) that the transaction may offer. The FDIC makes up the remaining shortfall by cash assistance to the acquiring institution.

The purchase and assumption transaction has a number of advantages as far as the FTC is concerned. First, it maximizes the going-concern value on both sides of the balance sheet: The acquirer picks up a deposit base, as in the case of insured deposit transfers, but also succeeds to a base of loan customers who are likely to return to the acquirer in the future for new financing. Second, by bundling the transfer of assets and liabilities, the purchase and assumption method saves on the costs of resolution. Third, the purchase and assumption transaction allows the failed institution to remain in operation, albeit in many cases under a different name, thus eliminating the danger that banking services will be disrupted and mitigating public concerns about bank failure. Fourth, purchase and assumption transactions remove some of the burden from the FDIC or RTC of collecting on the failed institution's assets. Finally, purchase and assumption transactions are sometimes said to be superior because they can provide protection for *all* depositors, even those with deposits in excess of the $100,000 insurance limit.

So strong are these advantages, at least in the view of the banking agencies, that there is a virtual presumption in favor of the purchase and assumption method of handling depository institution failures. The FDIC nearly always looks first to the possibility of a purchase and assumption transaction before seriously considering other options. Only if market conditions make a purchase and assumption infeasible—for example, if there are an insufficient number of qualified bidders interested in a purchase and assumption deal—will the FDIC vigorously pursue options such as deposit payoffs. This preference for purchase and assumption transactions is recognized and endorsed by the courts. See, e.g., FDIC v. Bank of Boulder, 911 F.2d 1466, 1475 (10th Cir. 1990), *cert. denied*, 499 U.S. 904 (1991); Gunter v. Hutcheson, 674 F.2d 862, 865 (11th Cir.), *cert. denied*, 459 U.S. 826 (1982).

Within the generic category of purchase and assumption transactions there are differences depending on the type and amount of assets and liabilities transferred to the acquiring institution. The acquirer may agree to take on the "whole bank"—that is, to assume all of the failed institution's liabilities and purchase all its assets. The FDIC, in its corporate capacity, writes a check to the acquiring institution to cover the difference in value between the assets purchased and the liabilities assumed, less any premium paid for the franchise and regulatory value of the failed institution. The whole-bank transaction is the simplest form of purchase and assumption deal, and has been in vogue at the FDIC in recent years because it "privatizes" the process of collecting on assets, including non-performing loans. Under a whole-bank transaction, it is up to the acquiring institution to go after recalcitrant debtors, thus reducing the burden on the FDIC of holding and enforcing bad loans.

Despite its conceptual simplicity, the whole-bank transaction is not the traditional purchase and assumption deal. The traditional form is so-called clean-bank transaction, under which the acquiring institution assumes all liabilities but purchases only the high quality assets, such as cash, government securities (which are marked to market), and well-secured, low-risk loans. The remaining "dirty" assets (nonperforming or questionable loans, risky securities, properties recovered in foreclosure proceedings, and so on) are "sold" by the FDIC-receiver to the FDIC-corporate; the "consideration" for these assets is the cash payment that the FDIC-corporate makes to the acquiring institution to cover the amount by which the liabilities assumed exceed the value of the assets assumed plus going-concern and regulatory value. See 12 U.S.C. §1843(c)(2)(A) (authorizing FDIC-corporate to purchase nontransferred assets), 12 U.S.C. §1823(d) (authorizing FDIC-receiver to offer such assets for sale).

Falling somewhere between whole-bank and clean-bank transactions are purchase and assumption deals in which the acquirer retains a "put" option with the FDIC. This option gives the acquirer the right to return assets to the FDIC within a specified time period. If the assets perform well for the acquirer, the acquirer will keep them, otherwise it can return them within a specified period of time and receive a refund from the FDIC, either in full or reduced by a "haircut" equal to some percentage of the purchase price.

## *QUESTIONS AND COMMENTS*

1. In a purchase and assumption transaction the acquiring institution usually takes over the failed institution's liabilities. This agreement is clearly intended to cover deposit liabilities. Does it cover all liabilities of any sort? What about legal claims against the failed institution that accrued prior to the receivership but that have not yet been filed? Holders of such claims would much prefer a claim against a solvent institution than one against a virtually valueless receivership. In theory, the answer to the question whether an acquiring institution assumes a given liability is a matter of contract. If the parties agree to transfer all liabilities, then the acquiring institution will be liable to all creditors of the failed institution. If some liabilities are excluded, then the acquirer will not assume them. But what if the contract is silent on whether the acquirer is assuming a given liability? What should the "default" rule be in such cases—what rule should a court adopt as reflecting the reasonable intent of the parties? The general rule appears to be that the acquiring institution assumes only those liabilities specifically mentioned in the contract. Do you agree with this default rule?

2. Are there any procedures by which a bank's former management can challenge a purchase and assumption transaction? Recall that under 12 U.S.C. §§203(b), 1464(d)(2)(D), the courts are generally prohibited from restraining or affecting the exercise of a receiver's powers except by means of an action to remove the receiver. One might easily infer that there is no statutory jurisdiction over an action against a receiver challenging its decision to consummate a purchase and assumption transaction. If, however, the decision to appoint a receiver was, in fact, inextricably connected with the question of which resolution procedure to use, there is some authority that a court may adjudicate the challenge. See Washington Federal Savings & Loan Association v. FHLBB, 526 F. Supp. 343, 393-394 (N.D. Ohio 1981).

3. One of the problems with a whole-bank purchase and assumption transaction is that the purchaser is asked to acquire a portfolio of assets that may be of uncertain quality. Because purchasers have difficulty in determining the actual value of the assets, they are likely to bid less than they might under conditions of perfect information in order to protect themselves against the risk that the assets will not perform adequately. How might a purchase and assumption transaction be structured to mitigate this risk?

4. The purchase and assumption procedure contemplates a process of competitive bidding for the failed institution. Should this bidding procedure be "standardized" so that all bids must follow the same format (for example, must be all cash bids, must include specified assets and no others, and so forth)? What are the advantages and disadvantages of standardizing a bid as opposed to allowing individualized negotiations with potential purchasers?

## 4. *Bridge Banks and New Banks*

Other resolution procedures used in recent years are "bridge banks" and "new banks." These are temporary institutions organized by the FDIC in order to take over the operations of a failed bank and preserve its going-concern value while the FDIC seeks a more permanent solution to its problems.

Under 12 U.S.C. §1821(m) the FDIC may establish a "new" national bank to take over the operations of failed institutions. The FDIC operates the new bank and provides it with sufficient cash to cover the insured deposits and reasonable operating expenses. The FDIC is then expected to solicit new private capital for the institution by a stock offering with prior subscription rights being given to the stockholders of the failed institution. 12 U.S.C. §1821(m)(15). If the stock offering fails, the FDIC must arrange a purchase and assumption transaction or wind up the affairs of the new bank within two years after the date of its organization.

Bridge banks, authorized under 12 U.S.C. §1821(n), are designed as temporary repositories of the business of a failed institution during a period in which the FDIC is attempting to arrange a permanent resolution of the institution. These institutions, chartered as national banks and insured by the FDIC, are managed by a board of directors appointed by the FDIC. They are not required to operate with any capital, although they may issue stock if necessary. Operating funds in lieu of capital are provided by the FDIC. Bridge banks acquire the assets and liabilities—or selected assets and liabilities—of the failed institution by means of purchase and assumption transactions.

Bridge banks are generally required to terminate operations within two years, either by purchase and assumption transaction with a solvent institution, "privatization" through sale of stock to nongovernmental entities, or dissolution by means of a receivership. Because a bridge bank is merely a temporary measure, it might more accurately be classified as a holding action rather than an independent resolution procedure, since it is evident that some other resolution procedure will be necessary at the end of the bridge bank's life.

*QUESTIONS AND COMMENTS*

What regulatory advantages do bridge banks provide that are not already provided by conservatorships? Compare the status of creditor claims against both types of institution.

## 5. *Choice Among Alternative Strategies: The Cost Test*

How is the FDIC to decide among the various alternatives available? The answer is clear in principle, although it is often obscure in fact: The agency is generally required to apply a "cost test" and adopt the resolution procedure that, all things considered, will impose the lowest costs on the deposit insurance funds. See 12 U.S.C. §1823(c)(4). In addition, a cost test is clearly implied by the fiduciary status of the FDIC; as a fiduciary, this institution has a duty to creditors (including the FDIC-corporate with respect to its claims as deposit insurer) and thus is obligated to take such actions as it believes will maximize the value of the assets under its control.

As fleshed out in the FDICIA, 12 U.S.C. §1823(c)(4), the FDIC, in resolving depository institution failures, must determine that the exercise of the authority in question is "necessary to meet the obligation of the [FDIC] to provide insurance coverage for the insured deposits," and that the total amount of the expenditures made and obligations incurred by the FDIC in connection with the resolution "is the least costly to the deposit insurance fund of all possible methods of meeting the [FDIC's] obligation. . . ." The statute instructs the FDIC to discount alternatives to present value and to document its analysis under the cost test and the assumptions on which that evaluation rests. In a potentially important provision, the FDIC is required, as of year-end 1994, to refrain from any action "that would have the effect of increasing losses to any insurance fund by protecting . . . depositors for more than the insured portion of deposits [or] creditors other than depositors." 12 U.S.C. §1823 (c)(4)(E)(i). Standing by itself, this provision might appear to cast serious doubt on the FDIC's habit of protecting all depositors of failed banks, insured or not. However, the statute goes on to provide that uninsured depositors may be protected in purchase and assumption transactions so long as the acquiring institution's commitment to honor the uninsured portion of the deposits does not increase the costs of the resolution as compared with the loss that would have been incurred had the institution been liquidated. 12 U.S.C. §1823(c)(4)(E)(iii).

Equally, if not more important, is the bearing of the cost test on the "too big to fail" doctrine. Historically, federal banking agencies have been unwilling to close banking institutions that were so large as to raise concerns about the stability of the banking system as a whole if they were closed. Continental Illinois National Bank & Trust Co., for example, was considered to be too big to fail when it ran into its difficulties in 1984; the federal regulators engineered an open bank assistance rescue largely because of their fear that the failure of such a mammoth institution would undermine public confidence in banks generally. The "too big to fail" doctrine has been extremely controversial, largely because it appeared to give a special benefit to large banks at the expense of smaller institutions that could be allowed to fail without risk to the banking system as a whole.

In the 1991 FDICIA legislation, Congress significantly restricted the scope of the "too big to fail" doctrine by applying the cost test to large as well as small failures, subject only to a narrow exception for failures involving "systemic risk." If an institution is considered too big to fail, so that the cost test cannot (in the view of the banking agencies) be narrowly applied without incurring excessive systemic risk, they may dispense with the cost text, but only if the board of directors of the FDIC (by two-thirds vote) and the Federal Reserve Board (by two-thirds vote) so recommend in writing, and the secretary of the treasury, in consultation with the president, determines that compliance with the cost test "would have serious adverse effects on economic conditions or financial stability" and that the planned action or assistance "would avoid or mitigate such adverse effects." 12 U.S.C. §1823(c)(4)(G). Any losses to an FDIC insurance fund stemming from a "too big to fail" rescue must be expeditiously recovered out of a special assessment on the members of the fund, and any such rescue must be investigated by the General Accounting Office. Id.

## *QUESTIONS AND COMMENTS*

1. Consider the following criticism of open bank assistance:

> the FDIC's current method of calculating costs is flawed. Under the current method, the FDIC compares the costs of open bank assistance directly with such other regulatory alternatives as liquidating the bank. The problem with this method of calculation is that it does not take into account error costs—the probability that the bank ultimately fails despite the FDIC cash infusion. When this happens, the ultimate costs to the FDIC of paying off shareholders must be layered onto the costs of the initial open bank assistance. While the insolvency costs may be mitigated to some extent by the earlier cash infusion, some significant costs are not overlapping. . . . Thus, once the FDIC reaches its initial calculation of the costs of using open bank assistance under its current methodology, it should then generate an estimate of the costs that the FDIC will incur if the open bank assistance program ultimately does not work, and then multiply this figure by the probability of such a failure occurring. This figure should then be added to the initial calculation of costs of using open bank assistance. . . .

Macey & Miller, Bank Failures, Risk Monitoring, and the Market for Bank Control, 88 Colum. L. Rev. 1153, 1177-1178 (1988). Do you agree with this analysis?

2. How reliable are the FDIC's estimates of the "least cost" resolution procedure? Is the FDIC's strong preference for purchase and assumption transactions consistent with the agency's responsibilities under the cost test?

3. What if a party believes that the FDIC has in fact not used the least cost approach to resolving a failure? Is there any way to challenge the erroneous decision in court on the ground that some other resolution procedure should be or should have been used? Most courts have held that the decision of what mechanism to use is within the FDIC's sole discretion. See, e.g., Super X Drugs v. FDIC, 862 F.2d 1252, 1255 (6th Cir. 1988); FDIC v. Bank of Boulder, 911 F.2d 1466, 1469 (10th Cir. 1990), *cert. denied,* 499 U.S. 904 (1991) (dicta).

4. As we will see, persons with claims against an insolvent institution stand to lose important rights and defenses if the FDIC decides to effect a purchase and assumption transaction. Does the potential loss of these rights and defenses create standing to challenge the FDIC's decisions? What policy might inform a judicial decision to deny borrowers standing in a case like this?

5. The FDIC must in theory sell a failed depository institution's assets in a fair auction to the highest responsible bidder. Does a disappointed bidder have any rights if the agency awards the assets to a competitor who may have submitted a lower bid? Getty v. FSLIC, 805 F.2d 1050 (D.C. Cir. 1986), was an action by a disappointed bidder claiming that the FSLIC had failed to consider applicable statutory priorities (which favored in-state bidders over out-of-state ones). The court agreed and required the agency to conduct a new auction. While *Getty* provides some solace for disappointed bidders, it should be noted that the case turned on the existence of explicit statutory priorities and on the FSLIC's failure to provide an adequate contemporaneous record indicating that it had actually considered the priorities. These are special factors that are not likely to arise in the standard purchase and assumption transaction in which the principal issues are the amounts of the bids and the responsibility of the bidders. The FDIC is likely to receive a great deal of deference from the courts with respect to its evaluation of these issues.

6. How significant do you think the FDICIA provisions will be in pruning back the reach of the "too big to fail" doctrine?

## D. MARSHALING OF ASSETS

### 1. *Introduction*

As we have noted, one of the principal jobs for a receiver is to marshal the assets of the failed institution. This means identifying all property of any value, including (among other things) ownership of real property, financial contracts, leasehold rights, contract rights, insurance claims, and potential legal claims for damages. The receiver must then liquidate the assets to obtain cash to pay out to the creditors. In disposing of failed bank assets, the FDIC is required to conduct its operations in a manner that, inter alia, "maximizes the net present value return from the sale or disposition" and "minimizes the amount of any loss realized in the resolution of cases." 12 U.S.C. §§1821(d)(3), 1821(d)(13).

For the most part the FDIC acts in a traditional receivership role in marshaling the assets. There are, however, a number of special problems or rules that are unique to banking law. We discuss three of these special situations: (1) insurance claims under directors and officers liability policies or bankers blanket bonds; (2) cross-guarantees between affiliates within a financial institution; and (3) banking rules applicable to the recovery of fraudulent conveyances.

## 2. *Insurance Litigation*

One of the more important assets the FDIC acquires when appointed as receiver or conservator of a failed depository institution is the legal claims that that institution may possess against officers, directors, and others who may have contributed to the institution's downfall. We discussed these claims in Chapter 7, insofar as they related to the enforcement of banking law and regulations. Now we consider them as they bear on the marshaling of assets under some failure regime.

The real party in interest in most of these cases is the former institution's insurance carrier, either under a bankers bond or under a policy of directors and officers liability insurance. Most depository institutions carry both types of coverage, which apply—in theory at least—to different forms of misconduct. Bankers bonds cover fraudulent or illegal conduct, but typically exclude all forms of negligence; directors and officers liability insurance covers negligence or gross negligence, but typically excludes intentional or criminal misconduct. Thus if an officer has embezzled funds, the loss will be covered by the bankers bond; if instead the officer has failed to exercise due diligence in the conduct of the institution's affairs, the loss will come from the directors and officers liability insurance policy.

Insurance companies, facing massive and unforeseen liabilities on their policies, have attempted under a variety of exclusions to avoid paying out on directors and officers liability insurance policies. Consider the following case.

### FDIC v. American Casualty Co.

***998 F.2d 404 (7th Cir. 1993)***

KANNE, J.: . . .

On February 26, 1986, Joe Gibson filed a shareholder derivative action against the then directors of the State Bank of Cuba ("Bank")—Wayne Grove, Linda Grove, Margie Zaborac, George Baylor, Henry Tarter, and Chester Jacobus—alleging that certain lending policies and practices constituted mismanagement of the Bank. When the Commissioner of Banks and Trust Companies of the State of Illinois subsequently determined that the Bank was insolvent and ordered it closed, the FDIC was appointed the Bank's receiver. By virtue of its status as receiver, the FDIC succeeded to the rights of the Bank and its shareholders, one of which is the ability to sue the Bank's directors and officers. The FDIC, in its corporate capacity, purchased from the FDIC, in its receiver capacity, all of the Bank's assets, including any claims against the Bank's directors and officers.

As a result of the receivership and the subsequent sale and assumption transaction, the FDIC was substituted as plaintiff in Joe Gibson's shareholder derivative claim and the case was removed to federal court. The FDIC filed a complaint alleging, as did Gibson's complaint, that the directors had negligently mismanaged the Bank. Ultimately, the FDIC obtained a default judgment in the amount of $1,194,822.27 against Wayne and Linda Grove, two of the director defendants.

However, the Groves filed for bankruptcy, and the FDIC was only permitted to seek satisfaction of the judgment from the Groves' insurer. . . . The Groves, as well as the other director defendants, were the subject of a directors' and officers' liability insurance contract ("Policy") between the Bank and [American Casualty Co. (ACC)]. The Policy provided coverage for losses stemming from "any actual or alleged error, misleading statement, act or omission, or neglect or breach of duty by the Directors and Officers in the discharge of their duties. . . ."

[T]he FDIC [attempted] to obtain Policy proceeds in satisfaction of the judgment against the Groves. . . . ACC asserted that the Policy did not cover the FDIC's judgment . . . ACC moved for summary judgment on the grounds that two provisions of the contract excluded coverage, the regulatory agency exclusion and the insured versus insured exclusion. . . .

The regulatory agency exclusion . . . provides as follows: "It is understood and agreed that the Insurer shall not be liable to make any payment for Loss in connection with any claim made against the Directors of [sic] Officers based upon or attributable to: any action or proceeding brought by or on behalf of the Federal Deposit Insurance Corporation, the Federal Savings & Loan Insurance Corporation, any other depository insurance organization, the Comptroller of the Currency, the Federal Home Loan Bank Board, or any other national or state regulatory agency (all of said organizations and agencies hereinafter referred to as "Agencies"), including any type of legal action which such Agencies have the legal right to bring as receiver, conservator, liquidator, or otherwise; whether such action is brought in the name of such Agencies or by or on behalf of such Agencies in the name of any other entity or solely in the name of any Third Party."

[The FDIC focuses] on the regulatory agency provision's language which excludes "any action or proceeding brought by or on behalf of the Federal Deposit Insurance Corporation." As mentioned, Gibson filed the original shareholder derivative action, and after its appointment as receiver, the FDIC was substituted as the plaintiff. . . . As such, the FDIC argues that it merely maintained Gibson's suit against the directors, and consequently the default judgment falls outside the language of the provision that excludes actions "brought" by the FDIC. . . . After reviewing the Policy as a whole, we agree . . . that the interpretation advanced by the FDIC is overly technical and unreasonable, and we hold that the regulatory agency provision unambiguously excludes coverage of the FDIC's judgment.

In addition to the regulatory agency provision, . . . the Policy contains an insured versus insured provision which excludes from coverage: "Loss . . . which is based upon or attributable to any claim made against any Director or Officer by any other Director or Officer or by the [Bank] . . . except for a shareholder derivative action brought by a shareholder of the Institution other than an Insured."

As a former director and officer, Gibson was considered an "insured" under the Policy. Consequently, even though his action was a shareholder derivative suit, if the FDIC had not been substituted as the plaintiff, the insured versus insured provision would have excluded from coverage any damages owed to Gibson by the Groves. In addition, the plain language . . . would have excluded from coverage an action by the Bank itself against the directors or officers. Finally, as earlier discussed, the regulatory agency provision without question excludes actions filed by the FDIC.

We refuse to conclude that, by excluding all losses resulting from claims filed by the FDIC and excluding all losses resulting from shareholder derivative claims made by insured shareholders, the parties intended to create a loophole in the exclusion that provided coverage for shareholder derivative actions filed by an insured shareholder and later maintained by the FDIC. Rather, when read in conjunction with the regulatory provision's latter phrase that excludes losses resulting from all legal actions the FDIC has a right to bring as receiver, the Policy's broad language excluding "any action or proceeding brought by or on behalf of the [FDIC]" can only be interpreted as excluding the default judgment at issue. . . .

The FDIC contends that even if the regulatory agency exclusion bars coverage of the current action, the court should not enforce that provision because to do so would violate federal public policy. . . . According to the FDIC, [FIRREA] codifies a federal public policy which prohibits the enforcement of the regulatory agency exclusion. The FDIC argues that it brought this action against the Bank through the powers granted by the following section of FIRREA: "The [FDIC] shall, as conservator or receiver, and by operation of law, succeed to (i) all rights, titles, powers, and privileges of the insured depository institution, and of any stockholder, member, accountholder, depositor, officer, or director of such institution with respect to the institution and assets of the institution." 12 U.S.C. §1821(d)(2)(A)(i). As the receiver, the FDIC possesses all the rights of the Bank's shareholders, including the right to sue directors and officers. Under the Policy, ACC would cover any loss relating to shareholder derivative claims. Thus, the FDIC reasons that when the FDIC obtained a judgment against the Groves in its capacity as shareholder, it should have been able to garnish the proceeds of the Policy to the same extent as could any other uninsured shareholder. According to FDIC, enforcing the regulatory agency exclusion would deprive it of the same rights afforded to shareholders under the Policy, in violation of a clear public policy embodied in §1821(d)(2)(A)(i).

[Enforcement of the regulatory agency exclusion does not violate public policy.] In enacting FIRREA, Congress considered and rejected the inclusion of "a provision that the FDIC could require contracts, including [director's and officer's] liability policies, to remain in effect even if the contract contained a provision terminating the contract upon the appointment of the FDIC as a conservator or receiver." . . . Instead, [in 12 U.S.C. §1821(e)(12)] Congress enacted the following provision:

"(A) In general. The conservator or receiver may enforce any contract, other than a director's or officer's liability insurance contracts . . ., entered into by the depository institution notwithstanding any provision of the contract providing for termination, default, acceleration, or exercise of rights upon, or solely by reason of, insolvency or the appointment of a conservator or receiver.

"(B) Certain rights not affected. No provision of this paragraph may be construed as impairing or affecting any right of the conservator or receiver to enforce or recover under a director's or officer's liability insurance contract or depository institution bond under other applicable law."

The enactment of §1821(e)(12) evidences Congress' intent to remain neutral on regulatory exclusions and completely rebuts the FDIC's argument that the enforcement of such clauses violates a public policy embodied in a different subsection of the same provision. . . . Consequently, the district court correctly held that enforcement of the regulatory exclusion does not violate any well-defined public policy. . . .

*QUESTIONS AND COMMENTS*

1. This case considers two of the most important exclusions in insurance coverage disputes when the FDIC sues former officers or directors of a failed depository institution: the insured vs. insured exclusion and the regulatory exclusion. These are standard in directors and officers policies, and accordingly they tend to receive a fairly uniform interpretation in the courts. Most if not all reported decisions are consistent with the excerpted case.

2. Another relevant exclusion in directors and officers policies is the exclusion for fraud, dishonesty, or criminal activity (such conduct is usually picked up by the bankers bond). Complicated coverage issues may arise under this exclusion if the director or officer is accused of

fraud, dishonesty, or criminality but is not finally adjudicated to have engaged in such behavior (note that the FDIC might not want the Department of Justice to prosecute bank officers or directors criminally if the consequence is to trigger the fraud or dishonesty exclusion).

3. Different issues arise under bankers bonds. These typically cover losses to the depository institution resulting directly from dishonest or fraudulent acts committed by bank employees (coverage extends to losses caused by any employee, not just officers and directors). The key coverage issues under bankers bonds include the following:

*Losses discovered during bond period.* Bankers bonds typically cover only losses actually discovered by the insured during the bond period. If the insured discovers an employee's defalcation only after the bond terminates, there is no coverage. Further, the bonds usually terminate immediately upon the appointment of a receiver or conservator. Thus if the FDIC discovers employee dishonesty only after being appointed as a fiduciary, there may be no coverage. Again, however, a court might refuse to enforce this limitation on grounds of public policy. The provision for coverage termination might also be challenged by the FDIC as an invalid ipso facto clause under 12 U.S.C. §1821(e)(12)(A), as discussed above.

*Losses resulting from employee "manifest intent."* Typically, bankers bonds cover only losses due to actions taken by an employee with "manifest intent" to cause the institution to sustain loss and to obtain financial benefit for a person or entity other than the institution. Coverage issues arise when the employee acted dishonestly but did not clearly seek a personal benefit. These problems can be particularly severe given that if the behavior was dishonest, it may fall within an exclusion from the directors and officers liability policy as well, leaving the depository institution bereft of coverage.

*Losses resulting directly from dishonesty or fraud.* Bankers bonds may exclude coverage for loan losses that are not directly the result of employee dishonesty or fraud. Because loan losses are usually the principal reason a depository institution fails, the FDIC is likely to push for reimbursement under the bond for loan losses on the ground that the loss was caused by an employee's dishonesty. The insurer may disclaim coverage on the ground that the loss was due to the borrower's default and not to employee dishonesty.

## 3. *Cross-Guarantees*

Failed depository institutions are often parts of bank holding companies. When a subsidiary bank within a holding company runs into difficulty, does the holding company itself or any of its other subsidiaries have any responsibility—or indeed, any power—to assist the subsidiary?

Outside the banking field, in the ordinary corporate law context, the general rule is that neither a parent firm nor any "siblings" have the obligation to support a failing subsidiary. Indeed, the parent institution will often lack the power to help out a subsidiary even if it wanted to. Such assistance might constitute a violation of fiduciary duties owed by the board of directors of the parent organization to the parent's shareholders (if the assistance is not in the best interests of the parent) or to minority shareholders in other subsidiary corporations (if the parent causes the assistance to come from a subsidiary).

If a corporate subsidiary fails, its creditors have claims only against the subsidiary's assets. The parent corporation will lose all value of its investment in the subsidiary, of course, but will not be required to dip into its own assets, or the assets of other subsidiaries, for the benefit of the subsidiary's creditors.

There are, of course, exceptions to this general rule. The creditors may attempt to "pierce the corporate veil" by claiming that the parent and subsidiary should be treated as one entity. American courts, however, are quite diligent at protecting the corporate form and will allow veil-piercing, even for wholly owned subsidiaries, only in unusual cases, such as when the subsidiary is grossly undercapitalized or corporate formalities have not been observed. Because of the highly regulated nature of banking, these conditions will rarely, if ever, be present in the case of a depository institution failure. Creditors of a failed subsidiary may also proceed against the parent's assets if they (or, in bankruptcy proceedings, the bankruptcy trustee) can establish the existence of a transfer from subsidiary to parent that satisfies the criteria for a fraudulent conveyance under the Uniform Fraudulent Conveyance Act, the Uniform Fraudulent Transfer Act, or the Bankruptcy Code. The Bankruptcy Code does not apply to depository institution failures, however, 11 U.S.C. §109(b)(2), and in general the provisions of the uniform acts will not be implicated because of the stringent regulatory restrictions on transfers between affiliates within a holding company structure under the Bank Holding Company Act.

In general, therefore, it might appear that creditors of a failed depository institution, including the FDIC-corporate, have little recourse against the assets of affiliates. However, this impression would not be entirely accurate. The Federal Reserve Board has long advocated a "source of strength" policy, under which a holding company is obligated to assist subsidiary depository institutions that were in danger of failing. The board asserted regulatory power to enforce this policy under its general authority to ensure that bank holding companies act in a safe and sound manner. When the source of strength policy was tested, however, it was repudiated by the Fifth Circuit Court of Appeals in the *MCorp* case, which we discussed in Chapter 7. The appeals court held that the policy was in excess of the board's regulatory jurisdiction and, if enforced, would require the holding company to violate fiduciary duties to its own shareholders. The Supreme Court, however, held that the lower courts lacked jurisdiction over the issue in the procedural posture in which the case arose, leaving the underlying substantive issue unresolved. See MCorp Financial, Inc. v. Board of Governors of the Federal Reserve System, 900 F.2d 852 (5th Cir. 1990), *reversed on other grounds,* 502 U.S. 32 (1991).

In a related policy, the FDIC sometimes attempted to obtain payments from solvent banks in a holding company structure for the losses associated with failures of other subsidiary banks. The FDIC claimed the right to discriminate among creditors, paying out only liquidation value on the claims of solvent affiliate banks while paying out significantly more—usually 100 percent—on other creditors' claims. In practice, the FDIC's policy sometimes ensured the failure of all banks in the holding company. This too was rejected by the courts. MBank New Braunfels v. FDIC, 721 F. Supp. 120 (N.D. Tex. 1989); Texas American Bancshares v. Clarke, 740 F. Supp. 1243 (N.D. Tex. 1990).

An important provision in FIRREA, however, fundamentally changed the ground rules in future cases. Under 12 U.S.C. §1815(e), any insured depository institution "shall be liable for any loss incurred by the [FDIC], or any loss which the [FDIC] reasonably anticipates incurring" in connection with the default of a commonly controlled insured depository institution, or any assistance provided by the FDIC to a commonly controlled depository institution in danger of default. The statute provides that this right of the FDIC is superior to the claims of the affiliated depository institution's shareholders, including the holding company and shareholders and creditors of the holding company. The FDIC's rights are also stated to be superior to debt claims by affiliates. The FDIC's claim under §1815(e) is junior to all other claims against the affiliated institution, including those of depositors, secured creditors, senior creditors, general creditors, and subordinated creditors. There are a series of transition rules for the phase-in of this "cross guarantee" provision. Supplementing the cross-guarantee rule is 12 U.S.C. §1821(i), giving explicit authority to the FDIC to discriminate among creditors so long as all creditors receive at least liquidation value.

## *QUESTIONS AND COMMENTS*

1. Observe that the source of strength doctrine was directed at the parent holding company, while the cross-guarantee provision is directed at affiliated depository institutions and not (directly) at holding companies. What forms of bank ownership are captured by the cross-guarantee rule that were not included in the source of strength policy?

2. Why didn't Congress codify the source of strength policy in FIRREA? Because the Federal Reserve Board was already enforcing it

administratively? Did Congress overlook the fact that the board's policy might not survive judicial scrutiny?

3. Do you see any constitutional difficulties with the cross-guarantee rule? How can the federal government simply insert itself in the priority hierarchy above existing interests without the payment of just compensation?

4. Is the cross-guarantee rule a good idea as a matter of policy? In light of the cross-guarantee rule, what is likely to happen to solvent banks within a holding company structure when another subsidiary bank runs into trouble? Does this consideration suggest that the cross-guarantee rule in FIRREA might actually indirectly accomplish something like the board's source of strength policy?

5. There is empirical evidence that depository institutions within substantial holding companies do better than other depository institutions. See Howell E. Jackson, The Superior Performance of Savings and Loan Associations with Substantial Holding Companies, 22 Journal of Legal Studies 405 (1993). Professor Jackson views the growth of holding company obligations as an important trend in American financial institutions law. See Howell E. Jackson, The Expanding Obligations of Financial Holding Companies, 107 Harvard Law Review 507 (1994). Professor Jackson argues that "[w]hether in the supervision of the bank and thrift industries or in the regulation of private pension plans, enhanced obligations are best understood as a response to real and often severe inadequacies in our current regulatory structure for financial intermediaries." The theoretical justification for such enhanced obligations, in his view, is that "these rules force financial holding companies to bear a greater share of the costs associated with the failures of regulated subsidiaries and that this cost-internalization prompts more efficient holding company supervision and control of risk-taking in those subsidiaries. Under this regime, primary-level oversight of financial institutions is provided by the holding companies, which can perform this function far more efficiently than government regulators." Id. at 612. What do you think of this theory? If expanding obligations work for financial institution holding companies, why not allow "veil-piercing" for wholly owned corporations generally? Wouldn't such a regime tend to internalize the costs associated with insolvency of the subsidiary in nonfinancial settings?

## 4. *Voidable Preferences and Fraudulent Transfers*

What if a depository institution in shaky financial condition pays off one of its creditors preferentially, to the detriment of other creditors after the institution has failed? Under 12 U.S.C. §91, transfers by a national bank "in contemplation of [insolvency], made with a view to . . . preference of one creditor to another . . . shall be utterly null and void. . . ." If such a transfer does occur, the receiver may institute an action to recover the amounts transferred in order to bring them back into the receivership estate.

Moreover, the FDIC as conservator or receiver and any other party appointed as conservator, may avoid a transfer by an institution-affiliated party, or by a debtor of the institution, or any obligation incurred by such parties, made within five years of the date of the appointment of the fiduciary if the purpose of the transaction was to "hinder, delay, or defraud" the institution or the appointed fiduciary. 12 U.S.C. §1821(d)(17). Thus, for example, if a person qualifying as an institution-affiliated party transfers wealth to a spouse, child, or other person to avoid having to pay money to the FDIC as receiver of a failed bank, the FDIC may be able to undo the transaction and recover the money.

There is also explicit statutory authority under FIRREA for the avoidance of security interests "taken in contemplation of the institution's insolvency or with the intent to hinder, delay, or defraud the institution or the creditors of such institution." 12 U.S.C. §1821(e)(11) (FDIC-insured institutions). Note that this language tracks 12 U.S.C. §91 with respect to interests created in contemplation of insolvency, but appears to go beyond the earlier statute by allowing avoidance of security interests created with the intent to "hinder, delay or defraud" the institution or its creditors.

In addition, it seems clear that the FDIC may exercise the traditional powers of receivers and conservators to avoid transfers made in contemplation of insolvency.

These powers to avoid conveyances in contemplation of insolvency have not generated much litigation in recent years, largely because in most purchase and assumption transactions all creditors have been made whole. The likelihood that all creditors will be made whole reduces the incentive an institution's officers might otherwise have to make a transfer in contemplation of insolvency; even if such transfers are made, there will be no damages unless some creditor is not paid in full. It appears, however, that the rules on transfers in contemplation of insolvency—and especially the rules respecting creation of security interests—will increase in significance as more and more insolvencies are resolved by means other than the purchase and assumption transaction in which all liabilities are assumed by the purchasing institution.

### *QUESTIONS AND COMMENTS*

1. You represent a lender that is considering whether to advance credit to a depository institution. Because the institution is in shaky financial condition, your client is unwilling to extend credit unless it is fully secured by marketable collateral. The potential borrower is quite

willing to pledge collateral for such a loan. What would you advise the lender regarding the potential legal risks incident to the transaction?

2. 12 U.S.C. §91 applies to transfers "in contemplation of [insolvency]" made "with a view to" frustrating the distribution scheme under the National Bank Act or preferring one creditor over another. What if after a transfer in contemplation of insolvency, the defendant claims that he did not intend to frustrate the statute or prefer one creditor over another? See FDIC v. Goldberg, 906 F.2d 1087 (5th Cir. 1990) (statute incorporates common law principle that one intends the natural and probable consequences of one's acts).

## 5. *Claims Against Bankrupt Debtors*

What happens when the debtor against whom the FDIC is asserting claims happens to be in the midst of bankruptcy proceedings? We then enter a complex maze of puzzles that relate federal depository institution receivership law with federal bankruptcy law. Courts have struggled to reconcile these two comprehensive statutory schemes.

The filing of a bankruptcy petition triggers an automatic stay of litigation affecting the debtor. 11 U.S.C. §362. Is the FDIC subject to this stay when it seeks to enforce claims against the bankrupt debtor—for example by foreclosing a mortgage? Under 12 U.S.C. §1821(j), no court may restrain or affect the FDIC's exercise of its powers as receiver. How, then, can the receiver be subjected to a stay by the bankruptcy court? On the other hand it would not appear sensible to allow the receiver to avoid a stay applicable to all other creditors of the debtor and thus obtain a priority to which it is not otherwise entitled. The statutes might be reconciled on the ground that the bankruptcy stay occurs automatically, by operation of law, and therefore there is no violation of the anti-injunction provision in §1821(j). If the receiver persists in ignoring the bankruptcy stay, however, the statutory conflict may be unavoidable because the bankruptcy trustee would then have no recourse but to attempt to enjoin the FDIC from proceeding.

Other problems concern jurisdiction of the respective bank failure and bankruptcy proceedings. Section 1823(d) establishes a comprehensive procedure for determining claims against the FDIC by creditors of failed depository institutions—a procedure which generally requires that claims be submitted first to the administrative process before they are adjudicated in court. When a *debtor* of a failed depository institution is in the midst of its own bankruptcy proceedings and asserts some right to offset against the receiver's or conservator's claim, the depository institution receiver may argue that the claim for offset must be submitted to the receivership for resolution. A requirement that the debtor exhaust its remedy in the depository institution receivership might interfere with the orderly disposition of the debtor's estate in the bankrutpcy process. See, e.g., Parker North American Corp. v. RTC, 24 F.3d 1145 (9th Cir. 1994). These issues are still being thrashed out in the courts, and clarification will undoubtedly take a long time.

## E. DISTRIBUTION TO CREDITORS

The previous section considered how a receiver marshals the assets of a failed institution. Once marshaled, how are these assets distributed to creditors? We address that general problem in this section. We look first at the statutory claims procedures, then at the standards for determining claims, and finally at the rules regarding the establishment of priorities among claimants.

### *1. Statutory Claims Procedures*

The procedures to be followed by the FDIC or RTC in depository institution receiverships are set forth in detail in 12 U.S.C. §1821(d). The first step is to determine what claims exist. To that end, the receiver publishes notices informing creditors of the receivership and inviting them to present their claims. The receiver also mails notice to creditors shown on the institution's books. 12 U.S.C. §1821(d)(3).

The next step is to determine whether or not the claim is valid, a matter of much controversy in recent years. In Coit Independence Joint Venture v. FSLIC, 489 U.S. 561 (1989), the Supreme Court held that creditors had the right to de novo judicial adjudication of claims against a federal savings and loan in FSLIC receivership. Thus creditors did not have to content themselves with judicial review of an administrative determination under the "arbitrary or capricious" standard. Although the Court's decision was formally based on statutory analysis, it was heavily influenced by constitutional concerns about vesting the core business of "Article III" federal courts in an administrative agency. As Justice O'Connor said for the Court, the relevant statutes "can and should be read to avoid these [serious constitutional] difficulties."

In a second part of its decision, the Court in *Coit Independence* ruled that a claimant was not required to exhaust administrative remedies. According to the Court, administrative remedies were "inadequate" because FSLIC had failed to adopt any procedures to guarantee prompt agency consideration of claims. Thus the claimant did not have to wait for the FSLIC to determine its claims administratively before seeking de novo judicial review.

A few months later, in FIRREA, Congress adopted a new claims procedure that addressed the problems identified in *Coit Independence.* First, Congress required that claims be presented in the administrative process. See 12 U.S.C. §1821(d)(6)(A) (requiring that before a lawsuit against an institution in receivership can be filed or continued, the claimant must have filed a claim with the receiver and received an initial determination); 12 U.S.C. §1821(d)(5)(C) (in general, claims not filed with the receiver in a timely fashion are forfeited); 12 U.S.C. §1821(d)(13)(D) (limiting judicial review to procedures expressly provided in 12 U.S.C. §1821(d)); 12 U.S.C. §1821(j) (generally prohibiting courts from restraining or affecting the exercise of powers or functions of the FDIC as conservator or receiver).

A somewhat different procedure appears to be established for judicial actions filed *before* a receiver or conservator is appointed, although, as with so much else in FIRREA, uncertainties abound. Under 12 U.S.C. §1821(d)(12), courts, upon request by the receiver, are required to stay for 90 days (45 days in the case of a conservatorship) any litigation to which the depository institution is a party at the time the receiver is appointed. Presumably the litigant must present its claim in the administrative process if a stay is granted. Section 1821(d)(5)(ii) provides that, subject to the provision for a stay of litigation, "the filing of a claim with the receiver shall not prejudice any right of the claimant to continue any action which was filed before the appointment of the receiver." The statute is not entirely clear as to the consequences if the receiver or conservator does not request a stay. Arguably the litigation should then proceed in court without regard to the statutory claims procedure, see Whatley v. RTC, 32 F.3d 905 (5th Cir. 1994), but some courts hold that claimants are required to present their claims in the administrative process even if the agency does not request a stay of preappointment litigation; this is equivalent to a conclusion that the statute does not establish any special procedures for preappointment lawsuits. See, e.g., Intercontinental Travel Marketing, Inc. v. FDIC, 45 F.3d 1278 (9th Cir. 1994).

As the second step in the claims procedure, Congress set forth relatively strict deadlines within which the receiver is required to act—an apparent response to the Supreme Court's opinion in *Coit Independence,* which had refused to require exhaustion of administrative remedies under prior law due to the lack of such deadlines. Under current law, the receiver must allow or disallow a claim within 180 days. 12 U.S.C. §1821(d)(5)(A)(i). The receiver makes its initial determination on the claim without hearing, but if the claim is disallowed, the receiver must send notice to the claimant stating the reasons for the disallowance and disclosing the available procedures for challenging the determination.

Third, once the initial determination is made, a new set of procedures for administrative or judicial review kicks in. A disappointed claimant may—but need not—seek administrative review of the initial decision by filing a petition with the agency. The receiver may grant a formal adjudicative hearing on the record, with judicial review under the Administrative Procedure Act. 12 U.S.C. §1821(d)(7)(A). Alternatively, the receiver and the claimant may agree to use an informal dispute resolution procedure (such as binding or nonbinding arbitration). 12 U.S.C. §1821(d)(7)(B). The statute also establishes an expedited claims process for persons who allege that they possess perfected security interests and that they will suffer irreparable injury if the standard procedures are used. 12 U.S.C. §1821(d)(8).

The claimant is not required to seek administrative review of the initial determination. Instead, a disappointed claimant may file suit (or continue an existing action) in the federal district court where the depository institution is located. 12 U.S.C. §1821(d)(6)(A). Although the statute does not provide so explicitly, it would appear that a court will review agency determinations de novo in such an action, as required under prior law in *Coit Independence.* De novo review would certainly satisfy the Supreme Court's constitutional qualms about divesting Article III judges of their core responsibilities; whether any less stringent standard of review would pass constitutional muster is uncertain. However, FIRREA also provided, mysteriously, that "[t]he receiver may disallow any portion of any claim by a creditor or claim of security, preference, or priority which is not proved to the satisfaction of the receiver," and "[n]o court may review the [receiver's] determination pursuant to [this authorization] to disallow a claim." 12 U.S.C. §1821(d)(5)(D)-(E).

Under FIRREA, jurisdiction over challenges to the receiver's disallowance of a claim will in almost all cases lie in federal court—even though in many cases the substantive basis of the claim will arise under state law. Under 12 U.S.C. §1819(b)(2)(A), "all suits of a civil nature at common law or in equity to which the [FDIC], in any capacity, is a party shall be deemed to arise under the laws of the United States." Thus jurisdiction over such suits is provided by 28 U.S.C. §1331 (giving federal district courts original jurisdiction over cases arising under federal law). The FDIC may remove such actions from state court to federal court. 12 U.S.C. §1819(b)(2)(B). There is only a limited exception to this federal jurisdiction for cases in which the FDIC acts as receiver for a state-*insured* depository institution; because almost all institutions are insured by the FDIC and not by the states, this proviso will almost never apply.

## *QUESTIONS AND COMMENTS*

1. Section 1823(d)(12)(B) provides that upon request by a conservator or receiver for a stay of any judicial action, the court "shall grant such stay as to all parties." Does this language really mean what it says?

What if the FDIC waits six months after being appointed receiver before requesting a stay? What if the plaintiffs are in danger of imminent and irreparable harm from delay and the FDIC would suffer no apparent prejudice if the litigation were allowed to go forward?

2. Could there be due process as well as Article III problems with allowing the FDIC as receiver to adjudicate claims against a failed institution, subject only to lenient judicial scrutiny under the Administrative Procedure Act? Why might a claimant distrust the FDIC's impartiality in this context?

3. What happens if the agency fails to act on a claim within 180 days? Should the claim be deemed allowed? Disallowed? Should the claimant be required to seek a judicial determination at this point?

## 2. *Determination of Claims*

In discussing the statutory procedures for determination of claims, we passed over for the moment the *grounds* on which a claim might be allowed or disallowed. In general, a claim is evaluated according to the same legal rules as would apply outside the receivership context. If the claimant has a good claim against the institution, the claim will be allowed. But if the claim is invalid for any reason—barred by the statute of limitations, unsupported by applicable law, factually unjustified, and so forth—it will be denied. There are, however, several special rules in this area of which the student should be aware.

First, traditional banking law states that the claim, to be provable against the receiver, must be "fixed" at the time of insolvency. If the claim is not fixed—arising from facts occurring prior to the insolvency and not dependent on post-insolvency events to establish its existence or amount—it might, under traditional banking law principles, be denied altogether.

Second, a most important exception to the general rule that claims are determined within receivership proceedings according to the same legal standards that would apply outside the receivership is the rule denying enforceability to certain agreements that tend to diminish or defeat the rights of the FDIC in receivership assets. We defer discussion of this rule to Section F of this chapter. We do so because the rule relates, not only to the resolution of claims *against* the receivership, but also to the validity of third party defenses to claims possessed *by* the receivership.

Third, as a practical matter the receiver may never reach the merits of whether or not a claim is valid, if the receiver concludes that the assets in the receivership are clearly insufficient to satisfy the claims of others that are both valid and superior to the particular claim in issue. Determination of the validity of the claim in these circumstances would be a fruitless waste of time since no money would be paid on the claim in any event. These cases are likely to arise fairly often in bank insolvencies because, as discussed below, Congress has given depositors in insured depository institutions a preference over other creditors. Courts typically exhibit great deference to the FDIC's assertion that a particular claim has no hope of obtaining any reimbursement out of the receivership estate.

Fourth, the claimant may lose out if the claim is not brought to the receiver in time for a particular distribution. The traditional rule in banking law, codified at 12 U.S.C. §1821(d)(10)(B), is that the FDIC has no liability for paying dividends on proved claims even if claimants whose claims are not proved do not share ratably in the distribution.

## 3. *Establishment of Priorities*

Those claims that have been proved must also be classified into their relative priorities. In bank failure, as in bankruptcy, one goal of the resolution proceedings, at least in theory, is to maintain the absolute priority of creditors over equity holders. The well-established rule is that creditors must be made whole from an insolvent corporation's assets before shareholders receive any distribution whatever.

The purposes behind this absolute priority rule are evidently to enforce expectations: Shareholders, in return for a residual claim on the institution's profits and assets, accept the risk of being placed last in priority in the event of insolvency; creditors, in return for giving up their claim on the institution's profits beyond the limits contained in their contracts with debtors, are assured that they will stand ahead of shareholders in the event of insolvency.

In addition to the absolute priority of debt over equity, the general objective in bank failure, as in bankruptcy, is to preserve the relative priorities among different types of claims within the general categories of debt and equity. Thus if a bank has issued subordinated debt, which is contractually subordinated to all other debt, that subordination agreement will generally be enforced in bank failure proceedings. This means that all the other debtholders will be paid off before the holders of the subordinated debt receive anything. Conversely, if the institution has any secured debt—debt secured by specific collateral—then in general bank failure proceedings the fiduciary will recognize the priority of the holder of the secured debt to receive the value of that collateral up to the amount of the lien.

Additional lien priorities may be established by state or federal law. In 1993 Congress amended §11(d) of the Federal Deposit Insurance Act to provide depositors with a preference over general and subordinated creditors of a failed bank or thrift when a receiver distributes the assets in a state that has not enacted a statute providing for such depositor preference. This amendment changed the previous law, under which depositors were paid on the same basis as general creditors in states without depositor preference laws. Effectively, Congress enacted a nationwide depositor preference law for insured institutions. 12 U.S.C. §1821(d)(11).

The flip-side of the priority rule—that priorities among suppliers of capital to an institution will be preserved in bank failure proceedings—is a rule of equal treatment or "ratable distribution." This rule is simply that all claimants on the institution's assets that are at the same level of priority should be treated equally. No common shareholder should be preferred over any other common shareholder; no unsecured creditor should be preferred over any other unsecured creditor at the same priority level. See 12 U.S.C. §194 (national banks).

Although these priority rules are easy to state, their application in practice can be difficult. Whenever a depository institution fails, and its liabilities are not assumed in full by a solvent institution in a purchase and assumption transaction, the creditors whose claims are not assumed will scramble to establish themselves in some type of priority position vis-à-vis other creditors. A variety of legal maneuvers have been attempted in order to boost the priority of particular claimants. As will be seen, these strategies are sometimes successful.

### a. Constructive Trusts

## Downriver Community Federal Credit Union v. FDIC

***879 F.2d 754 (10th Cir. 1989), cert. denied, 110 S. Ct. 1112 (1990)***

TACHA, Circuit Judge.

This appeal arises from a dispute between certain uninsured depositors in the insolvent Penn Square Bank, N.A. (PSB), and the Federal Deposit Insurance Corporation (FDIC), in its capacity as receiver, over the priority of the depositors' claims against the insolvent bank's assets. The district court found that PSB fraudulently induced the plaintiffs to deposit funds through issuing financial statements that were materially misleading as to PSB's financial condition. In the remedy phase of the trial, the district court imposed a constructive trust upon PSB's assets in favor of the plaintiff-depositors, thereby entitling them to recover the full amount of their deposits, rather than their pro rata share under the relevant provision of the National Bank Act, 12 U.S.C. §194. We hold that federal law limits these depositors' recovery to their pro rata share of the assets held by the receiver, and reverse.

I

The plaintiffs, Downriver Community Federal Credit Union (Downriver) and Wood Products Credit Union (Wood Products), were among the 140 credit unions, 48 savings and loans, and 47 commercial banks holding substantial uninsured deposits in PSB when the Comptroller of the Currency ordered PSB closed on July 5, 1982. . . .

The plaintiffs attempt to avoid the application of federal law to their claim . . . on the ground that their equitable right to the funds arose prior to insolvency. They contend that Oklahoma law governs the nature of their preinsolvency relationship with PSB, and that, because of PSB's fraud, their deposits never became part of PSB's assets, but were instead impressed with a trust relating back to the date of their initial deposits. The equitable fiction of the trusts relating back to the date that the plaintiffs deposited funds in PSB, however, does not change the fact that by purchasing a certificate of deposit in PSB, the plaintiffs intended a debtor and creditor relationship. Although the state law of contracts governs whether the parties intended to form a trust or a debtor/creditor relationship prior to insolvency, any attempt to recharacterize that relationship equitably after insolvency is governed by federal law.

The FDIC, as receiver, takes control of an insolvent national bank subject to the "rights and equities" existing prior to insolvency. . . .

Congress chose to achieve, through the National Bank Act, "a just and equal distribution of the assets of national banks among all unsecured creditors."

The Act's unfriendliness to special interests requires a claimant seeking a preference from pro rata distribution of assets to bear a heavy burden of proof. A national bank's fraudulent conduct may give rise to a constructive trust only when the plaintiff can show that the bank's fraud caused a particular harm that is not shared by substantially all other depositors, and that granting relief to the plaintiff does not disrupt the orderly administration of the receiver's estate. This general rule is exemplified in the cases involving constructive trusts imposed upon the assets of a hopelessly insolvent bank.

A bank receiving deposits after its officers know that the bank is hopelessly insolvent is deemed to commit fraud upon those depositors, entitling them to reclaim their deposits. . . .

Those who deposit funds after a bank is hopelessly insolvent can show a specific act of fraud that affects only them, and therefore they have a superior equitable position over others who deposited funds prior to hopeless insolvency with a hope or belief in the bank's future ability to repay the deposit. Furthermore, a hopelessly insolvent bank should have been closed by the Comptroller of the Currency as of the date of such insolvency, thereby preventing the receipt of further deposits. Equity therefore "regards that as done which should have been done," O'Neal v. White, 79 F.2d 835, 835 (4th Cir. 1935), *cert. denied,* 297 U.S. 706, 56

S. Ct. 501, 80 L. Ed. 994 (1936), and permits the rescission of deposit contracts made after the bank should have been closed.

Even in the case of hopeless insolvency, however, full restitution may be denied when it would sufficiently disrupt the orderly administration of the receiver's estate or otherwise result in inequitable treatment to other similarly situated depositors. . . .

Here, the application of these policies—preserving the orderly administration of the receiver's estate and achieving an equitable distribution among creditors—is not a question to be decided fortuitously because "a particular state happened to have the greatest connection in the conflict of laws sense." D'Oench, Duhme & Co., [v. FDIC, 315 U.S. 447, 473, 62 S. Ct. 676, 687 (1942)] (Jackson J., concurring). We refuse here to adopt Oklahoma law as the federal rule of decision because to do so would permit a constructive trust in favor of plaintiffs in contravention of the principles implicit in the National Bank Act.

In awarding a constructive trust in favor of the plaintiffs, the district court relied upon an Oklahoma statute providing that:

> [o]ne who practices a deceit with intent to defraud the public, or a particular class of persons, is deemed to have intended to defraud every individual in that class, who is actually misled by the deceit.

Okla. Stat. Ann. tit. 76 §4 (West 1987). The plaintiffs, having proved reliance upon PSB's published financial statements, were deemed to have been "actually misled" by PSB at the time they purchased PSB certificates of deposit, and accordingly the trial court ordered that they be allowed to recover all of their deposits. Such recovery violates both of the federal policies implicit in the National Bank Act.

Permitting recovery to the plaintiffs because they could prove reliance upon the financial statements, to the detriment of other uninsured depositors who could not or did not come forward to prove reliance upon PSB financial statements, fails to accord equal treatment to PSB creditors. . . .

Whether independently analyzing PSB financial statements, or relying upon money brokers who analyzed PSB's financial condition based upon the information contained in those statements, financial institutions other than the plaintiffs undoubtedly placed similar trust in PSB's misrepresented financial condition in assessing their risk of future loss. The National Bank Act precludes these depositors from being treated differently. . . .

Although the plaintiffs contend that we might avoid this unequal treatment by permitting all depositors situated similarly to the plaintiffs to sue as a class to establish constructive trusts, to allow such suits would potentially jeopardize the orderly administration of the receiver's estate that is required by the Act. We do not think that Congress would have intended to deluge the FDIC with the potentially crushing weight of claims for preferences on behalf of all the uninsured depositors who could allege that they relied upon misleading information that was available to all depositors. Allowing such a preference to be based upon a "race of diligence" among creditors would make "the equality promised to them by the [National Bank Act] . . . a mere mockery." . . .

Accordingly, the order of the district court imposing a constructive trust upon the assets of PSB in favor of the plaintiffs is reversed.

*QUESTIONS AND COMMENTS*

1. This case is another part of the fallout from the infamous Penn Square Bank failure. Observe that this case arose because the FDIC had not used a purchase and assumption transaction to resolve the Penn Square failure; instead it used a deposit payout procedure that left uninsured depositors (such as Downriver Community Federal Credit Union) with claims against the receivership estate.

2. What if Penn Square had been a state-chartered institution? Would the analysis of federal common law come out the same way? What weight do you give the Federal Deposit Insurance Act, which governs the FDIC's actions as receiver? The relevant part of 12 U.S.C. §1819, cited by the court in *Downriver Community Federal Credit Union,* now provides that "all suits of a civil nature at common law or in equity to which the [FDIC], in any capacity, is a party shall be deemed to arise under the laws of the United States," subject to a limited exception for cases in which the FDIC acts as receiver of a state-insured institution. 12 U.S.C. §1819(b)(2). Do you think this provision was intended to establish the applicability of federal common law, or might it have had some other purpose?

### b. Purchase and Assumption Transactions

Suppose the FDIC as receiver arranges a purchase and assumption transaction in which the acquiring firm assumes all the insured deposits and some, but not all, of the liabilities. What are the rights of the creditors whose claims have not been assumed by the acquirer?

Prior to 1989 such creditors might have argued that the requirement of ratable distribution in 12 U.S.C. §194 precludes treating one class of creditors better than another. Accordingly, it would have violated §194 to allow the payoff of some creditors in full and to remit others to a claim against the receivership where they are likely to receive much less.

Current law, as amended in FIRREA, provides that "[t]he maximum liability of the [FDIC or RTC], acting as receiver or in any other capacity, to any person having a claim against the [institution in receivership] shall equal the amount such claimant would have received if the [FDIC] had liquidated the assets and liabilities of such institution." 12 U.S.C.

§1821(i)(2). In addition, the FDIC is authorized "in its discretion and in the interests of minimizing its losses, [to] use its own resources to make additional payments or credit additional amounts to or with respect to or for the account of any claimant or category of claimants. The [FDIC] shall not be obligated, as a result of having made any such payment or credited any such amount . . . to make payments to any other claimant or category of claimants." 12 U.S.C. §1821(i)(3)(A). Do these provisions represent sound social policy?

#### c. Private Litigation

When a bank fails, the shareholders ordinarily will be wiped out. Facing such a prospect, shareholders—or lawyers anxious to represent them—may find it irresistibly appealing to convert part or all of their interests as shareholders into claims as creditors. An obvious route for accomplishing this result is for shareholders to bring suit against a party who may also be liable to the depository institution. If the shareholders succeed in maintaining such a lawsuit, they may be able to lay hands on assets that would otherwise pass to the bank or the receiver and be thereafter distributed to creditors. The practical effect is to enhance the priority of shareholders beyond a mere residual claim on the assets. Not surprisingly, the FDIC vigorously resists granting priority to shareholders through the device of private litigation.

Shareholder litigation as a device for boosting priorities raises two general issues. The first is whether the litigation itself is properly brought by shareholders in their individual capacities. The FDIC is likely to argue that the shareholder's lawsuit is properly framed as a shareholders' derivative action, rather than a direct action; if so, the recovery will redound to the benefit of the receivership, not the shareholders individually, and thus will go into the pool of assets payable to creditors. A subsidiary issue, but one with important practical consequences, is whether if the lawsuit is found to be derivative in nature, the FDIC can elbow the plaintiffs' attorneys aside on the ground that the prosecution should be conducted solely by the receiver and not by individual shareholders (whose attorneys are likely to win large attorneys' fees awards if successful). Consider the following case.

## Leach v. FDIC

***860 F.2d 1266 (5th Cir. 1988)***

GOLDBERG, Circuit Judge: . . .

Plaintiffs are minority shareholders of the Seminole State National Bank ("Bank"). The Appellees-Defendants include former directors and officers of the failed Bank, the Federal Deposit Insurance Corporation, in its capacity as Receiver of the failed Bank, and MBank Dallas, a creditor of the failed bank. According to the complaint, Plaintiffs' Bank stock lost all of its value because of mismanagement of the Bank by Defendant directors. . . .

The district court granted the Defendants' motions to dismiss for failure to state a claim for lack of standing. We agree, and hold that a minority shareholder cannot assert a claim as an individual under the circumstances of this case. Accordingly, we affirm the judgment of the district court.

### I. Factual Background

According to Plaintiffs' first amended complaint, they owned approximately 3,300 shares of the Bank's stock which constituted a minority ownership in the Bank. The directors and officers allegedly failed to manage properly the business matters of the Bank and failed to advise the Plaintiffs in a proper and timely manner of the true financial condition of the Bank. Plaintiffs allege that MBank concealed the true financial condition of the Bank from the plaintiffs when MBank Dallas knew of, and helped to conceal, the fraud and mismanagement perpetrated by the Defendant directors. Plaintiffs allege that they have suffered actual damage because they have lost the value of their stock as a direct result of the Defendants' misbehavior.

Our decision focuses on whether the Plaintiffs have standing to assert claims arising from the diminution in the value of their stock. The Plaintiffs filed their complaint on March 14, 1986. This was nearly two years after the Comptroller of the Currency declared the Bank insolvent and appointed the FDIC as Receiver of the Bark on March 16, 1984. Before filing their complaint, Plaintiffs did not make a demand on the FDIC-Receiver requesting the FDIC to file a direct action against the Defendant directors. As we shall see, this plays a significant role in our standing inquiry.[4]

### II. Discussion . . .

Essentially, standing analysis involves two separate prongs. The first prong is "injury in fact." . . . Our case does not involve this "injury in fact" prong. Plaintiffs have alleged a real and distinct injury—the loss of the value of their stock.

It is the second prong of standing law, what is sometimes referred to as the "zone of interest" test, that is the focus of our decision. "The zone of interest test is a guide for deciding whether . . . a particular

4. The FDIC-Receiver for the failed bank has advised us that it has sued the directors based upon the allegations in the Plaintiffs' complaint.

plaintiff should be heard to complain a particular" injury. Clarke v. Securities Industry Ass'n, 479 U.S. 388, 107 S. Ct. 750, 757, 93 L. Ed. 2d 757 (1987). "The test is not meant to be especially demanding; in particular, there need be no indication of congressional purpose to benefit the would-be plaintiff." *Clarke,* 107 S. Ct. at 757. . . .

To decide whether a plaintiff is arguably within the zone of interest recognized by a particular statute, it is necessary first to examine the statute itself to determine whether Congress intended to allow the plaintiff to sue. . . .

. . . Section 93(a) of the National Bank Act reads:

> If the directors of any national banking association shall knowingly violate, or knowingly permit any of the officers, agents, or servants of the association to violate any of the provisions of this chapter, all the rights, privileges, and the franchises of the association shall be thereby forfeited. Such violation shall, however, be determined and adjudged by a proper district or Territorial court of the United States in a suit brought for that purpose by the Comptroller of the Currency, in his own name, before the association shall be declared dissolved. And in cases of such violation, every director who participated in or assented to the same shall be held liable in his personal and individual capacity for all damages which the association, its shareholders, or any other person, shall have sustained in consequence of such violation. . . .

This statute on its face would appear to permit Plaintiffs to sue the Defendants for alleged mismanagement which allegedly caused Plaintiffs' stock to lose its value. The last sentence of section 93(a) states that "every director who participated [in a violation of the Bank Act] shall be held liable in his personal and individual capacity for all damages which the association, its *shareholders,* or any other person, shall have sustained in consequence of such violation" (emphasis added). However, even apparently plain words, divorced from the context in which they arise and in which their creators intended them to function, may not accurately convey the meaning the creators intended to impart. It is only, therefore, within a context that a word, any word, can communicate an idea.

Section 93(a) of the National Bank Act as enacted in 1864 was not created in a vacuum. In this pre-Erie v. Tompkins era, 304 U.S. 64, 58 S. Ct. 817, 82 L. Ed. 1188 (1938), it was commonly understood that there existed a general commercial common law. . . .

As part of the general commercial common law, it was understood that only the corporate body could sue misbehaving directors for wounds that the corporation suffered resulting from directors' misconduct. . . .

What we today term a shareholder derivative suit was a part of the general commercial common law when Congress enacted Section 93(a) in 1864. When writing Section 93(a), Congress relied upon the fact that injured shareholders did not possess a right of action against delinquent directors until the corporation itself had refused to bring suit. . . .

Plaintiffs in this case do not fall within either of the two exceptions to this notion that would allow them to sue derivatively: (1) where they make a demand upon corporation and the corporation refuses to sue; or (2) misbehaving directors or officers have "captured" the corporation so that any demand to sue would be a useless action. . . .

We have examined the historical context in which Congress passed 12 U.S.C. §93(a). From the context, we have learned that a general commercial law, specifically the genesis of the law of derivative suits, provides meaning to the terms of Section 93(a). Courts, before Erie v. Tompkins, relied on this general common law when interpreting Section 93(a). Modern courts have arrived at the same result. From all these sources, we conclude that minority shareholders who sue for "corporate" injury do not have standing to sue under Section 12 U.S.C. §93(a), unless one of the two exceptions authorizing derivative actions applies. . . .

This case . . . does not resemble such exceptional cases. Therefore, the judgment of the district court is affirmed.

## *QUESTIONS AND COMMENTS*

1. Can shareholders of a depository institution in receivership sue the former officers and directors directly under "civil RICO" for the loss in value of their shares? The courts are unanimous, or nearly so, that the rights under civil RICO in this situation are derivative. See, e.g., Crocker v. FDIC, 826 F.2d 347, 349 (5th Cir. 1987), *cert. denied,* 485 U.S. 905 (1988). What about uninsured depositors of a failed mutual savings and loan institution? See In re Sunrise Securities Litigation, 916 F.2d 874 (3d Cir. 1990) (same result).

2. A shareholder suit is brought against the directors of a solvent national bank under 12 U.S.C. §93(a) for mismanagement. The plaintiffs' attorney styles the suit as a derivative action and alleges that demand on the incumbent directors would be futile. After several months of vigorous litigation the bank fails, and the FDIC as receiver seeks to remove the plaintiffs' attorney on the ground that the FDIC should be in sole control of the litigation. What result? See Gaff v. FDIC, 814 F.2d 311, 315 (6th Cir. 1987) (shareholder asserting a derivative claim against a national bank had "no standing" to pursue the lawsuit as an individual after FDIC was appointed receiver; because the FDIC acquired every asset of the failed institution, it "effectively precluded individual shareholders from bringing derivative actions based on the same conduct"). Do you agree?

3. Obviously, from the point of view of the shareholders, it is highly desirable to locate some cause of action that will withstand a motion to dismiss on the ground that it is derivative in nature. The plaintiffs' bar

has identified a variety of such direct causes of action, the most important of which are actions arising under the federal securities laws. See, e.g., Howard v. Haddad, 916 F.2d 167 (4th Cir. 1990) (action under SEC Rule 10b-5 is direct, not derivative). Typically the plaintiffs will claim that the defendant directors caused the institution to issue false and misleading statements, on which the plaintiffs relied, about the financial condition of the bank. These securities law suits, however, benefit only persons who purchased or sold securities, see Blue Chip Stamps v. Manor Drug Stores, 421 U.S. 723 (1975), and accordingly do not offer a priority boost to shareholders generally. State law causes of action, such as complaints under "blue sky" laws, negligence law, or common law fraud, may be more successful at benefiting all shareholders.

4. Such lawsuits, however, may run into an additional bar. The FDIC as receiver may claim that it has priority over shareholders with respect to claims against solvent third parties. In FDIC v. Jenkins, 888 F.2d 1537 (11th Cir. 1989), the FDIC asserted such a priority as to assets of officers, directors, and other third parties who may have been responsible, at least in part, for the failure of Park Bank of Florida and for a subsequent purchase and assumption transaction by the FDIC. The court held that the FDIC was not entitled to a priority as insurer of bank deposits, rejecting the FDIC's argument that a purchase and assumption transaction is an absolute priority for the FDIC in suits against third parties in order to replenish its deposit insurance funds. The court was equally unconvinced by the FDIC's argument that its priority should be determined under federal common law: "Of course, it would be convenient to the FDIC to have an arsenal of priorities, presumptions and defenses to maximize recovery to the insurance fund, but this does not require that courts must grant all of these tools to the FDIC in its effort to maximize deposit insurance fund recovery. . . . We are not convinced that Congress considered collections against parties such as the bank-related defendants in this case as a necessary part of the recovery to the deposit insurance fund. Any such priority over third-party lawsuits will have to come from Congress, not this court. . . ."

Why wasn't the FDIC correct in believing that the Federal Deposit Insurance Act evinces a legislative intent to assist the FDIC in replenishing the insurance fund? And why wasn't it entitled to priority under federal common law? Isn't it in line with the general tenor and spirit of congressional policy in this area to give the FDIC, as stand-in for creditors, priority over the claims of shareholders against third parties?

### d. Setoffs

Let us now consider another important mechanism whereby priorities may be affected by special rules in the banking area: the right of "setoff" in bank insolvencies. Consider the following two situations:

1. Two banks, Bank A and Bank B, are in a correspondent relationship, pursuant to which Bank B maintains $100,000 in an account at Bank A and Bank A lends $100,000 to Bank B. Now Bank B fails and is placed in receivership. What is Bank A's recourse?

2. Bank A lends $500,000 to Borrower B, and Borrower B maintains a "compensating balance" of $500,000 in a checking account at Bank A. Bank A fails, and the FDIC as receiver pays off insured deposits and remits any uninsured deposits, including $400,000 of Borrower B's account, to a claim against the receivership. What is Borrower B's recourse?

Application of standard receivership principles would suggest that in both cases the party with a claim against the failed bank should share ratably with other creditors in the proceeds of the receivership. Thus in the first example, Bank A would be required to pay out Bank B's $100,000 deposit to the receiver on demand and be remitted to the position of a general creditor with respect to its claim for $100,000 against Bank B. In the second example, Borrower B would be liable to the receiver for the full amount of its indebtedness, $500,000, but must share ratably in the proceeds of the receivership for repayment of its $400,000 in uninsured deposits.

In all probability, these would not be the outcomes under banking law. Instead, the creditors of the failed bank may be able to take their claims against the bank and set them off against the claims the bank has against them. In the first example, Bank A could set off Bank B's deposit account in Bank A against Bank B's indebtedness to Bank A. Bank A can make itself whole by simply cancelling the deposit account. In the second example, Borrower B could set off its $400,000 in uninsured deposits against its indebtedness of $500,000 and thus owe the receiver only $100,000. Note that in both these circumstances the party dealing with the failed bank is able to use the setoff right to give itself a priority as compared with other general creditors.

The right of setoff in bank insolvency is relatively poorly defined. It is an area, however, that is likely to generate a substantial number of new problems and decisions. The following case, which is the leading Supreme Court precedent, is still good law.

## Scott v. Armstrong

*146 U.S. 499 (1892)*

[Farmer's and Merchant's State Bank issued a promissory note for $10,000 payable to the Fidelity National Bank. In exchange, Farmer's received $9,819.17 (reflecting a discount for interest), which, pursuant to a prior agreement, it deposited at Fidelity. Farmer's drew down $1,009.23 of the deposit, leaving an account balance of $8,809.94. Fidelity then became insolvent and the receiver brought an action on the note against Farmer's, to which Farmer's pleaded a setoff for $8,809.94.]

CHIEF JUSTICE FULLER, after stating the case, delivered the opinion of the court.

The Fidelity National Bank was closed by order of the bank examiner June 20, the receiver was appointed June 27, and the charter of the bank was forfeited and the bank dissolved by the decree of the Circuit Court, July 12, 1887. Title to its assets was necessarily thereby transferred to the receiver.

The note in controversy did not mature until September 7, 1887, but the deposit to the credit of the Farmer's Bank was due for the purposes of suit upon the closing of the Fidelity Bank, as under such circumstances no demand was necessary. The receiver took the assets of the Fidelity Bank as a mere trustee for creditors, and not for value and without notice, and, in the absence of statute to the contrary, subject to all claims and defences that might have been interposed as against the insolvent corporation before the liens of the United States and of the general creditors attached. . . .

In the case at bar the credits between the banks were reciprocal and were parts of the same transaction, in which each gave credit to the other on the faith of the simultaneous credit, and the principle applicable to mutual credits applied. It was, therefore, the balance upon an adjustment of the accounts which was the debt, and the Farmers' Bank had the right, as against the receiver of the Fidelity Bank, although the note matured after the suspension of that bank, to set off the balance due upon its deposit account. . . .

We are of opinion that the set-off should have been allowed. . . .

## *QUESTIONS AND COMMENTS*

1. This case illustrates a correspondent banking relationship in which a smaller bank, usually operating under state charter (like Farmer's and Merchant's) might keep funds on account at a larger bank, usually federally chartered (like Fidelity National), in order to facilitate the clearing of accounts (as well as for other purposes). Such a correspondent relationship was mutually beneficial to both banks. It was not uncommon for the larger bank to advance the smaller bank the funds to maintain the correspondent balances.

2. What is the source of the setoff right that the Court recognizes here?

3. What is the policy rationale for the setoff right? Is the Court implicitly recognizing the importance and economic value of correspondent banking relationships? If the rationale was to avoid penalizing corre-

spondent banking relationships, what does this say about the breadth of the setoff doctrine?

4. Is the Court's rationale that in a setoff situation like this one the debt is actually fictitious? If A lends B $10,000, and B lends A $10,000, arguably no debt relationship is created at all. The two "loans" are mere bookkeeping artifacts. The setoff right arguably erases the fictional debt and leaves behind only the "real" debt. If this is the rationale, how broadly should the setoff right be interpreted?

5. Is the Court's rationale, instead, that the parties to the transaction have implicitly *agreed* that setoff rights should exist in the event of either party's insolvency? Is the point here that Fidelity National implicitly secured Farmer's and Merchant's deposit account by the note that Farmer's and Merchant's gave to Fidelity National? Ordinarily, a security interest must be recorded or otherwise made known to subsequent creditors to be good against them. That wasn't done here, was it? In any event, if the existence of an implicit agreement was the basis of the decision, how broadly would you read the setoff right as recognized in the case?

6. The Court apparently endorses the proposition that where the mutual obligations have grown out of the same transaction, insolvency on the one hand justifies the setoff of the debt due upon the other. What are the contours of this mutuality requirement? What if there had been no understanding that Farmer's would deposit the loan proceeds at Fidelity National, but subsequently Farmer's did so to facilitate correspondent transactions? Would the case come out the same way?

### e. Executory Contracts

At the time of its failure, a depository institution will always be involved in a wide variety of ongoing contractual relationships in which some or all of the consideration called for under the contract is to be provided at a future date. The failed institution's obligations are obviously liabilities of the receivership, just as the other party's obligations under such contracts are assets. It will usually be impossible to separate these assets and liabilities since both depend on the performance of a single contract. The question, accordingly, is ordinarily whether the receiver should accept or disavow the contract as a whole.

Obviously, the preservation of priorities requires that the receiver have the power to repudiate "burdensome" executory contracts—that is, contracts in which the value to the receivership of the other party's promise is less than the costs to the receivership of performing the promises made by the failed institution. Otherwise, parties holding claims against the receivership embodied in executory contracts would receive super-priority, even though their proper status would ordinarily be that of general creditors.

Accordingly, the FDIC or RTC as conservator or receiver do have the power to repudiate executory contracts within a reasonable time when they determine that performance of the contracts is burdensome and that repudiation would promote the orderly administration of the institution's affairs. 12 U.S.C. §1821(e)(1). Under FIRREA, the general measure of damages for such a repudiation is limited to "actual direct compensatory damages" and does not include punitive damages, damages for lost profits, or awards for pain and suffering. 12 U.S.C. §1821(e)(3).

The statute sets forth special rules governing particular forms of executory contracts. In the case of leases in which the failed institution was *lessee,* the statute provides a draconian limitation on damages. In general, the bank's lessor has a claim only for rents accruing prior to the disaffirmation. 12 U.S.C. §1821(e)(4). Thus if a bank is party to a long-term, above-market lease—and, given reductions in real estate values, many banks may find themselves in such a situation—the receiver can repudiate the arrangement, and the lessor's only right in that case is for unpaid rents.

Far less onerous rules apply if the bank is a *lessor* of real property; the lessee may remain in possession for the term even if the receiver repudiates the lease, and has the right to offset lease rentals against any liability of the receiver for nonperformance of lease obligations. If, as is often the case in commercial real estate, the lease is a net lease under which the lessee is responsible for most of the costs of operation and upkeep, the receiver's repudiation could mean very little and might even benefit the lessee by providing a right of offset that was not present in the original lease. See 12 U.S.C. §1821(e)(5).

Another important class of executory contracts treated separately in the statute are "qualified financial contracts" such as forward contracts, repurchase agreements, and swap transactions. These are typically short-term money market instruments by which a bank obtains current funding or lays off risk. For example, the repurchase agreement ("repo") is a short-term secured loan structured as a sale of securities with an agreement to repurchase later at a higher price. The "seller" under a repo is in fact the borrower; the sales "price" is the loan amount; the resale price reflects the interest charge; and the securities themselves are the collateral. In legal form a repo contains an executory contract to repurchase at a higher price, which might be disaffirmed by the receiver of a bank "seller." But because the repo in substance is a secured loan, the statute creates a special set of rules that, in general, provide full protections to counterparties. See 12 U.S.C. §1821(e)(8).

### *QUESTIONS AND COMMENTS*

1. A bank has an outstanding contract with Acme Construction to renovate its building. The contract provides that Acme will be paid $1 million on completion of work, and that in the event that the bank

terminates the contract prior to the commencement of work at the site, the bank will be liable to Acme for $200,000 in liquidated damages. Acme expects that performance of the contract will cost it $900,000. In reliance on this contract, Acme expends $50,000 for specially cut marble that cannot be reused for any other purpose; it also turns down other work that it would otherwise have taken on and that would have earned it a profit of $300,000. Before any work is started at the site, the FDIC is appointed receiver and repudiates the contract. What is Acme's claim against the receivership?

2. What if Acme had performed half the contract at the time the bank is closed and claims a mechanic's lien arising under state law for $500,000, as well as damages for the remainder of the contract?

3. What is the policy rationale for limiting executory contracts in this manner? After all, if the bank had disaffirmed the contract prior to failure, it would appear that Acme would be able to assert the full measure of contract damages against the receivership estate, including lost profits or liquidated damages. Why limit contract rights so severely merely because a receivership has intervened?

4. Do you see any constitutional problems with limiting the rights of a contracting party to obtain damages for breach? Isn't it arguably a "taking" of property without just compensation for the government to tell a lessor that its leasehold rights shall henceforth be limited to the payment of accrued rents by a disaffirming receiver or conservator, and shall in no event include damages for lost future rentals?

5. Do the special rules on qualified financial contracts provide any possible legal avenue for assuring creditors of a shaky bank that they will be repaid notwithstanding the provision, discussed in a previous section, under which the FDIC as receiver or conservator may avoid security interests taken in contemplation of insolvency?

6. The FDIC seeks to repudiate as burdensome an apartment lease that is comprehensively rent-controlled under municipal ordinances. Can it do so? An argument could be made that the rent control ordinances so pervasively control the terms of the leasehold as to give the tenant a right of occupancy independent of any lease—and therefore free of the FDIC's power to repudiate leases. See RTC v. Diamond, 45 F.3d 665 (2d Cir.), *cert. denied,* 115 S. Ct. 2609 (1995) (concluding that the RTC could repudiate leases on a rent-controlled apartment in New York City).

## F. THE SIDE AGREEMENT RULE

We turn now to an enormously important topic, namely the rights that the FDIC or its assigns may possess in order to be free of claims or defenses based on "side agreements," whether oral or written, which are not contained in a depository institution's official files. Note that the side agreement rule applies both to claims *against* the institution in receivership, either by way of a direct action or a counterclaim, as well as to defenses against claims *by* the institution in receivership. The rule operates, accordingly, as both a sword and a shield for the agency and its assigns.

The side agreement rule is grounded in three separate, but closely related, legal doctrines: (1) the *D'Oench Duhme* case; (2) 12 U.S.C. §1823(e); and (3) the federal holder in due course doctrine. We first examine the sources of authority and the relationships between them, and then analyze how the side agreement rule operates in a variety of discrete factual settings.

## 1. *Sources of Authority*

### a. The *D'Oench, Duhme* Doctrine

### D'Oench, Duhme & Co. v. FDIC

*315 U.S. 447 (1942)*

Justice DOUGLAS delivered the opinion of the Court.

Respondent instituted this suit in the United States District Court . . . on a demand note for $5000, executed by petitioner in 1933 and payable to the Belleville Bank & Trust Co., Belleville, Illinois. Respondent insured that bank January 1, 1934; and it acquired the note in 1938 as part of the collateral securing a loan of over $1,000,000 to the bank made in connection with the assumption of the latter's deposit liabilities by another bank. Since 1935 the note had been among the charged off assets of the bank. The note was executed by petitioner in renewal of notes which it had executed in 1926. Petitioner, who was engaged in the securities business at St. Louis, Missouri, had sold the bank certain bonds which later defaulted. The original notes were executed to enable the bank to carry the notes and not show any past due bonds. Proceeds of the bonds were to be credited on the notes. The receipts for the notes contained the statement, "This note is given with the understanding it will not be called for payment. All interest payments to be repaid." Respondent had no knowledge of the existence of the receipts until after demand for payment on the renewal note was made in 1938. Certain interest payments on the notes were made prior to renewal for the purpose of keeping them "as live paper." Petitioner's president, who signed the original notes, knew that they were executed so that the past due bonds would not appear among the assets of the bank, and that the purpose of the interest payments was "to keep the notes alive." The original notes were signed in St. Louis, Missouri, were payable at petitioner's office there, and were delivered to the payee in Illinois. The evidence does not disclose where the note sued upon was signed, though it was dated at Belleville, Illinois, and payable to the bank there.

The main point of controversy here revolves around the question as to what law is applicable. The District Court held that Illinois law was applicable and that petitioner was liable. The Circuit Court of Appeals applied "general law" to determine that the note was an Illinois rather than a Missouri contract; and it decided that, under Illinois law, respondent was the equivalent of a holder in due course and entitled to recover. . . .

. . . [W]e are of the view that the liability of petitioner on the note involves decision of a federal, not a state, question under the rule of Deitrick v. Greaney, 309 U.S. 190. . . .

Sec. 12B(s) of the Federal Reserve Act, 12 U.S.C. §264(s), provides that "Whoever, for the purpose of obtaining any loan from the Corporation . . . or for the purpose of influencing in any way the action of the Corporation under this section, makes any statement, knowing it to be false, or wilfully overvalues any security, shall be punished by a fine of not more than $5,000, or by imprisonment for not more than two years, or both." Subdivision (y) of the same section provided, at the time respondent insured the Belleville bank, that such a state bank "with the approval of the authority having supervision" of the bank and on "certification" to respondent "by such authority" that the bank "is in solvent condition" shall "after examination by, and with the approval of" the respondent be entitled to insurance.

These provisions reveal a federal policy to protect respondent, and the public funds which it administers, against misrepresentations as to the securities or other assets in the portfolios of the banks which respondent insures or to which it makes loans. . . .

. . . [The National Banking Act also embodies a federal policy] to protect respondent, a federal corporation, from misrepresentations made to induce or influence the action of respondent, including misstatements as to the genuineness or integrity of securities in the portfolios of banks which it insures or to which it makes loans. Those principles call for an affirmance of the judgment below. . . .

Though petitioner was not a participant in this particular transaction and, so far as appears, was ignorant of it, nevertheless it was responsible for the creation of the false status of the note in the hands of the bank. It therefore cannot be heard to assert that the federal policy to protect respondent against such fraudulent practices should not bar its defense to the note. . . . If the secret agreement were allowed as a defense in this case the maker of the note would be enabled to defeat the purpose of the statute by taking advantage of an undisclosed and fraudulent arrangement which the statute condemns and which the maker of the note made possible. The federal policy under this Act of protecting respondent in its various functions against such arrangements is [clear and emphatic.]

Affirmed.

*QUESTIONS AND COMMENTS*

1. This case draws on "federal common law" to decide the FDIC's rights, there being no statute on point. It is an important precedent in the development of federal common law in the wake of the Court's holding in *Erie* that federal courts must apply the law of the appropriate state in diversity of citizenship cases. For treatments of federal common law, see Friendly, In Praise of Erie—and of the New Federal Common Law, 39 N.Y.U. L. Rev. 383 (1963); Mishkin, The Variousness of Federal Law: Competence and Discretion in the Choice of National and State Rules of Decision, 105 U. Pa. L. Rev. 797 (1957).

2. Why do you think D'Oench, Duhme & Co. executed this note in the first place?

3. What is the basis for the Court's decision here? Illinois law? Missouri law? The Federal Reserve Act? The National Banking Act? Something else?

4. Justice Jackson, in his concurring opinion (not excerpted), refers to the rule of this case as a doctrine of "estoppel." What did he mean?

5. What is the policy rationale underlying this decision? To penalize those who conspire with banks to inflate their assets? To assure persons who acquire the assets of a bank in a purchase and assumption transaction (here, the FDIC-corporate) that they can rely on the written files, without concern for side agreements located elsewhere? To impose losses on parties that can avoid them most cheaply? To preserve the assets of the FDIC insurance fund? To prevent the possibility of fraudulent defenses? To allow federal and state bank examiners to rely on the bank's official records in evaluating the safety and soundness of the institution prior to failure?

6. How broad is the rule of *D'Oench, Duhme?* Here, arguably, the parties had entered the side agreement in order to substitute a facially good asset (the notes) for a bad asset (the bonds), and thus bolster the bank's balance sheet. This arguably was intended as a fraud on the bank examiners and on creditors. But what if this element of bad intent is missing—for example, what if a bank, say, makes a bona fide oral promise to extend the maturity of a loan in order to allow the borrower time to raise additional funds from operations. If the borrower takes actions in reliance on this promise and the bank subsequently fails, is the FDIC bound by the agreement? Recall the Court's language in *D'Oench, Duhme:* "[t]he test is whether the note was designed to deceive the creditors or

the public authority, or would tend to have that effect." What should the result be in cases like this?

### b. Section 1823(e)

## Langley v. FDIC

*484 U.S. 86 (1987)*

Justice SCALIA delivered the opinion of the Court. . . .

I

The Langleys purchased land in Pointe Coupee Parish, Louisiana in 1980. To finance the purchase, they borrowed $450,000 from Planters Trust & Savings Bank of Opelousas, Louisiana, a bank insured by the FDIC. In consideration for the loan, they executed a note, a collateral mortgage, and personal guaranties. The note was renewed several times, the last renewal being in March 1982, for the principal amount of $468,124.41.

In October 1983, after the Langleys had failed to pay the first installment due on the last renewal of the note, Planters brought the present suit for principal and interest in a Louisiana state trial court. The Langleys removed the suit, on grounds of diversity, to the United States District Court for the Middle District of Louisiana, where it was consolidated with a suit by the Langleys seeking more than $5,000,000 in damages from Planters and others. The Langleys alleged as one of the grounds of complaint in their own suit, and as a defense against Planters' claim in the present suit, that the 1980 land purchase and the notes had been procured by misrepresentations. In particular, they alleged that the notes had been procured by the bank's misrepresentations that the property conveyed in the land purchase consisted of 1,628.4 acres, when in fact it consisted of only 1,522, that the property included 400 mineral acres, when in fact it contained only 75, and that there were no outstanding mineral leases on the property, when in fact there were. No reference to these representations appears in the documents executed by the Langleys, in the bank's records, or in the minutes of the bank's board of directors or loan committee.

In April 1984, the FDIC conducted an examination of Planters during which it learned of the substance of the lawsuits with the Langleys, including the allegations of Planters' misrepresentations. On May 18, 1984, the Commissioner of Financial Institutions for the State of Louisiana closed Planters because of its unsound condition and appointed the FDIC as receiver. The FDIC thereupon undertook the financing of a purchase and assumption transaction pursuant to 12 U.S.C. §1823(c)(2), in which all the deposit liabilities and most of the assets of Planters were assumed by another FDIC-insured bank in the community. Because the amount of the liabilities greatly exceeded the value of the assets, the FDIC paid the assuming bank $36,992,000, in consideration for which the FDIC received, inter alia, the Langleys' March 1982 note. . . .

## II

The Federal Deposit Insurance Act of 1950, §2(13)(e), 64 Stat. 889, as amended, 12 U.S.C. §1823(e), provides:

> No agreement which tends to diminish or defeat the right, title or interest of the [FDIC] in any asset acquired by it under this section, either as security for a loan or by purchase, shall be valid against the [FDIC] unless such agreement (1) shall be in writing, (2) shall have been executed by the bank and the person or persons claiming an adverse interest thereunder, including the obligor, contemporaneously with the acquisition of the asset by the bank, (3) shall have been approved by the board of directors of the bank or its loan committee, which approval shall be reflected in the minutes of said board or committee, and (4) shall have been, continuously, from the time of its execution, an official record of the bank.

### *A*

Petitioners' principal contention is that the word "agreement" in the foregoing provision encompasses only an express promise to perform an act in the future. We do not agree.

As a matter of contractual analysis, the essence of petitioners' defense against the note is that the bank made certain warranties regarding the land, the truthfulness of which was a condition to performance of their obligation to repay the loan. As used in commercial and contract law, the term "agreement" often has "a wider meaning than. . . . promise," Restatement (Second) of Contracts §3, Comment *a* (1981), and embraces such a condition upon performance. . . .

Quite obviously, the parties' bargain cannot be reflected without including the conditions upon their performance, one of the two principal elements of which contracts are constructed. It seems to us that this common meaning of the word "agreement" must be assigned to its usage in §1823(e) if that section is to fulfill its intended purposes.

One purpose of §1823(e) is to allow federal and state bank examiners to rely on a bank's records in evaluating the worth of the bank's assets. Such evaluations are necessary when a bank is examined for fiscal soundness by state or federal authorities, see 12 U.S.C. §§1817(a)(2), 1820(b), and when the FDIC is deciding whether to liquidate a failed bank, see §1821(d), or to provide financing for purchase of its assets (and assumption of its liabilities) by another bank, see §1823(c)(2), (4)(A). The last kind of evaluation, in particular, must be made "with great speed, usually overnight, in order to preserve the going concern value of the failed bank and avoid an interruption in banking services." Gunter v. Hutcheson, 674 F.2d, at 865. Neither the FDIC nor state banking authorities would be able to make reliable evaluations if bank records contained seemingly unqualified notes that are in fact subject to undisclosed conditions.

A second purpose of §1823(e) is implicit in its requirement that the "agreement" not merely be on file in the bank's records at the time of an examination, but also have been executed and become a bank record "contemporaneously" with the making of the note and have been approved by officially recorded action of the bank's board or loan committee. These latter requirements ensure mature consideration of unusual loan transactions by senior bank officials, and prevent fraudulent insertion of new terms, with the collusion of bank employees, when a bank appears headed for failure. Neither purpose can be adequately fulfilled if an element of a loan agreement so fundamental as a condition upon the obligation to repay is excluded from the meaning of "agreement." . . .

### *B*

Petitioners' fall-back position is that even if a misrepresentation concerning an existing fact can sometimes constitute an agreement covered by §1823(e), it at least does not do so when the misrepresentation was fraudulent and the FDIC had knowledge of the asserted defense at the time it acquired the note. We conclude, however, that neither fraud in the inducement nor knowledge by the FDIC is relevant to the section's application.

No conceivable reading of the word "agreement" in §1823(e) could cause it to cover a representation or warranty that is bona fide but to exclude one that is fraudulent. Petitioners effectively acknowledge this when they concede that the fraudulent nature of a *promise* would not cause it to lose its status as an "agreement." . . .

Finally, knowledge of the misrepresentation by the FDIC prior to its acquisition of the note is not relevant to whether §1823(e) applies. Nothing in the text would support the suggestion that it is: An agreement is an agreement whether or not the FDIC knows of it; and a voidable interest is transferable whether or not the transferee knows of the misrepresentation or fraud that produces the voidability. Petitioners are really urging us to engraft an equitable exception upon the plain terms of the statute. Even if we had the power to do so, the equities petitioners invoke are not the equities the statute regards as predominant. While the borrower who has relied upon an erroneous or even fraudulent unrecorded representation has some claim to consideration, so do those who are harmed by his failure to protect himself by assuring that his agreement is approved and recorded in accordance with the statute. Harm to the FDIC (and those who rely upon the solvency of its fund) is not avoided by knowledge at the time of acquiring the note. The FDIC is an insurer of the bank, and is liable for the depositors' insured losses whether or not it decides to acquire the note. Cf. 12 U.S.C. §1821(f). The harm to the FDIC caused by the failure to record occurs no later than the time at which it conducts its first bank examination that is unable to detect the unrecorded agreement and to prompt the invocation of available protective measures, including termination of the bank's deposit insurance. See §1818. Thus, insofar as the recording provision is concerned, the state of the FDIC's knowledge at that time is what is crucial. But as we discussed earlier, §1823(e) is meant to ensure more than just the FDIC's ability to rely on bank records at the time of an examination or acquisition. The statutory requirements that an agreement be approved by the bank's board or loan committee and filed contemporaneously in the bank's records assure prudent consideration of the loan before it is made, and protect against collusive reconstruction of loan terms by bank officials and borrowers (whose interests may well coincide when a bank is about to fail). Knowledge by the FDIC could substitute for the latter protection only if it existed at the very moment the agreement was concluded, and could substitute for the former assurance not at all.

The short of the matter is that Congress opted for the certainty of the requirements set forth in §1823(e). An agreement that meets them prevails even if the FDIC did not know of it; and an agreement that does not meet them fails even if the FDIC knew. It would be rewriting the statute to hold otherwise. . . .

A condition to payment of a note, including the truth of an express warranty, is part of the "agreement" to which the writing, approval, and filing requirements of 12 U.S.C. §1823(e) attach. Because the representations alleged by petitioners constitute such a condition and did not meet the requirements of the statute, they cannot be asserted as defenses here. The judgment of the Court of Appeals is affirmed.

### *QUESTIONS AND COMMENTS*

1. Congress expanded the scope of §1823(e) in FIRREA. The current provision states:

> No agreement which tends to diminish or defeat the interest of the [FDIC] in any asset acquired by it under this section or [12 U.S.C. §1821] . . . either as security for a loan or by purchase or as receiver of any insured depository institution, shall be valid against the [FDIC] unless such agreement—(1) is in writing, (2) was executed by the depository institution and any person claiming an adverse interest thereunder, including the

> obligor, contemporaneously with the acquisition of the asset by the depository institution, (3) was approved by the board of directors of the depository institution or its loan committee, which approval shall be reflected in the minutes of said board or committee, and (4) has been, continuously, from the time of its execution, an official record of the depository institution.

In addition, Congress provided that the FDIC may not not compromise claims based on agreements that fail to satisfy §1823(e). 12 U.S.C. §§1821(d)(3)(A), 1821(d)(9). And Congress explicitly extended the §1823(e) protections to bridge banks. 12 U.S.C. §1821(n)(4)(I). In what ways does the recent amendment to §1823(e) expand its scope?

2. What policy rationales for §1823(e) does the Court identify in *Langley?* Do you find these rationales convincing?

3. Should one draw any negative inferences about the scope of §1823(e) from the fact that Congress explicitly extended the protections of that statute to bridge banks but did not address a variety of other coverage issues (such as whether the protection of §1823(e) applies to parties acquiring assets from the FDIC)?

### c. The Federal Holder in Due Course Doctrine

## FSLIC v. Murray

*853 F.2d 1251 (5th Cir. 1988)*

W. Eugene Davis, Circuit Judge:

The makers of promissory and collateral mortgage notes appeal the district court's ruling on summary judgment that Federal Savings and Loan Insurance Corp. (FSLIC) could recover on the notes despite a number of defenses, including one based on evidence that Alliance Federal Savings and Loan Association (Alliance), the savings and loan holding the notes, had altered them fraudulently. We affirm.

#### I

Four married couples formed a general partnership called the Eastway Group to acquire real estate in Louisiana for commercial development. To finance this purchase, they borrowed $3.6 million in August 1984 from Alliance. All borrowers signed a $3.6 million promissory note in their individual capacities; this note was secured by a $5 million collateral mortgage on the purchased property. The borrowers admit receiving the proceeds from the $3.6 million loan. The Hintons eventually sold their interest in the partnership to the remaining partners, who agreed to indemnify them from liability on this loan.

In January 1985, the Federal Home Loan Bank Board (FHLBB)

appointed the FSLIC receiver of Alliance, and through a purchase and assumption transaction FSLIC became the holder of this note. When FSLIC filed suit against the makers, two of the four couples who signed the note filed individual bankruptcies. The two remaining couples, the Hintons and the Salvaggios, defended on several grounds: (1) they thought the Eastway Group would be liable for the note rather than them personally; (2) Alliance misrepresented the property's value and violated several oral side agreements; (3) they had signed several blank signatory pages that Alliance later misused; and (4) Alliance fraudulently and materially altered the notes after the makers signed them. Alliance did alter the notes. The defendants made the following pretrial stipulation:

> The hand note was . . . altered after the closing. Mary Anne Murray Lepore and John Lepore were made restrictively liable in the amount of $1,225,937.37. Alice Jayne Glaser Hinton and Gerry E. Hinton were made restrictively liable in the amount of $984,189.00, Marliene Salvaggio and Philip M. Salvaggio were made restrictively liable in the amount of $256,500.00, and Doris Schwartz Smart and Donald R. Smart were made restrictly liable in the amount of $1,175,592.00. Again, each wife was made restrictively liable "in conjunction with" her husband for the quoted amounts.

The parties agree that Alliance altered the notes without the makers' knowledge or permission, apparently in an attempt to deceive the federal regulatory authorities. Alliance may have sought to bolster the appearance of the note to bank examiners by limiting each debtor to his net worth. In addition, the alteration may have permitted Alliance to claim compliance with FHLBB restrictions on the dollar amount Alliance could loan to any one borrower. The parties suggest that Alliance altered the notes because the single $3.6 million loan to the Eastway Group exceeded that limit, and that Alliance's alterations changed the note in FHLBB's eyes from one loan for over three million dollars to four separate loans well within the FHLBB restrictions.

The defendants argued that the fraudulent and material alterations to the notes rendered them unenforceable under Louisiana law. The district court nontheless granted FSLIC's motion for summary judgment on grounds that federal common law precluded the defendants from asserting this defense against FSLIC. The court found the Hintons and Salvaggios solidarily liable to FSLIC for the note's entire amount. Finally, the court found that the Salvaggios were bound to indemnify the Hintons for their share of the judgment under their contract of sale of the Hintons' partnership interest.

The Salvaggios and the Hintons appeal the summary judgment in favor of FSLIC and the imposition of solidary liability. The Salvaggios appeal the indemnification order. We address each argument in turn.

**II . . .**

. . . Appellants defend enforcement of the note because Alliance, without authority, added a phrase after each name limiting each maker's liability on the hand note to a specific amount. Appellants argue that Louisiana commercial law provides an absolute defense because in the hands of anyone but a holder in due course, "alteration [of a note by a] holder which is both fraudulent and material discharges any party whose contract is thereby changed unless that party assents." La. Rev. Stat. Ann. §10:3-407(2)(a). A subsequent holder in due course, however, "may in all cases enforce the instrument according to its original tenor." Id. §10:3-407(3). Because we determine that FSLIC has at least the rights of a holder in due course when it acquires a negotiable instrument in a purchase and assumption transaction, appellants cannot use Alliance's alterations to defeat FSLIC's enforcement rights.

A holder in due course takes an instrument for value, in good faith, and without notice of any defense against it or claims to it. FSLIC does not meet the technical requirements of a holder in due course in this case because it acquired these notes in bulk through a purchase and assumption transaction, rather than in the normal course of business. Nonetheless, the sensitive federal interests implicated when FSLIC rescues an insolvent savings and loan lead us to conclude that FSLIC should enjoy at least holder in due course status as a matter of federal common law.

Most of the case law developed under *D'Oench* has in effect extended holder in due course to federal banking regulators in purchase and assumption situations. . . .

. . . [P]roviding FSLIC with at least the status of a holder in due course promotes the necessary uniformity of law in this area while it counters individual state laws that would frustrate a basic FSLIC objective: promoting confidence and stability in financial institutions. Moreover, clothing FSLIC with at least holder in due course status does not trample commercial expectations of note makers such as appellants. A maker must anticipate that his note may be transferred to a holder in due course; the maker therefore suffers no prejudice if the FSLIC is granted those rights.

Denying holder in due course status to FSLIC in this case also would create an unjustified windfall to the maker. Appellants' defense, if allowed, would absolutely bar enforcement of the note against the makers and would relieve them of their obligation to repay the $3.6 million they received. Any sums these appellants are excused from repaying comes at the expense of either the failed institution's depositors, its other creditors, or the taxpayers.

Finally, a uniform role such as this serves the goals of predictability and rationality more effectively than the alternative of invalidating individual defenses as they arise. Establishing at least holder in due course status for FSLIC allows it, the public and the courts to draw on a well-developed body of commercial law when determining which state law defenses are clearly unenforcible [sic] against FSLIC. Accordingly, we look to the Model Uniform Commercial Code for the substance of this uniform standard, and to "those cases which best supplement the UCC and further its purposes and design."

Louisiana law and the model UCC produce the same outcome in this case. Giving holder in due course status to FSLIC bars appellants' alteration defense. Thus, we hold that FSLIC is entitled to recover against the makers according to the terms of the note as it was originally signed. . . .

For the reasons discussed above, the judgment of the district court is in all aspects affirmed.

Affirmed.

### *QUESTIONS AND COMMENTS*

1. The holder in due course doctrine protects certain parties ("holders in due course") against certain defenses that a maker of a negotiable note might have against the party with whom the maker originally dealt. In general, under the Uniform Commercial Code (UCC), a party qualifies as a holder in due course if he or she is a holder of a negotiable instrument who took it for value, in good faith, and without notice of any claim or defense. UCC §3-302(1).

A holder in due course enjoys important rights as against the maker and other parties. He or she takes the instrument free from all claims to it on the part of any person, and all defenses of any party to the instrument with whom the holder has not dealt, except the following: (1) infancy, to the extent that it is a defense to a simple contract, (2) such other incapacity, or duress, or illegality of the transaction, as renders the obligation of the party a nullity, (3) such misrepresentation as has induced the party to sign the instrument with neither knowledge nor reasonable opportunity to obtain knowledge of its character or its essential terms, (4) discharge in insolvency, and (5) any other discharge of which the holder has notice when he or she takes the instrument. UCC §3-305. Accordingly, the holder in due course takes free of so-called personal defenses on the instrument, such as failure of consideration, breach of warranty, unconscionability, and fraud in the inducement (the type of fraud that was alleged in the *Langley* case).

Persons who do not qualify as holders in due course are not so lucky. They take the instrument subject to (1) all valid claims to it on the part of any person, (2) all defenses of any party that would be available in an action on a simple contract, (3) the defenses of want or failure of consideration, nonperformance of any condition precedent, nondelivery, or delivery for a special purpose, and (4) the defense that the holder, or a person through whom he or she holds the instrument, acquired it by theft, or that payment or satisfaction to the holder would be inconsistent with the terms of a restrictive indorsement. U.C.C. §3-306.

2. Would the FDIC ordinarily qualify as a holder in due course in depository institution insolvency proceedings? The answer, under the UCC, is clearly no. The FDIC as receiver of an insolvent bank does not take the bank's assets "for value"; it simply succeeds to the rights of the closed institution. Thus a claim or defense good against the closed institution ought, under the UCC, to be good against the FDIC as receiver as well. The FDIC does acquire assets for value in a purchase and assumption transaction; the assets are those not taken by the acquiring institution, and the value is the payment that the agency makes to cover the shortfall of assets to liabilities. Even so, under standard UCC law these agencies would not be holders in due course. Under UCC §3-302(3)(c), a holder does not become a holder in due course of an instrument "by purchasing it as part of a bulk transaction not in regular course of business." Clearly the assets acquired by the FDIC in a purchase and assumption transaction are obtained as part of a bulk transaction within the meaning of §3-302(3)(c). For the same reason, it would appear that an acquiring institution does not qualify as a holder in due course with respect to the assets it obtains in a purchase and assumption transaction. Comment 3 to §3-302 states that §(3)(c) "has particular application to the purchase by one bank of a substantial part of the paper held by another bank which is threatened with insolvency and seeking to liquidate its assets."

3. Nevertheless, a number of cases recognize that the FDIC and RTC *do* qualify for holder in due course status under federal common law, at least in the FDIC's corporate capacity and probably in its receivership capacity. Moreover, it seems clear that if the FDIC qualifies as a holder in due course, so do any transferees from the FDIC. This follows from the "shelter" rule of UCC §3-201(1), which provides that

> [t]ransfer of an instrument vests in the transferee such rights as the transferor has therein, except that a transferee who has himself been a party to any fraud or illegality affecting the instrument or who as a prior holder had notice of a defense or claim against it cannot improve his position by taking from a holder in due course.

Thus an acquiring institution in a purchase and assumption transaction would ordinarily qualify as a holder in due course to the same extent that the FDIC or RTC did so.

4. Professors White and Summers state the rationale for the holder in due course doctrine as follows:

> [i]n theory at least, the holder-in-due-course doctrine facilitated all kinds of transactions. First, it facilitated the flow of capital from large lenders to the seller to an individual consumer. In theory it did that by causing the lenders to purchase consumer paper and thus to use their capital to allow individual lenders and merchants to do business with the consumer. Second, the doctrine theoretically facilitates the transfer of checks and arguably makes one more willing to accept the checks if he knows he can be a holder-in-due-course of that instrument and take it free of defenses that might have existed between the buyer and the seller in the underlying transaction.

J. White & R. Summers, Uniform Commercial Code 613-614 (3d ed. 1988). Do similar policies underlie the federal holder in due course doctrine recognized in *Murray?*

5. Was it necessary for the *Murray* court to draw on a special federal holder in due course rule? Wasn't this a messy doctrinal approach, especially given that the federal rule deviates from the rule applicable under the UCC? Why couldn't the court simply have decided this case on the basis of *D'Oench, Duhme?*

6. What are the limits of the federal holder in due course doctrine, given that at least some of the technical requirements of the UCC are evidently inapplicable? What if the instrument in question is not "negotiable" under UCC §3-104? Ordinarily the holder could not be a holder in due course. Would the same result apply in the banking context? If the FDIC could be treated as a holder in due course, even though the note had not been negotiated, could ordinary contract rights be brought within the federal holder in due course doctrine? What if the FDIC or its transferees have notice of a claim or defense under UCC §3-304? Would they still qualify as holders in due course under federal common law? If we begin to stretch the doctrine in these ways, why call it a holder in due course doctrine at all—why not just call it general federal common law under *D'Oench, Duhme?*

#### d. Relationship Among Authorities

What happened to the *D'Oench, Duhme* doctrine when Congress enacted §1823(e) in 1950? One could easily argue that §1823(e) displaced *D'Oench, Duhme* entirely; Congress intended to codify the case, and—as in many other situations in which a legislature enacts a statute to govern relationships previously subject to the common law—the common law must give way. If §1823(e) were held to displace *D'Oench, Duhme,* it could actually reduce the protections available to the FDIC under the federal common law, to the extent it was interpreted as narrower in scope than prior law.

The courts have not followed this route. Some have stated that *D'Oench, Duhme* and §1823(e) are coextensive and, accordingly, have rejected the argument that the statute limits protections otherwise available under the common law. Other courts avoid the potential narrowing effect of §1823(e) by treating *D'Oench, Duhme* as an independent and alternative source of legal rights. See, e.g., FDIC v. Kasal, 913 F.2d 487, 491 (8th Cir. 1990), *cert. denied,* 498 U.S. 1119 (1991) (*D'Oench, Duhme* provides a "viable independent basis for invalidating collateral agreements against the FDIC even after the enactment of [the statute]").

The thesis that *D'Oench, Duhme* remains a viable, independent source of law raises other questions. Is *D'Oench, Duhme* broader in any respect than §1823(e)? If not, then its continued viability is a matter of theoretical interest only. If *D'Oench, Duhme* is broader in some respects, what are those respects? The reported decisions are murky.

For the most part, courts treat the three bases of authority as a single unitary doctrine, without bothering to distinguish the sources of the rights asserted by the FDIC or its assigns. See, e.g., FDIC v. Newhart, 892 F.2d 47 (8th Cir. 1989). We will not venture to tear asunder the polygamous marriage many courts have celebrated between *D'Oench, Duhme,* §1823(e), and the federal holder in due course doctrine. Rather, we follow the majority of reported decisions by treating these three bases of authority, for the most part, as if they are combined into a single, unified "side agreement" rule, without attempting to delineate the borders between them.

## 2. *Elements of the Rule*

### a. Beneficiaries of the Rule

Clearly under §1823(e) (as amended by FIRREA), the FDIC is entitled to the benefits of the side agreement rule in its capacities both as deposit insurer and as receiver of failed depository institutions. The courts are also in accord that the doctrine extends to other agencies such as the now defunct FSLIC and RTC, which played a role similar to that occupied by the FDIC, and that acquiring firms in purchase and assumption transactions can assert any side agreement defense that would have been available to the FDIC or RTC as receiver—at least if the acquiring firm has no actual or constructive knowledge of a claim or defense.

Other situations are less well understood. Take, for example, an institution that has received open bank or open thrift assistance from the FDIC. If such assistance involves the transfer of assets from the depository institution to the FDIC as security for loans or in exchange for a capital infusion, it would appear that the side agreement rule would protect the FDIC with respect to the assets so acquired. See FDIC v. WH Venture, 607 F. Supp. 473 (E.D. Pa. 1985). Any assets that remain in the hands of the depository institution, however, as well as any assets that are transferred to another institution without first being "laundered" through the FDIC, may not be so protected. The law in this area is unclear.

Coverage issues may also arise with respect to "new banks" authorized under 12 U.S.C. §1821(m). While the authorization for bridge banks contains an express side agreement rule, see 12 U.S.C. §1821(n)(4)(I), the new bank authorization contains no such language, an omission that a court might find significant.

What about claims or defenses that arise while an institution is operating under conservatorship or in the form of a bridge bank or new bank? Arguably, even if the side agreement rule cuts off claims arising *prior* to the establishment of the conservatorship, new bank, or bridge bank, the rule would not apply to claims or defenses against these institutions arising while they are operating under federal stewardship. On the other hand, the agencies may argue that the policies underlying the side agreement rule justify its application in this context as well.

Consider also whether the side agreement rule would bar claims and defenses arising after the establishment of a bridge bank, new bank, or conservatorship if the FDIC subsequently placed the institution in receivership and transferred its assets either to the FDIC-corporate or to some acquiring institution in a purchase and assumption transaction.

There is likely to be litigation on many of these issues during the years to come.

### b. The Requirement of an "Agreement"

What sorts of arrangements constitute "agreements" subject to the rule? The *Langley* case excerpted above establishes that the concept of an agreement is not to be construed narrowly or technically. As you will recall, the petitioners in that case borrowed money from a bank to purchase land, executing a note and other guarantees in exchange. The petitioners defended against the FDIC's suit on the note with the argument that the bank had fraudulently misrepresented the quantity of the land and the value of associated mineral assets. The Supreme Court held that this defense of fraud in the inducement was barred under the side agreement rule, stating:

> [a]s a matter of contractual analysis, the essence of petitioner's defense against the note is that the bank made certain warranties regarding the

> land, the truthfulness of which was a condition to performance of their obligation to repay the loan. . . . As used in commercial and contract law, the term "agreement" often has "a wider meaning than . . . promise," . . . and embraces such a condition on performance. . . . Quite obviously, the parties' bargain cannot be reflected without including the conditions upon their performance, one of the two principal elements of which contracts are constructed.

Langley v. FDIC, 484 U.S. 86, 90-91 (1987).

## *QUESTIONS AND COMMENTS*

1. Do you agree with the Court's analysis? Do you think there was any meeting of the minds between the bank and the borrower on whether the bank warrantied the information about the value of the property? If not, how was there an "agreement" on this matter?

2. Isn't the more natural construction to view the bank's alleged fraud not as a breach of contract, but rather as a tortious act of misrepresentation? Did the Supreme Court in effect hold that contracts with banks implicitly incorporate the common law background of tort liability?

3. Would the result have been the same in *Langley* if the "warranty" had been expressly included in the loan agreement? What does this suggest about how loan contracts with banks should be written in the future?

4. Isn't it virtually impossible to include all conditions to contractual performance in writing? The contract would have to be a thousand pages long, wouldn't it? The ordinary approach under contract law is to supply "background" or "default" terms when the parties have not explicitly specified some element of their agreement. Does *Langley* exclude defenses or claims based on such background terms? Wouldn't a more sensible result be to exclude only oral or side agreements that *deviate* from the default rules that would otherwise apply in the absence of express contractual language?

5. Suppose a contract with a depository institution contains ambiguous language on a particular question, and a party in litigation with the FDIC seeks to introduce extrinsic evidence to prove the meaning of the words in question. The agency claims that the evidence should not be admitted because it represents an attempt to prove an oral side agreement. What result? See Security Savings Bank v. Green Tree Acceptance, Inc., 739 F. Supp. 1342 (D. Minn. 1990) (allowing the proof).

6. Suppose a potential borrower signs a note and loan agreement with the bank, but the loan is subsequently refused. The borrower fails to retrieve the documents from the bank. Later the bank fails and the FDIC sues on the note. What result? See FDIC v. McClanahan, 795 F.2d

512 (5th Cir. 1986) (failure to recover the note was conduct likely to deceive bank examiners and, accordingly, was subject to side agreement rule). Suppose that the borrower fills out documents in blank, which the bank fraudulently alters? See FSLIC v. Murray, 853 F.2d 1251 (5th Cir. 1988) (same result). Do you agree with these cases?

7. While a depository institution is solvent, its officers fraudulently misrepresent its financial condition, inducing X to buy stock in the institution. After the institution fails, X sues the FDIC as receiver, claiming that the FDIC succeeded to the liabilities of the old institution. The FDIC cites the side agreement rule. What result? Compare Vernon v. Resolution Trust Corporation, 907 F.2d 1101 (11th Cir. 1990) (side agreement rule doesn't apply to tort claims) with Timberland Design v. First Service Bank for Savings, 932 F.2d 46 (1st Cir. 1991)(side agreement rule applies to tort claims).

### c. The Requirement of Right, Title, or Interest

In addition to the necessity of an agreement, it is also necessary for the FDIC or its assigns to have some right, title or interest that may be defeated or diminished by the side agreement in question. This element of the rule has raised a host of problems. For a sampling, consider the following:

1. The maker of a note alleges that the payee bank procured the note through fraud, and files suit against the bank to void the obligation. While the suit is under way the bank is placed in receivership, and the FDIC raises the side agreement defense. What result? This issue is decided favorably to the FDIC in the *Langley* case excerpted above.

2. A thrift institution purchases a share of a participated loan. Later it sues the original lender for misrepresentation and obtains a judgment of rescission. While the case is on appeal, the original lender is placed in receivership, and the receiver sues on the participation agreement. What result? See Olney Savings & Loan Association v. Trinity Bank Savings Association, 885 F.2d 266 (5th Cir. 1989) (because trial court had entered a judgment voiding the participating agreement, the receiver acquired no right, title or interest). Is there a significant difference in policy between this case and the previous one?

3. A real estate developer borrows money from a bank and executes a promissory note. Later the developer, with the full knowledge of the bank, sells the project to another developer, who pledges the same note to the bank as security for new loans. After the bank is placed in receivership, the FDIC sues the first developer on the note and raises the side agreement bar to the defendant's claim that the purchaser of the project has assumed its obligation on the note, with the bank's consent. Nothing in the loan file indicates such an assumption and release. What result?

See FDIC v. Prann, 694 F. Supp. 1027 (D.P.R. 1988), *aff'd sub nom.* FDIC v. Bracero & Rivera, Inc., 895 F.2d 824 (1st Cir. 1990) (because the first developer's obligation had been extinguished, the side agreement rule did not bar the defense). Does this square with the policy rationales behind the side agreement rule? Compare FDIC v. Hoover-Morris Enterprises, 642 F.2d 785 (5th Cir. 1981) (rejecting borrower's defense of accord and satisfaction where the parties had never consummated the agreement by delivery of a deed).

4. A bank president fraudulently induces a borrower to sign a loan guarantee, and then whites out the name of the ostensible beneficiary of the guarantee and inserts the name of another bank as beneficiary. In an action on the guarantee by the FDIC as receiver for the second bank, the guarantor claims that he was induced to sign the instrument without knowledge or reasonable opportunity to obtain knowledge of its essential terms. What result? See FDIC v. Turner, 869 F.2d 270 (6th Cir. 1989) (defense of fraud in the factum survived the side agreement bar). Does this suggest that the so-called real defenses that are good against a holder in due course under the UCC are also good against the FDIC, RTC, or their assigns under the side agreement rule?

5. A customer files suit against a bank, claiming breach of an agreement to extend credit. The agreement is contained in a letter from a bank officer, but is not reflected in the bank's official records. The FDIC is appointed receiver and raises the side agreement bar. The customer responds that the side agreement rule applies only to agreements that tend to diminish the FDIC's interest in *specific* assets; since the agreement to extend credit did not affect any particular asset of the bank, but rather the bank's total worth, the side agreement rule did not apply. What result? See Bell & Murphy & Associates, Inc. v. InterFirst Bank Gateway, 894 F.2d 750 (5th Cir.), *cert. denied,* 498 U.S. 895 (1990) (side agreement rule applies even if no specific asset is affected).

6. Customer A takes out a certificate of deposit in a bank. Later the customer assigns the certificate of deposit to Customer B and informs the bank. The bank fails and the FDIC sets the liability on the certificate of deposit off against a debt owed to the bank by Customer A. It asserts the side agreement rule to defeat Customer B's claim for the proceeds. What result? See Villafane-Neriz v. FDIC, 20 F.3d 35 (1st Cir. 1994) (side agreement rule applies only to *assets* of a failed institution, not liabilities).

#### d. Notice

Even if there is an agreement that tends to defeat the FDIC's right, title, or interest, the rule applies only if the agreement in question is a *side* agreement. If the agreement is approved by the depository institution's board of directors or loan committee, is embodied in writing, and included in the appropriate official records of the institution, it will be fully enforceable since there is no tendency for such an agreement to mislead the FDIC or its assigns about the nature of the institution's assets. But under what other conditions (if any) is the agreement sufficiently memorialized in the institution's records to provide the requisite notice? Consider the following fact patterns:

1. Suppose that the FDIC's bank examiners learned of a claim or defense during a routine examination. Should this knowledge be attributed to the FDIC to defeat the side agreement bar? Courts hold such knowledge to be irrelevant. See, e.g., FDIC v. Merchants National Bank of Mobile, 725 F.2d 634, 640 (11th Cir.), *cert. denied,* 469 U.S. 829 (1984):

> [s]ound policy reasons dictate against holding [the] FDIC liable for its knowledge of side agreements as well as the hidden meaning of bank assets. In the ordinary course of business examiners from [the] FDIC's open-bank division regularly visit all insured banks and even more frequently visit failing banks. If in undertaking a purchase and assumption transaction [the] FDIC's closed-bank division were held to matters of which the open-bank examiners had actual knowledge, . . . [a]ny asset would be subject to challenge based on the alleged knowledge of bank examiners. The resulting uncertainty would undercut [the] FDIC's ability to value assets quickly and precisely when conducting a purchase and assumption transaction.

2. What if a party can show that the FDIC's *closed bank* department was aware of a claim or defense at the time a receiver was appointed? See FDIC v. Gulf Life Insurance Co., 737 F.2d 1513 (11th Cir. 1984) (under federal common law, if the FDIC's closed bank department actually knows of a defense such as estoppel, waiver, or unjust enrichment at the time of the purchase and assumption transaction, it is subject to the defense); FDIC v. Turner, 869 F.2d 270, 273 (6th Cir. 1989) (suggesting in dictum that the FDIC might not be protected if it had actual notice of defenses before the purchase and assumption transaction transpired). But see Campbell Leasing, Inc. v. FDIC, 901 F.2d 1244 (5th Cir. 1990) (FDIC entitled to holder in due course status even though it had notice that a note was overdue, a factor that would defeat holder in due course status under UCC §3-302).

3. What if a defense is based on a bilateral obligation in the instrument that the FDIC seeks to enforce, even though the FDIC has no notice of any defense? See Howell v. Continental Credit Corp., 655 F.2d 743, 748 (7th Cir. 1981) ("the fact that the court must go outside the [instrument] to test the *strength* and *validity* of the defense [ ] is not fatal where the *foundation* and *basis* of that defense is in a document arguably meeting the nonsecrecy requirements of §1823(e)") (emphasis in original). What does this suggest about litigation strategy? About drafting agreements with banks?

4. In litigation with the FDIC, an obligor on a note held by the FDIC claims that the failed bank violated a commitment to finance third-party purchasers of the borrower's properties. The obligor introduces 71 official bank records, including the bank's written loan commitment to a third party purchaser that the bank repudiated on the day before the scheduled closing. None of the documents, however, expressly promises to fund such third-party purchasers as consideration for the note or otherwise. What result? See Beighley v. FDIC, 868 F.2d 776 (5th Cir. 1989) (documentation was inadequate to remove the side agreement bar).

5. The side agreement rule is often justified on the ground that the customer is in a good position to protect itself by ensuring that all its agreements with a depository institution are in writing and contained in the bank's official files. But is this realistic? What if the customer takes every possible precaution to ensure that the agreement is in writing, but the bank fails to submit it to its loan committee, as required by §1823(e)? What if the bank submits the agreement to its loan committee, but the committee's approval is not entered into the minutes of its meeting? What if the bank negligently or deliberately expunges an otherwise sufficient agreement from its official records at some time after the agreement is signed? Will these unilateral actions by bank officials redound to the disadvantage of the customer? Should they? What theory could a customer devise in such cases to avoid the side agreement rule?

### e. Scope of the Remedy

A final set of problems under the side agreement rule concerns the scope of the remedy. It is quite clear that the rule bars claims or defenses of a bank's customers that are directly related to particular instruments held by a bank. But a variety of fact patterns can arise in which the FDIC or its assigns might attempt to apply the side agreement rule more broadly. Consider the following:

1. The president of Bank B informs a long-standing customer that he has reached his lending limit, but that if the customer obtains the signatures of relatives on notes as accommodation parties, the bank can extend additional funds, providing that the loan payments are made directly to the president rather than to the bank. The parties agree orally that the bank will not look to the relatives for payment on the notes. The deal is consummated, and the customer makes regular principal and interest payments, which the president converts to his own use. The bank fails and the FDIC as receiver seeks payment from the cosigners on the notes, which according to the bank's records are in default. The cosigners defend on the grounds that (a) the bank agreed not to look to them for repayment, and (b) in any event the bank has been paid. What

result? See FDIC v. Kasel, 913 F.2d 487 (8th Cir. 1990), *cert. denied,* 498 U.S. 1119 (1991) (side agreement rule barred the defense).

2. Can a third party get around the side agreement rule by means of a setoff? Suppose Bank A sells a $1 million certificate of deposit to Bank B. Bank B fails, and in an action on the certificates of deposit by the receiver, Bank A claims a setoff for certain nonperforming notes that Bank A purchased from Bank B as a result of Bank B's fraudulent inducement. What result? See FDIC v. Texarkana National Bank, 874 F.2d 264 (5th Cir. 1989), *cert. denied,* 493 U.S. 1043 (1990) (setoff barred by side agreement rule).

3. Even if a borrower cannot obtain relief based on a side agreement by means of a setoff, is the borrower entirely out of luck? Suppose that in addition to a defense on the note, the borrower has lender liability claims against the bank based on the same transaction. Are these forfeited under the side agreement rule? See Campbell Leasing, Inc. v. FDIC, 901 F.2d 1244, 1249 (5th Cir. 1990) (borrower's claims against the bank for tortious interference with contract, breach of a security agreement, and intentional infliction of emotional distress not barred completely by side agreement rule; rather, borrower could obtain a judgment against the bank and share with other creditors in distributions from the receivership). Do you agree with this case? Compare Fair v. NCNB Texas National Bank, 733 F. Supp. 1099 (N.D. Tex. 1990) (side agreement rule applies to bar claims based on bank's alleged fraudulent representations made to induce the sale of assets held by the bank after foreclosure).

4. A borrower goes into Chapter 11 bankruptcy reorganization and the FDIC, as receiver of a lender bank, files a proof of claim. The bankruptcy trustee seeks equitable subordination of the FDIC's security interest in the collateral on the ground that the defunct bank had engaged in wrongful conduct towards the debtor by reneging on an oral promise to provide additional financing. The FDIC raises the side agreement bar. What result? See Matter of CTS Truss, Inc., 868 F.2d 146, 149-150 (5th Cir. 1989) (dictum) (side agreement rule bars subordination).

5. A borrower executes a note and mortgage to a bank in exchange for a loan and thereafter files for bankruptcy. The mortgagee bank fails, and the FDIC is appointed receiver. After the mortgage is foreclosed, the bankruptcy trustee claims priority in the proceeds of the mortgage sale on the ground that the mortgage and note were given in contemplation of insolvency for inadequate consideration. The FDIC sets up the side agreement rule. What result? See In re Kanterman, 108 Bankr. 432 (S.D.N.Y. 1989) (side agreement rule inapplicable, at least in the absence of reckless conduct by the bankrupt that could be attributed to the trustee, because trustee's rights arose by operation of law rather than pursuant to any agreement).

6. Suppose a borrower alleges that the failed bank induced her to execute promissory notes to underwrite the sale of overvalued bank

stock, and that the bank's actions were in violation of SEC Rule 10b-5 (generally outlawing false or misleading statements in connection with the purchase or sale of securities). Can the FDIC as receiver set up the side agreement rule against the borrower's suit for rescission of the notes? See Kilpatrick v. Riddle, 907 F.2d 1523 (5th Cir. 1990), *cert. denied sub nom.* Rogers v. FDIC, 498 U.S. 1083 (1991) (claim barred). Do you agree that the side agreement rule should trump the federal policy of good faith and fair dealing in securities transactions, which is embodied in Rule 10b-5? The dissenting judge in the *Kilpatrick* case argued that the policies of the securities law should prevail.

# 9 INTERNATIONAL BANKING

## A. INTRODUCTION

Banking is an industry that is peculiarly well suited to operating in international markets because its principal commodity is money, and because technology has now made it possible for banks and companies to send money across borders without delay and at very low cost. Moreover, international trade is of great importance to the economic well-being of most countries, including the United States.

International banking may be considered under three headings: (1) the U.S. activities of foreign banks; (2) the foreign activities of U.S. banks; and (3) international regulatory structures. We discuss these in turn.

## B. FOREIGN BANKS IN THE UNITED STATES

It may come as a considerable surprise to the ordinary consumer of banking services to discover what a large presence foreign banks have developed in the United States. Most of us do our personal business with a domestic institution and have little contact with foreign financial firms. We might assume that such firms occupy only a marginal niche in the U.S. banking market. But the facts are otherwise. Foreign bank operations in the United States are very big business, and, accordingly, the law relating to their operations is an important part of the overall scheme of U.S. banking regulation.

In considering how a nation's regulatory authorities should treat foreign firms doing business within its borders, it is useful to keep six possible regulatory models in mind. The purpose of this exercise is only to clarify ideas: the actual situation is never as neat or well organized as this kind of ideal type analysis would suggest. The models are these:

1. *Home country regulation.* The United States could allow a foreign bank to conduct business here under the same terms and conditions as those that apply to the foreign bank in its home country. Under this scheme, foreign banks would often operate in the United States under a very different regulatory scheme than that which applies to the U.S. operations of U.S. banks.
2. *National treatment.* Foreign banks operating in the U.S. would be treated just as if they were U.S. banks, subject to the same terms and conditions of operation.
3. *Special dispensation.* Foreign banks would be given special powers of operation in the United States, powers not enjoyed by domestic banks and not tied to any regulatory system in the foreign bank's home country.
4. *Special control.* Foreign banks would be regulated more strictly than domestic banks with respect to their U.S. operations, again without regard to the foreign bank's home-country regulations.
5. *Reciprocity.* Foreign banks would be allowed to conduct operations in the United States to the same extent that the foreign bank's home country permits U.S. banks operating in that country to conduct them.
6. *Multinational regulation.* Banks from all over the world would be subject to regulation by a multinational regulatory body with authority to control their international operations.

Which of these models appears the most sensible to you? Will any of them work in the pure form described above? What are their advantages and disadvantages?

As noted, the actual system of foreign bank regulation does not fit neatly into any of the six models. As a broad generalization, we can say that the regulatory system has been in the midst of a profound transformation. Prior to 1978, foreign banks enjoyed a degree of special dispensation when operating in U.S. markets, both with respect to their ability to expand geographically and to the stringency of regulation imposed on them here. That year witnessed a move towards the domestic regulation (national treatment) model, epitomized by an epithet from the dual banking system—"competitive equality." More recently still, small but significant elements of the special control model have been introduced into the system; in some respects, foreign banks operate in the United States under special regulatory constraints not applicable to their domestic competitors. At the same time, a degree of multinational regulation has entered the picture with the increasingly important activities of the Basel Committee of the Bank for International Settlements. The trend is toward more stringent regulation.

Because of this rapidly changing regulatory philosophy, the scheme of foreign bank regulation in the United States can best be understood through an analysis of the changes that have occurred over the past two decades. There are three key periods or events to keep in mind.

*Before 1978.* Prior to 1978, foreign banks typically operated in the United States by means of branches supervised by state regulators. Nothing in U.S. law stopped a foreign institution from establishing a subsidiary bank in the United States, but there were significant costs in doing so. By establishing a subsidiary bank in the United States, the foreign bank would become a bank holding company subject to regulation by the Federal Reserve Board, and its subsidiary would be regulated as a bank by state or national authorities, depending on the nature of the charter. Moreover, some foreign institutions may have faced difficulties under their own law in creating subsidiary corporations.

This state of affairs was quite advantageous to foreign institutions. They could, and did, branch across state lines whereas their domestic counterparts could not; by 1978, 63 foreign banks operated banking facilities in more than one state. Foreign banks, moreover, could engage in a wide variety of equity investments and could own stakes in U.S. securities firms. They were not subject to U.S. capital adequacy rules, and their home-country capital regulations were often less stringent. They were not subject to the system of interest rate controls that applied to all domestic U.S. banks and thrifts. They were not required to obtain federal deposit insurance and pay assessments; and, unlike state-chartered banks, they did not need to offer insured deposits in order to conduct their operations, which mostly involved financing of foreign trade.

*The International Banking Act of 1978.* All this changed in 1978 with the enactment of the International Banking Act (IBA). The policy of the IBA was competitive equality. It established mandatory federal jurisdiction over the domestic operations of foreign banks, and it vested regulatory responsibility in the Federal Reserve Board. The board requires foreign banks to hold reserves, and it examines branches and agencies of foreign banks. 12 U.S.C. §3105.

Foreign banks were also brought under the BHCA, which prohibited them from engaging in activities not so "closely related to banking or to managing or controlling banks as to be a proper incident thereto." See

12 U.S.C. §3106. These restrictions, which apply to the nonbanking activities of foreign banks that have U.S. branches even if those activities take place outside the United States, can be avoided if the foreign bank obtains a determination from the Fed that it is a "qualified foreign banking organization." An organization qualifies for this exemption if, disregarding its U.S. banking operations, more than half of its worldwide business is banking and if more than half of its banking business is outside the United States. 12 C.F.R. §211.23. If a foreign bank is a qualified foreign banking organization, it can engage in activities of any kind outside the U.S. and can engage in activities within the United States that are incidental to its activities outside this country. What sort of political compromise do you think this provision reflects?

In furtherance of the policy of competitive equality between foreign and domestic banks, the IBA required foreign banks to select a "home state" in the United States. If the foreign bank is entering de novo, the home state is the state where the foreign institution has its initial bank or branch. 12 U.S.C. §3103(c); 12 C.F.R. §211.22(a)(1-3). A foreign institution that had banks or branches in more than one state in 1978 could choose its home state from among the states where it was then doing business. 12 U.S.C. §3103(c).

The IBA also regulated the process by which foreign institutions establish branches and agencies in the United States. See 12 U.S.C. §3102. An agency is a place of business where the firm may pay checks, make loans, and maintain credit balances incidental to or arising out of the exercise of banking powers, but which does not accept deposits from citizens or residents of the United States. 12 U.S.C. §3101(1). A branch of a foreign bank is an office or place of business where deposits are received. 12 U.S.C. §3101(3). The Comptroller's approval is required for all new branches or agencies. 12 U.S.C. §3102(a). Such branches and agencies are required to comply with applicable federal law as well as the law of the state in which they are located. 12 U.S.C. §3106a.

Foreign branches are not required, under the IBA, to obtain federal deposit insurance so long as they operate only on a wholesale basis or restrict their deposit operations to foreign activities. However, if the branch accepts deposits of less than $100,000, it must obtain federal deposit insurance (subject to limited grandfather rights for certain branches in operation in 1991). See 12 U.S.C. §3104(c).

An office of a foreign bank that does not fall within the definition of branch, agency, or subsidiary is referred to as a "representative office." Such offices may be established in the United States only with the prior approval of the Fed. 12 U.S.C. §3107(a).

*The Foreign Bank Supervision Enhancement Act of 1991.* The IBA established a basic charter for foreign bank operations in the United States that is still, in substantial part, the governing law. Important changes occurred in 1991, however, largely as a result of the infamous scandal involving the Bank of Credit and Commerce International (BCCI). The following material gives some background on this extraordinary fraud.

## The BCCI Affair: A Report to the Committee on Foreign Relations, U.S. Senate

***Senator John Kerry and Senator Hank Brown***
***102d Congress, 2d Session (December 1992)***[1]

BCCI's organization, growth, collapse, and criminality, are inextricably linked with the personality of its founder, Agha Hasan Abedi. Abedi himself was a product of the unique conditions of Moslem India in the final period of British rule prior to partition, and of the Islamic professional class who fled India for Pakistan in the first years after partition. . . . Abedi was especially suited to succeed in the post-colonial environment, given his family's experience in northern India . . . where his father had served the Rajah. At the Rajah's court, Abedi was exposed to great wealth and to the concept that access to it could be had for anyone who managed to make himself indispensable to that person who controlled such wealth. Abedi also learned that the previously immutable laws of the British colonial power could be changed, at whim, by the new Indian and Pakistani rulers that followed. Indeed legal obstacles to any goal could be eliminated if they interfered with the plans of a sufficiently important political figure. These were lessons which Abedi applied throughout his career as a banker, and [they are] critical to BCCI's unique history. . . .

Press accounts of Abedi's life from the 1970's and 1980's typically note Abedi's wish for his success to be seen as a Pakistani version of a Horatio Alger story: success in the material world as being merely the logical reward for piety, hard work, sobriety, discipline, and loyalty. . . . By all accounts—ranging from statements made by Bert Lance to Jimmy Carter to the Pakistani bankers who went to work for him at BCCI—[Abedi] was a man of extraordinary personal charisma. That charisma was the glue which held BCCI together. . . . According to [a former BCCI official], Abedi was a man whose personality dominated all those around him, who could simultaneously turn great personal powers to good and to evil[:] "I remember looking in his eyes and seeing God and the Devil balanced equally in them.". . . [Another reported Abedi's attitude about the law as follows: "The only laws that are permanent are the laws of nature. Everything else is flexible. We can always work in and around the laws. The laws change."]

[The report focuses at length on the relationship between Abedi and

1. The text of this report has been edited and rearranged for clarity of presentation. Some information from other sources has been added to the bracketed text.

Sheikh Zayed bin Sultan Al Nahyan of Abu Dhabi, once an impoverished desert Bedouin, who had become one of the richest men in the world as a result of Abu Dhabi's fabulous oil wealth. The report portrays the sheikh as well-intentioned but naive in financial matters; even in the late 1970s, the sheikh "would on trips abroad routinely write checks for $100,000 or $200,000 at a time for members of his retinue to spend as they liked, written on the back of a matchbook or a piece of toilet paper." He reportedly had 14 wives, although never more than four at a time, and at least 19 sons and 22 daughters. An acquaintance described the sheikh as follows: "He would pray or listen to the news. He had a court jester-type person who made him laugh and told him poetry. He was a simple man, simple but shrewd. On a trip to Spain which lasted 2 weeks, his retinue spent $20 million, but he only spent $400 on himself the entire trip for two dogs whose price he negotiated down from $1,000."]

[Abedi earned Sheikh Zayed's trust and eventually his substantial financial support.] As a result of the Abedi-Zayed Agreement, Abedi now had essentially unlimited resources to create BCCI. He could now act simultaneously as manager of billions of dollars of Sheikh Zayed's personal wealth, as banker to the United Arab Emirates of which Sheikh Zayed was chief of state, and as chairman of a new bank that had guaranteed assets of hundreds of millions of dollars from its inception. . . . With Abedi relying on the Sheikh's resources to finance his rapid expansion, BCCI's finances quickly became so intermingled with the finances of Abu Dhabi that it was difficult even for BCCI insiders to determine where one left off and the other began. . . .

[The report describes Abedi's banking practices, which made it nearly impossible for anyone save Abedi himself and his deputy to understand the true condition and operations of the bank. These included extensive, nearly obsessive use of nominees and front men to shield the real parties in interest to transactions; a corporate structure with a complexity approaching that of fractal geometry; Abedi's refusal to locate BCCI's principal activities in any one country; the extensive use of Luxembourg and the Grand Caymans as havens for bank secrecy and confidentiality; the decision to divide the bank's annual audits between two different accounting firms, neither of which was given full information on the affairs of the consolidated institution; massive use of kickbacks and bribes; the intimidation of witnesses; and the retention of politically connected insiders to discourage governmental action.]

BCCI's entry into the United States was inevitable, given Abedi's desire to make BCCI into a global bank, and the size and importance of the United States financial and banking markets. . . . As a foreign bank, BCCI could not legally accept deposits from U.S. citizens, or itself become an FDIC member bank. But if BCCI could find a way to enter the FDIC system, it would be able to offer a whole new, and highly valued, service to its customers—U.S. government guaranteed deposit insurance. Abedi decided that he would first acquire legitimate banks in the United States for BCCI, and then determine later how to merge BCCI into them.

BCCI's initial strategy for the United States was to infiltrate the U.S. banking system through purchasing beachhead banks in major banking centers, and then to expand the beachhead operations until BCCI had U.S. banking operations of sufficient size that they could ultimately merge with BCCI itself. . . . In the end, BCCI was successful in acquiring four banks, operating in seven states and the District of Columbia, with no jurisdiction successfully preventing BCCI from infiltrating it.

[The report describes how Abedi paid court to Bert Lance, who had previously headed the National Bank of Georgia (NBG), an institution previously owned by the Financial General Bankshares group (FGB), a Washington, D.C., bank holding company. Lance, whom the report refers to as "the most notorious banker in the United States," had recently been forced to leave his position as head of Jimmy Carter's Office of Management and Budget under a cloud of allegations about his management of NBG. Lance was represented at congressional hearings by prominent attorney Clark Clifford and his partner Robert Altman.]

[At the time that he met Abedi, Lance was deeply in debt. He was also under a compelling need to sell his interest in NBG. Eventually, a sale of NBG was arranged to Saudi Arabian businessman Ghaith Pharaon. As it turned out, Pharaon was operating essentially as a stand-in for BCCI.]

[At roughly the same time, BCCI arranged for other Middle Eastern nominees to purchase FGB, the Washington, D.C., holding company that had once owned NBG. Ostensibly, these investors were acting as individuals, not as a unified group. Each of the individual purchases was limited to 4.9 percent of the stock, just under the level that would have required them to identify themselves to the SEC—an arrangement that thinly disguised the fact that the investments were part of a coordinated plan orchestrated by a single hand. A federal judge enjoined Lance and others from violating the securities laws and indicated that there was evidence that BCCI was behind the transaction. The Federal Reserve then sought and received assurances from BCCI, from the ostensible investors, and from their attorneys that BCCI was not orchestrating the purchase. Eventually, after extended litigation by dissident shareholders, the Federal Reserve Board approved the acquisition. Perhaps to further disguise its foreign ownership, FGB changed its name to First American Bankshares.]

[The report contains an extensive discussion of the activities of Clark Clifford and Robert Altman. Clifford and Altman at various times represented Lance, First American, the investors in FGB, and BCCI, among others. Clifford was also later made chairman and director of First American and director of its holding company. Altman functioned as a director and president of First American and director of its parent companies, in addition to providing legal services to these institutions. The other directors of First American were two of Clifford's old and prominent friends. The Federal Reserve and others have alleged that Clifford and Altman were allowed to purchase shares in First American's bank holding company at a bargain, using nonrecourse loans from BCCI backed only by the shares being purchased; BCCI also allegedly promised that if Clifford and Altman wanted to sell their shares, BCCI would arrange for the shares to be purchased by interested buyers "in such manner, amount, and at such prices as BCCI and [Clifford or Altman] shall mutually determine."]

[Eventually, the frauds at BCCI came to light. In June 1991 the Bank of England received a report from the accounting firm of Price Waterhouse that set forth details of the fraud by BCCI's top management. The Bank of England quickly consulted regulatory agencies in other jurisdictions. On July 5, 1991, regulators from eight nations closed all BCCI offices within their borders. These closures were coordinated, but each occurred under the law of the particular jurisdiction in the absence of any international standards for closure of a global bank. Within a few weeks, 44 jurisdictions had shut down BCCI operations. At the time of its collapse, BCCI was one of the larger banks in the world, with assets of approximately $20 billion and operations in 69 countries.]

[The costs of the collapse were borne largely by BCCI's sponsors in Abu Dhabi, but many individual investors in England and other countries also lost money. Tragically, these were often small depositors from Pakistan and other Islamic countries, many of them living in England, who believed Abedi's rhetoric about Third World development and economic self determination. BCCI and others pleaded guilty to criminal charges in the United States, and bank regulators in other parts of the world brought enforcement proceedings as well.]

[The Senate Committee Report sums up its principal conclusions as follows.] BCCI's unique criminal structure—an elaborate corporate spider-web with BCCI's founder, Agha Hasan Abedi and his assistant Swaleh Naqvi, in the middle—was an essential component of its spectacular growth, and the cause of its eventual collapse. The structure was conceived by Abedi and managed by Naqvi for the specific purpose of evading regulation or control by governments. It functioned to frustrate the full understanding of BCCI's operations by anyone.

Unlike any ordinary bank, BCCI was from its earliest days made up of multiple layers of entities, related to one another through an impenetrable series of holding companies, affiliates, subsidiaries, banks-within-banks, insider dealings and nominee relationships. By fracturing corporate structure, record keeping, regulatory review, and audits, the complex BCC family of entities created by Abedi was able to evade ordinary legal restrictions on the movement of capital and goods as a matter of daily practice and routine. In creating BCCI as a vehicle fundamentally free of Government control, Abedi developed in BCCI an ideal mechanism for facilitating illicit activity by others, including such activity by officials of many of the governments whose laws BCCI was breaking.

BCCI's criminality included fraud by BCCI and BCCI customers involving billions of dollars; money laundering in Europe, Africa, Asia, and the Americas; BCCI's bribery of officials in most of those locations; support of terrorism, arms trafficking, and the sale of nuclear technologies; management of prostitution; the commission and facilitation of tax evasion, smuggling, and illegal immigration; illicit purchases of banks and real estate; and a panoply of financial crimes limited only by the imagination of its officers and customers.

Among BCCI's principal mechanisms for committing crimes were its use of shell corporations and bank confidentiality and secrecy havens; layering of its corporate structure; its use of front-men and nominees; guarantees and buy-back arrangements; back-to-back financial documentation among BCCI controlled entities; kick-backs and bribes; the intimidation of witnesses and the retention of well-placed insiders to discourage governmental action. . . .

BCCI systematically relied on relationships with prominent political figures in most of the 73 countries in which BCCI operated. In most cases, these relationships were secured through payments by or financial benefits from BCCI to the officials in a country whose assistance BCCI needed. . . . The result was that BCCI had relationships that ranged from the questionable, to the improper, to the fully corrupt with officials from countries all over the world including Argentina, Bangladesh, Botswana, Brazil, Cameroon, China, Colombia, the Congo, Ghana, Guatemala, the Ivory Coast, India, Jamaica, Kuwait, Lebanon, Mauritius, Morocco, Nigeria, Pakistan, Panama, Peru, Saudi Arabia, Senegal, Sri Lanka, Sudan, Surinam, Tunisia, the United Arab Emirates, the United Kingdom, the United States, Zambia, and Zimbabwe. . . .

BCCI cannot be taken as an isolated example of a rogue bank, but a case study of the vulnerability of the world to international crime on a global scope that is beyond the current ability of governments to control. Its multi-billion dollar collapse is merely the latest in a series of international financial scandals that have bedeviled international banking this century. While BCCI's size and scope of criminality dwarfed previous scandals, its techniques and its associations with government officials, intelligence agencies, and arms traffickers, were neither new nor unique.

## *QUESTIONS AND COMMENTS*

1. Among other alleged misdeeds of BCCI was its alleged role in facilitating the drug trafficking and money laundering activities of former Panamanian strongman General Manuel Noriega.

2. Clifford and Altman's law firm, Clifford & Warnke, was a well-

known and highly respected Washington firm, reputed to have excellent connections with the political establishment and to hire only highly accomplished young attorneys. Although the firm itself was not accused of wrongdoing aside from the handling of the BCCI affair, it could not withstand the scandal and rather quickly dissolved.

3. Altman was criminally prosecuted for his role in the BCCI affair, but acquitted. Claiming to have been dupes of Abedi's fraud, both Clifford and Altman have steadfastly denied that they participated in BCCI's illegal transactions, engaged in any unethical conduct, or profited improperly from the operation of First American Bankshares.

4. Clifford's support of a Middle Eastern investment in an American banking firm may have come, in part, from his perspective as a presidential advisor over many years. In a hearing before the Federal Reserve Board on the FGB takeover, he stated that "[i]t is in the interest of our country that an effort is made to bring back to the United States as many of the dollars as we can that through the years we send over to the OPEC countries." Is this a valid consideration?

5. Abedi and his deputy, Naqvi, were indicted by New York and federal grand juries but evaded U.S. justice. Abedi suffered a heart attack in 1988 and gave up operational responsibility for the bank to Naqvi. Abedi reportedly moved to Karachi, Pakistan, where he was unavailable to U.S. authorities. He died in 1996. Naqvi, reportedly being held in Abu Dhabi, was also unavailable to U.S. authorities.

6. How would you characterize the BCCI affair? Was the problem one of clashing cultures? Of too much wealth pouring into the hands of a relatively unsophisticated if well-intentioned Middle Eastern ruler? Of regulatory shortfalls? Of lack of checks and balances? Was this an example of Lord Acton's adage, "power corrupts, and absolute power corrupts absolutely"?

7. Although by far the biggest scandal in international banking at this time, BCCI was not unique. There were also problems with certain letters of credit issued by the Atlanta agency of an Italian bank, the Banca Nazionale del Lavoro, and with the activities of the Greek National Mortgage Bank's New York representative office. Public concern about these different events precipitated the next important phase in the evolution of U.S. regulation of foreign banks, the Foreign Bank Supervision Enhancement Act of 1991 (FBSEA), which as we have noted was enacted as part of the comprehensive FDICIA legislation of that year.

## NOTE ON THE FOREIGN BANK SUPERVISION ENHANCEMENT ACT OF 1991

The FBSEA requires foreign banks to obtain the permission of the Federal Reserve Board before establishing a branch or agency or a commercial lending company in the United States. 12 U.S.C. §3105(d). The Fed may not approve such an application unless the foreign bank, in the Fed's judgment, receives "comprehensive supervision or regulation on a consolidated basis" in its home country. In addition, the foreign bank must provide the Fed with "adequate assurances" that the bank will make available such information on the operations and activities of the foreign bank and any affiliates that the Fed may require in order to ensure compliance with applicable U.S. banking laws. The FBSEA also eliminated a provision of the IBA that had exempted foreign banks in the United States from compliance with section 3 of the BHCA. Thus, prior board approval is now required for acquisitions by foreign institutions of more than 5 percent of the outstanding shares of any class of voting securities of a U.S. bank or bank holding company. See 12 C.F.R. §225.11(f).

To insure comprehensive oversight of any activities of foreign banks within the United States, the FDICIA gives the Federal Reserve Board the authority to examine the branches, agencies, and other offices of foreign banks, and it subjects foreign branches and agencies to the same lending limits as the branches and agencies of national banks.

The FBSEA also provides that the Federal Reserve Board may order a foreign bank to terminate the activities of any existing branches, agencies, or commercial loan subsidiaries if the foreign bank is not subject to comprehensive supervision or regulation on a consolidated basis in its home country. The Fed may also close a foreign bank's U.S. branches, agencies, or subsidiaries, if there is "reasonable cause to believe" that the foreign bank or any of its affiliates has violated the law or engaged in an unsafe or unsound banking practice in the United States in such a way that "as a result of such violation or practice, the continued operation of the foreign bank's branch, agency, or commercial lending company subsidiary in the United States would not be consistent with the public interest or with the purposes of the [relevant banking statutes.]" 12 U.S.C. §3105(e)(1)(B)(2). We include below an excerpt from the Federal Reserve Board's dramatic use of this exclusion authority against Daiwa Bank.

### *QUESTIONS AND COMMENTS*

1. The literature on BCCI and the regulatory response to the scandal is vast. For a sampling, see Raj Bhala, Tragedy, Irony, and Protectionism After BCCI: A Three-Act Play Starring Maharajah Bank, 48 Southern Methodist University Law Review 11 (1994); William B. Glidden, The Regulation of U.S. Bank's Operations Abroad, 108 Banking Law Journal 108 (1991); Daniel M. Laifer, Putting the Super Back in the Supervision of International Banking, Post-BCCI, 60 Fordham Law Review S467 (1992); Joel P. Trachtman, Recent Initiatives in International Financial

Regulation and Goals of Competitiveness, Effectiveness, Consistency and Cooperation, 12 Northwestern Journal of International Law and Business 241 (1991).

2. Do you think the problems at BCCI establish a need for a regulatory structure such as that adopted in the FBSEA? Even if not necessary, is such a structure desirable?

3. Under FBSEA, the foreign bank applicant must prove that it is comprehensively supervised in its home country. How effective will this process be? How often does a nation's system of bank regulation look inadequate *on paper?* Aren't most of the shortfalls ones of enforcement? Won't these often be hidden or swept under the table? If the Fed's response is that the applicant must prove that the regulatory system in the home country is effective in practice as well as in law, how can the applicant possibly do so?

4. The FBSEA appears to require that the presence of adequate supervision in the home country must be proved each time. Does this make sense? Wouldn't it be much more efficient for the Fed to issue a list of countries found to provide adequate comprehensive supervision? What precedential force, if any, should the Fed give to prior orders recognizing that the system of supervision in a particular country is sufficiently comprehensive to satisfy the FBSEA?

5. The FBSEA requires that foreign banks, in connection with applications to establish new offices in the United States, provide assurances that they will provide "such information on the operations or activities of the foreign bank or any affiliate of the bank that the Board deems necessary" to determine and enforce compliance with U.S. laws and regulations. How will this provision interact with foreign bank secrecy laws, which are often more stringent than laws applicable in the United States? The Fed has tried to balance the interest of the foreign sovereign in enforcing its bank secrecy regime with the interest of the United States in enforcing domestic banking laws.

6. What is meant by "comprehensive consolidated supervision"? The Basel Committee has defined the minimal acceptable level of supervision as one that "requires that the home country supervisor of a bank or banking group (a) receive consolidated financial and prudential information on the bank's or banking group's global operations, have the reliability of this information confirmed to its own satisfaction through on-site examination or other means, and assess the information as it may bear on the safety and soundness of the bank or banking group; (b) have the capability to prevent corporate affiliations or structures that either undermine efforts to maintain consolidated financial information or otherwise hinder effective supervision of the bank or banking group; and (c) have the capability to prevent the bank or banking group from creating foreign banking establishments in particular jurisdictions." Ann

Misback, The Foreign Bank Supervision Enhancement Act of 1991, 79 Federal Reserve Bulletin 1 (1993).

7. Another regulatory response to the BCCI affair came out of the Bank for International Settlements in Basel, referred to in the previous note. Basel Committee on Banking Supervision, Minimum Standards for the Supervision of International Banking Groups and their Cross-Border Establishments (June 1992). In some respects, the new Basel standards track the FBSEA quite closely. They recommend that all international banks be subject to consolidated supervision by home regulators. The standards require that an international bank must receive permission from both its home-country and host-country regulators before opening a cross-border banking establishment. In determining whether to approve a foreign operation, the host-country regulator can consider the bank's strength of capital, organization, and operating procedures for risk management. See Duncan E. Alford, Basle Committee Minimum Standards: International Regulatory Response to the Failure of BCCI, 26 George Washington Journal of International Law and Economics 241 (1992).

8. Host countries generally worry less about maintaining the safety and soundness of foreign banks operating through subsidiaries than those operating through branches. When foreign banks operate through subsidiaries, the subsidiaries are subject to the safety and soundness rules of the host country. The host country does not have to be concerned to a great extent about the safety and soundness of the foreign parent of the host-country subsidiary. If the parent becomes insolvent, there may be a transfer in ownership of the subsidiary, but this does not necessarily mean that the subsidiary's safety or soundness is in jeopardy. In contrast, when a foreign bank operates through branches, the host country must be concerned with the safety and soundness of the foreign bank, because if the bank fails its branches fail also.

Nevertheless host countries might prefer foreign banks to operate through branches. Many host countries would prefer that local deposits be backed by the entire capital of the bank, as is the case with branch deposits, rather than the capital of the local subsidiary, the case with subsidiary deposits. Also, foreign bank branches may be more competitive than subsidiaries in host-country markets because the loan capacity of a branch in the host country is a function of the bank's worldwide capital. See Hal S. Scott, Supervision of International Banking Post-BCCI, 8 Georgia State University Law Review 487 (1992). In a study concluded in December 1992, the Treasury Department and the Federal Reserve Board determined that requiring all foreign banks to operate in the United States only as subsidiaries is "neither necessary nor desirable," since "if the United States were to require that foreign banks conduct their U.S. operations in subsidiaries, the availability of credit in the United States market could be reduced, perhaps substantially."

## In the Matter of Daiwa Bank, Ltd., Osaka, Japan, and Daiwa Bank, Ltd., New York Branch

*Board of Governors of the Federal Reserve System, October 2, 1995, Docket No. 95-028-B-FB*

### Notice of Charges and of Hearing Issued Pursuant to the Federal Deposit Insurance Act, as Amended

[The Board of Governors alleged:]

[Daiwa Bank Ltd., Osaka, Japan ("Daiwa")] has informed the Federal Reserve Bank of New York (the "Reserve Bank") that a senior official of the New York Branch, Toshihide Iguchi ("Iguchi"), submitted a written confession to the President of Daiwa. The written confession detailed Iguchi's unauthorized trading of U.S. Treasury securities in which, over an 11-year period, he lost approximately $1.1 billion. The written confession detailed how he secretly traded U.S. Treasury securities in an unauthorized manner and then misappropriated securities from Daiwa, as well as from customers of the branch for whom the New York Branch was acting as custodian, in order to cover the losses. The confession also described how Iguchi falsified branch records and lied to examiners and auditors in order to hide the trading losses. . . .

According to Iguchi, during the time period in which he was responsible for the New York Branch's U.S. Treasury trading operations, he was also the head of the branch's custodial department which held securities, including U.S. Treasury securities, for the branch's customers, as well as those which the branch held for its own accounts. Consequently, at times pertinent to the charges herein, Iguchi asserts that he was responsible for the New York Branch's U.S. Treasury securities trading and for the actual securities that the branch held, as a fiduciary, for its customers as well as for its own accounts. Iguchi also asserts that he was able to influence the performance of the New York Branch's backroom operations for U.S. Treasury securities trading activities.

According to Iguchi's written confession, from 1984 until the middle of 1995, he cumulatively lost about $1.1 billion in trading of U.S. Treasury securities. Due to the lack of controls necessary for a safe and sound trading operation, Iguchi asserts that he was able to hide the losses from others at the branch, auditors, and examiners from the Reserve Bank and the Superintendent. Iguchi states that, because he was responsible for the branch's custodial department, he was able to sell securities from Daiwa's own accounts, as well as securities of customers for which the branch acted as custodian, in order to cover his losses. Iguchi further states that, because he was able to influence the performance of the branch's backroom operations, he was in the position to falsify accounting and other branch records in order to hide from auditors and examiners the trading losses and the misappropriation of securities.

In November 1992 and again in November 1993, the Reserve Bank and the Superintendent criticized the poor internal controls at the New York Branch. Both the Reserve Bank and the Superintendent were led to believe by Iguchi and other officials at the New York Branch that lines of authority were changed in November 1993 so that Iguchi no longer was responsible for both the branch's trading and custodial operations. The Board of Governors has reasonable cause to believe that Daiwa and the New York Branch did not change the reporting lines and that, in fact, Iguchi continued to exercise control over the branch's custodial operations as well as some of its U.S. Treasury securities trading operations.

By at least July 1995, Daiwa and the New York Branch were aware of Iguchi's unauthorized trading, the resulting losses of about $1.1 billion, the misappropriation of securities from Daiwa's accounts and from its customers' accounts, the falsification of branch records and the misrepresentations to auditors and examiners. . . . Daiwa and the New York Branch failed to provide the regulators with timely and adequate notice of this matter.

*QUESTIONS AND COMMENTS*

1. On November 1, 1995, Daiwa consented to the issuance of an order terminating Daiwa's U.S. banking activities by February 2, 1996. See Board of Governors of the Federal Reserve System, In the Matter of Daiwa Bank, Ltd., Osaka, Japan, Docket No. 95-028-B-FB, March 18, 1996. The case sent shock waves around the financial world.

2. Does this case remind you at all of the BCCI affair? Note that the regulators had reason to doubt the adequacy of the internal controls in effect at Daiwa and were informed that the necessary reforms had been implemented, when in fact they had not. In BCCI, the regulators requested assurances that the group of Middle Eastern investors that was attempting to acquire an American bank was not acting in concert and that BCCI had no involvement as principal in the transaction. In each case, the U.S. authorities received the requested information, and in each case it was false. If someone is out to commit a serious fraud, why would they balk at lying to regulators? But if the regulators can't rely on the representations they receive, what recourse do they have?

3. This case differs from BCCI in important respects, however. Note that unlike BCCI, Daiwa operated under comprehensive consolidated supervision—by the highly respected Japanese Ministry of Finance. But this wasn't enough to catch the problem. What does this suggest about the efficacy of the FBSEA?

4. Federal Reserve Board Chairman Alan Greenspan reported to Congress on another aspect of the Daiwa fiasco: "We understand that some officials at the Japanese Ministry of Finance were informed in early

August about Daiwa's losses. They did not instruct Daiwa to inform the U.S. authorities; nor did they themselves do so. This lapse on the part of the Ministry of Finance is regrettable because open communication and close cooperation among supervisory authorities are essential to the maintenance of the integrity of the international financial system. Finance Minister Takemura has acknowledged the ministry's failure in this regard and has pledged that in the future the ministry will promptly and appropriately contact U.S. authorities on such matters of U.S. interest. We have been assured that the ministry is taking steps to implement this pledge. In addition, we have been pleased that once the Daiwa problem was disclosed, the Japanese authorities have fully cooperated with U.S. supervisors in dealing with the consequences." Statement by Alan Greenspan, Chairman, Board of Governors of the Federal Reserve System, before the Subcommittee on Financial Institutions and Consumer Credit of the Committee on Banking and Financial Services, U.S. House of Representatives, December 5, 1995. Why did the Japanese Ministry of Finance delay notifying the U.S. authorities? Was there some thought that the scandal could be hidden? Was the ministry consulting with others in the Japanese government? Was it attempting to verify the information it had received? Whatever the motive, wasn't Greenspan correct that the ministry was at fault for its delay, given that the fraud occurred in the United States? Note the chairman's carefully chosen characterization of the ministry's lapse as "regrettable." In the super-polite world of international financial diplomacy, this was the equivalent of a spanking.

5. Why should the United States be concerned if a Japanese bank loses over a billion dollars in trading on U.S. treasuries? Shouldn't the United States be happy at the windfall?

6. Why didn't Daiwa catch the fraud, which had apparently been going on for many years?

7. In addition to consenting to leave the United States, Daiwa pled guilty to 16 criminal charges and paid $340 million in fines. Back in Japan, Daiwa's chairman, president, and several other top officers resigned over the scandal.

## C. INTERNATIONAL ACTIVITIES OF U.S. BANKS

### 1. *Regulation by the Federal Reserve Board*

The Federal Reserve Board is the primary regulator of domestic banks that seek to do business abroad. The Federal Reserve is responsible for approving the establishment of foreign branches by member banks and for regulating the activities of these branches. In addition, it is responsible for regulating banks' foreign investments. Finally, the Federal Reserve regulates export trading companies and Edge Act corporations. We will look at each of these in turn.

#### a. Member Banks

National and state-chartered Federal Reserve bank members that have capital and surplus in excess of $1 million are eligible to apply to the Federal Reserve for permission to open a branch in a foreign country. The FDIC regulates the international banking activities of state nonmember banks, but the international activities of such banks are trivial. Banks with foreign branches are required to keep accounts separate from their home office accounts and from the bank's accounts at its other foreign branches. Separate books and records, including separate profit and loss statements, must be maintained.

#### b. Export Trading Companies

An export trading company is a company engaged in exporting, importing, marketing, advertising, obtaining orders, and arranging insurance for goods for overseas export or import. In 1982, as a response to the rather dubious argument that the growing U.S. trade deficit was caused by a lack of financial intermediaries to finance the export operations of domestic manufacturing firms, Congress amended §4(c) of the Bank Holding Act to permit bank holding companies to invest in firms specializing in financing exports and international trade.

Bank holding companies, and Edge Act subsidiaries of bank holding companies, can invest up to 5 percent of their capital and surplus in export trading companies. Except in extreme cases, the Federal Reserve cannot disapprove applications by bank holding companies wishing to invest in an export trading company. In particular, the statute provides that the Federal Reserve may withhold its approval only (1) to prevent unsafe or unsound banking practices, or undue concentration; or (2) to avoid an adverse impact on the financial or managerial resources of the bank holding company; or (3) if the holding company fails to provide the Federal Reserve with adequate information. 12 U.S.C. §1843(c)(14). Export trading companies have not been popular investments for bank holding companies, and few have been created.

### c. Edge Act Corporations

By contrast, Edge Act corporations, which have been around since 1916, have proved far more popular, largely because they enabled banks to avoid state law restrictions on interstate banking. An Edge Act corporation is a domestic subsidiary of a U.S. bank that is engaged in international banking and finance, including that which takes place in the United States. An Edge Act corporation may have branches and subsidiaries in foreign countries and in states that the bank holding company would not be allowed to enter any other way. Thus banks have found it attractive to establish Edge Act corporations because such corporations may take international deposits and conduct other international business across state lines. However, as the restrictions on interstate banking have eroded (recall the discussion in Chapter 5), so too has the general desirability of establishing an Edge Act corporation.

There are two basic kinds of Edge Act corporations. *Banking Edges* accept deposits, provide foreign exchange services, and offer financing for international trade. *Investment Edges* don't accept deposits, but rather make investments in foreign firms that are not engaged in the business of buying or selling goods in the United States.

U.S. banks may invest up to 10 percent of their capital and surplus in Edge corporations. These corporations engage in traditional banking activities like borrowing and lending money, issuing guarantees, notes, drafts, and checks, receiving deposits both outside the United States and inside the United States, so long as the domestic deposits are incidental to or for the purpose of carrying out transactions in foreign commerce. 12 U.S.C. §615.

### d. International Banking Facilities

In the early 1980s, Congress became quite concerned about both the rapid expansion of foreign banks doing business within the United States and the increasing tendency of U.S. banks to move their banking operations offshore (usually to the Caribbean) to avoid reserve requirements on foreign deposits and taxes on foreign banking operations. Congress responded by passing the International Banking Act of 1978, which prompted the Federal Reserve to promulgate enabling regulations to authorize "International Banking Facilities." Any bank may create an International Banking Facility, which is simply a fictitious set of international extensions of credit and time deposit accounts from foreign depositors that are recorded on the books of a U.S. bank, Edge corporation, or foreign bank. 12 C.F.R. §204.8. An International Banking Facility is able to avoid reserve requirements and state taxes so long as it does not accept deposits from or conduct banking activities with U.S. residents. Deposits at International Banking Facilities, which must be in amounts of at least $100,000, are not insured by the FDIC and not subject to the FDIC's insurance assessments.

Inevitably, banks attempt to book loans and deposits through their International Banking Facility despite the fact that such loans and deposits are not truly "international." Thus, line drawing problems arise. Suppose, for example, that a bank books a loan through its International Banking Facility to a foreign airline whose planes serve U.S. airports. Is this loan sufficiently "international" to merit inclusion on the books of the International Banking Facility? Fed. Res. Board, Interpretation 2451, CCH Banking L. Rep. ¶30499B (Nov. 9, 1981).

## 2. *Regulation by Other Agencies*

While the Federal Reserve authorizes overseas branches and promulgates the regulations that govern the activities of such branches, the Multinational Banking Department of the Office of the Comptroller of the Currency does most of the hands-on regulating of overseas banking, including on-site examinations. Federal deposit insurance does not apply to bank deposits that are "payable at an office of such bank located outside of the States of the United States." 12 U.S.C. §1813(1)(5)(A). Thus if a U.S. bank records a foreign deposit at its home office or at a branch within the United States, that deposit is covered by deposit insurance, and the bank must include the deposit when calculating the amount owed to the FDIC. If the deposit is recorded and payable only at the foreign branch, then it is not covered by deposit insurance, and no assessment must be paid. Interestingly, the Glass-Steagall Act, which prevents U.S. banks from engaging in the business of buying, selling, and dealing in securities, does not apply to the banks' overseas activities. Consequently, U.S. banks can buy, sell, and underwrite securities through their international offices subject only to the usually minimal restrictions that the foreign host countries impose on such activities.

In addition to the Federal Reserve and the Comptroller, banks involved in international trade frequently encounter regulations promulgated by the Department of Commerce, which regulates and licenses the exports of U.S. manufacturing firms and enforces U.S. boycotts and defense-related export controls. The activities of the office of the U.S. Trade Representative and the Department of the Treasury are also of interest to international bankers since these agencies conduct trade negotiations with foreign governments and implement trade sanctions imposed on our trading partners by Congress or the president.

## 3. *Financing Assistance for International Banking Activities*

U.S. banks can receive financing assistance for their international banking activities through the Export Import Bank, which is designed to facilitate international trade by U.S. firms. Among its other activities (which include lobbying foreign governments for reduction of their export subsidies), the Export Import Bank guarantees loans made by U.S. banks to foreign purchasers who are buying U.S. products and subsidizes bank loans that are made to finance U.S. exports. Finally, the Overseas Private Investment Corporation is a government agency that provides banks with insurance to cover the political risks associated with their foreign banking activities. Such insurance covers the risks associated with war, expropriation, nonconvertibility, and repatriation.

The International Monetary Fund (IMF) is an international agency of great importance to international bankers. The IMF has played a major role in persuading foreign governments that have received large loans from the international banking community to improve their domestic economic situation (for instance, by reducing budget deficits, increasing productivity, reducing inflation, and reducing subsidies to locally favored industries) so that they will be better able to repay their outstanding international bank loans and attract new credit. Negotiations between the IMF and foreign sovereign debtor nations often are conducted simultaneously with negotiations by private bankers on debt rescheduling. Banks "look to IMF as a leader in beginning the process of negotiations and creating the atmosphere for reschedulings and new lending." A. Pollard, K. Ellis, J. Possaic, Jr., & J. Daly, Banking Law in the United States 484 (1988).

## 4. *U.S. Bank Loans to Foreign Countries*

During the 1980s, U.S. bank loans to certain foreign countries became a source of concern to regulators. In 1983 the International Lending Supervision Act was passed to address this problem, at least to some degree. 12 U.S.C. §3904. The act requires U.S. banks to add to their loss reserves to protect against the risks involved with outstanding loans to certain countries. In addition, the act contains technical rules regarding loan restructurings, general capital requirements, and new disclosure obligations for banks involved in international lending to foreign countries. The act further requires banking institutions that receive fees associated with rescheduling or restructuring loans to amortize these fees over the life of a restructured loan to the extent that the fees exceed administrative costs incurred by the bank in connection with the rescheduling or restructuring.

## 5. *Home Bank Liability for Foreign Branch Deposits*

The issue of whether a U.S. bank's home office will be liable for deposits originating in its foreign branches is a recurring theme in international banking law. The emergence of new, sophisticated technologies for effectuating international interbank transfers has, in some instances, made the legal issues surrounding home office liability even more difficult than before. Deposits can be kept in overseas branches of U.S. banks in the form of Eurocurrency deposits, and these deposits can be transferred among branches and among banks almost instantaneously through the Clearing House Interbank Payments System (CHIPS). This section will consider a variety of issues in connection with assessing whether home banks assume liability for deposits in their foreign branches.

### a. The Deposit Contract in International Banking

Despite the formal rule that the FDIC does not cover deposits in foreign branches of U.S. banks, and despite the fact that U.S. banks do not pay premiums to the FDIC for foreign-branch deposits, the FDIC traditionally extended insurance coverage to such deposits, at least where the bank involved actually becomes insolvent. The Federal Deposit Insurance Corporation Improvement Act of 1991 prohibits regulators from making any payment or taking any other action that would result in satisfying a claim against a bank that is not assessed for FDIC insurance purposes because it is at a foreign branch of a U.S. bank. One of the reasons the FDIC does not insure foreign branch deposits is that foreign branches are exposed to political risks of expropriation that do not affect deposits in U.S. banks. Because these deposits are uninsured, the Federal Reserve Board does not regulate these deposits as stringently as domestic deposits. Moreover, the Federal Reserve has officially advised member banks against guaranteeing foreign branch deposits.

If a foreign depositor has agreed to look only to the assets of his local branch for repayment of his deposit, then the home bank should be free of liability if the foreign branch is unable to make payment. However, the fact that foreign banking operations are branches rather than separately incorporated subsidiaries suggests that depositors should be able to recover against the home office. In the early part of the twentieth century, courts began to modify the traditional rule in favor of home office liability for deposit obligations of foreign obligations by treating foreign branches as separate legal entities rather than as a part of the bank itself. See Hannigan, United States Home Bank Liability for Foreign Branch Deposits, 1989 U. Ill. L. Rev. 735, 742. Recently, however, the separate entity doctrine has begun to erode.

## Citibank, N.A. v. Wells Fargo Asia, Ltd.

*495 U.S. 660 (1990)*

At issue here is whether the home office of a United States bank is obligated to use its general assets to repay a Eurodollar deposit made at one of its foreign branches, after the foreign country's government has prohibited the branch from making repayment out of its own assets. . . .

. . . Respondent Wells Fargo Asia Limited (WFAL) is a Singapore-chartered bank wholly owned by Wells Fargo Bank, N.A., a bank chartered by the United States. Petitioner Citibank, N.A., (Citibank), also a United States-chartered bank, operates a branch office in Manila, Philippines (Citibank/Manila). On June 10, 1983, WFAL agreed to make two $1 million time deposits with Citibank/Manila. The rate at which the deposits would earn interest was set at 10%, and the parties agreed that the deposits would be repaid on December 9 and 10, 1983. The deposits were arranged by oral agreement through the assistance of an Asian money broker. . . .

. . . A few months after the deposit was made, the Philippine government issued a Memorandum to Authorized Agent Banks (MAAB 47) which provided in relevant part:

> Any remittance of foreign exchange for repayment of principal on all foreign obligations due to foreign banks and/or financial institutions, irrespective of maturity, shall be submitted to the Central Bank [of the Philippines] thru the Management of External Debt and Investment Accounts Department (MEDIAD) for prior approval.

Ibid. According to the Court of Appeals,

> [a]s interpreted by the Central Bank of the Philippines, this decree prevented Citibank/Manila, an "authorized agent bank" under Philippine law, from repaying the WFAL deposits with its Philippine assets, i.e., those assets not either deposited in banks elsewhere or invested in non-Philippine enterprises.

Ibid. As a result, Citibank/Manila refused to repay WFAL's deposits when they matured in December 1983.

WFAL commenced the present action against Citibank in the United States District Court for the Southern District of New York, claiming that Citibank in New York was liable for the funds that WFAL deposited with Citibank/Manila. . . .

Little need be said respecting the operation or effect of the Philippine decree at this stage of the case, for no party questions the conclusion reached by both the District Court and the Court of Appeals that Philippine law does not bar the collection of WFAL's deposits from the general assets of the Citibank in the State of New York. The question, rather, is whether Citibank is obligated to allow collection in New York, and on this point two principal theories must be examined. The first is that there was an agreement between the parties to permit collection in New York, or indeed at any place where Citibank has assets, an agreement implied from all the facts in the case as being within the contemplation of the parties. A second, and alternative, theory for permitting collection is that, assuming no such agreement, there is a duty to pay in New York in any event, a duty that the law creates when the parties have not contracted otherwise. . . .

The Court of Appeals appears to have relied upon the first theory we have noted, adopting the premise that the parties did contract to permit recovery from the general assets of Citibank in New York. Yet the District Court had made it clear that there is a distinction between an agreement on "repayment," which refers to the physical location for transacting discharge of the debt, and an agreement respecting "collection," which refers to the location where assets may be taken to satisfy it, and in quite specific terms, it found that the only agreement the parties made referred to repayment.

The Court of Appeals, while it said that this finding was not clearly erroneous, appears to have viewed repayment and collection as interchangeable concepts, not divisible ones. It concluded that the agreement as to where repayment could occur constituted also an agreement as to which bank assets the depositor could look to for collection. . . . As the Court of Appeals itself acknowledged, the record contains ample support for the District Court's finding that the parties agreed that repayment, defined as the wire transfers effecting the transfer of funds to WFAL when its deposits matured, would take place in New York. The confirmation slips exchanged by the parties are explicit: the transfer of funds upon maturity was to occur through wire transfers made by the parties' correspondent banks in New York.

As to collection, the District Court found that neither the parties' confirmation slips nor the evidence offered at trial with regard to whether "an agreement concerning the place of collection could be implied from custom and usage in the international banking field" established an agreement respecting collection. Upon review of the record, we hold this finding, that no such implied agreement existed based on the intent of the parties, was not clearly erroneous. The confirmation slips do not indicate an agreement that WFAL could collect its deposits from Citibank assets in New York; indeed, Citibank/Manila's confirmation slip, stating that "[a]t maturity *we* remit US Dlr 1,049,444.44 to your account with Wells Fargo Bank Intl Corp NY *through Citibank New York,*" tends to negate the existence of any such agreement. The telexes from the money broker who arranged the deposits speak in terms of repayment, and indicate no more than that repayment was to be made to WFAL's account with its correspondent bank in New York; they do not indicate any agreement about where WFAL could collect its deposits in the event that Citibank/Manila failed to remit payment upon maturity to this account.

Nor does the evidence contradict the District Court's conclusion that the parties, in this particular case, failed to establish a relevant custom or practice in the international banking community from which it could be inferred that the parties had a tacit understanding on the point. Citibank's experts testified that the common understanding in the banking community was that the higher interest rates offered for Eurodollar deposits, in contrast to dollar deposits with United States banks, reflected in part the fact that the deposits were not subject to reserve and insurance requirements imposed on domestic deposits by United States banking law. This could only be the case, argues Citibank, if the deposits were "payable only" outside of the United States, as required by 38 Stat. 270, as amended, 12 U.S.C. §461(b)(6) and 64 Stat. 873, as amended, 12 U.S.C. §1813(*l*)(5). It argues further that higher rates reflected the depositor's assumption of foreign "sovereign risk," defined as the risk that actions by the foreign government having legal control over the foreign branch and its assets would render the branch unable to repay the deposit.

WFAL's experts, on the other hand, testified that the identical interest rates being offered for Eurodollar deposits in both Manila and London at the time the deposits were made, despite the conceded differences in sovereign risk between the two locations, reflected an understanding that the home office of a bank was liable for repayment in the event that its foreign branch was unable to repay for any reason, including restrictions imposed by a foreign government.

A fair reading of all of the testimony supports the conclusion that, at least in this trial, on the issue of the allocation of sovereign risk there was a wide variance of opinion in the international banking community. We cannot say that we are left with "the definite and firm conviction" that the District Court's findings are erroneous. Because the Court of Appeals' holding relies upon contrary factual assumptions, the judgment for WFAL cannot be affirmed under the reasoning used by that court. . . .

The judgment of the Court of Appeals is vacated, and the case remanded for further proceedings consistent with this opinion.

## *QUESTIONS AND COMMENTS*

1. On remand, the Court of Appeals held that New York law applied to the transaction and that under New York law, unless the parties agree to the contrary, a creditor may collect a debt at a place where the parties have agreed that it is repayable. Thus, the funds deposited in the Philippine branch *could* be recovered by the depositor from Citibank's assets

in New York, absent any restriction on the situs of collection in the deposit agreement. Wells Fargo Asia, Ltd. v. Citibank, N.A., 936 F.2d 723 (2d Cir. 1991), *cert. denied,* 505 U.S. 1204 (1992).

Who was the plaintiff in this case? Is there any reason to believe that the plaintiff could not protect itself contractually from the actions taken by the Philippine government? When the panel for the Second Circuit remanded this case to the district court to clarify the initial basis for its judgment, it ordered the district court to make supplemental findings of fact as to whether the parties had agreed where the debt could be repaid and whether they had agreed that the deposits were collectible only in Manila. How were these questions relevant?

2. The court draws a distinction between repayment and collection. What is the difference between these two? Is there any legal significance to this distinction? How did the district court's approach to the distinction differ from the circuit court's approach?

3. Consider the district court's conclusion that there was no express or implied agreement or understanding either between the parties, or in the Eurodollar market generally, on the issue of where depositors are entitled to look for satisfaction of their claims in the event that the branch where the initial deposit was booked is unable to make the required wire transfers to effectuate repayment? If you were deciding this case, would it be relevant to your inquiry that different branches of the same banks pay different rates of interest on Eurodollar deposits, and that the interest rate differentials are systematically related to the political instability in the countries where the branch offices booking the loans are located?

4. In Citibank v. Wells Fargo Asia, the Court was unable to figure out what the parties had agreed to with respect to repayment and collection. As circumstances become less foreseeable, relying on the parties' express or implied understanding becomes more difficult. Sometimes, however, the contingency at issue is easy to foresee. In such cases, we should not lose sight of the fact that the basic undertaking is one of contract interpretation.

In Garcia v. Chase Manhattan Bank, 735 F.2d 645 (2d Cir. 1984), a Cuban citizen purchased a certificate of deposit from Chase Manhattan's Havana branch shortly before the National Bank of Cuba seized the bank and froze all of its accounts. When the CD was sold, Chase officials in Cuba assured the purchaser that the debt was an obligation of Chase Manhattan's home office in New York as well as one of the Havana office. Indeed, the purpose of the agreement at issue in *Garcia* was "to ensure that, no matter what happened in Cuba, including seizure of the debt, Chase would still have a contractual obligation to pay the depositors upon presentation of their CDs." Id. at 650. Under these facts, the Second Circuit ruled that Chase's home office should be liable for the debt of its branch.

A different result was reached in Perez v. Chase Manhattan Bank,

61 N.Y.2d 460, 463 N.E.2d 5, 474 N.Y.S.2d 689 (1984), another case involving an attempt by a Cuban national to obtain repayment on certificates of deposit purchased in Cuba from U.S. banks' branches in that country. Here the court reasoned that Chase Manhattan was not liable on its branch's debt despite the fact that, under the terms of the contract, the debt owed on the certificate of deposit was payable at any Chase bank in the world. The key feature in *Perez* appears to be the fact that the original purchaser of the certificates of deposit was Rosa Manas y Pineiro, the wife of a former cabinet minister of General Fulgencio Batista, the Cuban dictator overthrown by Fidel Castro in 1959. Unlike the situation in *Garcia*, the law resulting in Chase Manhattan's refusal to pay here was not a general law nationalizing bank assets, but a particular law aimed at effectuating the recovery of property that had been "removed from the national wealth" under the Batista regime. Prior to its being nationalized, Chase's Cuban branches were directed to freeze accounts belonging to certain former government officials and their families. It was pursuant to this decree that Chase declined to pay the amounts owed on the CDs in *Perez*. Chase remitted the proceeds owed under these CDs to the Castro government. A year later the bank's Cuban branches were nationalized. Should this potential "double loss" to Chase be dispositive here? If not, what factors should be dispositive? The court reasoned that Chase satisfied its obligation under the certificates of deposit when it paid the amounts owing under the certificates to the Cuban government. Do you agree? A certificate of deposit is, of course, simply a contract between a depositor who agrees to make a loan to a bank and a bank that agrees to make repayment of principal and interest at a certain date in the future. Do you think the court's result in *Perez* represents the actual understanding between the parties to this particular contract?

### b. Transfer Risk, the Act of State Doctrine, and Sovereign Immunity

As noted above, when banks deal with firms and individuals in foreign countries, in addition to managing the usual credit risks that lenders must contend with, they also must contend with the risks associated with actions of foreign governments, which, on occasion, may decide that they do not want the obligations owed to certain foreign firms to be repaid. Here, a major bar to recovery is the act of state doctrine, a principle which holds that U.S. courts will decline to involve themselves in the conduct of the foreign policy of a sovereign nation. The act of state doctrine is similar to the doctrine of sovereign immunity in that it "shares with the immunity doctrine a respect for sovereign states." Banco Nacional de Cuba v. Sabbatino, 376 U.S. 398, 438 (1964). As the following case illustrates, however, applicability of the act of state doctrine often requires courts to consider aspects of a transaction that implicate contractual issues.

## Callejo v. Bancomer, S.A.

*764 F.2d 1101 (5th Cir. 1985)*

This suit is one of several arising from the promulgation by Mexico of exchange control regulations on August 13, 1982, and from the subsequent nationalization of privately-owned Mexican banks on September 1, 1982. The exchange control regulations mandated that all deposits in Mexican banks, however denominated, be repaid in Mexican pesos at specified rates of change. Because the dollar rate of exchange was well below the market rate, the regulations constituted a Montezuma's revenge on American investors who had dollar deposits in Mexican banks. A number of these indisposed investors, including the plaintiffs in the present suit, have brought claims against Mexican banks for breach of contract. . . .

### I. Facts

William Callejo and his wife Adelfa are United States citizens who reside in Texas. Beginning in 1979 or 1980, the Callejos purchased certificates of deposit ("CDs") issued by Bancomer, S.A., a then privately-owned Mexican bank. The record is unclear about how this business relationship originated—in particular, whether it resulted from Bancomer's solicitations in Texas. During the course of the Callejos' relationship with Bancomer, however, Bancomer regularly engaged in commercial activity in the United States, operating a branch office in Los Angeles and an agency in New York City. In Texas, Bancomer maintained accounts with both Republic Bank Dallas and Laredo National Bank. . . .

The four certificates of deposit at issue in the present suit were purchased by the Callejos on May 31 and June 3, 1982. Two were renewals of prior certificates and two were new certificates; all had terms of three months, were denominated in United States dollars, and called for payment of principal and interest in United States dollars. Together, they had a value of approximately $300,000. Like the other certificates of deposit purchased by the Callejos, they specified on their face Mexico City as the place of payment.

In August 1982, facing a severe monetary crisis brought on by a decline in the world price of oil, the Government of Mexico promulgated exchange control regulations. These were supplemented by further regulations in September 1982. The regulations required Mexican banks to pay principal and interest on U.S. dollar-denominated certificates of deposit in pesos rather than dollars, at a specified rate of exchange. The regulations also required that payment be made in Mexico and limited the number of pesos that foreigners could remove from the country. On September 1, 1982, the Government of Mexico nationalized all privately-owned Mexican banks, including Bancomer.

Pursuant to the new exchange control regulations, on August 13, 1982, Bancomer notified the Callejos that it would pay the principal and interest on the Callejos' four certificates of deposit in pesos at a rate of exchange substantially below the market rate. To forestall this, the Callejos renewed the two certificates of deposit due to mature on August 31, 1982, and filed the present suit.

As amended, the Callejos' complaint alleged breach of contract and securities act violations and sought either rescission of the sale of the certificates of deposit or money damages. In response, Bancomer filed a motion to dismiss, which the district court granted on February 27, 1984. The district court held that the Callejos' suit was not based on Bancomer's commercial activities and that therefore Bancomer, as an instrumentality of the Mexican Government, was entitled to sovereign immunity. The Callejos then brought the present appeal.

### II. Sovereign Immunity

Along with other privately-owned Mexican banks, Bancomer was nationalized by the Mexican Government on September 1, 1982. Consequently, Bancomer is now an "agency or instrumentality of a foreign state" within the meaning of 28 U.S.C. §1603(b)(2), and would ordinarily be entitled to immunity from the jurisdiction of American courts under the Foreign Sovereign Immunities Act [FSIA], 28 U.S.C. §1604. The FSIA, however, contains a number of exceptions to the jurisdictional immunity of foreign states. One of these is found in 28 U.S.C. §1605(a)(2), which states:

> (a) A foreign state shall not be immune from the jurisdiction of courts of the United States or of the States in any case—. . .
>
> (2) in which the action is based [1] upon a commercial activity carried on in the United States by the foreign state; or [2] upon an act performed in the United States in connection with a commercial activity of the foreign state elsewhere; or [3] upon an act outside the territory of the United States in connection with a commercial activity of the foreign state elsewhere and that act causes a direct effect in the United States.

The Callejos claim that this exception applies in the present case, since their suit is based upon a commercial activity by Bancomer that was both carried on and caused a direct effect in the United States. . . .

In determining whether Section 1605(a)(2) applies, two questions are relevant:

(1) Is the Callejos' suit "based upon a commercial activity" by Bancomer?
(2) If so, did this commercial activity have the required jurisdictional nexus with the United States? . . .

Under the FSIA, sovereign immunity depends on the nature of those acts of the defendant that form the basis of the suit. Here, the act complained of was Bancomer's breach of its contractual obligations to the Callejos, not the promulgation by Mexico of exchange control. . . .

These contractual obligations were commercial in nature; they were of a kind that a private individual would customarily enter into for profit. Indeed, at the time that Bancomer sold the certificates of deposit, it was a private entity and did so as part of its general commercial activities. The fact that Bancomer was later nationalized is, in the current context, irrelevant. Even if Bancomer had remained a private entity, it would have been obligated under Mexican law to breach its contractual obligations to the Callejos. Its actions in doing so were not actions that only a sovereign could perform, but were instead commercial. . . .

Nor does Bancomer acquire any derivative immunity by virtue of the fact that, in breaching the terms of the certificates of deposit, it was merely complying with the sovereign decrees of the Mexican Government. . . .

Because we hold that Bancomer's activities were neither themselves sovereign nor entitled to derivative immunity by virtue of being compelled by Mexican law, we conclude that the district court erred in dismissing the suit on the ground that the suit was based on sovereign, not commercial, activity. We therefore turn to the other prong of Section 1605(a)(2); that the commercial activity have the required jurisdictional nexus with the United States.

### *B. JURISDICTIONAL NEXUS*

Section 1605(a)(2) grants an exception from sovereign immunity for suits based upon a commercial activity by an instrumentality of a foreign state, but only if the commercial activity had a sufficient connection with the United States. Section 1605(a)(2) identifies three such connections:

> (1) commercial activity carried on in the United States; (2) commercial activity carried on outside the United States, with acts performed in the United States in connection with that activity; and (3) commercial activity

> carried on outside the United States that has direct effects in the United States.

The Callejos claim that Bancomer's commercial activities were carried on and had direct effects in the United States, and that therefore the first and third of these jurisdictional bases exist. We agree with the latter claim—namely, that the breach of the certificates of deposit had direct effects in the United States—and therefore do not address whether Bancomer's activities in connection with the certificates were "carried on in the United States" within the meaning of the FSIA. . . .

. . . Since the Callejos were located in the United States, the effects of Bancomer's breach were inevitably felt by them there. Moreover, these effects in the United States were foreseeable. Unlike the cases where an American was injured abroad, here the fact that effects were felt in the United States was not fortuitous. Bancomer had engaged in a regular course of business conduct with the Callejos over a several-year period. It was well-aware that it was dealing with American investors—it called them in the United States, mailed the certificates to them there, and remitted payments through an American correspondent bank. Given these factors, we do not perceive any material difference whether the legal place of payment was Mexico or the United States. In either case, Bancomer's breach was closely and foreseeably tied to the effects felt by the Callejos in the United States. . . .

In the present case, we fail to perceive why jurisdiction should not be exercised. Mexico's interest is not so great—the suit is based on commercial not sovereign acts—nor American's interest so weak—Bancomer had engaged in a longstanding business relationship with residents of the United States which caused them substantial financial harm—that the United States must defer to Mexico. Under these circumstances, we believe that Section 1605(a)(2) applies and that jurisdiction is consequently not barred by sovereign immunity.

### III. Act of State . . .

The act of state doctrine received its classic expression in Underhill v. Hernandez, 168 U.S. 250, 18 S. Ct. 83, 42 L. Ed. 456 (1897):

> Every sovereign state is bound to respect the independence of every other sovereign state, and the courts of one country will not sit in judgment on the acts of the government of another, done within its own territory. Redress of grievances by reason of such acts must be obtained through the means open to be availed of by sovereign powers as between themselves.

Id. at 252, 18 S. Ct. at 84. . . . Under the doctrine, the courts exercise jurisdiction but decline to decide certain issues. . . .

In the present case, Bancomer claims that Mexico's promulgation of exchange control regulations constituted an act of state, and that consideration of the Callejos' claims would require us to inquire into the validity of those regulations. The Callejos argue, in response, that the act of state doctrine is inapplicable for three reasons: (1) Mexico's promulgation of the exchange control regulations was a commercial act, not an act of state; (2) the "treaty exception" to the act of state doctrine applies, since the exchange control regulations violate Mexico's obligations under the Articles of Agreement of the International Monetary Fund; and (3) the situs of the certificates of deposit was Texas rather than Mexico, and therefore the certificates are not governed by the Mexican decrees. We consider each of these arguments in turn.

### A. *THE COMMERCIAL ACTIVITY EXCEPTION* . . .

. . . In the present case, we need not decide whether to adopt the commercial activity exception, since Mexico's actions were clearly sovereign and not commercial in nature. For act of state (as opposed to sovereign immunity) purposes, the relevant acts are not merely those of the named defendants, but any governmental acts whose validity would be called into question by adjudication of the suit. Here, although the specific act complained of by the Callejos was Bancomer's breach of contract, not Mexico's promulgation of the exchange control regulations, adjudication of the breach of contract claim would necessarily call into question the Mexican regulations. Under these regulations, Bancomer has discharged its obligation to the Callejos by paying off the certificates in pesos at the established rate of exchange. Thus, we could require Bancomer to honor the terms of the certificates only by disregarding the regulations. . . .

The power to issue exchange control regulations is paradigmatically sovereign in nature; it is not of a type that a private person can exercise. . . .

. . . Were we to disregard the exchange regulations by enforcing the Callejos' certificates of deposit, we would render nugatory the attempts by Mexico to protect its foreign exchange reserves. While we are doubtful of our ability to foresee what will vex the peace of nations, we have no doubt that disregarding the Mexican regulations would be very vexing indeed. We therefore reject the Callejos' commercial activity argument. . . .

### B. *THE TREATY EXCEPTION*

The act of state doctrine is premised not only on an unwillingness to apply American public policy to invalidate foreign laws but also on a pessimism about the competence of the judiciary to ascertain norms of international law. Potentially, international law as well as American public policy could serve as a touchstone for evaluating foreign acts of state: if an act of state were contrary to international law we could treat the act as invalid and adjudicate the plaintiff's claim. This approach would allow us to review foreign acts of state without engaging in the dubious practice of evaluating these acts against the potentially parochial norms of American public policy.

The Court, however, in large part foreclosed this avenue of review in Banco Nacional de Cuba v. Sabbatino, 376 U.S. 398 (1964). There the Court was asked to review the validity of Cuba's expropriation of a Cuban sugar company owned by United States residents. The Court declined to do so, holding that this country's response to Cuba's acts should be fashioned and implemented by the executive, not the judiciary. Id. at 431-32. Although the Court admitted that Cuba's acts might have violated international law, it held that international opinion was sufficiently divided that international law did not provide a firm basis for adjudicating the validity of Cuba's acts. . . .

Here, the Callejos claim that the Mexican exchange control regulations violate the Articles of Agreement of the International Monetary Fund ("Fund Agreement"), . . . to which Mexico is a party. In particular, they claim that the regulations violate Article VIII, Section 2(a), which forbids members from imposing exchange control regulations on "current international transactions" without the prior approval of the International Monetary Fund ("IMF" or "Fund"). The Callejos argue that because the Fund Agreement is "a treaty or other unambiguous agreement" the act of state doctrine does not apply. . . .

In the context of the present case, however, we need not pass on this question in the abstract, since the IMF has itself clarified the meaning of the Fund Agreement as it applies to the Mexican regulations by indicating that they are consistent with the Agreement. On May 3, 1983, in response to an inquiry from Bancomer's counsel, the Director of the Legal Department of the Fund specifically stated that "the 'provisions of Mexico's Currency Regulations (enacted in August and continuing in effect today) which require repayment of deposits in Mexican banks to be made in Mexican pesos regardless of the currency in which the deposits are denominated' . . . do not violate and are not inconsistent with the Articles of Agreement of the International Monetary Fund." 2 Rec. at 428. This determination at once renders the Fund Agreement unambiguous in its application to the present case, but also defeats, on the merits, the Callejos' Article VIII, Section 2(a) claim.

We consider the Funds' interpretations to be persuasive authority on the meaning of the Fund Agreement. The Fund Agreement is a complex regulatory document whose sense is often obscure. In interpreting it, we defer to the greater expertise of the Fund.

### C. THE SITUS OF THE DEPOSITS

The final argument advanced by the Callejos for not applying the act of state doctrine is that the situs of their CDs was Texas rather than Mexico. The Callejos argue that under traditional choice-of-law rules pegging the choice of law to the situs of the property, Texas law should govern the certificates. Application of the act of state doctrine, they contend, would improperly give extraterritorial effect to the Mexican decrees. . . .

Here, the incidents of the certificates of deposit clearly place them in Mexico. The certificates of deposit were issued by Bancomer's Nuevo Laredo branch, where the Callejos' deposits were carried, and called for payment in Mexico. This grouping of contacts, when viewed through the gloss of the policies underlying the act of state doctrine, places the debt in Mexico and calls for the application of Mexican law.

The Callejos contend, however, that although the specified place of payment was Mexico, the course of conduct of the parties altered this agreement since the Callejos regularly received their payments in Texas. The Callejos, however, mistake remittances for payments. Although Bancomer remitted its payments to the Callejos in Texas, this did not mean that the place of payment was Texas. . . .

To hold otherwise would throw a monkeywrench into the wheels of international finance, whose smooth operation depends in large part on the lubricating influence of correspondent banks. It would mean that the deposits held by a bank would have different situses depending on the locations of the correspondent banks that first received them. Potentially a bank would have to comply with different laws for different deposits at a single branch. Rather than open this Pandora's box, banks would almost certainly attempt to receive deposits directly, without the services of a correspondent bank.

For these reasons, therefore, we reject the view that the situs of these deposits was Texas rather than Mexico. Indeed, we note that under Texas law, Bancomer, as a foreign bank, did not even have the power to receive deposits in Texas. Moreover, holding that Mexico rather than Texas was the situs of the deposits furthers the general policies of the act of state doctrine. Given Mexico's interest in these certificates of deposit, which were issued by a Mexican bank and payable in Mexico, disregarding Mexico's exchange regulations would be a serious affront. We decline to take this course. Instead, we apply the act of state doctrine and affirm the dismissal of the suit. . . .

### *QUESTIONS AND COMMENTS*

1. One factor that seems to have entered into the court's decision-making process was its recognition that, as a practical matter, a regulatory

action that can be accomplished wholly within the borders of a foreign country cannot be successfully challenged in court since it would almost certainly be disregarded within the borders of the foreign state. See Allied Bank International v. Banco Credito Agricola de Cartago, 757 F.2d 516 (2d Cir. 1985). What difference should this consideration make? If the plaintiffs in one of these cases have gone to the expense of bringing suit in the United States, why not rely on this fact to resolve the issue of whether the court's judgment will have force or effect?

2. Of what relevance is it where the situs of the property in question is located? Does the nature of the property in question—bank deposits—really lend itself to this sort of inquiry?

3. To what extent do contractual considerations influence the court's decision in *Callejo?* If the case had been decided on purely contractual grounds without reference to the act of state doctrine, would the result have been the same?

4. Of what relevance is it that, at the time the certificates of deposit were sold, Bancomer was privately owned, as opposed to government-owned? Should the fact that the government of Mexico nationalized Bancomer shortly after promulgating the exchange control regulations that are at the heart of this suit influence the court's decision? If this same sequence of events occurred in the United States, wouldn't they clearly violate the Fifth Amendment's prohibitions on takings without just compensation?

5. The court of appeals overturned the district court's determination that Mexico was entitled to sovereign immunity on the grounds that the underlying cause of action arose because of Bancomer's commercial activities under the Foreign Sovereign Immunities Act, which provides that a foreign sovereign shall not be immune from the jurisdiction of U.S. courts in any case based on a commercial activity that caused a direct effect in the United States or was carried on in the United States. What was the district court's argument against the applicability of the Foreign Sovereign Immunities Act?

6. Despite finding that Bancomer's activities were commercial in nature for the purposes of sovereign immunity, the court of appeals found that the act of state doctrine shields the Mexican government from liability because "Mexico's actions were clearly sovereign and not commercial in nature." How can Mexico's activities be commercial for purposes of sovereign immunity but noncommercial for purposes of the act of state doctrine?

7. At about the same time as the Fifth Circuit was deciding Callejo v. Bancomer, the Second Circuit was deciding another important international banking law case involving the act of state doctrine, Allied Bank International v. Banco Credito Agricola de Cartago, 757 F.2d 516 (2d Cir. 1985). In this case, three Costa Rican banks, all of which were owned by the Costa Rican government, issued promissory notes to a consortium

of U.S. banks. These promissory notes were payable in U.S. dollars in New York City. The Costa Rican banks defaulted on these promissory notes because the Central Bank of Costa Rica issued a series of regulations that essentially suspended all external debt service payments. While the Central Bank of Costa Rica did permit external debt to be repaid by Costa Rican debtors who obtained express approval from the Costa Rican government, the Central Bank refused to authorize any foreign debt payments in U.S. dollars.

In accordance with the terms of the promissory notes, Allied Bank International, as agent for the 39 U.S. banks that owned these promissory notes, accelerated the amounts owed on the notes and sued for the full amount of principal and interest outstanding. Of the 39 original creditors, all but one, Fidelity Union Trust Company of New Jersey, reached an agreement with Costa Rica's Central Bank that called for the banks to reschedule their debt. Allied Bank International prosecuted the litigation in Allied Bank International v. Banco Credito Agricola de Cartago on behalf of Fidelity Union.

In the litigation before the Second Circuit, the executive branch of the United States filed an amicus curiae brief objecting to Costa Rica's actions. The U.S. government argued that debt resolution procedures should follow the model established by the International Monetary Fund (IMF). The IMF model is grounded in the understanding that parties are free to renegotiate their obligations, but that the underlying obligations nevertheless remain valid and enforceable. The executive branch argued that Costa Rica's unilateral restructuring of its private obligations was inconsistent with the IMF model of international cooperation and negotiation, and thus inconsistent with U.S. policy.

Before receiving the amicus brief from the U.S. government, the Second Circuit declined to consider whether the act of state doctrine applied to the litigation because the court determined that the actions of the Costa Rican government were fully consistent with the laws and policy of the United States. On the basis of this determination, the court reasoned that principles of comity between the judiciary and the executive compelled the court to recognize the validity of the Costa Rican government's refusal to permit its banks to pay their outstanding obligations. The executive branch's amicus brief caused the Second Circuit to reconsider its earlier decision.

Because of the executive branch's amicus brief, the outcome in *Allied Bank International* could not be based solely on considerations of comity between the judiciary and the executive branches. Instead, the court had to determine whether the act of state doctrine precluded judicial examination of the Costa Rican decrees. The court reasoned that the act of state doctrine would only bar Allied's suit if the situs of the underlying debts was in Costa Rica. The court held that the fact that the Costa Rican banks were obligated to repay the debts in U.S. dollars in New York meant that the situs of the debts was not Costa Rica, but the United States. The Second Circuit reasoned that the United States has an interest in maintaining New York's status as one of the foremost commercial centers in the world, and that this interest rendered the act of state doctrine inapplicable.

On what basis can *Allied Bank International* be distinguished from *Callejo?* Why do you suppose that 38 of the 39 members of the original loan syndicate agreed to renegotiate the Costa Rican debt? The one recalcitrant bank, Fidelity Union Trust, litigated this case for over 20 years. How would this fact enter into your decision about whether to litigate or renegotiate? Would the Costa Rican government have an incentive to block this repayment of foreign debt even if it knew that their effort ultimately would be unsuccessful?

8. How is the decision in these cases likely to influence the way that U.S. banks negotiate loans to foreign firms? Many banks find that bringing suit in a foreign jurisdiction is quite chancy. Moreover, even if the U.S. bank successfully litigates its claim in the foreign country, the judgment generally will be payable in the local currency even though the original loan was denominated in dollars. This may be undesirable under existing foreign exchange and currency exchange conditions. Clearly, where there is uncertainty surrounding the economic or legal climate in a particular foreign country, it is desirable to stipulate that the law of another country should govern the transaction. This was done in Allied Bank International v. Banco Credito Agricola de Cartago: The banks originally agreed to jurisdiction over the promissory notes in New York City.

9. First National City Bank v. Banco Para el Comercio Exterior de Cuba, 462 U.S. 611 (1983), pitted Citibank against the government of the Republic of Cuba. Citibank won. The issue concerned the establishment by the Cuban Government of the Banco Para el Comercio Exterior de Cuba (Bancec), which was formed as an independent corporate entity with full juridical capacity to facilitate the financing of Cuba's foreign trade.

Bancec sought to collect on a letter of credit issued by Citibank in support of a contract to deliver Cuban sugar to a buyer in the United States. Within days after Citibank received Bancec's request for payment on this letter of credit, all of Citibank's assets within Cuba were seized by the Cuban government. Citibank sought to avoid paying on its letter of credit by arguing that the amount owed should be set off against the value of Citibank's Cuban branches, which had been confiscated. Bancec sued in the U.S. District Court for the Southern District of New York in a diversity action, arguing that its separate juridical status shielded it from liability for the acts of the Cuban government. The district court rejected Bancec's arguments, finding that Bancec lacked independence from the Cuban government and was, in fact, a mere instrumentality or alter ego of that government and therefore not entitled to separate status.

The Second Circuit reversed, holding that Bancec was not an alter ego of the Cuban government for the purposes of Citibank's efforts at obtaining a setoff. The court held that independent entities created by foreign governments should be respected by courts except where the subject matter of the litigation against the state involves "state conduct in which the instrumentality had a key role." Banco Para el Comercio Exterior de Cuba v. First National City Bank, 478 F.2d 191 (2d Cir. 1973). Since Bancec had no direct role in the nationalization of Citibank's Cuban branches, the Second Circuit reasoned that its status as a separate juridical entity should be respected.

The Supreme Court reversed. The Court began by observing that government instrumentalities established as juridical entities distinct and independent from their sovereign should normally be treated as such. The Court noted that separate juridical entities normally are run as distinct economic enterprises. They have the power to sue and be sued, to own property, and to enter into binding contracts. These features permit government instrumentalities to conduct their operations with flexibility and independence from close political control and to eliminate uncertainty over whether an instrumentality's assets would be diverted to satisfy a claim against the sovereign, thereby reassuring third parties who might extend credit to the government instrumentality.

Despite the general rule respecting separate juridical entities created by foreign sovereigns, the Court held that the separate status of such firms will be disregarded in order to prevent injustice. In particular, where the immunities created by the establishment of a separate juridical entity are being used to defeat legislative policies, U.S. courts should disregard the corporate form of the foreign sovereign's subsidiary.

The Court noted that shortly after Citibank's assets were confiscated, Bancec was dissolved and its capital was distributed among other state-owned enterprises. As a consequence, the Court reasoned, the real beneficiary of a decision favorable to Bancec would, in fact, be the Cuban government, which of course was responsible for confiscating and then nationalizing Citibank's assets. Thus, the Court reasoned, giving effect to Bancec's separate juridical status would cause an injustice by benefiting the Cuban government. Is this sound reasoning?

After First National City Bank v. Banco Para el Comercio Exterior de Cuba, what is the rule for determining when the separate juridical status of a government instrumentality will be respected? The Court declined to articulate a mechanical rule and instead suggested that lower courts should apply "internationally recognized equitable principles to avoid the injustice that would result from permitting a foreign state to reap the benefits of our courts while avoiding the obligations of international law." 462 U.S. 611, 614 (1983).

10. Chuidian v. Philippine National Bank, 976 F.2d 561 (9th Cir. 1992), presented the following fact pattern. A Philippine bank issued a letter of credit, nominating its U.S. branch to service the letter in an

advisory role, with the power to pay on a properly presented draft under the letter but otherwise "possessed of the least possible amount of authority and discretion." The Philippine government directed that the letter not be paid. The holder of the letter sued in U.S. courts to obtain payment from the U.S. branch. The court of appeals held that the place for performance of the letter was the Philippines and that the designation of the U.S. branch as paying agent did not alter this conclusion. Since performance was illegal in the Philippines, the holder was out of luck. The case was widely hailed in international banking circles as clarifying—and limiting—the potential liability of banks operating as paying agents on international letters of credit.

## D. INTERNATIONAL REGULATORY STRUCTURES

As is the case in the United States, banking is a highly regulated industry throughout the world. U.S. banks doing business in foreign markets must comply with local laws and regulations. In 1990 the staff of the House of Representatives' Committee on Banking, Finance and Urban Affairs and the Subcommittee on Financial Institutions Supervision, Regulation and Insurance prepared a useful overview of the various regulatory environments that govern banking throughout the world. The four basic models, the American holding company model, the British universal banking model, the German and European Community (EC) universal banking model, and the Japanese compartmentalized banking model should provide something of a flavor for the various regulatory structures that U.S. banks face when they venture into the international arena.

### Staff of House Committee on Banking, Finance and Urban Affairs, 101st Cong., 2d Sess., An International Comparison of Banking Regulatory Structures

*Comm. Print 101-3 (June 1990)*

The liberalization of financial structures around the world is having an effect on the competitiveness of United States financial institutions. Banking regulations are generally designed to promote growth and stability. However, in an increasingly interdependent global financial system, regulation in some countries can be a source of competitive advantage and potential instability.

Among the Western industrialized nations, only the United States does not have a system of nation-wide banking. While the U.S. is moving toward a system of national banking, the European Community (EC) in its project "1992" is moving toward the provision of international banking across the borders comprising the twelve member, EC countries.

While in theory Japanese banks operate under a framework similar to that of the U.S., in practice, Japanese banks operate under a network of securities, insurance and commercial firm partnerships different from anything in the U.S. Additionally, Japan has displayed signs of moving toward British-style universal banking with its current consideration of altering its separation of commercial and investment banking.

The U.S. and Japan stand alone as the only countries which extensively limit the products and services that particular classes of financial institutions may offer. However, Japan is currently considering alterations to its financial structure. The EC is moving toward the most liberal financial structure in the world. The difference in structure in the U.S. will only become more pronounced as these developments progress.

By examining the different financial structures of the industrialized nations, one can more easily visualize the options within the U.S. policy debate, and their expected impact. . . . Four core issues in the U.S. public policy arena provide a useful framework for comparing the financial systems of many of the countries around the world. The four issues are:

1) the separation of banking and commerce;
2) the separation of banking and nonbanking financial services;
3) the safety net and supervisory structure; and
4) access to central bank funds and liquidity facilities.

With as many as 54 different supervisors (including the 50 states) regulating sometimes overlapping areas of the financial system, the United States has the most complex financial supervisory structure in the Western world. While the U.S. is moving toward regulating along functional lines, most foreign countries have a few, but all-encompassing supervisory bodies that regulate along institutional lines. For instance, in the United States, the Securities Exchange Commission (SEC) supervises securities activities, and the Federal Reserve, Comptroller of the Currency (OCC), and Federal Deposit Insurance Corporation (FDIC) supervise differently chartered banks. In Japan, the Ministry of Finance supervises both securities and banking activities.

In most of the Western industrialized world, banking organizations and their securities affiliates generally have access to the payment, account and liquidity facilities of their respective central banks. Japan, even with its Glass-Steagall type of law (Article 65), allows the major securities firms to hold accounts at the Bank of Japan and to access the discount window for funds in extreme circumstances.

Overall, many of the banking and financial sector laws around the world are changing. It is important to understand the implications for the United States.

### The Banking Models

Four basic models of banking exist in the Western world:

1) American holding company banking;
2) British-style universal banking;
3) German and EC-style universal banking; and
4) Japanese compartmentalized banking.

The British-style universal banking model is the basis for the financial structures of the countries with close historic ties to the United Kingdom, like Canada and Australia; the West German style of "one-stop-shopping" universal banking is similar to that in the Netherlands, Switzerland, France and Italy; and the United States and Japan are similar yet different in their extensive segmentation.

#### *AMERICAN HOLDING COMPANY BANKING*

The bank or financial services holding company is largely unique to the United States. In the U.S., holding companies are almost always the financial and managerial nerve center of the overall entity. A bank holding company is an organization (corporation, partnership, or association) that holds controlling stock in one or more commercial banks. . . .

Bank holding companies are formed in the U.S. to circumvent geographic restrictions, and to engage in certain activities that are not allowed to banks. Included in these certain activities are: mortgage banking, consumer finance, leasing, data processing, courier services, certain management consulting activities, insurance underwriting (in connection with credit, life, accident and health insurance), and discount brokerage. . . .

Holding companies, where they exist outside the U.S., are used more to link banking and commerce than to integrate financial services. Because universal banking countries are permitted a wide range of in-house powers, financial institutions in those nations do not need holding companies to place banking and securities activities under common control. In countries like Canada, Sweden and the U.K., where ownership ties between banks and securities firms occur through subsidiaries more often than through holding companies, generally a bank is the ultimate parent. Similarly, holding companies are not the primary vehicle for financial integration in Belgium, since banks there may conduct several in-house securities activities and may set up nonbank financial subsidiaries. . . .

### BRITISH-STYLE UNIVERSAL BANKING

The British-style of universal banking primarily differs from the U.S. holding company structure by: 1) the definition and scope of activities which may be conducted in-house or in the financial group; and 2) the nature of the regulations limiting or preventing various classes of transactions or relationships between various members of the entity as a whole (for example, "Chinese" walls in Britain, which are generally information flow controls, and "firewalls" in the U.S., which are generally capital flow controls).

Since the mid 1980s, financial service integration and true universal banking has been emerging in the U.K. Although the U.K. does not have a separation of commercial and investment banking or banking and commerce, few combinations of banking and commercial firms exist. The large commercial banks often have merchant banking subsidiaries, but few merchant banks have commercial bank subsidiaries. Additionally, life insurance and banking have become increasingly integrated in the U.K.

Merchant banks are typically wholesale oriented, rarely have branches, but accept deposits and make loans. They tend to focus on investment banking activities and compete largely with securities firms. Securities firms are unable to accept deposits. The majority of the securities firms in the U.K. are subsidiaries of foreign investment banks. In addition, the U.K. has specialized financial institutions like building societies (a British counterpart to U.S. savings and loans), finance companies, and trustee savings banks which service specific market niches. . . .

### GERMAN AND EC-STYLE UNIVERSAL BANKING

Germany operates under a wide-open style of universal banking that is arguably the most liberal in the world. Any institution engaging in banking activity is defined as a bank. Included in the permissible activities of a German bank are the taking of deposits, consumer and commercial lending, securities underwriting and trading, mutual fund operations, and investment counseling. With a banking license, any entity is permitted to hold large equity shares in commercial, industrial and insurance companies. However, by law all these activities must be engaged in within different departments of the bank. . . .

In general, the German-style universal banking system differs from the British-style universal banking system in three main areas: 1) Germany has fewer separate legal subsidiaries; 2) bank holding of commercial firms is far more common; and 3) combinations of banking and insurance firms are far more frequent.

Within the European Community as a whole, the German banking system is generally perceived to be the model. The recently adopted Second Banking Directive, which takes effect on January 1, 1993, permits EC banks to employ a single banking license to automatically branch or cross-border market their services to any of the other EC countries. In addition, the directive provides for uniform prudential standards and the international policy of "national treatment."

By including restrictive equity investment limits, however, the EC does not envision controlling ownership of commercial firms by banks. However, it is important to note that industrial-banking integration is not prohibited. Additionally, the EC's implementation of the universal banking model is expected to expedite and magnify German-style arrangements elsewhere within Europe.

### *JAPANESE COMPARTMENTALIZED BANKING*

Next to the United States, Japan currently maintains the greatest separation of financial services among the major industrialized countries. Along with institutional separation, Japan limits financial integration through ownership links, with banks and securities firms not permitted to own controlling interests in each other or to be owned by the same company. The common ownership of banks and insurance companies is restricted as well.

Japan, like the United States, has a strict separation of commercial and investment banking. Article 65 of Japan's Securities and Exchange Act of 1948 is modeled after the Glass-Steagall Act of 1933. The Japanese law prohibits banks from engaging directly in the domestic securities business and similarly, securities firms cannot participate in commercial banking activities like accepting deposits or making loans other than for securities purchases.

While the aim of Article 65 seems identical to that of Glass-Steagall, there are some differences. Although Japanese anti-monopoly law prohibits banks from holding more than five percent of the stock of any corporation, including securities companies, bank affiliations with securities firms are not restricted. Many foreign banks have asserted that antitrust law in Japan is relatively nonexistent. A Japanese bank is permitted to own shares in a securities firm (up to the five percent limit) and vice versa. Moreover, the five percent limit does not apply to a bank's affiliates, and banks generally have many affiliates that often form the basis for tight cultural relationships within an industrial group.

Traditionally, the Japanese financial system has been highly fragmented and compartmentalized by law, with each particular type of institution participating in a narrow range of activities. Due to the legal separation of banking, securities activities, and commerce, Japanese banking services are provided by commercial banks and various specialized financial institutions for long term lending, small business, agriculture, forestry and fishery. Securities firms have traditionally performed the underwriting, dealing and brokering in the capital markets and licensed insurance companies have had the exclusive right to broker and underwrite insurance products.

In practice, however, the Japanese financial firms operate through the "keiretsu" system of partnerships with other financial and non-financial companies. Because the five percent ownership restrictions do not apply to bank affiliates in Japan, industrial groupings of informal partnerships have come to comprise the marketplace. These partnerships are not based on majority stock ownership or holding company affiliations and may involve banks, securities firms, insurance companies, and many other non-financial firms in manufacturing and service oriented businesses like paper, petroleum, chemicals, metals, mining, shipping, textiles, real estate, and construction.

Through this system of partnerships, the Japanese financial institutions are guaranteed corporate demand for products and services and foreign firms are effectively discouraged from entering and competing in Japan. The keiretsu groups can act as a cartel providing a large obstacle for foreign competition. . . .

Securities firms perform traditional securities activities like underwriting, brokering and dealing in corporate securities markets. Their ability to engage in commercial banking is strictly prohibited, except for their offshore affiliates, which are permitted to engage in commercial banking.

This compartmentalization and specialization, however, is becoming increasingly blurred over time. With the introduction of new products and instruments in Japan, regulators are liberalizing regulations on a case-by-case basis. This Japanese consideration of drastic changes to Article 65 will further eliminate the strict delineation between the financial institutions. . . .

## Safety Net Comparisons

Banking stability has a positive effect on a market economy. For this reason, financial institutions are subject to a higher degree of regulation and supervision than is the case for most other types of private businesses. While the system of regulation and supervision may vary across borders, the rationale for such oversight is common among all Western industrialized nations. . . .

With the exception of the Herstatt Bank failure in 1974 in Germany, it is extremely difficult to find any cases in which any of the authorities around the world have been willing to permit the sudden and disorderly failure of an important banking or nonbanking failure. While size does not appear to be a major factor in letting an institution fail, disruption to the market does.

For this reason, the vast majority of the major industrialized countries, like the United States, subscribe to the "too big to fail" policy. It is generally perceived that if any of the largest banking institutions in any of these countries were in danger of failing, the domestic authorities would intervene to prevent market disruption.

### *DEPOSIT INSURANCE*

Deposit insurance protection schemes exist in almost all Western industrialized nations. While coverage limits exist as a matter of general practice, authorities in almost all industrialized nations have gone to considerable lengths to protect depositors from loss. Where depositor losses have occurred, they have generally been limited to isolated incidents of failure or incidents where the depositors had other relationships with the failed institution, like being a shareholder.

The private sector plays a much larger role in the deposit insurance schemes of foreign nations than in the United States. In the United States, with the Federal Deposit Insurance Corporation, the deposit insurance scheme is government operated and overseen. . . .

With the exception of Canada, almost all other Western industrialized nations operate mixed public/private controlled deposit insurance schemes, or completely private deposit insurance systems. Japan operates a deposit insurance plan which is mandatory for all banks and under mixed public/private control. Japanese premiums are assessed at a rate of .012% of deposits and depositors are insured to 10 million yen (approximately $69,000).

Canada maintains the Canada Deposit Insurance Corporation, a government run, mandatory bank enrollment scheme that insures depositors to C$60,000 (approximately $50,000 U.S.). Annual premiums are assessed as .001% of insured deposits, but unlike most schemes, Canada's deposit insurance covers interbank deposits.

The U.K. operates the Deposit Protection Fund, a mandatory bank enrollment, public/private enterprise which insures depositors to 75% of 20,000 pounds (75% of approximately $34,000). Annual premiums depend on payments made by the Fund in the prior year.

Germany operates a private and voluntary deposit insurance system in which banks are charged annual premiums of .03% of deposits. The maximum protection per depositor is 30% of the bank's capital and disclosed reserves. The German deposit insurance scheme also includes coverage for deposits in foreign branches of domestic banks, a feature which is rare.

France and Italy, like Germany, operate private and voluntary deposit insurance schemes. Maximum depositor protection in France is FF 400,000 (approximately $70,000). Italy, however, maintains coverage on a sliding scale of 100% of the first 200 million lira (approximately $161,000); 90% of the next 800 million lira (up to approximately $805,000); and 80% of the next two billion lira (up to approximately $2.5 million). French bank premiums are not annual, but assessed based on a bank's total deposits only when the fund makes payments to depositors.

***CENTRAL BANK AND PRIVATE SECTOR ROLE IN SAFETY NET***

In a number of prominent cases around the world, the central banks have moved swiftly and decisively to intervene in the cases of troubled bank and nonbank financial institutions. With no true correlation of central bank intervention and size of the troubled institution, public intervention appears to be largely motivated by concerns about systemic risk. The primary difference between central bank role in the U.S. and central bank roles around the world in relation to the safety net for financial institutions largely involves the moral suasion abilities of the central banks. The Federal Reserve largely lacks the persuasive abilities of the other central banks around the world.

The financial institution rescue efforts undertaken by the authorities around the world usually entail a joint effort between public officials, the central bank and the private sector, except in the United States. Foreign authorities seem to have greater authority and power to call upon private entities in rescue operations and private institutions in foreign countries are either more willing, or feel more compelled, to participate in stabilization and rescue efforts around the world.

***SUPERVISORY STRUCTURE***

. . . In virtually all other major industrialized countries, . . . one authority regulates the banking, securities and insurance activities in the country. Most frequently, the banking supervisor is the predominant and principal regulator, and in the vast majority of major industrialized countries outside the United States, fewer financial institutions exist, so supervisory relationships can be more focused and informal.

Like the United States, most countries have at least some areas of longstanding supervisory overlap. Because the central banks tend to have a role of lender of last resort, they usually have some supervisory role in maintaining liquidity levels and rules and oversight of the capital markets.

In most of the major industrialized countries, a single supervisor is responsible for both banking and securities firms. . . . That primary regulator is either a banking commission in the cases of Belgium, France,

Germany, Sweden, and Switzerland, or the central bank in the cases of Italy and the Netherlands. Because the banking commissions and the central banks in these countries do not set different rules or capital standards for banking and securities activities, functional supervision is not a broadly applied principle.

However, in the U.K., Canada, and Japan, regulatory segmentation is somewhat greater. These countries have separate supervisors for banking and securities activities. In the U.K., the Bank of England (the British central bank) supervises U.K. banks and firms engaged in wholesale money market activities while the Department of Trade and Industry, the Securities Investment Board (SIB) and, under SIB oversight, self-regulatory organizations are responsible for supervising firms engaged in securities activities.

To streamline supervision, however, the U.K. has introduced the concept of a "lead" regulator. An agreement between the Bank of England and the SIB assigns supervisory responsibility for the overall safety and soundness of the financial group to the regulator who covers the bulk of the group's business.

In Canada, banks are supervised by a federal regulator, the Office of the Superintendent of Financial Institutions (OSFI), and the Bank of Canada can require the OSFI to examine individual institutions. However, provincial authorities along with the self-regulatory organizations supervise securities firms.

In Japan, the Ministry of Finance (MOF) oversees both banks and securities firms, but the individual bureaus within the Ministry operate with some independence. The Banking Bureau of the MOF is the principal supervisor of banks, while the International Finance Bureau oversees the banks' international and foreign exchange business, and the Securities Bureau oversees their government bond business. The Securities Bureau is the principal supervisor of securities firms. In addition, the Bank of Japan (the Japanese central bank) supervises banks and a number of securities firms, including the largest ones, in connection with their accounts at the central bank.

In Canada, Japan, and the U.K., however, functional supervision is an emerging approach. Because permitted powers of banks and securities firms have begun to overlap in these countries, the authorities are moving toward functional supervision. For instance, in Japan, as new domestic markets for instruments such as swaps and commercial paper have developed, both securities firms and banks have been allowed to deal in them, and the MOF has expressed interest in common regulations. . . .

### Conclusion

Among the four basic banking models (from which most of the financial regulatory environments among the major industrialized countries are derived), the German universal banking model is the most permissive with respect to activities within one financial institution, and the United States' fragmented approach is the most restrictive. The United Kingdom and Canada, once proponents of a restrictive system not unlike that of the United States, have recently introduced universal banking on a lesser scale than that of Germany. Japan, like the United States, maintains a segmented, restrictive regulatory structure. However, Japan is slowly moving toward a more liberal structure, and it is currently considering altering its overall structure so as to permit more activities within banks. Although the United States may not necessarily be moving in this direction, the global trend in the financial regulatory structures is unquestionably moving toward greater liberalization and permissiveness in activities.

Most major industrialized countries strictly limit the interaction of banking and commerce. The U.S. and Japan limit holdings to 5% interests, yet Germany allows unrestricted interaction and ownership. Commercial ownership of banks is not the predominant form of integration in any country. With the exception of Germany, bank control of commercial enterprises is not a prominent feature in any economy. In nations allowing the common ownership of banks and commercial firms by a single holding company, regulatory policy is aimed at insuring the independence of the bank.

The strict limitation and separation of financial services found in the U.S. has a counterpart today only in Japan. Some Western nations have long permitted a single institution to provide directly both banking and securities activities. In other countries, like Canada and the U.K., recent legislation has expanded the integration of banking and securities activities through increased institutional powers or ownership affiliations.

In contrast to the United States, the private sector plays a much greater role in the safety nets around the world. Deposit insurance exists in almost every major industrialized country, but most often the private sector has a much larger role than that in the United States. While the United States maintains a deposit insurance system that is government operated and overseen, most other countries operate private or public/private mixed deposit insurance schemes.

Additionally, the central banks around the world have a much greater role in maintaining the safety net. While the central banks of the major industrialized countries appear most concerned with systemic risk, the primary difference between the United States' Federal Reserve and the other central banks lies in the moral suasion abilities of the foreign central banks. Foreign central banks generally have greater authority, power, and persuasive abilities with which to convince private entities to participate in financial institution rescue operations.

Although consolidated reporting and capital adequacy assessment have been adopted by banking regulators throughout the world, securities firms not affiliated with a bank are not generally subject to similar requirements. In countries with segmented supervisory authority, like the U.S., functional supervision has emerged. Where extensive application of functional supervision is intended, as in the U.K., it is not seen as a substitute for consolidated supervision. To streamline supervision, the U.K. has introduced the concept of a "lead" regulator. Generally, the supervisory structures in foreign countries are fewer in number, more streamlined, and less complex.

While most countries limit access to the central bank to commercial banks, Japan allows access to some securities firms it supervises, and the Bank of Canada lends to some securities firms. Additionally, the lender of last resort function is utilized differently in different countries. In the universal banking countries, securities problems can conceivably spill into the banking safety net, and moral suasion abilities are heavily relied upon.

The financial services world is moving in a clear direction toward liberalization. Current proposals to alter the financial structure in the U.S. would bring the integration of banking and securities activities, and possibly the integration of banking and commerce, closer to the level prevailing within the industrialized world.

## *QUESTIONS AND COMMENTS*

1. What are the chief differences between the four basic models of banking described in the preceding congressional study? Which of these models do you think is best?

2. How much of the difference in regulatory patterns among nations can be attributed to cultural differences? How much to historical factors? How much to interest group pressures?

3. How important is it that international banks have the same (or substantially similar) capital requirements to ensure fair international competition? As noted above, the Basel Accord of July 1988, represents an agreement among the central banks of the leading industrial countries as to minimum capital standards among major international banks. The ability of the world's bankers to reach this important accord has been attributed to the "sustained redistribution of market share towards Japanese banks," which created pressure for "defensive and aggressive reregulation around the world." E. Kane, Competitive Financial Reregulation: An International Perspective, in R. Portes & A. Swoboda, eds., Threats to International Financial Stability 138 (1987).

4. It is interesting to note that the private sector plays a much larger role in the deposit insurance schemes of foreign nations than it does in the United States. Similarly, coverage limits in the U.S. are higher than

those in many other countries. What effects do you think this has on U.S. banks' efforts to compete for international deposits?

5. Why do you suppose it is that foreign authorities appear to have more clout than U.S. authorities in calling on private entities to participate in rescue operations and stabilization efforts? The congressional study excerpted above contains the claim that the Federal Reserve "lacks the persuasive abilities of the other central banks around the world." Does this make sense? What factors other than "persuasive ability" might account for the greater authority of foreign central bankers?

6. In most major industrialized countries besides the U.S., a single regulator is responsible for banking and securities firms. Do you think this integrated regulatory structure gives firms in those countries an advantage over their U.S. rivals?

# TABLE OF CASES

*Principal cases are italicized.*

# TABLE OF STATUTES AND REGULATIONS

## State Statutes

*California Financial Code Annotated*



*California Civil Code Annotated*



*Florida Statutes Annotated*



*New York Banking Law*



*South Dakota Laws*



## Model and Uniform Acts

*Uniform Commercial Code*



*Uniform Partnership Act*



## Regulations

*Code of Federal Regulations*

*Federal Register*

# TABLE OF AUTHORITIES

Hu, Misunderstood Derivatives: The Causes of Informational Failure and the Promise of Regulatory Incrementalism, 102 Yale L.J. 1457 (1993), 316-19

Hu, Swaps, the Modern Process of Financial Innovation and the Vulnerability of a Regulatory Paradigm, 138 Penn. L. Rev. 333 (1989), 322

Hughes, Law Firm Kaye, Scholer, Lincoln S&L and the OTS, 7 Notre Dame Journal of Leg. Eth. and Pub. Pol. 177 (1993), 344

International Organization of Securities Commissions, Operational and Financial Risk Management Control Mechanisms for Over-the-Counter Derivatives Activities of Regulated Securities Firms (1994), 322

Jackson, The Expanding Obligations of Financial Holding Companies, 107 Harv. L. Rev. 507 (1994), 639

Jackson, Reflections on Kaye, Scholer: Enlisting Lawyers to Improve the Regulation of Financial Institutions, 66 Southern Calif. L. Rev. 1019 (1993), 344, 346

Jackson, The Superior Performance of Savings and Loan Associations with Substantial Holding Companies, 22 Journal of Leg. Studies 405 (1993), 639

Johnston & Schecter, Introduction, Kaye, Scholer and the OTS—Did Anyone Go Too Far?, 66 Southern Calif. L. Rev. 977 (1993), 344

Judd, Competition Between Commercial Paper Markets and Commercial Banks (Staff Paper, Fed. Reserve Bank of San Francisco), 524

E. Kane, Competitive Financial Reregulation: An International Perspective, in R. Portes & A. Swoboda, eds., Threats to International Financial Stability (1987)

E. Kane, The Gathering Crisis in Federal Deposit Insurance (1985), 298

Kawasaki, Liability of Attorneys, Accountants, Appraisers and Other Independent Contractors Under the Financial Institutions Reform, Recovery, and Enforcement Act of 1989, 42 Hastings L.J. 249 (1990), 343

Kostant, When Zeal Boils Over: Disclosure Obligations and the Duty of Candor of Legal Counsel in Regulatory Proceedings after the Kaye Scholer Settlement, 25 Akron State Bar J. 487 (1993), 344

Laifer, Putting the Super Back in Supervision of International Banking, Post-BCCI, 60 Fordham L. Rev. S467 (1992), 693

Langevoort, Interpreting the McFadden Act: The Politics and Economics of Shared ATMs and Discount Brokerage Houses, 41 Bus. Law. 1265 (1986), 424

Langevoort, Statutory Obsolescence and the Judicial Process: The Revisionist Role of the Courts in Federal Banking Regulation, 85 Mich. L. Rev. 672 (1987), 511-12

D. Leinsdorf, Citibank (1973), 409

R. Litan, What Should Banks Do?, 298

Luban, Social Responsibilities of Lawyers: A Green Perspective, 63 George Washington L. Rev. 955 (1995), 344

Macey, The Political Science of Regulating Bank Risk, 49 Ohio St. L.J. 1277 (1989), 512

Macey, Special Interest Groups Legislation and the Judicial Function: The Dilemma of Glass-Steagall, 33 Emory L.J. 1 (1988), 506-09, 511

J. Macey & G. Miller, Costly Policies: State Regulation and Antitrust Exemption in Insurance Markets (1993), 131

Macey & Miller, Bank Failures, Risk-Monitoring, and the Market for Bank Control, 88 Colum. L. Rev. 1153 (1988), 450, 630

Macey & Miller, Kaye, Scholer, FIRREA and the Desirability of Early Closure: A View of the Kaye, Scholer Case from the Perspective of Bank Regulatory Policy, 66 Southern Calif. L. Rev. 977 (1993), 344, 347

S. Maisel, Risk and Capital Adequacy in Commercial Banks (1981), 292
K. Marx, Theses on Feuerbach, in K. Marx & F. Engels, 1 Selected Works 15 (1969), 71
M. Malloy, I The Corporate Law of Banks, 107, 108
Marisco, A Guide to Enforcing the Community Reinvestment Act, 20 Fordham Urban L.J. 165 (1993), 220
Miller, Interstate Branching and the Constitution, 41 Bus. Law. 337 (1986), 430
Miller, The Future of the Dual Banking System, 53 Brook. L. Rev. 1 (1987), 112-17
Miller, Legal Restrictions on Bank Consolidation: An Economic Analysis, 77 Iowa L. Rev. 1083 (1992), 410
Misback, The Foreign Bank Supervision Enhancement Act of 1991, 79 Fed. Res. Bull. 1 (1993), 695
Mishkin, The Variousness of Federal Law: Competence and Discretion in the Choice of National and State Rules of Decision, 105 U. Pa. L. Rev. 797 (1957), 663
Murton, A Survey of the Issues and the Literature Concerning Risk-Related Deposit Insurance, FDIC Banking & Econ. Rev. 11 (Mar. 1986), 293

Note, A Conduct Oriented Approach to the Glass-Steagall Act, 91 Yale L.J. 102 (1981), 506
Note, Commercial Bank Mergers: The Case of Procedural and Substantive Deregulation, 95 Harv. L. Rev. 1914 (1982), 449
Note, The Line of Commerce for Commercial Bank Mergers: A Product-Oriented Redefinition, 96 Harv. L. Rev. 907 (1983), 474-75

Peltzman, Entry into Commercial Banking, 8 J.L. & Econ. 11 (1965), 100
A. Pollard, K. Ellis, J. Passaic, Jr. & J. Daly, Banking Law in the United States (1988), 702
R. Posner, Economic Analysis of Law (3d ed. 1986), 366

Render, Virtual Payment Systems: Legal Issues of Electronic Cash (1995), 41-42
Restatement (Second) of Contracts (1979), 222
Restatement (Second) of Torts (1979), 237
Robertson, The Comptroller and Bank Supervision (1968), 91
Rose & Talley, Bank Transactions with Affiliates: The New Section 23A, 100 Banking L.J. 423 (1983), 399

Saxon, Branching Powers and the Dual Banking System, 101 Comp. Curr. Ann. Rep. 316 (1963), 416
Scott, Deposit Insurance and Bank Regulation: The Policy Choices, 44 Bus. Law. 907 (1989), 288, 299
Scott, In Quest of Reason: The Licensing Decision of the Federal Banking Agencies, 42 U. Chi. L. Rev. 235 (1975), 91, 94
Scott, Supervision of International Banking Post-BCCI, 8 Georgia State University L. Rev. 487 (1992), 695
Scott, The Dual Banking System: A Model of Competition in Regulation, 30 Stan. L. Rev. 1 (1977), 118
Scott, The Uncertain Course of Bank Deregulation, 5 Regulation 40 (May/June 1981), 449
Seiberg, Maryland Thrift in Redlining Statement Insists That It Had Done Nothing Wrong, American Banker, August 24, 1994, 210
Short, Bank Problems and Financial Safety Nets, Economic Review of the Federal Reserve Bank of Dallas (Mar. 1987), 288
Shugart, A Public Choice Perspective on the 1933 Banking Act, in the Financial Services Revolution (England & Huertas, eds. 1988), 511
M. Singer, Funny Money (1985), 276
Staff of the House Committee on Banking, Finance & Urban Affairs, 101st Cong., 2d Sess., An International Comparison of Banking Regulatory Structures, Comm. Print 101-3 (June 1990), 720-30
Swire, Bank Insolvency Law Now That It Matters Again, 42 Duke L.J. 469 (1992), 608

Swire, Safe Harbors and a Proposal to Improve the Community Reinvestment Act, 79 Virginia L. Rev. 349 (1993), 218-19

Thorup, Injunctions Against Payment of Standby Letters of Credit: How Can Banks Protect Themselves?, 101 Banking L.J. 6 (1984), 168

Tiabi, Banking, Finance, and Community Economic Empowerment: Structural Economic Theory, Procedural Civil Rights, and Substantive Racial Justice, 107 Harv. L. Rev. 1465 (1994), 220

Trachtman, Recent Initiatives in International Financial Regulation and Goals of Competitiveness, Effectiveness, Consistency and Cooperation, 12 Northwestern J. of Intl. L. & Bus. 241 (1991), 694

United States Department of Justice and Federal Trade Commission, 1992 Horizontal Merger Guidelines, 451-53, 473-74, 480-82, 490-91

United States Department of the Treasury, Modernizing the Financial System: Recommendations for Safer, More Competitive Banks (1991), 280

United States General Accounting Office, Derivatives: Actions Needed to Protect the Financial System (1994), 322

Volcker, Congressional Testimony, 71 Fed. Reserve Bull. 430 (1985), 448-49

Wallace, The Uses of Usury: Low Rate Ceilings Reexamined, 56 B.U. L. Rev. 451 (1976), 97

Watt, After FDICIA, Is There Life for Dual Banking?, 11 Banking Policy Report (1992), 122

Weinstein, Remarks Delivered at Southern Methodist University (Sept. 13, 1990), 336

Weinstein, Attorney Liability in the Savings and Loan Crisis, 1993 U. Ill. L. Rev. 53 (1993), 344

L. White, Free Banking in Britain: Theory, Experience and Debate 1800-1845 (1984), 86

J. White & R. Summers, Uniform Commercial Code (3d ed. 1988), 673

Wilkins, Making Context Count: Regulating Lawyers After Kaye, Scholer, 66 Southern Calif. L. Rev. 1145 (1993), 344, 346, 347

Wilmarth, Too Big to Fail, Too Few to Serve? The Potential Risks of Nationwide Banks, 77 Iowa Law Review 957 (1992), 410-11

Wilmarth, The Potential Risks of Nationwide Consolidation in the Banking Industry: A Reply to Professor Miller, 77 Iowa Law Review 1133 (1992), 411

Wilmarth, Too Good to Be True? The Unfulfilled Promises Behind Big Bank Mergers, 2 Stanford Journal of Law, Business and Finance 1 (1996), 411

Zubrzycki, Note, The Kaye, Scholer Case: Attorneys' Ethical Duties to Third Parties in Regulatory Situations, 6 Georgetown J. of Leg. Eth. 977 (1993), 344

P. Zweig, Belly Up: The Collapse of the Penn Square Bank (1985), 276

# INDEX